Sports Economics

David Berri

Southern Utah University

worth publishers
Macmillan Learning
New York

Vice President, Social Sciences: **Charles Linsmeier**
Director of Content and Assessment: **Shani Fisher**
Executive Program Manager: **Simon Glick**
Marketing Manager: **Andrew Zierman**
Marketing Assistant: **Morgan Ratner**
Development Editor: **Lukia Kliossis**
Associate Media Editor: **Emily Schmid**
Editorial Assistant: **Courtney Lindwall**
Director, Content Management Enhancement: **Tracey Kuehn**
Managing Editor: **Lisa Kinne**
Content Project Manager: **Won McIntosh**
Director of Design, Content Management: **Diana Blume**
Cover Designer: **Vicki Tomaselli**
Interior Designer: **Patrice Sheridan**
Photo Editor: **Cecilia Varas**
Senior Workflow Project Manager: **Paul Rohloff**
Media Producer: **Daniel Comstock**
Composition and Illustrations: **Lumina Datamatics**
Printing and Binding: **King Printing Co., Inc.**
Cover photo: **Pete Saloutos/Getty Images**

ISBN-13: 978-1-319-28221-9
ISBN-10: 1-319-28221-0

Library of Congress Control Number: 2017940592

First printing
Printed in the United States of America

Worth Publishers
One New York Plaza
Suite 4500
New York, NY 10004-1562
www.macmillanlearning.com

Eileen Treanor

About the Author

David Berri is the lead author of two books—*The Wages of Wins* (with Martin Schmidt and Stacy Brook; Stanford University Press) and *Stumbling on Wins* (with Martin Schmidt; Financial Times Press)—written for a general audience on the subject of sports and economics. In addition, he has had more than 40 papers accepted and/or published in refereed journals in the field and at least a dozen additional papers published in academic collections. Beyond this academic work, Berri has written more than 100 articles for the popular press, including *The New York Times*, *Time.com*, *Atlantic.com*, *Vice Sports*, and the *Huffington Post*.

Berri has also served as president of the North American Association of Sports Economics (NAASE) and currently sits on the editorial board of the *Journal of Sports Economics* and *International Journal of Sport Finance* (the two journals in sports economics). Beginning in 2004, he has helped organize meetings of NAASE at the Western Economic Association, which is the world's largest gathering of sports economists annually.

Berri has taught sports economics since 1999, starting at Coe College and then moving on to California State University-Bakersfield. He has taught at Southern Utah University since 2008.

Contents

Vision and Story of *Sports Economics*

Let's begin with two simple observations. Sports are obviously fun. Yet economics is often referred to as the "dismal science."[1] Today, students sitting in introductory economics classes might see economics as "dismal" because these courses often emphasize abstract reasoning that many students struggle to find relatable. And economics courses seldom present the empirical studies that connect economics to the world students observe. Traditional sports economics texts have mostly relied on teaching through the use of models and microeconomic theory.

Sports economics as a discipline, and this text in particular, attacks each of these shortcomings. Many students don't just watch sports. They invest hours studying sports in detail, so they definitely relate to the subject matter. Sports also come with numbers that fans frequently cite, and these numbers have allowed economists to conduct many empirical studies testing a host of different economic theories. There is no other industry where we have so much data on both workers and firms. Sports economics is, in fact, far from "dismal"!

Sports economics isn't just a fun way to learn economics. Sports offer an abundance of amazingly detailed numbers on the productivity of individual workers. Unlike other firms we could study, in sports like baseball and basketball, we have detailed productivity information on every player on every team. And in a sport like baseball, this data set extends back to the 19th century. So although you would have no way of knowing the most productive worker for each of the leading firms in the United States in 1888, we can look at a site like baseball-reference.com and learn that Cap Anson of the Chicago White Stockings led all National League hitters in productivity that season.[2]

With such data in hand, we can address such big questions as:

- Do firms exploit workers?
- How would one investigate racial discrimination and does racial discrimination persist?
- How are women and men treated differently by firms and markets?
- What role does government play in business?
- Are economic decision makers rational?

These are questions that economists have pondered for decades. And with the abundance of data provided by sports, these questions can finally be addressed. So sports economics isn't just fun. It's important!

Sports economics is also closely linked to the fastest-growing field in economics — behavioral economics. In contrast to the standard neoclassical model of human behavior, behavioral economists argue that people are not fully rational. My own research and that of others cited in the text likewise indicate that decision makers in sports often fall short of the rational ideal.

With the rise of sabermetrics, sports economics has become increasingly driven by statistics and more open to behavioral economics. This shift away from traditional theory is reflected in this text, as I use sports statistics to walk students through how recent researchers have reached their conclusions. Finally, throughout this text, I have worked hard to present anecdotes and information that offer a cohesive story. Because if students aren't reading the textbook, what's the point?

I wish you and your students great success and real enjoyment as you use this text!

---

[1]This label "dismal science" can be traced back to the writing of Thomas Carlyle, who first penned the term in 1849. Many believe that Carlyle was addressing the argument advanced by Thomas Malthus: Because the number of people in a society would always grow faster than a society's food supply, most members of any society were destined to live a life of poverty. However, Carlyle was actually addressing was the claim put forth by John Stuart Mill and Adam Smith that slavery was wrong. Because Carlyle was a vehement racist, he believed that economics — the field of study inspired by the works of Smith and Mill — was "dismal."

[2]If we measure productivity with OPS (on-base plus slugging). See http://www.baseball-reference.com/players/a/ansonca01.shtml.

Engaging Students in the Study of Sports Economics

Sports Economics engages students with real-world sports stories and incorporates empirical research and statistical analysis to introduce the application of basic statistics, standard economic theory, and behavioral economics.

Empirical Focus and Statistical Analysis

Sports economics inherently has an abundance of data. This book draws on recent empirical research to shed light on the study of sports economics. And it also emphasizes what every student of statistics should learn. When people see numbers, there is a strong temptation to conclude that such numbers decisively "prove" an argument. But as any student of statistics learns, statistical studies come with confidence intervals. In other words, statistical analysis often just suggests an answer. This empirical focus is repeatedly emphasized throughout the text.

Narrative Approach

This book is built around real-world sports stories. This approach not only takes advantage of sports being a relatable subject matter, but also helps explain the foundational theory and math while keeping readers engaged.

Dedicated Women in Sports Chapter

Unlike other books on the market, an entire chapter devoted to women and sports is included here. It goes beyond examining market forces to explain how public policy and historical perceptions have driven the outcomes of gender and sports. Gender coverage is not limited to this chapter but highlighted throughout the text.

Historical Emphasis

Throughout the book, a number of historical anecdotes shed light on the economic theory that underlies sports. Sports economics also reveals much about the history of economics, and profiles of prominent economists are presented in marginal boxes to showcase their contributions to the field.

SAEED KHAN/Getty Images

Asking Questions to Elicit Engagement

Each chapter is designed to tell a story. This brief table of contents provides the basic questions designed to engage students in *Sports Economics*.

Powerful Support for Instructors

Instructors are supported in their teaching of *Sports Economics* by the following resources, all accessible via Macmillan Learning's catalog at www.macmillanlearning.com.

- An **Instructor's Resource Manual** offers teaching materials and tips to enhance the classroom experience, along with outlines, test questions, in-class activities, and additional resources.

- A **Solutions Manual**, prepared by the author of this text, provides detailed solutions to the end-of-chapter problems.

- **Image Slides** give access to every image, figure, and table in high-resolution format.

- **Lecture Slides** provide brief, yet comprehensive, outlines of key chapter concepts, designed to assist with lecture preparation and presentations.

Enhanced Value; Affordable Options

Affordability weighs heavily when choosing course materials. Worth Publishers is making it easier for instructors and students alike to select the highest-quality published material written by renowned economics educators, researchers, and policymakers at affordable prices. To better incentivize you to consider choosing Worth's valuable and cost-effective products, you and your students have the option to purchase *Sports Economics* as a printed paperback text in black and white or to select a full-color e-Book from one of Worth's e-Book partners. For more information, visit the Macmillan catalog at http://www.macmillanlearning.com.

Acknowledgments

The first person I must thank is Justin Wolfers, who originally suggested I write *Sports Economics*. Without Justin, this book would not have happened.

Sports Economics is a textbook designed to bring academic research into the classroom. Obviously, this book owes a debt to all the authors of all the studies cited. For my own academic research, I need to acknowledge my debt to my many co-authors and other individuals who helped me in this research. Such a list includes (in alphabetical order) Stacey Brook, J. C. Bradbury, Robert Brown, Brian Burke, Babatunde Buraimo, Corrine Coates, Lindsey Darvin, Christian Deutscher, Erick Eschker, Aju Fenn, Rod Fort, Bernd Frick, Arturo Galletti, Tiffany Greer, Jill Harris, Brad Humphreys, Todd Jewell, Anthony Krautmann, Young Hoon Lee, Michael Leeds, Eva Marikova Leeds, Michael Mondello, Lisle O'Neill, Ann Pegoraro, James Peach, Joe Price, Joshua Price, Dan Rascher, John Robst, Ryan Rodenberg, Giambasttista Rossi, Martin Schmidt, Rob Simmons, Brian Soebbing, Coby Vance, Jennifer Van Gilder, Roberto Vicente-Mayoral, Peter von Allmen, and Steve Walters.

I would also like to thank all the economists who have participated in sessions on sports economics at the Western Economic Association and with the North American Association of Sports Economists. These sessions have been of tremendous help in developing the stories in this text.

In addition, several people read early drafts of chapters and made many valuable suggestions:

Ross Booth, *Monash University*

Stacey Brook, *University of Iowa*

Karl Einolf, *Mount St. Mary's University*

Stanley Engerman, *University of Rochester*

Aju Fenn, *Colorado College*

John Fizel, *Penn State-Erie*

Nancy Jianakoplos, *Colorado State University*

Yvan Kelly, *Flagler College*

David Kiefer, *University of Utah*

Philip Lane, *Fairfield University*

William Lee, *Saint Mary's College*

Daniel Marburger, *Arizona State University*

Chris Maxwell, *Boston College*

Kris McWhite, *University of Georgia*

Phil Miller, *Minnesota State University, Mankato*

Jim Peach, *New Mexico State University*

Kevin Quinn, *St. Norbert College*

Allen Sanderson, *University of Chicago*

Lee Van Scyoc, *University of Wisconsin, Oshkosh*

The staff at Macmillan Learning — specifically, Chuck Linsmeier, Shani Fisher, Bruce Kaplan, Lukia Kliossis, Sarah Nguyen, Carlos Marin, Won McIntosh, Paul Rohloff, Emily Schmid, and Courtney Lindwall — have all been extremely patient and helpful. I'd also like to thank the copyeditor Patti Brecht and proofreader Cosmas Georgallis for their attention to detail on this project.

Finally, I need to thank my wife Lynn and my daughters Allyson and Jessica. This book would not be possible without the three most important women in my life.

It's Just Supply and Demand

What Determines Ticket Prices in Professional Sports?

To answer this question, Chapter 1 will explore the following:

1. **Application of the Marshallian Method:** Sports comes with numbers, so math is part of the story. But as Alfred Marshall observed more than 100 years ago, math is just the beginning. For analysis to be worthwhile, it must be "important to real life." Thus, any math we consider must be part of a story — a story that hopefully helps us understand the math.

2. **The Marshallian Cross or Standard Supply and Demand Model:** To determine what determines prices, economists turn to the standard supply and demand model. Here, we will introduce and review its basic elements.

3. **Deductive Reasoning:** Because economists historically had very little data to work with, economists have generally deduced the essence of a theory from a collection of basic principles. The standard supply and demand model is one of the best examples of deductive reasoning.

"There is no research setting other than sports where we know the name, face, and life history of every production worker and supervisor in the industry." In 2000, Lawrence Kahn[1] made this observation: And in one sentence, it captures the unique nature of sports economics. There simply is no industry where we have so much data on both workers and firms. Consequently, no other industry exists in which the application of economic theory and statistical techniques can yield so many insights.

The application of economic methods to the study of sport only goes back a few decades. The purpose of this textbook is to detail the many insights we have learned from such an application. Our specific approach will emphasize the two research approaches economists have taken.

Deductive reasoning, or moving from the general to the specific, is historically the approach economists have taken in all fields, and such was the initial approach in sports economics as well. Essentially, when we don't have data — and/or lack computing power — we rely on theoretical models to understand how the world functions.

Within sports economics, there is certainly much research that follows this traditional approach. But sports also come with many numbers. And that means a second approach, inductive reasoning, is possible.

Because sports economics relies on both inductive and deductive reasoning, the study of sports allows us to see how these approaches interact in the study of economics. For many of the stories told, we will begin by identifying our expectations with regard to deductive reasoning. We will then often move on to the story as told through the analysis of all its numbers. By looking at issues from both perspectives, we will encounter instances where the data:

- confirm economic theory
- don't seem to support economic theory
- leave us unsure where the answer ultimately lies

In sum, economic theory and data analysis shed much light on the study of sports and economics. But at times — and it is crucial that we recognize this — all of our analysis doesn't provide definitive answers (and there is thus a need for further research).

It is important to emphasize that the study of sports and economics does more than improve our understanding of sports. It also allows us to demonstrate how economists use data and statistical techniques to understand the surrounding world. Consequently, although our discussion will include economic theory, we will not lose sight of the numbers that make this industry so valuable to economists focused on empirical analysis. Specifically, it is easy to look at the study

---

[1]Lawrence Kahn, "The Sports Business as a Labor Market Laboratory," *Journal of Economic Perspectives* 15, no. 3 (Summer 2000): 74–94.

of sports and economics and consider this effort to be simply a pleasant diversion from more "important" applications of economics. We will make a different argument. The study of sports doesn't just draw on the ideas of important writers in the history of economic thought; it also allows us to address important questions that simply cannot be examined easily elsewhere.

For example, Karl Marx and J. B. Clark — in the 19th century — debated the question of whether or not workers are paid what they are worth in a market economy. Outside of sports, where data on worker productivity are scarce, such a question cannot be addressed easily. In the world of sports, though, it is a very different story. Likewise, the data generated by sports allow us to consider such important topics as racial discrimination and the value managers have to a firm. These issues have important implications beyond the world of sports. And it is within sports that we find the data necessary to empirically address them.

1.1 In Sports, Perception and Reality Don't Always Match

Let's start with two simple questions with which sports fans should be familiar: Who plays sports and which sports are most popular?

Once upon a time, sports were primarily the occupation — as Thorstein Veblen noted in 1899 — of the leisure class.[2] This means that many sports were played primarily by wealthy white males.[3] As time went by, though, sports spread to everyone. For some, "everyone" simply meant men of all social classes. But sports really are for everyone (where "everyone" means men and women). Today in the United States, more than 4 million boys play high school sports each year and more than 3 million girls do the same.[4] In addition, sports are played by women and men in both the college and professional ranks.

Sports are not just played in the United States either. Sports are played and watched around the world. And the numbers are staggering. In 2014, the Seattle Seahawks and Denver Broncos played at the Super Bowl in front of a global audience of 160 million. In October of the same year, a regular-season

> **Thorstein Veblen (1857–1929)**
>
> Veblen is perhaps the first celebrity American economist. His *Theory of the Leisure Class* (1899), which introduced the term "conspicuous consumption," offered a highly critical description of the behavior of the very wealthy in American society. In economics, Veblen is also known for being one of the founders of the institutional school of economic thought. Whereas economists today primarily treat individuals as independent agents, Veblen emphasized that an individual is shaped by the institutions that exist in society. Therefore, to understand human behavior, we have to acknowledge the role of the setting the human beings find themselves within.

---

[2]Thorstein Veblen, *The Theory of the Leisure Class* (New York: Macmillan, 1899).

[3]For example, the early powers in college football were the teams at Yale and Harvard (http://www.collegefootballpoll.com/history_of_college_football.html).

Of course, we will note that despite Veblen's observation at the time, sports in the 19th century were also played by less wealthy whites (certainly in baseball), African Americans, and women.

[4]R. Vivian Acosta and Linda J. Carpenter, "Women in Intercollegiate Sport: A Longitudinal, National Study, Thirty-Seven-Year Update, 1977–2014." Unpublished manuscript. Available at www.acostacarpenter.org.

game between Real Madrid and Barcelona of the Spanish Primera Division had a global audience of 400 million.[5] Yes, 400 million soccer fans tuned in to watch a single regular-season game.

And again, these sports fans are not just men. Studies show that 45% of National Football League (NFL) fans are women. And at least 30% of fans of Major League Baseball (MLB), the National Basketball Association (NBA), National Hockey League (NHL), and NASCAR are also women. You may not see this fact reflected in the media, since only about 10% of sports reporters, columnists, and editors are women.[6] But it is definitely true that both men and women love sports.

But love of sports doesn't necessarily mean you fully understand how sports work on and off the field. To illustrate our point, in May 2010, famed NBA broadcaster Marv Albert asked then President Barack Obama what actions he would take if he were appointed commissioner of the NBA for a day[7]:

> The biggest change I'd probably propose right now is the commissioner needs to figure out how to price tickets so that ordinary people can go to the games. I mean, I think that ticket prices have gotten so high, and I understand that salaries are high, ticket prices are going to be high, but you know, you hate to think that the only person that can go to a game is somebody who's got a corporate account.

This quote illustrates two important aspects of sports.

- **Once again, sports are very important.** We do not often hear the president of the United States outline his possible actions were he appointed to lead a specific business. Sports, though, aren't an ordinary business. They are the only business with an entire section of most newspapers dedicated to their day-to-day operations. Despite being a relatively small business,[8] sports are a significant part of many people's lives.

---

[5]Amanda Jennings, "The Super Bowl vs. the World Cup. What Is the Real Football?," *The Ladies League,* February 17, 2016, http://www.theladiesleague.org/#!The-Super-Bowl-vs-The-World-Cup-What-Is-The-Real-Football/n7e5e/56c506090cf25df9371d31cb.

[6]This point is made at The Ladies League (http://www.theladiesleague.org/#!about/hlzky).

[7]http://thestartingfive.net/2010/05/26/notes-from-tnts-exclusive-interview-with-president-barack-obama/.

[8]Brad Humphreys and Jane Ruseski estimated that the economic value generated by sports ranged from $44 to $60 billion in 2005 ["Estimates of the Dimensions of the Sports Market in the US," *International Journal of Sport Finance* 4 (2009): 94–113]. To put that number in perspective, in September 2008, the U.S. government seized control of American International

* **Even very dedicated fans don't always get it right.** Although people spend a great deal of time thinking and talking about sports, what people seem to believe about sports isn't always consistent with the academic analysis of this industry. In other words, President Obama's misstatement in this area is hardly unique.

To understand where President Obama went wrong in his analysis, you need to know more than sports. You also need to know some economics. Specifically, you have to know something about **supply** and **demand**.

Thomas Carlyle, in the 19th century, noted, "Teach a parrot the terms 'supply and demand' and you've got an economist." Today, the terms supply and demand can be found in all sorts of places. Consider the following from sportswriter Pat Kirwan[9] prior to the 2012 NFL draft:

> The reality of the draft is that supply and demand play into talent selection. In plain English, if 15 teams are looking to fill the same position and all 32 draft boards say only 10 players are projected as eventual starters at that spot, you will see these 10 guys all gone earlier than predicted.

Kirwan argues that the supply of a particular type of player may be less than demand. Consequently, we can expect the price—or where the players are selected in the draft—to increase. It all sounds so simple. Going back to our discussion of ticket prices, President Obama argues that as players' salaries increase, ticket prices increase. There appears to be some sense to this analysis. If a firm faces higher costs, it will offer less output. And when supply is reduced, as Kirwan noted with offensive linemen, prices will go up.

1.2 The Marshallian Method

Does the prior discussion really describe how ticket prices work? To answer this question, we need to consider another writer from the 19th century.

supply To be in "supply" of a product, one must be willing and able to produce and sell a good or service (in different quantities at different prices).

demand To be in "demand" of a product, one must be willing and able to purchase a good or service (in different quantities at different prices).

Group, Inc. in a deal worth $85 billion (M. Karnitschnig, D. Solomon, L. Pleven, and J. Hilsenrath, J., "U.S. to Take Over AIG in $85 Billion Bailout; Central Banks Inject Cash as Credit Dries Up," *Wall Street Journal*, September 16, 2008). In sum, a government bailout of one troubled insurance company is worth more than one estimate of the value of the entire sports industry.

[9]Pat Kirwan, "Before Offensive Tackles Fly Off Draft Boards, Consider Supply and Demand," CBS Sports, April 7, 2012, http://www.cbssports.com/nfl/draft/story/18379951/before-offensive-tackles-fly-off-draft-boards-consider-supply-and-demand.

**Alfred Marshall
(1842–1924)**

Much of what we
know as micro-
economics can be
traced back to Mar-
shall's *Principles of
Economics* (1890).
This book intro-
duced such familiar
concepts as the
supply and demand
model (known as the
Marshallian Cross),
price elasticity, con-
sumer and producer
surplus, and optimi-
zation techniques,
and explained how
conclusions depend
on the time period
examined. Marshall
consistently qualified
his conclusions. He
emphasized that
economics is not a
religion; it is simply
an engine of inquiry
and often its answers
depend very much
on how you look at
the question. Much
of this book tries
to follow that same
approach.

The study of sports economics falls within the wider field of microeconom-ics. And much of what we understand about microeconomics can be traced back to the writings of Alfred Marshall. Before we get to Marshall's specific contributions, let's spend a moment examining Marshall's approach to the study of economics (an approach that motivates much of what you will encounter in our discussion of sports economics).

John Maynard Keynes, a student of Marshall's who made some fairly signif-icant contributions to economics himself, had this to say about Marshall after he passed away in 1924[10]:

> Marshall . . . arrived very early at the point of view that the bare bones of economic theory are not worth much in themselves and do not carry one far in the direction of useful, practical conclusions. The whole point lies in applying them to the interpretation of current economic life. This requires a profound knowledge of the actual facts of industry and trade.

Keynes was not talking about sports and economics, but the quote captures what this book is all about. The study of sports allows us to apply what we understand from economic theory to a specific industry. And this exercise clearly falls within the Marshallian tradition.

Marshall didn't just provide us with the theoretical foundations to our approach, he also — in a tongue-in-cheek fashion — provided a step-by-step guide to our basic method.

In a letter to A. L. Bowley in 1906, Marshall laid out his approach to economics[11]:

1. Use mathematics as a shorthand language, rather than as an engine of inquiry.

2. Keep to them till you have done.

3. Translate into English.

4. Then illustrate by examples that are important in real life.

5. Burn the mathematics.

6. If you can't succeed in (4), burn (3). This last I did often.

---

[10]John Maynard Keynes, "Alfred Marshall, 1842–1924," *The Economic Journal* 34, no. 135 (September 1924): 342.

[11]Ronald Coase, "Marshall on Method," *Journal of Law and Economics* 18, no. 1 (April 1975): 30.

1.3 Marshall and the Demand Curve

Let's apply Marshall's approach to the question posed at the onset of this chapter: What determines prices?

Marshall provided a simple model, the **Marshallian cross**, to answer this question. Today, we call the Marshallian cross the standard supply and demand model.[12] As the name implies, the model consists of two elements: supply and demand.[13]

Marshallian cross The standard supply and demand model.

Let's start our discussion with demand, and again, we will follow the basic Marshallian method.

Steps 1 and 2: Use mathematics as a shorthand language (and keep at it until you are done).

Demand for a good can be illustrated by the **demand curve**,[14] which is captured by the following equation[15]:

demand curve Tells us how much of a good is demanded at various prices.

$$P = a_0 - a_1 \times Q_d$$

where P = price of a good (say, tickets, baseball cards, player jerseys, etc.)

[12]Marshall was not the first to argue that both supply and demand influenced the price of a good. But prior to Marshall, writers tended to emphasize the primacy of supply factors or the primacy of demand factors. Marshall's contribution is to note that the importance of supply or demand depends on the circumstances of the market.

[13]The terms "supply" and "demand" refer to the two sides of a market transaction. Both must apply to be considered part of a market. In other words, if you are willing to buy World Series tickets, but are not able to (because you lack money), you are not in "demand." Likewise, if you are able to buy World Series tickets, but not willing to (because you do not like baseball), you are also not in "demand."

[14]The demand curve can be illustrated as an actual curve. But for our purposes, we will utilize an equation that is actually a straight line. We will still call this, though, a "demand curve."

[15]From a firm's perspective, prices determine demand. In other words, demand is thought of as the dependent variable (i.e., it depends on changes in price) and price is the independent variable. Joseph Schumpeter noted that we normally place independent variables on the x-axis or on the right-hand side of the equation [*History of Economic Analysis* (New York: Oxford University Press, 1954), p. 991]. Marshall, conversely, put price on the y-axis or on the left-hand side of the equation. As I tell my students, this is because Marshall was trying to explain prices. Or as I put it, Marshall wasn't in sales, so he didn't care as much about the factors that drive how much a firm sells.

$$Q_d = \text{quantity demanded of a good}$$
$$a_0 = y\text{-intercept}$$
$$a_1 = \text{slope coefficient}$$

Steps 3 and 4: Translate into English and illustrate by examples that are important in real life.

Some people are mathematically inclined and can think in the language of math. For many people, though, this language is difficult to comprehend. Hence, Marshall encouraged people to translate math into words that could be understood.

Let's make some simple statements about the above equation. We'll begin by noting that the sign on a_1, the slope coefficient, is negative. This simply means that price and demand move in opposite directions. There are two reasons why we expect this relationship. First, when a good, like tickets, becomes more expensive, people have an incentive to buy more of other goods. Economists call this the **substitution effect**, or the tendency consumers have to substitute other goods for the tickets (or whatever good we are considering) as the price of tickets goes up. Conversely, as the price of tickets falls, consumers have an incentive to substitute ticket purchases for the purchases of other goods and services.

In addition to the substitution effect, we have what economists label the **income effect**.[16] As a ticket becomes less expensive, the purchasing power of consumers goes up. In essence, it's as if consumers' income has increased, allowing individuals to buy more tickets (and more of other goods as well). Both of these effects underlie what we call the **law of demand**:

> *As the price of a good increases, quantity demanded for the good will decline, holding all else constant.*

The law of demand tells us that as price increases, quantity demanded will decrease. In terms of the corresponding graph (Figure 1.1), changes in prices lead us to move from one point on the curve to another point (i.e., to move along the curve).

All of this is illustrated by the negative sign in front of a_1. Of course, there is another element in this equation. The y-intercept, or a_0, also tells an important story. In an equation, the y-intercept reveals to us the value of the dependent variable (in this case, price) when the independent variable is zero (in this

---

substitution effect In general, an increase in a good's price makes other goods more attractive to the consumer (and a lower price makes other goods less attractive).

income effect In general, a decrease in a good's price increases the purchasing power of a consumer (and an increase will decrease his or her purchasing power).

law of demand As the price of a good increases, quantity demanded for the good will decline, holding all else constant.

---

[16]The total effect of the price change is captured by the substitution and income effect.

case, quantity demand). And by itself, decision makers should understand that value. After all, at this price—and any price above this point—the firm can expect to sell nothing.

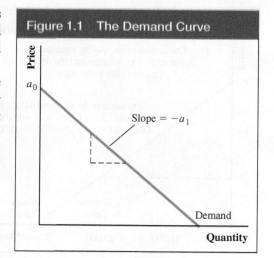

Figure 1.1   The Demand Curve

The y-intercept tells a bigger story. Our demand curve simply reveals to us the link between price and quantity demand. Other factors, though, impact demand for ticket prices. Coates and Harrison (2005)[17] studied attendance in MLB from 1969 to 1996. These authors found that higher prices led to less demand (as the law of demand would suggest), but demand wasn't just about prices. These authors considered a variety of additional factors, including (but not limited to):

- increase/decrease in the size of the market where the team played

- increase/decrease in per-capita income in the market

- move to a newer stadium

- increase/decrease in the capacity of the stadium

- improvement/decline in the quality of the team

To illustrate how one of these factors—in this case, improving the quality of the team—would impact a MLB team's demand, we begin by examining the following hypothetical demand curve

$$P = \$50 - 0.002 \times Q_d$$

At a price[18] of $25, this team would see demand for 12,500 tickets. Now, imagine the team acquired much better players, causing fans to believe the team would likely play much better in the future. We could illustrate this change by increasing the y-intercept as follows:

$$P = \$75 - 0.002 \times Q_d$$

[17]Dennis Coates and Thane Harrison., "Baseball Strikes and the Demand for Attendance," *Journal of Sports Economics* 6, no. 3 (August 2005): 282–302.

[18]According to the Team Marketing Report, the average MLB team charged $31.00 in 2016 https://www.teammarketing.com/public/uploadedPDFs/MLB_FCI_2016.pdf

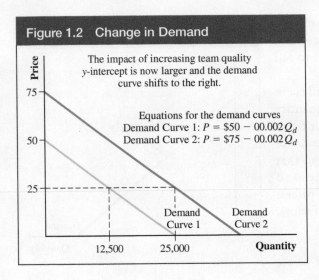

Figure 1.2   Change in Demand

The impact of increasing team quality y-intercept is now larger and the demand curve shifts to the right.

Equations for the demand curves
Demand Curve 1: $P = \$50 - 00.002 Q_d$
Demand Curve 2: $P = \$75 - 00.002 Q_d$

If the team keeps ticket prices at $25, it would then see demand increase to 25,000 tickets.

Again, to illustrate this change in team quality, we would increase the value of a_0. In other words, the y-intercept would increase in value and the demand curve would shift to the right, as demonstrated in Figure 1.2.

This simple example illustrates a key point about the demand curve. Our curve tells us the relationship between price and demand, holding all else constant. If something besides price changes, we illustrate this by moving the entire curve (i.e., changing the y-intercept). The following changes (noted earlier in the chapter) would cause an increase in demand:

- increase in the size of the market where the team played
- increase in the per-capita income in the market
- move to a newer stadium
- increase in the capacity of the stadium
- improvement in the quality of the team

And each of these changes would see the y-intercept for the team's demand curve increase. Likewise, if each of these factors moved in the opposite direction, the y-intercept would be lower.

1.4 Just a Matter of Time

One should note that the change in team quality led to a change in the demand for tickets.[19] How would this change the price? To answer that question, we need to discuss supply. Once again, we return to Marshall.[20] For Marshall, the story

---

[19]A "change in demand"—caused by a change in some factor other than the price of the product and results in a shift in the demand curve—should be contrasted with a "change in quantity demanded." This latter phrase only refers to a change in the price of the product and results in movement along the demand curve.

[20]The final two steps of the Marshallian method involve "burning the math"—and if we failed to find good examples from real life, burning our story as well. We are, however, going to skip

of how price impacts a firm's decision to supply a good or service depends on the time period one considers. To understand this point, let's briefly look at a baseball player who starred in the National League around the same time Alfred Marshall was teaching the world about supply and demand.

Honus Wagner's[21] career began with the Louisville Colonels of the National League in 1897. After three seasons in Louisville, Wagner was traded to the Pittsburgh Pirates in 1899. Over the next 18 seasons, Wagner managed to lead the league in OPS+ (on-base percentage + slugging percentage, adjusted for league averages and ball-parks)[22] for eight different seasons. When baseball's Hall of Fame came about in 1936, Wagner

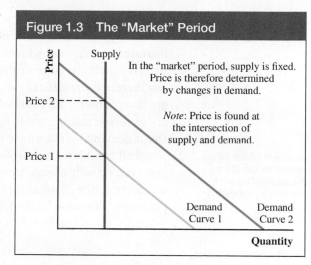

Figure 1.3   The "Market" Period

In the "market" period, supply is fixed. Price is therefore determined by changes in demand.

Note: Price is found at the intersection of supply and demand.

was one of its five original inductees. As great as Wagner's career was, today, he might be most well known for a photo taken of him in 1909. The American Tobacco Company issued a baseball card of Wagner. The story told, though, is that Wagner, not wanting to promote tobacco use in children, asked American Tobacco to halt production of his card. This request was granted, but not before a few cards had been printed.

At this point, the supply of these cards was clearly fixed. One can refer to such a time period where supply is fixed as the **market period**.[23] During this time period, prices are determined entirely by demand, as illustrated in Figure 1.3.

market period Period of time where firms cannot adjust supply so prices are determined entirely by the level of demand.

---

those last two steps. In other words, we will consider the math in our discussion (although we will strive to put the math into words). Furthermore, we will be connecting what we say to "real life."

[21]A good source of information on Wagner (and just about any other baseball player) is base-ball-reference.com.

[22]OPS+ is one measure of a player's overall hitting ability. Because worker productivity is an important part of economics, we will discuss in detail different measures of worker performance in sports in Chapter 6 and the statistics appendix of this book.

[23]The term "market period" comes from Landreth and Colander's (2002, p. 281). Marshall referred to this as "a market of very short period" (p. 312). As Marshall noted (p. 313): "Cost of production has for instance no perceptible influence on the day's bargaining in a fish-market." For a complete discussion, read Marshall's *Principles of Economics* (originally published in 1890). One can also consult Harry Landreth and David Colander, *History of Economic Thought*, 4th ed. (Boston: Houghton Mifflin, 2002), p. 281.

Figure 1.3 indicates that at Demand Curve 1, the price in the market—found where supply and demand intersect—is Price 1. Since 1909, incomes have increased among baseball fans. Higher incomes lead to more demand; therefore, we can expect the price of the Wagner baseball card to increase. And indeed it has increased dramatically in price. In 2013, one of the Wagner cards sold at public auction for $2.1 million.[24] What explains this high price? Again, the supply of these cards is entirely fixed, so the high price we observe today is entirely about demand. What we see in the market period can be contrasted with what Marshall considered a **short-run period**. In most markets,[25] given enough time, firms can actually change supply. How would this impact the price? Once again, we return to the Marshallian method. Let's begin with the equation for the supply curve, illustrated by the following general equation:

$$P = b_0 + b_1 \times Q_S$$

where P = price of a good (say, tickets, baseball cards, player jerseys, etc.)

Q_S = quantity supplied of a good

b_0 = y-intercept

b_1 = slope coefficient

short-run period Period when firms can change the supply of a good in response to a change in price.

law of supply As the price of a good increases, quantity supplied for the good will increase, holding all else constant.

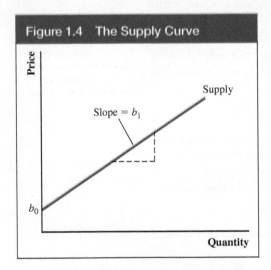

Figure 1.4   The Supply Curve

Notice in Figure 1.4 that the slope of the supply curve is positive. In words, we are arguing that in the normal period, higher prices lead firms to supply more of a good. This point is captured by the **law of supply**:

As the price of a good increases, quantity supplied for the good will increase, holding all else constant.

The law of supply is based on the simple notion that higher prices encourage firms to produce more of a product, while lower prices cause firms to produce less. This scenario may occur because firms have choices in production (think of farmers choosing between different crops). It can also occur because of the law of diminishing returns, which we will discuss in the next chapter.

---

[24]Darren Rovell, "Honus Wagner Card Sells for $2.1 M," April 6, 2013, http://espn.go.com/mlb/story/_/id/9140901/t206-honus-wagner-baseball-card-sets-21m-auction-mark.

[25]The operative word is "most." Obviously, in the market for Honus Wagner baseball cards, supply is not going to increase in the future.

1.5 The Marshallian Cross

Now that we have arrived at the supply curve, we can complete our picture of what was once called the Marshallian cross, shown in Figure 1.5—what we simply refer to as the supply and demand model in a normal time period.

Tim Tebow won the Heisman Trophy in 2007 as the quarterback for the University of Florida. He then led the Florida Gators to win the BCS National Championship in 2009. In 2010, the Denver Broncos selected Tebow in the first round of the NFL Draft and named him the starting quarterback in 2011 after a 1-4 start. Over the next 11 weeks, the Broncos won seven games, with three of these victories occurring in overtime and three others by a touchdown or less in regulation. The team's 8-8 record was good enough to land a playoff spot, where Tebow again led the Broncos to an overtime victory against the Pittsburgh Steelers [the defending American Football Conference (AFC) champions]. Although Tebow was not impressive statistically,[26] the Broncos' ability to win close games with Tebow in command greatly enhanced his reputation among sports fans.

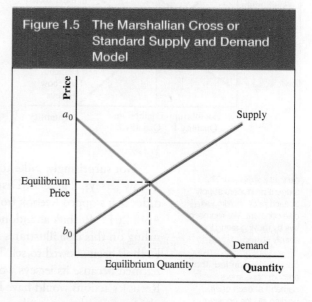

Figure 1.5   The Marshallian Cross or Standard Supply and Demand Model

Despite Tebow's reputation, after the season ended, the Broncos decided to go in a different direction. Peyton Manning was signed as a free agent by the Broncos. Then on March 21, 2012, Tebow was traded to the New York Jets. Within days of this trade, Nike replaced Reebok as the official supplier of NFL team uniforms. This means that Nike had the rights to sell Tebow's jersey with the Jets only. Reebok, though, ignored this point and decided to produce and sell New York Jets jerseys with Tebow's name on them. Let's use our simple Marshallian cross to illustrate how Reebok's decision would impact the market price.

The graph of Figure 1.6 begins with only Nike in the market selling Tebow jerseys. With Nike, we have Supply Curve 1. It intersects with Demand for Tebow Jersey at Equilibrium Price 1. Now what happens if Reebok also enters the market? The supply of Tebow jerseys increases. We represent this by shifting the supply curve to the right. At Equilibrium Price 1, there is now an excess

---

[26]Tebow only threw for 1,729 yards in 2011 and had more turnovers (13) than touchdown passes (12). We will explore more measures of quarterbacks in the book's statistics appendix.

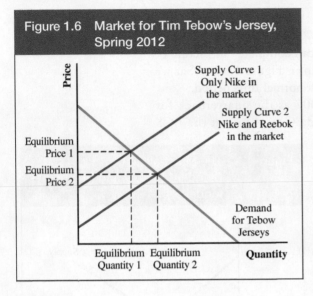

Figure 1.6   Market for Tim Tebow's Jersey, Spring 2012

supply of Tebow jerseys. In other words, at this price, **quantity supplied**[27] exceeds **quantity demanded**.[28]

The excess supply of jerseys causes the price in the market to decline. This decline leads the producers (i.e., Nike and Reebok) to reduce quantity supplied and also leads consumers to increase the quantity of jerseys demanded (in other words, the price change causes movement along both the demand and supply curves). These changes continue to happen until we reach a new equilibrium price where, once again, quantity demanded equals quantity supplied. One should note that the new equilibrium price (Equilibrium Price 2) is lower than the price that prevailed in the market without Reebok, so Reebok's actions cause the price that Nike can receive for its Tebow jerseys to be lower.

quantity supplied The amount producers supply at each price, holding all else constant. We represent this by moving along the supply curve.

quantity demanded The amount consumers demand at each price, holding all else constant. We represent this by moving along the demand curve.

Not surprisingly, Nike took Reebok to court to prevent Reebok from selling Tebow jerseys. The U.S. District Court in Manhattan soon issued a restraining order that stopped Reebok from manufacturing and selling Tebow merchandise. In April 2012, Reebok abandoned its efforts to produce and sell Tebow jerseys. The ruling on this case illustrates the simple story told by the Marshallian cross. Had Reebok been allowed to sell Tebow's New York Jets jersey, Nike would have been harmed because its jerseys would have been sold at a lower price. In other words, Reebok's actions would have harmed the economic interests of Nike. Beyond that observation, this story illustrates how supply and demand can come together to determine prices in the market.

On the other hand, changes in demand can also impact price. For example, imagine if Tebow were to lead a team to a win in the Super Bowl.[29] This would

---

[27]Quantity supplied should be contrasted with a "change in supply," which refers to how anything other than the price of the good impacts producers' supply. A "change in supply" is represented by moving the supply curve (or changing the y-intercept of the supply curve).

[28]Quantity demanded should be contrasted with a "change in demand," which refers to how anything other than the price of the good impacts consumers' demand. As noted earlier, a "change in demand" is represented by moving the demand curve (or changing the y-intercept of the demand curve).

[29]This seems unlikely, since Tebow did not play quarterback for any NFL team after 2012. Apparently, Tebow's inability to post "good" numbers for a quarterback reduced significantly the demand for his services. Tebow has since abandoned his football career and is now playing minor league baseball in the New York Mets' system.

increase the popularity of Tebow and demand for his jerseys. From our model, we would then expect the price of Tebow jerseys to rise.

1.6 What Determines Ticket Prices?

Now that we understand the basics of the Marshallian cross, let's return to the question posed at the beginning of this chapter. What determines ticket prices in the NBA? The answer to this question depends on whether we consider the market for tickets to be best characterized within the "market" or "normal" period. For an answer, consider the supply of tickets in the NBA. In 1967–68, the NBA began playing an 82-game regular season, with each team having 41 home games. The NBA has maintained this schedule ever since. Given the length of a fixed schedule, and the fact that stadium capacity for a team changes infrequently, one can argue that the supply of tickets for an NBA team is fixed. If supply is fixed, then Marshall's model of the market period applies. Given this argument, ticket prices in the NBA—and in any team sport where schedule length and stadium capacity don't frequently change—are determined solely by demand. That means former President Obama's argument about the link between player salaries and ticket prices is incorrect. Yes, salaries in the NBA have gone up over time, but that happened because demand for the NBA's product has increased over time.

Why has demand for the NBA increased? There are a number of factors that drive demand. Researchers have focused on the impact of income and market size. Both per-capita and population have increased in the United States over time. One should also note—as we will detail in Chapter 8—that there is more to the story. Sports leagues in their first several decades appear to be quite similar. This is true whether you look at baseball in the late 19th century, the NFL in the 1940s, the NBA in the 1960s, or the WNBA today: Sports leagues at the onset do not have nearly as many fans as we see in a league that is decades old. In sum (again, as we will detail in Chapter 8), familiarity in sports definitely leads to greater demand. And that leads to the following progression of events:

- greater demand for sporting events

- increases in the price of tickets

- with the revenue earned from these higher prices leading to more demand for professional athletes (the Marshallian cross, as we will detail, also applies to labor markets) and higher demand for players leading to higher salaries

In sum, our analysis indicates that the causation runs from ticket prices to salaries, not higher salaries to ticket prices.

If you happen to have a job, you can see that this must be true. Could you demand a higher salary at your current job and expect your employer to simply raise the prices of whatever the firm sells? Or let's imagine that a player like Kevin Durant really has this kind of power. If such is the case, why can't Durant then demand a salary of $1 billion? Or $1 trillion? If salary demands dictate ticket prices, we might expect there to be little to prevent players from demanding any sum to play sports. Our deductive analysis indicates that this cannot be the case. Teams do not charge higher ticket prices because players are expensive. Teams charge higher ticket prices because consumer demand makes this possible. In other words, because people are willing to pay the prices teams charge, teams charge those prices. What would happen if the players were somehow encouraged to take less money to play basketball? Again, our model says that demand for tickets determines the price. So prices would be unchanged by the players taking less money. In the end, all that would happen is that the owners will end up with more money.

1.7 "The Decision" Teaches Us How Market Impediments Have Unintended Consequences

Could the owners actually limit the salaries to players? Salaries (or wages) are simply the price of labor. Our supply and demand model allows us to understand what determines the salaries paid to players. At least it would, if supply and demand were allowed to determine the salaries of players.

> **price ceiling** A mandated price above which transactions cannot be made. Typically, it is the government that establishes such mandates (e.g., rent control laws in New York City). But we also find price ceilings in sports.

Consider the market for NBA players. In 1999, a **price ceiling** was introduced in the labor market for NBA players. The Collective Bargaining Agreement (CBA) that ended the 1998–99 labor dispute included a provision that limited the salary paid to any one individual player. This limit varied according to how many years of experience a player had in the NBA. As **Table 1.1** illustrates, the maximum salary ranged in 2016–17 from $22.1 million to nearly $31 million.[30]

Table 1.1 Maximum Salaries in the National Basketball Association: 2013–14 to 2016–17[31]				
Years in NBA	2013–14	2014–15	2015–16	2016–17
0–6	$13,701,250	$14,746,000	$16,407,500	$22,116,750
7–9	$16,441,500	$17,695,200	$19,689,000	$26,540,100
10+	$19,181,750	$20,644,400	$22,970,500	$30,963,450

[30]Very extensive details of the NBA's collective bargaining agreement can be found at a website maintained by Larry Coon: http://www.cbafaq.com/salarycap.htm.

[31]Larry Coon's "NBA Salary Cap FAQ" (http://www.cbafaq.com/salarycap.htm).

Figure 1.7 shows how a maximum wage impacts the labor market for NBA players. The maximum wage the NBA has instituted is below the wage that would prevail in an unrestricted market. The story of "The Decision" illustrates how we know this is true.

LeBron James was born in Akron, Ohio, and became a nationally known basketball star in high school. In 2003, LeBron graduated from high school and was selected by the Cleveland Cavaliers with the very first pick in the 2003 NBA draft. Seven years later, LeBron had twice been named league most valuable player (MVP) and the Cavaliers had advanced to the NBA Finals in 2007. But from 2008 to 2010, LeBron and the Cavaliers, despite averaging 57 regular-season wins, failed to return to the NBA Finals.

Figure 1.7   Impact of a Maximum Wage in the Labor Market for National Basketball Association Players

Despite a relative lack of team success, LeBron was a highly sought after free agent in 2010. Several teams hoped to acquire LeBron's services. On July 8, LeBron announced in a one-hour broadcast on ESPN — a broadcast known as "The Decision" — where he would play basketball in 2010–11 (and beyond).

In a free market, the highest bidder would secure LeBron's services, but in the NBA, with a price ceiling in place, no team could offer LeBron more money than the NBA maximum.[32] We know multiple suitors were willing to pay this maximum, so we can infer that the equilibrium wage — or the wage LeBron would have been paid in an unrestricted market — exceeded the NBA's maximum salary. How did LeBron decide? We cannot read minds and know for sure, but we know that the the choice wasn't dictated by wages. So what else could it be? Perhaps LeBron focused on the additional star power Miami employed. In addition to LeBron, the Heat also signed Chris Bosh and re-signed Dwyane Wade in the summer of 2010. Each of

---

[32]Actually, one team could offer somewhat more. The NBA's collective bargaining agreement allowed LeBron's previous team (i.e., the Cavaliers) to offer more money than anyone else to re-sign LeBron. We will discuss this issue in Chapter 5. For our purposes, the "Larry Bird Exception" that the Cavaliers could exploit does not dramatically change our story.

these players was selected in the first five picks of the 2003 draft.[33] Prior to the summer of 2010, these players also came together to appear in 17 NBA All-Star Games.

An average player will produce 0.100 wins per 48 minutes. As **Table 1.2** indicates, LeBron James, Dwayne Wade, and Chris Bosh were all above-average players prior to 2010.[34] By signing all three players, the Heat hoped to win an NBA title. In 2011, the Heat came very close, losing in the NBA Finals to the Dallas Mavericks. In 2012 and 2013, the Heat went beyond close. Both of these seasons, James, Wade, and Bosh each were on teams that won the NBA championship.

Table 1.2 Career Productivity of LeBron James, Dwayne Wade, and Chris Bosh Prior to the 2010–11 Season[35]		
Miami Heat Stars	Wins Produced	Wins Produced per 48 Minutes
LeBron James	109.3	0.241
Dwayne Wade	72.6	0.199
Chris Bosh	54.9	0.142

This story suggests that LeBron chose the Miami Heat to win an NBA title.[36] It also illustrates that interference in a market can have unintended consequences. As we will detail in Chapter 5, the maximum NBA salary is designed to prevent the richest NBA teams from assembling a team that would dominate the league. By forcing the price of stars below the equilibrium wage,

[33]LeBron James was the first player selected in 2003, Bosh was the fourth selection, and Wade was taken with the fifth pick.

[34] Wins produced data for these players (and all NBA players since 1977–1978 can be found at Box Score Geeks: http://www.boxscoregeeks.com/.

[35]Wins Produced is a measure of player performance for basketball players. It was originally noted in *The Wages of Wins* and detailed in Berri (2008) and *Stumbling on Wins*. One can see details of its calculations online at http://wagesofwins.com/how-to-calculate-wins-produced/. The model essentially argues that wins in basketball are primarily a function of how well a team acquires the ball without the other team scoring (i.e., rebounds missed shots of opponent, forces turnovers by opponent), maintains possession of the ball (i.e., rebounds own missed shots, avoids turnovers), and converts possessions into points (i.e., shoots efficiently). More will be said on this in Chapter 6 and in the statistics appendix to this book.

[36]The story has a happy ending for Cleveland. After the 2013–14 season, LeBron James returned to Cleveland. And in 2016, LeBron and the Cavaliers won an NBA title for the city of Cleveland.

all teams — whether relatively rich or poor — should be able to acquire top talent. Unfortunately, although the maximum wage does allow all teams to hire top talent, it also forces the star players to consider factors besides the wage in determining where they will play. In the case of James, Wade, and Bosh, these players seem to have considered whether or not they would contend for a title.[37] That means a policy designed to prevent a team from assembling a dominant group of players has apparently had the unintended consequence of motivating stars to play on a single team, therefore creating a squad that dominates the league.

1.8 What Is the "Right" Price?

Although the maximum wage in the NBA has not prevented the creation of dominant teams, it has reduced the price LeBron James and other stars receive for their services. Does this mean that NBA stars are paid the "wrong" price? People can look at the equilibrium price in a market and conclude that this is the "right" price and any deviation from it is wrong. From that perspective, LeBron's wage of $14.5 million in 2009–10 was wrong because it was less than what LeBron would have been paid in a market without a maximum salary restriction. On the other hand, other people might consider LeBron's wage of $14.5 million and wonder why a person who essentially bounces a ball for a living deserves so much money. Certainly, there seem to be many jobs in the economy that provide more benefits to society (i.e., teacher, police officer, doctor, nurse, etc.). From this perspective, LeBron's wage is also "wrong."

The discussion of whether a price is right or wrong harkens back to a discussion in economics from more than a century ago. Back in the 19th century, people argued that the distribution of wealth and income follows "natural" laws. Therefore, any attempts to help the poor are futile since these attempts violate natural laws.

In response to this line of reasoning, Jeremy Bentham, a 19th-century philosopher, referred to natural laws as "nonsense on stilts."[38] John Stuart Mill was

> **Jeremy Bentham (1748–1832)**
>
> Jeremy Bentham was a childhood genius (starting his study of Latin at age 3) and philosopher most frequently identified with Utilitarianism, or the concept that policies should be evaluated in terms of "utility." Specifically, policies ought to be assessed by looking at how well they increase happiness (i.e., utility) and/or decrease unhappiness. The concept of utility underlies much of the traditional economic theory of individual behavior.

---

[37]Because the NBA also has set a cap on payrolls, each of these players actually accepted a wage somewhat below the league maximum to play in Miami. That further indicates these players actually chose the Heat so they could contend for a title.

[38]For more on the original essay by Bentham, who can be thought of as teacher of John Stuart Mill, see Philip Schofield, "Jeremy Bentham's 'Nonsense Upon Stilts,'" *Utilitas* 15, no. 1 (March 2003): 1–26, http://journals.cambridge.org/action/displayAbstract?fromPage=online&aid=3372504.

**John Stuart Mill
(1806–1873)**

John Stuart Mill's *Principles of Political Economy* (1848) was the leading textbook on the subject of political economy in the mid-19th century. Mill was a disciple of Bentham, and the concept of Utilitarianism influenced a significant part of his writings on economics. He was also a well-known opponent of slavery and is today considered a feminist for his very vocal support of women's rights.

**John Neville Keynes
(1852–1949)**

Perhaps now best known as the father of John Maynard Keynes, John Neville Keynes was a writer of some repute before his famous son. J. N. Keynes stressed the importance of both deductive and inductive reasoning (concepts emphasized in this textbook). And he also defined, as highlighted in the text, positive and normative science.

a bit more measured in his reply, arguing that the distribution of wealth was entirely a function of the "laws and customs of society"; furthermore, these law and customs are "very different in different ages and countries."[39] In sum, there is no such thing as "natural" laws.

A 21st-century translation — applied to sports — could read as follows: We can use math and statistics to measure how much LeBron produces. These measurements can be "objective" or non-arbitrary, but how much LeBron should be paid for this production reflects the conventions of society and the NBA. We can see that society has adopted a system that allows a professional athlete to be paid millions for bouncing a ball. This same society also allows musicians and actors to be paid millions for their work, while offering considerably lower wages, for example, to teachers or police officers. In addition, we can see that the NBA has adopted rules that reduce the wages paid to LeBron. Because LeBron is getting less, we can infer that other people in the Miami Heat organization (players, coaches, front office workers, and the owner) must be getting more than they would if the market for LeBron wasn't restricted. Although we can determine from our analysis what is and why that might be the case, our analysis doesn't tell us what should be. Or as John Neville Keynes (father of John Maynard Keynes) emphasized in 1890, we need to distinguish between positive science (i.e., the study of what is) and a normative science (i.e., the study of what ought to be).[40] J. N. Keynes' distinction between the study of "what is" — or positive economics — and "what ought to be" — or normative economics — must be remembered as we examine the economics of sports. Or as Steven Levitt and Stephen Dubner put it in *Freakonomics* (2005):[41] "Morality, it could be argued, represents the way that people would like the world to work — whereas economics represents how it actually does work." (p. 13)

In this book, we will try and concern ourselves primarily with how the world of sports and economics appears to work. How it should work will hopefully become the focus of many lively discussions that ought to take place once we have completed our review of "what is" in sports economics.

[39]See the original 1848 edition of John Stuart Mill, Principles *of Political Economy*, p. 182 (https://www.gutenberg.org/ebooks/30107).

[40]John Neville Keynes, *The Scope and Method of Political Economy* (Kitchener, Ontario: Batoche Books, 1999), reprint of 4th edition from 1917, p. 22.

[41]Steven D. Levitt and Stephen J. Dubner, *Freakonomics: A Rogue Economist Explores the Hidden Side of Everything* (New York: William Morrow, 2005).

1.9 The Many Lessons "The Decision" Teaches

Much of our discussion of "what is" in sports economics relates to the economic actors (i.e., players and team) associated with "The Decision." Although this book will touch upon a variety of professional sports, it is useful to emphasize the degree to which our discussion throughout uses the building of the championship team led by LeBron James as its example.

- Did the Miami Heat pursue LeBron James to maximize team wins or maximize profits? The motives of profit maximization and win maximization will be explored in Chapter 3.

- The dominance of the Miami Heat impacts the level of competitive balance in the NBA. Chapter 4 will explore the theoretical determinants of balance in a sports league and empirically how balance is measured.

- The maximum salary that limits LeBron's salary was a result of negotiations between the NBA's player's union and the owners of NBA teams. Chapter 5 will explore the economics of such labor negotiations and how institutions like a maximum player salary came to be.

- We noted that LeBron is a very productive player on the court in the NBA. Chapter 6 will explore how performance is measured in professional sports.

- Once we understand how productive a player is on the field of play, we can then turn to a subject just touched upon: Is a player overpaid or underpaid? The value of labor and talent is the subject of Chapters 5 and 6.

- LeBron James, Dwayne Wade, and Chris Bosh are all famous African American athletes. When the NBA was established in the 1940s, it was an all-white league. In other words, African Americans were not allowed to play. Such overt racism was common in professional sports in the first half of the 20th century. The story of discrimination will be explored in Chapter 7.

- As noted, the sports media tends to be dominated by men. And this was also true of the coverage of "The Decision." James was interviewed by Jim Gray and most commentators on basketball tend to be men. In Chapter 8, we will explore gender bias in sports (a topic that goes beyond inequities in how the media covers sports).

- Chapter 9 will focus on the National Collegiate Athletic Association (NCAA). LeBron James went directly to the NBA from high school. Both Wade and Bosh spent some time playing college basketball, where each player generated substantial revenues for their respective schools. The economics behind college sports is the subject of Chapter 9.

- The Miami Heat play their home games at the American Airlines Arena. This venue was not built by the Miami Heat organization, but by the city of Miami. Why do cities spend money on stadiums and arenas? That question will be addressed in Chapter 10.

- When we looked at Wins Produced, we saw that LeBron James and Dwayne Wade have historically been very productive, while Chris Bosh has been closer to average. Despite these differences, all three are considered "stars" and all three are paid a similar wage. The disconnect between perceptions of performance and actual productivity will be the focus of Chapter 11, which examines how what we have learned from behavioral economics applies to the subject of sports.

1.10 Deductive Versus Inductive Reasoning

Before we get to the stories told in this book, it is important to emphasize how they will be told. The Marshallian cross is an example of how economists have traditionally approached the study of human behavior. The analysis begins with basic principles—in this case, the law of demand and the law of supply—and from this we deduce how the world works. This approach, called **deductive reasoning**, makes sense when an economist doesn't have much data about the world. When data exist, an alternative approach can be employed. **Inductive reasoning**[42] begins with data about the world, and with these data we employ empirical techniques to understand how the world works. Back in the 19th century—when Marshall was writing—data were scarce and computing power didn't exist. Hence, economists traditionally employed deductive reasoning. As our discussion of ticket prices indicated, as well as our discussion of Honus Wagner's baseball card and Tim Tebow's jersey, deductive reasoning can be quite illuminating. In sports,

deductive reasoning Method whereby one begins with a general principle (or set of general principles) and then derives a theory.

inductive reasoning Method whereby one determines patterns in data and then derives a theory.

[42]There has been quite a bit written about the nature of deductive and inductive reasoning. There is a temptation to think one takes either a deductive or inductive approach. But in reality, the two approaches inform each other. Before one looks at data, one should engage in some deductive reasoning (i.e., theorize, based on some basic principles, what you think you might find). And of course, stopping with deductive reasoning seems like a poor idea if data exist to test your theory.

data are abundant. Thus, we can go beyond deductive reasoning and employ actual data to learn how both sports and economics work. As we do this, we do not want to lose sight of the basic approach advocated by Marshall,[43] noted in 1885:

> [David] Ricardo and his chief followers did not make clear to others, it was not even quite clear to themselves, that what they were building up was not universal truth, but machinery of universal application in the discovery of a certain class of truths. While attributing high and transcendent universality to the central scheme of economic reasoning, I do not assign any universality to economic dogmas. It is not a body of concrete truth, but an engine for the discovery of concrete truth.

This quote should be kept in mind as we proceed. Economics is not dogma, and it is not a collection of universal truths. The tools of economics, including both deductive and inductive reasoning, simply provide us with the means to uncover how the world appears to work.

---

[43]Alfred Marshall, "The Present Position of Economics" (1885), reprinted in A. C. Pigou, ed., *Memorials of Alfred Marshall* (London: Macmillan, 1925), p. 164. Marshall's observation was also noted by Milton Friedman, "The Methodology of Positive Economics," In *Essays in Positive Economics* (Chicago: University of Chicago Press, 1966).

Key Terms

supply (p. 5)
demand (p. 5)
Marshallian cross (p. 7)
demand curve (p. 7)
substitution effect (p. 8)
income effect (p. 8)
law of demand (p. 8)
market period (p. 11)

short-run period (p. 12)
law of supply (p. 12)
quantity supplied (p. 14)
quantity demanded (p. 14)
price ceiling (p. 16)
deductive reasoning (p. 22)
inductive reasoning (p. 22)

Problems

Study Questions

1. According to Thorstein Veblen, who primarily played sports in the latter 19th century?
2. How many boys and girls play high school sports today?

**David Ricardo
(1772–1823)**

David Ricardo's *On the Principles of Political Economy and Taxation* (1817) is a classic example of deductive reasoning and the primary text on economics from the early 19th century. It is best known for advancing the theory of comparative advantage. Building on Adam Smith's *An Inquiry into the Nature and Causes of The Wealth of Nations* (1776), though, it also details the body of work we would today refer to as classical economics.

3. How does viewership of the Super Bowl (the biggest game in American football) compare to viewership of a regular-season soccer match (international football) in Spain?

4. What percentage of sports fans are women? What percentage of the sports media are women?

5. According to former President Barack Obama (and he was far from alone in making this argument), what is the relationship between player salaries and ticket prices?

6. According to Humphreys and Ruseski (2009), what is the size of the U.S. sports market?

7. According to John Maynard Keynes, what is the purpose of economic analysis (according to Alfred Marshall)? What does an economist need to engage in such an analysis? If we apply this perspective to the study of sports economics, what does an economist need to study sports?

8. What are the tongue-in-cheek steps to the Marshallian method? How can they be applied to the question that was the starting point for this chapter?

9. What are the key words in the definition of supply and demand?

10. With respect to the demand for baseball tickets, what are factors that:
    a. cause movement along the demand curve?
    b. cause the demand curve to shift?

11. What part of the demand curve changes when the curve is shifted? What part of the demand curve should not change?

12. What has determined the price of Honus Wagner's baseball card over time? Be able to illustrate this story (i.e., draw a supply and demand graph).

13. How is the market period different from the normal period in Marshall's analysis of prices?

14. Why did Nike take Reebok to court over the production of Tim Tebow jerseys in the Spring of 2012? Be able to illustrate this story.

15. According to Marshall's supply and demand model, what determines the price of tickets in the NBA? Be able to illustrate this story.

16. How does the NBA's salary cap impact quantity demand and quantity supplied of labor in the NBA's player market? What is the intent of this cap? According to the text, what is the actual impact of this cap?

17. Is there a "right" price for labor? Utilize the perspective of John Stuart Mill in answering this question.

18. What is the difference between positive and normative economics (according to John Neville Keynes)? How are "morality" and "economics" summarized by Steven Levitt and Stephen Dubner?

19. What is deductive reasoning? What is inductive reasoning?

20. According to Marshall, what is the basic approach to economics?

Math Questions

1. Define the elements of the following equation: $P = a_0 - a_1 \times Q_d$.
2. Given $P = \$150 - 0.005 \times Q_d$ as the demand for a professional sports team:
   a. If $P = \$60$, what is Q_d?
   b. If $P = \$40$, what is Q_d?
3. Imagine these two possible changes from the demand curve listed in Question 2:
   a. $P = \$175 - 0.005 \times Q_d$
   b. $P = \$125 - 0.005 \times Q_d$

   For each, identify whether Question 3(a) or 3(b) would be consistent with the following stated changes:
   i.   increase in the size of the market where the team plays
   ii. decrease in the per-capita income in the market where the team plays
   iii. move to a newer stadium
   iv. decline in the quality of players employed by the team
4. Define the elements of the following equation: $P = b_0 + b_1 \times Q_s$.

Dave Reginek/Getty Images

Market Size and Wins

Two Approaches to the Same Question

Does Market Size Dictate Outcomes in Sports?

To answer this question, Chapter 2 will explore the following:

1. **Market Size and Outcomes, a Deductive Approach:** This chapter will begin with the deductive model of profit maximization. This model will not only explain how a sports team determines profit-maximizing prices; it will also indicate that teams in larger markets are able to earn more revenue. These revenues should allow teams in larger markets to field better teams, and in sum, the deductive approach suggests that teams in larger markets should be more successful.

2. **Market Size and Outcomes, an Inductive Approach:** As we noted in Chapter 1, the deductive approach is powerful, but this doesn't tell us everything. Sports come with numbers, and it is the basic statistical analysis of those numbers that makes the field of sports economics so very interesting. We begin our study of these basics by looking at the statistical link between market size and team wins. This discussion will introduce such concepts as the *t*-statistic and *R*-squared.

3. **Explaining Wins in Sports:** Our deductive approach argues that more spending leads to more wins. To address this claim, we will consider two models: The first links payroll to team wins, and the second links what happens on the field of play to team wins. These two approaches will illustrate how well teams in North American sports are able to "buy" wins.

4. **A Simple Guide to Evaluating Statistical Models:** This chapter concludes with a simple guide to evaluating statistical models. While statistical analysis does not necessarily reveal the "truth," to understand what statistical models tell us, we need to consider such issues as a model's underlying theory, model specification, economic significance, and robustness to interpret statistical models. This list is not complete, but it provides a good starting point in discussing any statistical model we review.

Growing up in Detroit in the 1970s, I was taught two lessons by my father:

1. Our family loves the Tigers.

2. Our family hates the Yankees.

Why did my father hate the Yankees?

My father was born in 1926, and from 1926 to 2016—across 91 seasons—the New York Yankees:

- made the playoffs 49 times, or 54% of the time

- appeared in the World Series 37 times, or 41% of the time

- won the World Series 26 times, or 29% of the time

In contrast, across the same 91 seasons, the Detroit Tigers:

- made the playoffs 13 times, or 14% of the time

- appeared in the World Series 8 times, or 9% of the time

- won the World Series 4 times, or 4% of the time

One could make a similar comparison between the Yankees and any Major League Baseball (MLB) team and reach the same conclusion. It looks like the Yankees have some advantage over other baseball teams, and for fans of the other teams, this seems "unfair."

The source of the Yankees' advantage doesn't seem difficult to identify. Because the Yankees play in the largest market in North America, this team has more potential fans and therefore will likely earn more revenue than the other teams in MLB. Those greater resources allow the Yankees to succeed more often than their competitors.

To understand this argument, we need to talk about team revenue. According to Team Marketing Report, the New York Yankees had an average ticket price in 2016 of $51.55, and according to ESPN.com, the Yankees had 3,063,405 fans come through the gate at Yankee Stadium that season. Given these two numbers, the Yankees' gate revenue in 2016 was nearly $157.9 million. In contrast, the Detroit Tigers only charged $28.88 for a ticket and about 2,493,859 fans attended their games. Consequently, the Tigers' gate revenue for the season was $72 million or less than half of what the Yankees earned from the gate.[1]

2.1 From the Law of Demand to Team Revenue

Why do the Yankees do so well at the gate? The answer to this question depends on our understanding of the nature of demand and revenue. From the previous chapter, we learned that the demand curve has the following form:

$$P = a_0 - a_1 \times Q$$

Apply this equation to baseball and we see that as a team lowers ticket prices, attendance increases. This statement depends on all else being held constant, and when we compare Detroit and New York, we are not holding everything constant.

For the moment, let's ignore the obvious differences between markets and focus on the story told from our simple demand curve. We already noted that a team's revenue is found by simply multiplying price times quantity. Given this observation and our simple demand curve (which defines price in terms of quantity), a team's revenue function must be as follows:

$$\text{Revenue} = P \times Q = [a_0 - a_1 \times Q] \times Q = a_0 \times Q - a_1 \times Q^2$$

As Figure 2.1 indicates, as a team initially increases attendance, revenue for the team will increase. As the firm continues to lower prices to increase attendance, revenue will fall at a certain point.

The equation below should illustrate this process. Imagine a team faced the following demand curve:

$$P = \$75 - 0.0015 \times Q$$

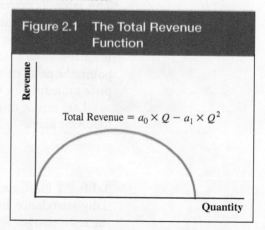

Figure 2.1   The Total Revenue Function

Total Revenue = $a_0 \times Q - a_1 \times Q^2$

Revenue

Quantity

---
[1] Data from Team Marketing Report https://www.teammarketing.com/public/uploadedPDFs/MLB-FCI-2016.pdf

From this demand curve:

- if the team charged $60, it would have 10,000 fans and gate revenue of $600,000

- if the team lowered its price to $45, attendance would rise to 20,000 and gate revenue would rise to $900,000

- if the team wanted more revenue, it could lower its price to $37.50 and see attendance increase to 25,000 and gate revenue continue to rise to $937,500

What if the team decided to keep lowering the price? As **Table 2.1** illustrates, at a price of $22.50, attendance will rise to 35,000. Gate revenue, though, will fall to $787,500.

Table 2.1 Ticket Prices, Attendance, and Revenue if the Demand Curve is $P = \$75 - 0.0015 \times Q$		
Ticket Price	Attendance	Revenue
$60.00	10,000	$600,000
$45.00	20,000	$900,000
$37.50	25,000	$937,500
$30.00	30,000	$900,000
$22.50	35,000	$787,500
$15.00	40,000	$600,000

This table illustrates a key lesson from the law of demand. Revenue depends on both price and quantity (i.e., attendance). Lower prices do lead to more attendance, but they also lead to less revenue. Initially, the attendance effect will dominate and lower prices will cause revenues for the team to increase, but at some point, the price effect overwhelms the attendance effect and further decreases in price cause revenue to actually decline.

Let's repeat this exercise, but now let's imagine the demand curve has the following form:

$$P = \$120 - 0.0015 \times Q$$

Table 2.2 illustrates what happens as this team lowers ticket prices. Again, initially attendance and revenue continue to rise with lower ticket prices. When the team charges $60 per ticket, attendance reaches 40,000 and gate revenue is $2.4 million. And again, as the team keeps lowering ticket prices—in this case, going below the $60 mark—gate revenue starts to fall.

Table 2.2 Ticket Prices, Attendance, and Revenue if the Demand Curve is $P = \$120 - 0.0015 \times Q$

Ticket Price	Attendance	Revenue
$105.00	10,000	$1,050,000
$90.00	20,000	$1,800,000
$75.00	30,000	$2,250,000
$60.00	40,000	$2,400,000
$45.00	50,000	$2,250,000
$30.00	60,000	$1,800,000

The story told by both these demand curves is the same with respect to how lower prices impact revenue, but there is an important difference. Although the proposed link between attendance and price—or the slope coefficient—is the same for both teams, one team seems to be doing much better at the gate. The first team maximizes revenue at $937,500, while the second team is able to reach $2.4 million in per game revenue.

What explains the difference? The key is the y-intercept or constant term. For the first team, a price above $60 results in only 10,000 fans showing up at the park. For the second team, price has to reach $105 for attendance to fall to 10,000. How can one team charge much higher prices? Now we have to return to factors that impact demand beyond the price for the ticket.

Again, let's talk Detroit and New York. There are three demand factors that are clearly different between these two teams:

- **Market Size:** We would expect that playing in a larger market leads to more demand. The Census Bureau tells us that the Yankees play in a market with about 18.9 million people. Meanwhile, the Tigers play in a market with only 4.3 million people.

- **Team Quality:** The Yankees—as we have noted—have a history of success, and although the Tigers have enjoyed some success, no one could believe the Tigers have been as successful across time as the Yankees.

- **Stadium Characteristics:** The Tigers play in Comerica Park, a stadium that opened in 2000 and seats 41,255 fans. Although Comerica is considered one of the more attractive parks in MLB, the new Yankee Stadium (1) opened in 2009 (so it is newer) and (2) it is much larger, with a seating capacity of 50,291.

These characteristics are not exactly independent of each other. Because the Yankees have a history of winning and playing in a larger market, it is not surprising that they would build a larger stadium.[2] Each of these factors will cause the *y*-intercept of the demand curve to be higher, and the higher the *y*-intercept (given the same slope coefficient), the more revenue a team can earn from a given level of attendance.

We can further illustrate this observation by noting the point where each hypothetical team will maximize revenue. This illustration requires that we discuss **marginal revenue**, or the amount of revenue a firm gains from an additional sale. Again, the law of demand says that a team, holding all else constant, can only sell more tickets by lowering the price. That means the amount of revenue from each sale is not a constant. This is clear if we go back to the total revenue curve described in Figure 2.1. Initially, the slope—again, this is marginal revenue—is positive. As a team increases attendance (by lowering the price), revenue continues to rise. The slope of the total revenue curve gets flatter (i.e., the slope declines). Eventually, revenue is maximized and at that point, the slope of the total revenue function is zero. Beyond that point, the slope is negative.

To illustrate, let's return to our first hypothetical demand curve:

$$P = \$75 - 0.0015Q$$

Given this demand curve, the total revenue curve will be:

$$TR = P \times Q = (\$75 - 0.0015 \times Q) \times Q = \$75Q - 0.0015Q^2$$

Applying a bit of calculus,[3] we can see that the slope of the total revenue curve then is simply:

$$MR = \$75 - 0.003Q$$

> marginal revenue The amount of revenue a firm gains from an additional sale and also the slope of the total revenue curve.

---

[2] Furthermore, this list is hardly inclusive. Other factors that may impact demand include the average income in the market (New York, relative to Detroit, has a higher average income) and the number of alternative entertainment choices consumers face (New York has more, which may depress demand for the Yankees).

[3] Marginal revenue can also be defined as the derivative of total revenue with respect to quantity. Here are some simple rules about taking a derivative.

If $TR = \$75$, then the derivative with respect to quantity would be 0 (since there is no quantity in this function).

If $TR = \$75Q$, then the derivative with respect to quantity would be 75 (since each 1-unit increase in quantity would increase revenue by \$75).

If $TR = -0.0015Q^2$, then the derivative with respect to quantity would be $(2 \times -0.0015) \times Q$ or $-0.003Q$.

This last calculation can be generalized.

If $TR = aQ^b$, then the derivative with respect to quantity would be $(b \times a) \times Q^{b-1}$.

So if $TR = 75Q - = -0.0015Q^2$, then the derivative with respect to quantity would be $MR = 75 - 0.003Q$.

Notice from the equation for marginal revenue — and from Figure 2.2 — that the demand curve and marginal revenue curve have the same y-intercept. The slope for the marginal revenue curve, though, is twice as large.

Given a linear demand curve, this will always be the case. For our second hypothetical example, the total revenue and marginal revenue equations will be as follows:

$$TR = \$120Q - 0.0015Q^2$$
$$MR = \$120 - 0.003Q$$

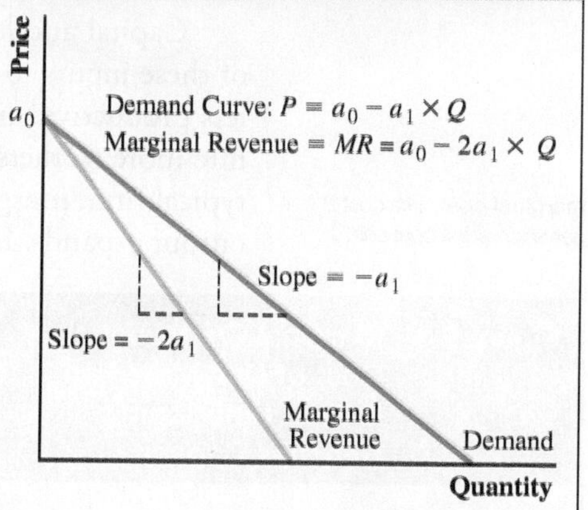

Given these two equations, where will each team maximize revenue? Again, revenue is maximized where the slope is zero, so to find the level of attendance that maximizes revenue, we set each marginal revenue equation equal to zero and solve for Q.

For Team 1,

$$\$75 - 0.003Q = 0$$
$$Q = 25,000$$

For Team 2,

$$\$120 - 0.003Q = 0$$
$$Q = 40,000$$

Figure 2.2   Demand and Marginal Revenue

Demand Curve: $P = a_0 - a_1 \times Q$
Marginal Revenue $= MR = a_0 - 2a_1 \times Q$

Slope $= -a_1$

Slope $= -2a_1$

Marginal Revenue   Demand

2.2 Debating Team Costs

Of course, revenues are only part of the story. Decision making requires that teams look at both benefits (i.e., revenues) and costs. This section will cover the debate on how one should model the cost of increasing attendance for a professional sports team, but let's start by discussing how economists think about a typical firm's costs. Just as Alfred Marshall argued that time impacts how we should think about the supply of a good, time also impacts how economists think about a firm's costs.

A firm requires land, capital (i.e., machinery), and labor to produce a good. In the long run, all these inputs can be varied by a firm, while in the short run, land and capital tend to be fixed and only labor can be varied. Because the other inputs are not changing in the short run, the productivity of additional labor will not be constant. More specifically, just as the law of demand motivated our discussion of a firm's revenue, the **law of diminishing returns** motivates our

law of diminishing returns As a firm hires more workers, holding all else constant, the amount of output from each additional worker a firm adds will eventually decline.

discussion of a firm's cost since it *simply states that as a firm hires more workers, holding all else constant, the amount of output from each additional worker a firm adds will eventually decline.*

Capital and land are fixed in the short run, so additional workers have less of these inputs to work with. Consequently, we expect additional workers to be less productive, and that means that a firm's cost per unit will rise as it seeks to hire more workers and expand output in the short run. This all means that for a typical firm, **marginal cost**, or the cost per each additional unit,[4] will increase as output expands. In other words, marginal cost is upward-sloping.

marginal cost The cost per each additional unit.

On the other hand, the short run in sports may be a different story. With respect to sports, output is attendance. Imagine a team is not at capacity. What is the cost of admitting one more fan? One could argue—as Ferguson *et al.* (1991)[5] did—that this cost is essentially zero,[6] since it doesn't cost a team anything to have one more fan sit in the stands. And that means marginal cost might look like what we see in Figure 2.3.

Notice that once marginal cost reaches capacity, it essentially becomes infinite. That is not entirely accurate, although the cost of expanding attendance beyond capacity in the short run is certainly quite large (since a team cannot simply expand the capacity of a stadium in a single day!). This representation suggests that the law of diminishing returns doesn't apply to a sports team when looking to expand attendance. However, it has also been argued that the cost of adding an additional fan in the short run isn't exactly zero.[7] For example, as attendance expands, a team will have to hire additional staff to manage and serve the larger crowds. Given this possibility, marginal cost for a team may appear as illustrated in Figure 2.4, which is similar to what we would typically see in non-sports industries.

Regardless of the exact shape of the marginal cost curve, the story of how a team would choose the ticket price to maximize team profits is the same. To find this price, a team must consider benefits and costs. Benefits, in this case, are the

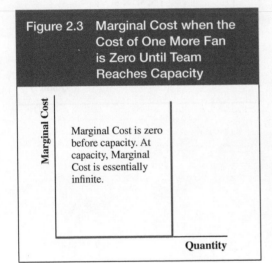

Figure 2.3   Marginal Cost when the Cost of One More Fan is Zero Until Team Reaches Capacity

Marginal Cost is zero before capacity. At capacity, Marginal Cost is essentially infinite.

Marginal Cost

Quantity

---

[4]One should note the similarity between the definitions of marginal revenue and the definitions of marginal cost. Marginal cost is also the slope of the total cost function.

[5]D. G. Ferguson, K. Stewart, J. C. H. Jones, and A. Le Dressay, "The Pricing of Sports Events: Do Teams Maximize Profits?," *Journal of Industrial Economic* 39, no. 3 (March 1991): 297–310.

[6]This argument also appears in Michael Leeds and Peter Von Allmen, *The Economics of Sports*, 4th ed. (Reading, MA: Addison-Wesley, 2010).

[7]This argument is presented by Rodney Fort in *Sports Economics*, 3rd ed. (Upper Saddle River, NJ: Prentice Hall, 2010).

team's marginal revenue and the costs are the team's marginal cost. There are three possibilities for a team:

- Marginal revenue could exceed marginal cost; or the amount of revenue earned from the last ticket sold exceeds the cost of that ticket.

- Marginal revenue could be less than marginal cost; or the amount of revenue earned from the last ticket sold is less than the cost of the ticket.

- Marginal revenue could equal marginal cost; or the amount of revenue earned from the last ticket sold is equal to the cost of the ticket.

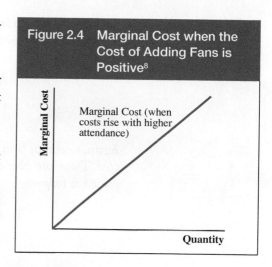

Figure 2.4   Marginal Cost when the Cost of Adding Fans is Positive[8]

In which scenario is a team maximizing profits?

Well, it can't be the first scenario. In such a scenario, the team could increase profits by selling more tickets. By simply lowering price, thereby increasing attendance, the team would see profits go higher because the revenue of these ticket sales would be greater than the cost. Consequently, if the first scenario were true, the team could not be profit-maximizing. In the second scenario, each ticket sale costs the team more than the revenue the sale earns. That means the firm could increase profits by raising ticket prices, which causes attendance to decline. Once again, because the team can change ticket prices and see profits rise, it cannot be profit-maximizing if this scenario holds. Therefore, by the process of elimination, it must be the case that the team maximizes profit, as Figure 2.5 illustrates, where marginal revenue equals marginal cost. In this instance, raising or lowering price will cause profits to fall.

Figure 2.5 illustrates the case where the marginal cost rises with increases in quantity. Again, profit is maximized where marginal revenue equals marginal cost. The firm takes this quantity—and the demand curve—to determine the profit-maximizing price.

We can also look at the former case, where marginal costs are zero until a team

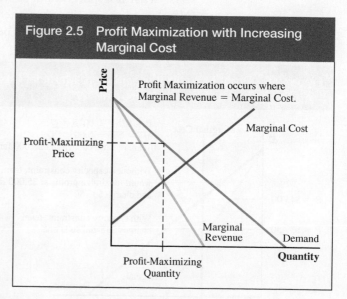

Figure 2.5   Profit Maximization with Increasing Marginal Cost

---

[8]At capacity, the marginal cost curve will become vertical.

reaches capacity, but let's first tell that same story with simple equations. Imagine a team facing the following equations for price, marginal revenue, and marginal cost:

$$P = \$75 - 0.0015Q$$
$$MR = \$75 - 0.003Q$$
$$MC = \$0$$

Again, a team or firm maximizes profits where marginal revenue equals marginal cost. Therefore, this team's profit-maximizing price and profit would be determined as follows:

$$\text{Profit-Maximizing Output: } MR = MC$$
$$\$75 - 0.003Q = \$0$$
$$Q = 25,000$$

If attendance is 25,000, the price must be:

$$P = 75 - 0.0015 \times (25,000) = \$37.50$$

This is the same outcome we saw earlier when we were looking at the level of attendance that maximized revenue. But what if the team doesn't have 25,000 seats? What if a sports team, as we see in the National Basketball Association (NBA), reaches capacity when attendance is 20,000? If that is the case, then the profit-maximizing solution would be, as Figure 2.6 illustrates, for the firm to set its price at $45 with attendance of 20,000.

We can see this is the best the team can do by considering a few prices greater than $45.00. As Table 2.3 indicates, prices higher than $45 would lead to less team revenue. Consequently, the team is worse off charging prices that do not result in a team selling out.

Such analysis explains an interesting puzzle in professional sports. MLB teams often fail to sell out, while teams in the NBA frequently play in front of capacity crowds. One might wonder then, why don't baseball teams simply lower their prices to sell those extra tickets? And if NBA teams are playing at capacity, why not charge even higher ticket prices?

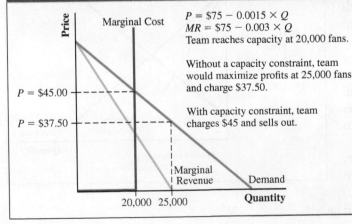

Figure 2.6   Profit Maximization with Zero Marginal Cost and a Capacity Constraint

Marginal Cost

$P = \$75 - 0.0015 \times Q$
$MR = \$75 - 0.003 \times Q$
Team reaches capacity at 20,000 fans.

Without a capacity constraint, team would maximize profits at 25,000 fans and charge $37.50.

With capacity constraint, team charges $45 and sells out.

P = $45.00

P = $37.50

Marginal Revenue

Demand

20,000 25,000

Price

Quantity

Table 2.3 Ticket Prices, Attendance, and Revenue if the Demand Curve is $P = \$75 - 0.0015 \times Q$ and the Team Reaches Capacity at 20,000 Fans

Ticket Price	Attendance	Revenue
$67.50	5,000	$337,500
$63.75	7,500	$478,125
$60.00	10,000	$600,000
$56.25	12,500	$703,125
$52.50	15,000	$787,500
$48.75	17,500	$853,125
$45.00	20,000	$900,000

The analysis of **Table 2.3** indicates that both teams in baseball and basketball may be profit-maximizing.[9] At least, it may be the case that baseball teams maximize their profits by setting a price that results in attendance short of the stadium's capacity, while NBA teams may maximize their profits by setting a price that results in persistent sellouts.

2.3 Why Do the Yankees Dominate?

Let's return to the subject of why fans of the Yankees tend to be happier than fans of the Tigers. Although we have looked at some numbers, what we have so far is a simple deductive model. This model of revenue and costs makes it clear why the Yankees have an advantage over the Tigers. The story is as follows:

- Because the Yankees play in a bigger market, the team's demand curve—relative to the Tigers—is further to the right.

- This means the Yankees are able to maximize profits at a point where they charge higher prices for their tickets and earn more revenues (again, relative to the Tigers).

- Higher levels of revenue allow the Yankees to spend more money on their players.

- A higher payroll means the Yankees are able to acquire better players.

- And, better players mean the Yankees win more often than the Tigers.

---

[9]Notice we are using the words "may be profit-maximizing." The question of whether or not teams actually try to maximize profits will be explored in the next chapter.

Again, this model is entirely deductive, and all of this follows our simple theories of demand and cost. We began the discussion with the laws of demand, supply, and diminishing returns; then considered some specifics with regard to professional team sports; and arrived at a story that explains why the New York Yankees dominate baseball (and the Detroit Tigers do not). Outside of sports — where data are relatively scarce — our story might end at this point. But sports come with numbers. Our next step is to thus approach this same question inductively.

2.4 Market Size and Wins: The Data from MLB

Early economists generally did not spend much time collecting or analyzing data, so deductive reasoning was the only game in town. By the 20th century, data collection — leading to inductive reasoning — became possible. Also known as data analysis, inductive reasoning can change how we see the world.

To illustrate, let's consider what we have learned so far via deductive reasoning. We have shown that teams in larger markets will win more games in professional sports, which all seems perfectly clear. Many people certainly believe that teams in New York have a clear advantage over teams in smaller markets, but what do we learn when we use inductive reasoning?

Table 2.4 reports the average winning percentage of each MLB team from 1998 to 2016.[10] It also reports the market size where each team plays. As one can see, the New York Yankees continue to dominate MLB. The Yankees won close to 59% of their regular season games across these 19 seasons, and they made the playoffs 15 times. The dominance of the Yankees is certainly consistent with what our deductive model has indicated. The team in the largest market should be able to purchase the best talent; therefore, it ought to be the most successful.

On the other hand, the Mets play in the same market but have ranked 12th in average winning percentage, and have made the playoffs only five times since 1998. Meanwhile, the St. Louis Cardinals — in the 22nd biggest market — have the 2nd highest average winning percentage. The Cardinals have also made 12 trips to the post-season since 1998.

Notice that the data seem to offer conflicting stories, but all we have done so far is tell a few anecdotes. Anecdotes are no substitute for systematic

---

[10]MLB added a franchise in Tampa Bay in 1998, thus creating a 30-team league. From 1998 to 2016, it continued to include 30 teams.

Team	Rank (winning percentage)	Winning Percentage	Rank (market size)	Market Size[a] (in millions)
New York Yankees	1	0.586	1	18.897
St. Louis Cardinals	2	0.555	22	2.813
Boston Red Sox	3	0.550	14	4.552
Atlanta Braves	4	0.548	12	5.269
Los Angeles Angels of Anaheim	5	0.534	3	12.829
Los Angeles Dodgers	6	0.533	3	12.829
San Francisco Giants	7	0.532	15	4.335
Oakland Athletics	8	0.527	15	4.335
Texas Rangers	9	0.513	7	6.372
Cleveland Indians	10	0.511	28	2.077
Philadelphia Phillies	11	0.508	8	5.965
New York Mets	12	0.507	1	18.897
Toronto Blue Jays	13	0.505	10	5.583
Chicago White Sox	14	0.505	5	9.461
Seattle Mariners	15	0.492	19	3.440
Chicago Cubs	16	0.491	5	9.461
Houston Astros	17	0.490	9	5.947
Arizona Diamondbacks	18	0.488	18	4.193
Minnesota Twins	19	0.486	20	3.280
Cincinnati Reds	20	0.483	27	2.130
San Diego Padres	21	0.478	21	3.095
Detroit Tigers	22	0.478	17	4.296
Montreal Expos/Washington Nationals[b]	23	0.472	13	4.703
Milwaukee Brewers	24	0.469	30	1.556
Florida Marlins	25	0.468	11	5.565
Baltimore Orioles	26	0.466	24	2.710
Tampa Bay Rays	27	0.462	23	2.783
Colorado Rockies	28	0.462	25	2.543
Pittsburgh Pirates	29	0.453	26	2.356
Kansas City Royals	30	0.445	29	2.035
Averages		**0.500**		**5.810**

Table 2.4 Average Winning Percentage and Market Size in Major League Baseball: 1998–2016

[a]Market size is taken from the U.S. Census and represents the number of people in the Metropolitan Statistical Area (http://www.census.gov/popest/data/metro/totals/2011/index.html). It is important to note that MSA is larger than the population in the actual confines of each city. For the Canadian teams—Montreal and Toronto—data are taken from Statistics Canada, which reports the size of the Census Metro Area.

[b]The Montreal Expos moved to Washington, DC (and became the Nationals) after the 2004 season. Market size for this franchise is the average of the population in Montreal and Washington, DC.

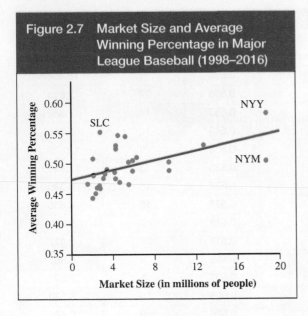

Figure 2.7   Market Size and Average Winning Percentage in Major League Baseball (1998–2016)

analysis, so our analysis begins with the scatterplot in Figure 2.7. On the *y*-axis, we see average winning percentage; on the *x*-axis, we see market size. There appears to be a relationship between these two factors.

Again, the Yankees (NYY) have the highest average winning percentage and play in the largest market. Of course, the Mets (NYM) play in the same market and are fairly close to average, meanwhile the Cardinals (SLC) are more successful in one of the smallest markets. Despite what we observe for the Cardinals and Mets, it appears, on average, that market size and average winning percentage have a positive relationship. In other words — as Figure 2.7's trend line indicates — as market size increases, the average winning percentage increases.

2.5 Modeling Market Size and Wins in Professional Sports

The equation for the trend line in Figure 2.7 is as follows:

$$\text{Average Winning Percentage} = 0.477 + 0.004 \times \text{Market Size} + e_t$$

This is an example of a simple regression line, and it is important that you understand each element of **regression analysis**.

In terms of our above model, this single equation argues that changes in average winning percentage (the **dependent variable**) are explained by differences in market size (the **independent variable**). The *y*-intercept in this equation, also known as the constant term, is 0.477. This could be thought of as a team's expected winning percentage if the market size was zero (keep in mind that no team could play in a market that did not have any people). The constant term is always the value we would expect for the dependent variable if all the independent variables (and in the text we will primarily consider models with multiple independent variables) were zero. This is almost always outside the realm of what we observe in the data; therefore, although a constant term typically needs to be included in the estimation of a regression line,[11] one shouldn't place too much emphasis on the estimated value of the constant term.

regression analysis A statistical technique that uses a single equation to attempt to "explain" movements in the dependent variable as a function of movements in the independent (or explanatory) variables.

dependent variable What we wish to explain with a regression model, or the *Y*-variable.

independent variable What we believe explains the dependent variable, or the *X*-variable.

---

[11]The constant term is included in any model to enforce the assumption that the error term (e_t) has a zero mean. Consequently, the constant term should be part of a model. But again it shouldn't generally be used in analysis.

We will emphasize the second number in this equation (0.004), called the slope coefficient. It indicates that if a team moves to a market with 10 million more people, the average winning percentage will increase by 4%.[12] Given a 162-game season, that means 10 million more people in a market is worth about 6.5 more wins. Another way to think about this slope coefficient is to compare Milwaukee—the smallest market in baseball—to New York. If the Brewers could move from Milwaukee (a market with 1.6 million persons) to New York (a market with 18.9 million persons), the Brewers can expect to win 11.1 more games. Of course, this is just an estimate since our regression line is not a perfect estimate of reality. In fact, most observations are not even on our line. In other words, there is clearly some error associated with our model.

The last term in our regression line (e_i) is called the error term. It represents the difference between what our model predicts and what we actually observe in the data. These differences exist because our simple model, which argues that market size is the sole determinant of average winning percentage, is not per-fectly consistent with reality. Other factors not included in our simple model also impact average winning percentage.

That being said, how well does market size explain outcomes? The answer to that question begins with the slope coefficient. Our slope coefficient certainly seems to indicate market size impacts wins, but before we reach that conclusion, we need to ask a very important question: Can we actually argue that the esti-mated slope coefficient is different from zero?

Why is this question important? Consider what it would mean if the slope coefficient was zero. In such a case, no relationship would exist between mar-ket size and winning percentage. Changes in market size would not lead to any expected change in winning percentage.

So how do we know if the coefficient is different from zero? Typically, research-ers report the t-statistic and/or the p-values. For the question we are asking—"Is the estimated coefficient statistically different from zero?"—the t-statistic—is simply the ratio of the estimated coefficient to the standard error of the coefficient. The general rule-of-thumb we follow is that the t-statistic should be, in absolute terms, greater than 2; in other words, the estimated coefficient should be at least twice the value of the standard error of the coefficient. If this is the case, we are confident—at about the 95% level[13]—that the estimated coefficient is not zero.

Again, all of this is just a rule-of-thumb. To be a bit more precise, we can also look at the p-value. The p-value for a t-statistic, as Studenmund notes, is

---

[12]Market size is measured in millions of people. The coefficient on market size is 0.004. So if market size increases by 10 million (or 10), winning percentage is predicted to increase by 0.04 or 4%.

[13]As noted in the appendix to this chapter, our rule-of-thumb is, as are all rules-of-thumb, an approximation.

"the probability of observing a *t*-stat this big or bigger (in absolute values) if the null hypothesis were true" (2006, p. 128).

For example, say your *t*-statistic has an absolute value of 2, which indicates that we are about 95% confident the estimated coefficient is not zero. In this instance, the *p*-value would be about 0.05. In other words, we are about 5% sure the true value of the estimated coefficient is not equal to zero.

What if the *p*-value is 0.01? Then we are 99% confident the true value of the estimated coefficient is not zero. What about a *p*-value of 0.25? Then our confidence level is only 75%. In general, researchers prefer *p*-values of 0.10 or smaller. In other words, researchers tend not to put much faith in results when we are not at least 90% confident the true value of the coefficient is not different from zero. And for many, the preferred confidence level must be at least 95% (hence our rule that the *t*-statistic should be greater than 2). It is immensely important that we emphasize the wording here: Although we are looking for the "truth," statistical analysis only provides estimates, so we should not present our estimations as if these are the "truth" or as if we have "proven" something. Estimates are simply estimates, and they are neither the truth nor proof. Because we wish to emphasize that regression results are estimates, and that *t*-statistics and *p*-values are important, we choose not to present them as a simple equation. The preferred presentation will be a table,[14] such as what appears in **Table 2.5**.

Table 2.5 Market Size and Average Winning Percentage in Major League Baseball: 1998–2016

Variable	Coefficient	*t*-Statistic	*p*-Value
Market size	0.004	3.33	0.002

The *t*-statistic for market size is 3.33 and the *p*-value of 0.002. So in this case, we have a *t*-statistic that is greater than 2 (in absolute value) and we are 99.8% sure the true value of the estimated coefficient is not zero. So that suggests we found something. But we must remember, what remains is just an estimate of the "truth."

So in baseball, it appears market size and outcomes are statistically related. What do we see when we look at other major North American sports? The National Football League (NFL) added its 32nd team (the Houston Texans) with the 2002 season. If we look at the NFL from 2002 to 2016, we see the relationship between market size and average winning percentage in **Table 2.6**.

---

[14]Regression results will be presented in two ways. Within the body of the text, only the variable being discussed—and the corresponding *t*-statistic—will be presented. In the appendix of each chapter, more information, such as results for the constant term, results for all other independent variables, *R*-squared, estimation techniques, etc., will be offered. To understand the stories told in this book, one only needs to understand the basic ideas of statistical significance (and later, economic significance). But for those who are interested, more statistical details will be offered.

Table 2.6 Market Size and Average Winning Percentage in the National Football League: 2002–16			
Variable	Coefficient	*t*-Statistic	*p*-Value
Market size	−0.0007	−0.17	0.865

The estimated slope coefficient is −0.0007, which says that teams in smaller markets should expect to have a higher winning percentage than those in a bigger market. Is that the "truth"? The *t*-statistic and *p*-value suggest this is not likely true. From the *p*-value, our confidence in our result is only about 13%, or well below the 90% or 95% threshold we prefer. And that means we conclude there is no statistical relationship between market size and average winning percentage in the NFL.[15]

It is important to remember that once we establish a result is not statistically significant, we should not engage in further discussion of the estimated coefficient. In other words, we should not talk about what a coefficient means once we establish that the coefficient is not statistically significant. All we should say is that the insignificance of the slope coefficient reported in Table 2.6 indicates market size in the NFL is not related to average winning percentage.

What do we see when we look at the NBA and National Hockey League (NHL)?[17] From **Tables 2.7** and **2.8**, we learn that baseball appears to be an

Table 2.7 Market Size and Average Winning Percentage in the National Basketball Association: 2004–05 to 2015–16			
Variable	Coefficient	*t*-Statistic	*p*-Value
Market size	−0.0021	−0.67	0.51

Table 2.8 Market Size and Average Points Percentage[16] in the National Hockey League: 2005–06 to 2012–13			
Variable	Coefficient	*t*-Statistic	*p*-Value
Market size	0.0007	0.46	0.65

---

[15]This means the "true value" of our coefficient could be positive, negative, or zero. And this means we do not know the direction of the relationship from this model.

[16]The NHL uses a point system, as opposed to winning percentage, to measure outcomes. Teams receive 2 points for a win and 1 point for an overtime loss. Given this system, points percentage is simply a team's standing points divided by a team's potential points (games played times 2). Average points percentage is calculated by summing the team's standing points from 2005–06 to 2011–12 and dividing by potential points.

[17]The NBA has had 30 teams since the 2004–05 season. The NHL model begins with the 2005–06 season. Due to a labor dispute (discussed in Chapter 5), the NHL did not play in 2004–05.

exception in North America. The estimated coefficient for market size in the NBA and NHL—judging from the *t*-statistics and *p*-values—are both statistically insignificant. So our models indicate that market size and average winning percentage are not related in the NFL, NBA, or NHL.

2.6 Modeling Payroll and Wins in Professional Sports

Evidence from the data appears to contradict the story we told when just relying on deductive reasoning, but perhaps this is not surprising. As we will see, a professional sports team's revenue is not simply about market size. Furthermore, because sports owners are not all equally wealthy, a rich owner in a smaller market may be able to outspend a relatively poor owner in a larger market. Consequently, we should not be surprised that wins are not about market size alone. What of the link between team spending and wins? Although market size may not be the sole determinant of team spending, does team spending dictate outcomes in professional sports? That's what deductive reasoning would seem to indicate. Now let's see what the data say.

The model we will employ has as its dependent variable a team's winning percentage in a given season. Because average payroll increases over time,[18] our independent variable will be a team's relative payroll, or a team's payroll in a season divided by the average payroll in the league that year:

$$\text{Winning Percentage} = b_0 + b_1 \times \text{Relative Payroll} + e_t$$

Team payroll data for MLB go back to 1988. From 1988 to 2016, we have 840 individual team observations. And across all these data, the results are reported in **Table 2.9**.

Table 2.9 Relative Payroll and Winning Percentage[19] in Major League Baseball: 1988–2013			
Variable	Coefficient	*t*-Statistic	*p*-Value
Relative payroll	0.0758	12.71	0.000
R-squared	0.16		

These results indicate that relative payroll has a statistically significant impact on winning percentage. In addition to this information, Table 2.9 also reports

---

[18]As noted, this is primarily because consumer demand has increased over time in professional sports.
[19]Data on payroll in Major League Baseball come from USAToday.com.

the *R*-squared (R^2)[20] of the model, or the percentage of the variation in winning percentage that the model explains. We see that relative payroll only explains 16% of the variation in winning percentage. Before we get to the implications of such a result, let's see what we find when we look at football, basketball, and hockey. See **Tables 2.10**, **2.11**, and **2.12**.

R-squared (R^2) The coefficient of determination, or the percentage of variation in the dependent variable (i.e. winning percentage) that is explained by all the independent variables (i.e. relative payroll).

Table 2.10 Relative Payroll and Winning Percentage in the National Football League: 2000–15[21]

Variable	Coefficient	*t*-Statistic	*p*-Value
Relative payroll	0.2701	3.84	0.000
R-squared	0.028		

Table 2.11 Relative Payroll and Winning Percentage in the National Basketball Association: 1990–91 to 2015–16[22]

Variable	Coefficient	*t*-Statistic	*p*-Value
Relative payroll	0.2631	9.72	0.0000
R-squared	0.111		

Table 2.12 Relative Payroll and Points Percentage in the National Hockey League: 2005–06 to 2015–16[23]

Variable	Coefficient	*t*-Statistic	*p*-Value
Relative payroll	0.1847	11.35	0.000
R-squared	0.223		

With respect to each sports league, relative payroll is statistically significant. What we see with respect to R^2 appears to depend on the league we are examining. For the NFL and NBA, relative payroll, relative to what we see in baseball,

[20]R^2 is explained in more detail in the appendix to this chapter.

[21]For 2000 to 2009, NFL payroll data derive from the *USA Today* website. For 2010, data were found at http://profootballtalk.nbcsports.com/2010/09/19/team-by-team-salary-cap-numbers-if-there-were-a-salary-cap/. For 2011 to 2013, data may be located at the following websites: http://www.osmguy.com/2011/12/2011-nfl-payrolls-by-team/, http://www.osmguy.com/2012/09/2012-nfl-salaries-by-team/, http://www.osmguy.com/2013/09/2013-nfl-payrolls-total-cap-spend-by-team/.
Data for 2014 and 2105 can be found at http://www.spotrac.com/nfl/cash/.

[22]Data on payroll in the NBA were taken from the website of Patricia Bender (http://www.eskimo.com/~pbender/).

[23]Data on NHL payroll derive from the *USA Today* website. It did not report payroll data for 2012–13.

explains less of the variation in winning percentage. In hockey, the amount explained is relatively higher.[24]

In general, we do observe the expected relationship. More spending does seem to lead to more wins, but much of the variation in wins is not explained by team spending.[25]

2.7 A Basic Model of Wins in Professional Sports

To put the wins/payroll results in perspective, let's take a different look at the link between talent and outcomes in professional sports. Our theory suggests that payroll should be a proxy for the level of talent on a team, but because this is sports, we also have a different measure of talent: the statistics tabulated for the players and the teams. The outcomes we observe in sports are solely the result of the actions the players and teams take on the field of play, so statistics, which tabulate those actions, also measure the ability of players and teams to impact outcomes. In other words, the numbers we see in sports should tell us something about talent. We will examine this idea in more detail in Chapter 6 and in the appendix at the back of the book. For now, let's look at a very simple model of wins in professional basketball:

$$\text{Winning Percentage} = c_0 + c_1 \times \text{Points Scored per Game} + e_t$$

The estimation of this model for the NBA yields the results reported in Table 2.13. From these results, we learn:

- If a team scored 1 more point per game, its winning percentage would increase by 0.011. Given an 82-game season, this means that a team which scored 1 more point per game would win 0.89 more games.

- Points scored per game explains 14% of the variation in winning percentage. This is a bit better than payroll, but still means that 86% of wins are not explained by our very simple model.

Table 2.13 Points Scored and Wins in the National Basketball Association: 1990–91 to 2015–16[26]			
Variable	Coefficient	t-Statistic	p-Value
Points scored	0.011	11.20	0.000
R-squared	0.14		

---

[24]Why there are differences across sports in this relationship is a topic to be discussed in future chapters.

[25]The lack of correlation between spending and wins will be explored in future chapters.

[26]Data on wins and team statistics for the NBA can be found at http://www.basketball-reference.com/.

Until now, all we have considered are models with one independent variable; such models are called **univariate models**. These tend to:

- help students see the very basics of regression analysis

- not help us understand much about the world

This latter observation is due to the fact that most things are explained by more than one factor. Consider wins in basketball: In Game 1 of the 1998 NBA Finals, the Utah Jazz scored 88 points. In Game 2 of the same series, the Jazz also scored 88 points. Which game, if any, did the Jazz win?

It would be easier to answer this question if you had one more piece of information. How much did Utah's opponent score in each game? As it turns out, the Chicago Bulls scored 85 points in Game 1 and 93 points in Game 2 (on their way to winning the series in six games). As this simple example illustrates, we can understand much more about winning if we know both points scored and points allowed. Consequently, a better model of wins would be the following:

$$\text{Winning Percentage} = d_0 + d_1 \times \text{Points Scored per Game} + d_2 \times \text{Points Allowed per Game} + e_t$$

Because this model has more than one independent variable, it is referred to as a **multivariate model**. When we estimate this model, we get the data listed in **Table 2.14**.

Table 2.14 Wins, Points Scored, and Points Allowed in the National Basketball Association: 1990–91 to 2015–16			
Variable	Coefficient	t-Statistic	p-Value
Points scored	0.0324	100.10	0.000
Points allowed	−0.0326	−103.97	0.000
R-squared	0.944		

When we consider both points scored and points allowed, we are able to explain 94% of the variation in winning percentage. Clearly, this model explains more of the variation in winning percentage than what we were able to explain when simply examining payroll or points scored per game.

We might wonder why the model reported in Table 2.14 doesn't explain 100% of the variation in winning percentage. It is important to remember that the model considers points scored and points allowed per game across an entire season. Except for games decided by just 1 point, every contest has points scored (or points allowed) that don't impact the outcome of the game. Across an 82-game season, all these excess points will tend to even out, but this process is not perfect in the NBA.

Beyond the issue of R^2, there is something else you should see from this simple model. The estimated impact of an additional point scored per game has changed. Our univariate model said one more point scored per game would result in less than one win across an entire season. Our multivariate model tells us that one more point scored per game, holding points allowed per game constant (and this is a key point), would result in winning percentage increasing by 0.033. Given an 82-game season, that means one more point scored per game, holding points allowed constant, would lead to about 2.7 more wins.

These two models demonstrate the importance of specifying your model. The simple univariate model looked like it was telling us something: Points scored per game in the univariate model were statistically significant. Because the univariate model didn't control for the impact of points allowed per game—and points allowed per game clearly impact the winning percentage—we obtained a very different result with respect to the impact additional scoring had on outcomes in basketball. It is important to note that our estimated coefficients reveal the relationship between the independent and dependent variable, holding the other independent variables constant. But if you don't include an independent variable in your model, then obviously there is no way for the model to take this missing independent variable into account. Consequently, your estimated coefficients can be very different.

Hopefully this simple exercise has illustrated that some effort must be made to include other "important" factors in your model. This is not the only issue we have to consider in formulating a model. Before we get to some of these other issues, let's look at another major North American sport via our simple model.

Table 2.15 reports the link between points scored per game, points allowed per game, and winning percentage in the NFL. These measures explain more of the variation in winning percentage than what was explained with market size or team payroll.

Table 2.15 Wins, Points Scored per Game, and Points Allowed per Game in the National Football League: 2002–15[27]			
Variable	Coefficient	t-Statistic	p-Value
Points scored per game	0.0017	36.05	0.000
Points allowed per game	−0.0018	−32.05	0.000
R-squared	0.85		

[27]Data on wins and team statistics for the NFL can be found at http://www.pro-football-reference.com/.

The R^2 for this model is only 85%, or less than what we observed in our study of the NBA. The difference between these two leagues can be understood by noting that the NFL's regular season is only 16 games, so the "evening out" process noted above has far less time to occur. Furthermore, blowouts are more common in the NFL. In other words, the margin of victory can be—relative to the NBA—quite large.

To illustrate, the Charlotte Bobcats of the NBA managed to only win 10.6% of their games in 2011–12. This was the worst performance by a team in NBA history. If we look at the game-by-game scores, the Bobcats scored at least 37.8% of the total points scored in every game played that season. In contrast, the New York Giants won the Super Bowl in 2012. During the entire 2011 regular season—when the team won 9 games and lost 7—it was actually outscored by 6 points, and when considering the season game-by-game, we see that the Giants played in four games where they actually failed to score 37.8% of the total points scored. In other words, of the Super Bowl champion's seven losses, four were bigger blowouts than any game played by the worst team in NBA history.

Baseball teams play a regular season almost twice as long as that in the NBA, so we might expect to see the "evening out process" work better in that sport. Nevertheless, baseball experiences the same problem we observed in football. The St. Louis Cardinals had a regular season record of 90-72 prior to winning the World Series in 2011. In 44 of these 72 losses, the Cardinals failed to score at least 37.8% of the total runs scored in the game, so the Cardinals were frequently defeated by margins bigger than anything we saw for the Bobcats in 2011–12.

Consequently, we should not be surprised by the findings in **Table 2.16**, which indicate that runs scored and runs allowed per game only explain 87% of the variation in team wins. Again, our explanatory power with player performance exceeds what we saw with market size or relative payroll.

Table 2.16 Wins, Runs Scored, and Runs Allowed in Major League Baseball: 1988–2016[28]			
Variable	Coefficient	*t*-Statistic	*p*-Value
Runs scored per game	0.0991	58.43	0.000
Runs allowed per game	−0.1015	−62.40	0.000
R-squared	0.87		

This is the same story we observed in the NHL, where the Los Angeles Kings won the Stanley Cup in 2012. In the regular season, this team only won 40 of

[28]Data on wins and team statistics for MLB can be found at http://www.baseball-reference.com/.

42 regular-season games, and in 30 of its games, the team lost and failed to score 37.8% of the total goals scored in the contest. With respect to the NFL, MLB, and relative to what we see in the NBA, blowouts are more common in hockey. Goals scored and goals surrendered, detailed in **Tables 2.17**, only explain 89% of the variation in standing points percentage.

Table 2.17 Points Percentage, Goals Scored, and Goals Allowed in the National Hockey League: 2005–06 to 2011–12[29]			
Variable	Coefficient	t-Statistic	p-Value
Goals scored per game	0.1687	33.23	0.000
Goals allowed per game	−0.1789	−38.27	0.000
R-squared	0.89		

Again, a model based on player performance trumps what we see from market size or relative payroll. That suggests a problem may exist in our deductive model. We argued that teams with higher payrolls would purchase better talent, yet this process seems imperfect. Payroll simply doesn't explain much about wins—at least not relative to a model based solely on the actions players take on the field.

There are a number of reasons for this discrepancy. The labor market in each of these sports leagues has several features (amateur drafts, reserve clauses, payroll caps, salary caps, etc.) that allow wages to deviate from what we would see in a free market. Furthermore, the link between player actions and outcomes does not always appear to be perfectly well understood by decision makers.

2.8 A Simple Guide to Evaluating Empirical Models

Much of this will be discussed in subsequent chapters as we review additional statistical (i.e., inductive) models, but beforehand we need to discuss a few issues to be considered in evaluating statistical models. It's important to note that beyond the first issue addressed, there is no specific order of importance to these guidelines. Rather, they are a collection of issues to keep in mind when reviewing a study.[30]

---

[29]Data on wins and team statistics for the NHL can be found at http://www.hockey-reference.com/.

[30]One should also note that this exercise merely serves as an introduction to the topic of model evaluation. For more information, one needs to take a class—or ideally, more than one class—in econometrics.

The Theoretical Foundation of the Model

We have already noted deduction and induction. One might conclude from this discussion that the latter is independent of theory, but that is not so.

Statistical analysis that is divorced from theory can produce some very odd results. Tyler Vigen created a program designed to find correlations between random data sets. As *Popular Science* detailed,[31] Vigen found there was 95% correlation between the consumption of mozzarella cheese and the number of civil engineering doctorates awarded. Vigen also noted that there is a 0.87 correlation between the age of Miss America and the number of people murdered by steam, hot vapors, and hot objects. Vigen's work illustrates that correlation does not imply causation, and this has to be remembered when looking at a regression model. A regression simply examines the link between a dependent variable (what you are trying to explain) and a collection of independent variables (what you think does the explaining). In choosing the independent variables, it is important to have some sort of theoretical construct.

Why is theory so important? Again, it's important to remember that statistical analysis can tell us about correlations. Causation is inferred from theory, so if you have no theory, it's not clear what your model reveals. And without a theory, it's not clear what other researchers and/or decision makers would ultimately do with your results. In essence (with very few exceptions), if you haven't got a theory, you haven't got a very useful model.[32] Thus, having a sound theory is important, but once it is certain a model has a clear theoretical foundation, there are a number of other issues to consider.

Specifying the Model

We have already noted the importance of specifying a model correctly. When we omit independent variables from a model, we can easily be led to incorrect conclusions regarding the direction, magnitude, and/or statistical significance of a specific independent variable. To illustrate, let's return to Table 2.13, which reports the link between points scored in basketball and winning percentage. The estimated coefficient for points in this regression is 0.011, and given the

[31]Colin Lecher, "Algorithm Reveals Link Between Sour Cream and Traffic Accidents: Visualizing the Unexpected Correlations That Surround Us," May 12, 2014, http://www.popsci.com/article/science/algorithm-reveals-link-between-sour-cream-and-traffic-accidents.

[32]A good example of this from sports is the plus–minus approach to player productivity utilized in both basketball and hockey. This approach looks at how a team performs with and without a player in the game. But this approach lacks any theoretical foundation. The results we see from this approach could come about because of the actions the player takes, or what other players happen to do when that player is in or out of the game. Since one cannot untangle the underlying causes, the results from plus–minus cannot tell us the actual impact of an individual player.

standard error of this coefficient, we are 95% confident that the "true" value of this coefficient falls between 0.009 and 0.013.

When we turn to Table 2.14, though, we see a different story. Looking at the link between points scored and wins in a model that also includes points surrendered, the estimated coefficient on points scored is 0.0324. This result is far outside the confidence interval we estimated when the model only included points scored.

It is important to emphasize what this simple exercise demonstrates: If you specify a model poorly, an estimated coefficient—even one that is statistically significant—can be quite "incorrect." That suggests a researcher should make every effort to specify a model as well as he or she can.[33] This also might suggest that one should include as many independent variables as one can find. Unfortunately, doing so is not that easy. Independent variables need to be independent of each other. If this is not the case, then you encounter the problem of **multi-collinearity**, or the problem of two or more independent variables having a linear relationship.

For example, imagine we were trying to explain a baseball team's attendance record (as covered in later chapters). One factor we would consider, as noted in Chapter 1, is the quality of the team by measuring a team's winning percentage. We could also consider how many runs a team scored and how many runs a team surrendered. If we decided to include all three factors, though, the model would have trouble distinguishing the separate effects. This is because winning percentage, as we have seen, is a function of runs scored and runs surrendered. Therefore, a model of team attendance could include winning percentage or runs scored and runs surrendered, but it shouldn't include all three of these variables.[34]

One can avoid issues of omitted variable bias and multi-collinearity by paying proper attention to theoretical foundations. Of course, different researchers can have different ideas about which independent variables are theoretically important. Hence, we should remember that regression analysis, as noted, does not necessarily establish the "truth." It can, though, help us see where the preponderance of the evidence might be located.

Statistical Significance and Economic Significance

After we understand the theory being tested, assuming the model was estimated properly with correct functional form, independent variables are independent,

> **multi-collinearity** The problem of two or more independent variables having a linear relationship.

---

[33]One should add that if the independent variables are completely independent of the missing variables, then the estimated coefficient should center on the "true" value even if the model is misspecified.

[34]If our model has multi-collinearity, we can expect the standard errors for the estimated coefficients to be higher and we are therefore more likely to conclude that a statistical relationship doesn't exist.

there are no other significant econometric issues,[35] and the like; we tend to look at the statistical significance of the estimated coefficients next. Again, statistical significance examines whether or not the estimated coefficients for the independent variables are different from zero. If they are, then the researcher might have found something.

Statistical significance, though, isn't everything. We also want to know the economic significance of the results. What this means is that we want to know how much each coefficient matters, and how much something matters is often a judgment call. Two researchers looking at the same model might reach different conclusions about how much something matters. Nevertheless, some effort should be made to discuss the magnitude, or economic significance, of a model's results.

Explanatory Power

Non-economists and students tend to get most excited about explanatory power or R-squared, but this excitement can be misplaced. If one is comparing two models that seek to explain the same thing, one might consider explanatory power in deciding which model is preferred. However, as emphasized in most econometric textbooks, just because one model can explain more does not mean it's the preferred model. A model with higher explanatory power, but with no theory behind it and/or serious econometric problems, is not a very good model.

In this text, we will review models where R-squared is over 90%, and we will review models where R-squared is less than 10%. Again, explanatory power tells us something, but it doesn't reveal everything.[36]

Robustness of Results

If we estimated the model differently, would we get substantially different results? When we pose this question, we are asking if the results are "robust."

Many issues we look at in this text have been considered by a number of researchers utilizing different data sets and different statistical techniques.

---

[35]The list of "other" econometric issues includes words like "heteroskedasticity" and "serial correlation." And the list goes well beyond these two terms. The purpose of the discussion here is to allow the reader to understand the regression results presented in the text. For those interested in actually using regression analysis to answer questions, a class in econometrics is highly recommended (more than one is probably preferable).

[36]Researchers might also consider whether or not the model has forecasting power, or can explain events beyond the sample considered to estimate the model. If a model doesn't have this characteristic (i.e., it can't explain something outside of the sample), then the value of the model might be limited. That being said, a model that appears to have predictive power but has no theoretical underpinnings is also limited in its usefulness.

If many of these researchers report the same result, then we can have confidence that something has been uncovered. In contrast, if multiple studies report conflicting results, then it is more difficult to reach firm conclusions. The issue of "robustness" must be kept in mind when reviewing a single study. Although the results may be statistically significant, we often wonder if a change to the study will offer a different result. This issue gets back to what we said earlier—we are not uncovering "the truth" in our analysis, we are simply trying to see in which direction the evidence might be pointing.

Prior Beliefs?

The last issue we wish to address is prior beliefs. Often, a person will look at the outcome of statistical analysis and see that it does not confirm what the individual believed, and when that happens, the results of the model are frequently dismissed.

Unfortunately, this is not the best way to look at research. A model isn't "good" because it told us what we already believed, and a model isn't necessarily "bad" because what we believed wasn't confirmed. The purpose of statistical analysis is to allow us to see more than we currently do. If prior beliefs are the yardstick used to measure what we see with the model, then the entire process is rather pointless. We might as well just vote on our prior beliefs and let the winning idea in this election determine where the evidence is pointing.

This issue is especially important in the study of sports and economics. Students often come to this class with an extensive background in sports. Unfortunately, much of what the student has learned about sports before this class is not confirmed by the empirical evidence we will review. If one cannot suspend prior beliefs, then the amount one will learn in this class will be limited. Before moving on, let us emphasize that the above list is not a score sheet. It is not everything researchers might consider, but it should help students understand the various empirical models we will review in the text.

Key Terms

marginal revenue (p. 32)

law of diminishing returns (p. 33)

marginal cost (p. 34)

regression analysis (p. 40)

dependent variable (p. 40)

independent variable (p. 40)

R-squared (R^2) (p. 45)

univariate model (p. 47)

multivariate model (p. 47)

multi-collinearity (p. 52)

total sum of squares (TSS) (p. 59)

explained sum of squares (ESS) (p. 59)

residual sum of squares (RSS) (p. 59)

Problems

Study Questions (Deductive)

1. For any given price, how would the following changes impact a team's revenue?
   a. Increase in the size of the market
   b. Building a new stadium
   c. Decline in the quality of the team's roster
2. For a typical firm, what is the shape of the marginal cost curve? Why does it have this shape?
3. For a sports team, what might the shape of the marginal cost curve be? Why does it have this shape?
4. What is the profit-maximizing rule?

Study Questions (Inductive)

5. Given Wins $= a_0 + a_1 \times$ Population $+ e_i$ what is the regression term that describes each element in this equation?
   a. Wins
   b. a_0
   c. a_1
   d. Population
   e. e_i
6. What is a "constant term?" Why is this term included in a regression equation and what information does it convey?
7. We have a rule-of-thumb that a t-statistic should be, in absolute value, greater than 2. Explain the reasoning behind this rule.
8. How do we calculate R-squared? What does this tell us?
9. What is the relationship between market size and win in North American pro sports? Answer this question using both deductive and inductive analysis.
10. Use the following econometric model and results to answer this question:

Dependent Variable: Team Winning Percentage from the WNBA (1997–2013)

   a. Interpret each slope coefficient.
   b. For which variables are we at least 95% certain that the coefficient is different than zero?
   c. Explain the reasoning behind your answer.
   d. For which variables are we not at least 95% certain that the coefficient is different than zero? Explain the reasoning behind your answer.
   e. Calculate the R^2 and interpret your answer.

Independent Variables	Coefficient	Standard Error	t-Statistic
Points per game	0.0315	0.0010	
Points surrendered per game	−0.0311	0.0011	
Constant	0.4712	0.0553	
Observations: 220			
Total sum of squares	5.56520		
Residual sum of squares	0.95645		

11. What is the relationship between payroll and wins in MLB, the NFL, NBA, and NHL? Is the deductive study consistent with the inductive study? Why or why not?
12. When we estimate the model in question 10 for the NBA, we see a higher explanatory power than what we do for MLB, the NHL, and NFL. Why is explanatory power higher for the NBA? Why are we unable to explain 100% of the variation in winning percentage with points scored and points surrendered per game?
13. What factors should we consider in evaluating a regression? Should we make sure the regression conforms to prior beliefs?
14. What is the difference between statistical significance and economic significance?

Thought Questions

1. Why do NFL, NBA, and NHL teams tend to sell out while MLB teams do not?
2. According to deductive reasoning, how successful should the New York Mets be on the field relative to the Detroit Tigers? From 1962 to 2016, the Mets won 48.1% of their regular season games while the Tigers won 49.9% of their contests. Do these records match your deductive reasoning? Why or why not?
3. Consider the following regression for the WNBA:

$$\text{Wins} = b_0 + b_1 \times \text{Points per Game} + e_i$$

Dependent Variable: Team Winning Percentage from the WNBA (1997–2013)

    a. What is the 95% and 99% confidence interval around (b_1)?
    b. Is (b_1) statistically significant?
    c. According to the results below, what is the chance that (b_1) could equal 0.0315?
    d. What lesson do we learn when we compare the results below to the results from Question 12 above?

Independent Variables	Coefficient	Standard Error	t-Statistic
Points per game	0.00954	0.00154	
Constant	−0.1892	0.1120	
Observations: 220			
Total sum of squares	5.5652		
Residual sum of squares	4.7360		

Math Questions

1. If $P = a_0 - a_1 \times Q$, what is the equation for total revenue?
2. If $P = \$150 - 0.005 \times Q$, what is the equation for total revenue?
3. Complete the following table:

Ticket Prices, Attendance, and Revenue if the Demand Curve is $P = \$50 - 0.005 \times Q$		
$10.00		
$15.00		
$20.00		
$25.00		
$30.00		
$35.00		
$40.00		
$45.00		

4. If $P = \$50 - 0.005 \times Q$,
   a. what is the equation for marginal revenue?
   b. how many tickets will the team sell when it maximizes revenue?
   c. what will the price be when the team maximizes revenue?
   d. how much revenue will the team earn when it maximizes revenue?
5. Given the demand curve in Math Question 4, if marginal cost for a sports team is zero,
   a. how many tickets will the team sell when it maximizes profit?
   b. what will the price be when the team maximizes profit?
   c. how much revenue will the team earn when it maximizes profit?
6. How would your answers to Math Questions 5(a), 5(b), and 5(c) change if the team's capacity was 5,000 seats less than your answer to Math Question 5(a)?

Appendix A
Very Basic Regression Analysis

The study of sports economics often requires the review of regression analysis. In the text, we noted some elements of this analysis. In this appendix, we provide a few more details.

We begin with the first regression noted in Chapter 2: The relationship between average winning percentage and market size. In the text, we emphasized whether or not there was a statistically significant relationship between these two variables (i.e., the t-statistic). In Table 2A.1, we note more aspects of this regression.

Table 2A.1 Market Size and Average Winning Percentage in Major League Baseball: 1998–2016				
Variable	Coefficient	Standard Error	t-Statistic	p-Value
Constant	0.4769	0.0087	54.58	0.000
Market size	0.0040	0.0012	3.33	0.002
R-squared	0.28			
Total sum of squares	0.0337			
Explained sum of squares	0.0096			
Residual sum of squares	0.0241			
Observations	**30**			

Remember, we already know that our simple model doesn't explain everything. R-squared is reported to tell us how much of the variation in the dependent variable (in this case, average winning percentage) is explained by our model. R-squared (or R^2) is a percentage, so it will fall between 0% or 0.00 (i.e., our model explains none of the variation in the dependent variable) and 100% or 1.00 (i.e., our model explains everything).[37]

In this case, our model explains 28% of the variation in average winning percentage. To arrive at this result, we needed to know three items (also reported in the table above)[38]:

---

[37]Both extremes are a problem. If our model explains nothing, that isn't very helpful. If our model explains everything, though, then we have just estimated an identity. And again, we don't need regression analysis for identities.

[38]Again, it is important to translate math into words. When we say

$$TSS = \sum (Y_i - \text{Mean of } Y)^2$$

we are indicating that to calculate TSS, we need to subtract the mean of the dependent variable from each observation of the dependent variable. We then square this value for each

- **Total sum of squares (TSS):** This is how much variation in the dependent variable there is to explain, or $\sum(Y_i - \text{Mean of } Y)^2$.

- **Explained sum of squares (ESS):** This is how much variation in the dependent variable the model explained, or $\sum(\hat{Y} - \text{Mean of } Y)^2$.

- **Residual sum of squares (RSS):** This is how much variation in the dependent variable the model did not explain, or $\sum e^2$.

Given these definitions, it should be clear that the following is true:

$$TSS = ESS + RSS$$

In simple words, how much variation the model explained (i.e., ESS) and how much variation the model did not explain (i.e., RSS) must equal the amount of variation there was to explain.

Given these definitions, R^2, or the percentage of the variation in the dependent variable (i.e., TSS) that we are explaining, is simply calculated as follows:

$$R^2 = \frac{ESS}{TSS}$$

One can also calculate this measure with RSS:

$$R^2 = 1 - \frac{RSS}{TSS}$$

It is tempting for students to conclude that the higher the R^2, the better. But that is not necessarily true. And as we go along, this point is going to be emphasized again and again.

total sum of squares (TSS) How much variation in the dependent variable there is to explain, or $\sum(Y_i - \text{Mean of } Y)^2$.

explained sum of squares (ESS) How much variation in the dependent variable the model explained, or $\sum(\hat{Y} - \text{Mean of } Y)^2$.

residual sum of squares (RSS) How much variation in the dependent variable the model did not explain, or $\sum e^2$.

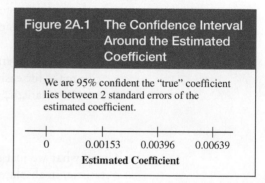

Figure 2A.1   The Confidence Interval Around the Estimated Coefficient

We are 95% confident the "true" coefficient lies between 2 standard errors of the estimated coefficient.

| 0 | 0.00153 | 0.00396 | 0.00639 |

Estimated Coefficient

---

observation, and then sum across all observations. After we have done this, we have measured the amount of variation in the dependent variable.

When we say

$$\sum(\hat{Y} - \text{Mean of } Y)^2$$

we are indicating that to calculate ESS, we need to subtract the mean of the dependent variable from the value of the dependent variable our model predicts. Again, we square this value for each observation and sum across all observations. After we have done this, we have measured the amount of variation in the dependent variable our model has explained.

When we say

$$\sum e^2$$

we are indicating that to calculate RSS, we need to square the error for each observation. The error is simply the difference between the actual value of the dependent variable and the value of the dependent variable our model predicts. After we square the error term, we again sum across all observations. And after we have taken that step, we have measured the amount of variation in the dependent variable our model has not explained.

Beyond R^2, we should also note more details about the t-statistic. Let's go back to our rule-of-thumb. As we noted, we are 95% confident that the true value of the coefficient is within 2 standard errors of the estimated slope coefficient.[39] To illustrate, the standard error of the estimated slope coefficient is 0.00119. That means we are 95% confident that the true value of this slope coefficient, as illustrated below, is between 0.00153 (2 standard errors below 0.00396) and 0.00639 (2 standard errors above 0.00396). So, what have we learned from our confidence interval?

We are 95% confident that the "true coefficient" is not a negative number and it is not zero. How do we know this? The confidence interval, 0.00153 to 0.00639 (as noted in Figure 2A.1), does not include zero or negative numbers.

This is important because by eliminating values of the opposite sign from our coefficient, we have established evidence that we have captured the direction of the relationship (in this case, larger markets lead to more wins). Since zero is not in our confidence interval, we have evidence that a statistical relationship exists. In general, we are 95% confident that we have a relationship (i.e., the "true" value of the coefficient is not zero) when our estimated slope coefficient is at least twice the size of the standard error.

To make life easier for us, statistical packages will report for each slope coefficient the t-statistic, which is calculated as follows:

$$t\text{-Statistic} = \frac{\text{Slope Coefficient}}{\text{Standard Error}}$$

Given what we just said about the slope coefficient and standard error, if the t-statistic, in absolute terms, is greater than 2, then we are about 95% confident that the true value of the slope coefficient is not zero.[40] That means we believe we have found something.

For the purpose of this text, understanding statistical significance (t-statistics and p-values), R-squared, and economic significance (which we review in the next chapter) should be sufficient to understand the empirical results discussed.

And for those who want more information, the appendices to each chapter will provide more information on the estimation of the models reviewed. For the models discussed in Chapter 2, the models were each simple linear models. So there isn't much more to add beyond the estimation results for each model.

---

[39]This statement is not perfectly precise. The 95% confidence interval is actually 1.96 standard errors in each direction (not 2 standard errors).

[40]Again, this statement is not perfectly precise. The 95% confidence interval is actually 1.96 standard errors in each direction (not 2 standard errors). So, the value of 2 is only a rule-of-thumb.

Tables 2A.2 through 2A.13 are full regression results that are summarized in Chapter 2. They are included here for reference.

Table 2A.2 Market Size and Average Winning Percentage in the National Football League: 2002–15

Variable	Coefficient	Standard Error	t-Statistic	p-Value
Constant	0.5032	0.0265	18.95	0.000
Market size	−0.0007	0.0043	−0.17	0.865
R-squared	0.001			
Observations	**32**			

Table 2A.3 Market Size and Average Winning Percentage in the National Basketball Association: 2004–05 to 2015–16

Variable	Coefficient	Standard Error	t-Statistic	p-Value
Constant	0.5112	0.0225	22.75	0.00
Market size	−0.0021	0.0032	−0.67	0.51
R-squared	0.02			
Observations	**30**			

Table 2A.4 Market Size and Average Points Percentage in the National Hockey League: 2005–06 to 2015–16

Variable	Coefficient	Standard Error	t-Statistic	p-Value
Constant	0.5548	0.0121	45.98	0.00
Market size	0.0007	0.0016	0.46	0.65
R-squared	0.007			
Observations	**30**			

Table 2A.5 Relative Payroll and Winning Percentage in Major League Baseball: 1988–2016[41]

Variable	Coefficient	Standard Error	t-Statistic	p-Value
Constant term	0.4241	0.0064	66.78	0.00
Relative payroll	0.0758	0.0060	12.71	0.00
R-squared	0.16			
Observations	**840**			

---

[41]Data on payroll in Major League Baseball come from USAToday.com.

Table 2A.6 Relative Payroll and Winning Percentage in the National Football League: 2000–15[42]

Variable	Coefficient	Standard Error	t-Statistic	p-Value
Constant term	0.2298	0.0708	3.25	0.00
Relative payroll	0.2701	0.0703	3.84	0.00
R-squared	0.028			
Observations	**510**			

Table 2A.7 Relative Payroll and Winning Percentage in the National Basketball Association: 1990–91 to 2015–16[43]

Variable	Coefficient	Standard Error	t-Statistic	p-Value
Constant term	0.2369	0.0276	8.5838	0.0000
Relative payroll	0.2631	0.0271	9.7182	0.0000
R-squared	0.1113			
Observations	**756**			

Table 2A.8 Relative Payroll and Points Percentage in the National Hockey League: 2005–06 to 2015–16[44]

Variable	Coefficient	Standard Error	t-Statistic	p-Value
Constant term	0.3657	0.0167	21.91	0.000
Relative payroll	0.1847	0.0163	11.35	0.000
R-squared	0.22			
Observations	**450**			

[42]For 2000 to 2009, NFL payroll data come from the *USA Today* website. For 2010, data were found at http://profootballtalk.nbcsports.com/2010/09/19/team-by-team-salary-capnumbers-if-there-were-a-salary-cap/. For 2011 to 2013, data may be located at the following websites:

http://www.osmguy.com/2011/12/2011-nfl-payrolls-by-team/, http://www.osmguy.com/2012/09/2012-nfl-salaries-by-team/, http://www.osmguy.com/2013/09/2013-nfl-payrolls-total-cap-spend-by-team/.

[43]Data on payroll in the NBA were taken from the website of Patricia Bender (http://www.eskimo.com/~pbender/).

[44]Data on NHL payroll were found at the *USA Today* website. It did not report payroll data for 2012–13.

Table 2A.9 Points Scored and Wins in the National Basketball Association: 1990–91 to 2015–16

Variable	Coefficient	Standard Error	t-Statistic	p-Value
Constant term	−0.578	0.0964	−6.00	0.000
Points scored	0.011	0.0010	11.20	0.000
R-squared	0.14			
Observations	**756**			

Table 2A.10 Wins, Points Scored, and Points Allowed in the National Basketball Association: 1990–91 to 2015–16

Variable	Coefficient	Standard Error	t-Statistic	p-Value
Constant term	0.522	0.0268	19.49	0.000
Points scored	0.032	0.0003	100.19	0.000
Points allowed	−0.033	0.0003	−103.97	0.000
R-squared	0.94			
Observations	**756**			

Table 2A.11 Wins, Points Scored per Game, and Points Allowed per Game in the National Football League: 2002–2015

Variable	Coefficient	Standard Error	t-Statistic	p-Value
Constant term	0.5339	0.0279	19.15	0.000
Points scored per game	0.0017	0.0000	36.05	0.000
Points allowed per game	−0.0018	0.0001	−32.05	0.000
R-squared	0.85			
Observations	**510**			

Table 2A.12 Wins, Runs Scored, and Runs Allowed in Major League Baseball: 1988–2016

Variable	Coefficient	Standard Error	t-Statistic	p-Value
Constant term	0.5105	0.0087	58.56	0.000
Runs scored per game	0.0991	0.0017	58.43	0.000
Runs allowed per game	−0.1015	0.0016	−63.40	0.000
R-squared	0.87			
Observations	**840**			

Table 2A.13 Points Percentage, Goals Scored, and Goals Allowed in the National Hockey League: 2005–06 to 2015–16				
Variable	Coefficient	Standard Error	t-Statistic	p-Value
Constant term	0.5877	0.0202	29.07	0.00
Goals scored per game	0.1687	0.0051	33.23	0.00
Goals allowed per game	−0.1789	0.0047	−38.27	0.00
R-squared	0.89			
Observations	330			

For the Money or the Glory?

Do Teams Profit-Maximize?

To answer this question, Chapter 3 will explore the following:

1. **Classic Model of Human Behavior:** We begin with how economists have typically described human beings. This description suggests that human beings seek to maximize utility and are capable of determining what actions achieve that end.

2. **Revenue and Profits in Sports:** Economists have traditionally posited that firms seek to maximize profits. To see if this is true in sports, we first discuss the data on revenue and profits. Those data reveal that professional sports in the United States and United Kingdom look quite different when we focus on profits.

3. **The Monopoly Model:** Sports in the United States (and North America) are built on the monopoly model, which can be traced back to 19th-century baseball. The story of how sports developed more than 100 years ago will reveal why professional sports in North America are unique.

4. **Promotion and Relegation:** If we look beyond North America, leagues are typically built around the institution of "promotion and relegation." Under this

institution, sports around the world are quite a bit more competitive than those in North America.

5. **Elasticity: Theory and Empirical Evidence:** To address the subject of profit maximization, researchers often turn to the concept of "elasticity." The final sections of this chapter introduce it and provide empirical estimates of price elasticity uncovered from sports studies.

Why do people buy professional sports franchises? We need to first ask how they make choices. Historically, economists have assumed that decision making by human beings has the following characteristics:

utility The level of satisfaction or happiness a person is able to achieve.

- Individuals seek to maximize **utility**. Utility can be thought of as the level of satisfaction or happiness a person is able to achieve.[1]

- The pursuit of utility is subject to constraints. Two common constraints are time and money. In simple words, people seek to make themselves as happy as possible given the circumstances of their life.

- Uncertainty exists, but human beings are able to maximize expected utility by assigning probabilities to different possible outcomes.

marginal benefits The value derived from the decision being made.

marginal cost The charge associated with the decision being made.

To maximize utility, people must consider **marginal benefits** (or the value derived from the decision being made) and **marginal costs** (or the charges associated with the decision being made); this process is described in Appendix A to this chapter. Here, we will emphasize that a person increases consumption of a good up until the point where the marginal benefit of the last unit consumed just equals the marginal cost of this unit. Obviously, before someone can know these are equal, that person would have to be able to estimate both marginal benefits and marginal costs.

opportunity cost The value of the next best alternative cast aside in making a decision.

Marginal costs also are not the only costs to be considered. Decision makers must also consider **opportunity costs**, or the value of the next best alternative cast aside in making a decision. To make the best decisions, the opportunity costs of all alternatives must be assessed and considered.

sunk costs Charges that are not impacted by the decision at hand.

For example, to know if you are maximizing utility by going to a baseball game tonight, you would need to know the benefits of attending the game, the costs associated with doing so, and also the value of how else you might spend your evening. And we are not quite done. Decision makers also have to ignore sunk costs. **Sunk costs** are charges that are not impacted by the decision at

[1]Typically, it is defined in terms of consumption of goods and services. The concept can be thought of more broadly as the satisfaction one derives from the outcome of any decision a person makes. In other words, winning a game enhances a person's utility (unless he or she was rooting for the opponent, and then it reduces utility).

hand. Because sunk costs cannot be changed by a decision, these costs should be considered irrelevant.

Say you purchased tickets for tonight's game last week and the price of those tickets cannot be refunded. Whether you go to the game or stay home instead, you are not getting that money back. In this instance, the price of the tickets is a sunk cost and that price should be ignored in deciding whether to attend the game. Now should you go to the game? You need to consider the benefits of going to the game, the costs you will incur by doing so (time spent at the game, parking, travel-related inconveniences, etc.), and what other ways you might spend your evening. Because it has already been purchased, the price of the ticket is no longer relevant to your decision.[2] At least, that is the story told by traditional economics.

Economists have traditionally argued that people behave in the fashion just described. In making decisions, human beings supposedly consider marginal costs and opportunity costs while ignoring sunk costs. And economists go even farther. Traditionally economists assume human beings are "rational." What does it mean to be "rational"? Berri et al.'s *The Wages of Wins* summarized the rationality assumption[3]:

> If people are rational they might start with a view of the world that is incorrect, but as new information becomes available, people change their perspective. If people do not change their ways, then they will lose to other people who adopt the new information. So either people change, or they lose. Whether people change their ways or simply lose out to those that do, the survivors in the game must know what they are doing. (p. 213)

Economists assume people know what they are doing, and such is not a recent assumption. More than a hundred years ago, Thorstein Veblen summarized how economists view human behavior.[4] In reading this quote, remember that Veblen is being sarcastic. In other words, like North, Veblen does not believe human beings are really rational.

---

[2]Beyond all these issues, economists also assume that human beings are consistent. For example, if you say you prefer the NFL to the NBA and also the NBA to the NHL, then we can infer that you must prefer the NFL to the NHL. In other words, economists assume preferences are transitive (which simply means that if you prefer A over B and B over C, then you must prefer A over C). In addition, economists also assume that people prefer more choices to fewer choices, and such choices can be ranked by a decision maker. Behavioral economists, note that people do not always prefer more choices.

[3] This summary is taken from p. 213 of *The Wages of Wins* [David J. Berri, Martin B. Schmidt, and Stacey L. Brook, *The Wages of Wins* (Stanford, CA: Stanford University Press, 2006).] As *The Wages of Wins* notes, this discussion of rationality is merely a re-writing of the original words of Douglass North, "Economic Performance Through Time," *American Economic Review* 84, no. 3 (1994): 360.

[4]Thorstein Veblen, "Why Is Economics Not an Evolutionary Science," *The Quarterly Journal of Economics* 12 (1898): 373–397.

> The hedonistic conception of man is that of a *lightning calculator of pleasures and pains* who oscillates like a *homogeneous globule of desire of happiness* under the impulse of stimuli that shift him about the area, but leave him intact. (italics added to the original; p. 389)

The idea that human beings are both "lightning calculators of pleasures and pains" and "homogenous globules of desire" suggests that the economic model of human beings is not entirely realistic (or even flattering). The idea that people have the "right model" does not — as we will discuss in detail later in the text — always stand up to scrutiny. Nevertheless, one must remember that economists employ models to describe reality, and for models to work, models must simplify reality.

At times, these simplifications do not change the basic story told. When these simplifications make a difference . . . well, then we have a different story to tell.

3.1 Revenues and Profits in Major Professional Team Sports Leagues

For now, we are going to think of people behaving in a fashion described by classic economics. Individuals are presumed to make decisions so that each individual's happiness will be maximized. What happens when we apply this approach to firms? We need to contemplate what makes a firm "happy." For economists, happiness for a firm is all about profits. And standard economic theory says that people who own a business are primarily motivated by the desire to maximize profits, but do owners purchase teams to maximize profits?

Owners often tell a different story. When Tom Gores purchased the Detroit Pistons in 2011, he described his purchase as follows: "This is a community asset. If all I do is make a few bucks and the community isn't happy, that's not good. The beauty of this is that the fans are the customers. If you buy a company, you have to make the customers happy . . ."[5]

Such a statement is not unique to Gores. Owners frequently argue that winning is their primary motivation. Of course, as Gores notes, winning is related to demand, so maybe these objectives aren't entirely different.

To help shed more light on this issue, let's examine some recent data on revenue and operating income for the four major North American sports. Before looking at the numbers, we should note that for the most part, professional

---

[5]http://www.forbes.com/sites/stevenbertoni/2011/09/21/tom-gores-on-buying-the-detroit-pistons/#176a573d67dc.

sports teams in North America are privately held firms. Consequently, these organizations are not required to release information on revenues, costs, and profits. The numbers we have come from Forbes.com. The writers at Forbes estimate revenues and costs from the information that is available. This information includes data on attendance, ticket prices, player salaries, and broadcasting agreements. Although there is a wealth of data on these issues, we should emphasize that the numbers reported below do not come directly from the teams, so these can be thought of as estimates of each team's revenue and operating income.

With this qualification in mind, let's begin with the National Football League (NFL). As enumerated in Table 3.1, Forbes.com reports that NFL teams earned $12.2 billion in revenue in 2015 and recorded an operating income of $2.9 billion. Furthermore, no team had an estimated operating income that wasn't positive. It appears that the NFL is, in general, a profitable business.

Table 3.1 Revenue and Operating Income for the National Football League[6]		
NFL Team, 2015	Total Revenue (in millions)	Operating Income (in millions)
Dallas Cowboys	$700	$300
New England Patriots	$523	$212
Washington Redskins	$447	$115
San Francisco 49ers	$446	$154
New York Giants	$444	$133
New York Jets	$423	$102
Houston Texans	$416	$129
Philadelphia Eagles	$407	$105
Green Bay Packers	$391	$101
Denver Broncos	$387	$82
Chicago Bears	$385	$104
Baltimore Ravens	$378	$103
Seattle Seahawks	$377	$67
Pittsburgh Steelers	$376	$68
Carolina Panthers	$362	$53
Miami Dolphins	$359	$58

(continued)

[6]Data from http://www.forbes.com/nfl-valuations/list/.

Table 3.1 *(continued)*		
NFL Team, 2015	Total Revenue (in millions)	Operating Income (in millions)
New Orleans Saints	$358	$77
Arizona Cardinals	$348	$95
Cleveland Browns	$347	$53
San Diego Chargers	$344	$59
Jacksonville Jaguars	$344	$92
Tennessee Titans	$342	$73
Tampa Bay Buccaneers	$341	$75
Kansas City Chiefs	$340	$62
Indianapolis Colts	$336	$68
Atlanta Falcons	$336	$69
Cincinnati Bengals	$329	$60
Buffalo Bills	$326	$26
Detroit Lions	$321	$64
Los Angeles Rams	$317	$67
Minnesota Vikings	$306	$51
Oakland Raiders	$301	$46
TOTALS	**$12,157**	**$2,923**

A similar story can be told about Major League Baseball (MBL). Only three teams have an operating income in the negative range. Baseball revenues — at $9 billion — are not quite as high as those reported for the NFL. Nevertheless, baseball in 2015, like the NFL, appears to be profitable. See Table 3.2.

Turning to the National Basketball Association (NBA), we again see evidence of widespread positive operating incomes (Table 3.3). Forbes.com only reports a negative operating income for three teams in 2015–16. We should note that these numbers stand in stark contrast to comments made by NBA Commissioner Adam Silver in June 2015.[7] As Silver stated:

> I don't know the precise number and don't want to get into it, but a significant number of teams are continuing to lose money and they continue to lose money because their expenses [payroll, arena and practice facility costs, and sales and marketing infrastructure] exceed their revenue. . . .

[7]Scott Davis, "NBA Commissioner Adam Silver Says a 'Significant Number' of Teams Are Losing Money," *Business Insider*, July 15, 2015, http://www.businessinsider.com/adam-silver-nba-teams-losing-money-2015-7.

Table 3.2 Revenue and Operating Income for the Major League Baseball[8]		
MLB Team, 2016	Total Revenue (in millions)	Operating Income (in millions)
New York Yankees	$526	$39
Los Angeles Dodgers	$462	−$21
Boston Red Sox	$434	$79
Chicago Cubs	$434	$84
San Francisco Giants	$428	$78
Los Angeles Angels of Anaheim	$350	$68
New York Mets	$332	$32
Philadelphia Phillies	$325	$88
St Louis Cardinals	$310	$41
Washington Nationals	$304	$38
Houston Astros	$299	$76
Texas Rangers	$298	$19
Seattle Mariners	$289	$12
Toronto Blue Jays	$278	$23
Atlanta Braves	$275	$15
Detroit Tigers	$275	−$36
Cleveland Indians	$271	$47
Chicago White Sox	$269	$42
Pittsburgh Pirates	$265	$51
San Diego Padres	$259	$23
Arizona Diamondbacks	$253	$47
Baltimore Orioles	$253	−$2
Minnesota Twins	$249	$30
Colorado Rockies	$248	$27
Kansas City Royals	$246	−$1
Milwaukee Brewers	$239	$58
Cincinnati Reds	$229	$16
Oakland Athletics	$216	$26
Miami Marlins	$206	−$2
Tampa Bay Rays	$205	$32
TOTALS	**$9,027**	**$1,025**

[8]Data from http://www.forbes.com/nba-valuations/list/.

Table 3.3 Revenue and Operating Income for the National Basketball Association[9]		
NBA Team 2015–16	Total Revenue (in millions)	Operating Income (in millions)
New York Knicks	$376	$141
Los Angeles Lakers	$333	$119
Golden State Warriors	$305	$74
Houston Rockets	$244	$63
Cleveland Cavaliers	$233	−$40
Chicago Bulls	$232	$46
Brooklyn Nets	$223	$16
Miami Heat	$210	$21
Boston Celtics	$200	$60
Dallas Mavericks	$194	$40
Toronto Raptors	$193	$46
Oklahoma City Thunder	$187	−$8
San Antonio Spurs	$187	$18
Los Angeles Clippers	$185	−$12
Portland Trail Blazers	$178	$41
Phoenix Suns	$173	$26
Detroit Pistons	$172	$22
Atlanta Hawks	$169	$20
Orlando Magic	$166	$45
Sacramento Kings	$164	$18
Utah Jazz	$164	$36
Charlotte Bobcats	$158	$9
Denver Nuggets	$157	$21
Indiana Pacers	$157	$24
New Orleans Pelicans	$156	$17
Memphis Grizzlies	$155	$0
Washington Wizards	$155	$7
Minnesota Timberwolves	$154	$26
Milwaukee Bucks	$146	$24
Philadelphia 76ers	$140	$18
TOTALS	**$5,866**	**$938**

[9]Data from http://www.forbes.com/nba-valuations/list/.

Silver and other NBA owners have a clear incentive to make an argument that contradicts the numbers reported by Forbes.com. Later in the text, we will detail owners' involvement in labor disputes with players and the owners' pursuit of public subsidies to build stadiums and arenas. In both areas, a report of significant profits makes it more difficult for the owners to argue that players and the public should make concessions to keep these teams in operation.

Again, we will discuss all of this in later chapters. For now, let's review the data for the fourth major North American sports league: revenue and operating income for the National Hockey League (NHL) in 2015–16 (Table 3.4). Overall, Forbes also shows this league to be profitable. However, seven teams appear to have an operating loss and the overall level of revenue and profits falls short of what we observed for the NFL, MLB, and NBA.

Table 3.4 Revenue and Operating Income for the National Hockey League[10]		
NHL Team, 2015–16	Total Revenue (in millions)	Operating Income (in millions)
New York Rangers	$219	$75
Montreal Canadiens	$202	$77
Toronto Maple Leafs	$186	$68
Pittsburgh Penguins	$178	$26
Chicago Blackhawks	$173	$34
Boston Bruins	$169	$34
Philadelphia Flyers	$160	$25
Vancouver Canucks	$146	$30
Dallas Stars	$144	$21
Los Angeles Kings	$142	$0
San Jose Sharks	$141	$7
Detroit Red Wings	$137	$6
Washington Capitals	$136	$12
Minnesota Wild	$136	$6
St Louis Blues	$129	$3
Tampa Bay Lightning	$127	$3
New Jersey Devils	$126	−$1
Anaheim Ducks	$121	−$1

(continued)

[10]Data from http://www.forbes.com/nhl-valuations/list/.

Table 3.4 *(continued)*		
NHL Team, 2015–16	Total Revenue (in millions)	Operating Income (in millions)
Calgary Flames	$121	$18
Ottawa Senators	$118	$6
Edmonton Oilers	$117	$15
Buffalo Sabres	$116	$1
Nashville Predators	$116	−$2
Colorado Avalanche	$115	$6
New York Islanders	$114	$3
Winnipeg Jets	$112	$11
Arizona Coyotes	$101	−$8
Columbus Blue Jackets	$100	−$2
Florida Panthers	$100	−$15
Carolina Hurricanes	$99	−$15
TOTALS	**$4,101**	**$441**

The general story appears to be clear — recent data on professional sports teams suggest most teams earn a profit, but this does not mean the teams are "profit-maximizing." It does suggest that owning a sports team is not the worst business venture one could enter into.

One should note that North Americans are not the only people who enjoy professional sports. Table 3.5 reports the revenue and profits for the 2012–13 English Premier League (EPL, a professional league for men's association football clubs).[11] As you can see, revenue in the EPL is comparable to what we observed in the NBA and NHL. Unlike what was the case in the four North American sports, negative profits were far more common in the EPL in 2012–13.

We should note that after 2012–13 the picture for the EPL changed. In both the 2013–14 and 2014–15 seasons,[12] the majority of teams in the EPL reported a profit; if you add profits across all teams in the league, you will get a number greater than zero. This change in circumstances may be linked to the

---

[11]The data come from David Conn of *The Guardian* (https://www.theguardian.com/football/2014/may/01/premier-league-accounts-club-by-club-david-conn).

[12]The data for 2013–14 can be found at https://www.theguardian.com/football/2015/apr/29/premier-league-finances-club-by-club; that for 2014–15 at https://www.theguardian.com/football/2016/may/25/premier-league-finances-club-by-club-breakdown-david-conn.

Table 3.5 Revenue and Profit for the English Premier League				
EPL Team, 2015–16	Revenues (in millions of British pounds)	Profit Before Tax (in millions of British pounds)	Revenue (in millions of U.S. dollars)	Profit Before Tax (in millions of U.S. dollars)
Manchester United	£363	−£9	$570.42	−$14.14
Arsenal	£283	£7	$444.71	$11.00
Manchester City	£271	−£52	$425.85	−$81.71
Chelsea	£260	−£56	$408.56	−$88.00
Liverpool	£206	−£50	$323.71	−$78.57
Tottenham Hotspur	£147	£4	$231.00	$6.29
Newcastle United	£96	£10	$150.85	$15.71
West Ham United	£91	−£4	$143.00	−$6.29
Everton	£86	£2	$135.14	$3.14
Aston Villa	£84	−£52	$132.00	−$81.71
Sunderland	£76	−£13	$119.43	−$20.43
Norwich City	£75	£1	$117.85	$1.57
Fulham	£73	−£2	$114.71	−$3.14
Southampton	£72	−£7	$113.14	−$11.00
West Bromwich Albion	£70	£6	$110.00	$9.43
Stoke City	£67	−£31	$105.28	−$48.71
Swansea City	£67	£21	$105.28	$33.00
Queens Park Rangers	£61	−£65	$95.86	−$102.14
Reading	£59	−£2	$92.71	−$3.14
Wigan Athletic	£56	£1	$88.00	$1.57
	£2,563	−£291	$4,027.49	−$457.28

Financial Fair Play Regulations established by the Union of European Football Associations (UEFA). These rules, which we will address in Chapter 5 when discussing labor market restrictions, limited the wages EPL teams could pay their players.

Prior to these rules, though, profit rates in the EPL lagged behind what we tend to see in North American sports leagues. To understand why this is the case, we need to consider just how differently North American sports leagues are structured compared to other leagues around the world. And that review begins with some important history.

3.2 Monopoly Comes to American Sports

The sport of baseball is referenced in a number of documents from the 18th century, including a mention by John Adams (born in 1735 and the second president of the United States) who refers to playing "bat and ball" as a child.[13] Many of the formal rules of the game were not established until the Knickerbocker Club was founded in 1842. Led by Alexander Joy Cartwright, the Knickerbocker Club set such rules as the number of players on each side and the distance between bases. While Cartwright and the Knickerbockers established some of the regulations that still apply today, there is one aspect of the game we all know that did not exist back in the 1840s. The game of baseball was initially played by amateurs and tickets were not required to view the game.[14]

The practice of charging admission dates to 1858. To see a game between All-Stars from New York and Brooklyn, 4,000 fans were charged 50 cents apiece.[15] Once fans were charged and teams began to collect revenue, another issue immediately surfaced. What should the players—whom the fans had obviously come to watch—receive for their efforts? The National Association of Base Ball Players (NABBP) came into existence the same year fans were first charged admission to games. According to the NABBP, players should not be paid. Although the NABBP sounds like an organization designed to promote the interest of players, it was actually created by elite clubs in New York City[16] and those elite clubs had a clear financial interest in not paying their players.

Revenues continued to grow in spite of this policy. Just 10 years later, the eight largest clubs in baseball earned a combined income of $100,000.[17] As revenues increased, the ban on paying players became harder and harder to enforce. To understand this, consider the simple deductive model we reviewed in the previous chapter. Teams that win more games will see an increase in revenue. To win more games, you need better players. How does a team convince better players

---

[13]This story was told in Stefan Szymanski and Andrew Zimbalist, *National Pastime: How Americans Play Baseball and the Rest of the World Plays Soccer* (Washington, DC: Brookings Institution Press, 2005), p. 220.

[14]The story of the Knickerbocker Club and Alexander Joy Cartwright appears in Szymanski and Zimbalist (2005, pp. 16–17).

[15]This story appeared in Ron McCulloch, *How Baseball Began* (Los Angeles: Warwick), p. 37 and was retold in Szymanski and Zimbalist (2005, p. 220).

[16]The story of the NABBP may be found in Szymanski and Zimbalist (2005, p. 19). The association was founded by the presidents of the Knickerbockers, Gothams, Empires, and Eagles.

[17]This was noted by Harold Seymour, *Baseball: The Early Years* (New York: Oxford University Press, 1960), p. 50 and was retold by Szymanski and Zimbalist (2005, p. 20). According to the data presented at eh.net (and www.measuringworth.com/), $100,000 in 1868 was worth about $1.55 million in 2016.

to play for it? Paying the players more money helps. Such payments were in violation of the NABBP rules, though. In consequence, initial payments were made "under the table."[18] Eventually, the paying of players became a regular part of the game of baseball. In 1869, the first entirely professional baseball team was established in Cincinnati. The Red Stockings had a payroll of $9,300, with an average wage of $930. This roughly translates into $15,223 in 2015 dollars,[19] so it may not seem like much of a salary today. But in 1869, nominal per-capita income was $203.78.[20] Thus, earning $930 to play baseball was considered a very good deal.[21] The following year, the deal for professional baseball players got even better when the Chicago White Stockings paid an average salary of $1,200.[22]

In 1871, the NABBP split into the National Association of Amateur Base Ball Players (NAABBP) and the National Association of Professional Base Ball Players (NAPBBP). The NAABBP only existed for four seasons and the NAPBBP for five, but the NAPBBP had a lasting impact on professional sports in North America. Obviously, an organization that exists for just five years has experienced some significant internal conflicts and crises. In reaction to one of these problems, William Hulbert, owner of the Chicago White Stockings, decided to create a new sports league.

The new sports league story centers on Davy Force. From 1871 to 1873, Force posted a batting average of 0.361. He also led the National Association with a 0.418 average in 1872.[23] In 1874, Force had his worst season up until that point in his career. Nevertheless, Hulbert's Chicago White Stockings wished to make sure Force didn't leave for another team for the 1875 season (Force had already played for four teams over four professional seasons). The White Stockings thus decided to sign Force to a new contract. Unfortunately, league rules specified that a team could not sign a player to a new contact during the regular season. In November 1874, the White Stockings signed Force to a new contract,

---

[18]Szymanski and Zimbalist (2005, p. 20) offer some details of how teams got around the NABBP rules. In addition to the practice of giving players jobs outside of baseball, these authors also note that some teams simply paid their players a wage.

[19]This calculation is based on the GDP deflator reported at https://www.measuringworth.com/datasets/usgdp/result.php. This site reports data on the GDP deflator in 1869 (with 2015 as equal to 100) that indicates the deflator was 6.03. To calculate real output, we perform the following: [(Nominal Income/Price Index) × 100] or ($930/6.03) × 100 = $15,423.

[20]Data on the price level and nominal income in 1869 can be found at http://www.measuringworth.com/.

[21]Szymanski and Zimbalist (2005, pp. 21–22) tell the story of the 1868 Red Stockings.

[22]Szymanski and Zimbalist (2005, p. 22).

[23]Statistics for 1872 can be found at http://www.baseball-reference.com/leagues/NA/1872.shtml. Force finished 2nd in batting average in 1872. In addition, Force finished 3rd in on-base percentage, 4th in slugging average, and 3rd in OPS (on-base percentage plus slugging average).

but the organization backdated it to September of the same year. No matter the backdating, the contract was still in violation of league rules.

As the White Stockings had violated the rules, Force's contract with Hulbert's team was viewed as invalid. In December 1874, the Philadelphia Athletics signed Force to a separate contract. With Force signed to two different contracts, the league had to decide on which team Force could play. In the end, the Philadelphia contract was upheld by the league's Association Council, a deliberative body led by an official from the Philadelphia franchise.[24]

This incident motivated Hulbert's decision to create a new baseball league. Hulbert's new league—the National League—transformed professional sports in North America. The National League was organized much as North American sports leagues are organized today. In 1876, the league consisted of the following eight teams:

- Boston Red Stockings
- Chicago White Stockings
- Cincinnati Reds
- Hartford Dark Blues
- Louisville Grays
- Philadelphia Athletics
- New York Mutuals
- St. Louis Brown Stockings

Today's baseball fan might regard this list as unfamiliar. Five of the teams listed folded by the end of the 1877 season and the Reds ceased to exist after the 1880 season.[25] Only the Red Stockings (who eventually became the Atlanta Braves) and White Stockings (who eventually became the Chicago Cubs) survived the first few years of the National League.

Although many of the teams failed to endure, a crucial structure of the National League did. If you carefully review the list above, you will see that in 1876 there were eight teams in eight different cities. This means that the National League granted each franchise a local **monopoly**, which is crucial to our understanding of North American sports. A monopoly is simply a firm that

monopoly A firm that is a sole seller in a market.

---

[24]The story of Force's contracts in 1874 is told at http://www.sportsecyclopedia.com/mlb/nl/hulbert.html (a site affiliated with *USA Today*). After his decision to sign Force, Hulbert then proceeded to sign several stars from other teams. This was a clear violation of NAABBP rules
[25]Today's Cincinnati Reds began as the Cincinnati Red Stockings in the American Association in 1882.

is a sole seller in a market. The advantage of being the sole seller is that the firm can establish and maintain a price above the cost of providing the product. This power can be illustrated with the following example.

Imagine there are two firms selling tickets to a sporting event online.[26] The tickets being sold are essentially identical (from the same section of the arena) and cost each firm $50 to acquire and sell; this cost includes not just the price of the ticket, but also the money to pay each firm's employees and the costs of each site, while giving a normal rate of return to the site's owner.[27] People buying the tickets understand that both firms are selling essentially identical tickets. What price can each firm charge?

If each firm decides to price the tickets at $70, each firm is making $20 in above-normal profits. And each firm is essentially splitting the market. Therefore, the path to gaining an advantage in the market is quite simple. If one firm charged a lower price—say, $65—then we would expect consumers to flock to the website of the low-priced seller. Of course, the high-priced site would quickly see this movement and lower its price. How long would this process continue? Eventually, each firm would be forced to accept a price of $50. In other words, competition forces each firm to charge a price that is equal to the cost of the good.

What if one of these firms could eliminate the competition in the market? Then that firm would obviously be able to charge a higher price. It is important to emphasize that a single firm cannot charge any price it likes. The firm is still constrained by the market demand curve, which, as we have noted, does indicate that a certain price demand will be zero. Even if only one firm is selling tickets to a game, people can still choose not to attend the game, and as the price increases, more people will make that decision.

Nevertheless, from a firm's perspective, a monopoly is preferable to competition. From society's perspective, however, monopolies have a number of problems. Higher prices are not one of these issues. Higher prices are simply a redistribution of income from buyer to seller. If you are the buyer, you are worse off, while the seller is better off. Since both are part of society, society as a whole is not worse off because of higher prices.

How those higher prices are achieved is a problem, though. Monopolies are still subject to the demand curve, so to charge a higher price, the seller must restrict output. This lost output represents a loss to society. Monopolized markets will offer less than competitive markets, and this means society is worse off. We can see such a loss when we look at the distribution of sports teams. William Hulbert constructed the

---

[26]The model with two firms selling identical products is called a Bertrand duopoly.

[27]A normal rate of return is defined as a return that is sufficient to maintain the owner's interest in the firm. If the return is lower than the "normal rate," we can expect the owner to divest from the firm.

National League so that each of its eight teams had control of a market. Eventually, a city like New York did violate the one-team-per-city rule. But even though New York did get more than one team, the numbers of teams was set by the league, not the market. We will next see that a different approach was taken in England.

Before we get to that story, let's note another issue with monopoly power that will demonstrate how Hulbert's innovation in the 19th century still impacts sports in the 21st century. In 2004, the city of Charlotte was given an NBA team, the Bobcats. Across the next 13 seasons, the Bobcats failed to win 40% of their games in five different years. In only three seasons did the Bobcats win more than half their games. But fans of this team have only seen three play-off wins in franchise history. And although the Bobcats are now known as the Hornets, Charlotte fans have yet to see a series win in this team's history.

In a competitive market, the unsuccessful are eliminated, but Hulbert's monopoly model, which was adopted by every other major North American sports league, prevents the Bobcats/Hornets from going out of business. A better team can't enter the Charlotte market, so if you wish to consume NBA basketball in Charlotte—and see the talents the NBA employs (which are primarily employed by teams located outside of Charlotte)—you have no choice but to go see this team. The story of the Charlotte Bobcats/Hornets, and other teams that lose consistently over time, illustrates a key feature of monopoly power. When competition is removed from the marketplace, firms have little incentive to produce a quality product. Such inefficiencies, labeled **x-inefficiency**,[28] mean that not only do monopolies produce less than competitive markets, what the monopolies produce can often be far less desirable to the consumer.

> **x-inefficiency** What happens when monopolies do not have an incentive to produce as efficiently as possible because they do not face competition.

Hulbert did not stop at giving the National League teams substantial monopoly power in the marketplace. He also took action, as we will discuss in detail in the next two chapters, to control player cost. In sum, Hulbert's league model was designed to maximize revenues in the local market and minimize player costs. This approach is consistent with the assumption of profit maximization.

3.3 Europeans Embrace Competition

In contrast to their development in North America, professional sports in the United Kingdom evolved on a very different path.

The sport of soccer, or football, appears to be a bit older than baseball. We know that such a game existed in medieval England, primarily because Edward III

---

[28]This term is used in Colander's *Microeconomics* textbook. It broadly refers to the inefficiencies associated with a monopoly, which persist because the discipline of market competition does not exist. David Colander, *Principles of Microeconomics*, 10th ed. (Dubuque, IA: McGraw-Hill, 2017), p. 335.

(1349), Richard (II) (1389), and Henry IV (1401) passed laws prohibiting soccer.[29] Despite these laws, the game survived. In the 19th century, English public schools began to play the game. Problems soon arose because common rules governing the game did not exist; games between teams from different schools became difficult to play. In 1846, rules were adopted at Cambridge, but it was not until 1863 that common rules—and the Football Association (FA)—were created.[30]

The FA was an organization created by amateurs, but just as in the United States, conflict arose between amateurs and professionals in the sport of soccer. In North America, such a conflict resulted in amateurs and professionals going their separate ways. Although the conflict between amateurs and professionals wasn't quickly resolved within the FA, by the mid-1880s a compromise had been reached. The professional clubs would be allowed to exist, but within the confines of the FA. As Szymanski and Zimbalist (2005) observed, this solution created an "integrated administration for the game at all levels. . . . In American terms, it would be the equivalent of a person, such as the commissioner of baseball, being responsible for the health of the game at all levels within the United States, not merely the interest of the major league teams" (p. 39). Szymanski (2009, p. 23) noted this compromise meant that soccer was governed by both national and international organizations that essentially controlled every aspect of the sport. Such control extended to the professional game.[31] In sum, the sport of soccer became subject to government control. Surprisingly—and in stark contrast to what we observed in North America—this government control led to leagues governed by competitive forces.

Before we delve into the competitive nature of European sports, let's detail how little power is held by the owners of European sports franchises. The FA and organizations like it don't just govern the sport. These organizations also impact the ability of teams to earn a profit. As Szymanski (2009) notes, the FA established rules that would be surprising to those familiar with North American

---

[29]As noted in Szymanski and Zimbalist (2005, p. 34). As these authors note, each of the kings referred to in the text passed a law against soccer or football in an effort to get people to focus on archery. There is evidence this focus was somewhat successful. In the battle of Agincourt (1415), Henry V (son of Henry IV) led a much smaller force of English soldiers to victory over 20,000 French soldiers. The key to victory was the English longbow. With a range of 250 yards, the English archers were able to decimate the French ranks. When the battle was over, about 6,000 French soldiers had died. The English, on the other hand, lost fewer than 500 men. For more on this, see http://www.history.com/this-day-in-history/battle-of-agincourt.

[30]Szymanski and Zimbalist (2005, pp. 34–35).

[31]Stefan Szymanski, *Playbooks and Checkbooks: An Introduction to the Economics of Modern Sports* (Princeton, NJ: Princeton University Press, 2009).

sports. Payments of profits to owners were historically restricted and salaries to team directors not allowed. Essentially, the profit motive for clubs was removed. In addition, the English Football League (EFL, founded in 1888) took an approach to league organization that is also unfamiliar to fans of North American sports. Recall that the National League in America restricted the number of franchises in an effort to create monopoly power. Although this approach has been adopted by every other North American league, the EFL used a different tactic. In order to include as many teams as possible, the EFL was organized into multiple divisions. At the end of each season, the worst-performing clubs were demoted to a lower division and the top-performing teams (in the lower divisions) were promoted to a higher level. The promotion and relegation system was adopted by leagues everywhere—at least everywhere except in North America.

Promotion and relegation systems make professional sports outside of North America very different, and it is important to consider these differences. In North America, professional sports are private ventures. In general, when we think of firms in the private sector, we think of market competition, but the story of teams like the Charlotte Bobcats make it clear that professional sports teams in North America are often shielded from some of the more dire consequences of competition. In contrast, public organizations are not frequently regarded as competitive. However, the institution of promotion and relegation has resulted in a system that subjects professional soccer teams in Europe to significant consequences when these teams do not succeed on the field.

The impact of promotion and relegation can be seen by reviewing the location of teams in the English Premier League (EPL)—the top division of football in England—in 2016. Remember, the National League in 1876 had one team per city. And even today, no city has more than two teams in Major League Baseball (or any other major sport).

In contrast, as **Table 3.6** shows, London hosts five different teams in the EPL, and Manchester and Liverpool each have two teams.

Table 3.6 Location of English Premier League Teams: 2016–17[32]		
EPL Team, 2016–17	Location	Population (in thousands)
Arsenal	London	8,250
Chelsea	London	8,250
Crystal Palace	London	8,250
Tottenham Hotspur	London	8,250
West Ham United	London	8,250
Everton	Liverpool	552

(continued)

[32]Population taken from the 2011 Census (https://www.citypopulation.de/UK-Cities.html).

Table 3.6 (continued)		
EPL Team, 2016–17	Location	Population (in thousands)
Liverpool	Liverpool	522
Manchester City	Manchester	511
Manchester United	Manchester	511
Leicester City	Leicester	444
Hull City	Kingston upon Hull	284
Stoke City	Stoke-on-Trent	271
Southampton	Southampton	254
AFC Bournemouth	Bournemouth	188
Swansea City	Swansea	179
Middlesbrough	Middlesbrough	175
Sunderland	Sunderland	174
Watford	Watford	132
Burnley	Burnley	82
West Bromwich Albion	West Bromwich	73

In addition, market size is not necessarily driving the location of teams. Two teams are located in cites with fewer than 100,000 people. Meanwhile, the following cities in England (see Table 3.7) had at least 300,000 people and did not have an EPL team in 2016–17. And there were another 10 cities with at least 200,000 people and no team. In sum, of the 23 cities in England with at least 200,000 people, only seven cities could claim a team in the top division of English soccer.

Table 3.7 Locations without an English Premier League Team: 2002–03 to 2012–13[33]	
English Cities with 300,000+ People and without an EPL Team, 2016–17	Population (in thousands)
Birmingham	1,086
Bristol	536
Sheffield	518
Leeds	475
Bradford	350
Coventry	326

[33]Population taken from the 2011 Census (http://www.citypopulation.de/UK-Cities.html).

The promotion and relegation system in the EPL—where the three worst teams in each season are demoted and the three best teams in the lower division promoted—explains the location of teams in the League. Any team from any location can play its way into and out of the EPL.

What is interesting is how much movement this system creates. Each season, 20 teams compete in the EPL and the top 17 will return the next year. Despite the fact that 85% of teams avoid demotion, over time the promotion and relegation system creates significant turnover in the League. For example, of the 20 teams that began the 2012–13 season, only 11 avoided demotion and were still playing just five years later. And 16 more teams appeared for at least one season during these same five years—with Leicester City, a team that only joined the League in 2014–15, winning the EPL title in 2015–16.

Winning and losing in English football have real consequences. Demotion to a lower level means the team is going to earn substantially lower revenues, and that means player contracts, which might have made sense at a higher level, may no longer be financially viable. Consequently, not only does a team suffer from losing, but players also stand to lose their jobs.

The promotion and relegation system has been adopted in soccer leagues around the world, outside the United States. Sports leagues in the United States—including the Major League Soccer—still employ the Hulbert model.

Again, the monopoly model appears to insulate teams from losses. Consider the case of the Los Angeles Clippers. The Clippers moved from San Diego to Los Angeles in 1984. Across the next 27 years (until the end of the 2010–11 season),[34] the Clippers only won 26.8% of their games. In 24 of these 27 seasons, the Clippers finished with a losing record. In a league where 16 teams make the playoffs, the Clippers only appeared in the post-season five times. In addition, the Clippers were rated one of the three worst teams in the NBA in nine different seasons. So the Clippers would have been demoted nine times (i.e. removed from the league nine times!) if the NBA used a system of promotion and relegation.

But that is not the consequence of poor play in the NBA or the other three major North American sport leagues. The Clippers, like other teams in North American sports, receive preferential treatment in the amateur drafts each league employs following each losing season.

---

[34]In 2011, with the help of the NBA, the Clippers acquired Chris Paul. Behind Paul, the Clippers have finally become a competitive team. It should be emphasized, though, that the NBA did assist the Clippers' acquisition of his services by nullifying a deal that would have sent Paul to the Los Angeles Lakers.

We will discuss the issue of player drafts in the next chapter. For now, we want to return to the question posed at the onset of this chapter: North American sports teams have taken actions to increase profitability, but can we argue that these teams are profit-maximizing?

3.4 Elasticity of Demand

Imagine you are hired by a sports team that is contemplating an increase in ticket prices. Given all that you know from the first three chapters of this book, will such an increase in prices cause ticket revenue to increase or decrease?

We know that

$$\text{Ticket Revenue} = \text{Price} \times \text{Ticket Sales} \qquad (3.1)$$

An increase in ticket prices will cause ticket sales to decrease, but because prices and ticket sales are moving in the opposite direction, the change in revenue is unknown. Of course, such a response won't make your employer happy. To offer a better response, you need to determine how much prices and tickets are changing. And to learn this, it is helpful to know how ticket sales respond to changes in price. We know that when prices go up, sales will go down, but by how much will sales decline? In other words, how responsive are sales to price changes?

When economists talk about "responsiveness," they use the term **elasticity**.[35] Elasticity is simply the ratio of the percentage change in a dependent variable (in this case, ticket sales) to a percentage change in an independent variable (in this case, price). The intuition behind this concept is not difficult to understand. There are essentially three possibilities with respect to price and sales. See Table 3.8.

elasticity The ratio of the percentage change in a dependent variable to a percentage change in an independent variable.

1. *The percentage change in sales exceeds the percentage change in prices.* In this case, the elasticity, in absolute terms, will be greater than 1. If prices decline, sales will increase by a larger percentage and revenue will rise. Likewise, a price increase will cause sales to decline by so much that revenue will also decline.

2. *The percentage change in sales is less than the percentage change in prices.* In this case, the elasticity, in absolute terms, will be less than 1. If price

---

[35]Elasticity can be defined as the responsiveness of some factor Y to a change in a factor X. It is always helpful to just think of elasticity as "responsiveness." And yes, this would probably be easier to understand if economists simply used the word "responsiveness" instead.

Table 3.8 Relationship Between Sales and Price			
Relationship Between Sales and Prices	Elasticity	If Price Declines	If Price Increases
% Change in Sales > % in Prices	> 1	Increase Sales ➔ Increase Revenue	Decrease Sales ➔ Decrease Revenue
% Change in Sales < % Change in Prices	< 1	Increase Sales ➔ Revenue Continues to Fall	Decrease Sales ➔ Revenue Continues to Rise
% Change in Sales = % Change in Prices	= 1	Increase Sales ➔ Same Revenue	Decrease Sales ➔ Same Revenue

declines, the resulting increase in sales will not be sufficient to prevent revenue from falling. Likewise, a price increase will cause sales to decline but not enough to stop revenue from rising.

3. *The percentage change in sales is equal to the percentage change in prices.* In this case, the elasticity, in absolute terms, will equal 1. If price declines, the ensuing increase in sales will result in revenue not changing. The same story is told for a price increase.

So what does any of this mean? Elasticity and revenue tell a very important story about profits. Consider a case where sales are not responsive to price. In that instance, elasticity, in absolute terms, is less than 1.

Given what we know about elasticity, how would an increase in prices impact total revenue?

- First, an increase in price would cause sales to decline, and with an elasticity that is less than 1, we know that the percentage change in sales is less than the percentage change in prices.[36]

- Since we are increasing prices—and the percentage change in price is larger than the percentage change in sales—it must be the case that revenue is increasing.

- But there is more to the story. Not only will revenue rise, we can also expect profits to increase. How do we know this? We have noted that in sports, the

[36]Remember, elasticity is a ratio. Since percentage change in sales appears in the numerator and percentage change in price is in the denominator, it must be the case that the percentage change in sales is less than the percentage change in price for the value of this ratio to be less than 1 in absolute terms.

marginal cost of a ticket sale may be zero or positive. If zero, a reduction in ticket sales will not change costs. If positive, a reduction in ticket sales will lower costs. In either case, more revenue means more profit.

How long will a price increase result in higher profits? This will be the reality as long as sales remain unresponsive to price. As noted in Appendix B, as prices go up, the responsiveness of sales to price changes increases, so eventually elasticity will no longer be less than 1. As long as elasticity remains less than 1, we can make a simple observation: *If a team (or any firm) has a price that is inelastic or unresponsive, then it simply has to increase price to increase profits. Therefore, a firm with an inelastic price is not profit-maximizing.*

3.5 Price Elasticity and Sports

Now let's move away from the story of elasticity and profits to examine real data from actual sports teams. In 2006, Stacey Brook[37] examined the link between attendance and ticket prices in the NFL. Ticket price was one element of this demand function. The estimated coefficient from this model is shown in Table 3.9.

Table 3.9 Estimated Link Between Ticket Prices and Attendance in the National Football League[38]			
Independent Variable	Coefficient	*t*-Statistic	*p*-Values
Ticket prices	−5,115.46	−2.49	0.014

Brook's results indicate that higher prices lead to lower attendance, after one controls for factors like team performance, per-capita income, market size, and so forth. Given these results, we can also calculate the price elasticity of demand.

Across the data set Brook employed, average ticket prices were $44.80 and average attendance was 487,594.192. Given the above results, the estimate of price elasticity, at the point of means, is an inelastic −0.47.[39] This thus indicates that NFL teams are not profit-maximizing. Such a result is not unique. Table 3.10 reports the results of 10 studies that indicate demand in professional sports is often inelastic, suggesting that sports teams are not profit-maximizing.

---

[37]Stacey Brook, "Evaluating Inelastic Ticket Pricing Models," *International Journal of Sport Finance* 1 (2006): 140–150.

[38]This table originally appeared in Brook (2006, p. 145).

[39]As explained in Appendix B, for a linear demand function, Elasticity = [ΔAttendance/ΔPrice] / [Average Price/Average Attendance] = −5,115.46 × (44.80/487,594.192) = −0.47.

Table 3.10 Literature Background Regarding Price Elasticity[40]

Author and Date	Sports	Estimate of Price Elasticity of Demand
Demmert (1973)	MLB	−0.93
Noll (1974)	MLB	Inelastic
Siegfried and Eisenberg (1980)	MLB	−0.25
Bird (1982)	English Soccer	−0.2
Scully (1989)	MLB	−0.61
Coffin (1996)	MLB	−0.11 to −0.68
Depken (2001)	NFL	−0.58
Garcia and Rodriguez (2002)	Spanish Soccer	−0.3 to −0.9
Hadley and Poitras (2003)	MLB	−0.21
Winfree et al. (2003)	MLB	−0.06

Or does it? Various writers have offered a number of explanations for these results.

- **Teams do not profit-maximize:** The most obvious explanation was noted above. Teams are simply not profit maximizers. There is some evidence to support this hypothesis. Frank Gamrat and Raymond Sauer (2000)[41] and Ramon DeGennaro (2003)[42] both examined the racehorse market, and both offer evidence that decision makers are not entirely motivated by profits.

- **Home field advantage:** David Boyd and Laura Boyd (1998)[43] argue for what one could call the 12th man effect. Teams often credit their fans (in football, this is called the 12th man) with their success. Following this reasoning, more fans could lead to more success on the field, and more success on the field could lead to more revenue for the team. In essence, teams are paying their fans with lower prices in return for their help in winning games.

---

[40]Table originally appeared in Anthony Krautmann and David J. Berri, "Can We Find It at the Concessions? Understanding Price Elasticity in Professional Sports," *Journal of Sports Economics* 8, no. 2 (April 2007): 184.

[41]Frank Gamrat and Raymond Sauer, "The Utility of Sport and Returns to Ownership: Evidence from the Thoroughbred Market," *Journal of Sports Economics* 1 (2000): 219–235.

[42]Ramon DeGennaro, "The Utility of Sport and Returns to Ownership," *Journal of Sports Economics* 4 (May 2003): 145–153.

[43]David Boyd and Laura Boyd, "The Home Field Advantage: Implications for the Pricing of Tickets of Professional Team Sporting Events," *Journal of Economics and Finance* 22 (1998): 169–179.

- **Public choice story:** As we will note later in the text, professional sports in North America frequently receive substantial public subsidies. Rodney Fort (2000)[44] argues that ticket prices are perhaps kept low to encourage local governments to help fund the stadiums and arenas where teams play.

- **Team revenue is not just about the gate:** The studies of price elasticity have focused on the link between attendance and the price of a ticket, but as anyone who has gone to a game understands, the price of a ticket tends not to be the only cost of attending a game. Fans generally purchase food, drinks, and perhaps souvenirs at games. Consequently, researchers[45] have argued that teams keep prices low to get fans into the stadium. Once in the stadium, the team sells food and drink to fans at prices that reflect the team's monopoly power with respect to concessions.[46]

Beyond all these issues, Roger Noll (2013)[47] raises a statistical issue with each of the above estimations. Think back to the basic supply and demand model. This model notes how factors that impact revenue (i.e., demand) and cost (i.e., supply) come together to determine the price in a market. The above models only consider demand issues. As Noll makes clear:

> Because the price coefficients have opposite signs in supply and demand equations, endogeneity[48] causes an upward bias in the price coefficient and the implied price elasticity of demand is more inelastic than is in fact the case. (p. 118)

---

[44]Rodney Fort, "Stadiums and Public and Private Interests in Seattle," *Marquette Sports Law Journal* 10 (Spring 2000): 311–334.

[45]A sample of research taking this approach would include Ronald L. Heilmann and Wayne R. Wendling, "A Note on Optimum Pricing Strategies for Sports Events," in Robert Engel Machol and Shaul P. Ladany (eds.), *Management Science in Sports* (New York: North Holland, 1976), pp. 91–100 and Anthony Krautmann and David J. Berri, "Can We Find It at the Concessions? Understanding Price Elasticity in Professional Sports," *Journal of Sports Economics* 8, no. 2 (April 2007): 183–191.

[46]Teams charge a relatively high price for food and drinks inside the stadium once you are in the stadium, your only choice is to purchase food and drink from the team (or go hungry).

[47]Roger Noll, "Endogeneity in Attendance Demand Models," in Placido Rodriguez, Stefan Kessenne, and Juame Garcia (eds.), *The Econometrics of Sport* (Northampton, MA: Edward Elgar Press, 2013), pp. 117–134.

[48]The term "endogenous" refers to factors that are determined by your model. In contrast, "exogenous" terms are determined outside the model. In estimating a model, we need our independent variables to be exogenous. If they are endogenous, or determined by other factors in our model, then our estimated coefficients will be biased.

Noll's argument suggests that the empirical analysis we have cited is not correct. Consequently, despite all the numbers we have seen, those numbers do not tell us teams are not profit-maximizing. So does that mean teams are profit-maximizing? The study of elasticity initially suggested that teams may not be profit-maximizing, but we have cast doubt on the validity of such studies. It is tempting to argue that teams are profit-maximizing, since we have evidence (and will offer quite a bit more) that teams, especially in North America, take actions to enhance their profits. But even if we believe teams are interested in profits, we do not know that teams are seeking to maximize profits. In fact, the author of the text suspects that owners of teams are interested in more than just profits. Taking actions to win games and titles — even if that doesn't enhance profits — likely increases the utility of owners.[49]

What have we learned? We started this chapter with a simple question, yet in the end, we don't have a simple answer. Teams in sports appear to be interested in profits, but we cannot say if teams are profit-maximizing. Although that answer may seem unsatisfying, it is important nonetheless. As we will see going forward, sometimes — even after all our deductive and inductive powers are fully employed — we still don't arrive at a definitive answer to the question posed. That doesn't mean, though, that our efforts have taught us nothing.

---

[49]Malcolm Gladwell in "The Psychic Benefits and the NBA Lockout" (http://www.grantland .com/story/_/id/6874079/psychic-benefits-nba-lockout) details the benefits an owner of a professional sports team derives beyond the simple difference between team revenues and team costs.

Key Terms

utility (p. 66)	sunk costs (p. 66)
marginal benefits (p. 66)	monopoly (p. 78)
marginal cost (p. 66)	x-inefficiency (p. 80)
opportunity cost (p. 66)	elasticity (p. 85)

Problems

Study Questions

1. Imagine you purchased a ticket to attend a baseball game. With respect to the decision to attend the game (after the ticket has been purchased), what are the benefits and costs? What cost(s) should be ignored in making such a decision?

2. How did Thorstein Veblen describe decision making (according to classical economists) in 1898?

3. How "profitable" are sports in North America and the United Kingdom?

4. When did baseball become a commercial product? What was the initial position of the NABBP with respect to players' pay?

5. What was the first team to entirely employ professionals? What year did this happen?

6. Who was Davy Force? What role did he play in the creation of the NL?

7. What "innovation" did William Hulbert introduce that still defines North American sports? How does this innovation impact profits in North American sports?

8. How many of the original National League teams survive today?

9. Which medieval English kings banned soccer? What impact did this have on the battle of Agincourt?

10. How was the conflict between amateurs and professionals resolved in North American sports? How was this same conflict resolved in England?

11. If demand is inelastic, what can a team do to increase profits? Why?

12. What is the elasticity of ticket demand in professional sports according to the sports economics literature?

13. Review the following explanation for inelastic demand in professional sports.
    a. Motive to maximize profits
    b. Home field advantage
    c. Public choice theory
    d. Nongate revenue
    e. Endogeneity of models

14. If $MU_{tickets}/P_{tickets} < MU_{food}/P_{food}$, what action will a utility-maximizing consumer take? Explain.

15. What is Gossen's first law?

16. What is Gossen's second law?

17. What does an economist mean when he or she argues that a person's decision making is consistent? Why would this property not apply when we talk about wins and losses in sports (in other words, can we apply this property to the ranking of teams)?

18. What is the promotion and relegation system? Review the past 10 seasons of standings in the MLB, NFL, NBA, and NHL. Which teams would have been removed each year if the worst three teams were relegated? Which team in each league would have been demoted most often? Standings data for each league can be found at http://www.baseball-reference.com/, http://www.pro-football-reference.com/; www.basketball-reference.com/, and http://www.hockey-reference.com/.

19. Referring to the EPL standings (http://www.premierleague.com/tables), answer the following:
    a. How many EPL teams in 2006–07 managed to survive to 2016–17 without being demoted?
    b. How many EPL teams in 2006–07 were demoted over the next 10 seasons but managed to return to the EPL?

20. In 2017–2018, how many EPL teams were located in London? How many were situated in markets with fewer than 200,000 people? How many markets with more than 200,000 people did not have a team in 2017–18?

Math Questions

1. Given these demand curves for the Utah Jazz, answer the following questions:

   $P = 90 - 0.0025Q$ $Q = 12,000$
   $P = 90 - 0.0025Q$ $Q = 18,000$
   $P = 90 - 0.0025Q$ $Q = 24,000$

   a. Calculate the own-price elasticity of demand for each demand curve.
   b. If the firm decreased its price by $10, what would happen to total revenue for each demand curve?
   c. If the Jazz decreased its price by $10, what would happen to the profit for each demand curve?

2. Given these scenarios for the Jazz, answer the following questions:
   • Ticket price increases by 10%, quantity demand falls by 5%.
   • Ticket price increases by 5%, quantity demand falls by 15%.
   • Ticket price decreases by 10%, quantity demand increases by 5%.
   • Ticket price decreases by 5%, quantity demand increases by 15%.
   a. What will be the impact of this change on total revenue?
   b. What will be the impact of this change on profit?

3. Given the following information:
   • Own-price elasticity of ticket demand = -0.5
   • Own-price elasticity of ticket demand = -0.8
   • Own-price elasticity of ticket demand = -1.5
   • Own-price elasticity of ticket demand = -2.4

a. If price increased by 10%, what would happen to:
    i. total revenue?
    ii. profit?
b. If price decreased by 10%, what would happen to:
    i. total revenue?
    ii. profit?
4. The Jazz learns that when it sells 15,000 tickets per game, total revenue is $1,000,000 per game. When it sells 16,000 units, total revenue is $900,000. From this information, what do we now know about marginal revenue and own-price elasticity? Explain.
5. The Jazz learns that own-price elasticity is −0.75. What does this tell us about total revenue and marginal revenue? Explain.
6. Given the following:
    a. $MU_T = 25$ $MU_F = 20$ $P_T = \$50$ $P_F = \$20$
    b. $MU_T = 210$ $MU_F = 20$ $P_T = \$70$ $P_F = \$5$
    c. $MU_T = 180$ $MU_F = 40$ $P_T = \$90$ $P_F = \$40$
    where T = ticket prices, F = food, MU = marginal utility, and P = price. For (a), (b), and (c):
    i. What action would a utility-maximizing consumer take with respect to the consumption of food and tickets?
    ii. How would the action proposed in (i) impact the marginal utility of food and tickets?

Appendix A
The Utility-Maximization Model

**Hermann Gossen
(1810–1858)**

Hermann Gossen's *The Development of the Laws of Exchange among Men and of the Consequent Rules of Human Action* was published in German in 1854. This book predates by about two decades the marginal revolution in economics credited to Stanley Jevons, Carl Menger, and Leon Walras in the 1870s. Gossen's work gives us both the law of diminishing marginal utility and a description of how consumers maximize utility. Today, these concepts are generally explained to students in principles of microeconomics everywhere!

We noted that economists argue that people maximize utility by considering marginal benefits and marginal costs. This appendix offers a few more details on such a process.

There are two approaches to explaining this model. One approach, which you may have observed in the principle of microeconomics, involves drawing indifference curves and budget constraints. Another approach involves telling a simple story.

Once upon a time, there was a writer named Hermann Gossen. In 1854, he published *Development of the Laws of Human Relationships*. Gossen's work introduced two important "laws" that have become central to our discussion of microeconomics. Gossen's first law is what we now know as the concept of diminishing marginal utility. This is simply the idea that the more you consume of a good, the less utility or happiness you will derive from each additional unit consumed.

Applying this to the world of sports, Gossen's first law explains why the per-unit cost of season tickets to a team tends to be less than the per-unit cost of attending a single game. This difference can be understood when we understand how much happiness you derive from each additional game you attend, with the first game giving a person more happiness than that same individual would derive from the 50th game attended. Because utility declines as you consume more of a good, demand curves—which tell us that for people to consume more of a good, prices must decline—are negatively sloped.

Gossen's second law allows us to understand how people decide to allocate their budgets; or for sports fans, how much of their budget should be spent on sports and how much on food, clothing, housing, and other items. Here is how Gossen described this second law[50]:

> Man obtains the maximum of life pleasure if he allocates his earned money between the various pleasures in such a manner that the last atom of money spent for each pleasure offers the same amount of pleasure. (p. 88)

A simple tale and some basic math should make this statement clear. Imagine a consumer has two goods: tickets (to sporting events) and food.[51] How does the consumer decide how much to spend on each good?

---

[50]Mark Blaug, *Great Economists Before Keynes* (Englewood Cliffs, NJ: Prentice Hall, 1986), p. 88.

[51]With these two goods, a sports fan can survive. Yes, he or she would be homeless. But assuming "food" includes a beverage, the sports fan will continue to live and get to see sports.

The key issues are the utility (Gossen uses the word "pleasure") the person derives from each good and the price of each good. Let's imagine we can actually measure utility. And let's imagine this measurement yields the following data:

> Marginal utility from tickets
> (i.e., utility derived from each ticket purchased) = 100
> Marginal utility from food
> (i.e., utility derived from each unit of food purchased) = 30

From these numbers, it looks as if a person would be happier with more tickets. But before we reach that conclusion, we need to determine prices. Let's imagine the price of each good is as follows:

> Price of each ticket: $25
> Price of each unit of food: $10

From this, we can now see that per dollar spent, the consumer derives 4 units of happiness (economists call these units of happiness "utils") from tickets and 3 units of happiness from food.[52] So per dollar spent, tickets to sporting events will make this person happier.

That means there is clear path for this person to increase his or her happiness. If this individual allocated more money toward buying tickets—and less money toward food—his or her overall happiness would go up. Gossen's first law also tells us what would happen as this person re-allocated his or her budget. As he or she consumed more tickets, the marginal utility derived from ticket consumption would decline. And as this person consumed less food, the marginal utility from food consumption would increase. Given these changes, such a consumer would continue to reallocate his or her budget until the last unit of money spent for tickets gives the same marginal utility as the last unit spent for food.

This basic story can be generalized to a world where people buy much more than tickets to sporting events and food. And that generalization tells us that a consumer will maximize utility across n goods when the following holds:

$$\frac{MU_1}{P_1} = \frac{MU_2}{P_2} = \cdots = \frac{MU_n}{P_n}$$

In words, *a consumer will maximize utility when the utility received per dollar spent is the same for all goods consumed.*

---

[52]This can be seen by dividing marginal utility by price. So for tickets, we divide 100 by 25. For food, we divide 30 by 10.

Again, Gossen's work is central to our understanding of microeconomics. Mark Blaug described it as follows[53]:

> It is not easy to see who influenced Gossen, . . . he went so far beyond his sources that he has absolutely no equal for originality in the entire history of economic thought. (p. 88)

Blaug is not the only one to have such a high opinion of Gossen's work. Gossen himself argued that he would do for economics what Copernicus did for astronomy.[54] Unfortunately, Gossen's contemporaries did not share his opinion and his book was not well received. And when Gossen died in 1858, his approach to consumer behavior had not been accepted by many people.

Gossen's approach, though, is widely accepted today. And that is because in the 1870s, a revolution in economics took place. Led by such writers as Stanley Jevons,[55] Leon Walras, and Carl Menger, economics embraced the marginal analysis we encounter in every principles class today.

It is important to note that this analysis is entirely deductive. We cannot actually measure utility. But this deductive reasoning does seem to correspond to what we can measure. Demand curves do seem to slope downward. And diminishing marginal utility suggests that people will prefer to consume a wide variety of goods, which also seems to be true.

Appendix B
The Math of Elasticity

The concept of elasticity or responsiveness is one that can be understood intuitively with just a couple of words. But for a few, math may help.

So let's consider a simple linear demand model:

$$\text{Ticket Sales} = a - b \times \text{Ticket Prices} \qquad (3B.1)$$

This looks similar to the standard demand curve, except now sales or quantity is on the left-hand side (as opposed to the right) and prices are on the right

---

[53]Blaug (1986).

[54]Blaug (1986, p. 88).

[55]It is Stanley Jevons who actually seems to have saved Gossen's work. Jevons came across it in the 1870s and graciously acknowledged that Gossen's efforts predated his own work.

(as opposed to the left).[56] Let's imagine that we examined data on sales and prices, and determined that the values of a and b were as follows:

$$\text{Ticket Sales} = 50{,}000 - 666.67 \times \text{Ticket Prices} \qquad (3B.2)$$

This model says that a 1-unit increase in ticket prices will cause sales to drop by 666.67 units. Do ticket prices thus have a "large" or "small" effect on ticket sales?

To answer this question, we need to do more than just look at the slope coefficient.[57] We also have to know how "responsive" ticket sales are to ticket prices.

To determine responsiveness, researchers often turn to the concept of elasticity, which we noted in this chapter as follows:

$$\text{Elasticity} = \text{Percentage Change in } Y/\text{Percentage Change in } X \qquad (3B.3)$$

As one can see, this is simply a ratio. And such a ratio tells us how a percentage change in a specific X (e.g., ticket prices) impacts the percentage in Y (e.g., ticket sales).

Percentage change in any variable is calculated as follows:

$$\text{Percentage Change in } Y = (Y_2 - Y_1)/(Y_1) \qquad (3B.4)$$

Given the definition of elasticity, elasticity can be redefined as

$$\text{Elasticity} = [(Y_2 - Y_1)/(Y_1)]/[(X_2 - X_1)/(X_1)] \qquad (3B.5)$$

The above calculation only requires two observations of X and two observations of Y. And it indicates that the change in Y we observe is only caused by the change in X we observe.

---

[56]The traditional demand curve—revealed in Chapter 1 (and often presented graphically in any principles of microeconomics course)—was introduced by Alfred Marshall. Marshall asked this question: "What determines prices?" Consequently, Marshall placed price on the y-axis (since price was the dependent variable). A firm, though, wishes to know what determines quantity or sales. Hence, for analysis of sales, we employ the demand curve presented in equation 3B.2. This equation, where quantity or sales appear on the left-hand side of the equation, makes more sense when quantity or sales are our focus.

[57]To see why the slope coefficient is inadequate, imagine if equation (3B.3) was for the sale of candy bars that normally sell for $1. This model says that a $1 increase in price, or a doubling of price, would only cause the firm to lose 666.7 sales. Since candy manufacturers typically sell thousands (if not millions) of units, that suggests sales are not very responsive to prices. Now imagine this equation is for automobiles. Again, a $1 increase in price causes sales to fall by 666.7 units. Since automobiles sell for thousands of dollars, this same slope, when applied to an automobile manufacturer, suggests sales are very responsive to price changes. These two examples illustrate why the slope—by itself—doesn't tell us how responsive prices are to sales. Hence, the need to calculate elasticity is real.

Obviously, this approach is inadequate. We know from our discussion of regression analysis that we need a much bigger sample to draw inferences. Furthermore, we know that often observed changes in a dependent variable are caused by changes in multiple independent variables (hence the need for multivariate analysis).

To connect elasticity to our demand model, we have to take a few more steps. Let's begin by noting that $Y_2 - Y_1$ is simply a change in Y. In other words,

$$Y_2 - Y_1 = \Delta Y \qquad (3B.6)$$

$$X_2 - X_1 = \Delta X \qquad (3B.7)$$

Given this, our definition of elasticity can be rewritten as

$$\text{Elasticity} = [\Delta Y/Y]/[\Delta X/X] \qquad (3B.8)$$

and this can be reformulated as

$$\text{Elasticity} = [\Delta Y/\Delta X]/[X/Y] \qquad (3B.9)$$

This latest definition allows us to calculate elasticity from a simple linear demand function.

To illustrate, let's return to our simple model (equation 3B.2):

$$\text{Ticket Sales} = 50,000 - 666.67 \times \text{Ticket Prices} \qquad (3B.2)$$

If ticket prices are $30, then this model predicts that sales are 30,000. Given this information, this hypothetical team's elasticity would be

$$\text{Elasticity} = -666.67 \times 30/30,000 = -0.67 \qquad (3B.10)$$

And since this is a ratio, a 1% increase in ticket prices will yield a 0.67% decrease in ticket sales.

One can generalize the results to determine the elasticity of any factor (at the point of means) included in a linear model. As the following equation illustrates:

$$\text{Elasticity} = \text{Estimated Slope Coefficient} \times$$
$$(\text{Mean of Variable } X/\text{Mean of Variable } Y) \qquad (3B.11)$$

So once we have estimated a linear model, we can ascertain elasticities for each of the independent variables.

Researchers often avoid all this math by simply estimating the demand function as a double-logged model. When we take that step, the estimated coefficient is the elasticity. And obviously, that is much easier!

REUTERS/Alamy

The Competitive Balance Defense

How Important Is Competitive Balance to a Sports League?

To answer this question, Chapter 4 will explore the following:

1. **The Argument for Competitive Balance in a Sports League:** The chapter begins by defining competitive balance and explaining why sports leagues — since the 19th century — have argued that it is essential for a sports league's survival.

2. **Institutions Adopted by Sports Leagues to Promote Competitive Balance:** Sports leagues have adopted a number of institutions in the name of competitive balance. The institutions we will consider include the reserve clause, reverse-order draft, salary caps, luxury taxes, and revenue sharing. How these institutions impact competitive balance will be discussed, beginning with the seminal work of Simon Rottenberg.

3. **Measurement of Competitive Balance:** Much of this discussion will focus on the work of Roger Noll and Gerald Scully, but other measures will also be evaluated.

4. **Explanation for the Level of Competitive Balance in a Sports League:** The argument advanced by sports leagues is that balance is determined by a league's institutions. The empirical study of balance uncovers a different story.

5. **Sports Leagues' Desire for Competitive Balance:** This final discussion will focus on the impact competitive balance actually has on the demand of sports fans. The empirical evidence reviewed indicates that fans and sports leagues appear to have a different opinion regarding the importance of competitive balance.

We do not know for certain whether or not owners are, in fact, profit-maximizing, but evidence does indicate that owners desire an increase in profits. In the previous chapter, we discussed the impact of monopoly power, and in this chapter, we will examine the policies owners advocate with respect to the labor market. We begin with the following quote about professional baseball:

> The financial results of the past season prove that salaries must come down. We believe that players insisting on exorbitant prices are injuring their own interests by forcing out of existence clubs which cannot be run and pay large salaries except at a personal loss.[1]

It is common to hear owners of professional sports teams make pronouncements like this today, but the statement above was not made in the 21st century. More than 130 years ago, on September 19, 1879, National League (NL) owners argued that baseball players were being paid too much. Owners didn't just complain about salaries in 1879, they also took action. Two weeks after the above statement appeared in print, the NL released this statement:

> The principal cause of heavy losses to [NL clubs] is attributed to high salaries, the result of competition. . . . [I]t was proposed that each [club's] delegate be allowed to name five desirable players from his own club. . . . [C]hosen men should not be allowed to sign with any other club without permission. . . . The aim of the league is to reduce expenses so that clubs can live.[2]

reserve clause A policy that allowed teams to retain the right to a player even when that player was not explicitly under contract.

The **reserve clause**, a policy that allowed teams to retain the right to a player even when that player was not explicitly under contract, was thus born. As time

---

[1]This quote appeared in E. Woodrow Eckard, "The Origin of the Reserve Clause: Owner Collusion Versus 'Public Interest,'" *Journal of Sports Economics* 2, no. 2 (May 2001): 118. It originally appeared in D. A. Sullivan (ed.), *Early Innings: A Documentary History of Baseball, 1825–1908* (Lincoln: University of Nebraska Press, 1995).

[2]Originally appeared in *The Buffalo Commercial Advertiser*, October 3, 1879, and was reprinted in Sullivan (1995, pp. 114–115) and Eckard (2001, p. 118).

passed, the justification for the policy shifted, and while the NL initially focused on player costs, about 10 years later a different justification emerged.

In 1889, the NL issued this statement: "As a check on competition, the weaker clubs in the League demanded the privilege of reserving five players."[3] The statement went on: "[T]he necessity for such power of preserving the circuit of a league, by approximately equalizing its playing strength, is recognized by the [Players] League."[4]

Eckard argues that this statement from 1889 was the first to explicitly connect the institution of the reserve clause to competitive balance. Over time, this association became the standard defense of the institution, which leads us to ask and answer a few questions:

1. What do we mean by competitive balance?

2. What do leagues do to promote competitive balance?

3. Do the league's actions actually alter competitive balance?

4. Is competitive balance important to a league's welfare?

4.1 The Competitive Balance Argument

In 1964, Walter Neale[5] made the argument that for a sports athlete to earn money, he or she must have competition. And the better the competition, the more interest fans would develop, leading to an increase in the profits of competitors. To illustrate, Neale discussed the career of Joe Louis.

For those who are too young to remember (virtually everyone reading this book), Louis was world heavyweight champion from June 1937 to May 1949. He defended his title 25 times, and both the length of his reign and the number of defenses remain records to this day. In sum, Louis was one of the greatest fighters ever, but as great a boxer as Louis was, he needed something very important in the ring. As Neale noted, he needed an opponent. The better the opponent, the more people would pay Louis—and his opponent—to fight. As Neale put it, "[p]ure monopoly is a disaster" in sports (p. 7).

---

[3]Originally appeared in A. G. Spalding, *America's National Game* (San Francisco: Halo, 1911), pp. 174–175 and reprinted in Eckard (2001, pp. 118–119). Spalding's book work initially published in 1911.

[4]As Eckard notes, this statement from the National League was issued in response to the formation of the Players League.

[5]Walter Neale, "The Peculiar Economics of Professional Sports," *Quarterly Journal of Economics* 78, no. 1 (1964): 1–14.

One should contrast Neale's observation with what we observe for firms in non-sports industries. Outside of sports, firms do better if their competition is weak or nonexistent. In sports, though, the stronger the competition, the more interest one sees from the paying customer. Neale labeled this characteristic of sports demand as the **Louis–Schmeling paradox**,[6] which goes beyond the world of boxing and applies to all sports. Uncertainty of outcome is one of the factors that we believe drives the interest of fans. Certainly, if fans know — and we mean, literally know with certainty — the outcome of a contest before the game is played, their interest will be much lower. Ratings for ESPN Classic, the only channel devoted to reruns in sports and the least successful ESPN channel, illustrate clearly this point.[7]

The Louis–Schmeling paradox captures the importance of **competitive balance**,[8] or the idea that the distribution of wins in a league should be consistent with profit maximization across the league. In other words, we think a league does not want one team winning every game the team plays.

To make sure this doesn't happen, leagues have enacted various rules supposedly designed to promote competitive balance.

Louis–Schmeling paradox In sports, the stronger the competition, the greater the interest of a paying customer — in contrast to what is observed outside of sports, where firms do better if their competition is weak or nonexistent.

competitive balance The distribution of wins in a league so it is consistent with profit maximization across the league.

4.2 The Reserve Clause

The first rule enacted to promote competitive balance was the reserve clause. Again, this initially applied to only five players on each roster. By the end of the 1880s, the NL had expanded the list of players who could be reserved to every

[6]Max Schmeling was perhaps the most famous opponent of Joe Louis. In 1936, Schmeling defeated the previously undefeated Louis. Since Schmeling was German, this victory became part of Nazi propaganda. In 1938, Louis and Schmeling met in the ring again. This much-anticipated fight ended when Louis knocked out Schmeling in the first round. Needless to say, the Nazis did not find this second result very helpful in their propaganda efforts.

[7]As *The Wages of Wins* noted, according to Darren Rovell at ESPN.com: In 2005, ESPN was in 80 million homes in the United States, while ESPN Classic was only in 25 million houses. Apparently, people would rather watch a live game between two lesser contestants on ESPN than watch a classic game without uncertainty of outcome on ESPN Classic. David J. Berri, Martin B. Schmidt, and Stacey L. Brook, *The Wages of Wins: Taking Measure of the Many Myths in Modern Sport* (Stanford, CA: Stanford University Press, 2006).

[8]The term "competitive balance" doesn't appear to have a specific definition that is agreed upon. In fact, Blair refers to it as a "vague term" (p. 67). See Roger Blair, *Sports Economics* (New York: Cambridge University Press. 2012).

Leeds and von Allmen simply refer to competitive balance as "the degree of parity within a league" (p. 145). Michael Leeds and Peter von Allmen, *The Economics of Sports*, 4th ed. (Reading, MA: Addison-Wesley, 2011).

player on the roster. In addition, a clause was added to each player's contract explaining the nature of the reserve system.

From the 1920s to the 1950s, this clause read as follows:

> [If] the player and the club have not agreed upon the terms of such contract, then . . . the club shall have the right to renew this contract for the period of one year on the same terms, except that the amount payable to the player shall be such as the club shall fix in said notice.[9]

How would the reserve clause impact competitive balance? As we will note later, because some teams are richer than others, one might suspect that without this clause the richest teams would employ all the best talent. And that would make the league quite imbalanced. We will see later that preventing richer teams from acquiring all the "best talent" is the motivation behind many labor market institutions (the reserve clause, the reverse-order draft, salary caps, etc.). And we will see later that the defense of these institutions is not valid. Nevertheless, the argument that the reserve clause prevented the richest teams from dominating the sport was employed for nearly a century.

How did this clause prevent players from migrating to the richest teams? When we look back on how the reserve clause was written, one might think it only gave a team the right to renew a player's contract for one year. The owners argued that the renewed contract also contained the reserve clause. That meant the owners could perpetually renew a player's contract according to terms the club would determine. Such a clause would seem to be a clear restraint on trade. Certainly, such a clause doesn't seem to exist outside of sports. Despite antitrust laws that would suggest a reserve clause was illegal, baseball was able to maintain this system for nearly a century.[10]

The persistence of this institution was made possible by a court case involving Major League Baseball (MLB) and the Federal League (FL).[11] The American League (AL) came into existence in 1899 and declared itself a major league in 1901 (after the NL exited several markets). In 1903, these two leagues agreed to coexist and play a World Series each year to establish baseball's world champion.[12]

---

[9] This originally appeared in James Quirk and Rodney Fort, *Pay Dirt: The Business of Professional Team Sports* (Princeton, NJ: Princeton University Press, 1992), p. 185.

[10] In 1880, the NL's action may have been perfectly legal. But after the Sherman Antitrust Act passed in 1890, the NL's policy of reserving players would seem to have been illegal. As we will note, MLB was made exempt from federal antitrust laws.

[11] This case was ultimately decided by the Supreme Court in 1922 (in *Federal Baseball Club of Baltimore, Inc. v. National League of Professional Baseball Clubs*, 259 U.S. 200). The story of this case may be found in various places including Quirk and Fort (1992, pp. 184–185) and Andrew Zimbalist, *Baseball and Billions* (New York: Basic Books, 1992), pp. 8–10.

[12] A label that makes sense if the entire world in 1903 really consisted of the eastern United States.

In 1914, the dominance of the AL and NL was challenged by the FL. It wished to become a third major league. To accomplish this objective, the league signed several stars from the AL and NL. The AL and NL, though, did not wish to share the American MLB market. Consequently, after the 1915 season, two owners of FL teams were allowed to purchase existing NL teams. And most of the other FL owners were given cash to simply disappear.

The lone exception to this settlement was the ownership of the FL franchise in Baltimore. Not only were the Baltimore owners offered less cash than the other FL owners, the city of Baltimore was ridiculed by Charles Comiskey (owner of the Chicago White Sox of the AL). As Comiskey noted: "Baltimore is a minor league city and not a hell of a good one at that."[13] The Baltimore owners sued on antitrust grounds and the Indiana State Supreme Court agreed that MLB had violated antitrust laws. This ruling was overturned by the District of Columbia Court of Appeals in 1921. Then in 1922, the U.S. Supreme Court—in a unanimous decision—upheld the ruling of the appeals court. Justice Oliver Wendell Holmes offered the following explanation for the Court's decision:

> The business is giving exhibitions of baseball, which are purely state affairs. . . . [C]ompetitions must be arranged between clubs from different cities and States. But the fact that in order to give exhibitions the Leagues must induce free persons to cross state lines and must arrange and pay for their doing so is not enough to change the character of the business.[14]

In sum, the Supreme Court in 1922 argued that baseball was not subject to federal antitrust laws because baseball did not represent interstate commerce. This argument was made despite the fact that the Supreme Court was aware major league baseball was played by teams in different states. As Quirk and Fort observe: "This was to become a highly controversial ruling. Within 20 years, the Court's expansion of the scope of the commerce clause negated essentially every substantive point that was made in the Holmes decision" (1985).

In 1953, the Supreme Court was again presented with the argument that baseball had violated antitrust laws.[15] George Toolson, a minor league player in the Yankees system, refused a reassignment by the Yankees to a different minor league team on the grounds that the Yankees shouldn't be able to prevent Toolson from selling his labor in a free market. In Toolson's view, he could probably reach

---

[13]This quote appeared in Zimbalist (1992, p. 9).

[14]Quirk and Fort (1992, p. 185).

[15]This case—*Toolson v. New York Yankees*, 346 U.S. 356 (1953)—is discussed in Quirk and Fort (1992, pp. 188–189) and Zimbalist (1992, p. 15).

the major leagues with a different organization, but the Yankees, who dominated baseball in the early 1950s, continued to keep Toolson in the minor leagues as insurance against a possible injury to one of the star players the Yankees retained on their world championship roster.

There was some expectation that the Supreme Court might reverse its 1922 ruling, but in a 7-2 vote, the Court upheld its decision. The one-paragraph opinion noted that the 1922 decision could be reversed by an act of Congress. In other words, the Court in 1953 didn't necessarily agree with the Court in 1922, but thought Congress should correct the Court's earlier mistake. Nevertheless, there was no action by Congress in 1953. And meanwhile, the Supreme Court issued a few more rulings that indicated some inconsistent thinking on the subject.

In 1957, the Supreme Court issued a ruling in *Radovich v. National Football League* that contradicted its position with respect to MLB.[16] The National Football League (NFL) had blacklisted George Radovich, a former All-Pro guard with the Detroit Lions, and worked to prevent him from getting a coaching job with the Pacific Coast League when he retired from playing. Radovich sued on antitrust grounds but a lower court dismissed the case, citing the Supreme Court's rulings in the *Federal Baseball* and *Toolson* cases. The case did advance to the Supreme Court where it was ruled that football—unlike baseball—was not exempt from antitrust laws.[17]

The notion that other sports leagues are not exempt from antitrust laws was upheld in *Haywood v. National Basketball Association.*[18] Spencer Haywood was a star player at Trinidad State Junior College, the University of Detroit, and for the 1968 U.S. Olympic team. After completing his sophomore season, he signed with the American Basketball Association (ABA). Haywood only played one season in the ABA before signing with the Seattle Super Sonics of the National Basketball Association (NBA). Seattle's signing of Haywood violated the NBA's rule that a player could not enter the NBA until four years had passed from the date of his high school graduation. Haywood sued, arguing that the NBA's rule violated the Sherman Antitrust Act.[19] In March 1971, the Supreme Court agreed with Haywood.

---

[16]The *Radovich v. NFL* case was discussed in Quirk and Fort (1992, pp. 189–190).

[17]Quirk and Fort (1992, p. 190).

[18]Details of *Haywood v. NBA* may be found at findlaw.com (http://caselaw.lp.findlaw.com/scripts/getcase.pl?navby=CASE&court=US&vol=401&page=1204).

[19]The Sherman Antitrust Act was passed in 1890. "The Sherman Act outlaws 'every contract, combination, or conspiracy in restraint of trade,' and any 'monopolization, attempted monopolization, or conspiracy or combination to monopolize'" (https://www.ftc.gov/tips-advice/competition-guidance/guide-antitrust-laws/antitrust-laws).

Given the rulings in the *Radovich* and *Haywood* cases, one might suspect that the Supreme Court was prepared to end the precedence set by *Federal League* and *Toolson*. However, the inconsistency of the Supreme Court continued in the Curt Flood case. In 1969, the St. Louis Cardinals traded Curt Flood, a 12-year MLB veteran and three-time All-Star, to the Philadelphia Phillies. Flood did not wish to move to Philadelphia and subsequently asked Commissioner Bowie Kuhn to rescind the transaction. In Flood's letter to Kuhn, he stated the following[20]:

> . . . I do not feel that I am a piece of property to be bought and sold irrespective of my wishes. . . . I, therefore, request that you make known to all Major League clubs my feelings in this matter, and advise them of my availability for the 1970 season.

Kuhn did not honor Flood's request. Consequently, Flood took his case to court, and it eventually reached the Supreme Court. In June 1972, in its 5-3 decision on *Flood v. Kuhn*, the Supreme Court voted to uphold the precedence of *Federal Baseball* and *Toolson*.

Justice Harry Blackmun wrote the following in the majority opinion[21]:

1. Professional baseball is a business, and it is engaged in interstate commerce.

2. With its reserve system enjoying exemption from the federal antitrust laws, baseball is, in a very distinct sense, an exception and an anomaly. *Federal Baseball* and *Toolson* have become an aberration confined to baseball.

3. Even though others might regard this as "unrealistic, inconsistent, or illogical," see *Radovich*, 352 U.S. at 352 U.S. 452, the aberration is an established one. . . .

Justice Blackmun went on to note that other sports are not exempt. Congress has the power to revoke baseball's antitrust exemption by legislative action. In sum, the majority of the Supreme Court in 1972 agreed that baseball shouldn't be exempt from antitrust laws, but believed it was up to Congress to end this exemption.

---

[20]This quote appeared in Edmund Edmonds, *The Curt Flood Act of 1998: A Hollow Gesture After All These Years?*, 9 Marq. Sports L. J. 315 (1999) (http://scholarship.law.marquette.edu/sportslaw/vol9/iss2/8).

[21]https://supreme.justia.com/cases/federal/us/407/258/case.html.

Congress didn't take any action in 1972. In fact, Congress didn't address this issue until 1998. By then, the absolute power of the reserve clause had been ended for more than 20 years.

The beginning of the end of the reserve clause in baseball takes us back to 1966. That year, the Major League Players Association (MLPA) hired Marvin Miller, an economist who had worked previously with the United Steelworkers of America (USW), as its executive director. As Miller noted in his autobiography,[22]

> Before 1966, the owners had a unilateral right to do, literally, anything they pleased; they could change the rules in the middle of a player's contract and say, "Here are the rules that now apply to you." The owners routinely tied players to documents — the Major League Rules, the Professional Baseball Rules, the league constitutions and bylaws — without even giving them copies of what they were agreeing to be bound by.

In 1968, the MLPA and the owners in MLB reached baseball's first collective bargaining agreement. As part of this agreement, owners were required to give a player a copy of every document that was part of the player's contract. This was clearly just a small step, since the big change came in 1970. That agreement introduced impartial grievance arbitration. Again, prior to 1966, the owner's power in baseball was essentially unchecked. Once the owners agreed to arbitration, any dispute between the owners and players couldn't simply be settled according to the owner's wishes.

Four years later, the owners learned what this meant with respect to the reserve clause. The reserve clause, as noted earlier, stated that if an agreement was not reached between a player and a club, "The club shall have the right to renew this contract for the period of *one year* on the same terms, except that the amount payable to the player shall be such as the club shall fix in said notice" (italics added to original; reprinted in Quirk and Fort, 1992, p. 185). Again, the owners interpreted this clause as indicating a team held a player's rights for as long as the team wished. The renewed contract also contained this same clause; therefore, the club could just renew a contract over and over again. Of course, one could read this clause differently. The clause does say "the right to renew this contract for the period of one year," so one could argue that one year only means one year.

In 1974, the matter moved beyond a simple academic debate.[23] Prior to the 1974 season, Andy Messersmith of the Los Angeles Dodgers and Dave McNally

---

[22]Marvin Miller, *A Whole Different Game: The Inside Story of Baseball's New Deal* (New York: Simon & Schuster, 1991), p. 213.

[23]This story appeared in Miller (1991, pp. 238–253).

of the Montreal Expos signed one-year contracts with their respective teams. When the 1974 season ended, each player refused to sign a new contract. The key player in this dispute was Messersmith.[24] In 1974, Messersmith was 28 years of age and ranked among the top 10 pitchers in the NL in wins, earned run average (ERA), and wins above replacement (WAR).[25] Messersmith was willing to re-sign with the Dodgers, but only if the team included a no-trade clause. The Dodgers refused to add such a clause and Messersmith refused to sign.

In 1975, Messersmith continued with the Dodgers, and again, his 1974 contract included the one-year renewal. Messersmith again finished among the top 10 NL pitchers in wins, ERA, and WAR. The Dodgers still refused to include a no-trade clause. At the end of the 1975 season, when the one-year renewals had expired, grievances were filed on behalf of Messersmith and McNally. The owners argued that although neither player had signed a contract before the 1975 season, their current teams still held the rights to both players. The union argued that "one year" meant one year, and therefore, both players were free to sign with any team (i.e., as free agents).

Again, the 1970 collective bargaining agreement stated that disputes between owners and labor would be submitted to binding arbitration. The arbitration panel consisted of John Gaherin (representing the owners), Marvin Miller (representing the players), and Peter Seitz (an independent voice on the panel). Since Gaherin represented the interests of owners and Miller those of the union, it was obviously Seitz who would primarily decide the case. The initial hearing on this case was scheduled for November 21, 1975. As chance would have it, the current collective bargaining agreement between players and owners was set to expire on December 31, 1975. Consequently, Seitz recommended that the owners and labor settle this issue in the collective bargaining process, but the owners rejected such a suggestion; therefore, Seitz issued his ruling on December 23, 1975. His ruling was simple: The reserve clause did not extend beyond one year. Consequently, Messersmith and McNally became free agents, and Seitz's decision

---

[24]As Miller (1991, pp. 243–244) noted, McNally had pitched 13 seasons for the Baltimore Orioles. After 1974, though, he was traded to the Montreal Expos. McNally pitched 12 games for the Expos and then left baseball. McNally had never signed his contract with the Expos, so if the reserve clause was interpreted as being only for one year (as the union argued), McNally would be a free agent at the end of the season. From Miller's perspective, McNally was a great addition to the case because (1) it gave the union someone else to challenge the rule besides Messersmith (as Miller put it, a "relief pitcher" for the case) and (2) McNally did not intend to return to baseball so he could not be subject to any future retaliation.

[25]We will discuss statistical measures for individual athletes later in the text. This discussion will note that Wins and ERA are poor measures of a pitcher's contribution to team success. Nevertheless, these measures are generally considered as relevant to a pitcher's value and likely led Messersmith to finish second in Cy Young voting in 1974.

ended the strict reserve clause in baseball. Most baseball players were not signed to long-term contracts, so a large number of free agents were about to hit the market.

With that in mind, it is time to return to our basic supply and demand framework. Prices in a market are a function of supply and demand. If a supply increases, prices must fall. If owners were concerned about the high price of talent, they would want to encourage a large supply of free agents.

The owner of the Oakland A's, Charles Finley, understood the basic economics of the free-agent labor market.[26] Finley wanted to let all players become free agents after each season. Unfortunately for the owners, no other owner understood the basic supply and demand model. Consequently, the owners and union reached an agreement that limited the supply of free agents, and subsequently raised the costs of these players. The agreement reached in 1976 gave players the right to free agency after six years of Major League service. Players without this much experience would work under the reserve clause.[27] Hence, the reserve clause, at least for veterans, finally ended in baseball. It was not ended by the court system or the legislative action of Congress (although they did finally address the labor market in baseball in 1998).[28] Collective bargaining between the players and owners eventually ended the institution.

It is important to note that collective bargaining also allowed this institution to exist for players without enough experience to qualify. This is important because one might suspect that future players who did not participate in the collective bargaining negotiations in 1976 might hope to challenge the reserve clause again in the court system (after all, this is clearly a violation of the antitrust laws). To support this, the courts have ruled that players, whether in the union or not at the time an agreement was reached, are subject to the particulars of that agreement. As a consequence, professional sports in North America continue to have a collection of labor market institutions that do not exist in other industries.

---

[26]Story told in Miller (1991, p. 370).

[27]Players with more than two years of experience had the right to have their salary disputes referred to binding—final offer—arbitration. The term final offer arbitration is defined as follows: If a player and a team cannot agree to a contract, each side submits its final offer to an independent arbitration panel that selects either the offer made by the team or the offer made by the player. This system forces each side to be "reasonable" since an "unreasonable" offer is more likely to be rejected.

[28]The Curt Flood Act of 1998 ended baseball's exemption from antitrust laws with respect to labor issues. See John T. Wolohan, *The Curt Flood Act of 1998 and Major League Baseball's Federal Antitrust Exemption*, 9 Marq. SportsL. J. 347 (1999) (http://scholarship.law.marquette.edu/sportslaw/vol9/iss2/9) and Edmonds (1999).

4.3 The Reverse-Order Draft

One of the oddest institutions is the reverse-order draft. For example, upon completing your college education, you will move into the workforce, where you will play a role in choosing your future employer. Imagine that a prospective employer could simply acquire the rights to your labor. Upon acquiring your rights, the employer informs you that you will either work for it or you will simply not work at all. Furthermore, another right the employer has is the ability to force you to work in whatever place in the world it chooses.

Outside of sports, such an acquisition of rights doesn't happen. In professional North American sports, this process is real and has actually become a fairly popular television program in both the NFL and NBA. The person we blame for this odd institution is Bert Bell.[29]

The story of Bert Bell and the draft begins in 1935. That year, the Brooklyn Dodgers and Philadelphia Eagles of the NFL entered into a bidding war for the services of fullback Stanislaus Clarence ("Stockyard Stan") Kostka. For those unfamiliar with college football in the 1930s, Kostka was considered the star player of the "Hook 'Em Cows." For those unfamiliar with the Hook 'Em Cows, this is the name bestowed on the Minnesota Golden Gophers of 1934.

In the midst of the 1934 season, *Time*[30] wondered if the Hook 'Em Cows were not only the best team of 1934, but perhaps the greatest team in the history of college football (which at that point already dated back a few decades). Minnesota finished the 1934 season with a perfect 8-0 record and the mythical national championship. After seven games, *Time* noted the following statistics for the team:

- 236 points scored versus 38 points allowed

- 122 first downs versus 37 first downs for the opponent

- 2,418 rushing yards or more than 300 yards per game versus 533 rushing yards for the opponent

These impressive statistics do not convey the dominance of the team. In the first half of each game, Minnesota developed a habit of punting on second down. Only in the second half would they make every effort to score. Despite the odd policy of punting on a second down in the first half of games, Minnesota still

---

[29]The story of Bert Bell and the draft was reported in Quirk and Fort (1992, pp. 187–188) and Berri and Schmidt (2010, pp. 64–65).

[30]"Football," *Time*, November 26, 1934 (http://content.time.com/time/magazine/article/0,9171,882323,00.html).

dominated their opponents in 1934. The "hero" of this team was Stan Kostka, who "in the first six games of the season he accounted for 532 yd. or more than a quarter of Minnesota's total ground gained by rushing. Minnesota's greatest ground-gainer, he can run 100 yd. in 12 sec. in uniform."[31]

When the 1934 season ended, Kostka's college career was over. At that time, there was no college draft, so like many outstanding college graduates who reach the labor market, a bidding war ensued for Kostka's services. The winning team was the Brooklyn Dodgers (yes, the NFL team in Brooklyn—like the baseball team—was called the Dodgers). The Dodgers paid $5,000.

Relative to what players make in the NFL today, Kostka was not paid very much. According to the Bureau of Labor Statistics, $5,000 in 1935 was worth about $89,000 in 2017.[32] In 2017, the minimum salary for an NFL rookie was $465,000, so Kostka was only earning about 20%—in real terms—of what the worst rookies in the NFL are guaranteed today. Nevertheless, Kostka was being paid a salary similar to what Bronco Nagurski earned in the 1930s, and Nagurski was an NFL All-Pro in 1932, 1933, and 1934. The idea that a player with no NFL experience, even one dubbed "King Kong," should earn as much as an NFL star probably struck some people as problematic.

Bert Bell, owner of the Philadelphia Eagles, offered a solution to this problem. Bell argued that NFL teams should no longer compete for the services of college talent. In contrast, teams should conduct a reverse-order draft. Starting in 1936, Bell proposed that the worst NFL team should have first choice among the best college talent, the second worst would have the second choice, the third worst the third choice, and so on. Once a team selected a specific player, he would not be able to negotiate with any other team. In sum, the bidding war the NFL witnessed for Kostka would be eliminated since college players could only negotiate with one team.

Bell's proposal was adopted by the NFL, and in 1936 the worst team in the league—yes, Bell's Eagles—made the first choice in the first NFL draft. With this first choice, Bell selected Jay Berwanger of the University of Chicago (which no longer has a football program, but was once a football powerhouse). Berwanger won the very first Heisman Trophy in 1935, and upon drafting Berwanger, Bell traded his rights to the Chicago Bears.

Berwanger faced a different labor market than Kostka. We do not know the offer the Bears extended to Berwanger, only the fact that he cited the low pay in the NFL at the time in defending his decision to skip an entire professional

---

[31]"Football," *Time*, November 26, 1934 (http://content.time.com/time/magazine/article/0,9171,882323,00.html).

[32]http://www.bls.gov/data/inflation_calculator.htm (accessed April 23, 2017).

football career.[33] Yes, the first pick in the first draft never played in the NFL, and Berwanger wasn't the only drafted player to make that decision. The draft in 1936 had nine rounds and 81 selections overall. Of these 81 selections, only 28 players actually played in the NFL.[34]

Bell's NFL experience was quite a bit longer, and much more successful from the NFL's perspective.[35] Bell continued to own the Eagles until 1940 and then became co-owner of the Pittsburgh Steelers until 1946. After that, Bell served as commissioner of the NFL until his death in 1959. As commissioner, he dealt with the All-America Football Conference, a rival league that existed from 1946 to 1949. The subsequent merger brought the San Francisco 49ers and the Cleveland Browns into the NFL.

Although his work as commissioner had a lasting effect on the NFL, one could argue that Bell's reverse-order draft had the largest impact on professional sports in North America. This institution was part of the NBA when it was founded in 1947. In the 1960s, both the National Hockey League or NHL (in 1963) and MLB (in 1965) also adopted a reverse-order draft.

Later on, we will discuss decision making in the draft and how this impacts players, teams, and competitive balance. For now, we will move on to other institutions leagues have utilized to promote competitive balance.

4.4 Simon Rottenberg Defends the Free Market

After 1965, the labor market in baseball looked quite good from the perspective of owners. Most players entered the labor market via the draft.[36] Once the player signed with the team who drafted him, the team would hold his rights forever, or at least until the team decided it did not wish to employ the player. The league argued that the draft and reserve clause were necessary to promote competitive balance. But in 1956, Simon Rottenberg[37] told a different story in what many consider the first academic article on the subject

---

[33]http://athletics.uchicago.edu/history/history-berwanger.htm.

[34]http://www.pro-football-reference.com/years/1936/draft.htm. The aforementioned Kostka didn't play much in the NFL. In one season for the Dodgers, Kostka played in nine games and rushed for 249 yards (on 63 carries for a 4.0 per-carry average). After that debut, Kostka never played in the NFL again (http://www.pro-football-reference.com/players/K/KostSt20.htm).

[35]http://www.profootballhof.com/hof/member.aspx?PLAYER_ID=23.

[36]The exception were international players.

[37]Simon Rottenberg, "The Baseball Players' Labor Market," *Journal of Political Economy* 64, no. 3 (June 1956): 242–258.

of sports economics.[38] Rottenberg began by acknowledging the competitive balance story, or the argument that the reserve clause prevented the rich clubs from "taking all the competent players for themselves and leaving only the incompetent for the other teams" (p. 246).

Rottenberg then proceeded to show—via an entirely deductive argument—that this "premise was false." Rottenberg began by assuming that a league is made up of rich and poor teams. Next, let's assume that the labor market for players has no restrictions. Given these two assumptions, Rottenberg argued that many may think the very best players would be hired by the richest teams. One might think the result would be a league where the richest teams would dominate and outcomes would become much more certain. Rottenberg, though, asserted that this view is incorrect.

As Rottenberg argued, sports are quite different from other markets. In other industries, the elimination of competition is considered positive from the perspective of an individual firm. He notes, "No team can be successful unless its competitors also survive and prosper sufficiently so that the differences in the quality of play among teams are not 'too great'" (1956, p. 254). He further points out that

> when a team already has three .350 hitters—it will not pay to employ another .350 hitter. If a team goes on increasing the quantity of the factor, players, by hiring additional stars, it will find that total output—that is, admission receipts . . . will rise at a less rapid rate and finally will fall absolutely. At some point, therefore, a first star player is worth more to poor Team B than, say, a third star to rich Team A. (p. 255)

Given this result, Rottenberg states that a reserve system is unnecessary. Because of diminishing returns, a rich team is not going to get much benefit from hiring every single star player. In addition, he also indicates that although rich teams may want to win, because competitive balance is important to demand,[39] playing talent will not be hoarded by the wealthiest clubs. In fact, Rottenberg asserts "that a market in which freedom is limited by a reserve rule such as that which now governs the baseball labor market distributes players among teams . . . as a free market would" (1956, p. 255).

---

[38]In "College Athletics, Universities and the NCAA: Western Social Science Association Presidential Address," *Social Science Journal* 44, no. 1: (2007): 11–22, Jim Peach noted that Rottenberg was not exactly first. Thorstein Veblen devoted several pages to athletics in his most famous work, *The Theory of the Leisure Class* (1898), a point we noted in the first chapter to this book.

[39]Rottenberg did not offer an empirical study supporting the notion that competitive balance is important. As we will note, subsequent studies cast doubt on the significance of competitive balance to league attendance.

invariance principle
The distribution of talent in sports leagues moves to its highest-valued use regardless of who (either the players or the owners) receives the revenue generated by the players.

Coase theorem When there are zero transaction costs, the application of legal rights has no effect upon the allocation of resources among economic enterprises — in baseball, the allocation of players will be the same under the reserve clause (where owners have the legal right to sell a player's talent) and a free market (where players have the legal right to sell their services).

Not only is the reserve system unnecessary, Rottenberg closes his argument by noting that a free market is actually preferred. A free market and the reserve system would distribute talent in the same fashion, and this concept is known as Rottenberg's **invariance principle**. Here is how Rodney Fort (2003)[40] enunciated it: "The distribution of talent in a league is invariant to who gets the revenues generated by the players; talent moves to its highest valued use in the league whether player or owners receive (the revenues the player generates)" (p. 242). Rottenberg's invariance principle is similar to a theorem credited to Ronald Coase. In 1960, Coase published "The Problem of Social Cost," which he argued would be the "the most widely cited article in the whole of modern economic literature."[41] He later received the Nobel Prize in 1991 for what became known as the **Coase theorem**.

Oddly enough, this theorem was actually stated by George Stigler (a point Coase made in his lecture when accepting the Nobel Prize).[42] Stigler defined the Coase theorem as when there are zero transaction costs, the application of legal rights has no effect on the allocation of resources among economic enterprises.[43]

If we applied the Coase theorem to MLB, we would observe that this theorem argues that the allocation of players will be the same under the reserve clause (where owners have the legal right to sell a player's talent) and a free market (where players have the legal right to sell their services). In other words, the Coase theorem is essentially the same as the Rottenberg invariance principle. A hypothetical example might make the arguments of Rottenberg (and Coase) clearer. Imagine a player who generates $500,000 in Kansas City (a relatively small market) but $1 million in New York (a relatively large market). Because the player can't bargain with different teams, his earnings are restricted (let's imagine $200,000). So Kansas City would receive $300,000 extra by employing this player (i.e. $500,000 minus $200,000). But because the New York team would pocket $800,000 extra employing this player, New York has an incentive acquiring this player from Kansas City. So under the reserve clause the player tends to migrate to the larger market.

This is the same outcome, though, in a free market. In that market, the New York team would be willing to pay up to $1 million to acquire the free agent while Kansas City would only be willing to pay $500,000. So in a free

[40]Rodney Fort, *Sports Economics* (Upper Saddle River, NJ: Prentice Hall, 2003).

[41]"Ronald H. Coase—Autobiography" that can be found at the Nobel Prize Committee's website (http://nobelprize.org/economics/laureates/1991/coase-autobio.html).

[42]"Ronald H. Coase—Prize Lecture" (http://nobelprize.org/economics/laureates/1991/coase-lecture.html). Stigler was awarded the Nobel Prize in 1982 (although, not for articulating the Coase theorem).

[43]Samuelson, Paul. "Some Uneasiness with the Coase Theorem," *Japan and the World Economy* 7 (1995): 2. Samuelson noted that "Ronald Coase never wrote IT down." The original quote derives from George Stigler, *Memoirs of an Unregulated Economist* (New York: Basic Books, 1988).

market, the player also migrates to a larger market. But in a free market, the player pockets much more money.

Before moving on, let's make one more observation about Rottenberg and Coase. If you check the citations listed in the notes here, you will note that Rottenberg's article appeared four years before Coase's paper was published. Maybe Rottenberg should have received a Nobel Prize for his work on baseball![44] Although Rottenberg never impressed the Nobel Prize committee, he certainly impressed economists looking at the sports industry. In the 1950s, when baseball still operated under the reserve clause, Rottenberg argued that the distribution of labor in baseball did not depend on such labor market restrictions.

4.5 Salary Caps, Luxury Taxes, Revenue Sharing, Oh My!

When a free market finally came to professional team sports in the 1970s, sports leagues did not think life would stay the same. Again, leagues had for almost a century argued that an unrestrained labor market would lead to competitive imbalance. Consequently, professional sports leagues adopted a variety of institutions designed to promote balance (at least, that was their argument) by restricting how much teams can spend on players. The institutions adopted include caps on payrolls, caps on individual salaries, luxury taxes, and revenue sharing. Each of the four major professional team sports leagues in North America chose to adopt a selection of these measures, but the NBA is unique in adopting all.

Payroll Caps

Free agency came to the NBA at around the same time it arrived in baseball. In 1976, the NBA and Players Association settled the Oscar Robertson case. Six years earlier, when Robertson was head of the NBA's players union, it filed a suit to stop a merger between the ABA and NBA.[45] The existence of two leagues bidding separately for playing talent had bid up the price of players. A merger would obviously reduce the players' bargaining power.

---

[44]Then again, Deidre McCloskey (1998) observed that the original Coase theorem appeared long before the reserve clause was enacted by the NL. McCloskey (1998) went on to note that how the Coase theorem is interpreted is often incorrect. Economists frequently emphasize the idea that when transaction costs are zero, the assignment of legal right doesn't matter. But according to McCloskey, that argument emphasizes the wrong point. In the real world, transaction costs do exist. Therefore, one could also argue that when transactions aren't zero, the assignment of legal rights definitely matters. McCloskey also noted that this latter interpretation was supported by Coase. Deidre McCloskey, "Other Things Equal: The So-Called Coase Theorem," *Eastern Economic Journal* 24, no. 3 (Summer 1998): 367–371.

[45]http://www.cbafaq.com/salarycap.htm (Section 6).

In 1976, the players agreed to this merger in exchange for the implementation of limited free agency. Free agency was liberalized in subsequent negotiations, and by 1983, teams in the NBA were claiming financial losses. Consequently, the NBA made an apparently[46] novel proposal to the Players Association. In exchange for a guaranteed share of league revenue, the teams would be constrained by a salary cap. Players were guaranteed 53% of league revenues, while each team's payroll would be capped at $3.6 million.[47]

Theoretically, the salary cap should result in improved competitive balance. If it is the case that teams that spend more win more,[48] then rich teams will win more than poor teams. While the cap on payrolls limits the rich team's ability to take advantage of their increased resources, capped payrolls could also reduce the theoretical gap between the rich and poor on the field of play. The effectiveness of the cap depends on its enforcement. The NBA instituted a "soft" cap, which makes it possible for teams to have a payroll that exceeds the actual cap. One such exemption is referred to as the "Larry Bird exemption,"[49] which allowed teams to exceed the cap on payrolls in order to re-sign one of their own players.[50]

The Individual Salary Cap

Teams could exceed the cap on payrolls, so the efficacy of this institution was considered limited. Therefore, the NBA instituted two new caps, but before discussing these, we need to note an issue with labels. The cap on payrolls is called a "salary cap," but it is technically a cap on how much a team can spend on all its players. The NBA adopted two restrictions on the payment to individual salaries, and such restrictions should be thought of as salary caps.

The first salary cap, a rookie salary cap, was adopted in 1995. Glenn Robinson was the first player selected in the 1994 draft. After a holdout, Robinson eventually signed a contract worth $68.5 million over 10 years. Such

---

[46]"Apparently" is appropriate here. Larry Coon notes that the NBA had a cap on payrolls in 1946–47. http://www.cbafaq.com/salarycap.htm (Section 5).

[47]The story of how the salary (or payroll) cap came about in the NBA in 1983 was told in Paul Staudohar, "Salary Caps in Professional Team Sports," *Compensation and Working Conditions*, Spring 1998, pp. 3–11.

[48]And yes, we have already seen this is not entirely the case.

[49]It is believed that this exemption was put in place, so the Boston Celtics could re-sign Larry Bird. As Larry Coon notes, though, Bird signed a long-term contract before the salary cap went into effect. Thus, although this exemption bears Bird's name, it was never used on Bird. See http://www.cbafaq.com/salarycap.htm (Section 25).

[50]The exemption, however, soon led to some problems. In 1993, the Portland Trail Blazers were able to acquire Chris Dudley, a center whom a number of teams wished to acquire, for a one-year contract worth only $790,000 (a contract considered well below his market value). After this one-year contract expired, the Blazers then re-signed Dudley for a contract worth $4 million per year. The story of Dudley's contract was told in Staudohar (1998, p. 5).

a contract for a player who had never played in the NBA led the owners to ask for a rookie salary cap as part of the 1995 collective bargaining agreement.[51] This cap ended rookie holdouts in the NBA.

The next collective bargaining agreement introduced a cap on the salaries of veteran players. To date, the NBA is the only North American sports league with this restriction, which has created a collection of players known as "max players." The specific maximum salary cap depends on a player's years in the NBA. For example, a maximum salary for players with fewer than six years of service in 2013–14 is $13.7 million, while a player with more than 10 years of service is $19.2 million.[52]

The NBA's willingness to cap the pay of rookies and veterans illustrates a key feature of labor unions in sports. Rookies—who are not in the union until they actually sign—and elite veterans are not the primary members of unions. Consequently, we should not be surprised that unions would limit the pay of these two groups in negotiating with owners. More on labor unions in sports will be offered in Chapter 5. In 2013–14, it is believed that 16 players in the NBA were so-called max players.[53]

The Luxury Tax

Despite the cap on team, rookie, and individual veteran pay, the NBA decided further restrictions were necessary. The 1999 collective bargaining agreement imposed a luxury tax on teams. A luxury tax is essentially a secondary cap on payrolls, but it was not collected until the 2002–03 NBA season.[54] Historically, the system was simply a dollar-to-dollar tax, or a team paid a $1 tax for each dollar its payroll exceeded the luxury tax threshold. Starting with the 2013–14 season, the tax in the NBA became quite a bit harsher. That season, teams that exceeded the luxury tax threshold would have been charged as follows:

Amount Taxed ($) per Dollar over Threshold	Luxury Tax Threshold ($ millions)	Up to a Payroll of ($ millions)
1.50	71.7	76.69
1.75	76.69	81.69
2.50	81.69	86.69
3.25	86.69	91.69
$3.75	91.70	96.69
$4.25	96.70	101.69

*for every additional $5 million in team salary, the amount taxed increased by $0.50. So if the table were continued, the next $5 million would see a tax of $4.75.

[51]http://www.cbafaq.com/salarycap.htm (Section 49).

[52]http://www.cbafaq.com/salarycap.htm (Section 16).

[53]Chuck Myron (http://www.hoopsrumors.com/2013/08/maximum-salary-players.html).

[54]A complete history for luxury tax payments from Mark Deeks and ShamSports.com (http://www.shamsports.com/2013/07/complete-history-of-luxury-tax-payments.html).

To illustrate, consider the Brooklyn Nets of 2013–14.[55] The Nets led the NBA with a reported payroll of $101,291,208. Given this payroll and the luxury tax, an estimate of the Nets' luxury tax obligations in 2013–14 is provided in Table 4.1.

Table 4.1 Estimating the Brooklyn Nets' Luxury Tax Payment: 2013–14			
	Payroll (in millions)	Tax Rate	Tax Payment (in millions)
Luxury tax threshold	$71.70	$0.00	$0.00
First level	$76.69	$1.50	$7.49
Second level	$81.69	$1.75	$8.75
Third level	$86.69	$2.50	$12.50
Fourth level	$91.69	$3.25	$16.25
Fifth level	$96.69	$3.75	$18.75
Nets' payroll (before taxes)	$101.29	$4.25	$19.56
		Total Tax Payment	$83.29
		Total Payroll with Tax Payment	$184.58

These numbers indicate the Nets were the most expensive team in NBA history. We also need to make two more observations:

- The Nets were owned by Mikhail Prokhorov, a billionaire from Russia. Given Prokhorov's resources and desire to win an NBA title, the NBA's luxury tax system—which nearly doubled the Nets' payroll—does not seem likely to restrain Brooklyn's spending.

- In 2013–14, the Nets did not look at all like a championship team. When the season ended, the team's record was only 44-38, and its point differential of −1.0 suggests it was actually below average.

Revenue Sharing

Let's conclude our discussion of labor market institutions with a brief discussion of revenue sharing. Each of the major North American professional team sports leagues shares revenues to some extent, although it was only recently that the NBA moved beyond sharing national broadcasting revenue and began sharing

---

[55]Find NBA payroll data at http://hoopshype.com/salaries.htm.

local gate revenues. As of 2017, revenues are still not equalized across all teams. What if the NBA completely shared all revenue?[56]

One might believe that a league where all revenue was shared would result in the same spending on talent. Therefore, assuming that teams know precisely whom to hire (equal spending leading to equal talent on the field), leagues would be completely balanced. Such is not the case.[57]

Later in this chapter, we will note empirical evidence that should be somewhat obvious with regard to this false assumption. A win in a larger market is worth more than a win in a small market. More wins in the larger market will increase the pool of revenue, and hence increase the revenue share going to all teams. Both large and small market teams prefer teams in larger markets to win more games.

For now, let's conclude this discussion by enumerating the institutions (see Table 4.2) that reportedly exist to promote competitive balance in each of the four major North American sports.[58] Except for salary arbitration, the NBA has adopted all the institutions listed. In contrast, MLB has relatively few restrictions in its labor market. Now that we have briefly detailed the institutions employed, let's seek to understand whether or not these have the desired effect on competitive balance.

Table 4.2 Institutions in Each of the Major North American Sports Leagues

Institution	NBA	MLB	NFL	NHL
Payroll cap	Soft cap	No	Hard cap	Hard cap
Individual salary cap	Yes	No	No	Yes
Rookie salary restrictions	Yes	No	Yes	Yes
Luxury tax	Yes	Yes	No	No
Reverse-order draft	Yes	Yes	Yes	Yes
Salary arbitration	No	Yes	No	Yes

---

[56]For literature exploring the impact revenue sharing has on competitive balance in sports, see Stefan Kesenne, "Revenue Sharing and Competitive Balance in Professional Team Sports," *Journal of Sports Economics* 1, no. 1 (2000): 56–65; Stefan Kesenne, "Revenue Sharing and Competitive Balance: Does the Invariance Proposition Hold?," *Journal of Sports Economics* 1, no. 6 (2005): 98–106; Stefan Kesenne, "Revenue Sharing and Owner Profits in Professional Team Sports," *Journal of Sports Economics* 5, no. 8 (2007): 519–529; Helmut M. Dietl, Martin Grossmann, and Markus Lang, "Competitive Balance and Revenue Sharing in Sports Leagues With Utility-Maximizing Teams," *Journal of Sports Economics* 3, no. 12 (2011): 284–308.

[57]Leeds and von Allmen (2011, p. 163).

[58]Adapted from Daniel Rascher and Timothy DeSchriver, "Smooth Operators: Recent Collective Bargaining in Major League Baseball," *International Journal of Sport Finance* 7 (2012): 176–208.

<u>4.6</u> The Noll–Scully Measure of Competitive Balance

We need a measure of balance to ascertain whether or not these institutions alter competitive balance. Literature in sports economics provides a number of choices,[59] but let's begin with what is probably the easiest to calculate and understand.

If a league is relatively balanced, the difference between the teams should be relatively small. Likewise, a league that is relatively imbalanced would exhibit large differences in the teams. To ascertain the size of these differences, look back at the AL in 1932. **Table 4.3** reports the final standings from this season. As one can see, the New York Yankees easily won the pennant. At this time, there were no divisions or playoffs in the AL. The team that had the most wins in the regular season advanced to the World Series. In this season, the Yankees, led by Babe Ruth, advanced to the Fall Classic, where New York swept the Chicago Cubs (it was the last title won by Ruth as a player).

Table 4.3 American League Standings: 1932

AL Team	Wins	Losses	Winning Percentage
New York Yankees	107	47	0.686
Philadelphia Athletics	94	60	0.610
Washington Senators	93	61	0.604
Cleveland Indians	87	65	0.569
Detroit Tigers	76	75	0.497
St. Louis Browns	63	91	0.409
Chicago White Sox	49	102	0.322
Boston Red Sox	43	111	0.279

When we look at these standings, the dominance of the Yankees stands out, but we also see how poorly the White Sox and Red Sox performed. A glance at these numbers suggests the AL in 1932 was not very balanced, but upon closer examination, one can also measure disparity in the outcomes observed.

One way to measure disparity is to calculate the standard deviation. As explained in Appendix A of this chapter,[60] standard deviations allow us to see the

---

[59]The many choices have been detailed in Dorian Owen, "Measurement of Competitive Balance and Uncertainty of Outcome," in John Goddard and Peter Sloan (eds.), *Handbook on the Economics of Professional Football* (Cheltenham and Camberley, UK: Edward Elgar, 2015), pp. 41–59. Owen noted that the Noll–Scully measure detailed here is "the most widely used measure of competitive balance in sports leagues."

[60]See the explanation in Appendix A to intuitively understand how standard deviation is calculated.

average difference between each observation and the average value in the sample in a series of numbers. Standard deviation is both simple to calculate and easy to understand (again, read the appendix).

Standard deviation is a simple concept, but it poses a problem. Consider the average standard deviation of winning percentage for 10 recent seasons from the NL, AL, NBA, and NFL.

Table 4.4 10 Years of Average Competitive Balance		
League	Season	Average Standard Deviation
NL	2007–16	0.068
AL	2007–16	0.067
NBA	2006–07 to 2015–16	0.160
NFL	2006–15	0.197

Table 4.4 suggests that baseball is more competitive than the NBA or NFL, but an issue exists with this comparison. Roger Noll (1988)[61] and Gerald Scully (1989)[62] illustrated this issue by independently developing a measure of competitive balance that compared the standard deviation of winning percentage to what we would see if the teams in a league were of equal playing strength. A league of equal teams can be thought of as an "ideal league," and the level of balance in this ideal (i.e., the **idealized standard deviation**) is calculated as the ratio of the mean winning percentage in the league to the square root of a league's schedule length.[63] The calculation of the idealized standard deviation illustrates the importance of schedule length. The shorter a league's schedule, as Table 4.5 illustrates, the larger will be a league's standard deviation of winning percentage.

idealized standard deviation The ratio of the mean winning percentage in the league to the square root of a league's schedule length; illustrates the importance of schedule length.

[61]Roger Noll, "Professional Basketball," *Stanford University Studies in Industrial Economics*, No. 144, 1988.

[62]Gerald Scully, *The Business of Major League Baseball* (Chicago: University of Chicago Press, 1989).

[63]Quirk and Fort detail the Noll-Scully measure on pp. 244–245. Here is the math for the idealized standard deviation:

$$\sigma_{lt}^{ideal} = \frac{\mu(wp)_{lt}}{\sqrt{N}}$$

where $\mu(wp)_{lt}$ = the mean winning percentage in the league

N = the total number of regular-season games

Table 4.5 Idealized Standard Deviations for the Major League Baseball, National Basketball Association, and National Football League		
League	Schedule	Idealized Standard Deviation
MLB	162	0.039
NBA	82	0.055
NFL	16	0.125

The approach Noll and Scully took in constructing a competitive balance metric is called the **Noll–Scully measure**. It compares the observed standard deviation of performance to an idealized standard deviation given a league's schedule length.[64] As the actual standard deviation (the numerator) gets closer to the idealized standard deviation (the denominator), the value of the Noll–Scully measure will approach a value of 1. Therefore, values closer to 1 indicate greater competitive balance. As seen in **Table 4.6**, such a comparison indicates that across the last 10 seasons, the NFL and NHL have been the most competitive, and the NBA seems to have competitive balance problems.

Table 4.6 Average Noll–Scully Measure			
League	Season	Average Standard Deviation	Average Noll–Scully Competitive Balance Measure[65]
NL	2007–16	0.068	1.76
AL	2007–16	0.067	1.70
NBA	2006–07 to 2015–16	0.160	2.87
NFL	2006–15	0.197	1.57
NHL	2006–07 to 2015–16	NA[66]	1.33

[64]Here is the math for the Noll–Scully measure:

$$CB_{it} = \frac{\sigma(wp)_{it}^{actual}}{\sigma(wp)_{it}^{ideal}}$$

Dorian Owen and Nicholas King, "Competitive Balance Measures in Sports Leagues: The Effects of Variation in Season Length," *Economic Inquiry* 53, no. 1 (2015): 731–744 presents a simulation that indicates this metric does not completely control for the impact of schedule length.

[65]Calculated as the average standard deviation across 10 years divided by the idealized standard deviation for the league.

[66]Unlike the other major North American sports, the NHL doesn't rank teams by winning percentage but rather considers standing points. The current formula for standing points is as follows:

NHL Standing Points = 2 × Wins + 1 × Overtime Losses

4.7 A Simple Snapshot of League Institutions

What explains how competitive balance varies across team and across different leagues? Given our discussion thus far, one might suspect the primary factor determining competitive balance is the various labor market institutions sports leagues have employed. With that hypothesis in mind, our first attempt to explain what determines competitive balance involves evaluating the impact of various labor market institutions, via a series of before and after snapshots.

Table 4.7 reports average competitive balance before and after each institution was enacted. Note that this approach assumes the only factor impacting

Table 4.7 Balance Before and After Various League Institutions							
League	Event	Year	Seasons Since Event	Balance Before	Balance After	Balance Improved?	Statistically Significant?
AL	Reverse-order draft[a]	1965	51	2.49	1.81	Yes	Yes
NL	Reverse-order draft[a]	1965	51	2.30	1.75	Yes	Yes
AL	Free agency	1976	40	2.25	1.82	Yes	Yes
NL	Free agency	1976	40	2.20	1.72	Yes	Yes
AL	Luxury tax	2003	14	1.78	1.82	No	No
NL	Luxury tax	2003	14	1.73	1.73	No	No
NFL	Payroll cap	1993	23	1.55	1.52	Yes	No
NHL	Payroll cap[a]	2006	11	1.72	1.36	Yes	Yes
NBA	Payroll cap	1983	33	2.49	2.83	No	Yes
NBA	Salary cap	1999	17	2.88	2.78	Yes	No

[a]Result consistent with what proponents of institutional change predicted.

The Noll–Scully measure requires a slightly different approach. First, one needs to calculate the standard deviation for standing points. For example, from 2001–02 to 2011–12, the standard deviation for standing points in the NHL has been 14.1, on average. The average standing points across these 10 years have been 90.1. Given this value, and a schedule length of 82 games, the idealized standard deviation for the NHL has been 9.95, on average. And that means the average Noll–Scully measure of competitive balance has averaged 1.42.

One should also add, prior to the lockout of 2004–05, an NHL game could finish in a tie. If that happened, a team received 1 point for a tie (and 2 points for a win and 1 point for an overtime loss). And prior to the 1999–00 season, teams only received 2 points for a win and 1 point for a tie. The 2012–13 NHL season was shortened to 48 games by a lockout. For that season, the average standing points were 53.4, so the idealized standard deviation was 7.7. The actual standard deviation was 9.6, so the Noll–Scully measure of competitive balance was 1.25.

competitive balance is the institutional change. No other factor is considered and no other factor is controlled for in the analysis, so the picture is clearly incomplete.

All that said, looking beyond at whether or not balance improved after each institution was established, the table also reports whether or not the change was statistically significant. In the table, the row "AL" and column "Balance Before" indicate that in the 48 seasons since the reverse-order draft was instituted, competitive balance in the AL was 2.49 times the ideal. For the NL, we note an average mark of 2.30. After the draft was put in place, the ratio of the actual standard deviation to ideal declined in both leagues, and the difference is statistically significant.[67] This suggests that the draft improved competitive balance in baseball.

Such is what proponents of the draft would have predicted. Prior to the draft, amateur talent sold in a free market. In such a market, the richest teams would be able to sign the very best talent. After the draft was instituted, the weaker teams in baseball had access to the very best amateur talent. Consequently, the draft allowed the gap between the best and worst in baseball to narrow.

We should note again that the theoretical work of Rottenberg suggests that both the draft and free agency should have no impact on balance. Once again, whether the players own the right to sell their labor on a free market or whether the teams own the rights to this labor, Rottenberg argued that the distribution of talent (i.e. competitive balance) would be the same. Our simple snapshot approach—which again is incomplete—would suggest Rottenberg was not entirely correct.

In contrast, the institution of free agency in 1976 had the opposite effect. The end of the reserve clause gave the teams with the most money access to the best free agents. This should have allowed the gap between the rich and poor to grow and, consequently, competitive balance to decline, but the results indicate that balance in both the AL and NL improved after the strict reserve clause ended.

When we look at the other institutions established in North American sports over the past 30 years, we see more results that seem to defy expectations. Competitive balance in baseball hasn't been impacted by baseball's luxury tax, and a similar story can be told about the NFL payroll cap. However, competitive balance in the NHL has improved since the payroll cap was instituted in 2006.

Competitive balance has also been impacted by the NBA payroll cap instituted in 1983. On the other hand, the effect has been the opposite of what we might expect (balance worsened). In contrast, the salary cap instituted in 1999 within the NBA has led to better balance. In all, the impact of the institutions employed by professional sports is not completely consistent with the expectations of the people who designed these institutions.

---

[67]To test for the statistical significance of the change, we employ a *t*-test. SocialResearchMethods .net provides an intuitive explanation of this test (http://www.socialresearchmethods.net/kb/ stat_t.php). The *t*-test is a ratio. In the denominator is the difference in the two means. The numerator is the variability we observe in the data, or this is a ratio of the "signal" to the "noise."

4.8 Two Competitive Balance Stories

If institutions are not the reason, how do we explain the levels of competitive balance that we observe? There are two competitive balance stories we need to tell. The first is illustrated by Table 4.8.

Table 4.8 Noll–Scully Measure of Competitive Balance in Various Sports Leagues[68]					
League	Acronym	Sport	Years	Number of Observations	Average Level of Competitive Balance
Major League Soccer	MLS	Soccer	1996–2003	8	1.281
North American Soccer League	NASL	Soccer	1967–84	18	1.341
French Ligue 1	FL1	Soccer	1976–2003	28	1.391
Spanish Primera Division	SPD	Soccer	1976–2003	28	1.403
German Bundesliga 1	GB1	Soccer	1976–2003	28	1.424
Italian Serie A	ISA	Soccer	1976–2003	28	1.554
English Premier League	EPL	Soccer	1976–2003	28	1.581
Canadian Football League	CFL	Football	1960–2003	41	1.481
Arena Football League	AFL II	Football	1987–2003	17	1.561
National Football League	NFL	Football	1922–2003	82	1.562
American Football League	AFL I	Football	1960–69	10	1.578
National Hockey League	NHL	Hockey	1917–18 to 2002–03	86	1.850
World Hockey Association	WHA	Hockey	1972–73 to 1978–79	7	1.891
National League	NL	Baseball	1901–2003	103	2.072
American League	AL	Baseball	1901–2003	103	2.129
National Basketball Association	NBA	Basketball	1946–47 to 2002–03	57	2.542
American Basketball Association	ABA	Basketball	1967–68 to 1975–76	9	2.601

The table reports on the average Noll–Scully measure across a number of seasons for a variety of sports leagues. In general, the average level of competitive balance appears to vary by sport. The soccer leagues are the most balanced, followed by American football, hockey, baseball, and basketball. Despite these leagues having very different institutions, balance is remarkably similar between leagues in the same sport.

The second piece of evidence is illustrated in Figures 4.1 and 4.2[69] that show the downward trend of competitive balance in the AL and NL throughout the 20th century. In other words, balance in baseball improved across the century.

[68]Data from David J. Berri, Stacey L. Brook, Aju Fenn, Bernd Frick, and Roberto Vicente-Mayoral, "The Short Supply of Tall People: Explaining Competitive Imbalance in the National Basketball Association," *Journal of Economics Issues* 39, no. 4 (December 2005): 1029–1041.

[69]Originally appeared in Martin B. Schmidt and David J. Berri, "On the Evolution of Competitive Balance: The Impact of an Increasing Global Search," *Economic Inquiry* 41, no. 4 (October 2003): 692–704.

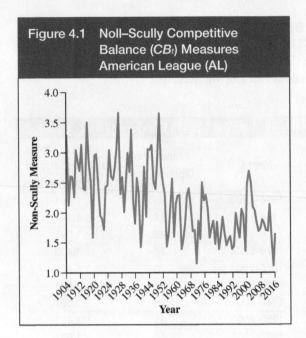

Figure 4.1   Noll–Scully Competitive Balance (*CB$_t$*) Measures American League (AL)

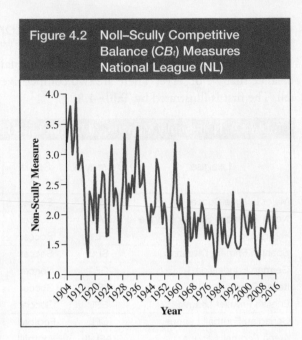

Figure 4.2   Noll–Scully Competitive Balance (*CB$_t$*) Measures National League (NL)

The same story is told in **Table 4.9**, which records the average level of balance across 10-year increments in both the AL and NL. In the early history of each league, balance looked very much like what we see in the NBA today, but in recent years, balance began to look similar to what is observed in the NHL.

A simple regression, originally reported in Schmidt and Berri (2003), is consistent with what we have seen in baseball. As shown in **Table 4.10**, time and balance have a negative and statistically significant relationship. Balance appears to have improved in baseball.

If we only consider our first piece of evidence, that level of balance is sports-specific, then our attention might focus on which aspects of these sports lead to more or less balance. One might argue that American Football is more balanced than basketball because American Football requires more players. Unlike what we observe in basketball, it is more difficult for one player in football to dictate the outcome of a contest.

The second piece of evidence, that balance can change over time, suggests the characteristics of the games being played may not be the story. Back in 1900, baseball had nine players on the field of play, just as teams do today, so the number of players cannot explain the changes we are observing.

Table 4.9 Competitive Balance Across Time in Baseball

Time Period	League	Average 10-Year Competitive Balance	League	Average 10-Year Competitive Balance
2007–16	AL	1.697	NL	1.756
1997–06	AL	2.061	NL	1.786
1987–96	AL	1.641	NL	1.640
1977–86	AL	1.898	NL	1.705
1967–76	AL	1.817	NL	1.841
1957–66	AL	1.980	NL	2.082
1947–56	AL	2.789	NL	2.215
1937–46	AL	2.400	NL	2.645
1927–36	AL	2.717	NL	2.432
1917–26	AL	2.299	NL	2.195
1907–16	AL	2.772	NL	2.673
1897–06	–	–	NL	3.037
1887–96	–	–	NL	2.685
1877–86	–	–	NL	3.032

Table 4.10 Connecting Competitive Balance to Time[70]

League	Sample	Variable	Coefficient	Standard Error	t-Statistic
AL	1911–2000	Constant	2.742	−0.109	−25.16
		Time	−0.012	−0.002	6.00
NL	1911–2000	Constant	2.439	−0.108	−22.58
		Time	−0.008	−0.002	4.00
AL	1960–2000	Constant	2.601	−0.335	−7.76
		Time	−0.011	−0.004	2.75
NL	1960–2000	Constant	2.721	−0.377	−7.22
		Time	−0.011	−0.005	2.20

4.9 Balancing Evolution

For an alternative explanation, we need to look in what might appear to be an unexpected place. We need to start thinking about the birthplace of players. Table 4.11 lists the birthplace of the primary starters at each fielding position for

---

[70]p-values were not reported in the original. Schmidt and Berri (2003).

Table 4.11 The Detroit Tigers Starting Lineups: 1912 and 2012

Position	1912 Detroit Tigers	Birthplace	2013 Detroit Tigers	Birthplace
1B	George Moriarty	Chicago, IL	Prince Fielder	Ontario, CA
2B	Baldy Louden	Pittsburgh, PA	Omar Infante	Puerto La Cruz, Anzoategui, Venezuela
SS	Donie Bush	Indianapolis, IN	Jhonny Peralta	Santiago, Santiago, Dominican Republic
3B	Charlie Deal	Wilkinsburg, PA	Miguel Cabrera	Maracay, Aragua, Venezuela
OF	Ty Cobb	Narrows, GA	Andy Dirks	Hutchinson, KS
OF	Sam Crawford	Wahoo, NE	Austin Jackson	Denton, TX
OF	Davy Jones	Cambria, WI	Brennan Boesch	Santa Monica, CA
C	Oscar Stanage	Tulare, CA	Alex Avila	Hialeah, FL

two Detroit Tigers teams 100 years apart.[71] Each of the 1912 Detroit Tigers was born in the United States; in fact, all but two of these players were born east of the Mississippi.

One hundred years later, the primary starters for the Detroit Tigers hailed from more diverse locations. In 2012, only one of these players was born east of the Mississippi in the United States, while half of the players were not born in the United States.

In addition, all the 1912 players would be regarded as Caucasians, while on the 2012 roster only Andy Dirks, Alex Avila, and Brennan Boesch are Caucasian. What does any of this have to do with competitive balance? To answer that question, we turn to the work of Stephen Jay Gould, an evolutionary biologist.

Looking back at the 1913 Tigers, we note Ty Cobb, who retired in 1928 and had a career batting average of 0.366, a career mark that still stands today. As Table 4.12 indicates, in three seasons Cobb surpassed the 0.400 mark. These three seasons were among the 24 times this ever occurred in the history of MLB.

Table 4.12 The 0.400 Hitter in Major League Baseball[72]

Player	Batting Average	Year
Ross Barnes	0.429	1876
Fred Dunlap	0.412	1884
Tip O'Neill	0.435	1887
Pete Browning	0.402	1887

(continued)

[71]As noted, the author is a Tigers fan. The 2012 Tigers were the last team Detroit sent to the World Series. These rosters and birthplaces are reported at baseball-reference.com.

[72]Data from baseball-reference.com.

Player	Batting Average	Year
Hugh Duffy	0.440	1894
Tuck Turner	0.418	1894
Sam Thompson	0.415	1894
Ed Delahanty	0.404	1894
Billy Hamilton	0.403	1894
Jesse Burkett	0.405	1895
Ed Delahanty	0.404	1895
Jesse Burkett	0.410	1896
Hughie Jennings	0.401	1896
Willie Keeler	0.424	1897
Ed Delahanty	0.410	1899
Nap Lajoie	0.427	1901
Ty Cobb	**0.420**	**1911**
Shoeless Joe Jackson	0.408	1911
Ty Cobb	**0.409**	**1912**
George Sisler	0.407	1920
George Sisler	0.420	1922
Rogers Hornsby	0.401	1922
Ty Cobb	**0.401**	**1922**
Harry Heilmann	0.403	1923
Rogers Hornsby	0.424	1924
Rogers Hornsby	0.403	1925
Bill Terry	0.401	1930
Ted Williams	0.406	1941

Table 4.12 shows that 15 of these seasons occurred in the 19th century, and 22 before 1930. After 1941, when Ted Williams batted 0.406, such a high batting average never happened again.

What became of the 0.400 hitter? Some have argued that since 1941 the hitters in baseball have simply declined in ability. Gould (1986, 1996)[73] argued that the opposite is the more likely explanation. Gould's argument begins with the proposition that the distribution of athletic talent in a population will follow a normal curve, as seen in Figure 4.3.

---

[73]Stephen Jay Gould, "Losing the Edge: The Extinction of the .400 Hitter," *Vanity Fair*, vol. 120, March 1983, pp. 264–278 and Stephen Jay Gould, "Entropic Homogeneity Isn't Why No One Hits .400 Any More," *Discover*, August 1986, pp. 60–66.

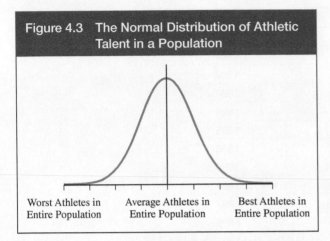

Figure 4.3   The Normal Distribution of Athletic Talent in a Population

Worst Athletes in Entire Population   Average Athletes in Entire Population   Best Athletes in Entire Population

At the far-left tail are individuals who have the least amount of athletic ability. In the middle is the average, with the largest number of individuals. The far-right tail shows the very best athletes.

Gould argues that the right tail does not just extend forever because the human body faces certain biomechanical limits. For example, someone may eventually surpass Usain Bolt's world record of 9.58 seconds in the 100-meter dash, but the limits of the human body tell us that someone is not going to beat this record by running the 100-meter dash in 3 seconds. Given the existence of biomechanical limits, athletes in the far-right tail tend to be fairly close to each other in athletic ability. If your population is large enough, most teams in a league will have access to athletes in the far-right tail. What if your population is smaller? Then, the supply of athletes in the far-right tail will also be smaller. Consequently, some teams will have to employ athletes who are closer to the population average.

How does this apply to the 0.400 hitter? Table 4.13 lists the Major League batting average for each decade since 1871. Across all 140 years, the league batting average has come close to the mark of 0.262. For a player to perform well beyond a typical hitter's rank, the player must be much better than an average player. In a league composed of many players from the far-right tail, a performance that greatly exceeds the one of the league's average player becomes far less likely. As the population of potential athletes increases, the 0.400 hitter vanishes.

Table 4.13 Average Batting Average in Major League Baseball History[74]

Decade	Total At Bats	Total Hits	Batting Average
1871–80	185,232	49,236	0.2658
1881–90	708,321	179,121	0.2529
1891–00	588,901	163,939	0.2784
1901–10	796,229	200,418	0.2517
1911–20	879,955	227,227	0.2582
1921–30	850,470	244,248	0.2872
1931–40	860,884	237,450	0.2758
1941–50	846,778	219,975	0.2598

(continued)

[74]Data from Sean Lahman.

Decade	Total At Bats	Total Hits	Batting Average
1951–60	842,680	217,649	0.2583
1961–70	1,128,458	280,768	0.2488
1971–80	1,355,482	349,021	0.2575
1981–90	1,384,416	357,539	0.2583
1991–00	1,503,476	399,761	0.2659
2001–10	1,665,280	439,821	0.2641
All Years	**13,596,562**	**3,566,173**	**0.2623**

Gould's argument does not just apply to the vanishing 0.400 hitter. As Schmidt and Berri (2003) discuss, it also explains why competitive balance in baseball improved in the latter half of the 20th century.

As mentioned before, the Tigers of 1913 were all born in the United States, most were born east of the Mississippi, and all players were Caucasian. However, starting in 1947, when Jackie Robinson took the field for the Brooklyn Dodgers, the population of MLB players began to change. Not only did baseball become racially integrated in the second half of the 20th century, baseball teams began to search for talent outside the United States.

As the population of available players expanded, the number of players in the far-right tail also expanded. The supply of amazing athletes expanded, and more teams employed such talents. That means contests between teams became increasingly competitive, and competitive balance thus improved.

Schmidt and Berri (2003) present evidence that the underlying population of talent is related to the level of competitive balance in baseball. The statistical evidence offered in their paper indicates that once you control for changes in population, factors like the rookie draft and free agency do not impact competitive balance.

It appears a similar story can be told about the NBA, which has persistently been the least balanced of the four major North American sports leagues. The same lack of balance was also seen in the brief history of the ABA. To understand this lack of balance, consider the typical athlete who plays professional basketball. The average height of an NBA basketball player is 6 feet, 7 inches. The U.S. Census[75] reports that 98.3% of males between the ages of 20 and 29 are 6 feet, 3 inches or shorter. In 2012–13, 80% of the NBA was taller than 6 feet, 3 inches, so the NBA draws much of its talent from a very small population. Following the analysis laid out in Gould's work, that indicates we could expect the NBA to experience low levels of competitive balance. In sum, the NBA suffers from a "short supply of tall people," and given the source of its

[75]http://www.census.gov/compendia/statab/2012/tables/12s0209.pdf.

competitive balance problem, we shouldn't be surprised that the policies the league adopts (e.g., salary caps, payroll caps, luxury taxes) do not appear to consistently alter the league's level of balance.

4.10 Do Leagues Want Competitive Balance?

The Louis–Schmeling paradox emphasizes how competitors in sports do not want to be too dominant. If fans know a competitor is going to win, then, it is argued, they are less likely to attend the contest. This was illustrated in Neale (1964) by examining the records for the New York Yankees in the 1950s. From 1947 to 1958, the Yankees won the AL pennant 10 times (and the World Series 8 times). In 1959, the Yankees finished in third place in the AL and were suddenly playing in front of larger crowds. This prompted Neale to say that the Yankees prayer must be, "Oh Lord, make us good, but not that good."

To illustrate Neale's argument, let's just look at the attendance data. The Yankees drew 2.18 million fans in 1947. Table 4.14 indicates attendance increased in 1948, but then declined every season until 1955. After small increases through 1957, attendance again declined in 1958.

Table 4.14 20 Years of Yankees' Attendance			
Year	Yankees' Attendance	Yankees' Winning Percentage	League Attendance without the Yankees
1947[a,b]	2,178,937	0.630	17,695,602
1948	2,373,901	0.610	18,546,941
1949[a,b]	2,283,676	0.630	17,931,689
1950[a,b]	2,081,380	0.636	15,381,597
1951[a,b]	1,950,107	0.636	14,176,569
1952[a,b]	1,629,665	0.617	13,003,379
1953[a,b]	1,537,811	0.656	12,845,986
1954	1,475,171	0.669	14,460,712
1955[a]	1,490,138	0.623	15,127,245
1956[a,b]	1,491,784	0.630	15,051,466
1957[a]	1,497,134	0.636	15,518,685
1958[a,b]	1,428,438	0.597	16,032,192
1959	1,552,030	0.513	17,591,949
1960[a]	1,627,349	0.630	18,284,140
1961[a,b]	1,747,725	0.673	17,146,793
1962[a,b]	1,493,574	0.593	19,973,115

(continued)

Year	Yankees' Attendance	Yankees' Winning Percentage	League Attendance without the Yankees
1963[a]	1,308,920	0.646	19,368,263
1964[a]	1,305,638	0.611	19,910,246
1965	1,213,552	0.475	21,257,308
1966	1,124,648	0.440	24,095,727

[a] Won American League pennant.
[b] Won World Series.

From 1947 to 1958, the Yankees only failed to win the AL pennant twice, but attendance declined by 34.4%. This suggests Neale's prayer for the Yankees wasn't being answered. Apparently, the Yankees were "too good."

Look at the last column in Table 4.14, and you will observe that there might be something else that explains part of the Yankees' attendance decline. League attendance, without the Yankees, reached 18.5 million fans in 1948. This was the highest mark in MLB history, but after reaching such a peak, baseball attendance declined and did not return to its 1948 level until the 1962 season. In sum, the Yankees were not the only team to see fewer fans in the 1950s.

A variety of factors could explain these data:

* The Yankees' dominance (i.e., lack of competitive balance) caused fans of baseball throughout the league to stay home.

* In the late 1940s, with the end of World War II, baseball attendance reached levels never seen before. That could have represented a temporary spike that leveled off in the 1950s.

* Racial integration, which began in 1947, could have caused some white fans to stay home in the 1950s.

Each of these stories fits what we see in the data. To ascertain which story "best" explains the evidence is somewhat difficult. This is especially true with respect to the second explanation, because we only have two examples in American baseball history of the nation returning from a global war (and two is a very small sample).[76]

"Testing" each explanation is difficult, but statistical analysis of the link between competitive balance and attendance is possible and has been done. Specifically, systematic analysis of the following questions has been completed:

* What is the relationship between league attendance and competitive balance?

* What is the relationship between team attendance and team performance?

[76]MLB attendance increased 40% from 1919 to 1920. Throughout the 1920s, baseball attendance gradually increased until declining sharply at the onset of the Great Depression.

To answer the first question, we must note that the Noll–Scully metric is not the only measure of competitive balance. Schmidt and Berri (2001)[77] employed the Gini coefficient to measure balance in baseball. The Gini coefficient has historically been used in studies of income distribution.[78] The Gini coefficient technically ranges from 0 to 1, with a value of 0 being complete equality (i.e., every team winning half their games). A value of 1 would occur if one team won all the games. This value cannot be achieved in sports since one team cannot appear in all games.[79]

The study examined the AL and NL from 1901 to 1999. Across these years, the average value for the Gini was 0.094 and 0.093, respectively, in the AL and NL. As we saw in the Noll–Scully measure, the Gini coefficient indicates that balance improved in both leagues during the 20th century. Prior to 1960, it was not uncommon to see values in excess of 0.100, but in the latter part of the 20th century, values were around 0.80 or lower.

We have already noted that balance improved in baseball over time. Now we wish to learn how this change impacted attendance. To answer this question, Schmidt and Berri looked at how attendance would change if a league went from the most balanced mark observed in the data to the least balanced mark. The results indicated that attendance would decline by about 1,000 fans per game, which works out to about a 4% decline in attendance. This result was based on examining competitive balance in each season. Schmidt and Berri also measured balance across three and five years. They assessed how persistent imbalance would impact attendance. The results indicated a stronger impact. Specifically, a

---

[77]Martin B. Schmidt and David J. Berri, "Competitive Balance and Attendance: The Case of Major League Baseball," *Journal of Sports Economics* 2, no. 2 (May 2001): 145–167.

[78]This measure was taken from Peter J. Lambert, *The Distribution and Redistribution of Income: A Mathematical Analysis* (Manchester, UK: Manchester University Press, 1993). The specific calculation employed in Schmidt and Berri (2001) is as follows:

$$G_i = \left(1 + \frac{1}{N_i}\right) - \frac{2}{N_i^2 \mu_{x_i}} \times (X_{N,i} + 2 \times X_{N-1,i} + 3 \times X_{N-2,i} + \cdots + N \times x_{1,i})$$

where

N = number of teams in the league

X_N = the winning percentage of team N

μ = the average value of x

i = the time period

In addition, teams are ranked in the data so that $x_N \geq x_{N-1} \geq \ldots \geq x_1$.

[79]This observation was made in Joshua Utt and Rodney Fort, "Pitfalls to Measuring Competitive Balance with Gini Coefficients," *Journal of Sports Economics* 3, no. 4 (November 2002): 367–373. One should note, though, that in a study of income inequality, a value of 1 is also not likely to be observed. Such a value would occur if one person in a society had all the income in a society. A society where one person gets everything and no one else gets anything is not likely to be observed (and not likely to last long if it was observed).

movement from the most balanced five-year measure to the least balanced would increase attendance by about 14% (or approximately 3,500 additional fans).

Humphreys (2002)[80] also looked at how balance affected league attendance. This study employed three different measures of balance[81]: the Noll–Scully measure, the Herfindahl–Hirschman index,[82] and competitive balance ratio (CBR). Each of these measures was employed in a model designed to explain league attendance.[83] This model controlled for such factors as population, the impact of wars, labor disputes, and television. The results indicated that 97% of the variation in league attendance could be explained by the independent variables employed.

When we turn to the competitive balance measures, only the CBR was found to be statistically significant.[84] When we turn to economic significance, we see that a movement from the highest to lowest observed level of balance would only result in about 4,000 additional fans per game.[85] In sum, both Schmidt and Berri and Humphreys found that the largest change in balance observed in baseball during the 20th century would not have a dramatic impact on league balance, despite looking at different measures of balance. Each of these studies examined aggregate league balance, and each presented evidence that balanced mattered in baseball, although the impact seemed small.

Another approach to this question is to look at how uncertainty of outcome impacts game-day attendance in baseball. Dan Rascher (1999)[86] explored MLB attendance in 1996. In a model with more than 40 different independent variables,[87] Rascher found that a better home team attracted more fans, but only up to a certain point. Attendance for the home team starts to fall when the home winning percentage surpasses the 60% to 70% range.

---

[80]Brad Humphreys, "Alternative Measures of Competitive Balance in Sports League," *Journal of Sports Economics* 3, no. 2 (May 2002): 133–148.

[81]Once again, there are many more measures of competitive balance.

[82]Often used in the field of industrial organization. Calculated as follows: $HHI = 10,000 \times \Sigma w^2$, where w = market share. Applied to sports, w could be the share of league championships.

[83]Estimated three times with each measure of balance employed separately.

[84]In the model employing CBR, the R^2 was 0.973. In the other two estimations, which employed the Noll–Scully and Herfindahl–Hirschman measures, respectively, the R^2 was 0.972. Interestingly enough, explanatory power in all three models was virtually identical.

[85]This calculation was not reported in Humphreys (2002), but was based on the data in that paper. It was reported in *The Wages of Wins* (Berri et al., 2006).

[86]Dan Rascher, "A Test of the Optimal Positive Production Network Externality in Major League Baseball," in John Fizel, Elizabeth Gustafson, and Larry Hadley (eds.), *Sports Economics: Current Research* (New York: Praeger, 1999), pp. 27–45.

[87]Rascher's study included such factors as the cost of attending the game, the time of the game, characteristics of the opposing pitchers, and local market characteristics (among other factors).

A more recent study told a different story. Beckman *et al.* (2012)[88] looked at game-day attendance in MLB from 1985 to 2009. Like Rascher (1999), the model employed included an extensive list of independent variables. The Beckman *et al.* model, with a larger sample than that which was employed in Rascher (1999), did not find evidence that home attendance declined if a team was "too good."

Each of these studies reviewed the data on baseball. Other sports have also been examined, and the results do not indicate that more competitive balance is what fans necessarily want.

- Coates and Humphreys (2010)[89] looked at game-day attendance in the NFL from 1985 to 2008. This analysis failed to uncover evidence that fans of the NFL prefer close contests.

- Forrest *et al.* (2005),[90] in their study of the English Premier League (EPL) in 1997–98, found that if teams were equal in playing strength, league attendance would decline.

- Coates and Humphreys (2012),[91] in a study of the NHL from 2005–06 to 2009–10, reported evidence that perfect competitive balance would result in less attendance.

Each of these studies reviewed game-day attendance. A similar story can be told from the examination of team revenue. Burgher and Walters (2003)[92] report that an additional win for a contending baseball team in New York was worth $3.62 million, in 1999. In contrast, an additional win for a contending baseball team in Milwaukee was only worth $0.562 million. A similar result may be seen for the NBA. Berri, Schmidt, and Brook (2004)[93] presented evidence

---

[88]Elise M. Beckman, Wenqiang Cai, Rebecca M. Esrock, and Robert J. Lemke, "Over Time Explaining Game-to-Game Ticket Sales for Major League Baseball Games," *Journal of Sports Economics* 13, no. 5 (2012): 535–555.

[89]Dennis Coates and Brad Humphreys, "Week to Week Attendance and Competitive Balance in the National Football League," *International Journal of Sport Finance* 5 (2010): 239–252.

[90]D. Forrest, R. Simmons, and B. Buraimo, "Outcome Uncertainty and the Couch Potato Audience," *Scottish Journal of Political Economy* 52 (2005): 641–661.

[91]Dennis Coates and Brad R. Humphreys, "Game Attendance and Outcome Uncertainty in the National Hockey League," *Journal of Sports Economics* 13, no. 4 (2012): 364–377.

[92]John Burger and Stephen Walters, "Market Size, Pay, and Performance: A General Model and Application to Major League Baseball," *Journal of Sports Economics* 4, no. 2 (2003): 108–125.

[93]David J. Berri, Martin B. Schmidt, and Stacey L. Brook, "Stars at the Gate: The Impact of Star Power on NBA Gate Revenues," *Journal of Sports Economics* 5, no. 1 (February 2004): 33–50.

that an additional win would have a different impact on team revenues in the NBA.

These studies of baseball and basketball suggest that leagues would not want to equalize wins across all teams. In other words, competitive balance is not what a profit-maximizing league would desire. What does all this mean for league policy? We turn back to Coates and Humphreys (2010), who noted leagues argue that when competitive balance declines, a league's revenues also begin to disappear. But, as Coates and Humphreys note, "Fans like to see games in which they expect the home team will win by a large margin. Fans do not buy tickets to see close games, or games that they expect the home team to lose" (p. 250).

In sum, the empirical study of sports leagues does not support the underlying justification of policies that are supposedly designed to promote competitive balance. Not only does the evidence suggest these policies do not work, but we also do not see much evidence that if these policies were successful, teams would be better off.

All this then leads to an obvious question: If policies like salary caps, payroll caps, and reverse-order drafts do not promote competitive balance, why are they put into place? The answer to that question will be the subject of the next chapter.

Key Terms

reserve clause (p. 100)
Louis–Schmeling paradox (p. 102)
competitive balance (p. 102)
invariance principle (p. 114)

Coase theorem (p. 114)
idealized standard deviation (p. 121)
Noll–Scully measure (p. 122)

Problems

Study Questions

1. What did the owners of the NL in 1879 argue must happen to player salaries for the league to survive? What did the NL do to reduce salaries at this time?

2. How did the justification for the reserve clause change over time?

3. Who was involved in the *Federal League* case? What did the Supreme Court 1922 ruling in this case establish? Why was that important?

4. What issues were involved in the 1953 *Toolson* case? How was it decided and was this decision justified? Why didn't the Supreme Court reverse its 1922 ruling in the *Federal League* case?

5. In what year was the first collective bargaining agreement reached in MLB? What were owners required to do with respect to a player's contract as a result of this agreement? What was introduced with the 1970 collective bargaining agreement?

6. In 1975, what ruling did an arbitration panel issue in the case of Andy Messersmith and Dave McNally? Why did this ruling introduce free agency?

7. How did Charles Finley, owner of the Oakland A's, think baseball should respond to free agency?

8. Why was the "reverse-order draft" invented?

9. Why does Simon Rottenberg argue that a reserve clause is not necessary to prevent rich teams from accumulating talent?

10. With respect to the NBA, MLB, NFL, and NHL, which labor market institutions exist?

11. The text presents a "simple snapshot" of how league institutions impact competitive balance. What is the basic story of this snapshot?

12. What two pieces of evidence must a theory of competitive balance be able to explain?

13. According to Stephen Jay Gould, why did the 0.400 hitter vanish in baseball?

14. Why did balance improve in baseball and the NHL?

15. Why does the NBA have less balance than other major North American sports?

16. Why did Walter Neale believe the Yankees must pray, "Oh Lord, make us good, but not that good?" Do the data confirm Neale's analysis?

17. According to Schmidt and Berri (2001) and Humphreys (2002), what is the relationship between competitive balance and attendance Major League Baseball?

18. According to Coates and Humphreys (2010), do fans want the competitive balance that various league institutions are designed to create? What do these authors think fans really want? How does that analysis change the traditional view economists (i.e. Rottenberg and Neale) have of how competitive balance impacts demand in sports?

19. We have seen that competitive balance is not quite as important to the demand of sports leagues. But let's say you were charged with improving the balance we see in a league. Given what was learned in the text, what policies would you advocate to accomplish this objective?

20. Imagine you were named league commissioner and were charged with maximizing the profits of the league. Given what you learned in this chapter, what policies would you advocate to accomplish this objective?

21. **Competitive Balance Problem** Given the following standings data from the AL and NBA, which league is more competitive in terms of the standard deviation and the Noll–Scully ratio? *Note:* Baseball played 154 games in 1954. The NBA's schedule was 72 games long in 1953–54.

    Hint: You might copy these data into Excel to do the calculations.

AL: 1954	Wins	Losses	Winning Percentage
Cleveland Indians	111	43	0.721
New York Yankees	103	51	0.669
Chicago White Sox	94	60	0.610
Boston Red Sox	69	85	0.448
Detroit Tigers	68	86	0.442
Washington Senators	66	88	0.429
Baltimore Orioles	54	100	0.351
Philadelphia Athletics	51	103	0.331

NBA: 1953–54	Wins	Losses	Winning Percentage
Minneapolis Lakers	46	26	0.639
New York Knickerbockers	44	28	0.611
Rochester Royals	44	28	0.611
Boston Celtics	42	30	0.583
Syracuse Nationals	42	30	0.583
Fort Wayne Pistons	40	32	0.556
Philadelphia Warriors	29	43	0.403
Milwaukee Hawks	21	51	0.292
Baltimore Bullets	16	56	0.222

Appendix 4A
Standard Deviation Made Simple

Standard deviation is a measure of disparity in outcomes. And our intuitive explanation begins by looking at the average difference between each team's outcome and the average performance in the league. For example, consider **Table 4A.1**.

Table 4A.1 Comparing Each American League Team in 1932 to the League Average		
AL Team	Winning Percentage	Difference Between Team WPCT and Average WPCT
New York Yankees	0.686	0.189
Philadelphia Athletics	0.610	0.113
Washington Senators	0.604	0.107
Cleveland Indians	0.569	0.072
Detroit Tigers	0.497	0.000
St. Louis Browns	0.409	−0.088
Chicago White Sox	0.322	−0.175
Boston Red Sox	0.279	−0.218
Average	**0.497**	**0.000**

The table shows us that the Yankees' winning percentage (WPCT) was 0.189 higher than the average in the AL in 1932. In contrast, the Red Sox were 0.218 below average.

The average difference across the league, though, is 0.000. And that is what we would find regardless of the disparity in final standings. In other words, average differences don't reveal anything.

However, we can take a different approach that will essentially tell us about average differences. We begin, as Table 4A.2 illustrates, by:

1. Squaring the difference between each team's winning percentage and the average winning percentage in the league.

2. We then sum these squared differences across all teams. This gives us 0.151.

3. This number is then divided by 7 ($n - 1$, where n is the number of teams). That gives us 0.022.

4. Finally, we take the square root of our result from Step 3. This gives us 0.147.

Table 4A.2 First Steps in Building a Simple Measure of Competitive Balance			
AL Team	Winning Percentage	Average Difference Between Team WPCT and Average WPCT	Difference Squared
New York Yankees	0.686	0.189	0.036
Philadelphia Athletics	0.610	0.113	0.013
Washington Senators	0.604	0.107	0.011

(continued)

AL Team	Winning Percentage	Average Difference Between Team WPCT and Average WPCT	Difference Squared
Cleveland Indians	0.569	0.072	0.005
Detroit Tigers	0.497	0.000	0.000
St. Louis Browns	0.409	−0.088	0.008
Chicago White Sox	0.322	−0.175	0.031
Boston Red Sox	0.279	−0.218	0.047
		Summation	**0.151**

The steps describe the process by which one calculates standard deviation. And as one hopefully sees, standard deviation is one way to get at "average disparity." Our first approach—just averaging the differences—didn't work because the positive and negative values cancel each other out. The calculation for standard deviation circumvents this issue by first squaring all our differences, which removes the negative signs. We then average our squared differences. And by taking the square root of these "average" squared differences, we are essentially coming back to the "average disparity" in the numbers.

Labor Negotiations in Sports

Are Professional Athletes Overpaid?

To answer this question, Chapter 5 will explore the following:

1. **A Worker's Value and Exploitation:** The answer to this question begins with a common approach (i.e., comparing what athletes get paid to what non-athletes receive). This approach, though, doesn't exactly answer the question. To understand this, we offer a simple discussion of how economists measure a worker's value and what we mean by "exploitation."

2. **A 19th-Century Debate:** Our answer to this question isn't just of interest to sports economists. This is a question that actually allows us to address a debate between Karl Marx and J. B. Clark more than a century ago.

3. **The Power of Labor:** How much an athlete is paid depends on his or her bargaining power. Under the reserve clause, bargaining power was limited. That changed with the rise of labor unions in professional sports. The impact of these unions, though, varies from sport to sport.

4. **The Lack of Power for Fans:** The dispute between owners and workers in sports clearly makes fans angry. But can fans do anything about this? Although fans might think they can, the data on attendance tell a very different story. And some simple economics explains why fans are unable to stop labor disputes in professional sports.

In 1920 — at the age of 25 — Babe Ruth hit 54 home runs for the New York Yankees. Only one team, the Philadelphia A's, managed to hit that many home runs that season. Hall-of-Famer George Sisler hit the second-most home runs that season, but his 19 home runs was barely a third of Ruth's total.

Throughout the 1920s, Ruth and the Yankees dominated baseball. The Yankees won the American League (AL) pennant six times and were world champions in 1923, 1927, and 1928. In 1930 — at the age of 35 — Ruth still managed to hit 49 home runs and lead baseball in slugging average and on-base percentage plus slugging average (OPS).

Despite this performance, though, people still wondered why Ruth was paid $84,098 to play baseball. In 1930, nominal per-capita income was only $748.[1] And the president of the United States, Herbert Hoover, earned a mere $75,000. Consequently, many asked Ruth why he was being paid more than the president. Ruth's reply: "I had a better year than Hoover."

Relative to the average person and the president, it appears that Ruth was well compensated in 1930. But $84,098 then is only worth $1.21 million today. To put those numbers in perspective, the minimum salary in Major League Baseball (MLB) in 2017 was $535,000 and the average salary in 2016 was $4.4 million.[2] Such numbers suggest that Ruth — relative to baseball players today — wasn't paid much in 1930.

To understand why Ruth was paid far less than players today, we return to the subject of the reserve clause. When Ruth negotiated his salary with the New York Yankees, he could not negotiate with anyone besides the New York Yankees. With only one buyer, Ruth's bargaining power was limited.

We can see evidence of this when considering how the maximum salaries paid to MLB players have changed across the past 100 years. Although Ruth's salary in 1930 garnered quite a bit of attention at the time — and is still remembered today — Table 5.1 indicates that it was not much different from the wage paid to Ty Cobb in 1927. Furthermore, the wage paid to Ruth remained the highest salary paid (in nominal terms) to a baseball player until 1949.

When Joe DiMaggio was paid $100,000 in 1949, Ruth's salary record was broken. But in real terms, DiMaggio's wage in 1949 still lagged behind Ruth's. The same story can be told about Ted William's record mark in 1959. And when we turn to the 1960s, we see that the highest paid player, Curt Flood, was paid a nominal salary below what Williams earned nearly 10 years earlier.

Thus, we see that Ruth was not paid well relative to players today. But it was not until the 1970s that a player received in real terms a wage that eclipsed

---

[1] One can find historical data on per-capita income at http://www.measuringworth.com/usgdp/. In real terms, $748 is worth $10,727 in 2017. This website presents real per-capita income. One can also utilize the inflation calculator from the Bureau of Labor Statistics, consulted for this story (http://www.bls.gov/data/inflation_calculator.htm).

[2] http://www.espn.com/mlb/story/_/id/15126571/study-mlb-average-salary-44m-44-pct-rise

Decade	Highest-Paid Player	Team	Year	Nominal Salary	Real Salary
1910s	Frank Chance	New York Yankees	1913	$20,000.00	$488,341.41
1920s	Ty Cobb	Philadelphia Athletics	1927	$80,000.00	$1,111,397,70
1930s	Babe Ruth	New York Yankees	1930	$84,098.33	$1,217,305,70
1940s	Joe DiMaggio	New York Yankees	1949	$100,000.00	$1,015,668.07
1950s	Ted Williams	Boston Red Sox	1959	$125,000.00	$1,038,354.81
1960s	Curt Flood	St. Louis Cardinals	1968	$111,000.00	$771,032.16
1970s	Mike Schmidt	Philadelphia Phillies	1977	$561,500.00	$2,239,782.73
1980s	Orel Hershiser, Frank Viola	Dodgers, Twins	1989	$2,766,666.00	$5,393,414.56
1990s	Albert Belle	Baltimore Orioles	1999	$11,949,794.00	$17,338,606.00
2000s	Alex Rodriguez	New York Yankees	2009	$33,000,000.00	$37,182,660.00
2011–16	Clayton Kershaw	Los Angeles Dodgers	2016	$34,571,429.00	$34,571,429.00

Table 5.1 Highest-Paid Players in Major League Baseball History[3]

Ruth's salary in 1930. As we noted in the last chapter, it was in the 1970s that the reserve clause in baseball finally ended. The demise of this clause allowed Mike Schmidt to negotiate with more teams than the Philadelphia Phillies in 1977. This increase in Schmidt's bargaining power landed him a wage that was — in nominal terms — five times higher than Flood's salary just nine years earlier. And in real terms, it was nearly twice the salary paid to Babe Ruth in 1930.

As one can see, this was just the beginning. Salaries in baseball have continued to increase. The maximum salary nearly doubled again by 1989. By 1999, the maximum salary (relative to 10 years earlier) had nearly tripled. And in 2009, the maximum salary (relative to 1999) had more than doubled again.

Clearly, the end of the reserve clause has dramatically changed wages in baseball. Has this resulted in players being "overpaid"?

The answer to this question will be provided in the next two chapters. In this chapter, we will lay out how wages are determined in professional sports. Part of this story has already been told when we discussed such institutions as the reserve clause, the reverse-order draft, and free agency in Chapter 4. That discussion, though, primarily focused on the owners. In this chapter, we will explore

---

[3]Source for 1910s to 1990s: Michael Haupert, "The Economic History of Major League Baseball," in Robert Whaples (ed.), EH.Net Encyclopedia, December 3, 2007, https://eh.net/encyclopedia/the-economic-history-of-major-league-baseball/.
Source for 2009 and 2016: http://www.baseball-reference.com/leaders/leaders_salaries.shtml. Real salaries determined from information available at http://www.bls.gov/data/inflation_calculator.htm (accessed November 23, 2016).

the player's side of the negotiations, a discussion that primarily focuses on the lessons economic theory teaches about workers' valuation and the impact of labor unions.

With this story told, we will then, in Chapter 6, move on to a discussion of the data. It is this review that will ultimately reveal how many players are overpaid — and underpaid — in North American sports.

5.1 Differing Views on the Overpayment of Professional Athletes

Player salaries have not just increased in baseball. Salaries have also risen in all major North American team sports. And this increase, as noted, can be attributed at least partially to the actions of unions. So while fans have been made unhappy by the conflict between labor and management in sports, this conflict—one can argue—has benefited the players.

But are the players now getting paid too much? For many people, the answer to this question is obvious. Just consider what athletes are paid in each of the four major North American sports leagues, as shown in **Table 5.2**.

Table 5.2	Salaries in the Major North American Sports				
League	Year	Maximum Salary	Average Salary	Median Salary	Minimum Salary
NBA	2016–17	$30,963,450[a]	$5,150,000[b]	$2,330,000[b]	$543,471[a]
MLB	2016	$33,000,000[e]	$4,381,980[d]	$1,500,000[d]	$507,500[c]
NFL	2016	$24,200,000[f]	$2,467,438[d]	$940,132[d]	$450,000[g]
NHL	2015–16	$14,300,000[h]	$2,803,043[d]	$1,600,000[i]	$575,000[h]

[a]http://www.cbafaq.com/salarycap.htm#Q16.
[b]http://hoopshype.com/salaries/players/.
[c]http://www.espn.com/mlb/story/_/id/14161690/mlb-minimum-salary-remains-507500-2016.
[d]http://www.espn.com/mlb/story/_/id/15126571/study-mlb-average-salary-44m-44-pct-rise (reported NHL data from 2014–15, reported NFL data derive from 2015).
[e]http://www.usatoday.com/sports/mlb/salaries/2016/player/all/.
[f]http://www.spotrac.com/nfl/rankings/ (this number is what is charged to the NFL's salary cap).
[g]https://www.spotrac.com/blog/nfl-minimum-salaries-for-2016-and-the-veteran-cap-benefit-rule/.
[h]http://www.puckreport.com/2009/07/nhl-minimum-wage-maximum-wage-by-year.html.
[i]http://www.usatoday.com/sports/nhl/salaries/2013/player/all/ (reported NHL data from 2013–14).

To put these numbers in perspective, median household income in the United States was estimated to be $56,516 in 2015.[4] So Clayton Kershaw, who made $33 million in 2016, had an income, as Table 5.3 illustrates, that was nearly 550 times larger than the income of the median household in the United States.

Table 5.3 Professional Athlete's Salaries Relative to the Income of the Median Household in the United States					
League	Year	Maximum Salary	Average Salary	Median Salary	Minimum Salary
NBA	2016–17	547.9 to 1	91.1 to 1	41.2 to 1	9.6 to 1
MLB	2016	583.9 to 1	77.5 to 1	26.5 to 1	9.0 to 1
NFL	2016	428.2 to 1	43.7 to 1	16.6 to 1	8.0 to 1
NHL	2015–16	253.0 to 1	49.6 to 1	28.3 to 1	10.2 to 1

Then again, the United States is an immensely rich nation. According to the World Bank, gross domestic product (GDP) in the world was about $74.3 trillion in 2015.[5] The World Bank noted that the United States had a gross domestic product of about $18 trillion in 2015. That means that approximately 24% of the world's GDP is from the United States.

And this means that median income in the world is quite a bit lower than what we observe in the United States. One estimate from 2013 placed median family income in the world at $9,733.[6] When we consider this number, we see that Clayton Kershaw took home more than 3,300 times what a typical family throughout the rest of the world lives on. And he gets all this for playing a game!

So maybe it is obvious that Kershaw was overpaid in 2016. In fact, even if we consider the earnings of a minimum-wage player in baseball, we note that a minimum-wage player makes more than 50 times what a median family in the world takes home. So maybe all baseball players are overpaid!

On the other hand, when we compare median family income in the United States to that in the rest of the world, we see that the former takes home nearly six times what the latter does. Maybe most people in the United States are overpaid.

In the end, these kinds of comparisons aren't going to get us anywhere. For virtually everyone, there is someone in the world who makes more and someone who makes less. The question of who is "overpaid" and who is "underpaid" requires a bit more thought.

---

[4]http://money.cnn.com/2016/09/13/news/economy/median-income-census/.

[5]http://data.worldbank.org/indicator/NY.GDP.MKTP.CD.

[6]http://www.gallup.com/poll/166211/worldwide-median-household-income-000.aspx.

So let's begin with a simple definition of what we mean by underpaid or exploited. Joan Robinson argued in 1933 that exploitation occurs when a worker is paid a wage less than the worker's marginal revenue product.[7]

What do we thus mean by marginal revenue product? When we think about hiring workers, we understand that the cost of the worker to the firm is generally captured by the worker's wage. The benefit of hiring an additional worker is related to two issues. First, the firm needs to consider the productivity of hiring that additional worker, or the worker's **marginal product (MP)**. Second, the production of that worker needs to be sold in the marketplace. And we have already seen that the benefit of selling additional output is captured by a firm's marginal revenue. If we multiply an additional worker's MP by the firm's marginal revenue, we have determined the benefit of hiring a worker, or the worker's **marginal revenue product (MRP)**:

$$\text{Marginal Revenue Product of Labor } (MRP_L) =$$
$$\text{Marginal Product of Labor } (MP_L) \times \text{Marginal Revenue of Output } (MR_Q)$$

Let's use these definitions to discuss a specific athlete. Albert Pujols was paid $13.87 million to play baseball in 2008. Again, relative to the average person in the United States and the world, Pujols appears to be dramatically overpaid. Then again, in 2008, Pujols hit 37 home runs, had a batting average of 0.357 and OPS of 1.114, and was named the most valuable player (MVP) in the National League (NL). And according to a study conducted by J. C. Bradbury[8] (a study we will discuss in Chapter 6), all the miracles Pujols worked on the baseball diamond (or the MRP of Pujols) was worth $24.72 million. In other words, according to the definition of exploitation offered by Robinson, Pujols was "exploited."

5.2 Unrestricted and Restricted Labor Markets[9]

Such a result may not have surprised a rather famous economist (or more specifically, a philosopher) from the 19th century. The writings of Karl Marx,

---

marginal product (MP) The productivity of hiring that additional worker.

marginal revenue product (MRP) Marginal product of labor multiplied by marginal revenue of output.

---

[7]Joan Robinson, *The Economics of Imperfect Competition*, 2nd ed. (London: Palgrave Macmillan, 1969), pp. 281–282. Originally published in 1933.

[8]John C. Bradbury, *Hot Stove Economics*, (New York: Copernicus Books, 2011). This study builds on the work of Gerald Scully ["Pay and Performance in Major League Baseball," *American Economic Review* 64 (1974): 917–930], whom we will also discuss in Chapter 6.

[9]This section is not only designed to explain the concept of MRP. It is also intended to explain that the study of sports economics allows us to explore some of the more important questions asked by economists (even those who may not like sports!).

which inspired millions around the world, argued that capitalism leads to the exploitation of workers. In other words, Marx posited that workers (and Albert Pujols would be classified as a worker) in a capitalist society tended to produce more value than they were paid by their employers.

Marx died in 1883. In 1899, J. B. Clark published *The Distribution of Wealth*. This work argued that workers under capitalism are paid according to their marginal productivity (a concept Clark helped to develop that we will explore in more detail momentarily). Therefore—contrary to what Bradbury found with respect to Pujols in 2008—there is no exploitation in the capitalist system. J. M. Clark, the son of J. B. Clark, affirmed that his father's statements about the ethical implications of marginal productivity "are oriented at Marx, and are best construed as an earnest, and not meticulously qualified, rebuttal of the Marxian exploitation theory."[10]

The arguments of Marx and Clark appear to capture two different views of capitalism. Marx argued that workers are paid less than they produce; therefore, capitalism is a "bad" system. Clark argued workers are paid what they are worth; therefore, capitalism is a "good" system.

Data were relatively scarce in the 19th century. So neither Marx nor Clark presented much empirical evidence supporting their respective views. Today, though, data are far more abundant—at least in the world of sports.

Before we get to the data, we need to master some basic labor economic theory. Once we understand the story told by the theory (reviewed in this chapter), we can then turn to the story told by the data (a story that begins in the next chapter).

Let's start with why Clark believed workers would be paid their MRP in a competitive labor market: The labor market in baseball, like the labor market in each of the major North American sports, has a variety of features that prevent every team from bidding on a player's services (i.e., the market is not often perfectly competitive). Furthermore, predicting performance is difficult. Nevertheless, let's imagine for a moment that the labor market was competitive and everyone knew the future performance of each player. In such a world, what would each player be paid?

Consider a player like Miguel Cabrera of the Detroit Tigers. J. C. Bradbury argues that Cabrera was worth (i.e., his MRP was) $12.84 million in 2009. Given Cabrera's MRP, what salary should he be paid?

> ## Karl Marx (1818–1883)
>
> When Karl Marx died in 1883, eleven people showed up at his funeral. And it would be decades before any nations would reorganize their economies according to "Marxist" principles. Although not noticed much in his lifetime, Marx's writings did eventually have a profound impact on the world. His basic argument that history proceeded through class struggle led many people in the world to reject capitalism, a system that Marx argued was defined by owners of capital exploiting workers. In the 21st century, few nations remain that embrace "Marxist" principles. Still, Marx's critique of capitalism has had a lasting impact on how many think about economics.

[10]As noted in Harry Landreth and David Colander, *History of Economic Thought*, 4th ed. (Boston: Houghton Mifflin, 2002), p. 255 and originally appeared in J. M. Clark, "J. M. Clark on J. B. Clark," in H. W. Spiegel (ed.), *The Development of Economic Thought* (New York: Wiley), p. 610.

monopsony A market with
only one buyer.

Let's imagine a world where the Tigers decide to only pay Cabrera $10 million. This may seem like a reasonable amount given that Cabrera is simply playing a game. Although such an assertion may be true, another team might look at Cabrera's MRP and conclude that they would do well to offer more than $10 million. In fact, if the market for Cabrera's services was quite competitive (i.e., a large number of teams were bidding for his services), then we would expect Cabrera's salary to essentially equal his MRP.

What if the market, however, wasn't competitive? What if the Tigers could somehow prevent other teams from bidding on Cabrera's services?

Economists refer to a market with only one buyer as a **monopsony**. If there is just one buyer, we would expect a firm to pay a wage that was less than the worker's MRP. And perhaps the best example of a monopsonistic employer is what has been observed historically in professional sports.[11]

Let's return to life under the reserve clause. Established by the NL in the 19th century, this clause created a market where players could only negotiate with one employer. As we noted, the eventual justification for this clause was competitive balance. But as the NL claimed in 1879, the original purpose of restricting the market for labor is to "reduce expenses" (i.e., reduce wages). And economic theory is consistent with that argument.

To see this deductively, let's go back to the work of Simon Rottenberg (1956).[12] Rottenberg observed that "the reserve rule, which binds a player to the team that contracts him, gives a prima facie appearance of a monopsony to the market. Once having signed a first contract, a player is confronted by a single buyer who may unilaterally specify the price to be paid for his services" (p. 252).

[11]In two labor economic textbooks—Ronald Ehrenberg and Robert S. Smith's *Modern Labor Economics* (Reading, MA: Addison Wesley Longman, 2000) and George Borjas' *Labor Economics* (New York: McGraw-Hill, 1996)—the primary example of a monopsony employer is a coal mine in a remote area. Upon further reflection, however, this example doesn't work very well, as Ehrenberg and Smith (p. 82) actually observe. Although small coal mining towns may have had only one employer, people could actually leave the town and go work someplace else. So workers still had some bargaining power. Such was not the case in MLB under the reserve clause. Babe Ruth could only negotiate with the New York Yankees. He had no other employer for his baseball services. Consequently, one can argue that baseball under the reserve clause is the best example of a monopsonistic firm. One should note, though, that this choice undermines the way monopsonies tend to be modeled. The models noted in the aforementioned textbooks argue that a monoposonistic employer must pay its workers the same wage. This assumption appears to be made in an effort to create the two-dimensional graph employed. When we look at sports, such an assumption is quite inconsistent with the empirical evidence.

[12]Simon Rottenberg, "The Baseball Players' Labor Market," *Journal of Political Economy* 64, no. 3 (June 1956): 242–258.

In such a market, what can we expect a player to be paid? Rottenberg suggests that each player would have a "supply price," or a price that a team must meet to prevent the player from pursuing another occupation.[13] This supply price would vary from player to player, depending on:

- what the player can earn in nonbaseball work

- other income a player can earn from playing baseball (i.e., endorsements)

- how much the player enjoys seasonal employment

- how much the player dislikes (or enjoys) constant travel

- how much the player enjoys (or dislikes) the attention of fans

Again, these factors would vary from player to player. So the supply price would also vary from player to player. We would thus expect players to be paid different wages under the reserve system. But as Rottenberg notes, we wouldn't expect a player to command more than his supply price.

Despite this argument, Rottenberg observed a "paradox" in baseball:

> If baseball players have, on the average, no skills other than those necessary to play baseball proficiently, then their next best wage would be relatively low. Why are they paid so much more? (p. 252)

The answer, according to Rottenberg, is that players still have some bargaining power. For example, players could simply refuse to play. And in the reserve clause era, holdouts were not uncommon.

Although refusing to play was a possibility, there was also another action a disgruntled player could take. Workers are not machines. In other words, human beings decide how hard they are going to work. If a player is not happy with his wages, he could agree to play. But he could also decide to not try his best.

Teams, of course, can choose to replace a disgruntled player. It is the existence of replacement talent that gives the team the ultimate bargaining power. Rottenberg notes that all players (i.e., any given player and all his replacements) could demand their full value, and in this instance, teams would be unable to pay any player a wage less than his MRP. But as Rottenberg states: "[I]t is incredible that all players should, in fact, exact

---

[13]One might also call this the player's "reservation price" or "reservation wage."

their full worth, it follows from this analysis that at least some players are exploited" (p. 253).

Given such an argument, let's summarize how Rottenberg believed baseball's labor market would function with and without a reserve clause.[14]

- If there is a free market, wages should equal MRP (so Clark is right!).

- If the market is restricted (by the reserve clause and/or reverse-order drafts), wages should be less than MRP (so Marx is right!).

- Whether the labor market is free or restricted, the distribution of playing talent (i.e., the level of competitive balance) should be the same.

- A third possibility is that wages could exceed MRP. One possible explanation for this is the **winner's curse**.

winner's curse A tendency for the winner in a bidding process to be the person/ group that most over-values what is being bid upon. This happens when value can only be estimated and not known with certainty.

All of these arguments are derived via deductive reasoning. Does the empirical evidence confirm this reasoning?

We have already found evidence that Rottenberg's competitive balance argument is consistent with the empirical evidence. His arguments with respect to player's wages require that we analyze data on a player's MRP. Before we get to that data (in the next chapter), we need to discuss what life was like in baseball after the reserve clause ended.

5.3 The Economics of Labor Conflict

In the previous chapter, we introduced Marvin Miller, the head of the Major League Baseball Players Association (MLBPA) from 1966 to 1982. Although Miller dramatically changed the relationship between players and owners in baseball, he was not responsible for creating baseball's labor union. Organized labor actually has a long history in professional baseball. In 1885, John Montgomery Ward formed the Brotherhood of Professional Baseball Players. In 1900, the Players' Protective Association was established. This effort was followed by

---

[14]How could this happen?

When a team makes an offer to a player, they know what the player did in the past. But salaries are paid in the future in return for productivity in the future. This means that teams must estimate future performance. Obviously, the team that secures the rights to a player is the team that makes the highest offer. Since this offer is based on an estimate of the future, it is possible that the team with the winning bid is the team that most overestimated a player's future performance. And in this circumstance, wages would exceed MRP. We will explore the empirical evidence for the winner's curse. For now, though, we should note that it is possible owners in the NL in 1879 believed that the winner's curse was bankrupting the league.

the Fraternity of Professional Baseball Players of America in 1912 and then the American Baseball Guild in 1946.[15]

As evidenced by the persistence of the reserve clause, these early unions did not experience much success. Part of this failure might be linked to an inability to create a union that actually represented the players. To illustrate, consider the following comment[16]:

> If I might, Senator, preface my remarks by repeating the words of Gene Woodling . . . 'We have it so good we don't know what to ask for next.' I think this sums up the thinking of the average major league ballplayer today.

This quote was from Robert Cannon in 1964. Cannon was a lawyer representing the MLBPA. And Woodling—for those unfamiliar with baseball history[17]—was an outfielder who played from 1943 to 1962, including six seasons with the Yankees when his team won the World Series five times (from 1949 to 1953).

In an era when the reserve clause would appear to be a significant constraint on a player's earning power, one might expect the players, and their representatives, to be somewhat disgruntled. But the above quote indicates that for at least some players, and their representatives, baseball under the reserve clause was so wonderful that they didn't "know what to ask for next."

When Miller assumed control the MLBPA, the attitude of the union quickly changed. This is likely due to the fact that Miller came to the MLBPA from the United Steelworkers of America (USW). As a veteran of labor-management negotiations in the steel industry, Miller was more likely—relative to his predecessors in the MLBPA—to see the union and owners as adversaries.[18] And that adversarial relationship often led to conflict.

---

[15]Each of these early unions is listed at http://mlbplayers.mlb.com/pa/info/history.jsp.

[16]The following quote is taken from the Professional Sports Antitrust Bill of 1964. The quote was reprinted in James Quick and Rodney Fort, *Pay Dirt: The Business of Professional Team Sports* (Princeton, NJ: Princeton University Press, 1992), p. 193.

[17]One can see the details of Woodling's career at http://www.baseball-reference.com/players/w/woodlge01.shtml.

[18]To illustrate, Miller notes in *A Whole Different Game* that the aforementioned Robert Cannon advised the players' union in 1965 while campaigning to become the commissioner of baseball. As Miller observed, this would be the equivalent of the head of the United Automobile Workers (UAW) seeking to become president of General Motors (p. 65). If you are negotiating with a group of people (i.e., owners) you hope to lead in the future, you are probably going to be less adversarial. Marvin Miller, *A Whole Different Game: The Inside Story of Baseball's New Deal* (New York: Simon & Schuster, 1991).

And what was the conflict between workers and owners? The conflict was essentially the same one we observe in all firms. Consider the following steps a typical firm follows:

1. Capital and labor (and other inputs) come together to produce output.

2. The output is sold, which generates revenue for the firm.

3. The revenue is then distributed to the owners of the firm (who provide the capital and other inputs) and the workers (who provide labor).

When we arrive at Step 3, we must answer the following question: How much of the revenue should go to the owners and workers?

If the input and output markets are perfectly competitive, as J. B. Clark detailed above, the answer is simple. All inputs in a competitive market are paid according to their contribution to firm revenue. But what if the markets are not competitive? Then the inputs may not be paid according to their economic contribution. And in that case, the payment will depend on the bargaining power of the participants.[19]

We have seen that owners can increase their bargaining power via institutions like the reserve clause. The evidence presented so far (and more shall be presented later) is that when the owners' bargaining power is enhanced, they can seize a larger share of the revenue pie.

If the workers continue to bargain individually, it would be difficult, as we saw through decades of baseball history, for the workers to overcome the owners' constraint. But what if the workers organized and bargained as a group? Now the bargaining power of labor is increased and the workers might be able to claim a larger share of the revenue pie.

How do the workers exercise their collective power? Under Marvin Miller, the players learned about the power of the **strike**, which is simply workers refusing to work in an effort to change the agreement they have with their employer. If enough workers withdraw their contribution to the production process, and a firm cannot easily replace these workers, then production will stop.

strike Workers refusing to work in an effort to force employers to make changes to the worker/employer labor agreement.

---

[19]It should be noted that one characteristic of a competitive market is that participants do not have the power to set prices. In other words, a competitive market can be defined as a market where participants do not have bargaining power.

Table 5.4 History of Labor–Management Strife in Major League Baseball[20]			
Nature of Dispute	Year	Days	Games Lost
Strike	1972	14	86
Lockout	1973	12	0
Lockout	1976	17	0
Strike	1980	8	0
Strike	1981	50	712
Strike	1985	2	0
Lockout	1990	32	0
Strike	1994–95	232	920

This is what happened in baseball in 1972. And as **Table 5.4** details, it also occurred again in 1980 and 1981. And then after Donald Fehr took over for Miller as head of the MLBPA, strikes took place in 1985 and 1994–95.

It should be noted that MLB was not the only North American sports league to suffer a strike. As **Table 5.5** enumerates, player strikes have also occurred in the National Football League (NFL) and National Hockey League (NHL).

Table 5.5 History of Labor–Management Strife in the National Football League, National Basketball Association, and National Hockey League[21]			
League	Year	Nature of Dispute	Games Lost
NFL	1982	Player strike	98
NFL	1987	Player strike	56
NHL	1994	Player strike	442
NBA	1998–99	Lockout	424
NHL	2004–05	Lockout	1230
NBA	2011	Lockout	240
NHL	2012–13	Lockout	510

[20]This table is adapted from one that originally appeared in Andrew Zimbalist, "Labor Relations in Major League Baseball," *Journal of Sports Economics* 4, no. 4 (2003): 333.

[21]Except for noting the NHL lockout from 2012–13, this table is taken from David J. Berri, "Did the Players Give Up Money to Make the NBA Better? Exploring the 2011 Collective Bargaining Agreement in the National Basketball Association," *International Journal of Sport Finance* 7 (2012): 158–175. One should take note, though, that only disputes that cost regular-season games are listed in this table. The NFL did have a lockout in 2011 that was resolved without the cancellation of any regular-season games.

lockout Employers
refusing to allow workers
to work.

In addition to strikes, both Tables 5.4 and 5.5 note that these leagues have also experienced lockouts. A **lockout** occurs when the owners prevent the players from coming to work. Why would the owners take this action?

The answer to this question is related to when the owners and players are paid. A player's contract is for the regular season. Although small bonuses are paid for the playoffs and future contracts might be influenced by what happens in the playoffs, for the most part, players are paid for the regular season. In contrast, a league makes a substantial portion of its revenue from the playoffs. Consequently, the bargaining power of the players is strongest right before the playoffs begin. And the owners see their strongest bargaining position as occurring before the season starts. Therefore, lockouts tend to occur before the season begins and strikes tend to occur toward the end. Since 1995, every labor dispute in sports has been a lockout. So although a strike has not occurred in over 20 years, labor disputes still plague professional sports.

And as Tables 5.4 and 5.5 make clear, strikes or lockouts appear to occur very frequently in professional North American sports. In fact, they occur more often than in non-sports industries. To ascertain this, let's look at data from non-sports industries.[22] The U.S. Department of Labor tells us that the number of union workers declined from 17.7 million in 1983 to 14.5 million in 2012.[23] There are approximately 4,000 unionized athletes in the four major North American sports leagues.[24] From 1972 to 2012, there were 15 labor disputes in sports. If non-sports union members had experienced this many disputes, we would have seen 62,650 conflicts. The number of

[22]This analysis replicates the work of James Quirk and Rodney Fort (1999, p. 68). Their comparison of labor disputes in sports to those in other American industries looked at data from only 10 years (1987–1996). Over this time period, sports were 50 times more likely to experience a work stoppage. The Quirk–Fort study was also replicated in Berri, Schmidt, and Brook (2006), which considered stoppages from 1981 to 2004. The Berri *et al.* study found that workers in sports were 25 times more likely to be involved in a labor dispute. Finally, Berri (2012) examined work stoppages from 1981 to 2011 and determined that sports leagues were 26 times more likely to have a labor dispute. The lower number reported here reflects the fact that labor disputes in non-sports industries were more likely to occur in the 1970s. David J. Berri, Martin B. Schmidt, and Stacey L. Brook, *The Wages of Wins: Taking Measure of the Many Myths in Modern Sport* (Stanford, CA: Stanford University Press, 2006). Released in paperback in September 2007.

[23]These numbers came from http://www.bls.gov/news.release/union2.nr0.htm. This site notes that 1983 is the first year for which comparable data are available. If we assume that labor membership has a linear downward trend from 1972 to 2012, the average number of union members in each year was about 16.7 million.

[24]This estimate derives from James Quirk and Rodney Fort, *Hardball: The Abuse of Power in Pro Team Sports* (Princeton, NJ: Princeton University Press, 1999), p. 68.

disputes from 1972 to 2012, though, was only 3,367.[25] That means management and labor in sports are about 17 times more likely to be involved in a labor dispute.

Why are disputes so common in sports? To answer this question, let's spend a moment thinking about the basic economics of a strike. Our analysis is captured by Figure 5.1. This relatively simple model was developed by Sir John Hicks.[26] The *y*-axis is the increase in wages that the union and firm are negotiating; the *x*-axis represents the length of the strike.

As the Hicks model illustrates, workers initially demand relatively high wages and the firm offers relatively low wages. This difference causes the strike (or a lockout). As the strike continues, both parties lose out on their payment from the production process. Consequently, both parties have an incentive to change their initial offer. How quickly these offers converge dictates the length of the labor dispute.

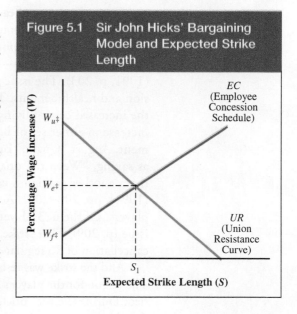

Figure 5.1   Sir John Hicks' Bargaining Model and Expected Strike Length

This pace of convergence depends on a number of factors. In non-sports industries, the issue for workers is whether or not they have an outside source of income from a strike fund, state unemployment benefits, and/or another job. For firms in non-sports industries, a list of factors would include the ability to have nonunion workers (i.e., management) and/or replacement workers take the place of the striking labor force.

When we turn to sports, though, it is a different story. The athletes in the four major North American sports tend to be the best in the world. So they cannot be easily replaced by managers and/or other workers. And that means these sellers of labor have monopoly power.

On the other side, the striking athletes in these sports cannot generally find employment that pays nearly as well as the salaries seen in the North American sports leagues. And that means the buyer of labor has monopsony power.

---

[25]For the number of labor disputes, see http://www.bls.gov/news.release/archives/wkstp_02082013.htm.

[26]John R. Hicks, *The Theory of Wages*, 2nd ed. (New York: St. Martin's Press, 1966), pp. 136–157. The discussion of Hicks presented follows from Ronald Ehrenberg and Robert S. Smith, *Modern Labor Economics* (Reading, MA: Addison Wesley Longman, 2000) pp. 495–499. One should note that this model has been somewhat simplified. Hicks hypothesized that initially workers would actually increase their wage demands (i.e., the union resistance curve would slope upward). After that initial increase, wage demands would decline.

Given the power of each group, who will prevail? In 1972, the owners were convinced their power would prove supreme.

The 1972 labor dispute, in the words of Marvin Miller, "was not only the first in baseball history—it was the first in the history of professional sports" (1991, p. 203). The issue in this dispute was not wages, but the players' pension and health benefits. The players' position was that these should rise with the increased cost of living. The owners' position was that there should be no increase in either set of benefits. Prior to the deadline for reaching an agreement, August "Gussie" Busch, owner of the St. Louis Cardinals, was quoted as saying, "We voted unanimously to take a stand. We're not going to give them another goddamn cent! If they want to strike, let them strike!" [Miller (1991), pp. 203–205]. According to Miller, Busch's quote served to rally the players. Of the 673 players asked to vote, 663 voted to go on strike over this issue (p. 209). That strike, as noted in Table 5.4, lasted 14 days and led to the cancellation of 86 regular-season games.

And the strike was resolved entirely according to the terms set by the players. The reason for the player's success was the inability of the owners to remain unified. During the very brief strike, some teams, in fact, opened their stadiums to the players for workouts.[27]

The player's triumph in 1972 was a harbinger of things to come for the owners. The 1972 strike appeared to teach the players that a unified front would be successful. In contrast, the divisions among the ownership ranks in baseball have been difficult to overcome. In disputes after 1972, the owners suggested institutions like a salary cap to control team spending and limit the wages paid to players. Such institutions would certainly benefit owners of small-market teams. But large-market teams could view such institutions as a constraint on their ability to sign the players perceived to be the most talented. In sum, the owners of small-market and large-market teams do not have the same incentives.

A story from 1996 illustrates this point. Baseball endured its worst labor dispute in 1994 and 1995. In 1996, Jerry Reinsdorf said, "We need some meaningful salary restraint and sharing of revenues, so everyone has a chance to compete."[28] Such a statement clearly echoed the owners' line during negotiations.

---

[27]This observation comes from Miller (1991, p. 220). Miller noted that the Chicago White Sox, Pittsburgh Pirates, and Philadelphia Phillies allowed players to work out at their facilities.

[28]Gerry Callahan, "Double Play: When He Signed Albert Belle, Jerry Reinsdorf Broke the Bank—and Maybe the Labor Impasse," *Sports Illustrated,* December 2, 1996, http://sportsillustrated.cnn.com/vault/article/magazine/MAG1009137/index.htm.

Often what matters is not what people say, but what they do. Just two weeks after Reinsdorf made this statement, his Chicago White Sox signed Albert Belle to a five-year, $55 million contract. At the time, this contract was worth $2.5 million more per year than the next richest contract. In sum, Reinsdorf, an owner of a large-market team, was a vocal supporter of "salary restraint" but also unable to ignore the incentive to use his resources to build the best possible team.[29]

The conflict between the incentives of small- and large-market teams in baseball, coupled with the unified front of the players, appears to be the primary reason baseball in 2017 does not have a cap on payrolls or individual salaries.

In contrast, workers in the NFL have faced a hard salary cap since 1992. And they have never seen unrestricted free agency. The outcome of the 1987 players' strike in the NFL illustrates why the league's Players Association has been unable to achieve the same level of success as their counterparts in baseball.

In 1987, the players in the NFL went on strike. The entire strike—the last in NFL history—only lasted three weeks. That is, for some players at least, it lasted three weeks. As Kevin Quinn (2012) notes,[30] 89 players crossed the picket lines. Some of them actually never went on strike but played in the games populated primarily by replacement players.[31] Again, the strike ended in just three weeks and the players returned without a new collective bargaining agreement.

So unions in baseball and football appear to have achieved different outcomes. What explains this difference?

An answer may be found in the stories of Ted Kluszewski and Jose Bautista.[32] In 1947, Kluszewski came to the Cincinnati Reds. Across the next six seasons, Kluszewski never hit more than 25 home runs in a season and never posted an OPS above 0.892. And then at 28 years of age—in 1953—Kluszewski suddenly became an All-Star. In 1953, Kluszewski hit 40 home runs and had a 0.950 OPS. The next season, he hit 49 home runs and had a 1.049 OPS. In sum, Kluszewski, after six years of major league experience in which he was not considered "great," suddenly morphed into an All-Star.

A similar story can be told for Bautista. Up until the age of 28, Bautista played for five different major league teams in six seasons. In none of these

---

[29]Callahan (1996).

[30]Kevin Quinn, "Getting to the 2011–12 National Football League Collective Bargaining Agreement," *International Journal of Sport Finance* 7 (2012): 141–157.

[31]Go to pro-football-reference.com for a list of players who crossed: http://www.pro-football-reference.com/blog/?p=6403.

[32]Player statistics for both Kluszewski and Bautista can be found at http://www.baseball-reference.com.

seasons did he hit more than 16 home runs or post an OPS above 0.757. And then—at the age of 29—Bautista hit 54 home runs with a 0.995 OPS. The next season his OPS increased to 1.056. In sum, like Kluszewski, Bautista suddenly became a star.

Now compare these stories to what generally happens in the NFL. In football, players are clearly segmented into positions. The star of each team tends to be the quarterback. These players tend to be the highest-paid and the primary focus of the fans. If a player is an offensive lineman, linebacker, or safety, he is never going to be a star quarterback. In other words, the NFL's labor market is fragmented. Some players are stars. Others are never going to be stars. This division undermines the unity of the union. After all, why should a nonstar hold out for a deal that will allow the stars to greatly increase their income?[33]

A similar story could be told about the National Basketball Association (NBA).[34] As we will note later, NBA players—relative to what is seen in football and baseball—are much more consistent with respect to performance from season to season. What this means is that the star players, athletes like LeBron James, Michael Jordan, Shaquille O'Neal, tend to remain stars. And those that are not stars—contrary to what we see in baseball—tend to remain nonstars. These differences might explain why the NBA has both a payroll cap (a soft cap, not an NFL hard cap) and a cap on individual salaries.

The NBA's first labor dispute, in 1998–99, illustrates this division. The outcome of the dispute was a cap on individual player salaries. No other North American team sport had agreed to such an institution. But the nature of player performance in the NBA suggests a simple explanation for why the majority of players in basketball would agree to this rule. Put simply, the majority of players in the NBA are never going to be considered maximum-salary players. Since most players cannot be a LeBron James or Michael Jordan, it is unrealistic for them to resist a deal that would limit the earning power of these stars.

The discussion of disputes in different sports illustrates a difference between sports and non-sports industries. The bargaining model from John Hicks argued that workers and firms bargained primarily over wage levels. But our discussion indicates that this model, as illustrated in Figure 5.2, should be modified when examining sports. Workers and owners in sports are not bargaining directly over wage levels. More often, they appear to be bargaining over the level of freedom in the marketplace, which would give the players the power to negotiate for higher wages.

And this is what makes sports so unusual. In a non-sports labor-management dispute, the owners will tend to prefer a labor market where they are free to pay

---

[33]This observation was made in Michael Leeds and Peter von Allmen, *The Economics of Sports*, 4th ed. (Boston: Addison Wesley, 2011), pp. 301–302.

[34]The following story was told in Berri (2012).

whatever wages the market might allow. In contrast, the union will bargain for higher wages (and other benefits). In sum, in non-sports negotiations, management generally prefers an unconstrained labor market and workers are in favor of some restrictions.

In sports, though, the story is reversed. Owners tend to be in favor of labor market restrictions that limit the bargaining power of workers. And workers in sports tend to prefer more freedom in the labor market. Or, workers in non-sports industries tend to bargain for specific wages that constrain the choices of owners. In sports, workers seek an environment that allows each worker to bargain for the best possible wage for him- or herself.

The contest between the workers and owners in sports is a game that doesn't seem to end. The reason for this is quite simple. Sports leagues generate billions of dollars in revenue that are divided among a small group of people. There simply are not many players and there are fewer owners. So each participant in each labor dispute is potentially fighting for large differences in income.

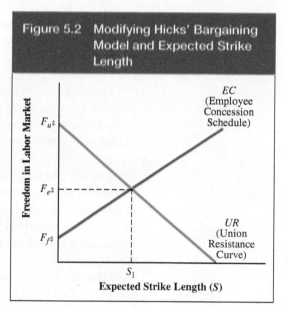

Figure 5.2   Modifying Hicks' Bargaining Model and Expected Strike Length

Consider the 1994–95 labor dispute in MLB. Unlike the aforementioned NFL players in the 1987 strike, the baseball players managed to stay on strike throughout the close of the 1994 season, the cancellation of the World Series, and the beginning of the 1995 season. Why were the players able to hold out? Beyond the issue of player unity, the money involved was quite large. Roger Noll argued that the owners' efforts to limit the growth in player salaries would have cost the players $1.5 billion over the lifetime of the proposed agreement. The strike, on the other hand, only cost the players $300 million.[35] Given these numbers, we can understand why the players refused to return to work in 1994 and why such disputes continue to plague professional team sports.

5.4 A History of Making Fans Angry

Fans of MLB, though, might tell a very different story from what we just described. Although the players "won" the dispute, the 1994–95 strike — from the fan's perspective — was the most costly in league history. And when a 2002 labor dispute threatened to cancel games again, the fans appeared to revolt.

[35]The analysis of Roger Noll appears in Quirk and Fort (1999, pp. 70–71).

The fans' attitudes were captured in the writings of Chuck Cavalaris of the *Knoxville New-Sentinel*.[36] His story begins with the following statement:

> The players ... and owners need to realize they are on the verge of ruining a great sport. Scores of people from across the country have joined our pledge to boycott major league baseball, if a strike wipes out the playoffs. We simply will not be held hostage any longer.

The key phrase in this statement is "scores of people." In 2001, MLB sold 72 million tickets. So finding "scores of people,"[37] in a market with millions of customers, is not impressive. In addition, many of the people responding to Cavalaris came from Tennessee. Since there has never been a MLB team in Tennessee, it is hard to imagine that the people writing to Cavalaris were actually buying many tickets.[38]

Despite these issues, fan surveys seemed to confirm the story told by Cavalaris. Joe Henderson (2002), in the *Tampa Tribune*, noted "one particular fan survey where 56 percent of baseball fans said they wouldn't attend another MLB game if there was a strike. Another 37 percent indicated that they would refuse to watch baseball on television."[39]

Such surveys made it clear. A player strike in 2002 would have had significant consequences for baseball. And there is some evidence that people in baseball believed these surveys were accurate. For example, Steve Kline, the player representative for the St. Louis Cardinals, had this to say when a deal was reached on August 30, 2002: "It came down to us playing baseball or having our reputations and life ripped by the fans. Baseball would have never been the same if we had walked out."[40]

---

[36]Chuck Cavalaris, "Fans Warn Against Baseball Stoppage," *Knoxville News-Sentinel (Tennessee)*, August 18, 2002, Sunday Final Edition, p. C2.

[37]For those unfamiliar with the term, a "score" is a group of 20.

[38]At this time, I was also interviewed by a local television station in Bakersfield, CA. In the interview, I noted my academic research (with Martin Schmidt) that indicated strikes and lockouts did not statistically impact attendance. The television station, though, also chose to interview men in a local Bakersfield bar. These men also claimed they would never attend another game if the players went on strike. Of course, there is also no MLB in Bakersfield. The television interviewer didn't raise this issue to the men in the bar.

[39]Joe Henderson, "Baseball Pushing Its Luck in Dispute?," *Tampa Tribune (Florida)*, August 18, 2002, Sunday Final Edition, Sports section, p. 1.

[40]http://sportsillustrated.cnn.com/baseball/news/2002/08/30/labor_friday/.

In spite of such sentiments, though, the data told a very different story. And because labor disputes have occurred in all the major North American sports, this story goes beyond what we observe in baseball. Let's talk about the NFL.

We begin with the history of paid attendance in the NFL.[41] Figure 5.3 reports the average regular-season attendance for each team from 1934 to 2015. As one can see, in the 1930s, the average team saw fewer than 100,000 fans across the entire regular season. Attendance during World War II was somewhat erratic, but as the war ended, average attendance spiked to 173,214 in 1946 and increased to 183,744 in 1947. But this spike was short-lived and attendance declined in the later 1940s. It was not until 1955 that the 1947 level was reached again. And then average attendance continued to rise, surpassing 250,000 in 1958, 350,000 in 1966, and 450,000 in 1978.

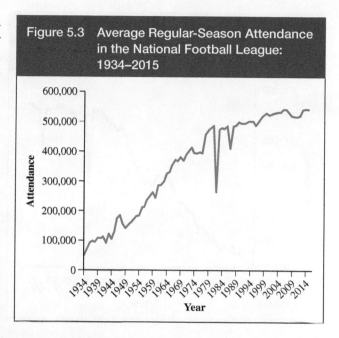

Figure 5.3   Average Regular-Season Attendance in the National Football League: 1934–2015

It is then that we see the impact of the NFL's labor disputes. In 1982, the schedule was reduced from 16 games to 9 games. This caused average attendance to decline from 485,964 in 1981 to 263,123 during the strike-shortened season. But the following year, average attendance was 474,187. The difference between average attendance in 1983 and 1981 is not statistically significant.[42]

A similar story may be told with respect to the 1987 labor dispute. In 1986, average attendance was 485,305. Again, a labor dispute reduced the number of games in 1987, so average attendance fell to 407,363. But in 1988, average attendance rebounded to 483,566. And again, the difference between 1986 and 1988 is not statistically significant.

Thus, our study of the labor disputes in the NFL fail to find evidence that fans held any grudge. The NFL, though, has not had a labor dispute since 1987. As Figure 5.4 illustrates, the same story cannot be told for the NBA.

---

[41]One can find these data on paid NFL attendance at http://static.nfl.com/static/content/public/image/history/pdfs/History/2013/536-538-Paid%20Attendance.pdf.

[42]This observation was made in Martin B. Schmidt and David J. Berri, "The Impact of Labor Strikes on Consumer Demand: An Application to Professional Sports," *American Economic Review* 94, no. 1 (March 2004): 344–357. It is derived from a model of NFL attendance that examined the impact of each labor dispute and the subsequent recovery in attendance. Similar models were estimated for the NHL and MLB.

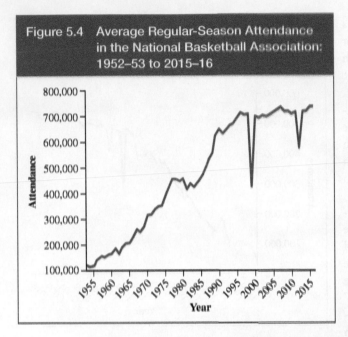

Figure 5.4   Average Regular-Season Attendance in the National Basketball Association: 1952–53 to 2015–16

Up until 1998, the NBA had the distinction of being the only major North American sports league to never lose a game to a labor dispute. This ended with the 1998–99 season. Prior to that season, attendance in the NBA had been steadily rising. In 1975–76, the average team surpassed the 400,000 mark. The 500,000 barrier was passed in 1986–87, while the 600,000 mark was exceeded just two years later. In 1995–96, the average team attracted more than 700,000 fans for the first time.[43]

Two years later, this average was 701,799. But then came the 1998 dispute, which cost teams 32 games. The next season, attendance was 691,674. Such a decline, though, is not statistically significant.[44]

The NBA was able to maintain labor peace for the next decade. But in 2011–12, the league again lost games to a labor dispute. This time, we see average attendance actually increasing after such an event. In 2010–11, average attendance was 710,086. In 2012–13, this mark was 710,677.

And when examining gate revenue,[45] we observe a similar increase. League gate revenue was $1.03 billion in 2010–11. In 2012–13, it was $1.11 billion, or 7.6% higher. Such numbers clearly suggest that NBA fans did not hold a grudge.

At this point, you may not be surprised to learn that the same story may be told for the NHL. The NHL did not lose games to a labor dispute until the 1994–95 season. That year, the league's schedule was reduced from 84 games in 1993–94 to 48 games. In 1995–96, the league adopted an 82-game regular-season schedule. With this shorter schedule, the league still saw the average regular-season attendance rise from 619,446 in 1993–94 to 655,447 in 1995–96. Clearly, this dispute did not permanently harm league attendance.

---

[43]Given the capacity constraints of the NBA, an average of 800,000 seems impossible. If every team sold out in 2015–16, the average team would attract 787,717 fans. As we noted in Chapter One, NBA teams have an incentive to price tickets so that sell outs are common. In 2015–16, the average team was at 93% of capacity.

[44]It also coincided with Michael Jordan's second retirement from the Chicago Bulls.

[45]Gate revenue is calculated by multiplying a team's attendance by a team's average ticket prices. Attendance can be found at ESPN.com. Average ticket prices are reported by Team Marketing Report at teammarketing.com.

The next labor dispute, though, promised to be more devastating. In 2004–05, the NHL lost an entire season to a labor dispute. Despite withholding an entire season from its fans, attendance in the NHL again increased. In 2003–04, the league had an average attendance of 677,872. In 2005–06, this mark increased to 695,139.

Given this reaction from fans, we probably should not be surprised that the NHL entered into another labor dispute in 2012–13. This dispute did not cancel the entire season, but did result in a schedule of just 48 games. In 2013–14, a full slate of games was again scheduled. And the returns suggest once more that NHL fans do not hold a grudge. The average team attracted 715,672 fans during the 2011–12 season. In 2013–14, the average team had 721,083 fans at their games. Yes, NHL fans again returned in larger numbers after a labor dispute. See Figure 5.5.

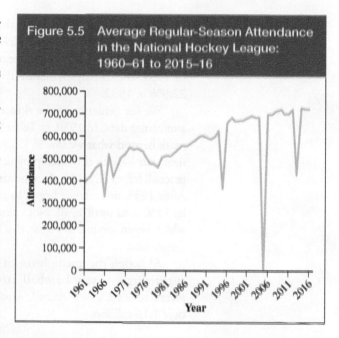

Figure 5.5   Average Regular-Season Attendance in the National Hockey League: 1960–61 to 2015–16

Next, we turn back to baseball. Again, the story told in the press was that labor disputes have a devastating impact on attendance. These disputes anger fans, and these fans impose costs upon leagues that dare to take away the games. So far we have not seen any evidence of this pattern in the NFL, NBA, and NHL. In baseball, though, it might appear that some evidence exists to back up the media's story. However, when we look at the entire history of baseball attendance, once again, such a spin doesn't stand up well to scrutiny.

To see this, consider Figure 5.6, which presents average regular-season attendance in MLB from 1901 to 2016. At the onset of the 20th century, teams generally attracted fewer than 500,000 fans during the regular season. It was not until 1920 that the average surpassed the half-million mark. As the economy plunged into the Great Depression, average attendance dipped back below the 500,000 mark.

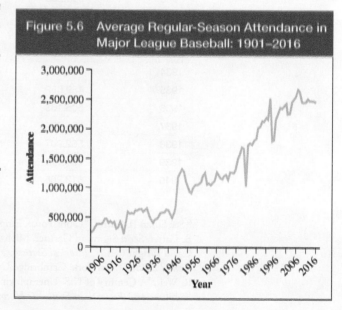

Figure 5.6   Average Regular-Season Attendance in Major League Baseball: 1901–2016

We should note, though, that the decline was not immediate. The Great Depression began in August 1929. Despite a well-publicized stock market crash in October, the unemployment rate only rose from 2.9% in 1929 to 8.9% in 1930.[46] In 1931, the unemployment rate spiked to 15.7% and then continued to rise to 22.9% in 1932.

We see evidence of the slow emergence of the Great Depression in baseball's attendance data. In 1930, as Table 5.6 reports, the average team drew 633,266 fans, a mark beyond what we saw in 1929 and a record at that point in baseball history. The next year—with the unemployment rate almost doubling—average attendance in baseball fell to 529,194. Average attendance continued to decline in 1932 and 1933. After 1933, attendance began to recover. But average attendance did not return to its 1930 level until 1940. Not coincidentally, it was the buildup toward World War II, which began around this time, that is credited for bringing the nation out of the Great Depression.

Although the unemployment rate fell back below 5% by 1942, the war—not surprisingly—saw baseball attendance fall. But in 1945, average baseball attendance set a new record. And in 1946, average baseball attendance spiked to over 1.16 million.

Table 5.6	Major League Attendance: 1929–52		
Year	Average MLB Attendance	Year	Average MLB Attendance
1929	599,261	1941	605,600
1930	633,266	1942	534,598
1931	529,194	1943	466,619
1932	435,910	1944	548,297
1933	380,564	1945	677,570
1934	435,232	1946	1,157,706
1935	459,082	1947	1,242,159
1936	505,163	1948	1,307,553
1937	558,754	1949	1,263,460
1938	562,907	1950	1,091,436
1939	561,111	1951	1,007,917
1940	613,968	1952	914,565

[46]See Susan B. Carter, "Labor Force, Employment, and Unemployment: 1890–1990," in Susan B. Carter, Scott Sigmund Gartner, Michael R. Haines, Alan L. Olmstead, Richard Sutch, and Gavin Wright (eds.), *Historical Statistics of the United States, Earliest Times to the Present: Millennial Edition* (New York: Cambridge University Press, 2006), Table Ba470–477. Also, David R. Weir, "A Century of U.S. Unemployment, 1890–1990: Revised Estimates and Evidence for Stabilization," *Research in Economic History* 14 (1992): 301–346.

As noted in the previous chapter, we do not know for certain that the jubilation associated with the end of World War II led to this increase.[47] We do know that attendance continued to rise until 1948, and then average attendance started to decline. Starting in the mid-1950s, though, average attendance began a slow ascent, finally returning to the level observed in 1948 with the 1976 season.

Understanding attendance in the first half of the 20th century in baseball is essential to understanding attendance in the era of labor strife. To see this, let's go back to 1976, or the year that baseball's free-agent market opened. With that event, baseball's labor problems seem to intensify. In 1981, the dispute between players and owners led to the loss of more than 700 regular-season games. Although the event was traumatizing to baseball fans, the impact it had on attendance is hard to see in the data. Yes, without games being played in 1981, attendance falls. But in 1982, as **Table 5.7** illustrates, average attendance actually surpassed what we observed in 1980 and marked an all-time record in baseball history.

Table 5.7 Major League Baseball Attendance: 1976–2016

Year	Average MLB Attendance	Year	Average MLB Attendance
1976	1,304,930	1996	2,146,335
1977	1,488,838	1997	2,256,025
1978	1,562,957	1998	2,353,372
1979	1,675,015	1999	2,337,979
1980	1,654,390	2000	2,378,630
1981	1,020,938	2001	2,419,370
1982	1,714,918	2002	2,246,336
1983	1,751,551	2003	2,254,350
1984	1,720,879	2004	2,432,298
1985	1,800,938	2005	2,497,527
1986	1,827,162	2006	2,535,959
1987	2,000,443	2007	2,650,106
1988	2,038,419	2008	2,619,704
1989	2,122,042	2009	2,446,167
1990	2,108,606	2010	2,435,127
1991	2,185,145	2011	2,448,384

(continued)

[47]Again, it is difficult to statistically test the impact of an event that only happens once.

Table 5.7 (continued)			
Year	Average MLB Attendance	Year	Average MLB Attendance
1992	2,148,864	2012	2,495,309
1993	2,509,212	2013	2,467,563
1994	1,786,072	2014	2,457,987
1995	1,802,473	2015	2,458,668
		2016	2,438,636

Across the next decade, baseball's attendance continued to grow. And then in 1993, the average team attracted more than 2.5 million fans. But then another labor dispute not only eliminated regular-season games. It also eliminated the 1994 World Series and then carried over into the 1995 regular season. So it was not until 1996 that baseball returned to a full slate of regular-season contests. And as one can see, average attendance in 1996 is below the record set in 1993.

Such a result suggests that the labor dispute of 1994 and 1995 had a negative impact on league attendance. And since attendance did not again reach its 1993 level until 2006, this particular labor dispute appears to have had a long-lasting impact.

A closer look at the data, however, reveals a somewhat different interpretation. From 1992 to 1993, baseball attendance increased from 2.1 million to 2.5 million. This 16.8% increase in attendance was the largest increase — one not associated with a labor dispute — since that World War II spike noted earlier. What explains this spike?[48]

The explanation begins with the Colorado Rockies and Florida Marlins. Both were expansion teams in 1993. And initially, each was very popular. Nearly 7.5 million fans saw these teams play. The Rockies, playing in Mile High Stadium (home of the Denver Broncos), set an attendance record with 4.4 million fans.

The attendance marks set by these two teams, though, were not permanent. Although the Rockies made the playoffs in 1995 and the Marlins won the World Series in 1997, neither team was able to come within 500,000 fans of the attendance record observed in 1993.[49] So it seems reasonable to conclude that the

---

[48]The following explanations appeared in *The Wages of Wins* (Berri *et al.*, 2006, p. 23).

[49]For the history of the Rockies' attendance from 1993 to 2012, go to http://www.baseball-almanac.com/teams/rockattn.shtml. One should note the Rockies moved into Coors Field, a smaller stadium, in 1995. Here, too, is the history of the Marlins attendance from 1993 to 2012: http://www.baseball-almanac.com/teams/marlins3.shtml.

portion of the 1993 spike associated with the Rockies and Marlins was not going to be observed in later years, regardless of the 1994–95 strike.[50]

The story of the Rockies and Marlins suggests that the attendance spike observed in 1993 wasn't likely to last. That means we should probably compare the 1996 level of attendance to what was observed in 1992. And since those marks were quite similar, we should suspect that even the 1994–95 labor dispute didn't have a lasting impact on fan interest.

So do fans hold a grudge? Certainly, some fans promise they will stay away when these disputes happen. But the data suggest that fans do not systematically respond to such disruptions. When the games return, the data tell us that fans also return.

5.5 Why Can't Fans Hold a Grudge?

All of this leads to two questions[51]:

1. Why do fans insist they will not come back after a labor dispute?
2. Why do fans consistently return after a labor dispute?

To answer them, let's employ our simple model of consumer behavior. We stated in Chapter 3 that people will consider marginal benefits and marginal costs when making a decision. With respect to tickets to sporting events, the marginal cost is the price of a ticket. Marginal benefits are the utility the consumer derives from attending the game.

If a person decides to attend a game, we can infer the following:

$$\text{Marginal Utility from Attending Game} \geq \text{Disutility of Paying the Price of Attending Game}$$

In simple words, sports make fans happy.

---

[50] *The Wages of Wins* (p. 23) observes that the top teams in baseball, like the Rockies, also played in football stadiums. Atlanta, Philadelphia, San Francisco, and Toronto all shared stadiums with football teams.

[51] The answer to these questions appears in *The Wages of Wins* (Berri *et al.*, 2006, pp. 24–25).

Now a labor dispute occurs and the fans' happiness is taken away. What action can the fans take? The problem for fans is that they are not explicitly part of the labor negotiations. All they can do when unhappy is make the following threat: If players and owners do not agree to end the labor dispute and give back the games to the fans, we will not attend games in the future. In simple words, the fans will take away the future earnings of the players and owners.

Is this a credible threat? It is reasonable to assume that in the future — when the games are ultimately played — the sports fan will still think that the marginal utility of attending the game exceeds the disutility associated with paying the price of attending the game. So when fans threaten to not return when the games return, they are saying that in the future they will be willing to take an action that will make them worse off. In sum, this is not a credible threat.

That is what the data show. Fans do return when the games return. Of course, this means there is no way for the fans to stop labor disputes from taking the games away. So we can expect labor disputes to continue in the future. And the winner in these disputes dictates how much of each league's revenue goes to the owners or players.

But we are still left with our original question: Are professional athletes overpaid? This chapter began by comparing the pay of athletes to non-athletes. Such a comparison—as noted—doesn't really answer the question. To answer the question we need to first think about what determines the pay of athletes. So we have reviewed the bargaining between owners and players, and that review has revealed that via labor union negotiations, player's bargaining power has improved.

So pay for players has increased. But are they being paid too much? Too little? Deductive reasoning won't give us the answer to these questions. To answer these questions we need inductive reasoning. Yes, we need to look at some numbers.

Key Terms

marginal product (MP) (p. 148)
marginal revenue product
  (MRP) (p. 148)
monopsony (p. 150)

winner's curse (p. 152)
strike (p. 154)
lockout (p. 156)

Problems

Study Questions

1. What was Babe Ruth paid in nominal and real terms in 1930? Which player was the first to be paid more than Ruth in nominal terms? Which player was the first to be paid more than Ruth in real terms?

2. Can you determine "overpaid" and "underpaid" by just looking at the size of a worker's salary? Why or why not?

3. How does Joan Robinson define exploitation?

4. How did Karl Marx and J. B. Clark characterize the treatment of workers in a capitalistic system?

5. What is the winner's curse?

6. What is the primary source of conflict between owners and players in professional sports?

7. In what years did baseball see a labor dispute from 1970 to 2000? When was this dispute a "strike" or a "lockout?" How many times were games cancelled (and when)?

8. When have strikes and lockouts occurred in the NFL, NBA, and NHL? Why have lockouts become more common in recent labor disputes?

9. With respect to strikes and lockouts,
   a. briefly explain the difference between a strike and a lockout.
   b. at what point in a season are players likely to strike? Explain your answer.
   c. at what point in a season are owners likely to lock out the players? Explain your answer.

10. How does the frequency of strikes and lockouts in professional sports in North America compare to the rest of the economy? What explains the difference?

11. Why had baseball's labor union had more success than the NFL's player union?

12. According to Schmidt and Berri (2004), what has historically been the long-term impact of player strikes and lockouts on attendance in MLB, the NFL, and the NHL?

13. Attendance in baseball declined from 1993 to 1996. Why do Schmidt and Berri (2004) argue that this decline is not about the strike that occurred 1994–95?

14. Why do the fans tend to return when the players return from a strike or lockout?
15. If you really like free markets, whom should you support in labor-market negotiations in sports: the owners or the players?
16. Why have the owners in baseball often failed in their negotiations with players? How does the story of Jerry Reinsdorf and Albert Belle illustrate this point?

The Economic Value of Playing Talent

Are Professional Athletes Overpaid?

The previous chapter addressed the same subject, but we now turn from theory to an analysis of the data. To answer the question posed, Chapter 6 will explore the following:

1. **Measuring the Marginal Productivity of a Baseball Player:** Baseball is the sport most often examined by economists. And such an examination will touch upon hitters and pitchers, emphasizing that we must consider both explanatory power and consistency in evaluating a performance measure.

2. **Measuring the Productivity of Players in a "Complex Invasion Sport":** Unlike baseball, many sports (i.e., football, basketball, hockey, soccer) involve taking an object from one end of the field of play to another. As we will explain, the nature of these sports impacts how the productivity of an individual athlete is measured. Our discussion will emphasize the importance of using both deductive and inductive analysis and understanding how to specify a model.

3. **Measuring the Economic Value of an Athlete:** Measuring marginal productivity is important because it can be the first step toward measuring the dollar value of an athlete. Two approaches have been offered to measure an athlete's economic value. The first looks directly at the marginal productivity of a player and the marginal revenue created by this output; the second simply examines the salary determination process. Both approaches tell a similar story. Specifically, athletes are often underpaid in a restricted market and frequently paid what they are worth in a free market. Contrary to the story told by fans, economists do not generally see overpayment reflected in the theory or data.

How effective is the professor teaching this class? Judging by his or her choice of textbooks, you might suspect your teacher is brilliant. But perhaps there is more to teaching than the choice of textbooks. Alas, measuring all that a teacher does is difficult. And this can create problems with respect to how people perceive performance.

To illustrate, one survey — taken more than 30 years ago at the University of Nebraska — revealed that 94% of college professors thought they were better teachers than the average professor at that same institution.[1] Obviously, everyone can't be above average. But when performance is difficult to measure, it is easy for most people to believe they are "good."

For athletes in sports, however, this delusion is difficult to maintain. In December 2015, the Chicago Cubs signed Jason Heyward to an eight-year, $184 million deal.[2] With an average wage of $23 million, Heyward was much better paid than an average baseball player. And given what he accomplished in 2015, this deal made some sense. Heyward's on-base percentage plus slugging average (OPS)[3] of 0.797 ranked second on a St. Louis Cardinals team that led the National League (NL) with 100 regular-season wins.[4] But in the first year of this deal, Heyward's OPS of 0.631 was the second worst mark in the NL (among those with enough plate appearances to qualify for the league rankings).[5] In sum,

[1]Patricia K. Cross, "Not Can, But Will College Teaching Improve?," *New Directions for Higher Education* 1977, no. 17 (Spring 1977): 1–15. Although it took place more than 30 years ago, one suspects a similar result would be obtained today from a survey of professors at institutions around the world.

[2]See http://www.espn.com/mlb/story/_/id/14343750/chicago-cubs-add-offseason-haul-agreeing-jason-heyward.

[3]We will discuss this metric later in the chapter. One can find it at http://www.baseball-reference.com.

[4]Heyward was also considered an above-average defender, winning his third Gold Glove in 2015. This was noted at http://www.baseball-reference.com.

[5]http://www.baseball-reference.com/leagues/NL/2016-standard-batting.shtml.

in terms of OPS, Heyward was clearly below average in 2016. And we suspect, he would be inclined to acknowledge this reality.

In a world where performance can be measured, it is quite difficult to maintain the views illustrated in the survey of University of Nebraska professors. And in such a world, the Marx–Clark debate from the previous chapter would seem relatively easy to settle.

To settle this debate, though, we need to measure performance — or as Clark and other economists would put it — marginal productivity. Our discussion will begin with baseball. But we will also discuss performance in a variety of "complex invasion sports" (like hockey, basketball, etc.). Before we get started, it is important to emphasize the following. Because the literature in this area (from academics and non academics)[6] is vast, this chapter can only serve as an introduction to the measure of marginal productivity and marginal revenue product (MRP) in professional sports. It is our hope that this introduction will help you understand both the lessons these measures teach and the important considerations in evaluating a specific performance metric.

6.1 Measuring the Productivity of a Hitter in Baseball

Professional sports allow us to measure productivity because they track statistics for their players. Why did teams start recording this information in the first place?

Teams can see which organizations are successful and which teams are not. But what teams need to know is which players are primarily responsible for the outcomes observed. In other words, as noted in Berri and Schmidt (2010),[7] teams track numbers to "separate a player from his team. We know at the end of a contest who won. What teams don't know is which players were responsible for a team's success (or failure)" (p. 33).

This desire to separate a player from his teammates appeared to exist very quickly in the history of baseball. Alan Schwarz, in his *Numbers Game* (2004),[8]

---

[6]The focus of this chapter will be primarily what economists have offered on the subject. The statistics appendix at the back of the book will comment on some models offered by non-academics. There is one issue that must be emphasized: Because students often use performance measures in their research projects, it is important for them to understand how different metrics are constructed and how to evaluate the validity of these constructions.

[7]David J. Berri and Martin B. Schmidt, *Stumbling on Wins: Two Economists Explore the Pitfalls on the Road to Victory in Professional Sports* (Princeton, NJ: Financial Times Press, 2010).

[8]Alan Schwarz, *Numbers Game: Baseball's Lifelong Fascination with Statistics* (New York: Thomas Dunne Books, St. Martin's Press, 2004). This is a wonderful book detailing the history of numbers in baseball. Much of what is discussed in this section derives from this book.

noted that the first box score appeared in the *New York Morning News* on October 22, 1845. And people took this practice quite seriously. Henry Chadwick, the so-called "Father of Baseball", wrote in 1861[9]:

> In order to obtain an accurate estimate of a player's skill, an analysis, both of his play at the bat and in the field, should be made, inclusive of the way in which he was put out; and that this may be done, it is requisite that all . . . contests should be recorded in a uniform manner. (Schwarz, 2004, p. 6)

Schwarz observed (p. 11) that Chadwick had very high hopes for baseball statistics. Chadwick ultimately hoped that the numbers would help people identify which players helped a team win (or lose). As part of this effort, Chadwick seized upon a statistic developed in 1872 by H. A. Dobson. In 1870, *The Clipper* (a weekly publication out of New York) began to report at bats for players. Since hits were already known for players, Dobson devised a new way to evaluate players: hits divided by at bats or a batting average.

As Schwarz put it, Chadwick declared that this measure "trumped all others." In Chadwick's words, "According to a man's chance, so should his record be. Then what is true of one player is true of all."[10]

More than 150 years later, batting average is still arguably the most cited statistic for a hitter in baseball. Nevertheless, not everyone shared Chadwick's enthusiasm for batting average. F. C. Lane, writing in the early 20th century, argued batting average was "worse than worthless" since it ignored the fact that singles, doubles, triples, and home runs all had a different impact on team outcomes.[11] In 1916, Lane added, "Would a system that placed nickels, dimes, quarters, and 50-cent pieces on the same basis be much of a system whereby to compute a man's financial resources? And yet it is precisely such a loose, inaccurate system which obtains in baseball. . . ."[12]

---

[9]Chadwick was an early pioneer in the reporting and tracking of baseball games. Schwarz also noted that Chadwick's system of scoring baseball became the standard for the game. Chadwick would record each event in the game by using a number [for the fielder(s) who handled the ball] and/or a letter for the event. The letter Chadwick chose was often the last letter in the word (or nearly the last letter). So "L" was used for a foul ball and "K" was used for a strikeout.

[10]Schwarz (2004, p. 11).

[11]Schwarz (2004, p. 34).

[12]Schwarz (2004, pp. 34–35).

Lane clearly preferred a measure that would take into account a player's ability to do more than just hit singles.[13] Back in 1916, though, hitting for power wasn't a major part of the game. To illustrate, Wally Pipp, Dave Robertson, and Cy Williams each hit 12 home runs in 1916, a mark that tied for the lead in all of Major League Baseball (MLB).

In 1919, as noted in the previous chapter, Babe Ruth hit 29 home runs for the New York Yankees. And the next season, Ruth slugged 54 home runs.[14] Three seasons later (in 1923), John Heydler, president of the NL, added slugging percentage to the NL stat sheets.[15] This statistic is calculated as follows:

$$\text{Slugging Percentage} \equiv \frac{\text{Total Bases}}{\text{At Bats}} \tag{6.1}$$

where Total Bases ≡ Singles + 2 × Doubles + 3 × Triples + 4 × Home Runs

Slugging percentage ignores unofficial at bats, so it does not take into account walks, being hit by pitches, and sacrifice flies. Nevertheless, in the past, it was often the measure employed by economists who needed a measure of a hitter's productivity.[16]

Although economists have tried to measure productivity with slugging percentage, other measures do exist. And these other measures have considered factors like walks. Understanding the importance of walks, though, has not always been obvious to everyone. In fact, there is one baseball cliché that says, "You can't walk your way off the island." This statement—applied to prospects from the Caribbean—argues that walks will not land a player a professional baseball contract. It is hits that get people's attention.

---

[13]Schwarz (2004, pp. 35–36) notes that Lane never suggested tracking a player's slugging percentage, a measure that actually was cited back in the 1860s and 1870s. Lane, though, did suggest a different metric quite similar to the linear weights measure created by Pete Palmer in the 1970s.

[14]No team hit 54 home runs in 1916. The Chicago Cubs led all of baseball with 46 home runs that season.

[15]Schwarz (2004, p. 50). He goes on to note that it was not until 1946 that the AL officially added slugging percentage to the official stat sheets.

[16]Berri (2008) notes that more than 10 published studies from 1982 to 2002 still employed slugging percentage as the primary measure of player performance in baseball. Berri, David J. "A Simple Measure of Worker Productivity in the National Basketball Association." In *The Business of Sport*, eds. Brad Humphreys and Dennis Howard, 3 volumes, (Westport, Conn.: Praeger, 2008): 1-40.

We will address this subject in more detail later on (when we discuss *Moneyball* and behavioral economics in Chapter 11). For now, we will note that walks, and on-base percentage, have been increasingly cited in the evaluation of players.

The calculation of on-base percentage is as follows:

$$\text{On-Base Percentage} = [\text{Hits} + \text{Walks} + \text{Hit-by-Pitch}] / [\text{At Bats} + \text{Walks} + \text{Hit-by-Pitch} + \text{Sacrifice Flies}] \qquad (6.2)$$

This measure essentially turns batting average on its head. Whereas batting average measures the ability of a player to get a hit, on-base percentage measures a hitter's ability to avoid making an out. As Eric Walker, a vocal proponent of on-base percentage, observed[17]:

> In baseball, . . . But there's one number everyone knows and agrees with: three. Three outs and you're gone. Period. The end. All runners cancelled, all theories moot, all probabilities zero. That number must, in any rational evaluation of the game, dominate planning.

Such an argument was echoed by Pete Palmer[18]: "There are two main objectives for a hitter. The first is to not make an out. . . ." Palmer, along with Dick Cramer, introduced in 1972 a statistic called batting run average.[19] This measure simply multiplies on-base percentage by slugging average. A more famous approach to these two statistics — OPS, or adding on-base percentage and slugging average[20] — was also introduced by Palmer (along with John Thorn).[21]

---

[17]This quote originally appeared in Eric Walker, *The Sinister First Baseman* (Millbrae, CA: Celestial Arts, 1982) and was reprinted in Schwarz (2004, p. 215).

[18]This quote originally appeared in a 1973 issue of *Baseball Research Journal* published by the Society for American Baseball Research (SABR) and was reprinted in Schwarz (2004, p. 219).

[19]Schwartz (2004, p. 164) notes that Batting Run Average was introduced in an article originally published in the *Baseball Research Journal*. One can see the original article here: http://research.sabr.org/journals/batter-run-average.

[20]Zimbalist (1992a, 1992b) may have been the first economist to follow the lead of Palmer and Thorn when he utilized slugging percentage with a player's on-base percentage in the construction of a summary statistic Zimbalist labeled PROD. Andrew Zimbalist, "Salaries and Performance: Beyond the Scully Model," in Paul Sommers (ed.), *Diamonds Are Forever: The Business of Baseball* (Washington, DC: The Brookings Institution, 1992a), pp. 109–133; Andrew Zimbalist, *Baseball and Billions* (New York: Basic Books, 1992b).

[21]Palmer and Thorn introduced OPS in *The Hidden Game of Baseball: A Revolutionary Approach to Baseball and Its Statistics* (Chicago: University of Chicago Press, 1984).

Thus, there are a number of measures of a hitter's performance. Which of these, if any, should we prefer?

One factor we might consider is how well each measure explains outcomes. When it comes to hitters, the outcome we would take into account is runs scored. Consequently, one issue we might consider is how well each of the statistics tracked for hitters explains the variation in runs scored for the team.

In other words, to evaluate these metrics, we should estimate the simple regression reported in equation 6.3:

$$\text{Team Runs per Game} = a_0 + a_1 \times \text{Hitter Statistic} + e_t \qquad (6.3)$$

where Hitter Statistic = batting average, slugging average, on-base percentage, batting run average, or OPS

Equation 6.1 was estimated with 1,318 MLB team observations from 1969 to 2016.[22] Across this sample, we see the results reported in **Table 6.1**.

Table 6.1 Connecting Various Measures of a Hitter's Productivity to Runs Scored per Game

Independent Variable	Coefficient	*t*-Statistic	*p*-Value	*R*-squared
Batting average	36.38	50.70	0.00	0.661
On-base percentage	33.96	70.20	0.00	0.789
Slugging average	15.60	77.43	0.00	0.820
OPS	11.97	113.89	0.00	0.908
Batting run average	34.35	119.12	0.00	0.916

All these statistics are statistically significant. But the ability of these statistics to explain outcomes varies. Only 66.1% of the variation in runs scored per game is explained by a team's batting average. This is not exactly "worse than worthless" — as F. C. Lane argued about 100 years ago — but batting average explains less of the variation in runs scored than the other measures considered.

We can improve explanatory power by considering on-base percentage or slugging average. And we do even better by combining these two measures, as was done with batting run average and OPS.

Although batting run average and OPS consider more than simple batting average, these measures still omit some actions of a hitter. For example, stolen

---

[22]Data were found at http://www.baseball-reference.com.

bases, caught stealing, and grounding into double plays are ignored. Do these omissions matter?

To answer this question, we turn to the following model reported in Blass (1992)[23]:

$$\begin{aligned}
\text{Runs Scored per Game} = b_0 + b_1 \times 1B + b_2 \times 2B + b_3 \\
\times 3B + b_4 \times HR + b_5 \times NBB + b_6 \\
\times HBP + b_7 \times SB + b_8 \times (GDIP + CS) \\
+ b_9 \times SF + b_{10} \times OUTS + e_t
\end{aligned} \quad (6.4)$$

where
$1B$ = singles per game
$2B$ = doubles per game
$3B$ = triples per game
HR = home runs per game
NBB = non-intentional walks per game
HBP = hit-by-pitch
SB = stolen bases per game
$GIDP$ = ground-into-double-plays per game
CS = caught stealing per game
SF = sacrifice flies per game
$OUTS$ = outs per game

Equation 6.4 was estimated across the same 1,318 observations of team runs scored per game—and across the same years (1969 to 2016)—utilized to examine the measures reported in Table 6.1. The results of this estimation are given in Table 6.2.[24]

Blass' 1992 model, re-estimated with more recent data, offers some interesting insights into the game of baseball. For example,

- A double is not twice as valuable as a single. If a man is on second or third, both a single and double will frequently allow the man on base to score.

---

[23]Asher Blass, "Does the Baseball Labor Market Contradict the Human Capital Model?," *Review of Economics and Statistics* 74 (1992): 261–268. Blass built on earlier work from the sabermetrics community. And as Schwarz (2004, p.36) noted, F. C. Lane—without the benefit of regression analysis—argued in the early part of the 20th century that a single was worth 0.457 runs, a double 0.786 runs, a triple 1.15 runs, a home run 1.55 runs, and a walk 0.164 runs. Schwarz also noted that Pete Palmer (a leader in the sabermetrics community)—with a regression—came to very similar conclusions. And again, Blass built on the work of researchers like Palmer.

[24]The data for this model were taken from baseball-reference.com.

Table 6.2 Connecting Various Statistics for a Hitter to Runs Scored per Game			
Independent Variable	Coefficient	*t*-Statistic	*p*-Value
Single	0.53	46.30	0.00
Double	0.61	29.33	0.00
Triple	1.12	16.66	0.00
Home runs	1.42	66.37	0.00
Non-intentional walks	0.35	34.14	0.00
Hit-by-pitch	0.23	5.06	0.00
Stolen bases	0.17	10.52	0.00
Ground-into-double-plays + caught stealing	−0.25	−6.53	0.00
Sacrifice flies	0.67	8.10	0.00
Outs	−0.11	−7.18	0.00
Constant term	0.22	0.52	0.60
R-squared	0.940		
Observations	300		

- A single is worth more than a walk. Both get a player to first base. But again, a single can drive home a runner who is on second or third. A walk doesn't generally lead to another runner scoring (the exception is if the bases are loaded).

- A stolen base does not add as much as being caught stealing takes away. This issue will be explored in more detail in our discussion of behavioral economics in Chapter 11.

These are just some of the stories we can deduce from Blass' model. Beyond these issues, we should note that the above model explains more of the variation in runs scored than was explained by batting run average or OPS. Equation 6.2, though, is more complex than OPS or batting run average. And we might conclude that a more complex measure isn't worth such a small gain in explanatory power. In other words, explanatory power isn't the only issue we would consider in evaluating a productivity measure.[25]

---

[25]The list of metrics we considered for hitters is hardly complete. As Albert and Bennett (2003) reported: *"The 1999 Big Bad Baseball Annual alone listed over 20 systems for evaluating offensive performance"* (p. 148). A website like baseball-reference.com reports — in addition to batting average, slugging percentage, on-base percentage, and OPS — wins above replacement (WAR), adjusted OPS+, runs created, offensive win percentage, base-out runs added, and win probability added. And that list is also not complete. Baseball-reference.com offers yet more metrics, and even the list at this website isn't exhaustive. James Albert and Jay Bennett, *Curve Ball: Baseball, Statistics, and the Role of Chance in the Game* (New York: Copernicus, 2003).

6.2 Measuring the Productivity of a Pitcher in Baseball

Economists have not examined pitchers as often as hitters in baseball. And the following will help us understand why researchers tend to focus less on those throwing the baseball.

In 2010, Ubaldo Jimenez posted a 2.88 earned run average (ERA) — or average number of earned runs per nine innings[26] — for the Colorado Rockies. This mark ranked eighth in the NL that season. Playing in Colorado, however, put Jimenez at a disadvantage since baseballs tend to fly farther at a mile above sea level. When ERA is adjusted for the ballpark effect, we see that Jimenez ranked third in the NL in 2010.[27]

Midway through the 2011 season, though, Jimenez had an ERA of 4.46. Colorado then sent Jimenez to the Cleveland Indians (for a collection of players) and Jimenez proceeded to post a 5.10 ERA for Cleveland across the remainder of 2011. Jimenez had never posted an ERA above 4.28 in his career prior to 2011, and except for the 2007 season (essentially his rookie season), he had never posted above 3.99. Suddenly, Jimenez was no longer — in terms of ERA — a top major league pitcher. And this story is not unique to Jimenez. As we will see in a moment, ERA for pitchers tends to be quite inconsistent.

How does this impact the measurement of a pitcher's productivity? Back in 1974, Gerald Scully — in a paper that is considered the first empirical examination of sports offered by an economist — ignored ERA and measured a pitcher's productivity with a pitcher's strikeout-to-walk ratio (K/BB). Andrew Zimbalist (1992b) and Anthony Krautmann (1999),[28] though, argued that ERA is a better measure of pitcher quality because it has greater explanatory power.

The argument advanced by Zimbalist and Krautmann can be seen by estimating equation 6.5:

$$\text{Team Runs Surrendered per Game} = c_0 + c_1 \times \text{Pitcher Statistic} + e_t \quad (6.5)$$

where Pitcher Statistic = ERA or strikeout-to-walk ratio

---

[26]$ERA = 9 \times$ (Earned Runs/Innings Pitched). Or in words, earned run average is simply the number of earned runs a pitcher is charged with per nine innings pitched.

[27]Adjusted ERA is reported at baseball-reference.com.

[28]Anthony Krautmann, "What's Wrong with Scully Estimates of a Player's MRP?," *Economic Inquiry* 37 (April 1999): 369–381.

Equation 6.5 was estimated with MLB team data taken from 1996 to 2016 (626 observations). The results of this estimation are reported in Table 6.3.[29] As one can see, ERA explains 98% of the variation in a team's runs surrendered per game, while K/BB only explains 55%. It thus appears Zimbalist and Krautmann are correct.

Table 6.3 Connecting Two Measures for Pitchers to Runs Surrendered per Game				
Independent Variable	Coefficient	t-Statistic	p-Value	R-squared
ERA	1.02	160.69	0.000	0.976
K/BB	−0.96	−27.35	0.000	0.545

Then again, Bradbury (2008)[30] put forth a different argument. "What makes a performance metric good? Two factors are important: the accuracy of the measuring value and degree to which the metric reflects skill" (p. 48).

The first issue we have already explored. Batting average doesn't appear to be as good a measure as OPS because the former doesn't do as good a job of explaining outcomes. In other words, batting average appears to be a relatively poor measure of value. And it appears we are telling a similar story with respect to K/BB.

Connecting a measure to current outcomes, though, isn't everything. We are ultimately trying to measure the value of an individual player. This means we must separate the value of the actions the player takes from the actions of his teammates and/or from the random variation we observe in a game (i.e., luck).

To address this latter issue, Bradbury (2008) offered the following:

One method researchers can use for separating skill from luck is to look at repeat performance of players. If performance is a product of skill, then the athlete in question ought to be able to replicate that skill. If other factors, such as random chance or teammate spill overs are responsible for the performance, then we ought not observe players performing consistently in these areas over time. A common way to gauge the degree of skill contained in a performance metric is to observe its correlation year to year. If metrics for individual players do not vary much from year to year, then it is likely that players have a skill in that area. If there is no correlation, then

[29]Data for this regression can be found at http://www.baseball-reference.com.
[30]John C. Bradbury, "Statistical Performance Analysis in Sport," in Brad Humphreys and Dennis Howard (eds.), *The Business of Sport*, 3 vols. (Westport, CT: Praeger, 2008), pp. 41–56.

it is likely that other factors are heavily influencing the metric. In the latter case, even if a particular metric appears to have a powerful influence on the overall performance of the team, its utility as a measure of quality is quite limited. (p. 48)

To illustrate Bradbury's observation, consider **Table 6.4**. This table reflects the consistency in a baseball player's performance according to the various measures we have considered. For example, for hitters, Bradbury considered all players with a minimum of 400 plate appearances in consecutive seasons from 1980 to 2005. The results indicate that a hitter's batting average in the current season has a 0.47 correlation, or r, with a hitter's batting average in the preceding year. This means that 22% of the variation in a hitter's batting average in the current season (i.e., r^2) can be explained by the same hitter's batting average last season.[31]

Table 6.4 Consistency of Hitters and Pitchers in Baseball: 1980–2005[32]		
Statistic for Hitter	r	r^2
Batting average	0.47	0.22
On-base percentage (OBP)	0.64	0.41
Slugging average (SLG)	0.67	0.45
On-base percentage plus slugging average (OPS)	0.65	0.43
Statistic for Pitcher		
Batting average on balls put in play (BABIP)[33]	0.24	0.06
Earned run average (ERA)	0.37	0.14
Home runs per nine innings	0.47	0.22
Walks per nine innings	0.64	0.42
Strikeouts per nine innings	0.79	0.62

[31]As explained in Chapter 2, r^2 tells us how much of the variation in the dependent variable is explained by our model. In general, this is what we report in this book. Bradbury (2008), though, also reports the correlation coefficient (r), which allows us to note how r and r^2 are related. An r of 0.47 could be seen as somewhat high. But as one can see, that is only an r^2 of 0.22.

[32]Bradbury (2008, pp. 50 and 52).

[33]Batting average on balls put in play (BABIP) is calculated as follows:

$$\frac{[\text{Hits} - \text{Home Runs}]}{[\text{At Bats} - \text{Strike Outs} - \text{Home Runs} + \text{Sacrifice Flies}]}$$

This measures how often a ball hit into play (i.e. fair but not out of the park) becomes a hit.

Looking at the hitter's statistics, we see that batting average doesn't just do a relatively poor job of explaining runs scored per game. It also is relatively inconsistent. In sum, whether we consider Bradbury's first or second factors in evaluating a performance measure, we are better off using on-base percentage, slugging average, and OPS as our measure of a hitter's productivity.

When we turn to pitchers, though, it is a different story. Zimbalist and Krautmann argued that ERA was the superior metric. But when Bradbury considered pitchers who had at least 100 innings pitched in consecutive seasons from 1980 to 2005, a problem with ERA was uncovered. As Table 6.4 reports, only 14% of the variation in a pitcher's ERA in the current season can be explained by what the same pitcher did the previous season. Both walks and strikeouts — the measures Scully preferred — are much more consistent across time.

To illustrate, Table 6.5 offers additional statistics on Ubaldo Jimenez. In three seasons, Jimenez posted essentially the same K/BB. His ERA, though, varied from good (ranked 16th out of 46 qualifying NL pitchers in 2009), to spectacular (ranked 8th out of 45 qualifying NL pitchers in 2010), to below average (ranked 82nd out of 94 qualifying major league pitchers in 2011).

Table 6.5 Performance of Ubaldo Jimenez: 2009–11[32]		
Season	ERA	K/BB
2009	3.47	2.33
2010	2.88	2.31
2011 (both teams)	4.68	2.30

Bradbury (2008) noted that the inconsistency we see with respect to ERA occurs because the outcomes from balls in play are very hard to predict. One can see this by looking at the very low correlation for BABIP, and also by just contemplating how difficult it is to predict what will happen when a round stick hits a round ball. Yes, the very nature of baseball makes for a significant random element. When we add to this unpredictability the fact that balls in play generally have to be fielded by someone other than the pitcher, it is clear that much of what may be learned from ERA is not about the pitcher.[35]

If ERA does not adequately measure a pitcher's ability, how do we get at his marginal productivity? Voros McCracken[36] published an article in 2001 at

---

[34]Data from http://www.baseball-reference.com.

[35]Bradbury (2008) noted that 70% of plate appearances result in a fair ball being hit. So again, ERA for pitchers is going to be quite unpredictable.

[36]McCracken, Voros, "Pitching and Defense? How Much Control Do Hurlers Have?," *Baseball Prospectus*, January 23, 2001, http://www.baseballprospectus.com/article.php?articleId=878.

Baseball Prospectus[37] that advanced an alternative to ERA. Because the outcome from balls hit into play is influenced by the performance of defensive players and luck, McCracken argued that we should evaluate pitchers in terms of factors that do not involve the defensive players around the pitcher. More specifically, McCracken suggested that we consider Defensive Independent Pitching Statistics (DIPS) or statistics that others labels as Fielding Independent Pitching (FIP).[38] These include strikeouts, walks, and home runs.[39] As noted in Table 6.4, each of these factors is more consistent from season-to-season than ERA. Interestingly, McCracken showed that a pitcher's current FIP statistics did a better job of predicting his future ERA than a pitcher's current ERA.[40]

All this suggests that Scully's utilization of K/BB was better than the turn toward ERA advocated by Zimbalist and Krautmann.[41] If we wish to evaluate the productivity of an individual pitcher, we need to focus on the statistical factors that actually measure his ability. Because ERA is heavily influenced by the players around the pitcher and luck, it is simply not a good measure of the marginal productivity of a pitcher.

6.3 The "ERA Problem" in Hockey

The problem we see with respect to ERA is not confined to baseball: We observe similar problems in sports like football and hockey. The football story will be touched upon in Appendix A at the back of the book. Here, we will briefly discuss the evaluation of goalies in hockey.

A hockey goalie would seem to be the easiest position in team sports to evaluate. A goalie has a sole primary responsibility: to stop the puck from entering the net. Although the goalie has just one primary task, there is more than one measure to evaluate this player's productivity. A list of these measures would include:

- shot attempts (SA)

- goals against (GA)

---

[37]SABR is a group (made up of academics and non academics) dedicated to the statistical analysis of baseball. *Baseball Prospectus* is a sabermetric website.

[38]The FIP label is used by baseball-reference.com, and this is the label we will utilize in the text.

[39]Hit-by-pitch is also generally added to this list. These factors are all measures that do not involve defensive players.

[40]This result was also confirmed by Bradbury (2008). In Chapter 8, we will discuss how to construct a FIP measure for a National Pro Fastpitch (NPF) pitcher.

[41]This point was emphasized by J. C. Bradbury, "What Is Right with Scully's Estimates of Player's Marginal Revenue Product," *Journal of Sports Economics* 14, no. 1 (2013): 87–96.

- saves (or the difference between SA and GA)

- save percentage (saves/SA)

- goals against average (GAA), which is calculated as GA/(minutes played/60)

We observed in Chapter 3 that goals scored and goals against certainly explain outcomes in hockey. But when looking at consistency across time, as noted in **Table 6.6**, we see a problem in the evaluation of a goalie's marginal product.[42]

Table 6.6 reports the r^2 term from a simple regression of a goalie's current performance on the goalie's performance the previous season. Three measures are considered: save percentage or saves/shot attempts; goals against average, and shot attempts per minute. The middle measure, goals against average, has about the same level of consistency that we observed with respect to ERA for pitchers in baseball (see Table 6.4).

Table 6.6 Consistency of NHL Goalies: 2000–01 to 2016–17		
Statistic	r	r^2
Save percentage	0.23	5%
Goals against average	0.31	10%
Shots on goal, minute	0.60	36%

Again, ERA is inconsistent because this measure isn't just about the pitcher; it is also about the defenders around the pitcher. This appears to be the same story for goals against average. That measure is essentially linked to the other two measures in Table 6.6. The number of goals a goalie surrenders per 60 minutes is a function of how many shots the goalie faces and the goalie's save percentage. With respect to shot attempts, we see some consistency—at least, relative to goals against average. Shot attempts, though, is not a factor a goalie has much ability to control. We might think a goalie can stop such shots from actually entering the net, but when we turn to save percentage, very little consistency may be seen. Only 5% of a goalie's current save percentage is linked to the same goalie's save percentage the previous season.

----

[42]The data set used to construct Table 6.6 consisted of all goalies who had consecutive seasons of at least 1,000 minutes played from 2000–01 to 2016–17. In all, 361 goalies are included in the sample. The analysis in Table 6.6 builds upon a study originally reported in Berri and Schmidt (2010).

Berri and Schmidt (2010) described this inconsistency as follows:

> . . . Consider the top goalies—in terms of save percentage[43]—for each season from 1983–84 to 2007–08. Of the goalies ranked in the top ten across these 23 seasons, only 70—or about 30%—were able to repeat a top ten ranking in the next season. So 70% of top ten goalies in a given regular season will generally be out of the top ten the next regular season. (p. 46)

Why are goalies so inconsistent? One suspects the issue is that save percentage fails to control for the quality of defenders in front of the goalie. As the defense in front of the goalie varies, the quality of shots changes as well. And consequently, the goalie's save percentage changes. In sum, our measure of a goalie's performance fails to separate the player from his teammates. And therefore, our measures of a goalie's performance—save percentage and goals against average—are not good measures of his marginal product.

6.4 Measuring Worker Productivity in a Complex Invasion Sport: The Basketball Case Study

So far, our attempts to measure marginal productivity have been limited to hitters and pitchers in baseball and goalies in hockey. The appendix at the back of the book will briefly touch upon the problems associated with football.[44]

What story can be told about basketball players? One might suspect that this sport would encounter the same problems we saw with respect to the non hitters discussed above. The five players on the court for a basketball team seem to rely on each other to both score and prevent the other team from scoring. Given these interactions, measuring the marginal productivity of a basketball player must be difficult.

It turns out, however, that this is not exactly the case. And the analysis of basketball illustrates an important story about data analysis. We have discussed the deductive approach. We have also spent time discussing induction. Although one might believe that the choice between these approaches is either/or, such is not the case. As the analysis of basketball will highlight, one must think both deductively and inductively.

---

[43]The goalies had to play 1,000 minutes in a season to be ranked.

[44]The appendix notes that a football quarterback's performance is quite inconsistent, primarily because it depends on his teammates. Interestingly, wins in baseball, hockey, and football tend to be assigned to pitchers, goalies, and quarterbacks, respectively. In other words, three groups of players whose performance clearly depends on their teammates are given the entire credit for a team's wins and losses.

We begin with the consistency of the statistics tabulated in a typical National Basketball Association (NBA) box score. Table 6.7 reports the correlation (r) and corresponding r^2 between an NBA player's performance over two successive seasons.[45] As one can see, NBA players—relative to what we saw for hitters, pitchers, and goalies—are much more consistent across time.

Table 6.7 Consistency of National Basketball Association players: 1977–78 to 2011–12		
Statistic	r	r^2
Field goal percentage	0.70	0.49
Free-throw percentage	0.76	0.58
Turnovers, per minute	0.79	0.62
Steals, per minute	0.82	0.67
Personal fouls, per minute	0.84	0.70
Free-throw attempts, per minute	0.84	0.71
Points, per minute	0.86	0.75
Field goal attempts, per minute	0.87	0.75
Defensive rebounds, per minute	0.92	0.85
Offensive rebounds, per minute	0.93	0.86
Blocked shots, per minute	0.93	0.86
Assists, per minute	0.93	0.87
Total rebounds, per minute	0.95	0.90

To put this in perspective, consider the same analysis for baseball players reported in Table 6.4. The only statistic from Table 6.4 that is as consistent as anything reported in Table 6.7 is strikeouts per nine innings. And that statistic is only more consistent than field goal percentage and free-throw percentage.[46] With respect to every other basketball statistic, we see much more consistency than anything observed in baseball. And this suggests that the

---

[45]The data, which one can find at http://www.basketball-reference.com, span from 1977–78 to 2011–12 and consist of all players who appeared in at least 20 games and played at least 12 minutes per game in successive seasons. In all, 7,835 player observations were employed.

[46]One might suspect that field goal percentage is somewhat inconsistent because it depends on a player's teammates and the defense the player faces. Although there is some evidence that passing matters (as the construction of Wins Produced argues), the finding that free-throw percentage and field percentage are similar in consistency across time suggests that maybe shooting efficiency varies because it is just difficult to consistently throw a basketball through a hoop.

numbers for NBA players tend to capture the productivity of each individual NBA player.

How do we make sense of these numbers? There is a temptation to run a regression with wins as the dependent variable and a collection of the factors listed in Table 6.7 as independent variables. After all, that is essentially the afore-mentioned approach taken by Asher Blass in modeling runs scored in baseball. But as Bill Gerrard (2007)[47] argued, a "complex invasion sport" is different. Here is how these "invasion" sports are described by Gerrard (in a discussion of soccer, p. 222): "Invasion team sports involve a group of players cooperating to move an object (e.g., a ball or puck) to a particular location defended by opponents (e.g., across a line or between goalposts)."

Gerrard noted that invasion sports present special problems with respect to evaluating player performance. Again, it is tempting to just run a basic regression like the one we saw in our discussion of baseball. Gerrard, though, cautioned against such an approach:

> The problem with the statistical approach in invasion team sports is the hierarchical nature of the game with the higher-level actions, scores, and saves (i.e., the blocking of scoring attempts by opponents) dependent on lower-level actions to create scoring opportunities and limit opposition scoring opportunities. (pp. 223–224)

Gerrard illustrated the hierarchical nature of complex invasion sports with the following model of soccer (p. 225)[48]:

(Equation 1)   Own Shots at Goal = f(Own General Play)

(Equation 2)   Opposition Shots at Goal = f(Own General Play)

(Equation 3)   Goals Scored = Own Conversion Rate × Own Shots at Goal

(Equation 4)   Goals Conceded = (1 − Own Save-Shot Ratio) × Opposition Shots at Goal

(Equation 5)   League Points = f(Goals Scored, Goals Conceded)

where general play includes number of passes, pass completion rate, crosses, dribbles, tackles won, interceptions, blocks and clearances

---

[47]Bill Gerrard, "Is the Moneyball Approach Transferable to Complex Invasion Team Sports?," *International Journal of Sports Finance* 2 (2007): 214–228.

[48]In Chapter 1, we noted that equations should be translated into words. In words, equation 1 would read as follows: Own Shots at Goal are a function of Own General Play.

As one can see, Gerrard did not propose one equation to estimate the impact of players on team outcomes; rather, Gerrard proposed a system of equations. He began by noting that a team's shots on goal (as well as the opponent's shots on goal) are a function of a team's general play. How many goals a team scores then depends on shots on goal and a team's conversion rate. Then, league standing points are about goals scored and goals conceded.

Now let's apply this same approach to the study of basketball,[49] beginning with one simple equation. As we saw in Chapter 2, and as noted again in equation 6.6 and **Table 6.8**, points scored (PTS) and opponent's points scored (Opp.PTS) are all we need to explain winning percentage in basketball:

$$WPCT = d_0 + d_1 PTS + d_2 Opp.PTS + e_i \qquad (6.6)$$

Table 6.8 Connecting Wins in the National Basketball Association to Points Scored and Points Surrendered: 1987–88 to 2015–16			
Variable	Coefficient	*t*-Statistic	*p*-Value
Constant	0.516	22.32	0.000
PTS	0.032	107.73	0.000
Opp.PTS	−0.032	−110.29	0.000
R-squared	0.943		

So what explains points scored? As Gerrard (2007) noted, scoring totals are determined by a team's conversion rate and shots. This relationship is captured by equation 6.7:

$$PTS = EffFG \times FGA + FTper \times FTA \qquad (6.7)$$

where[50] $EffFG$ = (field goals made + 0.5 × 3-point field goals made) /field goals attempted
$FTper$ = free throws made/free throws attempted

---

[49]Gerrard (2007) did apply this approach to four years of English Premier League (EPL) data. But basketball data, as we will note, are far more abundant for a variety of leagues.

[50]Effective field goal percentage (EffFG) is a measure of shooting efficiency from the field that captures the impact of shooting from both a 2-point and 3-point range.

Equation 6.7 is an identity. Once we know how many shots a team takes and how often those shots go into the hoop, we know how many points a team scores. Given this identity, we can rewrite equation 6.6. But now we can connect wins to eight different statistics (instead of just two):

$$WPCT = f_0 + f_1 EffFG + f_2 FGA + f_3 FTper + f_4 FTA + f_5 Opp.EffFG$$
$$+ f_6 Opp.FGA + f_7 Opp.FTper + f_8 Opp.FTA + e_i \qquad (6.8)$$

The estimation of equation 6.8 is reported in Table 6.9. As one can see, this model explains wins as well as the simple model based solely on PTS and Opp.PTS. And again, that is not surprising. We simply replaced PTS and Opp.PTS with the factors that completely explain those two variables.

Table 6.9 Connecting Wins in the National Basketball Association to Shots and Shooting Efficiency: 1987–88 to 2015–16

Variable	Coefficient	t-Statistic	p-Value
Constant	0.547	7.40	0.00
EffFG	5.288	79.06	0.00
FGA	0.030	47.25	0.00
FTper	0.807	17.62	0.00
FTA	0.024	40.83	0.00
Opp.EffFG	−5.329	−73.50	0.00
Opp.FGA	−0.029	−47.40	0.00
Opp.FTper	−0.834	−9.62	0.00
Opp.FTA	−0.025	−43.56	0.00
R-squared	0.946		

Of course, players don't just take shots and make (or miss) shots. What about rebounds, turnovers, steals, assists, blocked shots, and personal fouls?

Well, we could just ignore Gerrard and add all these factors to equation 6.8. The results of such an exercise are reported in Table 6.10. The independent variables are segmented into three groups there. In the first grouping (after the constant term), we see the same factors as listed in Table 6.9. And just as we observed, each of these factors is statistically significant and of the same sign as reported before.

The next grouping—which includes offensive rebounds (ORB), defensive rebounds (DRB), steals (STL), and turnovers (TO)—are factors one can classify as possession statistics. That is because each of these factors gives a team (or costs a team) possession of the ball. And although one might think getting and

Table 6.10 Connecting Wins in the National Basketball Association to all Box Score Statistics: 1987–88 to 2015–16

Variable	Coefficient	t-Statistic	p-Value
Constant	0.62083	4.45	0.000
EffFG	4.88790	30.48	0.000
FGA	0.02106	6.30	0.000
FTper	0.73210	12.39	0.000
FTA	0.01966	12.08	0.000
Opp.EffFG	−4.96226	−27.02	0.000
Opp.FGA	−0.02162	−6.44	0.000
Opp.FTper	−0.76373	−7.49	0.000
Opp.FTA	−0.02029	−10.19	0.000
ORB	0.00719	1.75	0.081
DRB	0.00286	1.15	0.249
STL	0.00286	1.04	0.300
TO	−0.01077	−2.64	0.008
Opp.ORB	−0.00482	−1.12	0.262
Opp.DRB	−0.00267	−1.23	0.219
Opp.STL	−0.00047	−0.14	0.891
Opp.TO	0.00709	1.89	0.059
AST	0.00160	1.69	0.092
BLK	−0.00014	−0.08	0.938
PF	−0.00065	−0.30	0.764
Opp.AST	−0.00004	−0.03	0.976
Opp.BLK	−0.00476	−2.00	0.046
Opp.PF	0.00031	0.89	0.374
R-squared	0.947		

Note: Variables in bold are significant at the 5% level or better.

keeping possession of the ball are important, the results in Table 6.10 suggest otherwise. Except for turnovers, none of the possession factors (for the team or the opponent) are statistically related to wins.

The last group of variables—which includes assists (AST), blocked shots (BLK), and personal fouls (PF)—can be thought of as "help" variables. These variables help a team's offensive (AST), the team's defense (BLK), or the opponent

(PF).[51] And as one can see, except for the opponent blocking your team's shots, none of these factors are related to wins.

So what do we make of these results? Should we conclude that rebounds, steals, turnovers, assists, blocked shots, and personal fouls either don't matter or don't really matter much?

Table 6.9 makes it clear that these factors are not very important. But before we leap to such a conclusion, let's consider the factors that explain field goal attempts. To take a shot in the NBA, a team needs to first acquire the ball. This happens when the opponent makes a shot (Opp.FGM and Opp.FTM), the opponent misses, and your team grabs the defensive rebound (DRB), or the opponent turns over the ball (Opp.TO).

Once the team acquires the ball, it can make a field goal attempt. But that is not all it can do with the ball. A team can also turn over the ball (TO) or attempt a free throw (FTA). The team can also get additional shots by grabbing offensive rebounds (ORB).

All these factors are included in equation 6.9. And the estimation of this equation is illustrated in **Table 6.11**:

$$FGA = g_0 + g_1 DRB + g_2 Opp.FGM + g_3 Opp,FTM \\ + g_4 Opp.TO + g_5 ORB + g_6 FTA + g_7 TO + e_i \qquad (6.9)$$

The results tell a few important stories: Clearly, acquiring and maintaining possession of the ball are important. Contrary to what we saw in Table 6.10, rebounds and turnovers matter. If a team wishes to take a shot, it needs to have the ball.

---

[51]The classification of box score statistics into "possession" and "help" groupings goes back to Price and Wolfers' 2007 presentation (at the Western Economic Association meetings) of the following paper: Joseph Price and Justin Wolfers, "Racial Discrimination Among NBA Referees," *Quarterly Journal of Economics* 125, no. 4 (November 2010): 1859–1887.

These authors took the win score equation [detailed in Berri, Schmidt, and Brook (2006)] and rewrote this equation as follows:

Points + Possession Gained (rebounds, steals) − Possession Lost (turnovers,
field goal shots, ½ free throws) + ½ Offensive Help (assists)
+ ½ Defensive Help (blocks) − ½ Help Opponent (fouls)

David J. Berri, Martin B. Schmidt, and Stacey L. Brook, *The Wages of Wins: Taking Measure of the Many Myths in Modern Sport* (Stanford, CA: Stanford University Press, 2006).

Table 6.11 Modeling Field Goal Attempts in the National Basketball Association[52]			
Independent Variable	Coefficient	*t*-Statistic	*p*-Value
Constant	5.211	9.58	0.000
Defensive rebounds	0.968	78.58	0.000
Opponent's field goals made	0.986	130.59	0.000
Opponent's free throws made	0.452	42.73	0.000
Opponent's turnovers	0.968	58.06	0.000
Offensive rebounds	1.081	77.20	0.000
Free throws attempted	−0.445	−55.30	0.000
Turnovers	−0.950	−53.90	0.000
R-squared	0.982		

These results also suggest that shots are not "created" in the NBA: 98% of a team's shots are explained by a team's ability to acquire and maintain possession of the ball.[53] That tells us shots are just "taken."

Two anecdotes illustrate this story. In December 2006, the Philadelphia 76ers sent Allen Iverson to the Denver Nuggets. Iverson averaged 24.4 field goal attempts per game for the Sixers prior to the trade. This mark represented more than 30% of the team's 78.1 field goal attempts per game. If one believed Iverson "created" those shots, then the Sixers would have been in trouble without their All-Star guard. But after that trade, the Sixers averaged 78.2 field goal attempts per game.

A similar story can be told when we look at the Denver Nuggets's record before and after the trade of Carmelo Anthony to the New York Knicks in 2011. Prior to it, the Nuggets averaged 80.0 field goal attempts per game, with Anthony taking 19.3 of these shots (or nearly 25%). After Anthony left for the Knicks, the Nuggets averaged 82.2 field goal attempts per game.[54] So again, losing the star player did not result in fewer shots.

---

[52]This model was estimated with team data from 1987–88 to 2013–14. Data can be found at basketball-reference.com. As Berri and Schmidt (2010) noted, this model would explain virtually 100% of field goal attempts if we included factors like team rebounds that change possession and the outcomes of tip-offs.

[53]As noted in Berri and Schmidt (2010), this model does not include team rebounds. Team rebounds that change possessions are not explicitly tracked by the NBA, but one can — as Berri and Schmidt (2010) also explained — estimate this factor.

[54]With respect to the Iverson and Anthony trades, in both instances, the team losing the "star" also posted a higher adjusted field goal percentage after the trade.

Both these anecdotes help us see the importance of a team gaining and keeping possession of the ball. And as we observed in Table 6.7, basketball players tend to be fairly consistent (relative to what we see in other sports) with respect to turnovers, steals, and rebounds. So if you want to take shots, the key is to find players who help you get and keep possession. The importance of possession factors would be entirely lost if you simply estimated one model for wins in basketball that included all the box score statistics. Because shot attempts are a direct function of the possession factors, a single regression will not show how the possession factors matter when shots are also included in the model.

And all of this illustrates a story we have told before. Analysis requires a combination of deduction and induction. Each approach by itself can be misleading. Theories (i.e., deduction) must be tested. We thus need some sort of empirical testing (i.e., induction). But as witnessed in our attempt to model wins in basketball, if we do not truly understand what we are modeling (i.e., we have no theory), it is also easy to be led astray.

The discussion of complex invasion sports illustrates how measuring marginal productivity can be difficult. And as the appendix to this book highlights, missteps are not uncommon. But as the appendix also notes, when the Wins Produced measure (a metric built on the lessons just reviewed) for basketball is detailed, one can measure marginal productivity in a complex invasion sport like basketball.

6.5 The Scully Approach to Measuring Marginal Revenue Product

Of course, marginal productivity is only part of the story. To get at a worker's economic value — or marginal revenue product (MRP) — we have to do more. Specifically, a worker's value to a firm is not just about the quantity produced. The firm has to sell this output in the marketplace. In other words, the amount this production is worth in the marketplace, or the worker's MRP, also matters.

To measure a player's MRP, we turn to one of the very first empirical papers written in sports economics. In 1974, Gerald Scully published a paper investigating the relationship between a player's salary and his economic value to the firm (or his MRP).

The Scully approach involves estimating two models. The first of these models links wins to player performance. The second model links wins to team revenue.

To illustrate Scully's approach, let's spend a bit more time with baseball history. We have already noted the history of baseball's reserve clause and the beginning of free agency in 1977. One of the very first free agents — and the player signed to the largest contract in 1977 — was Reggie Jackson.

Reggie Jackson is known today as Mr. October, primarily for his post-season exploits with the New York Yankees (the team that signed Jackson in 1977). Prior to arriving in New York, Jackson played nine seasons with the Athletics (in both Kansas City and Oakland) and one year with the Baltimore Orioles.

For each of these teams, Jackson toiled under the reserve clause. Because his bargaining power was limited, we suspect Jackson was paid less than what he was worth. Was this true? And if true, how much less?

To answer these questions, we need to consider Jackson's marginal productivity and the value this productivity has in the marketplace. For the former, we will employ the basic approach offered by Blass.[55] Specifically, we are going to re-estimate Blass' model with data from MLB for the years 1964 to 1985. This time period covers both the years before the end of the reserve clause and a few years after free agency commenced.

The results, outlined in Table 6.12, are essentially what Blass reported with data from 1976 to 1986. Applying this model to Reggie Jackson's 1973 season — the only year Jackson was named the American League's (AL's) most valuable player (MVP) — we obtain the results given in Table 6.13.

Table 6.12 Connecting Various Statistics for a Hitter to Runs Scored per Game: 1964–85[56]			
Independent Variable	Coefficient	t-Statistic	p-Value
Constant term	−0.17	−0.28	0.776
Single	0.50	29.81	0.000
Double	0.65	16.51	0.000
Triple	1.05	10.47	0.000
Home runs	1.44	41.18	0.000
Walks	0.32	20.38	0.000
Hit-by-pitch	0.51	5.07	0.000
Stolen bases	0.13	5.52	0.000
Ground-into-double-plays and caught stealing	−0.25	−4.49	0.000
Sacrifice flies	0.56	4.43	0.000
Outs	−0.08	−3.88	0.000
R-squared	0.93		

[55]Blass (1992) takes the same approach as Scully (1974). Blass estimates two relationships. The first links player statistics to outcomes (runs scored and ultimately wins). The second links wins to team revenue. From these two models we can estimate MRP.

[56]Data for regression can be found at http://www.baseball-reference.com.

Table 6.13 Calculating Reggie Jackson's Production of Runs: 1973[55]				
Variable	Reggie Jackson's Production per Game	Coefficient	Runs Created per Game	Runs Created per Game Played[a]
Single	0.636	0.50	0.315	47.6
Double	0.185	0.65	0.121	18.3
Triple	0.013	1.05	0.014	2.1
Home runs	0.212	1.44	0.305	46.1
Walks	0.503	0.32	0.162	24.4
Hit-by-pitch	0.046	0.51	0.024	3.6
Stolen bases	0.146	0.13	0.019	2.9
Ground-into-double- plays	0.139	−0.25	−0.035	−5.3
Sacrifice flies	0.046	0.56	0.026	3.9
Outs	2.523	−0.08	−0.214	−32.4
			Total Runs Created	111.3

[a]Jackson played 151 games in 1973. Runs Created per Game Played is simply the number of Runs Created per Game for each statistic multiplied by 151. For example, Jackson's production of singles produced 0.315 Runs Created per Game. So his singles created 47.6 Runs Created per Game.

Jackson's reputation was built on his ability to hit a long ball, and in 1973 he led the AL with 32 home runs. But in terms of run creation, the Blass model indicates that Jackson's singles were, in the aggregate, slightly more valuable.

Although the story of Jackson's ability to create runs is worthy of consideration, teams are ultimately interested in producing wins. So to measure Jackson's marginal productivity, we need to know how many wins Jackson's hitting production created. We learned in Chapter 2 that the relationship between runs and wins can be captured with the regression[58] reported in **Table 6.14**.

The model illustrated in Table 6.14 is specifically the regression of winning percentage (or wins per game) on both runs scored and runs allowed per game.

---

[57]Data for Reggie Jackson may be found at http://www.baseball-reference.com.

[58]Blass (1992) employed a more complex functional form to estimate this relationship. As he noted, his results are robust to other functional forms. And the linear form, employed in Table 6.13, makes the discussion of MRP easier to follow.

Table 6.14 Wins, Runs Scored, and Runs Allowed in Major League Baseball: 1964–85[57]

Variable	Coefficient	t-Statistic	p-value
Constant term	0.496	41.30	0.000
Runs scored per game	0.108	47.56	0.000
Runs allowed per game	−0.107	−45.97	0.000
R-squared	0.87		

Since all the variables in the regression are per-game measures, one can interpret the coefficient of 0.108 as indicating that each additional run scored leads to 0.108 additional wins. Or, it takes 10.8 additional runs to create one more win.[60]

It is tempting to simply multiply Jackson's runs creation by the value of these runs in terms of wins.[61] But if we take that approach, what is the value of a pitcher? Pitchers only allow runs. Clearly, some allow more than others. But all pitchers allow runs. If we simply multiply what a player does by the impact that action has on wins, we would then conclude that hitters, who only create runs, produce a positive quantity of wins. And pitchers, who only allow runs (except when they bat in the NL), produce a negative quantity of wins.

So we have to do a bit more than just multiply runs created by the value of these in terms of wins. One possible approach is to compare Jackson's production to what we would see from an average player. This involves the following steps:

1. Determine how many wins an average player would produce given the same opportunities: In 1973, hitters produced 17,060 runs in 148,584 plate appearances. So per plate appearance, the average player produced 0.115 runs. Given this result, an average player with Jackson's 629 plate appearances would have created 73.5 runs in 1973. And these runs would be worth 4.2 wins.[62]

---

[59]Data can be found at http://www.baseball-reference.com.

[60]Sabermetricians often note the basic result that 10 runs are worth a win. See http://www.fangraphs.com/blogs/win-values-explained-part-five/.

[61]This is the approach taken by Blass.

[62]To calculate average wins, we begin by noting that an average team would win half their games. If we assume that, on average, hitters produced half a team's wins and pitchers produce the other half, then a team of average hitters would be worth ¼ the number of games played. The Athletics in 1973 played 164 games, so if the team's hitters were average, they would have produced 41 wins. Since Jackson made 10.3% of the team's plate appearances, an average player with Jackson's plate appearances would be worth 4.2 wins.

2. Determine how much a player produced relative to the average player. According to Table 6.13, Jackson produced 111.26 runs in 1973 or 37.8 runs beyond average. If we multiply 37.8 by the value of a run (0.108 from Table 6.13), we see that Jackson produced 4.1 wins beyond average. And this means Jackson produced 8.3 wins in 1973.

Now, we have an estimate of Jackson's productivity.[63] To determine the value of this production, we need to connect wins to revenue. This can be done with the following model[64]:

$$\text{Revenue} = h_0 + h_1 \times \text{Wins} + h_2 \times \text{Wins Lagged} + h_3 \times \text{Market Size} + h_4 \times \text{New Stadium Dummy} + e_t \qquad (6.10)$$

where
Market Size ≡ the size of the standard metropolitan statistical area (SMSA)[65]
New Stadium Dummy ≡ 1 if the stadium is 8 years old or younger[66]

Before we get to the estimation of the model, let's provide a few details on the model's construction. First, the dependent variable (Revenue) is determined by multiplying average ticket price by a team's attendance. In addition, each team's local broadcasting revenue as well as its share of any national broadcasting deal was included.[67] Across the time period considered, the value of a dollar

---

[63]It should be noted that this is a somewhat crude estimate. More sophisticated measures would include park effects, specific productivity of players at each position, and defensive measures. One should note, though, the correlation between this measure of wins and the Win Shares measure of Bill James exceeds 0.95 (reported here: http://seamheads.com/baseballgauge/download.php).

[64]This model is a simple revenue model estimated in Berri, David J. and Anthony Krautmann. "Exploitation Before Free Agency. Revisiting the Original Scully Model." Presented at the Western Economic Association; Portland, Oregon; July, 2016.

[65]Data on population can be found in U.S. Census records. As http://www.peakbagger.com/pbgeog/histmetropop.aspx notes, the definition of SMSA is not fixed in time. And so the size of an SMSA can change as the Census expands a specific area. This appears to be the case with respect to New York, where the size of the SMSA took a major leap from 1980 to 1990. The aforementioned website, though, appears to offer a more consistent estimate for New York, so this information is what was employed in the Berri et al. (2015) study.

[66]This follows from J. C. Bradbury, Hot Stove Economics (New York: Copernicus, 2010).

[67]Data on average ticket prices, attendance, and broadcasting deals can be found at the website of Rodney Fort (https://umich.app.box.com/s/41707f0b2619c0107b8b). The data on average ticket prices were originally tabulated by Doug Pappas. The price data from Pappas ended in 1985 (hence, this is the last year examined). Finally, teams played a different number of games. So both revenue and wins are adjusted to what a team would see across 162 games.

changed, so the nominal value of revenue was adjusted to 1984 dollars with the consumer price index (CPI).[68] The results are reported in Table 6.15.[69]

Table 6.15 Estimated Total Revenue Function for Major League Baseball: 1964–85			
Independent Variable	Coefficient	t-Statistic	p-Value
Wins	114,866.00	12.53	0.000
Wins lagged	62,086.28	7.05	0.000
Market size	0.61	2.80	0.005
New stadium dummy	1,562,509.00	3.30	0.001
Constant term	−2,885,183.00	−1.36	0.174
R-squared	0.27		

The model includes both wins and lagged wins. That means a win this year will impact revenues in the current season as well as the revenues earned by a team next year. Because of the time value of money, the value of a win the next year has to be discounted.[70] And, according to this model, that means a win is estimated to be worth $173,996.

With this value in hand, we can now estimate Jackson's MRP. As Table 6.16 notes, Jackson's real MRP—calculated by multiplying the value of a win ($173,996) by the number of wins Jackson produced—was consistently above $1 million from 1973 to 1980.

Table 6.16 Reggie Jackson's MRP and Salary[69]: 1967–85						
Team	Year	Production of Wins	Jackson's Nominal Salary[70]	Jackson's Real MRP	Jackson's Real Salary	MRP − Salary
Kansas City Athletics	1967	0.70	$4,800	$121,396	$14,382	$107,014
Oakland Athletics	1968	7.00	$8,100	$1,217,189	$23,281	$1,193,908
Oakland Athletics	1969	10.65	$20,000	$1,853,750	$54,521	$1,799,228
Oakland Athletics	1970	5.03	$47,000	$875,190	$121,003	$754,187

(continued)

[68]This is done by simply multiplying the nominal value by the ratio of the CPI in 1984 (set equal to 100) by the CPI in the year examined.

[69]The model also indicates that a new stadium was worth $1.56 million in additional revenue while an increase by 1 million in market size would augment revenue by $0.61 million.

[70]The discount rate employed is 5%.

[71]Jackson also played in 1986 and 1987. Again, though, our revenue data set ends with 1985.

[73]The nominal salaries are the dollars Jackson actually saw. These data are reported at baseball-reference.com.

Table 6.16 (continued)						
Team	Year	Production of Wins	Jackson's Nominal Salary[70]	Jackson's Real MRP	Jackson's Real Salary	MRP − Salary
Oakland Athletics	1971	7.93	$45,000	$1,380,440	$111,158	$1,269,283
Oakland Athletics	1972	6.80	$55,000	$1,182,898	$131,554	$1,051,344
Oakland Athletics	1973	8.30	$70,000	$1,443,393	$157,569	$1,285,824
Oakland Athletics	1974	8.32	$135,000	$1,447,466	$273,739	$1,173,727
Oakland Athletics	1975	7.28	$140,000	$1,266,365	$260,102	$1,006,263
Baltimore Orioles	1976	6.49	$200,000	$1,129,122	$351,290	$777,831
New York Yankees	1977	7.62	$525,000	$1,326,183	$866,094	$460,090
New York Yankees	1978	6.34	$525,000	$1,102,952	$804,696	$298,256
New York Yankees	1979	6.50	$525,000	$1,130,827	$723,310	$407,517
New York Yankees	1980	8.75	$525,000	$1,522,972	$637,267	$885,704
New York Yankees	1981	3.18	$588,000	$552,930	$646,630	−$93,700
California Angels	1982	7.64	$1,103,000	$1,329,094	$1,142,614	$186,479
California Angels	1983	2.16	$975,000	$375,921	$979,083	−$603,162
California Angels	1984	3.77	$975,000	$656,796	$938,104	−$281,308
California Angels	1985	5.26	$1,058,894	$915,763	$984,102	−$68,340
Total		119.72		$20,830,647	9,220,501	$11,610,147

Comparing his MRP to his salary, we see that in real terms Jackson (again, according to this analysis) was underpaid by more than a million dollars seven different years, including 1973 (the year he was AL MVP). As noted, Jackson became a free agent in 1977. And with the Yankees, the difference between his MRP and salary lessened. And then after 1980, when Jackson was 34 years old, his salary finally exceeded his MRP.

Across these 19 seasons, it is estimated that Jackson produced $20.7 million while being paid—in real terms—$9.2 million. So he was "exploited" across his career. But in all his free-agent years, his salary and MRP were quite similar.

The basic pattern we see with respect to Jackson is consistent with recent research on this topic. Bradbury (2010) also employed the Scully approach to evaluate baseball players. And unlike Blass, Bradbury looked at both hitters and pitchers.

Bradbury began by connecting team revenue to run differential (i.e., runs scored minus runs surrendered), market size, and whether or not a team played in a new stadium.[73] With outcomes on the field connected to revenue, Bradbury then turned to measuring performance. And with respect to marginal productivity, he went well beyond the simple Scully approach. Specifically, for hitters, he considered:

- the total runs produced on offense by a player, calculated via "linear weights" (adjusted for park effects)[74]

- the total runs saved by a player's defense, calculated using the plus/minus fielding rating system

- a pitcher's ability to prevent runs, estimated with a FIP model [again, based on the earlier work of Voros McCracken (2001)]

In sum, Bradbury considered everything a hitter did on offense and defense.[75] And his analysis of pitchers was designed to separate the pitcher from the defenders around him.

Although Bradbury considered much more with respect to a baseball player's marginal product, his conclusions were quite similar to what Scully and Blass reported. As **Table 6.17** shows, Bradbury found that players without bargaining power (i.e., reserve players and arbitration-eligible players)—like Jackson before the advent of free agency—were underpaid. In contrast, it was not uncommon to see free agents be overpaid.

---

[73]Here is the specific team revenue model Bradbury estimated with data from MLB from 2003 to 2007:

$$\text{Team Revenue} = (W1 \times \text{Run Differential}) + (W2 \times \text{Run Differential2})$$
$$+ (W3 \times \text{Run Differential3}) + (W4 \times \text{Population})$$
$$+ (W5 \times \text{Honeymoon}) + \text{Constant}$$

Bradbury reported that each independent variable was statistically significant and the model explained 63% of the variation in team revenue.

[74]As noted in Berri and Bradbury (2010), linear weights was originally developed by operations research analyst George Lindsey in "An Investigation of Strategies in Baseball," *Operations Research* 11, no. 4 (1963): 477–501 and updated by sabermetricians John Thorn and Pete Palmer (1984). Linear weights estimate contributions to baseball events using play-by-play data to weigh the run-generating probabilities for individual events. Albert and Bennett (2003) demonstrated that the linear regression and linear weights methods yield similar results.

[75]Bradbury (2010) also noted that baseball-reference.com posts both the adjusted linear weights measure (adjusted batting runs) and an improved runs saved metric (defensive runs saved). As Bradbury observed, one simply needs to add the two together, add or subtract from the average, and you get the marginal product.

Table 6.17 The Overpaid and Underpaid in Baseball: 2006–09[76]		
Service Class	Median Percentage Difference from MRP for Hitters	Median Percentage Difference from MRP for Pitchers
Reserved players	−89%	−80%
Arbitration-eligible	−78%	−74%
Free agents	−13%	18%
All players	−68%	−66%

All this illustrates a basic story. Just as our theory suggested, the empirical evidence indicates that when a worker's bargaining power is limited, the wages paid to him or her will tend to be less than the worker's MRP.

6.6 The Promise and Reality of the Scully MRP Measurement

The analysis thus far has told a simple story. When a worker's bargaining power is limited, the wage paid to him or her will be less than the worker's MRP. But there is another story that the measurement of MRP also seems to tell. It appears that we can—via an examination of player statistics and the determinants of a team's revenue—objectively and exactly measure a player's MRP. In other words, we can measure a player's "true" economic value.

As noted, we can measure the marginal productivity of hitters in baseball and players in basketball.[77] However, even though marginal productivity can be measured in some sports, estimating the revenue function may present problems.

To illustrate, consider the following simple revenue function:[78]

$$\text{Revenue} = j_0 + j_1 \times \text{Wins} + j_2 \times \text{Wins}_{t-1} + j_3 \times \text{Population} + j_4 \times \text{New Stadium Dummy} + j_5 \times \text{Stadium Capacity} + e_t \qquad (6.11)$$

where the New Stadium Dummy $= 1$ if the stadium is 8 years old or younger[79]

---

[76]Originally reported by Bradbury (2010).

[77]It should also be possible to measure the marginal productivity of skaters in hockey. At least, some of the statistics tracked for skaters, as noted in Berri and Schmidt (2010), are quite consistent over time.

[78]This model is the simple revenue model estimated in Berri, *et al.* (2015). That work looked at revenue in MLB, the NBA, NFL, and NHL. David J. Berri, Michael Leeds, and Peter von Allmen, "Salary Determination in the Presence of Fixed Revenues," *International Journal of Sport Finance* (February 2015): 5–25.

[79]This follows from Bradbury (2010).

These results in Table 6.18 tell an interesting story. To see this, let's apply what we know about the NBA to the Miami Heat of 2010–11. Table 6.18 indicates that a win in the current season, given the coefficient on wins and wins lagged, is worth $808,277. LeBron James, in his first year in Miami, produced

Independent Variable	MLB,[81] 2002–11	NBA, 2002–11	NFL, 2002–11	NHL,[82] 2006–11
Wins	407,954.60[a] (4.99)	485,742.90[a] (7.96)	412,760.20[c] (1.96)	179,194.80[a] (2.58)
Wins lagged	227,912.40[a] (2.72)	338,660.70[a] (5.27)	211,906.60 (0.95)	140,486.80[b] (2.35)
Population	7.13[a] (6.1)	3.33[a] (11.54)	−0.08 (−0.11)	0.89[a] (2.48)
Stadium capacity	NA NA	3,161.27[a] (4.45)	3,759.95[a] (5.05)	6,861.60[a] (2.67)
New stadium dummy	17,900,000.00[a] (5.32)	4,929,099.00[b] (2.14)	8,758,291.00[b] (2.43)	−1,689,274.00 (−0.76)
Constant term	95,800,000.00[a] (7.40)	9,448,511.00 (0.70)	−38,100,000.00 (−0.70)	−66,500,000.00 (−1.40)
R-squared	0.49	0.60	0.45	0.48

Table 6.18 Estimating the Link Between Wins and Revenue for Major League Baseball, the National Basketball Association, National Football League, and National Hockey League[80]

Note: t-statistics reported in parentheses beneath each coefficient.

p-values not explicitly reported, but significance levels were noted as follows:

[a]Significant at the 1% level.

[b]Significant at the 5% level.

[c]Significant at the 10% level.

[80]This table originally appeared in Berri et al. (2015). Data on team revenue can be found at Forbes.com and the website of Rodney Fort (https://sites.google.com/site/rodswebpages/codes). Data on population come from the U.S. Census Bureau. Further data sources may be found in Berri et al. (2015).

[81]For baseball, stadium capacity was not included. Relative to other sports, baseball rarely sells out (as we noted in Chapter 2).

[82]For the NHL, standing points and lagged standing points were used instead of wins and lagged wins.

17.2 wins.[83] Given the value of a win, his estimated MRP was $14.05 million. When we look at salary, though, we note that James was paid $14.5 million. And this means LeBron James was overpaid.

Of course, James was a free agent. But the pattern of overpaid players is not just seen with respect to Miami's free agents. Every player whose salary we consider, with the exception of Erick Dampier, appears to be overpaid.

In looking at Table 6.19, it appears the key issue isn't the amount the Miami players were paid. The problem appears to be the estimate of what the

Table 6.19 Measuring the MRP of the Miami Heat: 2010–11				
Miami Heat, 2010–11	Wins Produced	MRP	Salary	MRP – Salary
LeBron James	17.21	$14,048,423	$14,500,000	−$451,577
Dwyane Wade	14.86	$12,124,201	$14,200,000	−$2,075,799
Chris Bosh	7.64	$6,233,156	$14,500,000	−$8,266,844
James Jones	4.76	$3,881,370	$1,069,509	$2,811,861
Mike Miller	2.72	$2,216,344	$5,000,000	−$2,783,656
Mario Chalmers	2.38	$1,939,094	$854,389	$1,084,705
Joel Anthony	2.26	$1,843,997	$3,300,000	−$1,456,003
Erick Dampier	2.00	$1,633,406	$1,129,469	$503,937
Eddie House	1.46	$1,194,841	$1,352,181	−$157,340
Zydrunas Ilgauskas	1.38	$1,129,736	$1,352,181	−$222,445
Carlos Arroyo	1.13	$925,183	$1,223,166	−$297,983
Udonis Haslem	1.12	$916,786	$3,500,000	−$2,583,214
Mike Bibby[84]	0.82	$667,083	no salary data	—
Jamaal Magloire	0.73	$592,614	$1,229,255	−$636,641
Juwan Howard	0.41	$333,012	$1,352,181	−$1,019,169
Jerry Stackhouse	0.00	−$2,364	$222,712	−$225,076
Dexter Pittman	−0.10	−$78,990	$473,604	−$552,594
Summation	**60.77**	**$49,597,893**	**$65,258,647**	**−$16,327,837**

[83]Wins Produced is the productivity model first introduced in Berri *et al.* (2006). See http://wagesofwins.com/how-to-calculate-wins-produced/ for more details on the calculation of this measure.

[84]Bibby was released by the Washington Wizards and signed by the Heat during the 2010–11 season. The terms of his deal with the Heat were not reported.

Heat players are worth. In 2010–11, the Heat team generated $158 million in revenues.[85] But the analysis of MRP indicates that, collectively, the Heat were worth less than $50 million. This means the Heat players were worth less than one-third of the team's revenue.

This story does not just concern the Heat. As **Table 6.20** notes, collectively, the Miami Heat produced more revenue than any other team.[86] But in terms of the ratio of MRP to real total revenue, the Memphis Grizzlies led the league with a mark of 38.6%.

Team	Actual Team Wins	Team Wins Produced	Total MRP	Real Total Revenue	MRP/Real Total Revenue
Miami	58	60.8	$49,119,827	$158,000,000	31.1%
Chicago	62	60.4	$48,850,638	$185,000,000	26.4%
LA Lakers	57	57.3	$46,284,850	$208,000,000	22.3%
San Antonio	61	56.1	$45,346,416	$139,000,000	32.6%
Orlando	52	55.5	$44,871,245	$140,000,000	32.1%
Boston	56	55.1	$44,560,625	$146,000,000	30.5%
Denver	50	53.4	$43,189,106	$113,000,000	38.2%
Dallas	57	52.0	$42,038,511	$166,000,000	25.3%
Oklahoma City	55	51.5	$41,608,919	$126,000,000	33.0%
Memphis	46	47.3	$38,236,446	$99,000,000	38.6%
Houston	43	46.9	$37,934,688	$150,000,000	25.3%
Philadelphia	41	45.2	$36,507,982	$116,000,000	31.5%
Portland	48	45.0	$36,369,692	$132,000,000	27.6%
New Orleans	46	43.6	$35,250,490	$109,000,000	32.3%
New York	42	43.0	$34,762,995	$244,000,000	14.2%
Phoenix	40	39.0	$31,536,817	$136,000,000	23.2%
Milwaukee	35	38.7	$31,256,259	$92,000,000	34.0%
Atlanta	44	38.6	$31,188,514	$109,000,000	28.6%
Indiana	37	38.0	$30,705,768	$101,000,000	30.4%

Table 6.20 National Basketball Association Team MRP and Revenues for the 2010–11 Season (teams ranked by total MRP)

(continued)

[85]According to Forbes.com.

[86]This is the story if you multiply Wins Produced by the value of a win. The Heat led the NBA in an efficiency differential (see the appendix to the book for its definition) in 2010–11. If we use actual wins, then the players on the Chicago Bulls would have produced the most revenue.

Team	Actual Team Wins	Team Wins Produced	Total MRP	Real Total Revenue	MRP/Real Total Revenue
Table 6.20 (continued)					
Utah	39	36.2	$29,284,651	$120,000,000	24.4%
Golden State	36	34.8	$28,134,364	$139,000,000	20.2%
LA Clippers	32	32.7	$26,400,226	$108,000,000	24.4%
Detroit	30	31.5	$25,479,179	$141,000,000	18.1%
Charlotte	34	30.3	$24,451,437	$101,000,000	24.2%
Sacramento	24	26.8	$21,644,660	$104,000,000	20.8%
New Jersey	24	24.7	$19,958,778	$89,000,000	22.4%
Toronto	22	24.2	$19,532,067	$134,000,000	14.6%
Minnesota	17	23.2	$18,755,662	$97,000,000	19.3%
Washington	23	21.4	$17,331,636	$109,000,000	15.9%
Cleveland	19	16.8	$13,588,137	$149,000,000	9.1%
Averages	**41.0**	**41.0**	**$33,139,353**	**$132,000,000**	**25.7%**

The collective bargaining agreement that governed the NBA's labor market in 2010–11 indicated players were to be paid 57% of league revenue. But the analysis of MRP shows that players were, on average, only worth 25.7% of revenue.

To understand this difference, we need to review a fundamental argument of the Scully approach. The approach argues that a player's marginal product is determined by his or her contribution to wins. Although this makes sense, in today's professional sports, a significant portion of team revenue is not related to team wins. For example, in 2008, the NBA signed a deal[87] with ESPN, ABC, and TNT that was scheduled to pay the league $7.44 billion over the next eight seasons.[88] The money a team receives from such a deal is not related to the team's success on the court. In other words, these are fixed revenues.[89]

The issue of fixed revenues is not confined to the NBA. Given the value of a win in MLB, the NFL, and the NHL (see Table 6.18), we can look at how the estimate of player MRP compares to league revenue in each of these sports. And

[87]For the details of this contract, see *USA Today* at http://usatoday30.usatoday.com/sports/basketball/2007-06-27-3096131424_x.htm (accessed January 18, 2013).

[88]In 2016, this deal was extended from 2016–17 to 2024–25. Across these additional nine seasons, the NBA would receive a reported $24 billion, or $2.66 billion per season (http://www.espn.com/nba/story/_/id/11652297/nba-extends-television-deals-espn-tnt).

[89]The implication of fixed revenues was noted in Berri *et al.* (2015).

as Table 6.21 indicates, in each league, we can link the percentage of revenue to the value of wins.[90]

Table 6.21	Team MRP and Revenues for Major League Baseball, National Football League, and National Hockey League (same sample as employed for Table 6.17)		
	MLB	NFL	NHL
Average real revenue	$195,000,000	$237,000,000	$95,100,000
Value of wins (or standing points)	$625,014	$412,760	$312,992
Average wins (or standing points)	81	8	91.5
Average team MRP	$50,618,224	$3,302,082	$28,645,700
MRP/real revenue	26.0%	1.4%	30.1%

As one can see, the Scully approach suggests that baseball and hockey players, collectively, produce about the same percentage of revenue as we see in the NBA. In the NFL, though, it is a different story. The NFL shares more revenue than any other league. This is why an NFL team can thrive in Green Bay, Wisconsin. The U.S. Census Bureau reports that only about 300,000 people reside in the metropolitan area of Green Bay, which is located more than 100 miles north of Milwaukee, Wisconsin.[91] No other major North American sports team survives in such a small market. And yet, the Packers both survive and consistently compete at the highest level. One reason this is possible is because the league shares so much of its revenue.

Because the NFL shares so much revenue, the link between revenue and wins is relatively weak. As Table 6.18 indicates, the coefficient on current season wins is only significant at the 10% level. And unlike what is observed in MLB, the NHL, and the NBA, lagged wins are not related to revenue in the NFL.

In addition to statistical significance, the value of an additional win is relatively low in the NFL. Consequently, if the Scully method was applied to NFL players, we would be hard pressed to explain how the Green Bay Packers were able to pay Aaron Rodgers an annual salary of $14.5 million.[92] Even if Rodgers

---

[90]One can link player production to wins in baseball and basketball. In hockey and football, this is a more difficult process. By using team wins, we assume that such a link can be made in all sports. It is certainly true that only the players on each field of play dictate outcomes, so theoretically, one should be able to link outcomes to individual player performance in all sports. But coming up with specific measures of marginal productivity (i.e., production of wins) is more difficult for players in the NFL and NHL.

[91]Milwaukee is hardly a large market. The U.S. Census Bureau estimates that its metropolitan area was only about 1.5 million in 2010.

[92]http://www.forbes.com/pictures/mli45ekfii/6-aaron-rodgers-13/.

was worth 16 wins to the Packers (or all the possible wins in a regular season), the value of a win from Table 6.21 suggests Rodgers would be worth less than $7 million. As one can see, focusing strictly on a player's contribution to wins appears to undervalue his or her impact on team revenues with recent data.

And going back to our earlier analysis of Reggie Jackson, we see the opposite problem. As **Table 6.22** indicates, whether we use the sample from 1964 to 1985 (employed to analyze Jackson) or the sample originally utilized by Scully (in 1974), the story is essentially the same. The total MRP generated by players actually exceeds the total revenue earned by teams. In sum, if you applied the Scully approach in the 1960s, 1970s, and 1980s, you might end up arguing that players generated more revenue than all the revenue their teams, in fact, earned.

Table 6.22 Team MRP and Revenues for MLB		
	MLB 1964–85 Sample	MLB 1968–69 Scully Sample[93]
Average real revenue[94]	$13,400,000	$12,461,972
Value of wins	$173,996	$178,552
Average wins	81	81
Average team MRP	$14,075,938	$14,462,729
MRP/real revenue	105%	116%

Before summarizing what this means for our measurement of MRP, let's consider one more data set. You will note that we have taken a look at baseball from 1964 to 1985, then again from 2002 to 2011. If we examine data from 1991 to 2001, yet another story emerges. Estimating the same model used from the other two data sets, we observe a kind of "goldilocks" spot in the data. From 1991 to 2001, the summation of player MRP, as **Table 6.23** records, is 55.6% of team revenue. According to *Financial World Magazine,* player costs were 53.7% of revenue in 1996.[95]

---

[93]Scully did not report the average revenue from his sample. From the sample used to examine 1964 to 1985, we see that real team revenue (in 1984 dollars) averaged $12.5 million. Scully estimated that a 1-point increase in team winning percentage (he did not consider lagged wins) would increase revenue by $10,330. Since one win increases winning percentage by 6.173 (over a 162-game season), one win, in 1968 and 1969 dollars, is worth $63,765. In 1984 dollars, that amount is worth $178,552.

[94]Real revenue is in 1984 dollars.

[95]These data can be found at the website of Rodney Fort (https://sites.google.com/site/rodswebpages/codes).

Table 6.23 Team MRP and Revenues for MLB: 1991–2001	
	MLB 1964–85 Sample
Average real revenue[96]	$115,000,000
Value of wins	$790,235
Average wins	81
Average team MRP	$63,984,961
MRP/real revenue	55.6%

Thus, if you were to study MRP in baseball with data from the 1990s, the results would indicate that players are paid, collectively, an amount similar to what the Scully model says they were worth. Does that mean our estimates of player value — calculated via the Scully model — are "correct" in terms of the 1990s?

Again, the promise of the Scully method is that we can use data on player statistics and team revenue to "objectively" measure the economic value of an athlete. But our study of team revenue tells a different story. The impact wins have on revenue appears to decline as we move forward in time. To understand why this might be happening, consider how the experience of going to a baseball game has changed over time.

As a child, in the 1970s, I would attend Tiger Stadium to watch the Tigers. At Tiger Stadium, you had a number of entertainment options, as long as the entertainment option you wanted was to see a baseball game. At today's stadiums, though, watching is only part of attending a game. Current stadiums offer a host of entertainment options (shopping, amusement parks, etc.) that can be enjoyed whether or not your favorite team is winning.

In addition to stadiums that minimize the importance of the home team winning, we still have fixed revenues. Teams earn money from national broadcasting deals whether they finish in first or last place. Such changes to the nature of consumer demand and the team's revenue streams have been beneficial to the owners. Wins in sports are a zero-sum game. No matter how well you manage your franchise, losing is going to happen. If your revenue depends primarily on winning, then your team finances depend on an outcome that is not entirely within your control. Thus, it is not surprising that teams have taken steps to diminish the importance of actually winning games.

Although it is tempting to think that the Scully approach can provide us with an objective measure of a player's worth, we see a different story when attempting to apply this same model to different sports at different times. What

---

[96]Real revenue is in 2013 dollars.

our model of revenue really captures is how important, in fact, winning games is to the revenues earned by teams. In the past in baseball, a team's ability to win games had a very large impact on its revenues. Today in all sports, winning is less important. These changes cast doubt on our ability to employ the Scully approach to objectively measure the value of a player's MRP.[97]

6.7 A Simpler Approach

We need to emphasize that the points just made do not undermine the basic argument of Scully (and others). Again, the story being told is that when a worker's bargaining power is limited, it is likely the worker's wage will be less than his or her MRP. Although measuring MRP exactly has its share of problems, we can unravel this same story with a simpler approach.

In 2014, Stefan Szymanski[98] looked at how much revenue was paid to athletes in three different sports: MLB, the NFL, and all four levels of the English Football League (EFL) (i.e., soccer). His analysis is reported in **Table 6.24**.

Table 6.24 Percentage of Revenue Paid to Athletes in Three Major Sports		
	1950s	Today
MLB, 1956 and 2012	17%	53%
NFL, 1956 and 2012	32%	52%
EFL, 1958 and 2013	38%	76%

Back in the 1950s, all three sports had institutions that limited the bargaining power of their athletes. And as one can see, the percentage of revenue paid to athletes was much lower than what we observe today. In more recent years, as we have detailed, the bargaining power of athletes in these leagues has increased. And as theory predicts, the percentage of revenue captured by the players increased.

The importance of bargaining power is especially highlighted by what we observe in the EFL. In European sports, institutions such as player drafts,

---

[97]The issue of how the value of a win varies across time is not the only issue with the Scully model. The model also fails to measure a player's contribution in practice. If the player doesn't play, according to the Scully model, the player has no value. In other words, all the time a player spends in practice is not captured by this approach.

[98]Szymanski's analysis can be found at the *Soccernomics* blog (http://www.soccernomics-agency .com/?p=639) and was based on data from the website of Rodney Fort (https://sites.google .com/site/rodswebpages/codes).

salary caps, and payroll caps do not exist. Without any of the institutions North American leagues utilize to limit player bargaining power, athletes in English football captured — according to the above calculations — more than three-quarters of league revenue.

In 2013, though, financial fair play rules were introduced. These rules restricted how much of the additional television money coming into the league could be paid to its players.[99] As a result, as Table 6.25 indicates, the percentage of revenue (which the English call "turnover") going to players declined. Prior to the rules being enacted, English Premier League (EPL)[100] players took home nearly 70% of league revenues. Afterward, that percentage declined at least 10%.

Table 6.25	Percentage of Revenue Paid to English Premier League Players: 2010–11 to 2014–15[101]		
Year	Wages	Turnover or Revenue	Wage as a Percentage of Turnover
2014–15[102]	£2,033	£3,367	60.4%
2013–14[103]	£1,889	£3,264	57.9%
2012–13[104]	£1,782	£2,563	69.5%
2011–12[105]	£1,626	£2,355	69.0%
2010–11[106]	£1,568	£2,284	68.7%

The financial fair play rules work much like a payroll cap. A payroll cap in North American sports prevents teams from giving revenue to players. The financial fair play rules do essentially the same thing. And this illustrates again how bargaining power impacts the wages of workers. Financial fair play rules limit how much revenue workers can bargain for in the negotiation process. As a result, the amount of revenue paid declines.

---

[99]http://www.theguardian.com/football/2015/apr/29/premier-league-clubs-profit-fair-play.

[100]The EPL is the top league of the English football leagues.

[101]Data come from various websites and from http://www.theguardian.com. The data from theguardian.com differ from the data reported by Szymanski in Table 6.24. This is because Szymanski looked at the levels of the EFL, and *The Guardian* only examined the EPL or top level of the EFL.

[102]http://www.theguardian.com/football/2016/may/25/premier-league-finances-club-by-club-breakdown-david-conn.

[103]http://www.theguardian.com/football/2015/apr/29/premier-league-finances-club-by-club.

[104]http://www.theguardian.com/news/datablog/2014/may/01/premier-league-club-accounts-debt-wages.

[105]http://www.theguardian.com/news/datablog/2013/apr/18/premier-league-club-accounts-debt.

[106]http://www.theguardian.com/news/datablog/2012/may/24/football-premier-league-club-accounts.

Again, this is a simple story. We did not need to run any regressions to see how institutions impact the bargaining power of athletes. All we had to do was look at the percentage of revenue actually paid to players.

6.8 The Free-Market Approach

This simple approach confirms the story told by economic theory. As bargaining power increases, the wages of workers increase. But it still fails to answer one question of interest. How much are workers "exploited" when bargaining power is limited?

Our last attempt to answer this question comes from the work of Anthony Krautmann (1999). This alternative he labels as the "free-market estimate" of a player's MRP. His approach is, in fact, quite simple. A market for free agents exists. If we assume that this market is efficient, then a player's MRP and salary will be equal. Given such an assumption, one can use what is learned from the free-agent market to evaluate the salaries of non free agents.

Specifically, the free-market approach involves estimating equation 6.12. The dependent variable is the free agent's salary, which again, we assume is the same as the free agent's MRP. The independent variables include measures of a player's performance (PERF) and a collection of non performance factors (Z):

$$MRP \text{ Free Agent} = \text{Salary Free Agent} = m_0 + m_1 \times PERF + m_2 \times Z + e_t \tag{6.12}$$

To illustrate, Krautmann, von Allmen, and Berri (2009)[107] presented a model (detailed in **Table 6.26**) of free-agent wages in MLB. In this example, PERF for

Table 6.26 Free-Agent Wages in Major League Baseball: 1997–2002 (dependent variable: log of wages in 2004 dollars)[108]

Variable	Coefficient	t-Statistic
Constant	9.488[c]	19.91
OPS	6.428[c]	9.80
POP	0.000014[a]	1.72

[107]Anthony Krautmann, Peter von Allmen, and David J. Berri, "The Underpayment of Restricted Players in North American Sports Leagues," *International Journal of Sport Finance* 4, no. 3 (August 2009): 155–169.

[108]This table originally appeared in Krautmann *et al.* (2009).

Variable	Coefficient	t-Statistic
CAT	0.287[b]	2.09
FIRST	0.121	0.71
SS	0.731[c]	4.45
THIRD	0.185	1.22
LF	−0.091	−0.51
CF	0.668[c]	3.54
RF	0.219	1.19
UTILITY	−0.524[c]	−3.73
R-squared	0.48	

p-values not explicitly reported, but significance levels were noted as follows:

[a]Significant at the 10% level.

[b]Significant at the 5% level.

[c]Significant at the 1% level.

a baseball hitter is captured with OPS. For Z, the model considered market size (POP) and then a series of dummy variables for different positions.

With this model estimated, one then turns to the non free-agent labor market. Utilizing the coefficients from the estimation of equation 6.12, one can predict what a non free agent would have earned had this player faced a free market for his services, as illustrated by equation 6.13:

$$\text{Predicted } MRP \text{ for Non free Agents} = m_0 + m_1 \times PERF + m_2 \times Z + e_t \tag{6.13}$$

The prediction from equation 6.13 is then compared to the actual wage of the non free agent. Krautmann *et al.* (2009) followed this simple approach for the labor markets in MLB, the NFL, and NBA. The results, reported in Table 6.27, indicate that non free agents in all three leagues are paid less than the player's estimated MRP.

One should note that the free-market approach assumes that free agents are paid their MRP. This approach thus does not allow us to examine the efficiency of the free-agent market (because it assumes this market is efficient). As we will note in Chapter 11, there are some problems inherent in such an assumption.

Putting aside these concerns for a moment, though, we do see that the free-market approach not only shows that workers with fewer bargaining rights are exploited. This approach also gives us an estimate of by "how much."

Table 6.27 Difference Between Estimated MRP and Wages (i.e., Surplus) for Non free Agents in Major League Baseball, the National Football League, and National Basketball Association (number of observations in each cell, 2004 constant dollars reported)[109]

		All		Starters	Utility
		Surplus	Wages as a % of $\widehat{MRP}$	Surplus	Surplus
MLB	Apprentices[a]	$1,217,000 (165)	19%	$1,676,000 (114)	$311,000 (51)
	Journeymen[b]	$221,000 (78)	86%	$304,000 (64)	=$158,000 (14)
NFL	Apprentices[c]	$492,000 (198)	50%	$575,000 (71)	$482,000 (127)
	Journeymen[d]	$264,000 (86)	77%	$551,000 (59)	$178,000 (27)
NBA	Apprentices[e]	$732,000 (272)	66%	$2,700,000 (83)	$564,000 (189)

[a]For MLB, apprentices refers to arbitration-ineligible players (mostly those with less than four years of experience).

[b]For MLB, journeymen refers to arbitration-eligible players (those with between four and six years of experience).

[c]For the NFL, apprentices refers to reserve players (those with less than three years of experience and playing under the reserve clause).

[d]For the NFL, journeymen refers to restricted free agents (those with three years of experience, and whose team can match any free-agent offer).

[e]For the NBA, apprentice refers to players with less than four years of experience.

6.9 Back to Marx and Clark

We began our discussion in the previous chapter with two important questions:

- Are workers "exploited" under capitalism, as Marx contended?
- Or, are workers paid exactly what they are worth under capitalism, as Clark contended?

As noted, neither Marx nor Clark did any comprehensive empirical analysis to establish their arguments. But the data from the world of sports allow us to empirically address these questions.

[109]This table originally appeared in Krautmann *et al.* (2009).

This chapter detailed three different approaches and all offered evidence consistent with what Marx argued. Specifically, if the bargaining power of workers is restricted, then the empirical evidence suggests that workers will be paid a wage that is less than their MRP. In other words, as noted above, when bargaining power is restricted, workers are likely to be exploited.

In contrast, we tend to believe that workers in a free market are paid a wage that is closer to their MRP. So if a worker faces a free market for his services, then he might expect to be paid what he is worth.

Thus, the data — and economic theory — suggest that both Marx and Clark are correct under certain circumstances. It is important to emphasize two points about these results:

- Outside the world of sports, where we do not have detailed measures of worker productivity, it would be difficult to address the claims of Marx and Clark. In this instance then, the analysis of sports data turns out to be quite important. Being able to address a debate that has existed for more than a century is something that makes the analysis of sports very valuable to economists.

- Even in the world of sports — where again, we have detailed measures of worker productivity — analyzing the link between MRP and wages is difficult. The Scully approach is problematic with respect to both the estimate of marginal productivity and the estimate of the impact wins have on revenue. The Krautmann approach, or "free-market" approach, can be applied to more sports but forces one to simply assume that free markets result in a wage equal to MRP.

This second observation illustrates once again how difficult it is to address these issues outside the world of sports. Even with many measures of productivity in sports, estimating MRP is a challenge. So outside the world of sports, where such measures are not readily available, one imagines that testing the ideas of Marx and Clark would not be easy. And we should add, it also means whether any worker is really paid what he or she is worth is hard to actually know.[110]

All of this illustrates a key point we emphasize with respect to empirical analysis. Inductive analysis can shed light on the arguments generated from deductive reasoning. But despite the light shed from inductivity reasoning, data

---

[110]So whether you and your boss are being paid what you are worth is not something we could easily ascertain outside the world of sports. And that means if you think your boss is overpaid . . . well, it may not be possible for your boss to prove this isn't true. Of course, it also might not be wise for you to express such a belief!

analysis doesn't always answer all our questions. And hence, there seems to always be a need for additional research.

Let's close this conversation by coming back to the questions we asked at the beginning of the previous chapter. Are athletes overpaid? Our analysis indicates that athletes are often underpaid. And in a free market, they can be paid what they are worth. But overpaid? Although fans frequently argue this is the case, the theory and data from sports economics suggest that such is not what is generally observed.

Problems

Study Questions

1. What is the purpose of tracking player statistics?
2. When did the first baseball box score appear? Who developed batting average and when was this introduced?
3. According to Pete Palmer, what is the first objective of a hitter?
4. According to the Asher Blass model, what is the relative value of a single, double, triple, and home run in baseball?
5. Which is the "better" measure of a pitcher's production: ERA or K/BB (and what are they)? Answer this question by referring to the work of Anthony Krautmann, Andrew Zimbalist, and J. C. Bradbury.
6. Relative to baseball players and hockey goalies, how consistent are basketball players from season-to-season? What explains this consistency?
7. According to Bill Gerrard, what is a "complex invasion sport"? What are examples of this kind of sport?
8. Why is it difficult to statistically model a complex invasion sport? What happens if you ignore the nature of complex invasion sports and simply attempt to estimate the impact of every player statistic in a single equation?
9. Do NBA players really "create" shots? Explain.
10. What is Gerald Scully's method for measuring MRP?
11. How do fixed revenues (define) impact our ability to measure the MRP of athletes in basketball and football?
12. What is a simpler approach to addressing the issue of whether players are overpaid or underpaid? What does the simpler approach tell us about athletes being overpaid or underpaid across time? What does this reveal about athletes around the world today?
13. Explain how Krautmann measured the MRP of a professional baseball player. What did he assume about the market for baseball free agents?

14. Krautmann's approach was applied to baseball, football, and basketball in Krautmann, von Allmen, and Berri (2009). Were athletes in these sports found to be overpaid or underpaid?

15. Karl Marx argued in the 19th century that capitalism exploits workers; J. B. Clark argued in the 19th century that workers are paid what they are worth in a capitalist system. How does the study of sports allow us to address the arguments of Marx and Clark?

16. Imagine you are hired by an NHL team. How much money would you suggest your team invest in a goalie?

17. Imagine you are hired by an NHL team. How would you measure the marginal product of a skater center or forward?

18. In 2016–17, Andrew Wiggins attempted 1,570 field goals for the Minnesota Timberwolves, a mark that led the team. His effective field goal percentage, though, was only 48.4%. This mark was below the league average and the Timberwolves average. So if Wiggins was removed from the team, what would likely happen to this team's offense?

Discrimination in Sports

Discrimination Historically was Part of Sports. Is that Still True Today?

To answer this question, Chapter 7 will explore the following:

1. **The History of Discrimination in Sports:** Studies of discrimination focus on data from the past half-century. But looking back at the early 20th century, we see that a study is simply not necessary. All major sports leagues historically only employed white players. So discrimination has been historically a part of sports.

2. **The Economic Theory of Discrimination:** Gary Becker originated the economic theory of discrimination of 1957. It is his work that guides many of the empirical studies of discrimination using sports data.

3. **The Empirical Evidence of Racial Discrimination:** There is a vast literature examining the empirical evidence of discrimination in sports. We will begin by looking at salary discrimination in the National Basketball Association (NBA), highlighting the challenges a researcher faces in examining racial discrimination in sports. We will also talk about, but are not limited to, the allocation of minutes, voting for post-season awards, and how referees call the game.

4. **Beauty and Discrimination:** The same approach utilized to study race's impact on player evaluation in basketball can be used to study a different kind of discrimination. Researchers have argued that a person's physical attractiveness can impact wages and employment outside of sports. A recent study also suggested a quarterback's physical attractiveness affects his wage. This result gives new meaning to the statement "he looks good out there."

The history of professional sports in the United States dates back to the 19th century, and in some ways, the decades have not changed very much. For example, we could talk about on-base percentage and slugging percentage for each baseball player who played in the 1870s, and although the history of the National Football League (NFL) and NBA doesn't extend quite as far, much of what we observe about the early days of these sports remains true today.[1]

There is one very large difference. The participants in Major League Baseball (MLB) were generally white until Jackie Robinson took the field for the Brooklyn Dodgers in 1947. The key word in the proceeding sentence is "generally." Although it is widely believed that Robinson was the first African American baseball player, the player now considered to hold that honor was Bud Fowler. From 1878 to 1895, Fowler played for a number of professional baseball clubs.[2]

Furthermore, Fowler was not the only African American player in the 19th century. The Walker brothers (Welday and Moses Fleetwood)[3] played in the American Association, during the 1880s regarded as a major league. But by the end of Fowler's career, blacks no longer participated in major or minor league baseball.

A similar story may be told about football. Back in 1904, Charles Follis became the first black professional football player when he signed with the Shelby Athletic Club.[4] For the next 30 years, 16 additional black players were signed,[5] but in 1933, the NFL adopted a color barrier and became an all-white league.[6] This barrier was removed in 1946 when the NFL Los Angeles Rams signed both Kenny Washington and Woody Strode. The Rams were required to integrate their team if they wished to lease the L.A. Coliseum.[7] Interestingly, the

---

[1]The study of racial discrimination in professional sports primarily focuses on baseball, basketball, and football. The National Hockey League (NHL) has had fewer than 50 black players since the 1970s. Willie O'Ree became the NHL's first black player in 1958, but he was the only black person to play in the NHL until the 1970s. See http://www.nhl.com/ice/page.htm?id=51822.

[2]For a list of teams on which Fowler played, go to http://www.baseball-reference.com/minors/player.cgi?id=fowler004joh. For the story of Fowler's professional career, consult Brian McKenna (http://sabr.org/bioproj/person/200e2bbd).

[3]For statistics on and photos of the Walker brothers, see http://www.baseball-reference.com/players/w/walkewe01.shtml and http://www.baseball-reference.com/players/w/walkefl01.shtml.

[4]Charles Ross, *Outside the Lines: African Americans and the Integration of the National Football League* (New York: New York University Press, 1999), p. 10.

[5]Ross (1999, p. 5).

[6]Ross (1999, p. 46)

[7]Ross (1999, p. 82).

Cleveland Browns, of the All-American Football Conference, also integrated in 1946 with the signing of Bill Willis and Marion Motley.[8]

The year that professional football integrated, the Basketball Association of America (BAA) came into existence as an all-white league. In 1949, the BAA merged with the National Basketball League (NBL) to form the National Basketball Association. For the 1949–50 season, the NBA remained all-white. Then in 1950, Earl Lloyd, Nat Clifton, and Chuck Cooper became the first African Americans to play in the NBA.

The story of how each of these leagues eventually integrated illustrates that race historically played a role in the hiring of professional athletes. Today, we might think race plays far less of a role in decision-making in sports.

But before we see if that is true, we do need to note something important about race. We might think that race is biological. Angela Onwuachi-Willig noted that race is "not biological" but rather a "social construct." She goes on to note: "...There is no gene or cluster of genes common to all blacks or all whites. Were race 'real' in the genetic sense, racial classifications for individuals would remain constant across boundaries... [Someone] categorized as black in the United States might be considered white in Brazil or colored in South Africa."[9]

This observation does not mean people's perceptions of race don't impact decision-making. Certainly the exclusion of blacks in much of the first half of the 20th century from professional sports highlights how race matters. Today, though we wonder, if that is still the case. Table 7.1 does, in fact, show that the current racial and ethnic composition of professional sports isn't dominated by whites. Over the past 20 years, the percentage of whites playing in MLB, the NBA, and NFL has declined.

Table 7.1 Racial and Ethnic Composition of Major League Baseball, the National Basketball Association, and National Football League[10]

	MLB	NBA	NFL
	2016	2015–16	2016
White	59.0%	18.3%	27.4%
African American	8.3%	74.3%	69.7%
Latino	28.5%	6.3%	0.8%
	MLB	NBA	NFL
	1991	1990–91	1991
White	68%	28%	36%
African American	18%	72%	61%
Latino	14%	0%	0%

[8]Ross (1999, pp. 82–85).

[9]Angela Onwuachi-Willig. "Race and Racial Identity Are Social Constructs," New York Times, June 17, 2015.

[10]Data for the MLB, NBA, and NFL from the Institute for Diversity and Ethics in Sports, directed by Richard Lapchick (http://www.tidesport.org/racial-and-gender-report-cards.html).

It is reasonable to conclude that although each of these sports clearly discriminated in the past, these leagues are rather diversified today — meaning, at least, in a world where African Americans comprise more than two-thirds of the NFL and nearly 75% of the NBA, race may not matter much. Whether or not race still impacts decision-making in sports, however, can't be determined by simply looking at various percentages.

There may be no subject that sports economists have addressed more frequently than the story of racial discrimination. Is it still an issue? More specifically, are white and black players truly treated the same in professional sports today? To answer this question, one must explore the allocation of wages, jobs, awards, and playing time, as well as the behavior of customers. Finally, discrimination is not just about race; it also includes gender, which will be addressed in the next chapter.

Given the vastness of the related literature, what follows is merely a sample of what economists have found. Reviewing this sample highlights how economists have addressed this issue in the past and, perhaps more importantly, how difficult it is to study discrimination even in an industry with an abundance of data on worker productivity.

7.1 The Economic Theory of Discrimination

We begin with work that established the theoretical approach that has driven most discrimination studies. Race and gender played a significant role in the functioning of labor markets in the United States, yet the issue of discrimination was not addressed by economists until Gary Becker's seminal work in 1957. In *The Economics of Discrimination*, Becker put forth an approach to this subject that still dominates how economists think about discrimination today.[11]

A simple example illustrates Becker's approach. Imagine we have an employer who faces a labor force consisting of both white workers (w) and black workers (b).[12] As Becker observes, if

* the white and black workers are perfect substitutes, and

* the labor market is perfectly competitive, and

* there is no discrimination,

then the wages of white and black workers would be the same.

---

[11]Gary Becker, *The Economics of Discrimination* (Chicago: University of Chicago Press, 1957).

[12]Economist Cass Sunstein observed (http://www.bloombergview.com/articles/2014-09-22/partyism-now-trumps-racism) that discrimination also applies to political preferences. The research Sunstein cited was from Shanto Iyengar, Gaurav Sood, and Yphtach Lelkes, "Affect, Not Ideology: A Social Identity Perspective on Polarization," *Public Opinion Quarterly* 76, no. 3 (2014): 405–431.

What if employers discriminated against black workers? Then employers will perceive the wages of each group as follows:

$$\text{Wages of White Workers} = MRP$$
$$\text{Wages of Black Workers} = MRP - dc$$

where MRP = the marginal revenue product
dc = the "discrimination coefficient"

Imagine a firm had two potential employees with the same MRP. If one was black and one was white, then the employer who discriminated against black workers would hire the white worker if both demanded the same wage. This is because the existence of Becker's **discrimination coefficient** (*dc*) reduces, in the mind of the discriminating employer, the value of the black work, which means the black worker can only be hired if she accepts a lower wage. Becker's approach allows us to measure how discrimination actually affects the wages of the discriminated group. Specifically, if discrimination exists the data would indicate that a black worker who is as productive as a white worker would be paid a lower wage.

discrimination coefficient (*dc*) A coefficient that measures how much discrimination exists in a market.

Remember, this is not just about wages. Discrimination appears in hiring, firing, allocation of positions, and playing time. In essence, if discrimination exists, we should see the discriminated group suffering worse labor outcomes (once we control for performance).

Competitive labor markets should theoretically eliminate discrimination over time. Imagine we have two firms: one operated by an employer with a taste for discrimination and a competing firm run by an employer who does not share this taste. The employer without the "taste" will be willing to hire workers from the discriminated group. Because of the other firm's discrimination, the non-discriminating firm will be able to hire these workers at a discount, thus increasing the non-discriminating firm's profit. In the long run, the discriminating firm will be driven out of business.

The work of Becker advances a collection of testable hypotheses. It argues that discrimination can come from employers, coworkers, and customers. It illustrates how discrimination manifests itself in the marketplace, and that competition in the marketplace can eventually eliminate discrimination.

Outside the world of sports, where productivity is difficult to measure, all of this is difficult to test. But with sports data, discrimination can be examined in a variety of different ways. What follows is a sampling of this variety in the literature.

7.2 The Empirical Evidence of Wage Discrimination in the NBA

In most industries, objective measures of individual productivity do not exist. Consequently, it is difficult for a researcher to know if differences in wages are due to race or simply reflect differences in productivity. In sports, this problem appears to be something we can overcome. Professional team sports offer an abundance of worker productivity data. As a result, there is an abundance of studies employing data from sports to ascertain whether or not race still plays a role in the evaluation of worker performance.

This research has examined a number of different aspects of worker evaluation. Perhaps the most popular choice in the literature is player salaries, specifically NBA player salaries.

Lawrence Kahn (1991)[13] noted that researchers typically estimate a regression with salary as the dependent variable and a collection of independent variables that include productivity measures and a dummy variable for race.[14] This approach is described by equation 7.1:

$$S = \beta_0 + \beta_1 \times R + \beta_n \times X_N + e_i \qquad (7.1)$$

where S = worker's salary

$\quad R$ = dummy variable for a worker's race

$\quad X_N$ = measures of worker productivity, a firm's characteristics, and other non-race factors that might affect a worker's salary

$\quad e_i$ = an error term

In general, if the researcher finds that β_1 is statistically significant, then he or she concludes that evidence of discrimination has been uncovered. Of course, if all other factors that may influence salary are not included in the model, then the estimation and interpretation of β_1 will be difficult.

The volume of published research in this area suggests such studies are not immensely difficult to complete and publish. This abundance doesn't just indicate that sports data allow such studies to be completed. It also indicates that even if we have measures of performance, the study of race is still

---

[13]Lawrence M. Kahn, "Discrimination in Professional Sports: A Survey of the Literature," *Industrial Labor Relations Review* 44 (April 1991): 395–418.

[14]This is not the only approach one can take. The Oaxaca–Blinder decomposition will be discussed when we review the issue of national origin bias.

fraught with challenges. Next is a review of some of the challenges researchers have confronted.

What Sample Should Be Employed?

If one is studying wage discrimination, the first obvious step is to collect data on player salaries. Which player salaries should one focus on?

The four studies in Table 7.2 found evidence of racial discrimination in the NBA in the 1980s.[15] Each of the studies follows Kahn's (1991) approach. Salaries were regressed on a collection of performance variables and a dummy variable for race. Each of these studies found a gap between black and white salaries, after controlling for performance.

Table 7.2 Four Studies of Wage Discrimination in the National Basketball Association in the 1980s			
Study	Sample	Year	Salary Gap
Wallace (1988)	229 players	1984–85	16.8%
Koch and Vander Hill (1988)	278 players	1984–85	11.0%
Brown, Spiro, and Keenan (1991)	227 players	1984–85	14.0%
Kahn and Sherer (1988)	226 players	1985–86	20.0%

Three of these studies look at data from the same season, while the Kahn and Sherer (1988) study just examines data from the next season. Each found a statistically significant gap, but the size of the gap varied, even for studies considering the same year. This is a reminder that statistical analysis provides estimates of relationships, but does not give us an "absolute truth."

The reliability of these estimates also depends on how the analysis was conducted. The four studies cited all took a very similar approach, in which salary data were collected from a specific year. Performance data were then collected from seasons prior to the year utilized for the salary data. But a problem exists with this approach.

---

[15]Wallace, Michael. "Labor Market Structure and Salary Determination Among Professional Basketball Players." *Work and Occupations* 15, no. 3 (August 1988): 294–312.

Koch, James V. and C. Warren Vander Hill. "Is There Discrimination in the Black Man's Game?" *Social Science Quarterly* 69, no. 1 (March 1988): 83–94.

Brown, Eleanor, Richard Spiro, and Diane Keenan. "Wage and Non-Wage Discrimination in Professional Basketball: Do Fans Affect It?" *American Journal of Economics and Sociology* 50, no. 3 (July 1991): 333–345.

Kahn, Lawrence M. and Peter D. Sherer. "Racial Differences in Professional Basketball Players' Compensation." *Journal of Labor Economics* 6, no. 1 (January 1988): 40–61.

Consider the case of Moses Malone. In 1982, Malone signed a six-year contract with the Philadelphia 76ers. At the time the contract was signed, Malone was 27 years old and had played for six years. Three of the aforementioned studies looked at salaries in 1984–85 and performance in 1983–84. With respect to Malone, the 1984–85 salary was determined in 1982. Consequently, researchers were actually examining the link between a player's salary (determined in 1982) and his future performance (what he did in 1984–85). Such an approach would be fine if one assumed that decision makers could forecast performance perfectly two or three years into the future. Even if players were evaluated correctly—and as we will note later, there is good reason to think this is not true in the NBA—decision makers would also have to forecast the impact of age and injury.

Jenkins (1996)[16] argued that the issue of multiyear contracts introduces "measurement error" in the aforementioned studies. Consequently, Jenkins advocated a different approach. Rather than looking at most players from a single season, Jenkins collected data on 368 veteran free agents from 1983 to 1994. This sample allowed Jenkins to look at the specific factors that were known about a player at the time he signed a professional contract, which addressed the following questions:

* From 1983 to 1994, after controlling for performance, was there evidence that blacks and whites received different free-agent offers?

* Via separate regression for white and black players, was the return to performance different for white and black players from 1983 to 1994?

* Is there any evidence of discrimination from 1983–84 to 1987–88 (a time period that includes the years other researchers examined)?

Regarding all three questions, Jenkins found no evidence of salary discrimination in the NBA.

Thus, we are left with two results. A collection of studies reported evidence of racial discrimination in the mid-1980s in the NBA. The size of the estimated gap was different, but the results were all statistically significant. The Jenkins (1996) study then focused on measurement error common to all these studies. When this measurement error was corrected, the evidence of salary discrimination no longer existed.

---

[16]Jeffery A. Jenkins, "A Reexamination of Salary Discrimination in Professional Basketball," *Social Science Quarterly* 77, no. 3 (September 1996): 594–608.

How Should the Researcher Measure Performance?

Sports come with a multitude of performance measures. Which measure should a researcher employ? For example, Jenkins (1996) employed "Points Created" as its measure of player performance. This measure is similar to the NBA Efficiency metric discussed in the appendix at the back of the book.[17] Like the NBA Efficiency metric, Points Created is not correlated with team wins. Does this represent a problem with the Jenkins study?

As we will note in our discussion of behavioral economics and sports in Chapter 11, perceptions of player value in basketball do not always match how player performance impacts wins. Given such differences, the researcher examining race should look at the measure that matches perceptions. After all, the study of race is about perceptions. Utilizing a measure that is linked more closely to wins but not the perceptions of performance may not allow one to correctly capture the link between race and worker evaluation.

How Should the Researcher Measure Race?

Beyond the productivity question is the issue of "measuring race." At first glance, one might believe we don't need to. A basketball player is either black or white[18]; consequently, a common approach in the literature has been to use a dummy variable to capture the impact of race. Rodney Fort and Andrew Gill (2000)[19] noted a problem with this approach:

> [R]ace and ethnicity perceptions are based on a bundle of individual characteristics (skin color, facial features, surname, etc.), so that a continuous measure may allow a more precise assessment of race/ethnicity effects. (p. 22)

What did these authors mean by a continuous measure? The basic approach was to ask a group of people to look at pictures on baseball cards. These people were then asked "how black" and "how Hispanic" each person appeared to be.

---

[17]Points Created was developed by Bob Bellotti [*The Points Created Basketball Book 1991–92* (New Brunswick, NJ: Night Work, 1992)]. His basic Points Created formula is

$$\text{Points Created} = \text{Points} + \text{Rebounds} + \text{Assists} + \text{Blocked Shots} + \text{Steals} - \text{Turnovers} - \text{All Missed Shots} - \tfrac{1}{2}\,\text{Personal Fouls}$$

[18]In recent years, players have been more ethnically diverse; for example, we've watched Asian stars like Yao Ming and Jeremy Lin. It is thus possible for players to be neither black nor white. But the vast majority are either black or white.

[19]Rodney Ford and Andrew Gill, "Race and Ethnicity Assessment in Baseball Card Markets," *Journal of Sports Economics* 1, no. 21 (February 2000): 21–38.

The rankings of the group were then averaged to arrive at final measure of each player's ethnicity.

The authors argue that this is an improved approach over the general practice of having only the authors of a study ascertain a person's race. The survey also provides for variation within a race, so the researcher can determine how difference in the skin tone of two black players affects outcomes.[20] The survey approach does present other problems, though. It is possible that the people in the survey will not see race in the same way that the people you are studying regard race (unless you survey the people you are studying).

Perhaps a simpler approach (or at least an approach that addresses the first concern noted above) is to actually measure skin tone. This approach, taken by Robst et al. (2011) would allow us to determine whether lighter and darker African Americans experience different outcomes.[21] Specifically, these authors

considered each player's RGB score in evaluating salary discrimination within the NBA.

To understand the RGB score, we must first note that there are three primary colors: red, green, and blue (hence, the acronym RGB). Using Adobe Photoshop, one can measure how much of these three colors appears in an image. The ranges for each color extend from zero (no color) to 255 (full intensity). A white image would give values of close to 255 for each of these colors. A black image would yield values closer to zero for each color (Wright, 2006).[22]

Consider the photo of Derrick Rose shown here. Rose's RGB score involves measuring three facial areas: the forehead, right cheek, and left cheek. **Table 7.3** indicates that the R's, G's, and B's for each area are averaged to eliminate significant variation of color over different sections of the face. Summing the average R, G, and B for the three areas yields a value of 380.7 (184.0 + 118.7 + 78.0).

---

[20]Specific results are reported in Fort and Gill (2000): *"Card prices reflect discrimination against Black and Hispanic hitters and Black pitchers when player characteristics are evaluated at the means"* (p. 33).

[21]John Robst, Jennifer Van Gilder, Corrine Coates, and David J. Berri, "Skin Tone and Wages: Evidence from NBA Free Agents," *Journal of Sports Economics* 12, no. 2 (April 2011): 143–156. This study built upon a literature examining how "colorism" (i.e. treating people with different skin tones differently) impacts economic outcomes.

[22]The methodology was detailed in S. Wright, *Digital Compositing for Film and Video* (Burlington, MA: Focal Press, 2006). For this study, all images were taken from the NBA website. Using Photoshop's image leveling tool, the players' photos are normalized to eliminate bias due to camera or photographic differences.

Table 7.3 Measuring RGB Score for Derrick Rose[22]			
	Red	Green	Blue	RGB
Left cheek	182.0	116.0	67.0	
Right cheek	190.0	133.0	112.0	
Forehead	180.0	107.0	55.0	
Averages	184.0	118.7	78.0	380.7

Utilizing the RGB measure, Robst et al. (2011) considered NBA free agents from 2001 to 2007. Examining NBA salaries, contract amount, and contract length (in three separate equations), this study did not report any evidence that a player's RGB score affected wages (a different story will be told when we look at the sports media's voting patterns for the NBA's Most Valuable Player or MVP Award).

Robst's result is quite similar to that of the Jenkins (1996) study reviewing data from the 1980s, so perhaps race no longer matters in the evaluation of NBA players.

Are the Results Robust? Part 1: The NBA Salary Story

Imagine you have constructed a study of racial discrimination, and you think you have put together an adequate sample of players to consider. You believe there are reasonable measures for performance, race, and anything else relevant to your study, so you estimate the regression and the results do indicate that evidence of racial discrimination exists. Does this mean you are finished? Not exactly. We would feel more comfortable with your finding if we thought it was "robust." In other words, if you take a slightly different approach to the study (i.e., different sample, different performance measures, different estimation technique, etc.), do you still get the same finding?

Peter Groothuis and James Richard Hill (2013) illustrated such a robust approach.[24] Using NBA data from 1990 to 2008, Groothuis and Hill (2013) addressed two questions. Did race impact whether or not a player was cut from a team? And did race impact a player's wage? With respect to the first question, the authors failed to find evidence that race impacted who made an NBA team. For the study of wages, the authors first estimated five separate

[23]Calculation provided by Jennifer Van Gilder.

[24]Peter Groothuis and James Richard Hill, "Pay Discrimination, Exit Discrimination or Both? Another Look at an Old Issue Using NBA Data," *Journal of Sports Economics* 14, no. 2 (2013): 171–185.

models examining a player's wage in the current season. Each of these considered experience, experience squared, where a player was drafted, draft number squared, points per season, rebounds per season, assists per season, and dummy variables for year (in addition to a dummy variable for whether or not a player is white).

The differences in the models are made clear in Table 7.4. It reports the results with respect to the dummy variable for white players. The results indicate that in the most complete model, reverse discrimination is uncovered. In other words, white players are paid less than black players for the same performance.[25]

Table 7.4 Impact of Race on Player's Wages: 1990–2008[26]			
Model No.	Considerations for Wage	Coefficient for White Dummy Variable	t-Statistic
I	No additional variables	−0.0125	0.34
II	Correction for survivorship bias	−0.0076	0.21
III	Correction for survivorship bias and a player's height	−0.0535	1.43
IV	Correction for survivorship bias and a dummy variable for foreign-born players	−0.00497	1.27
V	Correction for survivorship bias, a player's height, and a dummy variable for foreign-born players	−0.0864	2.17

Turning to a player's career earnings, the five models were estimated, again. Each of these models included, in addition to a dummy variable for white players, where a player was drafted and draft number squared.

Table 7.5 indicates that white players might be paid a premium. In the first three models, the white dummy variable is positive and significant at the 10% level. In the fourth model, which excludes the dummy variable for foreign-born players and player height, race is significant at the 5% level.

[25]Groothius and Hill (2013) only reported t-statistics. They did not report p-values.
[26]Groothius and Hill (2013, Table 3, p. 179).

Table 7.5 Impact of Race on Player's Career Earnings: 1990–2007[27]			
Model No.	Considerations for Career Earnings	Coefficient for White Dummy Variable	t-Statistic
I	Dummy variable for foreign-born players, a player's height, his body mass index, and average career points, rebounds, assists, steals, blocks, and turnovers	0.1574	1.65
II	Same as Model I, but excluded body mass index	0.1578	1.65
III	Same as Model I, but excluded both body mass index and the dummy variable for foreign-born players	0.1648	1.85
IV	Same as Model I, but excluded the body mass index, the dummy variable for foreign-born players, and player height	0.2080	2.46
V	Body mass index, the dummy variable for foreign-born players, and player height, but excluded all performance statistics	−0.1207	0.94

Again, Groothius and Hill (2013) note that results should be interpreted with caution. The authors note that depending on how the models are constructed and estimated there is evidence of discrimination against blacks and evidence of discrimination against whites. In other words, the results depend entirely on how the authors did the study. That suggests, as the authors emphasize, the limitations of their empirical methodology.

> We suggest the conflicting results are due to the limitations of the dummy variable technique. The results are not robust. Research that uses the residual method to measure discrimination must be viewed with a great deal of caution. (p. 183)

---

[27]Groothius and Hill (2013, Table 5, p. 182).

Are the Results Robust? Part 2: The NBA's MVP Story

A similar story was told in an investigation of the voting for the NBA's Most Valuable Player (MVP) Award. The study of salaries is complicated by the nature of this decision, since a team agrees to pay a player a salary in return for what that player will do in the future. The aforementioned studies of salary employ the past performance of a player as a measure of what the decision maker would likely consider a player's future output. It is possible that there is a disconnect between past performance and the decision maker's judgment of the future.

The study of voting for post-season awards requires one to examine the link between past performance and a decision. This might be a better approach to the study of racial bias, but even so, problems still arise.

Before we get to those problems, consider the nature of the sports media in the United States. In 2009, Scoop Jackson, an African American sportswriter, observed that sports media in the United States is predominantly white.[28] Jackson's observation highlights an interesting aspect of player evaluation in the NBA. The majority of players are black, but Jackson notes that an even larger percentage of writers are white. At the end of each season, these writers decide most of the awards bestowed on players.[29]

The specific model[30] employed is reported in **Table 7.6**. The dependent variable in this model is the number of voting points a player received.[31] This is related to a player's race, age, number of wins on a player's team, the size of the market where the player performs, dummy variables for whether a player is a frontcourt player (i.e., DBIG or center/power forward) or backcourt player (i.e., DGUARD or point guard/shooting guard), and MVP wins in the last five years.

---

[28]http://sports.espn.go.com/espn/page2/story?page=jackson/060713 (posted in 2009; accessed March 14, 2013). Looking at the number of black sports editors employed at APSE newspapers in the United States, only 4 out of 305 were found.

[29]Coaches decide on the members of the all-rookie teams and the all-defensive teams.

[30]David J. Berri, Jennifer Van Gilder, and Aju Fenn, "Is the Sports Media Color-Blind?," *International Journal of Sport Finance* 9 (2014): 130–148.

[31]The voting for this award works like so: Each voting sportswriter lists five players on his or her ballot. The first person listed receives 10 voting points, the second is worth 7 points, 5 points are awarded for third, with 3 and 1 point awarded for fourth and fifth places, respectively. Patricia Bender provides voting data at basketball-reference.com. Further details on how voting points were used in the study may be found in Berri et al. (2014).

Table 7.6 Explaining Sports Media's Vote for the National Basketball Association's Most Valuable Player Award	
Dependent Variable	Voting points for the MVP Award
Independent Variables	**Race of the Player**, measured with a simple dummy variable, RGB variable, or three dummies (Darker, Medium, Lighter)
	Productivity of the Player, measured with NBA Efficiency or Wins Produced
	Team Wins
	Age of the Player
	Market Size, or population of metropolitan area where the team is located
	Past MVP Winner, or number of MVP wins in the last five years
	Dummy Variable for Big Man, equal to 1 if a player is a center or power forward
	Dummy Variable for Guard, equal to 1 if a player is a shooting guard or point guard

Obviously, the key factor is the player's race. The estimated model employs different measures of race, and the first two are the standard dummy variable (equal to 1 if the player was black) and the RGB variable. In addition, three dummy variables — Darker, Medium, and Lighter — were also used. These are defined as follows:

- Darker is equal to 1 if a player is black and has an RGB score 300 or lower.

- Medium is equal to 1 if a player is black and has an RGB score between 301 and 350.

- Lighter is equal to 1 if a player is black and has an RGB score that is 351 or higher.

- The omitted or reference category is non-black players.

In addition to different measures of race, the model also considered two measures of performance: NBA Efficiency and Wins Produced. With three measures of race and two measures of performance, the model detailed in Table 7.6 was estimated six different times.[32] With respect to race, the results for all six estimations are reported in **Table 7.7**.

---

[32]The specific dependent variable was the log of voting points for the MVP Award, normalized for the number of voters. The dependent variable is zero for many of the players, so the estimation method was a censored TOBIT model with robust standard errors.

Table 7.7 Link Between Race and Voting for the National Basketball Association's Most Valuable Player Award[33]

Variable	Coefficient	t-Statistic
Dummy variable for race, NBA Efficiency	0.28[c]	1.84
Dummy variable for race, Wins Produced	0.58[a]	3.03
RGB score, NBA Efficiency	−9.44E−04[c]	−1.93
RGB score, Wins Produced	−2.52E−03[a]	−3.99
Dummy variable Darker, NBA Efficiency	0.47[a]	2.84
Dummy variable Medium, NBA Efficiency	−0.02	−0.14
Dummy variable Lighter, NBA Efficiency	0.24	1.41
Dummy variable Darker, Wins Produced	0.97[a]	4.75
Dummy variable Medium, Wins Produced	0.20	0.85
Dummy variable Lighter, Wins Produced	0.32	1.52

p-values not explicitly reported, butt significance levels were noted as follows:
[a]Significant at the 1% level.
[b]Significant at the 5% level.
[c]Significant at the 10% level.

The results reported in Table 7.7 indicate that sportswriters take race into account in voting for this award. Using the simple dummy variable approach, race is only significant at the 10% level (in some circles, that doesn't count) when we use NBA Efficiency as the measure of performance. When we consider the dummy variable for Darker, we do see that skin color matters. Darker players receive more consideration for the MVP Award. This suggests that sportswriters believe "blacker" players make better NBA players, independent of performance.

It seems as if we have a clear story with respect to race. Voters for the MVP Award think black players are better than white players at basketball, or voters think white players are worse. Either way, a racial stereotype seems to influence voting for the NBA MVP Award.

We could stop with this story, but let's look at one more approach reported in the Berri et al. (2014) article. Rather than simply employ NBA Efficiency or Wins Produced, one could also consider a collection of performance statistics.[34] Table 7.8 details how this approach yields a different story.[35]

[33]Berri et al. (2014, Table 2, p. 137).

[34]The collection included adjusted field goal percentage, free-throw percentage, points per game, rebounds per game, steals per game, assists per game, blocked shots per game, personal fouls per game, and turnover percentage.

[35]Table 7.8 is an abbreviated version of a table that originally appeared in Berri et al. (2014). The dependent variable is the log of voting points for the MVP Award, normalized for the number of voters, and this is a censored TOBIT model with robust standard errors.

Table 7.8 Another Look at Voting for the National Basketball Association's Most Valuable Player Award: Measuring Performance with an Assortment of Box-Score Statistics[36]

Variable	Coefficient	t-Statistic
Dummy variable for race	0.03	0.19
RGB score	=4.02E−04	−0.81
Dummy variable Darker	0.15	0.88
Dummy variable Medium	=0.06	−0.35
Dummy variable Lighter	=0.02	−0.08

None of these coefficients had a corresponding p-value that was less than 0.10.

In Table 7.8, none of the measures of race are statistically significant. As noted in Appendix A to this chapter, explanatory power with this approach increases. That suggests that with a measure of performance more closely aligned with perceptions, race is not important.

Once again, the results reported in Table 7.8 tell the story about robustness. Our analysis of racial discrimination seems to depend on both how we measure race and how we measure performance. Remember, outside of sports, it is difficult to measure the latter, and even in sports, where we can measure race and performance, such studies are difficult.

7.3 Learning from Implicit Bias

We know that at one point racial discrimination existed in professional sports. The studies conducted with recent data fail to report consistent evidence of discrimination. Can we thus conclude that racial discrimination in sports has ended?

The astronomer Carl Sagan once commented: "Absence of evidence is not evidence of absence." Because we have not found consistent evidence something exists (i.e., racial discrimination in sports), this does not mean that it definitely does not exist. It could be that our tools to uncover the existence of racial discrimination are simply not up to the task. It might also mean that discrimination in sports has ended[37]; there, in fact, is evidence that people can change their behavior.

---

[36]Berri et al. (2014, Table 3, p. 138).

[37]Moving past sports, there is evidence that discrimination has not ended. One of the best examples is the evidence that employer responses to submitted résumés can be altered by making applicants' names sound more "white." In other words, labor market outcomes for African Americans, even after controlling for performance (the résumés are identical for all applicants), are worse. Marianne Bertrand and Sendhil Mulainathan, "Are Emily and Greg More Employable Than Lakisha and Jamal? A Field Experiment on Labor Market Discrimination," *American Economic Review* 94, no. 4 (September 2004): 991–1013.

This story begins with the concepts of "explicit bias" and "implicit bias." The former is defined as "an attitude that somebody is consciously aware of having."[38] In other words, **explicit bias** refers to our conscious beliefs. In contrast, an **implicit bias** is a "positive or negative mental attitude towards a person, thing, or group that a person holds at an unconscious level."[39]

To test the existence of implicit bias, Anthony Greenwald, Mahzarin Banaji, and Brian Nosek devised the **Implicit Association Test (IAT)**. As these authors observed: "The IAT measures the strength of associations between concepts (e.g., black people, gay people) and evaluations (e.g., good, bad) or stereotypes (e.g., athletic, clumsy). The main idea is that making a response is easier when closely related items share the same response key."[40] The results of this test have been quite surprising, as Malcolm Gladwell noted in *Blink*[41]:

> [I]t shows our unconscious attitudes may be utterly incompatible with our stated values. As it turns out, for example, of the fifty thousand African American who have taken the Race IAT so far, about half of them, like me, have stronger associations with whites than with blacks. (p. 85)

In May 2007, the concept of "implicit bias" was introduced to fans of the NBA. Alan Schwarz' article "Study of NBA Sees Racial Bias in Calling Fouls" appeared on the front page of *The New York Times*.[42] Schwarz detailed a study by Joseph Price and Justin Wolfers[43] that utilized data from 1991 to 2002, and found that the racial composition of the three-person referee teams in the sport affected the calls black and white players would see in a game. For example, an all-white crew was more likely to call fouls on black players. Similarly, an all-black crew was more likely to call fouls on white players. Price and Wolfers (2010) conclude in their paper:

> These results are striking, given the level of racial equality achieved along other dimensions in the NBA and the high level of accountability and

---

[38]"FAQ on Implicit Bias" from the Stanford School of Medicine (http://med.stanford.edu/diversity/FAQ_REDE.html).

[39]"FAQ on Implicit Bias" from the Stanford School of Medicine (http://med.stanford.edu/diversity/FAQ_REDE.html).

[40]From https://implicit.harvard.edu/implicit/takeatest.html. One can also take a test at the aforementioned website.

[41]Malcolm Gladwell, *Blink* (New York: Back Bay Books, 2007).

[42]http://www.nytimes.com/2007/05/02/sports/basketball/02refs.html.

[43]The study was subsequently published: Joseph Price and Justin Wolfers, "Racial Discrimination Among NBA Referees," *Quarterly Journal of Economics* 125, no. 4 (November 2010): 1859–1887.

monitoring under which the referees operate. Although the external validity of these results remains an open question, they are at least suggestive that implicit biases may play an important role in shaping our evaluation of others, particularly in split-second, high-pressure decisions. (p. 1885)

The NBA was not pleased with this study. In the process of protesting the studies' conclusions,[44] David Stern, the league commissioner, announced in *The New York Times* article that a separate study commissioned by the league failed to find any evidence of bias.

Price and Wolfers examined the data utilized in the NBA study and, in a subsequent publication,[45] revealed a number of issues inherent in the NBA study. There was an issue with how the NBA's study coded the dummy variables employed. As noted before, a dummy variable is a variable that takes on a value of 1 or 0 depending on whether a specific condition holds. In a study of race, one could define a dummy variable as equal to 1 if a person is black and 0 if a person is white. Or, one could define the dummy variable as equal to 1 if a person is white and 0 if a person is black. The choice of the researcher is entirely arbitrary, and it makes no difference which choice the researcher makes. The results will be identical; all that will change is the sign on the dummy variable's coefficient.[46]

The authors of the study commissioned by the NBA failed to understand the fundamental nature of dummy variables. As Price and Wolfers (2012) note:

The first point that emerges from these tables is that many of the regression models that the NBA runs in their analysis are redundant. For example, models 5–8 are literally identical, with the only difference being which group is used as the omitted category. . . . In each case the coefficients on the player or referee race dummy variable are the same but with the opposite sign. (p. 322–323)

This was not the only problem Price and Wolfers (2012) uncovered with the NBA's study, and when all these problems were addressed, the NBA's study confirmed the earlier results reported by Price and Wolfers (2010).

---

[44]This study received attention beyond *The New York Times*. It was widely covered by CNN, ABC News, ESPN, NPR, Associated Press, and more than 100 different newspapers (http://users.nber.org/~jwolfers/research.php.

[45]Joseph Price and Justin Wolfers, "Biased Referees?: Reconciling Results with the NBA's Analysis," *Contemporary Economic Policy* 30, no. 3 (2012): 320–328.

[46]For example, if a model indicated that blacks were discriminated against and you coded your dummy variable as 1 for black and 0 for white, the coefficient for the race dummy variable would be negative and statistically significant. If the variable was 1 for white and 0 for black, the dummy variable would be in absolute value the same size (and statistical significance), but its sign would be positive.

The attention paid to this research created a natural experiment. In 2007, referees learned that they might be calling games with an implicit bias. Did that information affect their behavior?

Devin Pope, Joseph Price, and Justin Wolfers addressed this issue in a study of racial bias across three samples.[47] The first sample simply replicates the original study by Price and Wolfers (2010). Table 7.9 reports that players who face referees of the opposite race (relative to the player) see 0.192 additional foul calls per 48 minutes.

Table 7.9	Out-Group Racial Bias Among NBA Referees in Three Samples[48]	
Study	Coefficient	t-statistic
Original study: 1991–2002	0.192[a]	3.254
Out-of-sample: 2003–06	0.214[b]	2.000
Post-treatment period: 2007–10	−0.0002	−0.0022

p-values not explicitly reported, but significance levels were noted as follows:
[a]Significant at the 1% level.
[b]Significant at the 5% level.
[c]Significant at the 10% level.

In the second sample, Pope et al. looked at data from 2003 to 2006. These data came after the time period originally studied, but before the publicity from *The New York Times* article. Across this data set, the authors reported evidence of out-group bias.

The third sample tells a different story. This sample, from 2007 to 2010, was taken after *The New York Times* covered Price and Wolfers' original research. In this sample, the evidence of bias vanishes. The authors offered a variety of explanations for why the bias appeared to disappear. And although they could not rule out every possible explanation for why the evidence of implicit bias vanished, it does seem likely that NBA officials changed their behavior after being made aware of the bias.

The studies of implicit bias with respect to NBA referees combine to tell a powerful study. First, even in an environment where decision making is heavily scrutinized, evidence of implicit bias can be uncovered. As these authors noted, "NBA Commissioner Stern has claimed that these referees 'are the most ranked,

[47]Devin Pope, Joseph Price, and Justin Wolfers, "Awareness Reduces Bias," *Management Science* (forthcoming).

[48]These results were originally reported in Pope et al. (forthcoming), Table 1. There, out-group bias was defined by the authors as "extra fouls per 48 minutes when refereed by an out-group crew, relative to an in-group crew."

rated, reviewed, statistically analyzed and mentored group of employees of any company in any place in the world.'"[49] Despite this scrutiny, there was evidence of discrimination. However, it appears that if decision makers are made aware of such bias, there is evidence they are capable of overcoming this issue.[50]

7.4 National Origin Bias

The study of implicit bias and referees was encouraging, but we should still note that the study of discrimination with respect to race is problematic. Researchers must confront how difficult it is to define race in a fashion consistent with the perceptions of the decision maker. Race is simply not a factor that is clearly defined for each individual.[51]

In contrast, national origin is more easily defined. Either a person is a U.S. citizen, or he or she is not. One can't be 50% a U.S. citizen or 25% a citizen of Germany. National origin is very much an either/or issue. There is reason to suspect that national origin matters in the evaluation of basketball players, and such a story begins with the origin of basketball.

James Naismith invented basketball during the winter of 1891–92 at Springfield College in Massachusetts.[52] Springfield College[53] has noted that by 1905 the game was recognized as an official winter sport at various high schools and colleges. By 1936, basketball was introduced as an Olympic sport.[54]

The United States dominated the first Olympic basketball competitions, winning the gold medal at each of the 1936 to 1968 Summer Games. In 1972, the Soviet Union managed to win the gold medal, an outcome repeated by the Soviet Union in 1988. Professionals began playing basketball in 1992, which restored U.S. dominance. Except for the 2004 Olympics (at which Argentina

---

[49]Price and Wolfers (2010, p. 1859).

[50]It is important to note that psychologists who study this issue do not believe overcoming bias is a simple process. And it is possible to make this issue worse. But there is some evidence that one can train people to reduce bias. https://www.theatlantic.com/science/archive/2017/05/unconscious-bias-training/525405/

[51]As noted earlier, Angela Onwuachi-Willig noted how race is a "social construct" in *The New York Times*, June 17, 2015.

[52]According to the Springfield College website, Naismith was simply hoping to find something for students to do during the New England winter. For more on the story of the origins of basketball, visit the Springfield College website (http://www.springfieldcollege.edu/welcome/birthplace-of-basketball/index#.VFUn5_nF_h4).

[53]http://www.springfieldcollege.edu/welcome/birthplace-of-basketball/index#.VFUn5_nF_h4.

[54]http://www.sports-reference.com/olympics/sports/BAS/mens-basketball.html.

secured first place), the gold medal in basketball has gone to Team USA at each of the Olympic Games played from 1992 to 2016.

U.S. dominance in many international competitions suggests that players from the United States might have an inherent advantage. In other words, decision makers might favor players from the United States; therefore, players born elsewhere might face discrimination. This discrimination is called **national origin bias** (or **national origin discrimination**). In both the United States and Europe, such a bias is a violation of the law. To address whether or not it occurs, Berri, Deutscher, and Galletti (2015)[55] estimated the model described in **Table 7.10**.

national origin bias (or national origin discrimination) A preformed negative opinion or attitude toward a group of persons of the same race or national origin who share common or similar traits, languages, customs, and traditions.

Table 7.10	Explaining Minutes per Game in the National Basketball Association and Spanish Liga ACB
Dependent Variable	**Minutes per Game**
Independent Variables	**Productivity of Player,** or vector of player statistics, including points, adjusted field goal percentage, free-throw percentage, rebounds, turnover, steals, assists, blocks, and personal fouls
	Draft and Experience, or vector of variables interacting with draft position and experience
	Height of Player
	Games Played
	Age (and age squared)
	Dummy Variable for U.S.-Born Player (DUSA), equal to 1 if the player is born in the United States

In the previous chapter, we noted that this model indicated coaches overvalued scorers and had a difficult time ignoring sunk costs in allocating minutes. Now we turn to what the model says with respect to DUSA. This is a dummy variable, equal to 1 if a player was a U.S. citizen. The results indicate that after controlling for factors like player productivity, draft position, experience, etc. just being a U.S. citizen gets a player an estimated 1.16 additional minutes of playing time each game.

So far, our study of discrimination has followed the approach detailed earlier in equation 9.1; in it, a model that includes a dummy variable is estimated for race (or in this current discussion, national origin). Ronald Oaxaca (1973)[56] and Alan Blinder (1973) introduced a different approach, one often observed in non-sports studies, known as the Oaxaca–Blinder decomposition.

---

[55]David J. Berri, Christian Deutscher, and Arturo Galletti, "Born in the USA: National Origin Effects on Time Allocation in US and Spanish Professional Basketball," *Special Issue: National Institute Economic Review* 232 (May 2015): R41–R50.

[56]Ronald Oaxaca, "Male-Female Wages Differentials in Urban Labor Markets," *International Economic Review* 14 (October 1973): 693–709.

The Oaxaca–Blinder decomposition involves estimating a salary model for the discriminated group–in this case, players who are not U.S. citizens. It then employs the characteristics of the group that is not discriminated against, those born in the United States, to predict the earnings (via the aforementioned model) of the discriminated group. Finally, it compares these hypothetical earnings to the actual earnings of the group that is not discriminated against.

In the end, we are decomposing the gap in minutes between the two groups into an explained portion and an unexplained portion. Berri et al. (2015) noted that the explained portion, which captures differences in the endowments of each group, does not indicate non–U.S.-born players should receive fewer minutes. Table 7.11 shows that the unexplained portion (or the differences that we cannot explain by the performance of players) indicates players born in the United States receive 1.39 additional minutes. This suggests that coaches in the NBA favor players from the United States.

Table 7.11	Decomposition Results for the National Basketball Association: 2001–02 to 2013–14[57]	
Independent Variable	Coefficient	z-Statistic
U.S.-born player	24.08[a]	160.40
Non–U.S.-born player	22.77[a]	78.83
Difference	1.31[a]	4.03
Explained	−0.08	0.28
Unexplained	1.39[a]	6.91

p-values not explicitly reported, but significance levels were noted as follows:
[a]Significant at the 1% level.

The same study then moved on to an examination of how minutes were allocated in the Spanish Liga ACB, a premier basketball league in Europe that employs players from around the world. Just as was done with respect to the NBA, Berri et al. used two approaches to ascertain whether or not coaches considered national origin in allocating minutes.

The first approach involved estimating the model detailed in Table 7.10 for the Spanish ACB.[58] The results indicated that players born in the United States again received 1.79 additional minutes (after controlling for experience), and players born outside of Spain and the United States received 0.96 additional minutes per game.

---

[57]Berri et al. (2015), p. R5.

[58]Reverse-order drafts do not happen in Europe. The impact of draft position was not part of the Spanish ACB model.

Table 7.12 details the Oaxaca–Blinder decomposition approach, which tells the same story. Players born in Spain are treated differently with respect to both players born in the United States and players born outside of Spain (but not born in the United States). Some of this gap can be linked to explained differences, but in both cases, there is an unexplained portion of the gap that suggests discrimination.

Table 7.12 Decomposition Results for the Spanish Liga ACB: 2011–12 to 2013–14[59]					
Independent Variable	Coefficient	z-Statistic	Independent Variable	Coefficient	z-Statistic
Spain-born player	18.77[a]	43.9	Spain-born player	18.77[a]	43.9
non–Spain-born player	20.43[a]	71.83	U.S.-born player	22.05[a]	47.28
Difference	−1.66[a]	−3.23	Difference	−3.28[a]	−5.18
Explained	−0.42	−1.01	Explained	−1.75[a]	−3.5
Unexplained	−1.24[a]	−3.14	Unexplained	−1.53[a]	−3.01

p-values not explicitly reported, but significance levels were noted as follows:
[a]Significant at the 1% level.

In two different places, we see evidence of national origin bias, and in both cases, that bias favors players born in the United States. Berri et al. (2015) noted that these results suggest coaches are biased, but it could be that the bias originates in the fans who prefer to see players born in the United States. Alternatively, it could be that non=box-score factors, such as the ability to play defense, are different between the two groups and therefore coaches are justified in giving U.S.-born players more minutes on the court. In sum, even when finding evidence of discrimination, we need to consider what we have determined. And, of course, that is true for any results we uncover.

7.5 He Really Looks Good Out There!

We have seen evidence that discrimination occurs with respect to race and national origin, but these are not the only sources. Discrimination can occur due to gender, religious beliefs, and ethnicity. In addition, workers may also be favored for being "more attractive." Hamermesh and Biddle (1994) found that better-looking people, after controlling for other factors that might impact

[59]Berri et al. (2015, p. R7).

wages, are paid 5% more in the labor market.[60] Surprisingly, there is some evidence that beauty is an important consideration in sports.

To understand whether or not looks matter in professional sports, we first need to measure a player's appearance. One might think that beauty is in the eye of the beholder, but researchers in economics, sociology, and anaplasty (the application of reconstructive surgery) have argued that facial symmetry, which can be objectively measured,[61] is what defincs "better-looking" people. Since symmetry can be measured, it is thus possible to determine if attractiveness is related to wages in professional sports.

The study we will review[62] was published in 2011 and focuses on the labor market for NFL quarterbacks (see Table 7.13). The model is quite similar to

Table 7.13	Explaining Salaries of Quarterbacks in the National Football League
Dependent Variable	**Salaries of Quarterbacks**
Independent Variables	**Passing Yards,** in the prior season
	Career Pass Attempts
	Experience, or total years of experience (and experience squared)
	Dummy Variable for First Round of Draft, equal to 1 if the quarterback was drafted in the first round
	Dummy Variable for Second Round of Draft, equal to 1 if the quarterback was drafted in the second round
	Dummy Variable for NFL Veteran, equal to 1 if quarterback has played at least three years in the NFL
	Dummy Variable for Changing Teams, equal to 1 if the quarterback is with a new team this year
	Teammate Talent, measured with log of the team's non-quarterback offensive salary
	Pro Bowl, equal to 1 if the quarterback has appeared in the Pro Bowl
	Symmetry, or the measure of the quarterback's facial symmetry

[60]D. S. Hamermesh and J. Biddle, "Beauty and the Labor Market," *American Economic Review* 84 (1994): 1174–1194. Hamermesh later wrote a book on this same topic: *Beauty Pays: Why Attractive People Are More Successful* (Princeton, NJ: Princeton University, 2011).

[61]In 2002, Dave Davis, with the assistance of Mike Jones, developed Symmeter, a symmetry measurement tool. See http://www.symmeter.com for more information on this computer package.

[62]David J. Berri, Rob Simmons, Jennifer Van Gilder, and Lisle O'Neill, "What Does It Mean to Find the Face of the Franchise? Physical Attractiveness and the Evaluation of Athletic Performance," *Economics Letters* 111 (2011): 200–202.

that outlined in Berri and Simmons (2009).[63] As Tables 7.13 details, salaries of NFL quarterbacks[64] are related to passing yards from the prior season, career pass attempts, total years of experience in the league (as well as experience squared), whether the quarterback was selected in the first or second round of the NFL draft, the change in bargaining status after a player has completed three years in the NFL, the impact of changing teams, the talent surrounding the player,[65] and whether or not the player has ever appeared in the Pro Bowl. Let's add an additional measure—a quarterback's facial symmetry.

The results in **Table 7.14** indicate that facial symmetry does appear to matter. Not only is it statistically significant, but the model based on season data suggests that a 2 standard deviation change in symmetry from 1 standard deviation below the mean to 1 standard deviation above the mean (a 3.16 change in the symmetry score) would result in a salary increase of 11.8% ($378,000 at the mean salary). In the NFL, it appears that being better-looking pays off!

Table 7.14	Modeling[66] the Link Between Quarterback Salary and Facial Symmetry			
Variable	Coefficient (season model)	t-Statistic	Coefficient (career averages)	t-Statistic
Symmetry	0.038[b]	2.33	0.052[a]	2.61

p-values not explicitly reported, but significance levels were noted as follows:
[a]Significant at the 1% level.
[b]Significant at the 5% level.

One could argue that facial symmetry matters because quarterbacks literally are the face of a franchise. Certainly, quarterbacks are often asked to speak to the media, but it is also possible that teams simply have trouble evaluating a quarterback's contribution. As noted in Chapter 6, the statistics associated with a quarterback's performance can be quite inconsistent across time. This suggests

[63]David J. Berri and Rob Simmons, "Race and the Evaluation of Signal Callers in the National Football League," *Journal of Sports Economics* 10, no. 1 (February 2009): 23–43.

[64]Quarterbacks considered were not strictly free agents. NFL contracts are not guaranteed, so NFL players can essentially be considered free agents each year.

[65]The salaries of the offensive players around the quarterback are included to capture the performance of the quarterback's teammates.

[66]This table originally appeared in Berri et al. (2011). This paper noted that the model was estimated with data from 1995 to 2009. The salary data were logged and robust standard errors reported. In addition, year dummies were part of the model. Finally, the qualifying condition was that the quarterback had played at least one season (i.e., rookies were excluded).

that a quarterback's statistics are often about his teammates, which means that separating a quarterback from his teammates might be very difficult. When performance is hard to evaluate, factors like facial symmetry might be more likely to enter the decision maker's assessment.[67]

7.6 Challenges in the Study of Discrimination

Let's conclude by emphasizing the basic story told in this chapter. Discrimination is a topic that has been frequently examined by economists utilizing data from sports. As noted (more than once), sports comes with an abundance of player performance data. Consequently, economists have frequently utilized data from the sports industry to investigate this subject. Our discussion has only touched on a few of the studies in this vast literature. This chapter can serve as an introduction to the topic, but we should highlight that even when productivity data exist, investigating discrimination is fraught with challenges. These challenges mean that whatever results we uncover, we still have to think about what those results mean.

So is discrimination still a part of sports today? There is some evidence that discrimination is still part of the story. And there is some evidence that this has become less of an issue. What we can say with certainty is more careful research is needed on this topic.

Key Terms

discrimination coefficient
(*dc*) (p. 225)
explicit bias (p. 238)
implicit bias (p. 238)

Implicit Association Test (IAT) (p. 238)
national origin bias (or national origin
discrimination) (p. 242)

Problems

Study Questions

1. Who was the first African-American professional baseball player, and when did he play?
2. When did the NFL become an all-white league? Why (and when) did the NFL integrate?
3. When was the NBA an all-white league? Who were the first African American players in the NBA?

---

[67]For more on this story, NFL Films created an amusing short video describing the particular research: http://www.nfl.com/videos/nfl-films-presents/09000d5d823f6c54/NFL-Films-Presents-QB-glamour.

4. According to Gary Becker, why should we expect competition to eliminate discrimination?

5. Why is it difficult to study discrimination outside of the sports industry?

6. What measurement error in the study of salary discrimination in the NBA did Jenkins (1996) uncover? When this error was corrected, what impact did it have on the study's results?

7. How should a researcher measure performance in a study of discrimination?

8. How has race been measured in the sports economics literature? What is an RGB score?

9. What does it mean for a result to be robust?

10. What is implicit bias, and what was reported with respect to NBA referees?

11. When was basketball invented? How long after its invention was basketball made an Olympic sport?

12. How are non–U.S.-born players treated in both the NBA and Spanish Liga ACB? What are the potential sources of bias?

13. What is the link between facial symmetry and the pay of NFL quarterbacks?

14. According to a collection of studies examining salary discrimination in the NBA, what factor dominates player evaluation in the NBA?

15. According to this textbook, how did Derrick Rose win the NBA MVP Award in 2011?

16. Imagine a study examining whether or not Major League Baseball teams discriminated against shorter pitchers. If the study failed to find statistical evidence for discrimination, does this prove there is no discrimination?

17. The study of sports media bias used a single equation to investigate how race impacted the voting for the NBA's MVP. How would this study be different if the Oaxaca-Blinder decomposition were employed instead?

18. Discrimination takes many forms and can occur across many dimensions. With respect to sports, construct a list of
    a. all the player evaluations where discrimination might be found (i.e. wages, allocation of minutes, etc.)
    b. all the dimensions of discrimination one might see (i.e. race, gender, etc.)

Appendix A
Learning from Control Variables

The focus of Chapter 7 was discrimination. As noted, such studies include control variables. These are often not discussed in much detail (and generally were not in the text). In this appendix, though, we are going to spend some time looking at the complete models estimated with respect to the NBA's MVP Award and the salaries paid to NFL quarterbacks.

7A.1 The NBA's MVP Award

The model of the sports media's voting for the NBA's MVP Award begins with this equation:

$$VP_n = \beta_0 + \beta_N RACE + \beta_1 AGE + \beta_2 TMWINS + \beta_3 MARKET + \\ \beta_4 DBIG + \beta_5 DGUARD + \beta_6 MVPWINS + \beta_K PROD + e_i$$

$$(7A.1)$$

where VP = voting points
$RACE$ = simple dummy variable, RGB variable, or three dummies (Darker, Medium, Lighter)
$TMWINS$ = team wins
$MARKET$ = population of city where team is located
$DBIG$ = dummy variable, Big Man (center or power forward)
$DGUARD$ = dummy variable, Guard (points guard or shooting guard)
$MVPWINS$ = number of MVP titles won in last five years
$PROD$ = NBA Efficiency or Wins Produced

The model was estimated with data from 1995 to 2012. The sample included any player who reasonably could have been considered.[68] Since the number of voting points for many of these players is zero, the estimation method was a censored regression model (often referred to as a tobit model). The complete results reported in Berri et al. (2014)[69] are given in Table 7A.1.

---

[68]This is defined as all players who received some consideration for the All-NBA teams.
[69]Berri et al. (2014, Table 2, p. 137).

t-Statistics below each coefficient Variable	Model 1	Model 2	Model 3	Model 4	Model 5	Model 6
Table 7A.1 Estimation of Model for National Basketball Association Voting Points Dependent variable: log of voting points for the MVP Award, normalized for the number of voters[70] Years: 1995–2012						
Dummy variable, race	0.28^c			0.58^a		
	1.84			3.03		
RGB		−9.44E−04^c			−2.52E−03^a	
		−1.93			−3.99	
Dummy variable, Darker			0.47^a			0.97^a
			2.84			4.75
Dummy variable, Medium			−0.02			0.20
			−0.14			0.85
Dummy variable, Lighter			0.24			0.32
			1.41			1.52
Age	0.01	0.01	0.01	−0.06^a	−0.07^a	−0.06^a
	0.79	0.52	0.88	−3.32	−3.73	−3.39
Team wins	0.06^a	0.06^a	0.06^a	0.06^a	0.06^a	0.06^a
	9.69	9.65	9.67	8.01	7.97	8.01
Market size	−1.94E−08	−1.91E−08	−2.48E−08^c	−3.17E−09	−2.91E−09	−1.20E−08
	−1.56	−1.49	−1.89	−0.19	−0.17	−0.70
Dummy variable, Big Man	−0.66^a	−0.65^a	−0.62^a	−0.15	−0.12	−0.06
	−4.23	−4.13	−3.93	−0.74	−0.61	−0.29
Dummy variable, Guard	0.27^c	0.29^b	0.29^b	0.08	0.13	0.15
	1.83	1.96	1.97	0.38	0.64	0.76
MVP wins past 5 years	0.12^a	0.12^a	0.12^a	0.40^a	0.41^a	0.40^a
	3.90	3.91	3.86	9.07	9.20	8.94
NBA Efficiency per game	0.29^a	0.28^a	0.28^a			
	19.32	18.77	18.43			
Wins Produced				8.87^a	8.93^a	8.63^a
				7.07	7.11	6.97
Observations	**736**	**736**	**736**	**736**	**736**	**736**
Pseudo R-squared	**0.30**	**0.30**	**0.31**	**0.15**	**0.15**	**0.16**

p-values not explicitly reported, but significance levels were noted as follows:
^{a}Significant at the 1% level.
^{b}Significant at the 5% level.
^{c}Significant at the 10% level.

---

[70]This is a censored regression model. There were 463 left censored observations (i.e., observations where voting points were zero). There were 273 uncensored observations. Robust standard errors were estimated.

As noted in the text, this model was estimated with different measures of performance. Table 7A.2 reports what we see when box-score stats are used.

Table 7A.2	Estimation of Model for NBA Voting Points, All Stats Version[71] Dependent variable: log of voting points for the MVP Award, normalized for the number of voters[72] Years: 1995–2012		
Variable	Model 7	Model 8	Model 9
Dummy variable, race	0.03		
	0.19		
RGB		−4.02E−04	
		−0.81	
Dummy variable, Darker			0.15
			0.88
Dummy variable, Medium			−0.06
			−0.35
Dummy variable, Lighter			−0.02
			−0.08
Age	0.03^b	0.03^c	0.03^c
	2.03	1.87	1.79
Team wins	0.07^a	0.07^a	0.07^a
	10.70	10.70	10.68
Market size	$−3.20E−08^b$	$−3.21E−08^b$	$−3.47E−08^b$
	−2.47	−2.48	−2.56
Dummy variable, Big Man	0.04	0.05	0.07
	0.28	0.33	0.43
Dummy variable, Guard	0.35^a	0.36^a	0.37^a
	2.67	2.71	2.75
MVP wins past 5 years	0.03	0.04	0.04
	1.19	1.22	1.33
Adjusted field goal percentage	−0.24	−0.17	−0.25
	−0.17	−0.12	−0.17

(continued)

[71]Berri et al. (2014, Table 3, p. 138).

[72]This is a censored regression model. There were 463 left censored observations (i.e., observations where voting points was zero). There were 273 uncensored observations. Robust standard errors were estimated.

Table 7A.2 (continued)			
Variable	Model 7	Model 8	Model 9
Free-throw percentage	−0.04	0.02	0.07
	−0.06	0.02	0.10
Points per game	0.21[a]	0.21[a]	0.20
	12.99	12.88	12.83[a]
Rebounds per game	0.17[a]	0.17[a]	0.17[a]
	4.58	4.67	4.63
Steals per game	0.23[c]	0.22[c]	0.23[c]
	1.91	1.84	1.92
Assists per game	0.22[a]	0.22[a]	0.21[a]
	5.66	5.77	5.07
Blocked shots per game	0.45[a]	0.45[a]	0.43[a]
	4.47	4.43	4.26
Personal fouls per game	−0.41[a]	−0.43[a]	−0.41[a]
	−3.77	−3.88	−3.78
Turnover percentage	0.04[c]	0.05[b]	0.05[b]
	1.86	2.02	2.15
Observations	**736**	**736**	**736**
Pseudo *R*-squared	**0.35**	**0.35**	**0.35**

p-values not explicitly reported, but significance levels were noted as follows:
[a]Significant at the 1% level.
[b]Significant at the 5% level.
[c]Significant at the 10% level.

Unsurprisingly, the studies of discrimination tend to focus on how the factor that leads to bias (race, national origin, attractiveness, etc.) relates to the decision examined. The study of discrimination cannot simply focus on the decision considered and one factor. Other aspects of worker evaluation have to be taken into account, and although this is not often emphasized by researchers, the control variables frequently tell interesting stories.

Berri (2006)[73] examined 15 different studies investigating racial discrimination in the NBA. Each of these studies employed various box-score statistics to control for the skills of the players examined. When these control variables were reviewed, an interesting pattern emerged (see Table 7A.3).

[73]David J. Berri, "Economics and the National Basketball Association: Surveying the Literature at the Tip-off," in John Fizel (ed.), *The Handbook of Sports Economics Research* (Armonk, NY: M.E. Sharpe, 2006), pp. 21–48.

Table 7A.3 Impact of Box-Score Statistics in 15 Studies of Racial Discrimination in the National Basketball Association

Player Productivity Variable	Significant Coefficient	Insignificant Coefficient or Incorrect Sign	Not Tested
Points scored	14	1	0
Field goal percentage	4	5	5
Free-throw percentage	0	9	5
Offensive rebounds	0	7	7
Defensive rebounds	1	6	7
Total rebounds	5	3	7
Assists	6	6	2
Steals	0	9	6
Blocked shots	6	4	5
Personal fouls	1	5	8
Turnovers	0	0	14

In all but one study, total points scored were statistically significant. The results for the remaining box-score statistics were much more mixed. This suggested that scoring tends to dominate player evaluation in the NBA.

Consider the aforementioned study of bias in the sports media. It examined both player performance and team success, and if we move past statistical significance and look at economic significance, an interesting story emerges. Specifically, in Table 7A.4, the elasticity of each statistically significant factor employed[74] in the study of the sports media and the NBA MVP Award is reported. This table makes clear that the sports media is primarily influenced by two factors: points per game and team wins.

Table 7A.4 Elasticity[75] of Statistically Significant Factors from the Study of Sports Media Bias and the National Basket Association's Most Valuable Player Award

Variable	Model 7	Model 8	Model 9
Points per game	3.97	3.95	3.93
Team wins	3.41	3.41	3.41
Rebounds per game	1.19	1.19	1.20

(continued)

[74]Excluding the factors associated with race, which have already been discussed.

[75]Berri et al. (2014, Table 4, p. 140). Because this is a linear model, elasticity was measured by multiplying the estimated slope coefficient (from Table 7A.2) by the ratio of the independent variable to the dependent variable. For the aforementioned ratio, the average values of the independent and dependent variables were employed. In other words, elasticity was measured at the point of means.

Table 7A.4 (continued)			
Variable	Model 7	Model 8	Model 9
Personal fouls per game	−1.06	−1.09	−1.06
Assists per game	0.93	0.93	0.88
Age	0.77	0.72	0.72
Turnover percentage	0.57	0.61	0.66
Blocked shots per game	0.40	0.39	0.38
Steals per game	0.28	0.27	0.28
Market size	−0.15	−0.15	−0.17

Scoring and wins dominate this evaluation, so a player almost has access to a road map to win this award. To illustrate, Berri et al. (2014) noted the case of Derrick Rose. Prior to the 2010–11 season, Rose was asked about his level of confidence[76]:

> "It's high," Rose said of self-confidence. "The way I look at it within myself, why not? Why can't I be the MVP of the league," he asked. "Why can't I be the best player in the league? I don't see why [not]. Why can't I do that?"

At the time he made this statement, Rose's confidence seemed out of line with his actual accomplishments; he was only 21 years of age. He had only played two NBA seasons and had never received a single vote for league MVP. The Bulls had only won 41 games in each of Rose's first two seasons, so Rose was a young player on a mediocre team.

Between 2009–10 and 2010–11, changes were made to the Bulls' team. Table 7A.5 indicates that 13 players who played in 2009–10 were not employed in 2010–11. Players like Ronnie Brewer, Keith Bogans, Carlos Boozer, Kyle Korver, Omer Aski, and Kurt Thomas were added. These players came together to produce 27.7 wins in 2010–11.[77] Rose also improved (from 5.4 wins to 10.2 wins), but without this influx of talent, Rose and the Bulls would not have led the NBA in regular-season wins in 2010–11.

Rose changed his game by increasing his scoring average from 20.8 per game in 2009–10 to 25.0 points per game in 2010–11. This was not due to increased shooting efficiency. Rose's adjusted field goal percentage declined from 0.495 to 0.485. What changed was the number of shots he attempted. And since Rose was the team's point guard, he had significant say with respect to who got to shoot

[76]Nick Friedell, "Derrick Rose Has High Expectations," ESPNChicago.com, September 28, 2010, http://sports.espn.go.com/chicago/nba/news/story?id=5622446.

[77]More on Wins Produced is offered in the appendix to this book.

| Table 7A.5 The Chicago Bulls in 2009–10 and 2010–11[78] | | | | | |
| Chicago Bulls 2009–10 | | | Chicago Bulls 2010–11 | | |
Players Retained	Wins Produced	WP48	Players Retained	Wins Produced	WP48
Derrick Rose	5.4	0.090	Derrick Rose	10.2	0.161
Luol Deng	7.1	0.128	Luol Deng	9.3	0.139
Joakim Noah	8.8	0.219	Joakim Noah	8.4	0.255
Taj Gibson	5.8	0.127	Taj Gibson	5.2	0.143
James Johnson	0.1	0.005	James Johnson	−0.3	−0.110
Summation	27.1		*Summation*	32.7	
Players Lost	Wins Produced	WP48	Players Added	Wins Produced	WP48
Kirk Hinrich	4.9	0.095	Ronnie Brewer	9.1	0.245
John Salmons	3.2	0.091	Keith Bogans	4.4	0.146
Tyrus Thomas	2.4	0.171	Carlos Boozer	4.0	0.103
Hakim Warrick	1.0	0.089	Kyle Korver	3.4	0.098
Ronald Murray	0.5	0.036	Omer Asik	3.2	0.155
Acie Law	0.2	0.086	Kurt Thomas	2.7	0.111
Brad Miller	0.2	0.006	C. J. Watson	1.0	0.042
Chris Richard	0.2	0.041	Rasual Butler	0.0	0.085
Joe Alexander	−0.1	−0.118	John Lucas	−0.1	−0.268
Aaron Gray	−0.2	−0.207	Brian Scalabrine	−0.1	−0.076
Devin Brown	−0.4	−0.216			
Lindsey Hunter	−0.6	−0.231			
Jannero Pargo	−1.8	−0.104			
Summation players lost	9.6		*Summation players added*	27.7	
2009–10 Wins Produced total	36.8		**2010–11 Wins Produced total**	60.4	
Actual 2009–10 wins	41		**Actual 2010–11 wins**	62	

on the team. Rose's decision to take more shots increased his scoring. And with more productive teammates, Rose's team won many more games. As a direct result of these two changes, the 22-year old point guard went on to win the MVP Award in 2011.

---

[78]Berri et al. (2014, Table 5, p. 141).

The value of Rose was made clearer the next season. The lockout shortened the NBA season to 66 games in 2011–12. Rose missed 27 of these games, so he was only available for about 60% of the season. Despite the loss of the league's MVP, the Bulls in 2011–12 still finished with the best record in the NBA. Although Rose only produced 4.3 wins in 2011–12, the team managed to win 76% of their games behind the play of Joakim Noah (12.0 wins), Luol Deng (5.9 wins), Ronnie Brewer (5.7 wins), Kyle Korver (5.5 wins), Carlos Boozer (5.1 wins), and Omer Aski (4.8 wins).[79]

All this suggests that Rose was not the primary reason the Bulls suddenly became an above-average team. His ability to take shots and score seems to have altered perceptions. The real story is clear when we move past the focus of interest in our study (i.e., race) and look at what is revealed by the control variables.

7A.2 Learning from the Control Variables: The Salaries Paid to NFL Quarterbacks

Chapter 7 closed with the story of how facial symmetry can impact the salaries of NFL quarterbacks. The work of Berri et al. (2011) told yet more stories about the compensation of quarterbacks. Again, we begin with the model:

$$lnSAL = b_0 + b_1 \times PYARDS + b_2 \times CPASSATT + b_3 \times EXP + b_4 \times EXPSQ + b_5 \times DRAFT1 + b_6 \times DRAFT2 + b_7 \times VET + b_8 \times NEWTM + b_9 \times \ln OFFSAL + b_{10} \times PB + b_{11} \times SYMMETRY + e_t \tag{7A.2}$$

where

$PYARD$ = a quarterback's passing yards from the prior season

$CPASSATT$ = career pass attempts

EXP = total years of experience in the league as well as experience squared (EXPSQ)

$DRAFT1, DRAFT2$ = whether the quarterback was selected in the first or second round of the NFL draft

VET = a player has completed three years in the NFL

$NEWTM$ = the impact of changing teams

$lnOFFSAL$ = the talent surrounding the player

PB = whether or not the player has ever appeared in the Pro Bowl

---

[79]Wins Produced numbers for this team—and any NBA team back to 1977–78—can be found at www.boxscoregeeks.com.

This model[80] was estimated with data from 1995 to 2009, with data from individual seasons and career averages, and the results are reported in Table 7A.6.

Table 7A.6 Modeling the Link Between Quarterback Salary and Facial Symmetry[81]				
	Pooled OLS, $n = 621$		Career Averages, $n = 138$	
Variable	Coefficient	t-Statistic	Coefficient	t-Statistic
PYARDS	0.00027[a]	10.79	0.00058[a]	10.70
CPASSATT	0.00016[a]	4.62		
EXP	0.182[a]	4.22	0.170[a]	3.31
EXPSQ	−0.012[a]	5.12	−0.010[a]	3.60
DRAFT1	0.852[a]	9.09	0.888[a]	5.47
DRAFT2	0.180	1.06	0.081	0.37
VET	0.334[a]	3.09	0.162[b]	2.10
NEWTM	−0.430[a]	6.12	−0.592[a]	3.77
lnOFFSAL	0.421[a]	5.47	0.276[c]	1.83
PB	0.264[a]	3.73	0.144	1.02
SYMMETRY	0.038[b]	2.33	0.052[a]	2.61
R-squared	0.62		0.80	

p-values not explicitly reported, but significance levels were noted as follows:
[a]Significant at the 1% level.
[b]Significant at the 5% level.
[c]Significant at the 10% level.

We have noted the issue with facial symmetry, but we can also see that quarterbacks drafted in the first round continue to receive a higher salary even after their performance on the field has been observed. This suggests that NFL decision makers have trouble letting go of an initial assessment of a player. On the other hand, quarterbacks pay a penalty when they switch teams. If one team signals that it is about to move on from a quarterback, another team will then be able to sign that same player at a discount.

When we discuss models of discrimination, we tend to just focus on the issue of discrimination, but the other variables in these models can also tell stories. It is worthwhile to consider what those variables are trying to reveal.

---

[80]Berri et al. (2011). Salary data were logged and robust standard errors reported with year dummies as part of the model. Finally, the qualifying condition was that the quarterback played at least one season (i.e., rookies were excluded).

[81]Berri et al. (2015, Table 2, p. 201).

Women and Sports

Can Markets Explain Differences in Outcomes for Women and Men in Sports?

To answer this question, Chapter 8 will explore the following:

1. **The Demand for Women's Sports:** Traditionally, economists focus exclusively on supply and demand to explain outcomes in a market. But women's sports highlight how much public policy and historical perceptions drive the outcomes we observe.

2. **Wages Paid in Women's Sports:** The gap between the wages paid to women and men has been well documented outside of sports. Inside of sports, we also see such a gap in professional basketball. In addition to exploring this gap, this chapter will discuss the process by which wages are paid in women's sports.

3. **Leadership in Women's Sports:** Women are leaders of firms, universities, and nations. But in sports, women only seem to lead women's sports teams. It is very rare to see a woman lead a men's team. In contrast, men are often hired to lead women's teams. This suggests that many believe men are better leaders than women. The data in women's sports allow us to test this idea, a test that reveals no evidence of men and women having different leadership abilities.

Historically, sports have been played mostly by men. In 1971, 3.7 million boys played high school sports, while fewer than 300,000 girls did. The girls who played in high school had limited opportunities to continue doing so after graduation. In 1970, there were just 2.5 women's teams per school in the National Collegiate Athletic Association (NCAA); across all colleges, only about 16,000 women played sports.[1] And for the few women who got to play college team sports, their career almost always ended with their college graduation. The professional team sports leagues we see today in women's sports did not exist.

Forty years later, these numbers are quite different. As of 2013, there were 4.49 million boys playing high school sports and 3.2 million girls. So while boys' participation had increased by 21%, the participation rate among girls had increased by 966.7%. And upon high school graduation, many of these girls now find opportunities in college. In 2014, there were over 200,000 women playing college sports.[2] When these women leave college, some will find opportunities to play professionally. Women are now paid to play in a variety of sports: the Women's National Basketball Association (WNBA), National Women's Soccer League (NWSL), National Women's Hockey League (NWHL), and National Pro Fastpitch (NPF).

What explains these changes? The go-to explanation economists turn to is "market forces." If we follow that story, then in 1970, very few women and girls were interested in playing sports. And soon afterward, demand for sports changed dramatically and suddenly many women and girls loved sports.

Obviously, that story is somewhat ridiculous. A more plausible explanation begins with Title IX. Title IX is an amendment to the Civil Rights Act of 1964. Initially, the Civil Rights Act focused on discrimination with respect to race, color, religion, and national origin. But in 1972, the following was added: "No person in the United States shall, on the basis of sex, be excluded from participation in, be denied the benefits of, or be subjected to discrimination under any educational program or activity receiving federal financial assistance."[3]

Although Title IX does not explicitly mention sports, its impact on sports is clear. Zimbalist (2001)[4] noted that female participation in sports changed dramatically after the amendment was signed into law by President Richard Nixon. In 1971, 294,015 girls participated in high school sports. In 1973, this number

---

[1]R. Vivian Acosta and Linda J. Carpenter, "Women in Intercollegiate Sport: A Longitudinal, National Study, Thirty-Seven-Year Update, 1977–2014." Unpublished manuscript, 2014. Available at http://www.acostacarpenter.org.

[2]Acosta and Carpenter (2014).

[3]A discussion of the Civil Rights Act of 1964 and the specifics of Title IX can be found in Susan L. Averett and Sarah M. Estelle, "The Economics of Title IX Compliance in Intercollegiate Athletics, in Eva Marikova Leeds and Michael Leeds (eds.), *Handbook on the Economics of Women in Sports* (Cheltenham, UK: Edward Elgar, 2013).

[4]Andrew Zimbalist, *Unpaid Professionals* (Princeton, NJ: Princeton University Press, 2001).

increased to 817,073; by 1978, it was 2.08 million. Zimbalist (2001) observed a similar pattern at the college level. In 1971, only 31,852 women played college sports. By 1977, that number increased by more than 100% to 64,375.

The story of Title IX indicates that it takes more than market forces to explain women's sports. What appears to matter is the existence of opportunity. A brief story from the history of soccer further illustrates this point.[5] There is evidence that women were playing soccer in the 19th century. In 1881, the *Glasgow Herald* reported on a match between teams of women from Scotland and England. In 1895, the British Ladies' Football Club (soccer club) was founded.

During World War I, women's soccer in England took off. And the popularity of women's soccer didn't end when the war concluded in 1918. In 1920, 53,000 fans turned up to watch a women's soccer match (with another 14,000 reportedly turned away). Such demand exceeded what was typical for men's soccer at the time.

Although market forces seemed to indicate that women's soccer was economically viable, opportunity for this sport to grow was soon eliminated by non-market forces. In December 1921, the English Football Association (FA) declared that football was "quite unsuitable for women and not to be encouraged." Coaches and referees were told they would lose their licenses if women's games were allowed on men's fields. Yes, women's soccer was banned. And that ban stayed in place in England until 1972.[6]

The story of Title IX illustrates how government can create opportunity. And the actions of the English FA in 1921 illustrate how a governing body can take away that opportunity. Both stories highlight that we need to do more than just appeal to "market forces" in explaining why something does or does not happen.

8.1 The Lesson Learned — and Not Learned — from Demand Data

In 2016, the average WNBA team saw 7,655 fans at each game.[7] Meanwhile, the average National Basketball Association (NBA) team in 2015–16 managed to attract 17,864 fans.[8] The market has thus spoken. Women's professional basketball is not as popular as men's professional basketball.

---

[5]Amanda Coletta, "A League of Their Own: The Most Dominant Soccer Team in 1920 Was Full of Female Factory Workers," *The New York Times*, June 5, 2015, http://nytlive.nytimes .com/womenintheworld/2015/06/05/a-league-of-their-own-the-most-dominant-soccer-team- in-1920-was-full-of-female-factory-workers/.

[6]Coletta (2015).

[7]http://www.wnba.com/news/record-breaking-attendance-five-years-digital-social-retail/.

[8]http://www.insidehoops.com/attendance.shtml.

Once again, we need to work a little bit harder to draw a conclusion. Let's start with a bit of history. The WNBA was founded in 1997. With the conclusion of the 2016 season, the league has only existed for 20 years. The NBA began as the Basketball Association of America (BAA) in 1946–47.[9] The league's 20th season occurred in 1965–66. That season the Boston Celtics, led by the league's most valuable player (MVP) Bill Russell, won the NBA title. Wilt Chamberlain led the league in points, rebounds, and field goal percentage. NBA fans also were able to witness the talents of All-NBA players like Oscar Robertson, Jerry West, and Rick Barry. Despite this talent, though, the average team only drew 6,019 fans per game.[10]

To illustrate the popularity of the NBA around this time, in March 1962, Chamberlain scored 100 points in a game for the Philadelphia Warriors. This is a mark that has never been matched in NBA history. It was also a game that few people saw. The game took place in Hershey, Pennsylvania, nearly 100 miles outside of Philadelphia. The reported attendance was only 4,124.[11]

The NBA's lack of popularity early in its history was not unusual. In baseball, the National League (NL) came into existence in 1876. In 1895, the average team only drew 3,690 fans per game.[12] Six years later, the American League (AL) started to play. Twenty years into its history, the average AL team attracted 7,968 fans per game.[13] A similar story can be told about the National Football League (NFL). In 1941, the average NFL team played before 20,157 fans, about 30% of the gate an average NFL team sees today.[14]

Early in a league's history, attendance appears to be relatively low. Attendance is clearly not a function of only one factor.[15] But one factor that does seem important early on is familiarity—how familiar the media and fans are with the teams and players in a league. Neale (1964)[16] referred to this as the "fourth

---

[9]The NBA considers 1946 the year the league began. To illustrate, the 50th anniversary team was named in 1996. And three NBA franchises—the Knicks, Celtics, and Warriors—formed in the BAA in 1946.

[10]http://www.apbr.org/attendance.html.

[11]http://www.nytimes.com/packages/html/sports/year_in_sports/03.02.html.

[12]http://www.baseballchronology.com/Baseball/Years/1895/Attendance.asp.

[13]http://www.ballparksofbaseball.com/1920-29attendance.htm.

[14]https://sports.vice.com/en_us/article/how-the-wnba-compares-to-other-sports-leagues-at-age-20.

[15]Other issues we would consider is that population and incomes were lower in the past. That would depress attendance. Of course, there are many more entertainment options that would depress attendance today. And there is the possibility that women sports, in general, face customer discrimination. That being said, the history of sports suggests attendance in the early years of a league tends to be lower than what we see in later years.

[16]Walter Neale, "The Peculiar Economics of Professional Sports," *Quarterly Journal of Economics* 78, no. 1 (1964): 1–14.

estate benefit." Neale noted that one product of a sports league is coverage by the media. This essentially amounts to free advertising for the league.

Early in a league's history, however, such coverage might be relatively scarce. Consider once again Wilt Chamberlain's 100-point game. There was no television broadcast of this game. And after the game, media coverage was less than impressive. *Sports Illustrated* reported the story in one paragraph on page 67 of the magazine. Daily newspapers did not see this as a front-page story.[17]

Again, at the time, the NBA—despite having existed for 18 years—was not considered a major sport by the media. Unfortunately, the media tends to have the same attitude toward all of women's sports today. Cooky, Messner, and Musto (2015)[18] reviewed how much time the sports media spends examining women's sports. As Table 8.1 illustrates, historically, women's sports have received very little coverage. Local network coverage in Los Angeles, via KCBS, KNBC, and KABC, devoted only 5% of its sports coverage to women's sports in 1989. That percentage increased to 8.7% 10 years later. But after that, coverage of women's sports declined, so in 2014 there was even less coverage of women's sports than 25 years earlier.

Table 8.1 Coverage of Men and Women's Sports by KCBS, KNBC, and KABC: 1989–2014[19]

Year	Men	Women	Neutral
1989	92.0%	5.0%	3.0%
1993	93.8%	5.1%	1.1%
1999	88.2%	8.7%	3.1%
2004	91.4%	6.3%	2.4%
2009	96.3%	1.6%	2.1%
2014	94.4%	3.2%	2.4%

Cooky *et al.* (2015) tell a similar story for ESPN Sportscenter in 2014. That year, only 2% of ESPN's coverage was devoted to women's sports.

Perhaps such coverage simply reflects overall interest in women's sports. But first, we need to understand that most sports coverage is done by men. The Women's Media Center reported that, in 2015, only about 10% of sports reporters were women.[20]

---

[17]http://www.businessinsider.com/photos-in-1962-the-media-barely-noticed-that-wilt-chamberlain-scored-100-points-2012-3?op=1.

[18]Cheryl Cooky, Michael A. Messner and Michela Musto, "'It's Dude Time!' A Quarter Century of Excluding Women's Sports in Televised News and Highlight Shows," *Communication & Sport*, 2015, pp. 1–27.

[19]Cooky *et al.* (2015. p. 6).

[20]See Women's Media Center, "The Status of Women in the U.S. Media 2015," 2015, http://wmc.3cdn.net/83bf6082a319460eb1_hsrm680x2.pdf.

This percentage does not reflect the interest women have in sports. A 2015 Gallup poll indicated that 59% of adults consider themselves sports fans. Broken down by gender, 66% of men and 51% of women describe themselves as fans of sport.[21] This means that about 43% of the population of sports fans are women. Nevertheless, 90% of those reporting on sports for the media are men.[22]

Maybe all those men are actually reporting on women's sports as the market suggests they should. Unfortunately, the stories behind the sales of sponsorships and television rights suggest that the market doesn't always reflect values perfectly consistent with the data.

The 2015 Women's World Cup Final between the United States and Japan attracted 25.4 million viewers on Fox Television. An additional 1.3 million viewers watched the game in Spanish on Telemundo.[23] The audience of 26.7 million viewers was larger than for any soccer match in U.S. history. The match attracted more viewers than those who had tuned in to see:

- (in the United States) the 2014 Men's World Cup Final between Germany and Argentina[24]

- Game 7 of the 2014 World Series between the Kansas City Royals and San Francisco Giants[25]

- the decisive Game 6 of the 2015 NBA Finals between the Golden State Warriors and Cleveland Cavaliers[26]

Despite the spectacular ratings, sponsorships for the broadcast of the Women's World Cup seemed to be immensely undervalued. Whereas the Men's World Cup brought in $529 million for ESPN in 2014, Fox was only paid a reported $17 million for the broadcast of the Women's World Cup in 2015.[27]

---

[21]http://www.gallup.com/poll/183689/industry-grows-percentage-sports-fans-steady.aspx.

[22]The population of reporters is not the only issue. In 2016, Alison Overholt became the editor-in-chief of *ESPN The Magazine*. This was the first time a woman had been named editor of a major U.S. sports magazine. And yes, that means all the other editors of major sports magazines are men.

[23]http://www.nytimes.com/2015/07/07/sports/soccer/womens-world-cup-final-was-most-watched-soccer-game-in-united-states-history.html?_r=1.

[24]http://www.nytimes.com/2015/07/07/sports/soccer/womens-world-cup-final-was-most-watched-soccer-game-in-united-states-history.html?_r=1.

[25]http://www.nytimes.com/2015/07/07/sports/soccer/womens-world-cup-final-was-most-watched-soccer-game-in-united-states-history.html?_r=1.

[26]http://www.npr.org/sections/thetwo-way/2015/07/06/420514899/what-people-are-saying-about-the-u-s-women-s-world-cup-win.

[27]http://www.bloombergview.com/articles/2015-11-06/a-free-market-in-soccer-would-pay-women-more.

This disparity in sponsorship revenue does not seem consistent with the actual number of viewers. How is this possible?

Sponsorship deals are made in advance of a broadcast and are based on forecasts made by those involved in the transaction. As Mike Mulvihill, a senior vice president for Fox Sports, noted after the 2015 Women's World Cup: "No question, I underestimated where this would be. It's one of the most pleasant surprises we've ever had."[28]

The undervaluation of women's sports does not just concern soccer. We see a similar story with respect to the WNBA. In 2013, the average WNBA broadcast attracted 231,000 viewers on ESPN and ESPN2. Meanwhile, the average Major League Soccer (MLS) broadcast — on the same networks — attracted 220,000 viewers. Such numbers would suggest the WNBA was the better investment. But the WNBA television deal with ESPN, signed in 2012, only pays the league $12 million per season. In contrast, in 2014, ESPN paid MLS $75 million per year to broadcast its games and Univision agreed to pay another $15 million.[29]

Can anything be done to change how the media covers sports? Back in 2013, only 7% of the sports media coverage in France was devoted to women's sports.[30] At that time, Valerie Fourneyron, the French minister of sport, decided to allocate 1 million euros per year to help media outlets increase their coverage of women's sports. The government also mandated a day every year on which the sports media in France would exclusively focus on women's sports. Three years after these efforts, the coverage of women's sports in France has increased from 7% to 15%. This still does not reflect equality, but demonstrates substantial progress in a short period of time.

It is easy to look at attendance numbers and broadcasting deals and argue that those statistics simply reflect the market. But both history and perceptions of gender in sports drive the numbers we see.[31] And those numbers can be changed — for the better and worse — by non-market forces.

[28]http://www.nytimes.com/2015/07/07/sports/soccer/womens-world-cup-final-was-most-watched-soccer-game-in-united-states-history.html?_r=1.

[29]http://www.bloombergview.com/articles/2015-11-06/a-free-market-in-soccer-would-pay-women-more.

[30]http://www.sbs.com.au/topics/zela/article/2016/06/15/french-media-coverage-womens-sport-cause-celebre.

[31]Not only are women's sports able to attract audiences that rival what we see for men's sports, women are increasingly the fans watching men's sports. It is reported that of the NFL's 150 million fans, 45% are women. So women are not just supplying sports content, women are also often the consumers of this content (https://www.washingtonpost.com/business/economy/women-are-pro-footballs-most-important-market-will-they-forgive-the-nfl/2014/09/12/d5ba8874-3a7f-11e4-9c9f-ebb47272e40e_story.html).

8.2 The Gender Wage Gap in the WNBA

Francine Blau and Lawrence Kahn note that in 2014, women who worked full-time earned—on an annual basis—about 79% of what men earned.[32] There thus appears to be a gender-based wage gap in the U.S. economy.

In sports, we tend to see the same story repeat itself. The one clear exception is tennis. In tennis, women and men who win one of the four major[33] championships are awarded the same prize money.[34] The person responsible for making this happen was Billie Jean King. In 1972, King won the U.S. Open Women's Singles title and did not receive the same prize money as Ilie Năstase (who secured the Men's Singles title). King responded by informing the U.S. Open that she would not play in 1973 if the prize money was not equal. The U.S. Open consequently opted to make the prizes equal, a practice eventually followed by other major sports.

Two things should be noted about the process by which the gender wage gap was closed in tennis. First, women's and men's tennis are not that different in terms of popularity. A recent Harris poll revealed that women's tennis fans outnumber men's tennis fans.[35] And perhaps to illustrate this point, *Sports Illustrated* named Serena Williams its Sportsperson of the Year in 2015.

But beyond the popularity of women's tennis, we need to emphasize what Billie Jean King did in 1972. King didn't just ask for equal wages. King announced she would stop playing until it happened. In essence, King threatened to go on strike to change the labor market outcome. As noted in our discussion of labor economics, until baseball players unionized and threatened to strike, the labor market in that sport also didn't change.

The power labor has to withhold its services can be illustrated by the outcomes observed when this doesn't happen. Professional basketball has a sizable gender wage gap. The average NBA player in 2014–15 was paid

---

[32]Francine Blau and Lawrence Kahn, "The Gender Wage Gap: Extent, Trends, and Explanation," IZA Discussion Paper no. 956, January 2016. Paper to be published in the *Journal of Economic Perspectives*. It is important to note that this statistic does not mean that in every job women are paid 79% of what men make. And gender discrimination—although clearly part of the story—does not explain the entire difference. As Blau and Kahn (2016) indicated, approximately 38% of the gap may be attributed to discrimination.

[33]The four majors are the Australian Open, the French Open, Wimbledon, and the U.S. Open.

[34]This is not true in the non majors. In non majors, men and women are not always paid the same.

[35]http://espn.go.com/nba/story/_/id/14470482/michael-jordan-jordan-stays-atop-harris-poll-ahead-babe-ruth-muhamad-ali.

4.45 million.[36] In contrast, the average WNBA player was paid $75,000.[37] So these numbers suggest that women earned 1.7% of what men were paid to play professional basketball.

Obviously, such a comparison is misleading. There is a significant revenue gap between the NBA and WNBA. According to Forbes.com, in 2013–14, the NBA netted $4.7 billion in revenue.[38] Forbes.com does not report similar data for the WNBA, but Harris and Berri (2016)[39] offers an estimate of revenues from other sources. For example, we have already noted that the WNBA has a television contract that pays it $12 million per season.[40] We also know average attendance in 2014 was 7,578 per game[41] and that the average ticket price is at least $15.[42] With 204 home games, gate revenue for the 2014 season was at least $23.2 million. Of course, there are other sources of revenue (merchandise, sponsorships, playoff ticket sales, etc.). But we can estimate that WNBA revenues, as Table 8.2 details, were a minimum of $35 million in 2014.

Table 8.2 Estimate of Women's National Basketball Association Revenues: 2014[43]	
Revenue Factors	Revenue
Television revenue	$12,000,000
Average attendance	7,578
Average ticket price	$15
Gate revenue per game	$113,670
Total gate revenue for 204 regular-season games	$23,188,680
Total revenue	$35,188,680

[36]According to basketball-reference.com, total team payroll in 2014–15 was $2,190,680. There were 492 players logging minutes that season, so the average salary was $4,554,603.

[37]http://sportsday.dallasnews.com/dallas-mavericks/mavericksheadlines/2015/07/26/sefko-why-wnba-has-never-been-stronger-as-league-enters-dallas-market.

[38]http://www.forbes.com/nba-valuations/list/.

[39]Jill Harris and David Berri, "If You Can't Pay Them, Play Them: Fan Preference and Own-Race Bias in the WNBA," *International Journal of Sport Finance* 11 (August 2016): 163–180.

[40]http://www.sportsbusinessdaily.com/Daily/Issues/2013/03/28/Media/WNBA.aspx.

[41]http://www.sportsbusinessdaily.com/Journal/Issues/2015/09/21/Leagues-and-Governing-Bodies/WNBA.aspx.

[42]This was reported for 2011 in David J. Berri and Anthony Krautmann, "Understanding the WNBA On and Off the Court," in Eva Marikova Leeds and Michael Leeds (eds.), *Handbook on the Economics of Women in Sports* (Northampton, MA: Edward Elgar, 2013), pp. 132–155.

[43]Table originally appeared in Harris and Berri (2014, p. 249).

We have noted that the average salary in the WNBA is $75,000. There were 154 women who logged minutes in the league in 2014. So the WNBA paid $11,550,000 to its players in 2015. This means that the television deal was enough to pay every single WNBA player.

The NBA pays 50% of its revenue to its players. The above analysis, which underestimates league revenue, says the WNBA only pays 32.8% of its revenue to its players. And that means, WNBA players are only receiving about 70% of what NBA players would be paid.

There is additional evidence that the women in the WNBA are underpaid. The WNBA reports that in 2014, 101 women in the league supplemented their income by playing in women's basketball leagues in other countries.[44] The wages paid to the WNBA stars to play in these other leagues often dwarf what the WNBA offers. For example, Brittney Griner was paid $600,000 to play in the Women's Chinese Basketball Association in 2014. It was also reported that both Sylvia Fowles and Maya Moore were paid at least $600,000 to play in the same league.[45] Meanwhile, Diana Taurasi was paid $1.5 million by a team in the Russian Premier League and an additional sum—enough to at least cover her WNBA salary—to sit out the 2015 WNBA season.[46] Yes, Taurasi was paid to *not* play in the WNBA.

The Taurasi story suggests salaries in the WNBA are too low. And it doesn't appear that this will change soon. The current labor agreement between the WNBA and its players calls for a $121,500 cap on the maximum salary in the league in 2021.[47] What would that number be if the stars of the WNBA were paid like those of the NBA?

Again, the NBA pays 50% of its salaries to its players. Let's imagine that is the only restriction facing WNBA players. And let's argue that players are paid only for wins.

In 2015, league MVP, Elena Delle Donne, produced 8.3 wins for the Chicago Sky.[48] This mark led the league and represented 4.1% of all wins in

[44]http://www.wnba.com/archive/wnba/news/2014_overseas.html.

[45]http://www.businessinsider.com/brittney-griner-basketball-china-2014-4.

[46]http://espn.go.com/wnba/story/_/id/12272036/diana-taurasi-decision-sit-spark-wnba-salary-changes.

[47]The current maximum salary is $107,500 (https://sports.vice.com/en_us/article/basketballs-gender-wage-gap-is-even-worse-than-you-think). For the future value, see http://wnbpa-uploads.s3.amazonaws.com/docs/WNBA%20CBA%202014-2021Final.pdf.

[48]The calculation of Wins Produced follows the method described in Berri and Krautmann (2013), which followed earlier work reported in David J. Berri and Martin B. Schmidt, *Stumbling on Wins: Two Economists Explore the Pitfalls on the Road to Victory in Professional Sports* (Princeton, NJ: Financial Times Press, 2010), and David J. Berri, "A Simple Measure of Worker Productivity in the National Basketball Association," in, Brad Humphreys and Dennis Howard (eds.), *The Business of Sport*, 3 vols. (Westport, CT: Praeger, 2008), pp. 1–40.

2015. Following the same approach documented in Table 8.1, one can estimate league revenues in 2015 at $34.4 million.[49] If the players were paid 50% of the $34.4 million in league revenue, then Delle Donne was worth $700,754 in 2015, or nearly seven times the league's salary cap.

The NBA also has a cap on individual salaries. It stipulates that a player with less than seven years of experience can only be paid 25% of the league's cap.[50] Given a league payroll cap of $17.2 million going to players, each of the 12 teams could only pay $1,433,045 to its members. And 25% of that is $358,261. This number is about half of what we cited above, but still more than three times the salary Delle Donne was, in fact, paid in 2015.

Why are WNBA players paid so little? One issue may be that even though the WNBA has a union, it has never come close to threatening a strike. Again, the history of labor relations in sports suggests that outcomes improve for labor once labor is able to credibly threaten to withhold its services.

Two recent examples highlight the power of threatening to withhold labor. In 2015, the women's national soccer team in Australia, the Matildas, had advanced further in the World Cup than any of the men's teams in that nation's history. Despite their success, however, the Matildas were only paid $500 (Australian dollars) in match fees, while members of the men's soccer team received $7,500 (Australian dollars). The disparities in pay and financial support led the players on this team to skip a tour of the United States after the World Cup.[51] As a result of this strike, the members of the Australian women's soccer team did see their pay increase.[52]

A similar story took place with respect to the United States Women's National Hockey Team. In 2005, this team won its first gold medal in the International Hockey Federation Women's World Championship. This team then proceeded to win the gold medal again in 2008, 2009, 2011, 2013, and 2015.[53] Despite this success, the women who competed on these hockey teams were not well compensated. The women of the national team were only paid $6,000 every

---

[49]Television revenue was still $12 million in 2015. Average attendance was 7,318. If the average ticket price was still $15, then gate revenue was $22,393,080. And that means league revenue was $34,393,080.

[50]http://www.cbafaq.com/salarycap.htm#Q18.

[51]http://thinkprogress.org/sports/2015/09/10/3699819/heres-why-the-australian-womens-soccer-team-is-on-strike/.

[52]http://www.smh.com.au/sport/soccer/matildas-strike-vindicated-by-pay-increase-says-midfielder-hayley-raso-20151109-gkucdk.html.

[53]All-time tournament results can be found here: http://www.usawomenshockey.com/page/show/1429977-year-by-year-results

four years by USA Hockey.[54] Essentially, they received a small stipend to train for the Olympics. But they were asked to compete in tournaments outside the Olympics. And for those there was no compensation.

Prior to the 2017 World Championship, though, the women threatened to go on strike. USA Hockey responded by first trying to find replacement players.[55] But when this approach failed, USA Hockey turned to negotiations. In the end, the deal struck dramatically changed wages for these women. According to an ESPN.com report, annual pay for the women on the national team was increased to approximately $70,000.[56] So over a four year period, a woman on this team would receive about $280,000, or a 4,667% increase in pay.

Increasing athlete pay was not the only result of this strike. But the dramatic change in pay alone highlights the power of the labor strike. As we have noted, fans and the sports media frequently condemn labor disputes. However without such disputes, we often see inferior labor market outcomes for athletes in professional sports.

8.3 The Highest-Paid Women in Professional Team Sports in North America

We have seen that WNBA stars can command much higher wages outside of North America. Consequently, WNBA stars are not the highest-paid women in professional team sports in North America. That honor currently goes to Monica Abbott, a pitcher in the National Pro Fastpitch (NPF) league. In 2016, she agreed to a six-year contract with the Scrap Yard Dawgs (an NPF expansion team) worth $1 million.[57]

Why was Abbott paid so well? To begin with, she may be the greatest pitcher in NPF history. As the discussion of how to measure an NPF pitcher's performance indicates, Abbott—along with Cat Osterman and Jennie Finch—ranks

---

[54]see http://www.espn.com/espnw/voices/article/18908360/time-usa-hockey-wake-support-women-team

[55]http://www.espn.com/espnw/sports/article/19004695/usa-hockey-reaches-d-iii-players-rec-league-players-potential-replacements

[56]http://www.espn.com/olympics/story/_/id/19026627/usa-hockey-us-women-national-team-reach-agreement-avoid-boycott

[57]Abbott's contract calls for her to receive a base salary of $20,000 per year, with attendance bonuses adding $880,000 to her total six-year contract (http://espn.go.com/espnw/sports/article/15464430/pitcher-monica-abbott-signs-1-million-contract-national-pro-fastpitch-expansion-team).

among the top three pitchers in league history. But Abbott's pay is not just a function of her skill. After all, Delle Donne and the other stars of the WNBA are also amazingly skilled basketball players. There also seems to be an issue with the market for Abbott's services.

First of all, Abbott was a free agent when she negotiated this contract. According to the NPF website, "Players who are not currently under contract and have not been drafted are considered free agents. . . ."[58] Abbott's contract had expired with the Chicago Bandits (her 2015 team), so she was free to sign with the Scrap Yard Dawgs.

But why was this team willing to pay so much to sign her? A few factors were cited at the time of signing. The owner of the Scrap Yard Dawgs, Connie May, noted that the team was an expansion team and they wished to sign a player who would bring them immediate publicity. In other words, the Scrap Yard Dawgs had significant demand at this time for a star to give the team some needed media attention. There was also the issue of Abbott's other employment choices. The average college graduate has a starting salary of $50,000.[59] According to the NPF website, the average salary in the league is only $5,000 to $6,000. Since players are typically college graduates, they often leave the NPF to accept jobs outside of professional athletics. In addition, many NPF players play professionally in Japan, where they make more money than the NPF can offer. In sum, Abbott had other opportunities that would pay her more.

Abbott—as the discussion of measuring pitching performance illustrated—is also a unique talent. Only Cat Osterman and Jennie Finich rival Abbott's skill, and those players have retired. As Connie May noted: "We don't have another Monica, Cat Osterman or Jennie Finch coming up in the foreseeable future. So if we miss this opportunity, then it's on us."[60] Abbott can thus command a million dollar salary, while other NPF talents are paid considerably less.

The story of Abbott's contract highlights the importance of bargaining power in setting wages. On the demand side, the Scrap Yard Dawgs needed a major talent to attract publicity. The talent they wanted had other options and was unique in the market. All this shifted bargaining power to Abbott and allowed her to command a wage well beyond what other women in professional team sports in North America can.

---

[58]http://www.profastpitch.com/home/.

[59]http://time.com/money/3829776/heres-what-the-average-grad-makes-right-out-of-college/.

[60]http://www.foxsports.com/mlb/story/monica-abbott-million-dollar-deal-softball-landmark-womens-sports-050516.

History of the NPF

The 2015 Women's College World Series (WCWS) attracted 31% more television viewers than the Men's College World Series, with 1,196,000 average viewers.[61] Despite the relatively greater popularity of the WCWS, its participants who become professional softball players do not tend to experience the same outcome as the men who eventually sign on as Major League Baseball (MLB) players. As noted in previous chapters, MLB has existed for well over a century and, in 2015, more than 73 million fans attended MLB games. In addition, MLB games are broadcast on ESPN, Fox, and TBS. So although fewer fans see the men who play college baseball, many will watch the few college baseball players who eventually make a major league roster.

In contrast, women who become professional softball players in the United States graduate to the NPF league, which has been around since 2004. Like most new sports leagues, teams have entered, exited, and/or relocated. In all, 14 different franchises have played in the league, with no more than 7 playing in a given season. In 2015, those teams were the Akron Racers, Chicago Bandits, Dallas Charge, Pennsylvania Rebellion, and USSSA Pride (with their home field in Kissimmee, Florida). In 2016, the Scrap Yard Dawgs were added (with their home field in The Woodlands, Texas, just north of Houston). Of these teams, only Akron has existed since 2004. Chicago entered the league in 2005, while USSSA Pride began play in 2009. The remaining franchises all started in the last three seasons.

According to the league website, the league attracts between 1,500 and 2,500 fans per game.[62] In 2015, the 5-team league played a 48-game schedule, or had 120 home games. That means in 2015, the league attracted 240,000 fans for the entire season, or the approximate number of spectators a MLB team draws in about 8 games.

Of course, we need to put those attendance numbers in proper perspective. The NPF began its 13th season in 2016. In 1890, the NL was in its 15th season. That year, the league attracted 776,042 fans to the ballpark. With 8 teams and 66 home games per squad, the league averaged 1,469 fans per contest,[63] similar numbers to what the NPF draws today.

One should note that comparing attendance in 1890 in the NL to what we see today in the NPF is problematic. As noted earlier in this chapter, populations in the past were much smaller. But also we noted, there are now far more entertainment

---

[61]https://nfca.org/index.php?option=com_content&view=article&id=6281:record-viewership-at-the-2015-women-s-college-world-series&catId=109&Itemid=149.

[62]http://www.profastpitch.com/about/faqs/.

[63]http://www.ballparksofbaseball.com/1890-99attendance.htm.

options. So there are forces today that would make attendance larger (i.e. more population) and smaller (i.e. more entertainment options). The point made with this comparison is to highlight again how few people attended what we consider the major professional sports leagues when these leagues were in their first few decades of existence. The poor attendance we saw in the past in men's professional sports highlights how long it takes to build demand in a professional sports league.

Evaluating Pitchers in the NPF

There is a sense that when it comes to player statistics, baseball's numbers are the best at evaluating the performance of individual players. Although this might be argued for hitters in baseball,[64] it certainly can't be argued for pitchers. The standard metric for pitchers is earned run average (ERA). But as McCracken (2001) argued[65] — and as we noted in Chapter 6 — pitchers and the defensive players often work together to get the opponent out. As McCracken noted, ERA is a poor measure of a pitcher's performance.

A better approach is to focus on defensive independent statistics like walks, strikeouts, home runs, and hit batsmen. In other words, we should ignore statistics attributed to pitchers who partially depend on the actions of others. Obviously, this list begins with wins and losses since pitchers cannot win or lose a game by themselves. But it also includes hits allowed, sacrifice hits, sacrifice flies, and earned runs. All these partially depend on the action of fielders.

McCracken illustrated the issue by noting the consistency of a pitcher's performance with respect to these statistics. Bradbury (2007a)[66] highlighted McCracken's point by looking at the year-to-year correlation for major league hitters for strikeouts, walks, hit-by-pitch, home runs, ERA, and batting average allowed on balls in play (BABIP).[67] Bradbury (2007a) reported the following correlations:

- Strikeouts: 0.78

- Walks: 0.64

- Hit-by-pitch: 0.51

---

[64]Berri and Schmidt (2010) note problems with this argument for hitters.

[65]Voros McCracken, "Pitching and Defense: How Much Control Do Hurlers Have," January 23, 2001, http://www.baseballprospectus.com/article.php?articleid=878.

[66]J. C. Bradbury, "Does the Baseball Labor Market Properly Value Pitchers?," *Journal of Sports Economics* 8, no. 6 (2007a): 616–632.

[67]BABIP = (Hits – Home Runs) / (At Bats – Strikeouts – Home Runs + Sacrifice Flies). This simply measures how often batted balls that are not home runs actually become hits (http://www.fangraphs.com/library/pitching/babip/).

- Home runs: 0.47

- ERA: 0.35

- BABIP: 0.25

As McCracken noted, the factors that are independent of the defense around the pitcher are more consistent than those that rely partially on the performance of a team's defense.

This led McCracken to develop the defense independent pitching statistics earned run average (DIPS ERA) or what *Baseball Prospectus* refers to as fielding independent pitching (FIP).[68] Bradbury (2007b) presented the basic methodology.[69] A pitcher's ERA is regressed on the FIP factors (strikeouts, walks, hit-by-pitch, home runs) and BABIP.[70] And the results create a more stable measure of a pitcher's performance.[71]

This basic idea has been used to create a FIP measure for the NPF. The data employed included all pitchers in the NPF who pitched at least 50 innings from 2004 to 2016. The model involved regressing each pitcher's ERA on the defensive independent statistics (again, strikeouts, walks, hit-by-pitch, and home runs) and a defensive dependent measure (hits per ball in play or HperBIP).[72] The results, reported in Appendix A of this chapter, indicate that 89% of the variation in a pitcher's ERA may be explained by these factors.

To construct a FIP ERA measure for pitchers, we first multiply each player's defensive independent statistic by the corresponding coefficient. We then use the average value for HperBIP in the sample to construct each player's FIP ERA.

An example will help illustrate the process. The following table reports Monica Abbott's defensive independent statistics for 2016. In addition, the estimated coefficient from our model is reported.

---

[68]See http://www.baseballprospectus.com/glossary/index.php?search=FIP. As acronyms go, FIP sounds much better than DIPS. So, as we noted in Chapter Six, we will follow the lead of *Baseball Prospectus* and call this FIP.

[69]J. C. Bradbury, *The Baseball Economist: The Real Game Exposed* (New York: Dutton, 2007b).

[70]Bradbury (2007b) also controlled for age of the pitcher, league of the pitcher, and season played. His model explains 77% of the variation in a pitcher's ERA.

[71]In *Hot Stove Economics: Understanding Baseball's Second Season* (New York: Copernicus, 2010), Bradbury notes in a different study of pitchers that ERA has a 0.30 year-to-year correlation, while DIPS ERA has a 0.54 year-to-year correlation.

[72]BABIP, which Bradbury used, requires sacrifice flies. We do not have sacrifice flies for every year in the NPF. Consequently, we turn to HperBIP, or [Hits − Home Runs]/[Outs + Hits − Strikeouts − Home Runs]. This metric was originally used by McCracken; see http://sabr.org/research/many-flavors-dips-history-and-overview. Additionally, the model included team-specific fixed effects.

To calculate FIP ERA, we multiply the pitcher's statistic by the corresponding coefficient. We next sum the values. And then we add to this sum both the constant term and the impact of the HperBIP (i.e., the league average for HperBIP multiplied by its corresponding coefficient). The result is the pitcher's FIP ERA.

Defensive Independent Statistics	Value for Monica Abbott, 2016	Estimated Coefficient	Column 2 × Column 3
Strikeouts per 7 innings pitched	9.077	−0.123	−1.118
Walks per 7 innings pitched	1.619	0.195	0.315
Hit-by-pitch per 7 innings pitched	0.442	0.478	0.211
Home runs per 7 innings pitched	0.343	1.623	0.558
Defensive Dependent Statistics	NPF League Value		
NFP average hits per ball in play (per 7 innings pitched)	0.271	12.729	3.453
		Constant	−1.916
		FIP ERA	1.502
		Actual ERA	0.981

As one can see, Abbott's actual ERA in 2016 was 0.981, a mark that led the league. Her FIP ERA was a bit higher, but her mark of 1.502 also led the league.

To put Abbott's mark in perspective, the average ERA across the entire sample was 2.55. The average FIP ERA is also 2.55. Thus, Abbott in 2016 was much better than average. But as **Table 8.3** indicates, it was not her best mark or even among the top 10 marks in league history. Topping this list was Jennie Finch in 2007, who had a 0.105 ERA and a 0.302 FIP ERA. Both marks are the best measures — among pitchers with 50 innings pitched — in league history.

How good was Finch? Although her 2007 FIP ERA set the league record, her career FIP ERA was only 1.51. Yes, this is amazing. But both Cat Osterman (with a career mark of 1.35) and Abbott (with a career market of 1.25) were a bit better. In sum, the trio of Finch, Osterman, and Abbott makes for the three best pitchers in league history.

Although these three were the best, it was possible for NPF hitters to actually hit off their league's pitching. The same cannot be said of MLB players. In 2003, 2004, and 2005, Finch participated in a tour where she faced such legendary hitters as Albert Pujols, Barry Bonds, and Alex Rodriguez. None of

Table 8.3 Top 10 National Pro Fastpitch Seasons, by Pitching, in League History: 2004–15				
NPF Pitcher	Year	Team	ERA	FIP ERA
Jennie Finch	2007	Chicago Bandits	0.105	0.302
Cat Osterman	2009	Rockford Thunder	0.415	0.749
Monica Abbott	2015	Chicago Bandits	0.310	0.904
Monica Abbott	2011	Chicago Bandits	0.802	0.985
Monica Abbott	2013	Chicago Bandits	0.925	1.069
Monica Abbott	2010	Tennessee Diamonds	0.789	1.166
Alicia Hollowell	2007	Akron Racers	1.194	1.188
Lauren Bay	2005	Chicago Bandits	0.883	1.189
Jamie Southern	2005	Akron Racers	0.750	1.192
Christa Williams	2005	Texas Thunder	0.756	1.194

these hitters could get a hit off of Finch's pitches. In fact, Bonds, the best hitter at the time, could only hit the ball if Finch told him exactly which pitches were coming. And by "hit," all Bonds could do was "tap a meek foul ball a few feet."[73]

The same cannot be said for the women of the NPF. Yes, Finch was dominant. But women did get actual hits—and even home runs—off of her. So when you are watching NPF softball, remember: You are seeing women do something that major league hitters cannot!

8.4 Are Men Really Better Leaders?

Women make up roughly 50% of the population. But women tend to occupy only 20% of leadership positions. Such a result may be seen across a wide variety of industries and government positions. For example,[74] in 2013, women held:

- 24.5% of leadership positions in academia
- 23.5% of leadership positions in the arts and entertainment sector

[73]http://www.si.com/more-sports/2013/07/24/sports-gene-excerpt.

[74]The following derives from "Benchmarking Women's Leadership in the United States," a report prepared by the University of Denver, Colorado Women's College, in 2013 (http://www.womenscollege.du.edu/media/documents/BenchmarkingWomensLeadershipintheUS.pdf).

* 15% of executive positions in Fortune 500 businesses

* 10% of CEO positions at the top 10 banking companies

* 23.3% of leadership positions in journalism and media

* 23% of leadership positions in law

* 25.5% of leadership positions among medical school faculty, regulatory agencies, and public and private hospitals

* 20% of all leadership positions in the technology sector

* 22.8% of all political and governmental leadership roles

* 18% of seats in Congress

These percentages are much lower in men's professional and college sports. In fact, it is extremely rare for a woman to coach a men's sports team in North America. So both within and outside of sports, men are clearly favored for leadership roles. This suggests that people believe men are better leaders. Is there any empirical evidence, though, to support such a contention?

Let's start with college coaching. A recent study indicates that there are no female coaches of any male teams in all of Division I sports.[75] In contrast, today, male coaches are quite common in women's college sports, with males holding more than 55% of head coaching jobs.[76] There thus appears to be some disparity in the market for head coaching jobs in college sports.

According to Acosta and Carpenter, after Title IX was passed in 1972, more than 90% of women's teams were coached by women. But by 1978, that percentage had fallen to 58.2%. And since then, as Table 8.4 illustrates, the percentage has gradually declined. Today, less than 44% of women's teams are coached by women.

Once again, a similar table for men's sports would reveal that women are essentially shut out from coaching men's teams. So men are perceived to be qualified to coach women, but women are not perceived to be qualified to coach men.

The sports of softball and baseball highlight this difference. Softball is played by women and baseball is played by men. According to Acosta and Carpenter, 83.5% of softball teams were coached by women in 1977. In 2014,

---

[75]Kate Fagan and Luke Cyphers, "The Glass Wall: Women Continue to Shatter Stereotypes as Athletes. So How Come They Can't Catch a Break as Coaches?," *ESPN The Magazine*, 2015, http://sports.espn.go.com/espn/eticket/story?page=theGlassWall.
[76]Acosta and Carpenter (2014).

Table 8.4	Percentage of Women Coaching National Collegiate Athletic Association Women's Teams[77]		
Year	Percentage of Women Coaching Women's Teams	Year	Percentage of Women Coaching Women's Teams
2014	43.4%	1994	49.4%
2012	42.9%	1992	48.3%
2010	42.6%	1990	47.3%
2008	42.8%	1988	48.3%
2006	42.4%	1986	50.6%
2004	44.1%	1984	53.8%
2002	44.0%	1982	52.4%
2000	45.6%	1980	54.2%
1998	47.4%	1978	58.2%
1996	47.7%	1972	90%+

this percentage had dropped to 66.3%. Meanwhile, women do not coach any NCAA baseball teams.

Given the nature of the sports, though, this pattern might seem odd. The men who coach softball did not play softball in college. Again, this is a sport played by women. And yet, men, who presumably only have a background in baseball, are considered qualified to coach women's softball. But women, who only have a background in softball, are apparently not qualified to coach baseball.

Perhaps — as the aforementioned non-sports data seem to suggest — men are just "better" leaders. To address this issue, von Allmen (2013) examined how the gender of coaches affected outcomes in college softball.[78] The specific model von Allmen employed incorporated the dependent and independent variables listed in Table 8.5 (complete details of this model are reported in Appendix A of this chapter).

The key variable in this model is the dummy variable for gender. And Table 8.6 reports the estimated link between the gender of the coach and outcomes in college softball. As noted in the table, gender is not statistically significant. So it does not appear men are better than women at coaching softball.

---

[77]Acosta and Carpenter (2014).

[78]Peter von Allmen, "Coaching Women and Women Coaching: Pay Differentials in the Title IX Era," in Eva Marikova Leeds and Michael Leeds (eds.), *Handbook on the Economics of Women in Sports* (Northampton, MA: Edward Elgar, 2013), pp. 269–289.

Table 8.5 Evaluating Gender and Coaching in College Softball

Dependent Variable	**RPI:** Rank of team according to the rating percentage index (an index that considers both winning percentage and strength of schedule)
Independent Variables	**Gender:** dummy variable for gender of coach (1 = female, 0 = male)
	ShareExp: ratio of expenditures for each program to the expenses of all programs in the sample
	PAC-10: dummy variable for teams in the PAC-10, the dominant conference in softball
	WS10: number of World Series appearances over the 10-year period, 1996–2005

Table 8.6 Link Between Gender of Coach and Results in College Softball[79]

Variable	Coefficient	Standard Error	*t*-Statistic	*p*-Value
Gender	4.14	5.17	0.80	0.425

von Allmen (2013) also looked at team outcomes given team history and expenditure. A different approach is to directly examine how a coach affects the performance of individual workers.[80]

Specifically, we will discuss what impacts the performance of a college women's basketball player. For example, ESPN's website offers an abundance of data on men's college basketball. This includes box score statistics for every single player in NCAA Division I. But ESPN.com does not provide box score statistics for individual women playing college basketball. One can find such data at stats.NCAA.org, but complete data only exists back to the 2012–13 season (data for men's college basketball players goes much further back. However, since there are more than 300 women college teams in each year, there is more than enough data to conduct a study.

The study will employ the model detailed in Table 8.7. The dependent variable is the productivity of a woman in the current season per 40 minutes. This is regressed on a collection of independent variables: year in school, games played (to control for injury), productivity of teammates, position played, team expenditures per player, and past performance. Our focus, however, is the impact

---

[79]von Allmen (2013, p. 281).

[80]This study that follows is based on the work of Lindsey Darvin, Ann Pegoraro, and David Berri, "The Head Coach Role—Is It Only a Job for Men? An investigation of Head Coach Gender and Player Performance in the WNBA and NCAA Women's Basketball," working paper, 2016 followed the approach taken by David J. Berri, Michael Leeds, Eva Marikova Leeds, and Michael Mondello in "The Role of Managers in Team Performance," *International Journal of Sport Finance* 4, no. 2 (May 2009): 75–93, which looked at how player performance is impacted by coaches in the NBA.

Table 8.7	Evaluating Gender and Coaching in National Collegiate Athletic Association Women's Basketball
Dependent Variable	P40: Wins' productivity per 40 minutes or a player's overall productivity per 40 minutes played[81]
Independent Variables	Gender: dummy variable for gender of coach (1 = female, 0 = male)
	ClassID: equal to 1 if the player is a freshman, 2 if sophomore, etc.
	GP: games played last two seasons (to control for injury)
	TMPROD: productivity of players on team
	DBIG: dummy variable equal to 1 if the player is a power forward or center
	DGUARD: dummy variable equal to 1 if the player is a point guard or shooting guard
	TOTEXPPER: total expenditure on program per player
	LagP40: player productivity the previous season

of coaches' gender. And as one can see in Table 8.8, it appears that the gender of the coach does not impact the performance of individual players.

Table 8.8	Link Between Gender of Coach and Individual Player Performance in National Collegiate Athletic Association Women's Basketball[82]		
Coefficient on Gender	Standard Error	t-Statistic	p-Value
−0.0029	0.0034	−0.88	0.38

A similar study was conducted for the WNBA,[83] which has existed since 1997. From 1997 to 2015, there have been 56 coaches who coached at least one entire season. Of these, 29 have been men and 27 women. Thus, 48% of coaches in the WNBA are women. Given the slight preference for men in the WNBA, and the overwhelming preference for men in the NBA, we again wonder if male coaches have a larger impact on individual player performance.

---

[81]This is measured following the work of Berri and Krautmann (2013).

[82]The model, based on the work of Darvin et al. (2016), employed conference fixed effects. It also only considered players who played at least 200 minutes in consecutive seasons. Overall, 3,615 observations were employed.

[83]Darvin et al. (2016).

To answer this question, the factors listed in Table 8.9 were utilized in a model designed to see if the gender of a coach impacts the productivity of individual players.

Table 8.9	Evaluating Gender and Coaching in the Women's National Basketball Association
Dependent Variable	PROD40: A player's overall productivity per 40 minutes played[84]
Independent Variables	Gender: dummy variable for gender of coach (1 = female, 0 = male)
	Age: age of the player (squared term is included because this is not expected to be a linear relationship)
	GP: games played last two seasons (to control for injury)
	TMPROD: productivity of teammates
	NewTeam: dummy variable for moving to a new team
	NewCoach: dummy variable for moving to a new coach
	DBIG: dummy variable equal to 1 if the player is a power forward or center
	DGUARD: dummy variable equal to 1 if the player is a point guard or shooting guard

To estimate the model, data for each WNBA player were collected for 19 seasons, beginning with 1997 and ending in 2015.[85] Once again, as Table 8.10 details, the story seems to be the same as we saw in the study of women's college basketball. The gender of a coach in the WNBA is not related to player performance.

Table 8.10	Link Between Gender of Coach and Individual Player Performance in the Women's National Basketball Association[86]		
Coefficient on Gender	Standard Error	t-Statistic	p-Value
−0.0031	0.0043	−0.71	0.48

[84]This is measured following the work of Berri (2008) and Berri and Schmidt (2010).

[85]Data for each player were obtained through online databases such as archived team rosters, archived player profiles, and http://www.basketball-reference.com/wnba/. The model also included player fixed effects to control for characteristics such as the quality of the player.

[86]The model, based on the work of Darvin *et al.* (2016), employed player fixed effects. It also only considered players who played at least 200 minutes in consecutive seasons. Overall, 1,620 observations were employed.

So what have we learned? The market appears to suggest that being a man is helpful. And all these results make it very clear that having a male coach does not lead to higher player productivity.

We would prefer to see a similar scenario for the NBA. But in 2015–16, only two women, Becky Hammon and Nancy Lieberman, worked as coaches in that league. And both are only assistant coaches. Once again, there has never been a woman hired as a head coach in a major North American professional sport.[87]

Women are clearly underrepresented in every sector of the economy. But women do work as leaders of Fortune 500 companies, university presidents, governors of states, members of the U.S. Congress, and heads of nations. If women can lead in all these other settings, why are sports teams not hiring them to lead?[88]

One explanation sometimes offered is that women do not respond well to pressure. A paper by Cohen-Zada *et al.* (2016) cast doubt on such an explanation.[89] These authors looked at data from the four Grand Slam tennis tournaments of 2010. With a data set consisting of 4,127 tennis games for women and 4,153 games for men, they found that men consistently perform worse as competitive pressure increases.[90] In sum, men are more likely to choke. This same result was observed even when the authors considered a variety of different empirical approaches (i.e., the evidence appears to be robust).[91]

[87]Nancy Leiberman did coach an NBA Development League team from 2009 to 2011. And Becky Hammon coached the San Antonio Spurs summer league team in the summer of 2015 and 2016. Leiberman's team made the playoffs in 2011, while Hammon's team won the Las Vegas summer league title in 2015 (http://www.newsday.com/sports/columnists/barbara-barker/mike-francesa-s-rant-about-women-coaches-reflects-stone-age-thinking-1.13209552).

[88]If you talk to women who are sports fans, they often cite a common misperception. Men frequently question whether or not women truly understand sports—an observation shared by Molly Cosby (http://www.theladiesleague.org/single-post/2016/1/25/Should-Women-Go-Through-Stricter-Security-Screenings-to-Enter-Sporting-Events). Such an explanation both (1) greatly exaggerates how complicated sports might be to understand and (2) insults women. If you are a male who resorts to it . . . you really need to stop!

[89]Danny Cohen-Zada, Alex Krumer, Mosi Rosenboim, and Offer Moshe Shapir, "Choking Under Pressure and Gender," working paper, October 2016, https://www.researchgate.net/publication/308901292_Choking_Under_Pressure_and_Gender.

[90]The authors of this study note that the tennis matches examined were not mixed. They therefore suggest it is possible their results do not extend to competitive circumstances, where both men and women are participating at the same time.

[91]The authors note there may be a biological reason for this outcome. There is a literature that suggests cortisol levels increase more rapidly for men as pressures mount. Cortisol has been found to harm a mind's critical abilities.

The study of tennis suggests that when it comes to choosing leaders, the issue isn't how men and women respond to competition. A more likely explanation is that men are favored because women face discrimination. And there is a cost to such discrimination. As we will observe in Chapter 11, although most coaches do not appear to be capable of altering player performance, some have proved able to do this. As we noted in our discussion of discrimination, a team is less likely to find the best talent if it does not consider all qualified candidates.

8.5 To Understand Gender and Sports, You Need to Look Beyond Markets

Economists tend to focus on market forces as the explanation of the outcomes observed in the economy. And sometimes that focus is correct. But our discussion of women and sports has revealed we frequently need to look beyond the market to explain what we are observing.

Nearly 100 years ago, women's soccer was a popular sport in England, attracting thousands of fans. Then the Fédération Internationale de Football Association (FIFA), an organization led by men, shut it down.[92] Decades later, it was believed women simply didn't like sports. And then Title IX was passed in the United States, forcing schools to offer sports programs to women. Suddenly, we learned women did indeed enjoy playing and watching sports.

These stories highlight how non-market forces can impact outcomes. We encountered a similar story when we turned our attention to the compensation of athletes and assignment of leadership positions. Again and again, we have to do more than say, "This is simply a reflection of supply and demand."

---

[92]Today, women do participate in FIFA. But a recent vote illustrates that men still control the organization. As Julie Foudy of ESPN.com reported, the Asian Football Confederation held a vote in May of 2017 to fill a position for a female member of the FIFA Council. Four candidates ran for the position. The person most widely considered the most qualified was Moya Dodd, a woman and former player for the Australian National Team. The woman selected was Mahfuza Akhter Kiron. 27 of the 44 voters (all male) selected a woman who later revealed she did not know who won the last Women's World Cup in soccer. If one does not know the very basic facts about the sport one is leading, one is not likely to be able to do much to reform the sport. But this is who an all-male group decided was the best woman to help lead FIFA. As Foudy argued, such a vote doesn't exactly represent the best approach to equality in soccer. http://www.espn.com/espnw/voices/article/19364609/dear-fifa-do-better-support-equal-representation

Problems

Study Questions

1. What is Title IX, and when was it enacted??

2. How has the number of girls/women playing high school/college sports changed from before the passage of Title IX to today? What role have so-called market and non-market forces played in the participation rates?

3. How popular was women's soccer in England prior to 1921? How and why did this change in 1921?

4. How is FIP ERA calculated? Why do we believe this is a better measure of a pitcher's performance?

5. How does demand for the WNBA today compare to demand for the NBA today? How does demand for the WNBA today compare to what we saw in the NBA after 20 years?

6. According to Cooky, Messner, and Musto (2015), how does coverage of women's sports compare to that of men's sports? How has this changed over time?

7. How was the gender wage gap in professional tennis overcome?

8. How does the percentage of revenue paid to WNBA players compare to what we see for the NBA? What explains the difference in the two leagues?

9. In general, what percentage of leadership positions goes to men in the economy?

10. What role does the gender of a coach play in outcomes for college softball, women's college basketball, and the WNBA? Does the evidence support the idea that men are better leaders?

11. Who is better in the "clutch," men or women? Reference the study of Grand Slam tennis in answering this question.

12. We noted in the text that attendance is relatively low early in a league's time span. Design a model to predict attendance in a league. List and explain all independent variables that you believe might explain attendance.

13. Demand for college women's sports and international competition involving women's teams seems much higher than what we for professional women's sports leagues. What might explain this difference?

Appendix 8A

Econometric Models for Women's Sports

The chapter reviewed several empirical models designed to study gender and sports.

The first was our model to estimate FIP ERA for pitchers in the NPF. Table 8A.1 presents the results of that model's estimation.

Table 8A.1 Dependent Variable as a Pitcher's ERA (minimum 50 innings pitched): 2004-16[93]			
Variable	Coefficient	t-Statistic	p-Value
Strikeouts per 7 innings pitched	−0.123	−6.30	0.000
Walks per 7 innings pitched	0.195	4.89	0.000
Hit-by-pitch per 7 innings pitched	0.478	3.82	0.000
Home runs per 7 innings pitched	1.623	14.60	0.000
Hits per ball in play (per 7 innings pitched)	12.729	12.13	0.000
Constant	−1.916	−5.62	0.000
Observations	191		
R-squared	0.87		

The second model came from the work of von Allmen (2013). This study estimated the following model:

$$RPI = a_0 + a_1 \times ShareExp + a_2 \times WS10 + a_3 \times PAC\text{-}10 + a_4 \times GENDER \qquad (8A.1)$$

where RPI = rank of team according to the rating percentage index (an index that considers both winning percentage and strength of schedule)

$ShareExp$ = ratio of expenditures of each program to the expenses of all programs in the sample

$WS10$ = number of World Series appearances over the 10-year period, 1996-2005

$PAC\text{-}10$ = dummy variable for teams in the PAC-10 (the dominant conference in softball)

$GENDER$ = dummy variable for gender of coach (1 = female, 0 = male)

The estimation of this model is reported in Table 8A.2. As one can see, the model indicates that success in softball is linked to spending and past success. Such a result is consistent with what we will note in the next chapter. Success in college sports is heavily linked to past success, since it appears a school's past success in a sport influences the choices of today's recruits.

The third and fourth model both looked at how the gender of a coach impacts the performance of an individual player. We first examined this issue with respect to women's college basketball. The specific model[94] is detailed in equation 8A.2:

$$PROD40 = b_0 + b_1 \times DGENDER + b_2 \times lagPROD40 + b_3 \times CLASS + b_4 \times GM2 + b_5 \times TOTEXPPER + e_t \qquad (8A.2)$$

---

[93]Data for this estimation derive from http://www.profastpitch.com/home/.

[94]The model detailed in equation 8A.2 is derived from Darvin et al. (2016).

Table 8A.2 Explaining Success in College Softball[95]

Variable	Coefficient	Standard Error	*t*-Statistic	*p*-Value
Constant	92.01	7.91	11.63	0.000
Gender	4.14	5.17	0.80	0.425
ShareExp	−3,933.81	650.44	−6.05	0.000
WS10	−3.11	1.58	−1.97	0.052
PAC-10	−9.56	10.78	−0.89	0.378
Adjusted *R*-Squared	**0.41**			

where $PROD40$ = player productivity, per 40 minutes

$DGENDER$ = dummy variable for gender of coach (1 = woman, 0 = man)

$lagPROD40$ = PROD40, last season

$CLASS$ = equal to 1 for freshmen, 2 for sophomore, etc.

$GM2$ = games played last two seasons (control for injury)

$TOTEXPPER$ = total expenditure per player for team[96]

The model was estimated with conference fixed effects.[97] The results are reported in **Table 8A.3.**

Table 8A.3 Explaining Individual Performance in College Women's Basketball: 2012–13 to 2014–15[98]

Independent Variables	Coefficient	Standard Error	*t*-Statistic	*p*-Value
Gender	−0.0029	0.0034	−0.88	0.38
Class	0.0041	0.0019	2.13	0.03
GP	0.0023	0.0003	7.57	0.00
TMPROD	−0.0166	0.0464	−0.36	0.72
DBig	0.0188	0.0043	4.40	0.00
DGuard	−0.0030	0.0045	−0.66	0.51

(continued)

---

[95]von Allmen (2013, p. 281).

[96]These data come from the Department of Education (http://ope.ed.gov/athletics/Index.aspx).

[97]Fixed effects are dummy variables employed in panel data. As Peter Kennedy noted: "The dummy variable coefficient reflect ignorance—they are inserted merely for the purpose of measuring shifts in the regression line arising from unknown variables" (p. 222). *A Guide to Econometrics*, 3rd ed. (Cambridge, MA: MIT Press, 1996).

[98]This model is derived from the study reported in Darvin *et al.* (2016).

Table 8A.3 *(continued)*				
Independent Variables	Coefficient	Standard Error	*t*-Statistic	*p*-Value
TotExp	2.95E-08	3.72E-08	0.79	0.43
LagProd	0.5042	0.0191	26.34	0.00
Constant	−0.0816	0.0175	−4.67	0.00
R-squared	0.25			
Adj. *R-squared*	0.24			
Observations	3,615			
Minimum minutes	200			

The model was estimated with data from the 2012–13, 2013–14, and 2014–15 seasons. Although men's college basketball data exist back to 2002–03, women's data are less plentiful. ESPN.com does not even report data from the current season. The NCAA reports women's data back to 2009–10, but the minutes data are only correct from 2012–13 to the present.[99] This thus limits the study to some extent.

Despite this issue, the model—as detailed in the chapter—did suggest that the gender of a coach is not related to player performance. It also tells a few additional stories:

- Players do improve throughout their time in school, and the more games a player participates in, the better she performs. Obviously, this latter result may also indicate that better players get more games.

- It was hypothesized that player performance could be related to spending on players. The model indicates that such is not the case. This suggests team spending does not typically alter on-court productivity. One should note that conference fixed effects are included and these are related to team spending. So that might help explain the result observed with respect to spending.

The third model detailed in the chapter looked at coaching in the WNBA. The specific model[100] designed to explain productivity per 40 minutes in the WNBA[101] is noted in equation 8A.3:

---

[99]http://stats.ncaa.org/team/inst_team_list?sport_code=WBB&division=1.

[100]This model is based on the Darvin *et al.* (2016).

[101]This is measured following the methodology detailed in Berri and Krautmann (2013) without the adjustment made for position played. In other words, this is not Wins Produced (which includes an adjustment for position played). The position adjustment is necessary if you are

$$PROD40 \equiv b_0 + b_1 \times DGENDER + b_2 \times AGE + b_3 \times SQAGE + b_4$$
$$\times\ GM2 + b_5 \times TMPROD40 + b_6 \times DNEWTEAM + b_6$$
$$=\ DNEWCOACH + b_8 \times DBIG + b_9 \times DGUARD \quad\quad (8A.3)$$

where $PROD40$ ≡ player productivity, per 40 minutes
$\quad\ DGENDER$ ≡ dummy variable for gender of coach (1 = woman, 0 = man)
$\quad\quad\quad\ AGE$ ≡ age of player
$\quad\quad\quad\ GM2$ ≡ games played last two seasons (control for injury)
$\quad TMPROD40$ ≡ teammate productivity per 40 minutes
$\ DNEWTEAM$ ≡ dummy variable for new team
$DNEWCOACH$ ≡ dummy variable for new coach
$\quad\quad\ DBIG$ ≡ dummy variable for center or power forward
$\quad\ DGUARD$ = dummy variable for point guard and shooting guard

The model was estimated with player-specific fixed effects. The results, which are for players with at least 200 minutes in the current and past season, are reported in Table 8A.4.

Table 8A.4 Explaining Individual Performance in the Women's National Basketball Association: 1998–2015[102]				
Independent Variables	Coefficient	Standard Error	t-Statistic	p-Value
Gender	−0.0031	0.0043	−0.71	0.48
Age	0.0129	0.0071	1.82	0.07
Age, Sq.	−0.0003	0.0001	−2.12	0.03
GM2	0.0011	0.0004	2.97	0.00
TMPROD	−0.0941	0.0682	−1.38	0.17
DNewTeam	0.0033	0.0053	0.62	0.53
DNewCoach	−0.0141	0.0045	−3.11	0.00
DBig	0.0156	0.0102	1.52	0.13
DGuard	−0.0178	0.0095	−1.86	0.06
Constant	−0.0466	0.1077	−0.43	0.67

(continued)

comparing players at different positions. But in a study like this, you are only looking at how the performance of a specific player changes. In addition, the position adjustment is only an approximation. Clearly, some players are centers and some are guards. But where a specific player ends up on that spectrum is somewhat arbitrary and can change from year to year. Hence, as was shown in Berri *et al.* (2009), the position adjustment is not included.

[102]This study is based on the work reported in Darvin *et al.* (2016).

Table 8A.4 (continued)				
Independent Variables	Coefficient	Standard Error	t-Statistic	p-Value
R-squared	0.74			
Adj. R-squared	0.65			
Observations	1,620			
Minimum minutes	200			

In Chapter 8, we discussed the results with respect to gender. Here are some other stories told by this model:

* Both age and age squared are statistically significant and of the correct signs. The results indicate that a WNBA player tends to peak at 25 years of age. In addition, Table 8A.5 reveals how age generally impacts performance. If a player is average at her peak (at 25 years of age), then she will likely not dip below the 0.090 mark until 32 years of age. Such a result reveals that WNBA players appear to be less impacted by age than NBA players.

Table 8A.5 Impact of Age on Women's National Basketball Association Players[103]			
Age	WP48	Age	WP48
19	0.091	27	0.099
20	0.094	28	0.098
21	0.096	29	0.096
22	0.098	30	0.094
23	0.099	31	0.091
24	0.0997	32	0.087
25	0.1000	33	0.083
26	0.0997	34	0.079

* The results suggest that playing more games leads to higher productivity. Obviously, this can reflect the choices of coaches. But it also likely reflects the impact of injury. Ideally, we would include actual data on injuries.

* Although the gender of a coach did not matter, moving to a new coach generally saw a dip in productivity. This may indicate that it takes time for players to adjust to a new system.

[103]This table reports expected performance for a player who is average at the age of 25, or the estimated peak age for WNBA players.

The Economics of College Sports

How "Professional" are College Sports?

To answer to this question, Chapter 9 will explore the following:

1. **The Highest-Paid Public Employee in each State:** One might think the governor of each state would be the highest-paid public employee. But one would be wrong.

2. **History of the National Collegiate Athletic Association (NCAA):** The NCAA began as a safety institution. Today, it is an institution that has established rules which clearly lead to economic exploitation.

3. **Competitive Balance in the NCAA:** The NCAA has enacted rules to promote competitive balance. These rules, though, have contributed to competitive imbalance in both men's and women's sports.

4. **Worker Exploitation in the NCAA:** The NCAA refers to their employees as student-athletes. But the athletes are very much employees. And many of them generate far more revenue than the NCAA pays these employees.

5. **The Labor Market for College Coaches:** Many college coaches are paid as well as professional coaches, despite the fact that college sports

generate far less revenue than professional sports. Beyond the overpayment of coaches, there is also evidence of gender discrimination in the hiring of college coaches.

6. **Title IX Enforcement:** Title IX has existed since 1972. More than four decades later, though, Title IX is still not well enforced.

Who is the highest-paid public employee in your state? You might say it is the governor. If this is your guess, then no matter where you live in the United States, you would be incorrect. As the website Deadspin reported in 2013—and as the map shown here, based on the original at Deadspin, illustrates—in 40 of the 50 U.S. states the highest-paid public employee is either a football or basketball coach at a public university.[1]

[1] http://deadspin.com/infographic-is-your-states-highest-paid-employee-a-co-489635228. Randy Edsall was fired as head coach of the University of Maryland football team in October 2015. In 2016, Edsall was being paid $2.673 million to NOT coach the Maryland football team. And that salary made him the highest paid public employee in the state of Maryland in 2016. Yes, the highest paid public employee in the state of Maryland in 2016 was a football coach who wasn't even coaching! http://www.syracuse.com/sports/index.ssf/2017/05/randy_edsall_maryland_football_highest_paid_state_employee_fired.html

One of these states is Kentucky. In 2014–15, the three highest-paid NCAA men's basketball coaches who participated in the 2015 NCAA Men's Division I Basketball Tournament were John Calipari (Kentucky University, $6.0 million), Mike Krzyzewksi (Duke University, $6.0 million), and Rick Pitino (University of Louisville, $4.1 million).[2] The State of Kentucky thus committed more than $10 million to hiring two basketball coaches.

To put these wages in perspective, consider two pieces of information. First, it was reported that in 2014, the average National Basketball Association (NBA) coach was paid about $3 million.[3] Second, consider the data presented in Table 9.1.

Table 9.1   Revenues of Top 30 College Basketball Programs and National Basketball Association Teams: 2015–16

School, 2015–16	Total Revenue[4] (in millions)	NBA Team, 2015–16	Total Revenue[5] (in millions)
University of Louisville	$45.6	New York Knicks	$376
Duke University	$31.0	Los Angeles Lakers	$333
University of Kentucky	$27.2	Golden State Warriors	$305
Syracuse University	$26.9	Houston Rockets	$244
Indiana University-Bloomington	$23.1	Cleveland Cavaliers	$233
University of Wisconsin-Madison	$22.8	Chicago Bulls	$232
University of Arizona	$21.7	Brooklyn Nets	$223
University of North Carolina at Chapel Hill	$21.3	Miami Heat	$210
Ohio State University-Main Campus	$19.9	Boston Celtics	$200
The University of Tennessee, Knoxville	$18.6	Dallas Mavericks	$194
Marquette University	$18.3	Toronto Raptors	$193
University of Kansas	$18.0	Oklahoma City Thunder	$187
The University of Texas at Austin	$18.0	San Antonio Spurs	$187
Michigan State University	$17.6	Los Angeles Clippers	$185

(continued)

[2]Salary data were reported by *USA Today*. The numbers reported reflect what the school paid. *USA Today* has indicated that Calipari and Pitino received "other pay" that increased Calipari's total compensation to $6.4 million and Pitino's pay to $6.0 million (http://sports.usatoday .com/ncaa/salaries/mens-basketball/coach/).

[3]Ken Berger, "For Many NBA Assistants, the Road to Glory Is Well-Traveled," *CBS News*, September 24, 2014, http://www.cbssports.com/nba/writer/ken-berger/24723463/for-many-nba-assistants-the-road-to-glory-is-well-traveled.

[4]Data on men's college basketball revenue can be found at the Department of Education's website (http://ope.ed.gov/athletics/#/). These statistics were self-reported by the school.

[5]NBA revenue data can be found at http://www.forbes.com/nba-valuations/.

Table 9.1 (continued)			
School, 2015–16	Total Revenue[4] (in millions)	NBA Team, 2015–16	Total Revenue[5] (in millions)
University of Maryland, College Park	$17.1	Portland Trail Blazers	$178
University of Michigan, Ann Arbor	$16.8	Phoenix Suns	$173
University of Illinois at Urbana, Champaign	$16.7	Detroit Pistons	$172
University of Arkansas	$16.0	Atlanta Hawks	$169
University of Pittsburgh-Pittsburgh Campus	$15.8	Orlando Magic	$166
The University of Alabama	$14.4	Sacramento Kings	$164
Northwestern University	$14.1	Utah Jazz	$164
North Carolina State University at Raleigh	$13.6	Charlotte Bobcats	$158
University of Dayton	$13.5	Denver Nuggets	$157
University of Florida	$13.3	Indiana Pacers	$157
University of Minnesota-Twin Cities	$12.6	New Orleans Pelicans	$156
Xavier University	$12.3	Memphis Grizzlies	$155
Florida State University	$12.3	Washington Wizards	$155
Gonzaga University	$12.1	Minnesota Timberwolves	$154
University of Oklahoma-Norman Campus	$12.0	Milwaukee Bucks	$146
Auburn University	$11.7	Philadelphia 76ers	$140
	$554.6		$5,866

Table 9.1 reports that in 2015–16 the University of Louisville basketball program led the NCAA Division I men's basketball teams with $45.6 million in revenue. This mark is nearly $95 million less than the revenue earned by the Philadelphia 76ers, or the NBA team that earned the least amount of revenue in 2015–16. Overall, NBA teams earned nearly $6 billion in revenue in 2015–16. The top 30 college teams, on the other hand, only earned a bit more than $550 million, or about 10% of the revenue earned by 30 NBA teams. And if the revenues earned by all 347 Division I programs are added together, we see just $1.57 billion in revenues.[6]

The top NCAA basketball coaches thus earn salaries that are similar to those of many NBA coaches, but NCAA basketball teams generate far less revenue. Why would the state of Kentucky be willing to pay so much money to John Calipari? The answer to this question is related to the wage earned by Anthony Davis.

---

[6]College revenue data come from the U.S. Department of Education ("The Equity in Athletics Data Analysis Cutting Tool," http://ope.ed.gov/athletics/Index.aspx). NBA revenue data (as noted previously in the text) derive from Forbes.com.

Anthony Davis was the first player chosen in the 2012 NBA draft. Before entering the NBA, he had spent one year at the University of Kentucky. Davis was the most productive player employed by the University of Kentucky in 2011–12. In fact, his 12.96 Wins Produced was the highest mark for any men's college basketball player from 2002–03 to 2015–16.[7] For all this production, though, Davis received a one-year scholarship to the University of Kentucky — a scholarship that might be worth about $32,000.[8] NCAA rules prohibited the University of Kentucky from paying Davis any more than this amount. In sum, the labor market for college athletics has a price ceiling.

This price ceiling is a very big part of our story of sports on college campuses. And the history of this institution needs to be reviewed before we can understand why so many states spend so much money on the coaches of "amateur" sports teams.

9.1 Some History of the NCAA

It is likely that most students at universities in the United States take for granted the role that athletics play on our college campuses. Many students are often asked to pay fees to support athletics and a smaller population of students spend time rooting for the teams representing their school. Student athletes are expected to devote a great deal of time practicing and playing sports, and it is not expected that these athletes will be paid — beyond the value of a scholarship — for their efforts.

If we look around the world, though, it becomes very clear that the United States is an anomaly. Nowhere else in the world do we see colleges and universities making such a large investment of time and money in athletics. Around the world, college and universities actually focus their resources almost entirely on the education of students.

---

[7]The data needed to calculate Wins Produced for men's college basketball begin with the 2002–03 season.

[8]*USA Today* reported that the value of a scholarship at Kentucky in 2010–11 was $32,703. (http://usatoday30.usatoday.com/sports/college/mensbasketball/2011-value-of-college-scholarship.htm). This same article argued that a player at Kentucky also received about $110,000 in additional value, of which $70,000 was related to coaching. It is important to note, though, that this value is based on what private coaches charge at training facilities. It is not clear that John Calipari had this kind of impact on the performance of his players. In addition, one can argue that the cost of a scholarship overstates the actual cost of a player attending a school. Many students do not pay the full tuition cost of a school. In addition, the marginal cost of an additional student in many classes is essentially zero.

So how did the American system of commercialized college sports arise? Andrew Zimbalist, in *Unpaid Professionals*,[9] notes commercialism has been a part of the story from the beginning:

> Intercollegiate sports in the United States lost its innocence on day one. In 1852, at bucolic Lake Winnipesaukee in New Hampshire, the Harvard and Yale boat clubs gathered for a rowing contest. The setting was harmless enough, but already commercial interests were at work. The superintendent of the Boston, Concord, and Montreal Railroad organized the event, luring the Harvard and Yale rowing crews with "lavish prizes" and "unlimited alcohol" in order to attract wealthy passengers up to watch the event. In the 1855 boat race between Harvard and Yale the first known eligibility abuse occurred. The Harvard coxswain was not a student, but an alumnus. (pp. 6–7)

The story of collegiate rowing in the 1850s illustrates that commercialism has a long history in collegiate sports. And when collegiate football took off, commercialism became a much bigger part of college sports. Zimbalist (2001) reports that Princeton and Yale were able to attract about 40,000 fans to their football games in the late 1880s, games that generated more than $25,000 in gate revenues (or about $600,000 in 2016 dollars).[10]

The presidents of Princeton and Harvard both commented on the increasingly large role athletics were assuming on college campuses. In 1890, Woodrow Wilson (president of Princeton and eventually president of the United States) observed, "Princeton is noted in this wide world for three things: football, baseball, and collegiate instruction." President Charles Eliot of Harvard seemed to echo this sentiment, saying, "Colleges are presenting themselves to the public, educated and uneducated alike, as places of mere physical sports and not as educational training institutions."[11]

And the desire for success on the field gave schools a clear incentive to engage in behavior that would clearly be considered cheating today by the NCAA. For example, Yale in the 1880s had a $100,000 slush fund ($2.4 million in 2016) to help its football team. The problems with

---

[9]Andrew Zimbalist, *Unpaid Professionals* (Princeton, NJ: Princeton University Press, 2001).

[10]This calculation uses the GDP Deflator from 1888 noted at Louis Johnston and Samuel H. Williamson, "What Was the U.S. GDP Then?" MeasuringWorth, 2017 https://www.measuringworth.com/usgdp/

[11]Zimbalist (2001, p. 7).

nonstudents playing—and being paid—were also observed. Zimbalist (2001) notes two stories that would have definitely made headlines today:

- Fielding Yost, who became a Hall of Fame college coach for a number of schools, most prominently the University of Michigan, was involved in a significant scandal at Lafayette College. In 1896, Yost was a student at the University of West Virginia. That same football season, Lafayette College had a game scheduled against the University of Pennsylvania, a team that had won 36 consecutive games. To win the game, Lafayette College enrolled Yost as a student. He remained at Lafayette College for only two weeks, but it was sufficient time for Yost and the rest of the Lafayette team to end the University of Pennsylvania's winning streak.

- The story of James Hogan at Yale is perhaps even more amazing. In 1905, Yale lured Hogan to its campus by offering him "free meals and tuition, a suite in Vanderbilt Hall, a trip to Cuba, a monopoly on the sale of game scorecards, and a job as cigarette agent for the American Tobacco Company."[12]

In addition to such efforts to secure players, coaches were already becoming the highest-paid employees on college campuses in the 1890s.[13] In sum, college sports in the 19th century seemed to have many of the problems people report today. Only the problems in some way appear to have been much worse.

At present, the NCAA is often seen as the organization charged with policing college sports and preventing the abuses that have existed since the 19th century. Originally, though, the organization had a different purpose.

In 1905—after a number of people had been severely injured and/or died during college football games—President Theodore Roosevelt summoned representatives of Harvard, Yale, and Princeton[14] to the White House.[15] Out of this meeting developed an organization of universities that in 1910 would become the NCAA.

---

[12]Zimbalist (2001, p. 7).

[13]For more on Yale and Hogan, one can read the article at http://www.courant.com/opinion/op-ed/hc-op-commentary-goldstein-yales-walter-camp-bent--20140314-story.html.

[14]In 1905, these three schools were, in fact, football powerhouses.

[15]This story has been retold in a number of sources. Most recently, it could be found in Charles Clotfelter, *Big-Time Sports in American Universities* (New York: Cambridge University Press, 2011), p. 10.

Over time, the focus of the NCAA moved past issues of safety. Jim Peach (2007)[16] identified six specific functions. The first three, which he labeled non-controversial, included:

1. rule-making

2. historical record-keeping

3. conducting championship tournaments

To this list, Peach noted three functions that he labeled controversial:

4. making sure college athletes are "amateurs" (this term is difficult to define, but any definition would have to note that the wages of student-athletes are fixed)

5. making sure college sports programs maintain academic integrity

6. promoting competitive balance

What follows is a discussion of why these functions are "controversial." Before we get to this, though, it is worth noting that Peach (2007) described these functions as defined by "thousands of rules" that are detailed in a manual more than 500 pages in length. As he observed, international trade agreements make for shorter reading!

9.2 Competitive Balance and the NCAA

The "controversial" functions that Peach (2007) notes are actually related. Specifically, one reason college athletes are not paid more than the value of a scholarship is the notion that paying athletes would disrupt competitive balance. This story very much follows from our discussion of competitive balance in professional sports.

Sports are divided between rich and poor teams. If player pay is not restricted, the richest teams will purchase all the best talent. As a result, contests between rich and poor will not be uncertain and demand from consumers will collapse. We have already seen with respect to professional sports that this story fails from the perspective of economic theory and empirical evidence. What do

---

[16]Jim Peach, "College Athletics, Universities, and the NCAA," *Social Science Journal* 44 (2007): 11–22.

the data from the NCAA say? If competitive balance is what the NCAA believes it is creating, the data seem uncooperative.

Before we get to the data, though, let's comment on how to measure balance in college sports. Previously, we noted the Noll–Scully measure (i.e., the ratio of the actual standard deviation of winning percentage to the idealized standard deviation of win percentage) of competitive balance. Although this approach does appear to work for professional sports, it does not seem to work as well for college sports[17]. As Treber, Levy, and Matheson (2013) observed[18]:

> Unfortunately, the standard deviation of win percentage measure is of only limited use in college basketball because of the stratification of teams by conference and the limited amount of interaction between teams from different conferences. In the NCAA, teams are typically organized into conferences with other teams of similar ability, and teams play roughly half of their games against conference opponents, limiting the amount of contact between teams in different conferences. The standard deviation of winning percentage may simply capture the fact that teams are relatively balanced within their own conferences while failing to fully identify the possibility of wide discrepancies in talent between conferences. (p. 254)

Because conferences and schedules are unequal, we need to take a different approach. Jim Peach (2007) proposed that one examine competitive balance by looking at post-season outcomes. For example, as **Table 9.2** illustrates, the distribution of Final Four appearances and national championships has been quite unequal in men's college basketball.

Table 9.2 reports that 21 schools have captured 59.8% of all Final Four appearances since 1939. And these same 19 schools have also won 76% of all NCAA titles in men's basketball. In 2017, there were 351 schools participating in Division I men's basketball. The data indicate that just 6% of those schools dominate this sport.

---

[17]The issue with the Noll–Sully measure also applies to the aforementioned Gini coefficient, the Herfindahl–Hirschman measure, and the competitive balance ratio. Again, because conferences and schedules are so different, any measure of the dispersion of winning percentages would not work so well for college sports.

[18]Jaret Treber, Rachel Levy, and Victor Matheson, "Gender Differences in Competitive Balance in Intercollegiate Basketball," in Eva Marikova Leeds and Michael Leeds (eds.), *Handbook on the Economics of Women in Sports* (Northampton, MA: Edward Elgar, 2013), pp. 251–268.

Table 9.2 Distribution of Final Four Appearances in Men's College Basketball: 1939–2015[19]		
School	Final Four Appearances	National Championships
North Carolina Tar Heels	20	6
UCLA Bruins	18	11
Kentucky Wildcats	17	8
Duke Blue Devils	16	5
Kansas Jayhawks	14	3
Ohio State Buckeyes	11	1
Louisville Cardinals	10	3
Michigan State Spartans	9	2
Indiana Hoosiers	8	5
Michigan Wolverines	7	1
Arkansas Razorbacks	6	1
Cincinnati Bearcats	6	2
Oklahoma State Cowboys	6	2
Syracuse Orange	6	1
Connecticut Huskies	5	4
Florida Gators	5	2
Georgetown Hoyas	5	1
Houston Cougars	5	0
Illinois Fighting Illini	5	0
Oklahoma Sooners	5	0
Villanova Wildcats	5	2
Total of these 21 Division I schools	**189**	**60**
Total Final Four and titles since 1939 for all schools	**316**	**79**
Percentage from these 21 schools	**59.8%**	**75.9%**

A similar story can be told about college football. Unlike men's basketball, college football has only recently added a playoff. Historically, teams were simply ranked at the end of the season, most commonly by the Associated Press (AP). In 2016, 128 schools participated in the top division (the Bowl Championship Subdivision, BCS) in college football. As Table 9.3 indicates, though, nearly 50% of final ranking spots have been held by only 20 schools.

[19]http://www.sports-reference.com/cbb/.

Table 9.3 Distribution of Final Associated Press Rankings in College Football[20]		
School	Final AP Appearances	BCS Titles
Michigan	59	0
Ohio State	56	2
Oklahoma	56	1
Alabama	54	4
Notre Dame	52	0
Nebraska	48	0
USC	48	1
Texas	46	1
Tennessee	44	1
Penn State	41	0
LSU	39	2
Auburn	38	1
Georgia	35	0
Florida State	33	2
UCLA	32	0
Florida	31	2
Miami (FL)	31	1
Clemson	30	1
Arkansas	28	0
Total appearances/titles	801	19
All appearances/titles (all 2016 schools)	1,618	19
Percentage of top 20 programs	49.5%	100.0%

As noted, it is only recently that a title game was played in college football.[21] Of the teams that have won the 19 title games played, all 19 appear in Table 9.3. In sum, of the more than 100 schools not listed in Table 9.3, none have managed to win a title.

Peach (2007) found a similar pattern with respect to baseball and men's volleyball. And a lack of balance is not just confined to these sports. College wrestling—a sport Peach (2007) did not examine—has seen only four schools

---

[20]http://www.sports-reference.com/cfb/.

[21]From 1998 to 2013, the top two teams were selected for this game. Starting in 2014, a four-team playoff was used to determine the teams in the title game.

(Iowa, Oklahoma State, Minnesota, and Penn State) win all but one title from 1989 to 2017.[22] And since 1928, two of these schools, Oklahoma State and Iowa, have won 57 college wrestling titles.

The imbalance of college sports can be understood by looking at recruiting in men's college basketball. Consider the 2013 recruiting class in men's basketball at the University of Kentucky. Julius Randle, Andrew Harrison, Dakari Johnson, James Young, and Aaron Harrison all committed to John Calipari's Kentucky Wildcats. These five players occupied five of the first 11 slots in the Recruiting Services Consensus Index (RSCI) rankings.[23] A sixth signing, Marcus Lee, was the 16th player in the RSCI rankings.

When the season ended, Randle and Young declared for the NBA draft. But the 2014 class more than made up for these two defections. Karl-Anthony Towns (RSCI Rank No. 4), Trey Lyles (RSCI Rank No. 12), Tyler Ulis (RSCI Rank No. 18), and Devin Booker (RSCI Rank No. 23) committed to the Wildcats.

Because Alex Pothyress (RSCI Rank No. 8 in 2012) and Willie Cauley-Stein (RSCI Rank No. 39 in 2012) still played on the Wildcats team, the 2014–15 roster had 10 players ranked in the top 40 in their respected RSCI class. And that means the Wildcats had two lineups consisting entirely of top recruits. In other words, at any one time, the Wildcats had an entire lineup of top recruits sitting on their bench.

Why would all these players crowd onto one team? The answer relates to the price ceiling the NCAA has imposed. Because universities cannot pay anything beyond a scholarship, teams cannot use money to attract talent. Consequently, just as we see in the NBA, players appear to choose their university based on the likelihood that their school will be successful on the court. That means the best teams attract the best talent. Or in other words, the best teams get better, while the worst teams keep losing.

Although the 2013 and 2014 recruiting class for Kentucky represented a quite amazing lineup, Tables 9.2 and 9.3 make it clear that this story is not entirely unique in the history of college sports. The ability of a few teams to dominate each of the above sports suggests that players have consistently sorted themselves in the same fashion we observed for the basketball recruits

---

[22]In 2015, Ohio State won the title. This was the first time since 1988 that one of the top four teams did not win (Arizona State won in 1988). Ohio State defeated Iowa to take the 2015 crown. See http://www.ncaa.com/history/wrestling/d1 for the complete history of these champions.

[23]Each year, a number of different groups rank the top high school recruits in the nation. The rankings are summarized by the RSCI developed by RSCIhoops.com. The RSCI rankings reported come from basketball-reference.com (see, e.g., http://www.basketball-reference.com/awards/recruit_rankings_2014.html).

of John Calipari. Because college athletes cannot be paid, they appear to be choosing schools based on the probability of team success. So the best athletes in men's basketball seem to first consider Kentucky. The best wrestlers go to Iowa and Oklahoma State. And the best football players seem to prefer Alabama.

9.3 Even More Competitive Imbalance in Women's College Sports

So far our discussion of college sports has focused strictly on men's sports. And prior to 1972, men's college sports were essentially the only college game in town. But in 1972, Title IX was passed.

Title IX is an amendment to the Civil Rights Act of 1964. Initially, the Civil Rights Act focused on discrimination with respect to race, color, religion, and national origin. But in 1972, the following was added to the Act: "No person in the United States shall, on the basis of sex, be excluded from participation in, be denied the benefits of, or be subjected to discrimination under any educational program or activity receiving federal financial assistance."[24]

Although Title IX does not explicitly mention sports, its impact on sports is clear. Zimbalist (2001) noted that female participation in sports changed dramatically after the amendment was signed into law by President Richard Nixon. In 1971, 294,015 girls participated in high school sports. In 1973, this number increased to 817,073, and by 1978 it was 2.08 million. According to Acosta and Carpenter (2014), more than 3 million girls played high school sports in 2013.

Zimbalist (2001) noted a similar pattern at the college level. In 1971, only 31,852 women played college sports. By 1977, that number increased by more than 100% to 64,375. Acosta and Carpenter (2014) noted that in 2012, more than 200,000 women participated in college sports.

Because women also play college sports, many of the issues we examine for men's sports can also be examined with data from women's sports. And although we will comment on issues like coaching and Title IX enforcement, for now let's consider an interesting story about competitive imbalance in women's college sports.

---

[24]The discussion of the Civil Rights Act of 1964 and the specifics of Title IX can be found in Susan L. Averett and Sarah M. Estelle, "The Economics of Title IX Compliance in Intercollegiate Athletics," in Eva Marikova Leeds and Michael Leeds (eds.), *Handbook on the Economics of Women in Sports* (Cheltenham, UK: Edward Elgar, 2013).

Treber *et al.* (2013) looked at balance in men's and women's basketball. Two specific approaches were offered. The first examined the margin of victory in first-round games at the NCAA Tournament. As Table 9.4 illustrates, whether we take into account margin of victory or the winning percentage of the higher seeds, the women's game appears less competitive.

Seed	Win Margin, Men's Tournament, 1985–2011	Win Percentage, Men's Tournament, 1985–2011	Win Margin, Women's Tournament, 1994–2011	Win Percentage, Women's Tournament, 1994–2011
1	25.84	100.0%	39.97	98.6%
2	16.77	96.2%	27.50	100.0%
3	11.53	84.6%	19.76	100.0%
4	9.49	78.8%	16.00	93.1%
5	4.54	66.3%	7.61	77.8%
6	3.94	68.3%	7.22	70.8%
7	2.20	58.7%	5.36	65.3%
8	−0.16	48.1%	0.39	47.2%

Table 9.4 Margin of Victory in First-Round NCAA Basketball Tournaments[25]

Like Peach (2007), Treber *et al.* (2013) also looked at the distribution of championships. The specific approach taken by the latter was to calculate the Herfindahl–Hirschman index ratio (HHIR). As Treber and colleagues note, the HHIR is the difference between the HHI that is actually observed and the HHI that would exist if no team won more than one title.[26] The larger the ratio, the less balanced is the sport. As these authors reported, from 1982 to 2011, this ratio was 2.20 in the Men's NCAA Division I. In Women's NCAA Division I, however, the ratio was 4.47.

Previously, we suggested why men's college sports are competitively imbalanced. As noted, the cap on student-athlete pay appears to be promoting the imbalance observed. And that same issue applies to women's sports. Why does even more imbalance exist in women's college basketball?

Treber *et al.* (2013) focused on the underlying population of talent playing women's sports. As we noted in Chapter 4, as the underlying population of talent expands, the level of balance tends to improve. And conversely, if the underlying population is restricted, we can expect to see more balance.

[25]Treber *et al.* (2013, p. 255).

[26]As Treber *et al.* (2013) noted, the HHIR in their study is calculated by squaring the share of championships won by each school, adding together these squared values, and multiplying by 10,000.

Treber and colleagues cited two reasons why the underlying population of female basketball players is restricted (relative to what we see with respect to males). First, the history of women's basketball is relatively short. As Treber *et al.* (2013) noted, the first Olympic competition for men took place in 1936 and the NBA began in 1946. In contrast, women did not compete in basketball at the Olympics until 1976 and the Women's National Basketball Association (WNBA) was not formed until 1997. Because men have had a longer history and more opportunities to play, Treber *et al.* thus argued that it is not surprising the underlying talent pool is larger.

In addition to differences in the history of the game, these authors pointed to the differences in financial incentives. In 2011–12, the maximum salary for an NBA player with 10 or more years of experience was $18.1 million.[27] In the WNBA, though, the maximum salary in 2012 was only $105,000.[28] As Treber and colleagues argued, the much smaller financial rewards in the WNBA mean that fewer young women are willing to invest the time necessary to become an elite basketball player. And again, with a smaller population participating, the greater the level of imbalance.

Financial incentives aside, one might also note a disparity in media coverage between men and women's sports. Cooky, Messner, and Musto (2015)[29] indicated that in 2014, ESPN's Sportscenter devoted only 2% of its highlight show to women's sports. A similar story was told about 2009, 2004, and 1999.

This disparity can be highlighted by the coverage of the NBA and WNBA during the month of July. At this time, the WNBA is in the midst of its season, while the NBA season has ended. Despite the fact that the WNBA is actually generating news with every game played, stories on ESPN Sportscenter are 5 times more likely to be about the NBA (relative to the WNBA).[30] A similar story can be told about the Men's and Women's NCAA Basketball Tournament. In March 2014, ESPN was more than 10 times more likely to discuss the former versus the latter.[31]

In addition to differences in the quantity of coverage, Cooky, Messner, and Musto noted clear differences in the quality and enthusiasm of the coverage.

---

[27]http://www.cbafaq.com/salarycap.htm.

[28]http://usatoday30.usatoday.com/sports/basketball/story/2012-05-19/nba-wnba-basketball-salary-disparity/55079608/1.

[29]Cheryl Cooky, Michael A. Messner, and Michela Musto, "'It's Dude Time!' A Quarter Century of Excluding Women's Sports in Televised News and Highlight Shows," *Communication & Sport* 3, no. 3 (June 5, 2015): 1–27.

[30]Cooky *et al.* (2015, p. 11) noted that the NBA was the focus of 16 main stories in July 2014. In contrast, only 4 stories were about the WNBA.

[31]Cooky *et al.* (2015, p. 13) noted that the Men's NCAA Tournament was the focus of 83 main stories in March 2014. In contrast, only 8 stories were about the Women's NCAA Tournament.

This large disparity in both quantity and quality of coverage likely interacts with the lack of pay in women's basketball. In turn, both factors likely limit the population of girls willing to acquire the skills necessary to play basketball at a high level. And the limited population likely results in even less competitive balance.

9.4 Worker Productivity and Exploitation in the NCAA

In April 2010, the NCAA announced a 14-year deal with CBS Television and Turner Broadcasting[32] that would pay the NCAA $10.8 billion for the rights to broadcast the Men's Basketball Tournament. And yes, "billion" is the correct word.

It is not unusual to see large television deals for professional sports. But college basketball is not played by professionals. College basketball players are referred to as student-athletes. The student-athletes that people watch during the NCAA Men's Division I Basketball Tournament receive an academic scholarship to attend their respective schools. But other payments are prohibited because student-athletes are supposed to be amateurs.

Of course, it seems clear from the size of this television deal that these student-athletes are generating substantial revenues for their schools. In other words, we expect the marginal revenue product (MRP) of these student-athletes to be positive. However, does the MRP exceed the value of an academic scholarship? If the answer is no, then one could argue that student-athletes are "fairly" compensated for their effort. If the answer is yes, though, then we would argue that student-athletes are being exploited.

Remember, exploitation is defined as a worker's MRP exceeding his or her wage. To address whether or not exploitation exists, we need a measure of MRP to compare to the value of the student-athlete's scholarship.

One approach to this issue was offered by Robert Brown (1993, 1994).[33] Brown's approach was to estimate a revenue function for college sports that

---

[32]Turner Broadcasting is the parent company of TNT and TBS (among other companies).

[33]Robert W. Brown. "An Estimate of the Rent Generated by a Premium College Football Player." *Economic Inquiry* 31 (1993): 671–684.

Robert W. Brown. "Measuring Cartel Rents in the College Basketball Player Recruitment Market." *Applied Economics* 26 (1994): 27–34.

This approach was later updated in the following:
Robert W. Brown, and R. Todd Jewell. "Measuring Marginal Revenue Product of College Athletics: Updated Estimates." In F. Rodney and F. John (eds.), *Economics of College Sports* (Westport, CT: Praeger, 2004).

Robert W. Brown. "Research Note: Estimate of College Football Rents." *Journal of Sports Economics* 12 (2011): 200–212.

includes as an independent variable the number of draft picks employed by the team. For example, Brown (1993) indicated that having a National Football League (NFL) draft prospect on a college football roster was worth $583,760 in 1988 (or 1,191,514 in 2017).[34] Brown (1994) indicated that a future NBA player in 1988–89 was worth $871,310 to a college basketball team ($1,778,432 in 2017).[35]

Since a scholarship is worth much less, Brown's analysis suggests that players drafted into the NBA or NFL appear to be exploited by the NCAA. Most players, though, are not drafted. For example, 4,656 men participated in Division I college basketball in 2012–13. Of these, only 41 were selected in the 2013 NBA draft. This means that Brown's approach would not reveal the MRP of more than 99% of the population of men's college basketball.

More recent work by Lane, Nagel, and Netz (2012)[36] attempted to measure the MRP of all college basketball players. It directly followed the standard Scully approach (detailed in Chapter 6). First, a wins model was designed to capture the marginal productivity of a player. And then a revenue model was estimated to ascertain the value of a win.

Of course, as noted, there are difficulties with the Scully approach. And when we turn to college sports, the list of issues increases. Such a list would begin with fixed revenues. As we discussed previously, the Scully approach suffers when fixed revenues are large. The aforementioned $10.8 billion NCAA tournament television contract is not strictly a function of a team's wins. Therefore, a significant portion of team revenue is not going to be connected to what a player does on the court. The standard Scully approach will thus undervalue the MRP estimate of a player.

But the problems with the Scully model go beyond this one issue. It argues that the revenue model can capture—via the link between wins and revenue—the player's contribution to firm revenue. But as we noted in Chapter 6, this simply captures the fans' demand for wins. In the past, when baseball stadiums had fewer entertainment options, wins mattered much more to team revenue.

Beyond the revenue issues, we also have noted that the marginal product estimates only capture how a player impacts wins. So a player's star appeal is not included. In addition, the work a player put into practice is not valued. Finally, the fact that bench players are necessary to provide insurance against injury is not included.

---

[34]Calculation based on the inflation calculator found at https://data.bls.gov/cgi-bin/cpicalc.pl Comparison of September 1988 to April 2017. If the dollar figure comes after 1913, I have used the BLS calculator in the text. If it is before 1913, I have used the Measuring Worth site.

[35]Calculation based on the inflation calculator found at https://data.bls.gov/cgi-bin/cpicalc.pl Comparison of September 1988 to April 2017. If the dollar figure comes after 1913, I have used the BLS calculator in the text. If it is before 1913, I have used the Measuring Worth site.

[36]Erin Lane, Juan Nagel, and Janet Netz, "Alternative Approaches to Measuring MRP: Are All Men's College Basketball Players Exploited?," *Journal of Sports Economics* 15, no. 3 (June 2012): 237–262.

In sum, the Scully approach doesn't quite capture a player's MRP in sports. There are, however, other approaches to consider. Previously, we discussed how Krautmann (1999)[37] used the free-agent labor market to estimate the MRP of nonfree agents in baseball. More recently, Goff, Kim, and Wilson (2016)[38] utilized salary and performance data from the NFL and NBA to estimate what college players would earn in each respective sport.

The difficulty with the approaches put forward by both Krautmann (1999) and Goff *et al.* (2016) is that they require we assume salaries are a good approximation of MRP. But given the issues earlier raised about player evaluation in each sport, such may not be a good assumption. Nevertheless, we can follow the lead of these papers and utilize some basic characteristics of the professional labor market to approximate the MRP of a college athlete.

Let's illustrate by applying a few characteristics of the NBA's player market to a study of college basketball players. The last NBA collective bargaining agreement guaranteed the players 50% of league revenue. In addition, there are minimum salary thresholds.[39] The minimum salaries essentially acknowledge that a player who never sets foot on the court does contribute to a team's success by participating in practice and providing insurance in case another player is injured.

We should note that limiting the salaries paid to workers is a feature that is common in North American sports, but does not exist in a free labor market. Consequently, the characteristics of the NBA labor market suggest that players are not paid exactly what their MRP might be. Nevertheless, let's take what we know about the imperfect NBA market and estimate what MRP may look like in college basketball.

The team we will analyze is the 2014–15 men's basketball team at Duke University, who won the 2015 NCAA championship.[40] According to the Department of Education, the men's basketball team at Duke recorded revenues of $33,772,145 that season. Following the NBA's example, 50% of that revenue, or $16,886,073, would go to the players. Since 12 players logged minutes for this team, that works out to an average salary of $1,407,713. So if the college player

---

[37]Krautmann, A., "What's Wrong with Scully Estimates of a Player's MRP?," *Economic Inquiry* 37, no. 2 (April 1999): 369–381.

[38]Brian Goff, H. Youn Kim, and Dennis Wilson, "Estimating the Market Value of Collegiate Football Players Using Professional Factor Shares," *Applied Economics Letters* 24, no. 4 (2016): 233–237.

[39]There is also a maximum salary cap. In the example that follows, though, no player has an MRP that exceeds the maximum percentage thresholds established by the NBA.

[40]The analysis of the Duke University men's team in 2014–15 was first reported by David J. Berri, "Paying NCAA Athletes," *Marquette Sports Law Review* 26, no. 2 (2016): 479–491.

market was similar to the NBA market, the average college player at Duke would be paid far more than the cost of attendance.[41]

We can do more than just approximate what an average salary would be in the college market based on that number in the NBA. We can also use our knowledge of the NBA market to estimate each player's value if players were paid for their production of wins[42] and every player was guaranteed a minimum wage (which again compensates the player for participation in practice and insuring the team against the risk of injury).

In 2014–15, the average salary in the NBA was $4,603,659, while the minimum salary for a player with no experience was $507,336.[43] So in 2014–15, the minimum salary was 11% of the average salary in the NBA. We have already noted that the average salary for Duke University—if the team allocated 50% of its revenue to its players—would be $1,407,713. Following the NBA example, the minimum salary would then be $155,074. And since that clearly exceeds the cost of attendance, if Duke University followed the example of the NBA's labor market, even players who did not play in regular-season games would earn more than the cost of attending school.

Duke University had 12 players on its roster (who appeared at least once in a game) in 2014–15, and if all those players received this minimum wage, Duke University would have paid $1,860,892 to its players. This is $15,025,180 less than the 50% the NBA's rules would require the school to pay its players.

To allocate the remaining revenue, let's consider each player's Wins Produced. As explained in the appendix to this book, the box-score data collected by the NBA can be used to estimate each player's production of wins. These same box-score data are also tabulated by the NCAA. Therefore, we can employ the same methodology to estimate each college player's Wins Produced.[44]

---

[41]Duke University estimates the cost of attendance for out-of-state students in 2015–16 at $67,654 (https://financialaid.duke.edu/undergraduate-applicants/cost; last visited June 9, 2016). One should note that this figure exaggerates the cost of attendance, since the marginal cost of admitting one more student is far less than the stated tuition cost.

[42]As we have noted, such is not the case in the NBA. But the point of this exercise is to estimate the MRP. Therefore, we must begin with an estimate of the marginal product. And a player's production of wins can approximate it.

[43]See http://www.cbafaq.com/salarycap.htm. In addition to reporting the minimum salary in the NBA, this site also reports that players were paid $2.145 billion in 2012–13. With 469 players in the league, the average salary was thus $4,573,561.

[44]These data can be found at http://www.sports-reference.com/cbb/. This site, though, only has complete data for each Division I team going back to 2009–10. One can find box-score data at RealGM.com dating to 2002–03. Consequently, the Wins Produced of every men's college basketball player can be estimated back to that season.

In Table 9.5, we see the Wins Produced of each player on the Duke University team in 2014–15, and the corresponding estimate of each player's MRP.

Table 9.5 MRP Estimates for the Men's Basketball Team at Duke University: 2014–15[45]		
Player	Wins Produced	MRP Estimate
Tyus Jones	7.9	$3,755,823
Jahlil Okafor	6.5	$3,082,682
Quinn Cook	5.1	$2,406,018
Justise Winslow	4.9	$2,323,924
Amile Jefferson	4.9	$2,294,193
Marshall Plumlee	2.3	$1,076,578
Matt Jones	2.0	$923,584
Grayson Allen	0.7	$305,217
Rasheed Sulaimon	0.6	$252,831
Semi Ojeleye	0.0	$155,074
Sean Kelly	0.0	$155,074
Nick Pagliuca	0.0	$155,074
Team totals	**35.1**	**$16,886,073**

Once again, each player starts with the minimum salary. The remaining revenue allocated to the players (again, the NBA allocates 50% to its players) is then divided according to each player's contribution to wins.[46]

According to this approach, Tyus Jones was worth $3.76 million to Duke University.[47] And five more players were worth more than $1 million. Remember, exploitation is defined as wages being less than the MRP. So given this definition, one can argue that every single player was exploited by Duke University.

We should again emphasize: This approach underestimates each player's MRP. The estimate is based on characteristics of the NBA's labor market. This market, as noted, is still restricted. In an unrestricted market, as we see in European sports, players receive more than 50% of league revenue. So if the collegiate market were unrestrained, we would expect the MRP estimates to be even higher.

---

[45]Source of original data: http://www.sports-reference.com/cbb/. Wins Produced and the MRP estimate are author's calculations.

[46]One will note that two players have a negative Wins Produced. These players' MRP is set at the previously estimated minimum. The remaining players then see a small deduction in their MRP so that the sum stands at 50% of team revenue.

[47]Tyus Jones produced 7.9 wins in 2014–15, or about 22.5% of the team's Wins Produced. Consequently, he was allocated about 22.5% of the revenue that remained after each player was paid the estimated minimum wage.

9.5 Coaching College Sports

The analysis of the revenue generated by college basketball players can be repeated for any team in Division I-A college basketball. And such an exercise indicates that many players are producing more revenue for their respective schools than they are being paid. So who is getting the revenue the players are not seeing?

One possibility is the coaches. Previously, we discussed coaches' pay and revenue in basketball. Now let's turn to football. Table 9.6 reports the salaries of the head coaches, and corresponding team revenues, of the top 10 teams in college football in 2012 (ranked by revenue).

To put these numbers in perspective, Table 9.7 reports the salaries paid to the NFL's head coaches in 2013 (and the corresponding team revenues). As one can see, the average NFL team earns close to $300 million in revenue, while the top college teams barely earn more than $50 million.

Given this disparity in revenues, one might expect a similar disparity in the salaries paid to coaches. But that is not what we see. The average college coach at a top football program is only paid $1.5 million less than an average NFL head coach.

Table 9.6 10 Highest-Paid Head Coaches in College Football: 2015[48]

Head Coach	University	Salary of Head Coach, 2015	College Revenue, 2015	Percentage of Revenue Paid to Head Coach
Nick Saban	University of Alabama	$7,087,481	$97,023,963	7.3%
Jim Harbaugh	University of Michigan	$7,004,000	$88,251,525	7.9%
Urban Meyer	Ohio State University	$5,860,000	$83,547,428	7.0%
Bob Stoops	Oklahoma University	$5,400,000	$78,737,409	6.9%
Jimbo Fisher	Florida State University	$5,150,000	$70,321,194	7.3%
Charlie Strong	University of Texas	$5,100,270	$121,382,436	4.2%
Kevin Sumlin	Texas A&M University	$5,000,000	$62,199,166	8.0%
James Franklin	Penn State University	$4,400,000	$71,305,219	6.2%
Les Miles	Louisiana State University	$4,388,721	$86,312,831	5.1%
Hugh Freeze	University of Mississippi	$4,310,000	$53,399,653	8.1%
	Average	**$5,370,047**	**$81,248,082**	**6.6%**

---

[48]Source of salary data: *Fortune* (http://fortune.com/2015/12/12/heisman-colleges-coaches-2015/). College revenue data come from the Department of Education (https://ope.ed.gov/athletics/#/).

Head Coach	NFL Team	Salary of Head Coach, 2015	NFL Revenue, 2015	Percentage of Revenue Paid to Head Coach
Sean Payton	New Orleans Saints	$8,000,000	$358,000,000	2.2%
John Harbaugh	Baltimore Ravens	$7,500,000	$378,000,000	2.0%
Andy Reid	Kansas City Chiefs	$7,500,000	$340,000,000	2.2%
Bill Belichick	New England Patriots	$7,500,000	$523,000,000	1.4%
Jeff Fisher	St. Louis Rams	$7,000,000	$317,000,000	2.2%
Pete Carroll	Seattle Seahawks	$7,000,000	$377,000,000	1.9%
Tom Coughlin	New York Giants	$6,670,000	$444,000,000	1.5%
Chip Kelly	Philadelphia Eagles	$6,500,000	$407,000,000	1.6%
Bruce Arians	Arizona Cardinals	$6,000,000	$348,000,000	1.7%
Jason Garrett	Dallas Cowboys	$6,000,000	$700,000,000	0.9%
	Averages	**$6,967,000**	**$419,200,000**	**1.7%**

Table 9.7 Salaries of Head Football Coaches in the National Football League: 2015[49]

Again, the difference between the NFL and the college ranks seems obvious. The NFL pays its players close to 50% of team revenues. College teams — because of NCAA restrictions — do not have to share as much revenue with their players. And consequently, more revenue is able to be directed toward coaches.

Clearly, being a head coach at a top college team is a lucrative position. Unfortunately, we do not seem to have any research that reveals how to land one of these positions. Paul Holmes (2011),[50] though, did look at how a coach manages to keep such a job.

The model Holmes (2011) presented considered a variety of independent variables. The factors found to be statistically significant included:

- winning percentage
- winning percentage last season
- winning percentage two seasons ago
- winning percentage in conference
- record against rival

[49]Source of salary data: *Sportige* (http://sportige.com/79788-top-10-highest-paid-nfl-coaches/). NFL revenue data come from *Forbes*. One can find these data online at https://www.statista.com/statistics/193553/revenue-of-national-football-league-teams-in-2010/.

[50]Paul Holmes, "Win or Go Home: Why College Football Coaches Get Fired," *Journal of Sports Economics* 12, no. 2 (2011): 157–178.

- historical winning percentage (from 3 to 10 seasons ago)

- historical winning percentage (from 11 to 30 seasons ago)

- tenure with school

The results with respect to winning percentage the past three seasons (as well as record in conference and against rivals) were not surprising. If a coach wishes to keep his or her job, winning is better than losing. What may be surprising is the impact of a school's historical record. Holmes (2011) reports that the better a team has done historically, the more likely a coach will be fired today.

So the key to keeping a job as a college coach is to win, but if you happen to work for a school that has won historically, you better win quite a bit. Does that mean you are better off coaching at a school without much history? Perhaps not, since as Peach (2007) noted, college teams that have won in the past tend to win in the future. In other words, it is easier to win at a school that has won in the past. But if you do not win as much as fans expect, as Holmes (2011) suggested, your risk of losing your job will increase.

9.6 Title IX Enforcement: Myth and Measurement

Although the market for coaches does exhibit gender bias, we have seen, as previously noted, tremendous progress with respect to women participating in college athletics. One might suspect that if schools are devoting more resources to women's sports, men's sports, in turn, have suffered. The data, though, don't seem to tell that story.

Before getting to the real story, we need to discuss the enforcement of Title IX. As Averett and Estelle (2013) noted, initially it was not clear how Title IX would be enforced. Then in 1979, the Department of Health, Education and Welfare established what came to be known as the "three-prong test,"[51] described by Averett and Estelle as follows:

- **Proportionality Test:** "Provides a composition of athletic opportunities to men and women that is proportional to the gender composition of the student body"

- **Program Expansion Test:** "Demonstrate consistent program expansion for women"

- **Accommodation of Interest Tests:** "Show accommodation of student interests or abilities"

---

[51]Averett and Estelle (2013, p. 178).

This list leads one to wonder if schools, in fact, comply with Title IX and how this compliance is achieved.

In 2004, Deborah Anderson and John Cheslock published a study looking explicitly at how schools achieved compliance.[52] These authors began by noting that although satisfying any of the three prongs would indicate compliance, schools tend to focus on the first test. Specifically, people tend to focus on the proportionality gap:

$$\text{Proportionality Gap} = [(\text{Percentage of Undergraduates Who Are Female}) - (\text{Percentage of Athletes Who Are Female})] \times 100$$

As Anderson and Cheslock (2004) noted, the common rule is that a gap of 3 to 5 percentage points indicates a school is in compliance. In other words, a school doesn't have to be in perfect compliance. It just has to be close.

Unfortunately, not many schools are actually close. Anderson and Cheslock (2004) found that in 1995–96, about 7–10% of schools were in compliance. This number increased to 11–18% in 2001–02. But overall, the average gap was 13%.

Although most schools were not in compliance (and as we will see, that is also true with recent data), some progress has been made. To see how this progress has been made, Anderson and Cheslock (2004) ran four different regressions with the following dependent variables: net change in the number of athletes (separate regressions for male and female) and net change in the number of teams (separate regressions for male and female).

A collection of independent variables were considered.[53] But the primary focus of the study is how the proportionality gap impacted the number of teams and participants at the school. And as Table 9.8 indicates, Anderson and Cheslock failed to find statistical evidence that the proportionality gap impacted the number of men's teams at the school.

There is some evidence that schools reduce the number of men participants to achieve compliance. But as Anderson and Cheslock (2004) noted, the results indicate that a 5-percentage-point proportionality gap leads to 2.4 additional female athletes and a loss of only 1.2 male athletes. In sum, it appears that schools—to the extent that achieving compliance is a goal—primarily focus on adding teams and athletic positions for women.

---

[52]Deborah J. Anderson and John J. Cheslock, "Institutional Strategies to Achieve Gender Equity in Intercollegiate Athletics: Does Title IX Harm Male Athletes?," *American Economic Review* 94, no. 2 (2004): 307–311.

[53]As Anderson and Cheslock (2004) noted, the list of additional explanatory variables includes controls for public and private schools, history as a black college or university, geographic region, selectivity of school, endowment per student, level of tuition and fees, state funding of school, undergraduate enrollment, and division in which school competes.

Table 9.8 Impact of Proportionality Gap on Athletic Participation in the National Collegiate Athletic Association[54]

Dependent Variable	Proportionality Gap	t-Statistics	Proportionality Gap, Squared	t-Statistics
Change in men's teams	−0.0294	−1.729	0.00008	0.160
Change in women's teams	0.0371[b]	2.016	−0.00004	−0.080
Change in men participants	−1.698[b]	−2.041	0.046[b]	2.000
Change in women participants	−2.811[a]	−4.134	−0.040[b]	−2.105

Observations = 703.

p-Values not explicitly reported, but significance levels were noted as follows:

[a]Significant at the 1% level.

[b]Significant at the 5% level.

It is important to emphasize that most schools in the Anderson and Cheslock (2004) sample were not in compliance. More recent work by Averett and Estelle (2013) indicated this is still an issue. These latter authors noted that in 2009, the average proportionality gap for all schools was 15.668. And only 14.87% of schools had a proportionality gap of 5% or less. One issue Averett and Estelle (2013) raised is a lack of enforcement. Although Title IX states that schools will lose federal funding if they are not in compliance, Averett and Estelle (2013) noted that no school has ever suffered this punishment.

Thus, the evidence does not suggest men's collegiate sports have been substantially impacted by Title IX. Part of this is because schools have primarily added sports for women to reach compliance. But perhaps more importantly, the majority of schools are not actually in compliance with Title IX. And after more than 40 years, it seems unlikely this situation is going to change.

9.7 Profitability in College Sports

With respect to revenues and costs, we have come up against three stories in this chapter. First, college sports generate quite a bit of revenue. Second, the pay of athletes in both men and women's sports is severely restricted. And finally, most college and universities are not spending money to comply with Title IX. All of this would suggest that college sports are profitable. In other words, revenue should definitely exceed costs.

Looking at the top 30 college men's basketball teams, we generally see that revenues exceed expenses. For 2013–14, the U.S. Department of

---

[54]Anderson and Cheslock (2004, p. 309).

Education reported that the top 30 men's programs—in terms of revenue—had $527.2 million in revenues and only $269.2 million in expenses.[55] And Oklahoma State alone reported expenses in excess of revenues.

But if we look at the next 100 schools—again, in terms of revenue—the picture changes somewhat. The revenue of these schools was $579.5 million, while their combined expenses were $505.8 million. Although overall this group of schools had revenues in excess of expenses, such was not true for 48 of the schools in the sample.

When we turn to the top 100 college women's basketball programs (again, ranked in terms of revenues), a lack of profits becomes the norm. Overall, these programs report $237.4 million in revenue and $238.4 million in expenses. And for 86 schools, profits were either zero or below zero.

This suggests that college sports are not very profitable. But before we leap to this conclusion, let's note something odd about the sample. Of the 230 schools examined, 111 of them (or nearly half) report that their revenue and expenses are exactly the same. For example, Baylor University reports that it earned $6,238,722 in revenue from its women's basketball team. And it reports the exact same number (to the last dollar!) in expenses.

To explain this pattern, we turn to the work of H. R. Bowen (1980), who gave us the revenue theory of cost.[56] As Bowen noted, non-profits have an incentive to spend every increase in revenue. One reason for this tendency is that more spending can enhance the reputation of the institution. And this leads to what Martin (2009)[57] referred to as the revenue-cost spiral. In other words, as revenues rise, we see a corresponding increase in costs.

When looking at the data from the Department of Education, we see evidence of this spiral. Again, 48% of the schools noted above reported revenues and expenses that were identical. Since for nonprofits, there is no person who can claim a positive difference between revenue and expenses,[58] the schools

[55]College revenue data come from the U.S. Department of Education ("The Equity in Athletics Data Analysis Cutting Tool," http://ope.ed.gov/athletics/Index.aspx). They were reported to the Department of Education by universities.

[56]H. R. Bowen, *The Costs of Higher Education* (San Francisco: Jossey-Bass, 1980). This discussion of Bowen's work may be found in Chad McEvoy, Alan Morse, and Stephen Shapiro, "Factors Influencing Collegiate Athletic Department Revenues," *Journal of Issues in Intercollegiate Athletics* 6 (2013): 249–267.

[57]Robert E. Martin, "The Revenue-to-Cost Spiral in Higher Education," John William Pope Center for Higher Education Policy, July 2009, https://www.jamesgmartin.center/acrobat/revenue-to-cost-spiral.pdf.

[58]A nonprofit, by definition, is an organization that is not designed to earn a profit. So contrary to a for-profit organization, a non-profit does not have anyone in the organization who can lay claim to any positive difference between revenue and cost. And therefore, there is no one with an incentive to make sure revenues actually exceed costs (as you would see in a for-profit organization).

have every incentive to keep spending. So despite rapid increases in revenues across recent years, the NCAA can continue to claim that profits are uncommon. The lack of profits, though, does not indicate that sports are not good business for colleges and universities. The lack of profits simply reflects the realities of a nonprofit business. Beyond the issue of how non-profits behave, we should also circle back to the particular incentives facing universities. Universities have made it clear that they are not willing to pay student-athletes. If they schools report no profits or losses, it is easier to argue that there simply are no funds to pay players. Reporting profits, though, makes that argument more difficult.

In this chapter, we have noted that college sports are quite similar to professional sports. The main difference is that pay to student-athletes is set by the NCAA. And the result of this policy is competitive imbalance and the exploitation of many of the athletes it employs. The NCAA, though, would like to claim that it does not have the resources to increase their pay and to fully comply with Title IX. Our brief discussion of profits, however, indicates that such an argument is probably incorrect. The money does exist to solve the issues raised in this chapter. But for those issues to be solved, it is likely some of the people who benefit from college sports (and yes, coaches are on this list) would have to accept less. And since we expect that people respond to incentives, it seems unlikely—given the incentive in college sports—that the NCAA will voluntarily remedy these issues in the near future.

Problems

Study Questions

1. What public employee occupation tends to be the highest paid in each state?
2. When did college athletics become commercial? How many fans were attending football games at Princeton and Yale in the 1880s?
3. Which U.S. president called for the formation of the NCAA and what was its original purpose?
4. What is the competitive balance argument for why student-athletes should not be paid?
5. How does the ceiling on the pay to student-athletes impact competitive balance in college sports?
6. How does competitive balance in women's college basketball compare to that in men's college basketball? What explains this difference?
7. According to our definition of exploitation and the calculation of MRP offered in the text, how many players on the 2014-15 Duke men's basketball team were "exploited"? How many players on the Duke women's basketball team were exploited?

8. How do the revenues of the top 32 college football teams compare to the revenues of NFL teams? How do the salaries of the head coaches compare?

9. According to von Allmen (2013), who is the "better" coach, on average, in college softball: a man or a woman? How did he reach this conclusion?

10. What is the three-prong test to establish compliance with Title IX? Which of these "prongs" is focused on the most?

11. According to Anderson and Cheslock (2004), what do schools primarily focus on to achieve compliance with Title IX?

12. According to Averett and Estelle (2013), what percentage of schools is in compliance with Title IX? Why are more schools not in compliance?

13. Are college sports profitable? Reference data and theory in answering this question.

14. What is Bowen's revenue theory of cost? What is the revenue-cost spiral?

15. What has happened to the population of men coaching college women since 1972? What has happened to the population of women coaching college men during this same time period? How would you explain the difference in the observed pattern?

16. If schools decided to pay student-athletes in terms of their economic value, where would this money come from? Who would likely see their pay reduced if this were the case?

17. In some sports, the revenue generated by the athletes will not be enough to cover the cost of the scholarship. Should schools still extend these scholarships in a world where there are not restrictions on the pay of athletes?

Subsidizing Sports

Why do Governments Subsidize Sports?

To answer this question, Chapter 10 will explore the following:

1. **Government Spending's Impact on the Economy:** The majority of economists believe government spending can help an economy. A majority also agree, though, that government spending on sports does not tend to help it.

2. **Link Between Sports Spending and when a Study Is Completed:** There is a difference between studies done before an event (i.e., ex ante studies) and studies conducted after it (i.e., ex post studies). The former are generally offered by consultants who argue sports provide substantial benefits. The latter, conducted by independent economists, consistently disagree.

3. **Few Economic Benefits that Result from Hosting International Sports Events:** Cost–benefit analysis clearly suggests that hosting the Olympics or the World Cup does not generate enough economic benefits to justify the economic costs.

4. **Sports Make Us Happy!** Sports may not provide economic benefits, but governments do have another noneconomic reason to host sporting events.

In June 2013, Chris Hansen, a hedge fund manager from Seattle, contributed $100,000 to an organization seeking to prevent the construction of a new $448 million arena for the Sacramento Kings.[1] How a billionaire spends a few thousand dollars is probably not often the subject of major news stories. But in this case, Hansen's contributions sparked significant outrage.

To understand, we must go back and examine a few events that proceeded Hansen's donation. The ARCO Arena had been built for the Sacramento Kings in 1988. Over the next 25 years, several campaigns to build a new arena for the Kings were mounted, with many of these efforts involving public money. One of the most recent occurred in early 2012, when the owners of the Kings (the Maloof family) and the local government in Sacramento agreed to construct a $447 million arena, with $258 million coming from the city.[2]

A few months after this agreement was reached, however, the Maloof family backed out of the deal. It then proceeded to open negotiations to move the Kings to other locations and/or sell the team to Chris Hansen, who planned on moving the Kings to Seattle. In January 2013, Hansen and the Maloofs reached an agreement.

Soon after this agreement was reached, though, the city of Sacramento — with the help of software tycoon Vivek Ranadive — put together another offer to keep the Kings in Sacramento. In the end, Hansen's purchase offer was higher.[3] But the National Basketball Association (NBA) voted against relocating the Kings to Seattle, and ultimately, the Maloofs sold the team to Ranadive.

This deal, as noted, involved the city of Sacramento investing public money in the construction of a basketball arena. Such an investment leads one to ask the following questions:

1. How often does the public make an investment in professional team sports?

2. Why would a government vote to subsidize a professional sports team?

3. Do these subsidies produce enough benefits to justify their cost?

As we will see, the answer to these questions depends on whom you ask. Supporters of public subsidies frequently assert that this kind of spending creates jobs and economic growth. However — and this is a bit of a spoiler — independent sports economists often argue that these subsidies do not provide substantial benefits. Consequently, according to them, one could suggest that Hansen's contribution, in fact, helped the city of Sacramento.

---

[1] http://espn.go.com/nba/story/_/id/9575561/chris-hansen-gave-100000-group-opposing-new-sacramento-kings-arena.

[2] http://www.sacbee.com/2013/03/23/5287542/mayor-city-reaches-agreement-on.html.

[3] Hansen's offer placed the Kings' value at $625 million, while Randive's valued the Kings at $534 million (http://espn.go.com/nba/story/_/id/9575561/chris-hansen-gave-100000-group-opposing-new-sacramento-kings-arena).

To understand that point, though, we need to first review the story told by the research into the economics of public subsidies for professional sports. And that story begins by noting how many economists seem to agree with the independent sports economists.

10.1 Economists Agree?

George Bernard Shaw (the Irish playwright and cofounder of the London School of Economics)[4] once said: "If all economists were laid end to end, they would not reach a conclusion."

This quote captures the sentiment that economists have trouble making definitive statements on any particular subject; that on many subjects, economics is deeply divided. But as Gregory Mankiw reports at his website,[5] and explores in his principles textbooks, most economists agree on a number of areas.

Two subjects relate to the issue of public subsidies for professionals sports. First, Mankiw reports that 90% of economists agree "fiscal policy (e.g., tax cut and/or government expenditure increase) has a significant stimulative impact on a less than fully employed economy." In other words, 9 out of 10 economists believe that government spending can help an economy do better. And that certainly fits the story told by stadium enthusiasts. If the government helps build a sports stadium, shouldn't that help an economy create jobs and grow?

Economists — perhaps surprisingly (given what we just stated) — seem to disagree. Mankiw also reports that 85% of economists agree "local and state governments should eliminate subsidies to professional sports franchises."

This appears to be a contradiction. On the one hand, economists think that government spending can be helpful. On the other hand, economists think that government spending on sports is not helpful. Perhaps what we need, as President Harry Truman once said, are more one-handed economists.[6] Or perhaps many economists just don't like sports.

The key to this puzzle might be the phrase "less than fully employed economy." Back in the 1930s, both the United States and United Kingdom (and many other places in the world) saw their economies shrinking. John Maynard Keynes — a British

---

John Maynard Keynes (1883–1946)

In 1936, John Maynard Keynes published *The General Theory of Employment, Interest and Money*. This work changed how economists thought about recessions and the role of government in managing the economy. As Keynes argued, if the economy went into a recession because households and firms were spending less, an increase in government spending could bring an economy back to full employment. It should be noted that Keynes was definitely a supporter of free markets and didn't believe government should play a persistent active role in the macroeconomy. Nevertheless, Keynes' work clearly transformed how economists think about macroeconomic policy.

---

[4]Not George Howard Shaw, the starting quarterback for the Baltimore Colts in 1955.

[5]http://gregmankiw.blogspot.com/2009/02/news-flash-economists-agree.html. This blog is also the source for the two quotes that follow in the text.

[6]As we noted, President Truman appeared to grow frustrated with the advice he received from economists. All too often, an economist would state an opinion, only to continue with the phrase "on the other hand," then offering an alternative point of view. Consequently, Truman spoke of the need for economists who only had "one hand."

Paul Samuelson
(1915–2009)

Paul Samuelson made numerous contributions to economics in his lifetime. But it is two works that define his career. First is *Foundations of Economic Analysis* (1947), a book based on his Harvard dissertation that emphasizes how much of economic behavior can be described mathematically. It is this work that is often credited with turning economics from a discipline that relied primarily on words into one where math was central to the stories being told. His second contribution was his textbook, *Economics: An Introductory Analysis*. First published in 1948, this textbook went on to be the best-selling textbook in history and is likely the foundation of most leading textbooks today. This textbook popularized the notion of the neoclassical synthesis, the idea that microeconomic behavior can be explained with standard neoclassical economic theory while macroeconomic phenomena required an approach based on Keynesian macroeconomic theory.

economist (and student of Alfred Marshall, discussed in Chapter 1) — suggested there was a solution to this problem. If spending in the private sector was on the decline, an increase in government spending (or a cut in taxes, which might spur private sector spending) would stimulate the economy to grow.

In much the same way that the stats revolution was not embraced by decision makers in sports, what Keynes had to say in the 1930s was not immediately embraced by politicians. But when government spending increased dramatically in the buildup for World War II, economic growth in the United States increased and the nation's unemployment rate plummeted. Since the end of World War II, politicians, both Republicans and Democrats, have embraced fiscal policy whenever the nation was in a recession.[7] And again, most economists seem to think these policies are a fairly good idea.

Part of this story is the idea of a **multiplier**. Nobel Laureate Paul Samuelson, an early advocate of Keynesian economics, summarized this concept as follows in his classic textbook:

> The multiplier is the number by which the change in investment must be multiplied in order to present us with the resulting change in income. Samuelson argued that a multiplier would be greater than 1 so that $1 in increased spending led to more than a $1 increase in economic output. In defending this notion, Samuelson noted, "[B]y using ordinary common sense one can see why, when I hire unemployed resources to build a $1,000 garage, there will be a secondary expansion of national income and production, over and above my primary investment" (p. 212).[8]

Samuelson goes on to explain why an expansion beyond the initial $1,000 in spending occurs. The people hired to build the garage will spend a portion of this money on other goods and services.[9] The people selling these other goods

---

[7]To illustrate, President John F. Kennedy (a Democrat) advocated a tax cut to spur the economy in the 1960s. During the 1980s, President Ronald Reagan (a Republican) advocated a tax cut and an increase in government spending in response to a recession. President George W. Bush (a Republican) followed a similar policy, advocating a tax cut in the early part of his administration to spur an economic recovery. And President Barack Obama (a Democrat) also advocated a stimulus package in response to the recession that greeted him when he entered office in 2009.

[8]These quotes are from the 8th edition of Samuelson's *Economics* (New York: McGraw-Hill, 1970). This textbook was first published in 1948 and in the decades that followed remained the dominant textbook in the marketplace.

[9]The portion of income spent on income is called the marginal propensity to consume (MPC). If the MPC is 0.7, then the builders of the garage will spend $700 on new consumption. The people providing the goods and services will now have $700 in new income. If their MPC is 0.7, they will now spend $490 on new goods and services. And the producers of those goods and services will see their income go up $490. With an MPC of 0.7, these people will now increase their consumption by $343, and so on.

multiplier The number by which the change in investment must be multiplied to calculate the resulting change in income.

and services will now have extra income, which they will also be able to spend on new consumption. This new consumption becomes someone else's income, and a portion of that now becomes new consumption. This process continues from person to person, and thus the initial $1,000 in income multiplies through the economy.[10]

The key phrase in Samuelson's description is "when I hire unemployed resources." What if the same spending was observed in an economy at full employment? Then the resources hired to build Samuelson's garage would simply come from some other project in the economy. In other words, Samuelson's spending would **crowd out** other spending in the economy. Consequently, there would be no multiplier and no expansion in the economy.

Here then is the key to our story: If an economy is not at full employment, government spending can increase the output of an economy. But if it is at full employment, that is not going to happen.

Unfortunately, it appears that many advocates of government spending on sports fail to take this issue into account. Too often, they argue that sports will provide a tremendous economic benefit. Matheson (2008)[11] provided a list, reproduced in part in **Table 10.1**, of some of the official studies associated with such claims.

crowd out No change in output in spite of government spending in a fully employed economy.

Table 10.1 Examples of Mega-Event Ex Ante Economic Impact Studies[12]

Event	Year of Event	Sport	Impact	Source (and year of study)
Super Bowl (Atlanta)	1994	Football	$166 million	Humphreys (1994)
Super Bowl (Miami)	1999	Football	$393 million	Sports Management Research Institute, NFL (1999)
Super Bowl (San Diego)	2003	Football	$367 million	Marketing Information Masters, NFL (2003)
MLB All-Star Game	1999	Baseball	$75 million	Selig *et al.* (1999)
MLB World Series	2000	Baseball	$250 million	Comptroller of the City of New York, Ackman (2000)
NCAA Men's Final Four (St. Louis)	2001	Basketball	$110 million	St. Louis Convention and Visitor's Bureau, Anderson (2001)
U.S. Open	2001	Tennis	$420 million	Sports Management Research Institute, U.S. Tennis Association (2002)

---

[10]If the MPC is 0.7, the actual multiplier would be $(1)/(1 - 0.7)$ or 3.33. So $1,000 in income has a $3,333 impact on the economy. One should note this is a simple textbook calculation. The size of the multiplier associated with fiscal stimulus appears much smaller.

[11]Victor Matheson, "Mega-Events: The Effect of the World's Biggest Sporting Events on Local, Regional, and National Economies," in Brad Humphreys and Dennis Howard (eds.), *The Business of Sport*, Vol. 1 (Westport, CN: Praeger, 2008), pp. 81–100.

[12]Matheson (2008, p. 82).

These 12 studies were all conducted before the event in question. And all 12 suggested that each event would provide substantial economic benefit. The studies conducted after the event, though, told a very different story. And the reason for these different stories was the methodologies the ex ante studies had applied.

10.2 The Value of Sports: Industry Approach Versus Economic Theory

Baade and Matheson (2012)[13] noted that a typical economic impact study proceeds as follows: First, the direct economic impact of the event is calculated by multiplying the number of people who attended the event by the average spending of each fan. After the direct economic impact is determined, the researcher then employs a multiplier to capture the indirect impact this spending has on the local economy. As Baade and Matheson observed, typically, that multiplier is 2, which means the researcher doubles the direct economic impact to arrive at a figure that is supposed to represent the total economic impact of the sports event.

Baade and Matheson (2012) go on to point out that such an approach suffers from three theoretical deficiencies: the substitution effect, the crowding out effect, and the leakage effect. Here is a breakdown of each effect:

substitution effect What happens when consumers simply reduce their expenditure on other items to spend money on sports.

crowding out effect What happens when the crowds associated with a sporting event lead other people to avoid the event, thus reducing its economic impact.

- **Substitution effect:** Spending on sporting events comes out of a consumer's entertainment budget. It seems unlikely that sports will cause consumers to expand this budget. A more plausible explanation is that consumers who spend more money on sports simply spend less money on other entertainment options. Ex ante studies that just examine statistics on sports attendance ignore the limits of a consumer's entertainment budget.

- **Crowding out effect:** We have spoken about how government spending in an economy at full employment will crowd out private spending. With respect to sporting events, there is a different form of crowding out that is actually about "crowds." Baade and Matheson (2012) noted that the

[13]Robert Baade and Victor Matheson, "Financing Professional Sports Facilities," in Sammis White and Zenia Kotval (eds.), *Financing Economic Development in the 21st Century*, 2nd ed. (New York: Routledge, 2012), pp. 323–342.

number of tourists who arrived in August 2008 in Beijing, site of that year's Summer Olympics, was the same as the number of tourists who arrived in August 2007. But a review of data for the entire year indicates there were fewer tourists in 2008 than in 2007. Essentially, many of the tourists who normally visited Beijing found someplace else to go in 2008.[14]

• **Leakage effect:** The primary employees at professional sporting events tend to be the athletes people are paying to see. Consequently, much of the revenue these events generate go to the athletes. But as Siegfried and Zimbalist (2002)[15] have observed, professional athletes do not always live in the city where they are employed. This means that spending on sports tends to leak out of the community hosting the event. As Baade and Matheson (2012) noted, if the leakage is significant enough, then professional sports can actually reduce local income. After all, as we have noted, consumers have a limited entertainment budget. If the spending on sports displaces spending on local restaurants, which tend to employ people from the local area, then the community ends up worse off as their dollars exit the area.

leakage effect What happens when professional athletes employed by sports teams tend to live elsewhere, with spending then leaking outside the city hosting the team.

10.3 The Value of Sports: The Empirical Evidence

We have two basic approaches. The industry approach focuses on the spending associated with a sports event and with a multiplier forecasts economic impact. Economic theory, though, notes three theoretical issues with the industry approach. What do we observe when evaluating economic impacts after an event?

The findings from numerous academic studies examining the economic impact of various sporting events, as recorded in **Table 10.2**, indicate that the ex ante studies appear to exaggerate the benefits of sports. A few of the events listed are the same as those given in Table 10.1. When we compare the ex ante and ex post studies, quite a few differences become clear.

---

[14]Baade and Matheson (2012) also noted that Honolulu, which hosts the Honolulu Marathon and NFL Pro Bowl, does not see a large increase in tourists from either event. Although thousands attend each, it appears both events simply cause other tourists to stay away.

[15]John Siegfried and Andrew Zimbalist, "A Note on the Local Economic Impact of Sports Expenditures," *Journal of Sports Economics* 3, no. 4 (November 2002): 361–366.

Event	Years	Variable	Impact	Source
Table 10.2 Examples of Mega-Event Ex Post Economic Impact Studies[16]				
MLB All-Star Game	1973–97	Employment	Down 0.38%	Baade and Matheson (2001)
Super Bowl	1973–99	Employment	537 jobs	Baade and Matheson (2000a)
Super Bowl	1970–2001	Personal income	$91.9 million	Baade and Matheson (2006)
MLB playoffs and World Series	1972–2000	Personal income	$6.8 million/game	Baade and Matheson (2008)
NCAA Men's Basketball Final Four	1970–99	Personal income	Down $44.2–$6.4 million	Baade and Matheson (2004)
Daytona 500	1997–99	Taxable sales	$32–$49 million	Baade and Matheson (2000b)
Super Bowl	1985–95	Taxable sales	No effect	Porter (1999)
Multiple events (Florida)	1980–2005	Taxable sales	Down $34.4 million (avg.)	Baade, Bauamann, and Matheson (2008)
Multiple events (Texas)	1991–2005	Gross sales	Varied (positive and negative)	Coates (2006)
Multiple events (Texas)	1990–2006	Sales tax revenue	Varied (positive and negative)	Coates and Depken (2009)
NFL Pro Bowl	2004–08	Tourist arrivals	6,726 visitors	Baumann, Matheson, and Muroi (2009)
NHL regular-season games	1990–99	Hotel occupancy	Slight increase	Lavoie and Rodriguez (2005)

For example,

- The ex ante studies, on average, claimed that the Super Bowl would have a $308 million impact. The ex post studies from the academic literature found either no effect or much smaller economic impacts (537 more jobs in one study and $91.9 million additional income in another).

- The ex ante studies of the Major League Baseball (MLB) All-Star Game forecast an impact of $75 million. The ex post study, though, found a negative impact.

- The ex ante study of baseball's World Series predicted a $250 million impact. The ex post study determined an impact of $6.8 million per game, which means that a city would have to host about 38 games to achieve the expectation of the ex ante study.

- The ex ante study of the National Collegiate Athletic Association (NCAA) Men's Final Four promised an economic impact of $110 million. The ex post study found a negative economic impact.

The general pattern is that in almost every case, the promise of the ex ante studies is not held up in the ex post studies. And consequently, economists appear to believe government subsidies of sports are a bad idea.

10.4 Government Ignoring Economists — at the Local and Federal Level

Despite this position, governments have been ignoring economists for more than 70 years. In 1953, the Braves relocated from Boston to Milwaukee. This move was at least partially motivated by the construction of County Stadium, a facility built with public funds. Prior to Milwaukee's actions to attract the Braves, stadiums were almost always private ventures.[16] After the Braves' move to Milwaukee, governments frequently got into the stadium-building business.

Robert Baade and Victor Matheson (2012)[17] tabulated the extent of government involvement in the building of arenas and stadiums in each of the major North American sports leagues since 1990. The results, reported in Tables 10.3 to 10.7, indicate that government involvement in the United States is quite extensive.

Table 10.3 Subsidies to Build National Football League Stadiums: 1992–2011[19]					
Team	Stadium	Built	Cost (000s) (Nominal)	Public Cost (000s) (Nominal)	Public Percent
New Orleans	Superdome (repair and rehab)	2011	$505	$490	97%
New York Giants/ New York Jets	MetLife Stadium (part of Meadowlands Sports Complex)	2010	$1,600	$0	0%
Kansas City	Arrowhead Stadium (rehab)	2010	$375	$250	67%
Dallas	AT&T Stadium (formerly Cowboys Stadium)	2009	$1,150	$325	28%

(continued)

[16]There were three exceptions to this general rule. In an attempt to attract the Olympic Games, the cities of Los Angeles, Chicago, and Cleveland all built stadiums. These stadiums included the Los Angeles Coliseum (1923), Soldier Field in Chicago (1923), and Cleveland Municipal Stadium (1931). This observation was made in Ted Gayer, Austin Drukker, and Alexander Gold, *Tax-Exempt Municipal Bonds and the Financing of Professional Sports Stadiums*, Economic Studies at Brookings (Washington, DC: Brookings Institution, 2016). The same point was made originally in John J. Siegfried and Andrew Zimbalist, "The Economics of Sports Facilities and Their Communities," *Journal of Economic Perspectives* 14, no. 3 (2000): 95–114.

[17]Robert Baade and Victor Matheson, "Financing Professional Sports Facilities," in Zenia Kotval and Sammis White (eds.), *Financing Economic Development in the 21st Century*, 2nd ed. (Armonk, NY: M.E. Sharpe, 2012), pp. 323–342.

[18]Tables 10.3 through 10.7: Baade and Matheson (2012).

Team	Stadium	Built	Cost (000s) (Nominal)	Public Cost (000s) (Nominal)	Public Percent
Table 10.3 *(continued)*					
Indianapolis	Lucas Oil Stadium	2008	$720	$720	100%
Arizona	University of Phoenix Stadium	2006	$71	$267	72%
Philadelphia	Lincoln Financial Field	2003	$285	$228	80%
Green Bay	Lambeau Field	2003	$295	$251	85%
Chicago	Soldier Field	2003	$600	$450	75%
New England	Gillette Stadium	2002	$325	$33	10%
Houston	NRG Stadium (formerly Reliant Stadium)	2002	$300	$225	75%
Detroit	Ford Field	2002	$300	$219	73%
Seattle	CenturyLink Field (formerly Qwest Field)	2002	$300	$201	67%
Pittsburgh	Heinz Field	2001	$230	$150	65%
Denver	Sports Authority Field (formerly Invesco Field)	2001	$365	$274	75%
Cincinnati	Paul Brown Stadium	2000	$400	$400	100%
Cleveland	FirstEnergy Stadium (Browns Stadium)	1999	$283	$255	90%
Tennessee	Nissan Stadium (formerly LP Field)	1999	$290	$220	76%
Buffalo	New Era Field (formerly Ralph Wilson Stadium) (rehab)	1999	$63	$63	100%
Baltimore	M&T Bank Stadium	1998	$220	$176	80%
Tampa Bay	Raymond James Stadium	1998	$169	$169	100%
San Diego	Qualcomm Stadium	1997	$78	$78	100%
Washington	FedEx Field	1997	$250	$70	28%
Oakland	Oakland Coliseum (rehab)	1996	$200	$200	100%
Carolina	Bank of America Stadium	1996	$248	$52	21%
Jacksonville	Everbank Field	1995	$121	$121	100%
St. Louis	The Dome at America's Center (formerly Edward Jones Dome)	1995	$280	$280	100%
Atlanta	Georgia Dome	1992	$214	$214	100%
29 of 32 teams			$10,537	$6,380	61%

For example, with the exception of MetLife Stadium (part of the Meadowlands Sports Complex, created specifically for the New York Giants and Jets), every single stadium built for National Football League (NFL) teams received government spending. And 11 of these were entirely constructed with government money.

The lone exception in New York reveals the difference between public and private financing. In 2014, the Super Bowl was played at the MetLife Stadium. This was not the first time a Super Bowl was played in a cold-weather location. But when this had happened before, the game was played inside a domed stadium, so both players and fans remained quite warm in spite of the weather conditions outside.

The 2014 Super Bowl was, in fact, played outside. When asked why the MetLife Stadium did not have a roof, one of the owners of the New York franchises cited the expense of adding a roof. Of course, owners tend to watch games from a luxury box, so the cold does not impact their enjoyment of the game. But fans at the 2014 Super Bowl might have wondered why they were not having the same physically comfortable experience as those who attended the 2012 championship game, also played in a cold-weather location. The difference was that the fans in Indianapolis were seated inside a domed stadium. And as Table 10.3 notes, this domed stadium was built entirely with government money. In sum, if the owners are paying the bill, building a roof becomes a huge, perhaps insurmountable, expense. If the government is providing the funds, then building a roof is economically feasible.

One should emphasize, the NFL is not the only league to receive government assistance. Every baseball stadium constructed since 1991, as Table 10.4 notes, has used some government money; five stadiums alone have been built entirely through public financing.

A similar story may be told for the Major League Soccer (MLS, Table 10.5) and NBA (Table 10.6). Most of the facilities employed by teams in these sports received public financing.

Table 10.4 Subsidies to Build Major League Baseball Stadiums: 1991–2011					
Team	Stadium	Built	Cost (000s) (Nominal)	Public Cost (000s) (Nominal)	Public Percent
Miami	Marlins Field	2012	$525	$370	70%
Minnesota	Target Field	2010	$544	$392	72%
New York Mets	Citi Field	2009	$600	$164	27%
New York Yankees	Yankee Stadium	2009	$1,300	$220	17%
Kansas City	Kaufmann Stadium (rehab)	2009	$250	$175	70%
Washington	Nationals Park	2008	$611	$611	100%
St. Louis	Busch Stadium	2006	$365	$45	12%
San Diego	PETCO Park	2004	$457	$304	66%
Philadelphia	Citizens Bank Park	2004	$346	$174	50%

(continued)

Table 10.4 *(continued)*					
Team	Stadium	Built	Cost (000s) (Nominal)	Public Cost (000s) (Nominal)	Public Percent
Cincinnati	Great American Ball Park	2003	$325	$280	86%
Pittsburgh	PNC Park	2001	$262	$262	100%
Milwaukee	Miller Park	2001	$400	$310	78%
Detroit	Comerica Park	2000	$300	$115	38%
Houston	Minute Maid Park	2000	$265	$180	68%
San Francisco	AT&T Park	2000	$357	$15	4%
Seattle	Safeco Park	1999	$518	$392	76%
Arizona	Chase Field	1998	$349	$238	68%
Los Angeles Angels	Angel Stadium (rehab)	1998	$118	$30	25%
Tampa Bay	Tropicana Field	1997	$208	$208	100%
Atlanta	Turner Field	1997	$235	$165	70%
Oakland	Oakland Coliseum (rehab)	1996	$200	$200	100%
Colorado	Coors Field	1995	$215	$168	78%
Cleveland	Progressive Field	1994	$175	$91	52%
Texas Rangers ·	Globe Life Park in Arlington (formerly Ballpark at Arlington)	1994	$191	$135	71%
Baltimore	Camden Yards	1992	$110	$100	91%
Chicago White Sox	Guaranteed Rate Field (formerly U.S. Cellular Field)	1991	$167	$167	100%
26 of 30 teams			$9,393	$5,511	59%

Table 10.5 Subsidies to Build Major League Soccer Stadiums: 1999–2011					
Team	Stadium	Built	Cost (000s) (Nominal)	Public Cost (000s) (Nominal)	Public Percent
Houston	BBVA Compass Stadium (formerly Dynamo Stadium)	2012	$110	$50	45%
San José	Avaya Stadium (formerly Earthquakes Stadium)	2012	$60	$0	0%
Kansas City	Wizards Stadium	2011	$160	$80	50%
Portland	Providence Park (formerly PGE Park) (rehab)	2011	$31	$31	100%
Vancouver	BC Place Stadium	2011	$365	$365	100%
New York	Red Bull Arena	2010	$190	$90	47%

Team	Stadium	Built	Cost (000s) (Nominal)	Public Cost (000s) (Nominal)	Public Percent
Philadelphia	Talen Energy Stadium (formerly PPL Park)	2010	$120	$77	64%
Salt Lake	Rio Tinto Stadium	2008	$115	$16	14%
Colorado	Dick's Sporting Goods Park	2007	$131	$66	50%
Toronto	BMO Field	2007	$63	$63	100%
Chicago	Toyota Park	2006	$98	$98	100%
Montreal	Saputo Stadium	2006	$14	$0	0%
Dallas	Toyota Stadium (formerly Pizza Hut Park)	2005	$80	$80	100%
L.A. Galaxy/Chivas	StubHub Center (formerly Home Depot Center)	2003	$150	$0	0%
New England	Gillette Stadium	2002	$325	$33	10%
Seattle	CenturyLink Field (formerly Qwest Field)	2002	$300	$201	67%
Columbus	Mapfre Stadium (formerly Columbus Crew Stadium)	1999	$29	$0	0%
17 of 18			$2,340	$1,249	53%

Table 10.6 Subsidies to Build National Basketball Association Arenas: 1990–2010

Team	Stadium	Built	Cost (000s) (Nominal)	Public Cost (000s) (Nominal)	Public Percent
Orlando	Amway Center	2010	$480	$430	90%
Brooklyn	Barclays Center	2010	$637	$150	24%
Charlotte	Spectrum Center (formerly Time Warner Cable Arena)	2005	$265	$265	100%
Memphis	FedEx Forum	2004	$250	$250	100%
Phoenix	U.S. Airways Center (construction and rehab)	1992/ 2004	$157	$157	100%
Houston	Toyota Center	2003	$235	$192	82%
San Antonio	AT&T Center	2002	$186	$158	85%
Oklahoma City	Chesapeake Energy Arena (formerly Ford Center)	2002	$89	$89	100%
Dallas	American Airlines Center	2001	$420	$210	50%
Toronto	Air Canada Centre	1999	$265	$0	0%
Indiana	Bankers Life Fieldhouse (formerly Conseco Fieldhouse)	1999	$183	$183	100%

(continued)

Table 10.6 (continued)					
Team	Stadium	Built	Cost (000s) (Nominal)	Public Cost (000s) (Nominal)	Public Percent
Atlanta	Philips Arena	1999	$214	$63	29%
Denver	Pepsi Center	1999	$160	$35	22%
L.A. Lakers/Clippers	Staples Center	1999	$375	$59	16%
New Orleans	Smoothie King Center (formerly New Orleans Arena)	1999	$114	$114	100%
Miami	American Airlines Arena	1998	$213	$213	100%
Washington	Verizon Center	1997	$260	$60	23%
Golden State	Oracle Arena (rehab)	1997	$121	$121	100%
Philadelphia	Wells Fargo Center	1996	$206	$0	0%
Boston	TD Garden	1995	$160	$0	0%
Portland	Moda Center (formerly Rose Garden)	1995	$262	$35	13%
Seattle	Key Arena (rehab)	1995	$75	$75	100%
Cleveland	Quicken Loans Arena	1994	$152	$152	100%
Chicago	United Center	1994	$175	$0	0%
New York	Madison Square Garden (rehab)	1991	$200	$0	0%
Utah	Vivint Smart House Area (formerly EnergySolutions Arena)	1991	$93	$0	0%
Memphis	Memphis Pyramid	1991	$65	$65	100%
Minnesota	Target Center	1990	$104	$52	50%
27 out of 30			$6,115	$3,126	51%

A somewhat different story may be told for the National Hockey League (NHL), as seen in Table 10.7. Only 36% of NHL arena costs are paid by the public. One key difference is the substantial presence of teams in Canada. Except for the Ottawa franchise (which received only $6 million in public funds), Canadian teams have not been successful in any bid to get the public to pay for their arenas.[19]

In the United States, we also see that some cities do better than others. New York teams—relative to the rest of teams in the United States—often are not heavily subsidized. The New York Rangers, Knicks, Giants, and Jets received no subsidies for their arenas/stadiums. And the Yankees and Mets each received less than 30%.

[19]One should add that the NHL has seen a change in recent years. If you look at arenas built in the United States from 1997 to 2010, the public has contributed 48% of the cost.

Table 10.7	Subsidies to Build National Hockey League Arenas: 1991–2010				
Team	Stadium	Built	Cost (000s) (Nominal)	Public Cost (000s) (Nominal)	Public Percent
Pittsburgh	PPG Paints Arena (formerly Consol Energy Center)	2010	$321	$130	40%
New Jersey	Prudential Center	2008	$375	$210	56%
Arizona	Gila River Arena (formerly Jobing.com Arena)	2003	$180	$180	100%
Dallas	American Airlines Center	2001	$420	$210	50%
Columbus	Nationwide Arena	2000	$175	$ 0	0%
Minnesota	Xcel Energy Center	2000	$130	$130	100%
Toronto	Air Canada Centre	1999	$265	$ 0	0%
Atlanta	Philips Arena	1999	$214	$63	29%
Colorado	Pepsi Center	1999	$160	$35	22%
Los Angeles	Staples Center	1999	$375	$59	16%
Carolina	PNC Arena (formerly RBC Center)	1999	$158	$98	62%
Florida	BB&T Center (formerly Bank Atlantic Center)	1998	$212	$185	87%
Washington	Verizon Center	1997	$260	$60	23%
Nashville	Bridgestone Arena	1997	$144	$144	100%
Philadelphia	Wells Fargo Center	1996	$206	$ 0	0%
Ottawa	Canadian Tire Centre (formerly Scotiabank Place)	1996	$188	$6	3%
Buffalo	KeyBank Center (formerly HSBC Arena)	1996	$128	$55	43%
Tampa Bay	Amalie Arena (formerly St. Pete Times Forum)	1996	$160	$120	75%
Montreal	Le Center Bell	1996	$230	$ 0	0%
Vancouver	Rogers Arena	1996	$160	$ 0	0%
Boston	TD Garden	1995	$160	$ 0	0%
Chicago	United Center	1994	$175	$ 0	0%
St. Louis	Scottrade Center	1994	$170	$35	20%
Anaheim	Honda Center	1993	$123	$123	100%
San José	SAP Center (formerly HP Pavilion)	1993	$163	$133	82%
New York Rangers	Madison Square Garden (rehab)	1991	$200	$ 0	0%
26 out of 30			$5,451	$1,974	36%

A similar story can be told about teams in Los Angeles. One suspects that both stories are about bargaining power. Teams in New York and Los Angeles are quite valuable because of the respective size of their markets. Consequently, it would be difficult for owners to threaten to leave these markets in an effort to secure a better arena/stadium deal. Government officials in both cities would likely fail to find such a threat credible.[20]

The experience in the New York and Los Angeles markets gives us some insight into why the public spends so much on stadiums and arenas. Because North American sports team restrict which cities get teams, the teams have significant bargaining power in negotiating with city governments.

We should point out that this is also not just an issue for cities. Gayer, Drukker, and Gold (2016) observe that cities frequently finance stadium construction and renovation with tax-exempt municipal bonds. These authors estimate that since 2000 the federal government has lost approximately $3.2 billion in federal tax dollars because of such financing.

These same authors go on to note: "There . . . remains no economic justification for federal subsidies for sports stadiums. Residents of, say, Wyoming, Maine, or Alaska, gain nothing from the Washington-area football team's decision to locate in Virginia, Maryland, or the District of Columbia" (p. 6).

10.5 The Economic Cost of International Parties

Public subsidies of professional sports are not limited to North American sports. Substantial public spending also characterizes the Olympics and Fédération Internationale de Football Association (FIFA) World Cup. And again, if we believe the consultants, there are huge benefits to being a host country.

Zimbalist (2015)[21] notes that the ex ante projections suggest these events offer huge economic benefits. For example, he points to the following:

- The 2010 Vancouver Olympic Games were projected to create $10.7 billion in economic growth and 244,000 jobs.

- The 2002 World Cup in Japan was projected to increase income by $24.8 billion.

---

[20]The NFL did leave the Los Angeles market when the Rams moved to St. Louis and the Raiders moved back to Oakland. One should note that this move helped the NFL as a whole, since teams in other markets can now threaten to leave for this market. In addition, because so much of the revenue in the NFL is shared, the benefit of playing in the Los Angeles market is muted.

[21]Andrew Zimbalist, *Circus Maximus* (Washington, DC: Brookings Institution Press, 2015).

- The 2010 World Cup in South Africa was projected to increase income by $12.8 billion.

- The 2012 London Olympics was projected to increase income by $17 billion and create 31,000 jobs.

Just as we saw with public spending on North American sports, Zimbalist (2015) stresses that numerous ex post studies of hosting the World Cup and Olympics fail to find evidence of an impact similar to what was predicted in the ex ante studies. In many cases, as **Table 10.8** illustrates, there was no significant economic impact from hosting these sports events.

Table 10.8	Ex Post Studies of the World Cup and Olympics[23]			
Event	Year	Variable	Impact	Source
FIFA World Cup	1974	Employment	No significant impact	Hagn and Maennig (2008)
FIFA World Cup	1994	Income	Average income $712 million below trend	Baade and Matheson (2004)
FIFA World Cup	1994	Employment	No significant impact	Baumann and Engelhardt (2011)
FIFA World Cup	2006	Employment	No significant impact	Hagn and Maennig (2009)
FIFA World Cup	2006	Employment and income	No significant impact	Feddersen, Grotzinger, and Maennig (2009)
FIFA World Cup	2006	Economic growth and employment	No significant impact on growth, small impact on employment in hospitality sector	Feddersen and Maennig (2012)
FIFA World Cup	1998, 2006, and 2010	Hotel stays, income, retail sales	No significant impact for France, significant impact on hotel stays and income for Germany	Allmers and Maennig (2009)
FIFA World Cup	2010	Economic growth	0.1% increase for South Africa	du Plessis and Venter (2010)
FIFA World Cup	2011	Tourism	Tourism increases 40,000 to 90,000	du Plessis and Maennig (2011)
FIFA World Cup	Various years	Economic growth	Slower growth in host country	Szymanski (2002)
Summer Olympics	1972	Income and employment	Significant positive impact on income, but no statistically significant impact on employment	Jasmand and Maennig (2008)
Summer Olympics	1996	Employment	Statistical impact on employment	Feddersen and Maennig (2013)

(continued)

[22]Zimbalist (2015).

Table 10.8 (continued)				
Event	Year	Variable	Impact	Source
Summer Olympics	2000	Consumption	Household consumption reduced by $2.1 billion	Giesecke and Madden (2011)
Winter Olympics	2002	Employment	Short-run positive impact, no long-run impact	Baumann *et al.* (2012)
Summer Olympics	1996 and 2002	Sales, hotels, airports	No significant impact	Porter and Fletcher (2008)
Olympics	Various years	Economic growth	No long-term impact	Billings and Holladay (2012)
Olympics and World Cup	Various years	Economic growth	No meaningful lasting benefits	von Rekowsky (2013)

In addition to the general lack of economic benefits to the hosting nation, a number of substantial costs are imposed. As Zimbalist (2015) indicates, these include:

- *the cost of bidding for the games:* A host nation must pay either FIFA or the International Olympic Committee (IOC) for the right to host these events. And the bidding presentation itself is also expensive. Zimbalist (2015) notes that the City of Chicago spent $100 million on its failed bid for the 2016 Summer Olympics.

- *the cost of opening and closing ceremonies:* These spectacles are seen by people around the world, but the ceremonies are expensive to create and execute. Zimbalist (2015) notes that China spent $343 million just on its opening ceremonies in 2008.

- *the cost of security:* Zimbalist (2015) notes that security at the 2004 Athens Games cost $1.5 billion. The Olympic Games since 2004 also have reported security costs in excess of $1 billion.

- *a host of additional costs:* According to Zimbalist (2015), these include spending to maintain facilities, disruptions of local business, and the need to provide food and lodging to both athletes and executives of FIFA or the IOC.

Beyond these issues is the plight of workers hired to build the facilities needed to host such games. Reports indicated that migrant workers in Qatar—contracted for the 2022 World Cup—died at a rate of 1 every 2 days in 2014.[23]

---

[23]http://www.theguardian.com/world/2014/dec/23/qatar-nepal-workers-world-cup-2022-death-toll-doha.

Such workers are often hired to build the infrastructure needed to host these games. And this infrastructure imposes substantial short- and long-run costs. Zimbalist notes that the Bird's Nest in Beijing cost $460 million to build. Today, the venue is rarely used, but still costs $10 million per year to maintain. Other facilities built for these games have been completely abandoned.

A similar story can be told about the 2004 Summer Olympics in Athens. Four years after the Games, Athens continued to spend $784 million to maintain the facilities it had constructed for the Olympics, many of which were no longer used or significantly underutilized.[24]

When we consider the costs and benefits of these games, it appears—from the ex post studies—that the economic benefits are meager. But the costs, both in the short and long run, are substantial. In essence, as Szymanski (2009) notes,[25] the World Cup and the Olympics are parties that a nation throws for the world.

When we consider these events as parties, then we are less surprised to learn that the economic costs exceed the economic benefits. After all, few people throw a party to improve their economic fortunes. Parties are an expense. And just as the parties you throw at your own home do not make you financially richer, the parties that governments throw for the World Cup and the Olympics tend to leave the host nations financially worse off.

10.6 Sports Make Us Happy

So why do nations throw these parties? To answer this question, let's review some history.

Professional sporting events are not a modern invention. The term "bread and circuses" can be traced back to the Roman Emperor Augustus (who ruled Rome from 31 BCE to 14 CE). To keep the citizens of Rome reasonably well fed, Augustus gave away grain and controlled food prices. But one cannot live on bread alone! So Augustus also provided chariot races and contests between gladiators (i.e., circuses).

Although it is possible that Augustus claimed the circuses were necessary to promote economic growth, this certainly isn't the way the writer Juvenal (who lived from 55 CE to 127 CE) described these events. According to Juvenal, the bread and circuses served as a bribe of the masses. People who were fed and happy were less likely to riot.

---

[24]Mark Perryman, "Do the Olympics Boost the Economy?," Daily Beast, July 7, 2012, p. 7 [referenced in Zimbalist (2015)].

[25]Stefan Szymanski, *Playbooks and Checkbooks: An Introduction to the Economics of Modern Sports* (Princeton, NJ: Princeton University Press, 2009).

Such a perspective may seem very cynical. But Juvenal's insight from nearly 2,000 years ago gives us some insight into why governments are willing to spend so much on sporting events.

To illustrate, we turn to a study conducted by Georgios Kavetsos and Stefan Szymanski (2010).[26] These authors began by noting that the economic impact of sporting events does not seem to be substantiated by independent economic studies. So why do sports subsidies continue to be approved? One explanation might be found in surveys of life satisfaction.

In recent years, economists have been turning to these kinds of surveys. Traditionally, economists have focused on such issues as income to assess economic impact. The purpose of accumulating income, though, is to supposedly add to happiness (i.e., increase "life satisfaction"). With that in mind, some economists have looked to surveys of life satisfaction in an effort to address more directly the impact of policy changes.

With respect to the impact of sports, Kavetsos and Szymanski wondered how hosting and winning events would impact reported levels of happiness. Given this objective, the dependent variable in their study was the level of life satisfaction reported in surveys of people living in 12 different European nations. The independent variables included measures of the outcome of the sporting event; macroeconomic variables (such as GDP per capita, inflation, etc.); individual factors (like whether or not the person is employed, educational level, marital status, age, etc.); and a dummy variable for whether or not the person lived in the host nation.

One might suspect that athletic success would definitely make people happier. But Kavetsos and Szymanski (2010) only found weak support for that hypothesis. They uncovered stronger support for the hypothesis that hosting an event increases reports of life satisfaction. In fact, the magnitude of the effect is similar to the impact of a person getting married, although, as the authors indicated, the impact of hosting sports is short-lived (while the impact of marriage is much longer).

These results may help explain why subsidies keep happening. As Kavetsos and Szymanski (2010) noted, a paradox seems to exist in the economic literature. Studies consistently show that spending on sports doesn't lead to significant economic gains. Yet, politicians who authorize this spending are not penalized by voters. Maybe economists are focusing on the wrong outcome variables. Instead of concentrating on tangible income gains, perhaps what economists should focus on is the notion that sports simply cause people—especially those in the host nation—to feel good.

---

[26]Georgios Kavetsos and Stefan Szymanski, "National Well-Being and International Sports Events," *Journal of Economic Psychology* 31 (2010): 158–171.

As Kavetsos and Szymanski (2010) observed, their study only considered the impact of sports in Europe—with the focus primarily on the Olympics and football (i.e., soccer). At this point, similar studies of life satisfaction in North America have yet to be conducted. Such a study might help us understand why politicians in North America keep spending public money on the sports that make—at least the fans—happy.

Key Terms

multiplier (p. 322)

crowd out (p. 323)

substitution effect (p. 324)

crowding out effect (p. 324)

leakage effect (p. 325)

Problems

Study Questions

1. According to Gregory Mankiw, what percentage of economists agree with the following statements?
   a. "Fiscal policy (e.g., tax cut and/or government expenditure increase) has a significant stimulative impact on a less than fully employed economy."
   b. "Local and state governments should eliminate subsidies to professional sports franchises."
2. Which economist advocated expansionary fiscal policy as the solution to the Great Depression in the 1930s? Since the end of World War II, presidents of which political party in the United States have agreed with this approach to resolving recessions?
3. What is a multiplier? With respect to government spending, what is crowding out?
4. What do ex ante studies find with respect to public spending on sports?
5. According to Robert Baade and Victor Matheson, what are the problems with ex ante approaches to the study of public spending on sports?
6. What do ex post studies find with respect to public spending on sports?
7. Which stadium may be seen as marking the beginning of the move toward public funding of sports arenas and stadiums?
8. On average, how much does the public spend on building stadiums in the MLB, NFL, NBA, NHL, and MLS?

9. With respect to the World Cup and Olympics, what is the economic impact of these events from ex ante and ex post studies?

10. List and explain the short- and long-run costs incurred from hosting the World Cup or Olympics.

11. According to Juvenal, why did Roman emperors provide sporting events to the public?

12. According to Kavetsos and Szymanski (2010), why might governments subsidize sporting events? According to these authors, is it better to host an event or be the nation that wins the event?

13. Imagine developers wish to build a racing track. Two locations are considered. First is Los Angeles, California, a market with a host of entertainment options. The second is Visalia, California, a market with fewer entertainment options. How would the economic impact of the racing track differ between these two markets?

14. Imagine you were living in a city with high unemployment, and a sports team proposed that the government subsidize a new stadium for the team in the city. Discuss why this proposal might be good for the local economy and why it might not be.

Moneyball On and Off the Field

Is the Market for Talent in Sports Efficient?

1. **The *Moneyball* Story:** This chapter begins with the now classic *Moneyball* story from Michael Lewis. Published in 2003, *Moneyball* details the amazing tale of the Oakland A's, a team that managed to win many games without spending much money.

2. **The Rationality of Decision Makers:** The *Moneyball* story, though, is not just about the Oakland A's but part of a much broader debate in economics. One side of this debate argues that market participants tend to be "rational." A second argues that this is not entirely the case. Although this debate has been examined in non-sports settings, the data generated by the world of sports provide us with unique insights into a discussion that is often at the core of economics.

3. **The Baseball Labor Market:** The first data set we will examine comes from the baseball labor market. *Moneyball* argues that the A's were able to take advantage of market inefficiencies. The data, though, seem to tell a different story.

4. **The Labor Market in Complex Invasion Sports:** When we move on to the veteran labor market in complex invasion sports — like basketball and

football — we find that the evidence suggests decision makers do not behave in a fashion consistent with the traditional model. And when we move to the market for amateur talent, more evidence surfaces that decision making is not entirely rational.

5. **Rationality and Coaching:** *Moneyball* isn't just about the labor market. Researchers have also examined the on-field decision making of coaches in basketball, baseball, and football. In each case, on-field decisions have been found to be less efficient.

6. **Coaches and Player Productivity:** This leads us to wonder about the value of coaches. Studies have shown that coaches are not consistently different from each other. This doesn't mean coaches are without value. But it does suggest that most coaches are not able to alter player performance more than other coaches.

From 1993 until 1997, the Oakland A's finished with a losing record in each season and won only 44.2% of their games. And then in October 1997, the A's hired Billy Beane as the team's general manager.

As Table 11.1 notes, in 1998, the Oakland A's only had a winning percentage of 45.7%. But then the fortunes of this team changed. From 1999 to 2006, the A's won 58% of their games and consistently ranked in the top 10 in baseball in terms of winning percentage. But turning to how much the A's spent on talent, we see a team that consistently ranked toward the bottom of baseball's payroll rankings.

Table 11.1 The Oakland A's Winning Percentage and Payroll: 1998–2006[1]

Year	Winning Percentage	Winning Percentage Rank	Payroll (in millions)	Payroll Rank
1998	0.457	21st	$20.1	28th
1999	0.537	10th	$24.2	26th
2000	0.565	6th	$32.1	25th
2001	0.630	2nd	$33.8	29th
2002	0.636	2nd	$40.0	28th
2003	0.593	4th	$50.3	23rd
2004	0.562	9th	$59.4	16th
2005	0.543	9th	$55.4	22nd
2006	0.574	5th	$62.2	21st

[1]Bill Gerrard, "Is the Moneyball Approach Transferable to Complex Invasion Team Sports?," *International Journal of Sports Finance* 2 (2007): 214–228.

From 1999 to 2006, the New York Yankees also had great success. But as Table 11.2 reveals, the Yankees spent a great deal more on playing talent. While the A's only spent $357.4 million on payroll from 1999 to 2006, the Yankees spent $1.15 billion. All that additional spending, though, didn't result in many more wins. From 1999 to 2006, the Yankees won only 26 additional regular-season games. In fact, from 1999 to 2002, the A's won 383 regular-season games, or exactly the same number of regular-season games won by the New York Yankees.

Table 11.2 The Oakland A's and New York Yankees: 1998–2006[2]				
	Oakland A's		New York Yankees	
Year	Winning Percentage	Payroll (in millions)	Winning Percentage	Payroll (in millions)
1998	0.457	$20.1	0.704	$63.5
1999	0.537	$24.2	0.605	$85.0
2000	0.565	$32.1	0.540	$92.5
2001	0.630	$33.8	0.594	$109.8
2002	0.636	$40.0	0.640	$125.9
2003	0.593	$50.3	0.623	$149.7
2004	0.562	$59.4	0.623	$182.8
2005	0.543	$55.4	0.586	$208.3
2006	0.574	$62.2	0.599	$194.7

So how did the A's achieve the same regular-season results while spending so little on talent? That was the question Michael Lewis addressed in his best-selling book — and subsequent movie — *Moneyball*.[3] The story Lewis told centered on baseball statistics. Essentially, it was argued the A's were able to buy wins cheaply because the A's had developed a better understanding of how player performance relates to team wins. More specifically, it is reported that Billy Beane and the A's understood that baseball was undervaluing a hitter's ability to get on base (i.e., the ability of that hitter to draw a walk).

We will investigate the empirical evidence supporting this particular story later. First, though, we need to emphasize the implications this story has

---

[2]Gerrard (2007, p. 216).

[3]Michael M. Lewis, *Moneyball: The Art of Winning an Unfair Game* (New York: W.W Norton, 2003). The movie *Moneyball* was released by Sony Pictures in 2012 and starred Brad Pitt as "Billy Beane."

for economics. As noted previously, economists assume that individuals are rational utility-maximizers. Or as Thorstein Veblen[4] sarcastically put it:

> The hedonistic conception of man is that of a *lightning calculator of pleasures and pains* who oscillates like a *homogeneous globule of desire of happiness* under the impulse of stimuli that shift him about the area, but leave him intact. (p. 389; italics added to the original)

The *Moneyball* story calls into question the idea that decision makers in baseball are lightning calculators. To illustrate this argument, let's talk about the history of walks (more precisely known as the base on balls). Today, we think of a walk as what happens when a pitcher throws four balls to a batter. But prior to 1889, the National League (NL) awarded a base after as many as six, seven, eight, or nine balls. And in 1887, batting average, which currently is hits divided by at bats, was calculated as hits plus walks divided by at bats. This change had the predictable effect of encouraging players to try for walks. Such actions, though, lengthened the game and resulted in a longer experience for the fans (and some reported loss of fan interest).[5]

Although walks generated some interest in 1887, for most of baseball history, the walk was noted by statisticians but probably not noticed much by fans. For example, you may know that Barry Bonds set the all-time record for walks in a season with 177 in 2001.[6] But did you know that Bonds broke the record of 170 set by Babe Ruth in 1923? Or that prior to Ruth, this record was held by Jimmy Sheckard, who had 147 walks in 1911?[7]

Maybe you do know all this. But one suspects that most fans are not entirely familiar with the history of walks. Whether you know the story or not, though, the story of the season record for walks illustrates how long this particular statistic has been tracked. And if the *Moneyball* story is true, baseball collected a

---

[4]Thorstein Veblen, "Why Is Economics Not an Evolutionary Science," *Quarterly Journal of Economics* 12 (1898): 373–397.

[5]The story of the walk in the 1880s comes from Alan Schwartz, *Numbers Game: Baseball's Lifelong Fascination with Statistics* (New York: Thomas Dunne Books/St. Martin's Press, 2004), p.18. As Schwartz noted, the change in 1887 resulted in Tip O'Neill (a left-fielder for the St. Louis Browns of the American Association, not the Speaker of the House of Representatives from 1977 to 1987) leading professional baseball with a "batting average" of 0.492 (his actual batting average, from baseball-reference.com, was 0.435).

[6]Bond went on to break this record in 2002 and 2004. His mark of 232 is the current high mark in major league history (http://www.baseball-reference.com/leaders/BB_season.shtml).

[7]Data on the history of this record may be found at http://www.baseball-reference.com/leaders/BB_season.shtml.

number for more than a century, but before Beane came along, decision makers failed to understand how that number related to outcomes.

11.1 The First Sports Economics Article Proposes a Rationality Test

Sports economists tend to see the article authored by Simon Rottenberg in 1956 (discussed in Chapter 4) as the article that became the catalyst for the study of sports and economics. But eight years before Rottenberg's article appeared, Milton Friedman and L. J. Savage had utilized sports to illustrate an economic principle.[8]

Critics of the standard approach to economics (i.e., writers like Veblen) argue that people are not "lightning calculators" and do not have the ability to understand all that is necessary to behave as rational, profit-maximizing decision makers. Friedman and Savage, though, use the analogy of a billiards player to illustrate why critics of the standard economic approach might be wrong. The physics behind billiards is quite complex. But one doesn't have to understand the physics behind billiards to be successful. A player just has to perform as if he or she did understand this math.

Likewise, decision makers in economics — whether they are utility-maximizing consumers or profit-maximizing firms — do not need to be "lightning calculators" who fully understand the mathematics of consumer and firm economics. But successful consumers and firms must behave as if they fully understand the mathematical calculations necessary to achieve their ends.

Such an approach to a decision maker is captured by the concept of "instrumental rationality." As North (1994)[9] noted, instrumental rationality argues that the market process will punish people who have not arrived at the correct model. And when decision makers don't use the "right" approach at first, markets will continue to punish them until they get it right or exit the market. And that means eventually, people in a market must uncover the correct approach.

[8]Milton Friedman and L. J. Savage, "The Utility Analysis of Choices Involving Risk," *Journal of Political Economy* 56, no. 4 (August 1948): 279–304. These authors also argued that one should evaluate a model on the basis of its predictions, not its assumptions. That argument, though, is problematic. Although prediction is a desirable characteristic of a model, ultimately, scientists are trying to explain how the world works. So models need to explain what we are observing, not just make predictions about what we might see in the future.

[9]Douglass North, "Economic Performance Through Time," *American Economic Review* 84, no. 3 (1994): 359–368.

Do economic actors follow the dictates of instrumental rationality? As Friedman and Savage argued, one cannot criticize this idea by simply arguing that people do not understand the underlying mathematics. To refute the fundamental rationality assumption, one should show that people, in fact, fail to make rational decisions.

There has been quite a bit of work examining the rationality assumption in the laboratory. Specifically, students have been brought into laboratories at universities and asked to work through a variety of problems with academic applications.[10] Although such experiments are illuminating, a common criticism of any laboratory experiment is this: Life does not take place in a laboratory. The students participating in these studies know they are in a laboratory. And it is natural to wonder if their observed behavior would the same if the same study was conducted in a setting where consequences were real.

Such a setting can be seen in sports. In one sense, sports aren't reality. Whether or not your team wins or loses—and this may be hard for sports fans to accept—doesn't really matter to the lives of fans. But for the people employed in this industry, outcomes matter. Winners are rewarded and losers tend to get fired. And these are not the only outcomes. Losers in sports are open to public ridicule.

Consider George Steinbrenner, who bought the New York Yankees in 1973 (and continued to own the team until his death in 2010). When Steinbrenner purchased the Yankees, this franchise had not appeared in the post-season since 1964. For Yankee fans, such a playoff drought was surprising. Prior to 1969, Major League Baseball (MLB) had only allowed two teams in the post-season, and these two teams obviously played in the World Series. From 1921 to 1964, the Yankees had never gone more than three years without appearing in the World Series.

And in 1976, just four years after Steinbrenner assumed control of the Yankees, this team was once again in the playoffs. Over the next five seasons, the Yankees appeared to be back, appearing in the post-season in four of these five years.

But then the fortunes of Steinbrenner and the Yankees changed. From 1982 to 1993, the Yankees were completely shut out of the playoffs.[11] Such a losing streak led to clear consequences for the managers of the Yankees. From 1982 to 1993, the Yankees employed 10 different managers. Until Buck Showalter managed the team from 1992 to 1995, no manager employed by Steinbrenner had ever lasted more than three seasons.

---

[10]Dan Ariely, *Predictably Irrational: The Hidden Forces That Shape Our Decisions* (New York: HarperCollins, 2008) has conducted and detailed many of these laboratory experiments.

[11]Remember, the streak continued the next year because there were no playoffs in 1994.

Steinbrenner also experienced another consequence common to sports. He became the subject of public ridicule. This is an important point to make. If a firm fails outside of sports, the failure is often quite anonymous. Few people can name the executives who lead the most well-known firms in the American economy. But in sports, owners are known by the public. And when failure happens, the public is frequently not afraid to voice their displeasure.

This point was illustrated clearly in the classic television comedy *Seinfeld*. From 1994 to 1998, "George Steinbrenner" appeared in 10 different episodes.[12] In each, Steinbrenner was portrayed as a buffoon. And the reaction to this buffoon highlights the notion that decision makers in sports are not perfectly rational.

Consider what George Costanza said to Steinbrenner upon meeting him for the first time:

> I must say, with all due respect, I find it very hard to see the logic behind some of the moves you have made with this fine organization. In the past 20 years you have caused myself, and the city of New York, a good deal of distress, as we have watched you take our beloved Yankees and reduce them to a laughing stock. . . . (*Seinfeld*, "The Opposite," Season 5, 1994)[13]

In Season 7, a storyline was aired suggesting that George Costanza had died while employed by the Yankees. The character of "George Steinbrenner" then took it upon himself to notify George's parents of his death. Here are the first words out of the mouth of Frank Costanza (George's father) after hearing from Steinbrenner that his son had died:

> What the hell did you trade Jay Buhner for?! He had 30 home runs and over 100 RBIs last year. He's got a rocket for an arm. You don't know what the hell you're doin'! ("The Caddy," Season 7, 1996)

Although these statements are taken from a television show, they clearly illustrate two realities about sports. First—as anyone who listens to sports talk radio learns—fans are not convinced that decision makers in sports know what they are doing. Second, the failure to succeed as much as fans desire causes people to publicly question and ridicule decision makers in sports (again, sports talk radio also makes this clear).

---

[12]Steinbrenner was never shown on Seinfeld. Instead, his voice was portrayed by Larry David, who cowrote the show (see http://seinfeld.wikia.com/wiki/George_Steinbrenner).

[13]The quoted dialogue from *Seinfeld* may be found at http://www.seinfeldscripts.com.

The first point illustrates the debate between writers such as Thorstein Veblen and those who follow in the tradition of Milton Friedman. Do decision makers in sports actually behave like "expert billiard players"? Or do the data fail to confirm this prediction?

11.2 Testing the Moneyball Hypothesis in Baseball and Soccer

Michael Lewis provides no formal statistical test of his claims in *Moneyball*. He simply notes that the Oakland A's found success without spending much money. And he accepted the explanation given by the A's that this result was due to Oakland's approach to the evaluation of talent. But what story does the data tell? Our answer will discuss both the free-agent market for hitters and pitchers in baseball and the market for soccer players in Italy.

With respect to baseball's labor market, we begin with a study published by Jahn Hakes and Raymond Sauer in 2006.[14] These authors noted that the "Moneyball hypothesis" was not accepted by everyone:

> The publication of *Moneyball* triggered a firestorm of criticism from base-ball insiders (Lewis, 2003), and it raised the eyebrows of many economists as well. Basic price theory implies a tight correspondence between pay and productivity when markets are competitive and rich in information, as would seem to be the case in baseball. The market for baseball players receives daily attention from the print and broadcast media, along with periodic in-depth analysis from lifelong baseball experts and academic economists. Indeed, a case can be made that more is known about pay and quantified performance in this market than in any other labor market in the American economy. (p. 173)

This paragraph illustrates two issues:

1. Baseball is an ideal place to test Friedman's notions about decision making in the marketplace.

2. Baseball comes with an abundance of information on prices and productivity. So economists have the data necessary to evaluate the efficiency of decision making.

Such abundance, however, suggests that baseball's labor market should be efficient. In other words, we enter the study of baseball's labor market with the

---

[14]Jahn K. Hakes and Raymond D. Sauer, "An Economic Evaluation of the Moneyball Hypothesis," *Journal of Economic Perspectives* 20 (2006): 173–186.

expectation that decision makers in this industry should conform to Friedman's characterization of human decision making.

The Hakes–Sauer test involved looking at two specific relationships. First, the link between player statistics and wins was examined. This allowed researchers to establish which factors mattered most to a team's success on the field. The second step involved exploring how player statistics impacted player salaries. This examination established what decision makers were paying players to do on the field. If the decision makers conformed to the precepts of instrumental rationality, then teams would pay their players for the actions that impacted team wins.

To illustrate, let's begin with the following model of runs scored in baseball[15]:

$$\text{Runs Scored per Game} = a_1 + a_1 \times \text{Batting Average} + a_2 \\ \times \text{Isolated Power} + a_3 \times \text{Eye} + e_1 \qquad (11.1)$$

$$\text{Where Isolated Power} = \text{Slugging Average} - \text{Batting Average}$$

$$\text{Eye} = \frac{(\text{Walks} + \text{Hit-By-Pitch})}{\text{Plate Appearances}}$$

The three independent variables utilized in this model capture the three primary aspects of offensive performance.[16] Batting Average is the classic measure of performance (as previously detailed). And as noted, by itself, it leaves much of runs scored unexplained.

But if we add the two latter variables, we do better. Isolated Power captures the ability of a hitter to hit for power beyond his ability to hit for average. And Eye captures what the *Moneyball* story is supposed to be about. Specifically,

---

[15]This discussion of the free-agent market for hitters in baseball is based on Paul Holmes, Rob Simmons, and David Berri, "Moneyball and the Baseball Players' Labour Market," paper presented at Western Economic Association meetings, Denver, CO, 2014.

[16]The choice of variables derives from Hakes and Sauer (2006). These authors, though, primarily focused on on-base percentage and slugging average in this article and their earlier work published in 2006. They were not alone in making this choice. In "Assessing the Relative Importance of Inputs to a Production Function: Getting on Base Versus Hitting for Power," *Journal of Sports Economics* 14, no. 2 (2013): 203–217, Daniel Deli noted that a similar choice was made by Joseph Adler in *Baseball Hacks* (Sebastopol, CA: O'Reilly Media, 2006); J. C. Bradbury in *The Baseball Economist: The Real Game Exposed* (New York: Plume, 2007); and Wayne Winston in *Mathletics* (Princeton, NJ: Princeton University Press, 2009). As Holmes *et al.* (2014) observed, the correlation between team on-base percentage and slugging average is 0.79. In contrast, the correlation between Isopower and Eye is 0.43, Eye and Batting Average is 0.18, and Isopower and Batting Average is 0.08. Because on-base percentage and slugging average are highly correlated, it is more difficult for regression analysis to ascertain the corresponding impacts.

it was argued that the A's success hinged on their ability to take advantage of an undervalued asset (i.e., the ability to draw a walk).

This model was estimated with team data (i.e., Runs Scored per Game is the team's runs scored per game) from 1969 to 2016 in MLB. Because we are primarily interested in how much of an impact these factors have on outcomes, this model was estimated by taking the log of both the dependent and independent variables. By taking this step, the estimated coefficients are the elasticity of runs scored with respect to each independent variable. The results are reported in Table 11.3.

Table 11.3 Modeling Runs Scored with Batting Average, Isolated Power, and Eye[17]			
Independent Variables	Coefficients or Elasticities	t-Statistic	p-Value
Batting Average	1.779	84.17	0.000
Isolated Power	0.858	44.12	0.000
Eye	0.288	31.78	0.000

The R-squared for this model is 0.92, or quite close to what we observed with respect to the Blass model discussed in Chapter 6.[18] And since the estimated coefficients are elasticities, we can easily see that of these three factors, batting average has the largest estimated impact on runs scored. Furthermore, the ability to draw a walk has the smallest impact.

Now that we understand how these factors impact outcomes on the field, we turn to how these factors are valued in the marketplace. To address this issue, data were collected on free-agent hitters[19] from 1997 to 2012. The specific model, detailed in Table 11.4, involves regressing the log of free-agent salary[20]

---

[17] Data for this regression come from baseball-reference.com.

[18] When we estimate the Blass model across the same years utilized above, we see that the Blass model explains 94% of the variation in runs scored from 1997 to 2016. Now it is important to note that one cannot compare explanatory power in a linear model to the explanatory power we see in a logged model. This is because a linear and logged model have two different dependent variables (i.e., in one, we are looking at runs scored per game; in the other, the log of runs scored per game). However, if we reestimate equation 11.1 with a linear model, we see that explanatory power remains at 92%.

[19] The data set included all position players except catchers.

[20] The specific measure is the average value of a free-agent's salary across the length of the contract (adjusted for inflation). The Hakes and Sauer (2006) study referred to earlier considered the salary of all players. But because players sign multiyear contracts, such a study could involve connecting a player's performance on the field to a salary that was determined years before the performance took place. An alternative is to only look at free agents [a point originally made by Jeffrey Jenkins,

on a collection of nonlogged independent variables.[21] This model is thus what we call a semi-logged model (common in studies of salaries).

Table 11.4	Modeling Free-Agent Salary with Batting Average, Isolated Power, and Eye[22]		
Variable	Coefficient	p-Value	Elasticities[23]
Batting Average	13.883	0.000	3.72
Isolated Power	4.530	0.000	0.69
Eye	2.866	0.002	0.31

Perhaps surprisingly, the *Moneyball* story is not confirmed by this study of salaries. Once again, we have already seen that in order of impact on runs scored per game, Batting Average would be ranked first and Eye last. In Table 11.4, we see the same ordering. Batting Average has the largest impact on free-agent salaries. This is followed—again, exactly as we observed with respect to runs scored per game—by Isolated Power and Eye.[24]

All this suggests that the market for free-agent hitters in baseball conforms more closely with the vision of Milton Friedman and L. J. Savage. The valuation of hitters in terms of outcomes (i.e., runs scored per game) tends to correspond to what we see with respect to wages.

What about pitchers? For that position, we turn to a study by Bradbury (2007).[25] It examined an issue noted in both Chapters 6 and 8. Pitchers in baseball are often evaluated in terms of earned run average (ERA). But ERA depends on the fielders around the pitcher. Consequently, people have argued that a better approach is to consider defensive independent pitching statistics, which include strikeouts, walks, home runs, and hit batters. Although those who analyze stats in baseball make this argument, what do decision makers in baseball focus on?

"A Reexamination of Salary Discrimination in Professional Basketball," *Social Science Quarterly* 77, no. 3 (September 1996): 594–608]). Such an approach allows one to ascertain the link between a player's salary and his performance in the time period just before this salary was determined. Consequently, the link between pay and perceptions of performance can be better ascertained.

[21]This list of variables included plate appearances, age, and a measure of a player's speed.

[22]Holmes et al. (2014). *t*-Stats were not reported in this paper.

[23]This is a semi-logged model. So the elasticity—at the point of means—is simply the coefficient by the mean value of the variable.

[24]The Holmes et. al. paper looked at salaries from 1997 to 2012. The paper also considered whether or not the release of the Moneyball story in 2003 altered the market. The results do not suggest the book or movie changed the labor market in baseball.

[25]J. C. Bradbury, "Does the Baseball Player Labor Market Properly Value of Pitchers?," *Journal of Sports Economics* 8, no. 6 (December 2007): 616–632.

To answer this question, Bradbury (2007) looked at salaries for starting pitchers from 1987 to 2004.[26] Two specific models were estimated. One focused on factors independent of defenders (i.e., strikeouts, home runs, walks, and hit batters) and batting average on balls put in play (BABIP). The second model looked at the traditional "triple crown" of pitching statistics: ERA, wins, and strikeouts. As we have noted before, the defensive independent actors are more consistent across time and a better measure of a pitcher's value. Bradbury wanted to know if decision makers in baseball understood this story.

Bradbury (2007) began estimating his two models with the 1986 season. He then reestimated it for each season until 2004. Across these 19 years, we see, as Table 11.5 reports, that salaries are most consistently related to a pitcher's strike-outs. In contrast, ERA and winning percentage were hardly ever significant. This suggests that decision makers in baseball are often able to ignore factors beyond the control of the pitcher (i.e., ERA and winning percentage).

Table 11.5 How Often Do Various Pitching Statistics Explain a Pitcher's Salary? Years Examined: 1986–2004 (regression run for each model = 19)[27]

Independent Variable	No. of Times Independent Variable Was Statistically Significant
Model 1	
Strikeouts	16
Walks	5
Home runs	6
Hit batters	1
BABIP	3
Model 2	
Winning percentage	3
ERA	3
Strikeouts	11

Beyond demonstrating that the market for pitchers focuses primarily on the most consistent pitching statistics, Bradbury (2007) also noted some consistency between what we see with respect to a pitcher's impact on game outcomes and what a pitcher is paid. As Bradbury observed (2007, p. 627), the results from

[26]To be in the sample, a pitcher had to pitch more than 100 innings in back-to-back years to be included in the study. The sample is not restricted to free agents, but included all starters who met the innings limit. The author wishes to thank J. C. Bradbury for this discussion of his sample.

[27]Bradbury (2007, Tables 6 and 7, pp. 628–629).

both models (i.e., the salary model and game outcome model) indicated that the value of strikeouts, walks, and home runs in the labor market was similar to the impact these factors had on game outcomes.

Now we apply the same methodology to Italian soccer.[28] Once again, we need two models: a model for salaries and a model for game outcomes.

For the salary model, contract data, for newly signed contracts, were collected for defenders, midfielders, and forwards in Italian soccer from 2000–01 to 2013–14 seasons. The average salaries were then regressed on a collection of player characteristics and performance statistics. Across all three positions, one performance—shots on target—was consistently significant. And shooting efficiency was consistently insignificant. In sum, soccer players are primarily paid to take shots.[29]

When we consider game outcomes, obviously, wins are about goals scored and goals surrendered. And goals are determined entirely by shot attempts and shooting efficiency. So why do decision makers focus on the former and not the latter? One explanation is simply that shot attempts are consistent across time. As Berri, Buraimo, Rossi, and Simmons noted, a player's shot attempts this season have a 0.703 correlation with what the same player attempted last season. In contrast, shooting efficiency only has a year-to-year correlation of 0.171. Thus, teams have some ability to predict which players can attempt shots. But whether or not those shots go in the net is far less predictable. Consequently, the best strategy is to simply hire players who are consistently able to get shots. If your team consistently shoots more than your opponent, it is more likely you will win.

So in the market for pitchers, hitters, and soccer players, we see evidence consistent with the story told by Friedman and Savage. Perhaps this is not surprising. Performance data in baseball have existed for over a century. And the data that drive outcomes in soccer—shot attempts—are easy to track and notice.

11.3 Testing the Moneyball Hypothesis in Basketball

Basketball fans today are accustomed to looking at a box score and seeing data on offensive and defensive rebounds, steals, blocks, and turnovers. But the National Basketball Association (NBA) didn't start tracking these data for players until the 1970s.[30] So historically, unlike what we see in baseball, many performance stats were not available to decision makers.

---

[28]The study of Italian soccer is taken from David Berri, Babatunde Buraimo, Giambattista Rossi, and Rob Simmons, "Pay and Performance in Italian Football," paper presented at Western Economic Association meetings, Portland, OR, 2016.

[29]Full results of this model are reported in the appendix to this chapter.

[30]Offensive rebounds, defensive rebounds, steals, and blocks were first tracked for players in the NBA in the 1973–74 season. Turnovers were not tracked for players until the 1977–78 season.

In addition, even when these data were made available, interpreting them is difficult. One doesn't need regression analysis to know a home run is worth more than a single in baseball. But how does one more rebound compare to one more point? What about the relative value of shooting efficiency, turnovers, and blocked shots? Without statistical analysis, untangling the effects of each of the factors the NBA tracks to evaluate performance is quite difficult. In other words, functioning like a "lightning calculator" might be necessary to make decisions in a sport like basketball. And consequently, the vision of Friedman and Savage may not apply.

Once again, we turn to the same approach utilized to examine *Moneyball* in baseball and Italian soccer. We begin with how wins are determined in basketball. As noted in Chapter 6 and the appendix to this book, teams win because the team is able to acquire possession of the ball (i.e., grab defensive rebounds and force turnovers), maintain possession of the ball (i.e., avoid turnovers and grab offensive rebounds), and convert possessions into points (i.e., shoot efficiently). So the factors that drive wins are shooting efficiency, rebounds, and turnovers. Are these the same factors that drive player salaries? And does the estimated impact these factors have on wins correspond to the size of the impact these factors have on player salaries?

To answer these questions, we turn to a model of player salaries.[31] As detailed in the appendix to this chapter, the model we employ includes free-agent salaries[32] in the NBA to a collection of box-score statistics, as well as non-performance factors that might impact the wage a player receives. The results with respect to the player statistics are reported in **Table 11.6**.

Table 11.6 Modeling NBA Free-Agent Salaries: 2001–11[33]			
Variable	Coefficient	*t*-Statistic	Elasticity[34]
Points scored[a]	1.073	10.33	0.428
Rebounds[a]	1.202	5.78	0.210
Steals	0.697	0.61	

(continued)

[31]The model we utilize, detailed in the appendix to this chapter, is from David Berri, Michael Leeds, and Peter von Allmen, "Salary Determination in the Presence of Fixed Revenues," *International Journal of Sport Finance* 10, no. 1 (February 2015a): 5–25. This paper modeled free-agent salaries from 2001 to 2011 and it builds on the earlier model presented in David Berri, Stacey L. Brook, and Martin Schmidt, "Does One Simply Need to Score to Score?," *International Journal of Sport Finance* 2, no. 4 (November 2007): 190–205.

[32]This is the log of average salary across the length of the player's contract. Only players who signed for more than year are included in the sample.

[33]Berri *et al.* (2015a, Table 9, pp. 16–17).

[34]This is a semi-logged model. So the elasticity—at the point of means—is simply the coefficient by the mean value of the variable.

Table 11.6 *(continued)*			
Variable	Coefficient	*t*-Statistic	Elasticity[34]
Assists[a]	1.234	3.55	0.107
Blocked shots[a]	1.552	2.86	0.032
Turnover percentage[b]	0.006	2.03	0.074
Personal fouls[a]	−2.022	−3.24	−0.183
Adjusted field goal percentage[b]	0.490	2.00	0.242
Free-throw percentage[b]	0.220	1.87	0.166

p-Values not explicitly reported, but significance levels were noted as follows:
[a]Significant at the 1% level.
[b]Significant at the 10% level.

The story told in Table 11.6 is simple. When we consider the estimated elasticity of each factor, points scored is easily the most important factor. Nothing else a player does on the court has as large an impact on the wage he is paid.

To understand how important, consider how a 1 standard deviation in each box-score statistic impacts salaries. As **Table 11.7** indicates, a 1 standard deviation in points scored per minute is worth $833,913. If a free agent increased *both* his rebounds and shooting efficiency by 1 standard deviation, he still wouldn't

Table 11.7 Value of 1 Standard Deviation in each Box Score Statistic on Free-Agent Salaries: 2001–11[35]	
Independent Variable	Impact of 1 Standard Deviation Change
Points	$833,913
Total rebounds	353,616
Personal fouls	−$331,361
Assists	$313,706
Blocked shots	$170,419
Free-throw percentage	$151,544
Adjusted field goal percentage	$149,091
Turnover percentage	$141,272

[35]This table is derived from what is reported in Berri *et al.* (2015a). Because this is a semi-logged model, the slope for each independent variable can be estimated by multiplying the estimated coefficient from the model by the average value of dependent variable. For example, the estimated coefficient for points scored per minute is 1.0731, while the average value of the real player salary used in the model was $7,557,670. Consequently, the slope of points is $8,110,377.52. Multiplying this by the standard deviation of points (which is 0.1028) tells us the 1 standard deviation increase in points scored per minute is $833,913. Similar calculations yield all the values reported in Table 11.7.

see the same increase in his salary. In sum, scoring gets you paid in the NBA and that suggests a problem exists with player evaluation in basketball.

To understand why the focus on points scored suggests that NBA teams are not getting player evaluation exactly right, consider the story of Allen "The Answer" Iverson.[36] In 1996, the Philadelphia 76ers selected Iverson with the first pick in the 1996 NBA draft. At the conclusion of his first season, Iverson was named by every coach except one to the NBA All-Rookie First Team and was also named by sportswriters as the league's Rookie of the Year.

Iverson followed up this rookie campaign with a 14-year career in which he[37]:

* appeared in 11 All-Star games

* was named to the All-NBA First Team three times, All-NBA Second Team three times, and All-NBA Third Team twice

* led the NBA in points scored per game four times (and finished his career ranked 24th in total points scored)

* led the NBA in steals per game three times

* was named the league's most valuable player (MVP) in 2001

* was paid $154.4 million across his career

All this suggests Iverson was a great NBA player. He scored points in abundance. He was considered a star by fans and sportswriters alike. And NBA teams paid him a large sum of money to play basketball.

But if we consider everything Iverson did, there is some evidence that he wasn't quite as good as the above list of accolades suggests. For example, Iverson also finished his career:

* ranked 16th in turnovers, having led the NBA in this category in two different seasons

* ranked 18th in field goal attempts, having led the NBA in this category in four different seasons

* with a 45.2% effective field goal percentage, a mark well below average for an NBA player.

---

[36]The story of Allen Iverson was noted in *The Wages of Wins* and also David J. Berri, "Think You Know Basketball? You Need to Know the Numbers to Know the Game," for first issue of *Sports & Entertainment Review* 1, no. 1 (2015): 6-13. David J. Berri, Martin B. Schmidt, and Stacey L. Brook, *The Wages of Wins: Taking Measure of the Many Myths in Modern Sport* (Stanford, CA: Stanford University Press, 2006).

[37]Details of Iverson's career can be found at http://www.basketball-reference.com/players/i/iversal01.html and http://www.boxscoregeeks.com/players/544-allen-iverson.

In other words, Iverson scored many points because he took many shots, not because he was very good at actually converting shots into points. So when we look at everything, it appears Iverson did some things well and some things not so well. The question then is—as economics often asks—did the costs exceed the benefits?

When we consider Iverson's Wins Produced, it appears that his inability to avoid turnovers and consistently hit his shots was a significant problem. He finished his career with only 48.0 Wins Produced. To put that in perspective, Michael Jordan and Magic Johnson each had seasons where they produced more than 25 wins. And in 2015–16, the leaders in Wins Produced were Stephen Curry (21.5 wins), DeAndre Jordan (18.9 wins), Kawhi Leonard (17.8 wins), and Russell Westbrook (17.4 wins).

In addition, Iverson's career WP48 was only 0.056. As noted in the appendix to this book, an average NBA player posts a mark of 0.100. Iverson was an above-average player in two seasons. But of course—since he played 14 seasons—he was below par 12 times. Once again, Iverson's shooting inefficiency was a significant problem. This is a problem because, as we noted previously, shot attempts on a team are a finite resource.

A similar story can be told about Carmelo Anthony.[38] At the conclusion of the 2016–17 season, Anthony had played 14 years in the NBA. Across these years, he appeared in ten NBA All-Star games and was also named to the All-NBA Second or Third Teams six different times. In addition, he led the NBA in scoring (i.e., points scored per game) in 2012–13 and finished in the top 10 in points per game nine other seasons. His career earnings after 2016–17 stood at $205.8 million.

But when we turn to Wins Produced, we see a player who has only produced 40.6 wins across his 13-year career, with a WP48 of only 0.056 (again, the average WP48 is 0.100). Once more, shooting efficiency appears to be a problem. Anthony has a 48.2% career effective field goal percentage, a mark that is below average for an NBA player. Consequently, despite the accolades, points, and money, Anthony has been a below-average NBA player.

The Iverson and Anthony anecdotes serve to illustrate what we see when examining the systematic study of wins and salaries in the NBA. Players in the NBA have been primarily paid to score points. Scoring, though, is a function of both shot attempts and shooting efficiency. Thus, players can simply increase their scoring totals by "taking" more shots. The operative word is "taking" (as noted previously). Shot attempts do not change because a leading scorer is no

[38]Details of Carmelo Anthony's career can be found at http://www.basketballreference.com/players/a/anthoca01.html and http://www.boxscoregeeks.com/players/215-carmelo-anthony.

longer available. When scorers depart, other players simply get to take those same shots.

Therefore, the key issue in evaluating a player is whether or not his shot attempts are efficiently turned into points. But the study of salaries reported above indicated that from 2001 to 2011, shooting efficiency did not have nearly the impact on wages as scoring. This suggests that teams were not making decisions in a fashion consistent with the instrumental rationality framework.

One interesting aspect of this story is that it appears many economic actors in the NBA understand players are primarily paid for scoring. For example, consider the following from Glenn Robinson: In 1994, Robinson was selected with the first overall pick in the NBA draft. Just five games into his rookie season, Robinson said the following to Associated Press writer Jim Litke[39]:

> [A] lot of people that don't know the game, they think it's all about scoring. I look at it from a team perspective. We have to do well as a team. I don't need to go out there and score 30 points a game and have us lose.

Robinson added: "But I want to see all of us get something done." So a very young Robinson noted that while scoring might help him individually, it would not necessarily help the team. It is interesting that this quote captures the essence of the argument we make in this chapter. Scoring does help a player earn additional money. Wins, though, are about more than scoring.

Like players, owners also understand how scoring drives player evaluations. In the summer of 2013, the Wizards signed John Wall to an NBA maximum contract. The Wizards had chosen Wall with the 1st pick in the 2010 draft. In the summer of 2013, the Wizards still had an option to employ Wall under the terms of his original rookie contract. But they decided to resign Wall early and pay him the maximum allowed under the NBA's collective bargaining agreement. In defending this move, Ted Leonsis, owner of the Wizards, said the following: "One of the reasons we wanted to do this and do it early is to remove the I-need-to-get-stats. This is such a stats-oriented league and to have the focus on what the team needs to accomplish."[40]

---

[39]Jim Litke, "Big Dog's Big Push to Get Out of the Big Doghouse," Associated Press, November 16, 1994.

[40]http://www.csnwashington.com/basketball-washington-wizards/talk/leonsis-shows-hand-early-courting-wall.

These two quotes suggest that players and owners — the people involved in the negotiation of free-agent contracts — understand the story told by the above regression analysis. Scoring gets you paid. We also see evidence these people understand that a focus on scoring is inconsistent with winning basketball games.

One might argue, though, that scoring is what makes a player a star. And it is star power that attracts fans. This hypothesis was addressed by Berri, Schmidt, and Brook (2004).[41] As detailed in the appendix to this chapter, this article offered evidence that it is wins which attract fans, not star power. In other words, an inefficient star, like Iverson and Anthony, does not attract fans as much as simply fielding a team that wins games.

Given this result, teams should focus on a player's ability to produce wins. The above quote from Ted Leonsis indicates that such is indeed his focus. But the quote also reveals the incentives facing the players. Leonsis believed he had to sign Wall to a maximum contract so that Wall would not focus on his "stats." This is certainly an odd approach to worker compensation. Leonsis is arguing that first he needs to pay his worker, and then his worker will respond by focusing on the owner's objective (i.e., wins). Normally, though, one would suspect the order of events should be reversed. First, an employee demonstrates that he or she can be productive (i.e., focused on the owner's objective) and then the owner is willing to pay that worker.

To understand the perverse logic of the NBA, one has to understand the incentives facing the players. Players know — as the above quotes indicate — that more scoring leads to more pay. Imagine if Leonsis understood, though, that this was not true. Scoring totals alone did not lead to more wins, and therefore paying scorers who do not produce wins is not a good idea. But what if you believe your fellow owners don't understand this point. Furthermore, what if you think that John Wall has the potential to produce wins in large quantities in the future.[42] Then you may feel compelled to pay more than a player is worth today to secure his services in the future.

In sum, when we insist that decision makers in the NBA are not fully rational, we are not arguing that our concept of rationality does not apply at all. What appears to be the case is that decision makers fail to understand the value

[41]David J. Berri, Martin B. Schmidt, and Stacey L. Brook, "Stars at the Gate: The Impact of Star Power on NBA Gate Revenues," *Journal of Sports Economics* 5, no. 1 (February 2004): 33–50.

[42]After seven seasons with Washington, Wall had produced 52.1 wins in 18,033 minutes. This resulted in a WP48 of 0.139, or a mark that is above average. So although Wall did not quite produce wins at the level of LeBron James, Kevin Durant, or Stephen Curry, he did become an above-average player. Details on Wall's Wins Produced can be found at http://www.boxscore-geeks.com/players/348-john-wall

of the statistics tabulated to evaluate performance. But despite this limitation, we might still expect decision makers, both management and players, to behave "rationally" in the sense that each party seeks to maximize its gain. But there is an important constraint. Maximization occurs in the context of how decision makers understand the world.

11.4 Moneyball in the Draft

Thus far, we have discussed the salaries paid to veteran players in baseball and basketball. In such a market, the buyers would have already seen the player perform as a professional athlete. Consequently, we might expect players in this market to be evaluated correctly. But with respect to what may be observed in the study of basketball, we have found some inefficiencies.

Now we turn to a market where less information is available. As previously noted, each of the major professional team sports in North America employs a reverse-order draft in the market for nonamateurs. According to the leagues, this institution is designed to reward the worst teams (and of course, punish the best teams). The reward, though, depends on the ability of teams to identify the "best" talent.

Unlike the market for veteran talents, the players available in the draft in major professional team sports have yet to play against the talent that exists in major professional team sports. So decision makers in each sport have to infer a lot from what a prospective player does against mostly nonprofessional talent. Obviously, this task is more difficult than the job of evaluating veterans.

Decision Making in the MLB Draft

Our study of how well this task is completed begins with MLB. draft, an institution awash with uncertainty. Burger and Walters (2009)[43] reported that two-thirds of players drafted by major league teams never play baseball at the major league level. And 92% of drafted players fail to become "regular contributors."[44]

So this is a market where the odds of even finding a player capable of performing like an average major league baseball player are long. Despite these odds,

[43]John D. Burger and Stephen J. K. Walters, "Uncertain Prospects: Rates of Return in the Baseball Draft," *Journal of Sports Economics* 10, no. 5 (October 2009): 485–501.

[44]The two-thirds figure comes from Burger and Walters (2009) and is based on data from 1990 to 1997. These authors also noted that another 25% of players made it in the big leagues, but never became regular players. This leaves about 8% of players who were drafted and became regular contributors.

there is enough information to improve your chances. To illustrate, Burger and Walters looked at two different comparisons in the draft:

- high school players versus college players
- pitchers versus nonpitchers

In 1997, Burger and Walters (2007) noted that about 50% of the players drafted were selected out of high school. Fans of the NBA—where an age limit has been imposed to prevent a few players from making a leap from high school to the professional ranks—might be surprised to learn that baseball has always selected players directly from high school. And no movement has arisen to end this practice. Furthermore, players selected out of high school do not go to a major league roster. Instead, they go to the lowest levels of minor league baseball, where they must often play for years before reaching the highest ranks of professional baseball.

Of course, not all players choose to follow that path. Some players decide to play college baseball. These players are also selected by major league teams. So which is the better choice? Burger and Walters (2009) looked at the expected net revenue (i.e., difference between the average revenue generated by a specific class of player and the corresponding cost) of high school and college players. The data indicated that a player selected out of college had a 57% expected return. In contrast, the typical player selected out of high school only had a 36% expected return. Given this result, we should expect decision makers to prefer players with some college experience. Burger and Walters (2009), though, found that the selections of teams suggested they overvalued high school talent.

A similar story was told when the authors looked at pitchers and nonpitchers. Again, the expected net revenues of each class of player were estimated. The results indicated that pitchers had an expected return of 34%, while position players (i.e., nonpitchers) had an expected return of 52%. Such results should indicate that teams favor position players in the draft. Burger and Walters (2009), however, reported the opposite pattern. The selections of teams suggested that teams overvalue pitchers in the draft.

In *Stumbling on Wins*, the drafts from 1997 to 2006 were examined to see if the choices of major league teams had begun to change. The results, though, indicated that decision makers more often preferred high school players and pitchers (i.e., the players with lower expected returns).[45] Thus, it does not appear that decision makers in MLB are making the most efficient decisions possible with respect to the draft.

---

[45]David J. Berri and Martin B. Schmidt, *Stumbling on Wins* (Upper Saddle River, NJ: FT Press, 2010), p. 101.

Interestingly enough, Winfree and Molitor (2007)[46] offered evidence of more efficiency on the other side of this market. These authors specifically looked at the choices faced by those players selected out of high school. Such players have a choice: Start playing professional baseball or defer the professional ranks and play college baseball. Via an examination of expected lifetime earnings, Winfree and Molitor (2007) noted that high school players drafted earlier had higher earnings if they played professional baseball. In contrast, those selected later were better off going to college first. The evidence these authors presented suggests that players seem to understand the expected outcome of each choice. Players who would earn more by playing professional baseball tended to do this, while those who would earn more by going to college followed that path.

Such results indicate that not all decisions with respect to the MLB draft are inefficient. Apparently, high school students can make choices in a way consistent with the Friedman and Savage description of decision making. Those drafting high school players, though, are not quite as efficient.

Decision Making in the NBA Draft

The draft in the NBA is quite a bit different from the one in baseball. In the latter, most players drafted never appear on a major league roster. In the former, as Table 11.8 illustrates, more than 80% of players selected in the NBA draft (from 1995 to 2006) eventually play in the league, however brief that period of time may be. Part of this difference can be attributed to the fact that baseball teams are not only stocking their major league rosters, but also all their affiliated minor league rosters.

Beyond this issue, though, is the problem of forecasting baseball performance. As Table 11.9 shows, only 65.6% of players selected in the first round of the MLB draft ever appear in a MLB game. And misses (or players selected who never play) in the top 10 of the draft are not uncommon.

Table 11.8 Percentage of Players Drafted in the NBA Who Eventually Played: 1995–2006[47]			
Year	Drafted	Played in NBA	Percentage Played in NBA
1995	58	50	86.2%
1996	58	47	81.0%
1997	57	47	82.5%

(continued)

[46]Jason Winfree and Chris Molitor, "The Value of College: Drafted High School Baseball Players," *Journal of Sports Economics* 8, no. 4 (2007): 378–393.

[47]Based on data from basketball-reference.com.

Table 11.8 (*continued*)

Year	Drafted	Played in NBA	Percentage Played in NBA
1998	58	56	96.6%
1999	58	46	79.3%
2000	58	50	86.2%
2001	57	49	86.0%
2002	58	49	84.5%
2003	58	47	81.0%
2004	59	46	78.0%
2005	60	55	91.7%
2006	60	52	86.7%
Totals	**699**	**594**	**85.0%**

Table 11.9 Percentage of Players Drafted in First Round of MLB Draft Who Eventually Played in MLB: 1995–2006[48]

Year	Drafted in First Round	Played in MLB	Percentage Played in MLB
1995	30	19	63.3%
1996	35	23	65.7%
1997	52	31	59.6%
1998	43	30	69.8%
1999	51	24	47.1%
2000	40	23	57.5%
2001	44	26	59.1%
2002	41	27	65.9%
2003	37	27	73.0%
2004	41	33	80.5%
2005	48	37	77.1%
2006	44	32	72.7%
Totals	**506**	**332**	**65.6%**

This suggests that decision makers in the NBA have a better chance of identifying a player who can contribute something at the highest level. But establishing that NBA decision makers can locate their players in the draft isn't

[48]Based on data from baseball-reference.com.

enough. What we wish to know is how often the teams selecting first are, in fact, picking the "best" players.[49]

Consider the 2009 NBA draft. The "best" player selected that year was Stephen Curry. Across his first eight seasons, Curry produced 98.9 wins and his WP48 was 0.239 (again, the average is 0.100).[50] As noted earlier, in 2015–16, Curry produced 21.5 wins (a mark that led the league). In addition, he was named MVP of the league, the first unanimous selection in the history of the award. Curry's amazing 2015–16 season followed a 2014–15 campaign where he was also named MVP while leading his team to the 2015 NBA title.

Despite these accomplishments, people did not think Curry was the "best" player in the 2009 draft. In fact, he was not even considered the best point guard. In 2009, the Minnesota Timberwolves had both the 5th and 6th pick in the draft. Minnesota also believed it needed a point guard. So with the 5th pick, the team selected Ricky Rubio. At the time, though, Rubio was playing in Spain. And that meant he would not officially come to the NBA until the 2011–12 season.[51]

Because Rubio's move to the NBA was delayed, it might have made sense for the Timberwolves to select another point guard with their 6th pick. Again, Curry was available. But the Timberwolves went in a different direction, selecting Johnny Flynn from the University of Syracuse. In 2008–09, Syracuse finished with a record of 28-10 and advanced to the regional semifinal in the National Collegiate Athletic Association (NCAA) tournament. The leading scorer on that team was Flynn, a player who was ranked 20th in the nation as a high school player in 2007.[52] Curry also led his college team in scoring in 2008–09. But his team, Davidson, played in a much smaller conference (the Southern) and didn't even appear in the NCAA tournament in 2009. And Curry was never among the top 100 high school players and he was also almost a full year older.

Both Flynn and Curry started for their respective NBA teams in 2008–09. But after starting 81 times as a rookie, Flynn only started 10 more times across the rest of an NBA career that ended with the 2011–12 season. When it ended,

---

[49]The discussion of where players are selected in the NBA draft comes from David J. Berri, Stacey L. Brook, and Aju Fenn, "From College to the Pros: Predicting the NBA Amateur Player Draft," *Journal of Productivity Analysis* 35, no. 1 (February 2011): 25–35 and David J. Berri, Steve Walters, and Jennifer Van Gilder, "Stereotypes and Hiring Decisions: Lessons from the NBA Draft," paper presented at the Western Economic Association, San Francisco, CA, July 2012.

[50]Curry's stats taken from http://www.boxscoregeeks.com.

[51]Across his first six seasons, Rubio produced 44.2 wins and posted a 0.189 WP48. Not the same as Curry, but above average. Rubio's stats may be found at http://www.boxscoregeeks.com.

[52]http://www.basketball-reference.com/awards/recruit_rankings_2007.html.

Flynn had played for three NBA teams and produced −2.5 wins in his entire career. Clearly in hindsight, the Timberwolves made a mistake when they passed on Curry. Twice.

So where did the Timberwolves go wrong? To answer this question, let's consider some factors that might impact where a player is selected on draft night. A list of factors would include the player's performance on the court, the success of his college team, the conference where he played, how he was perceived before college, and various measurements taken at the NBA combine. Table 11.10 shows how these factors impact a player's draft position.

Table 11.10 What Determines where a Player Is Selected in the NBA Draft[53]: 2001–16	
Box-Score Statistics/Team Winning Percentage	1 Standard Deviation Increase
Points	−5.1
Assists	−2.0
Adjusted field goal percentage	−1.7
Steals	−1.6
Personal fouls	1.4
Total rebounds	−1.3
Blocked shots	−1.3
Winning percentage college team	−2.1
Combine Factors	
Height	−2.7
Maximum vertical leap	−1.9
Sprint time	1.8
Wing measure	−1.4
Dummy Variables and Age	**Impact**
Top 5 high school ranking	−7.1
Small conference	4.0
Age	4.0
Final Four appearance	−3.5

[53]These results come from a working paper by Berri, *et al.* (2012). The box-score statistics are per 40 minutes played. And except for adjusted field goal percentage, the box-score statistics and combined factors are adjusted for position played. This means a player is only above average in height if he is above average in height for the position he played.

We have already seen that scoring dominates the NBA free-agent market. And now we observe that when it comes to on-court performance, scoring has the largest impact on where a player is selected. A 1 standard deviation increase in scoring per 40 minutes improves a player's draft position by five slots. No other box-score statistic has half of this impact.

Beyond on-court performance, a player can place higher in the draft if he is taller and appears in the Final Four. It also helps to be a highly ranked high school player, younger, and to play for a team with a winning record. Except for playing for a winner, Curry met none of these other criteria. He was not unusually tall for his position. He never played in the Final Four. And he was not a highly regarded high school player. In 2009, he was a relatively older player from a team in a much smaller conference. Consequently, the best player in the 2009 draft did not hear his name called until the 7th pick.

The results with respect to the Final Four are especially interesting. As the working paper by Berri, Walters, and van Gilder (2012) noted, a Final Four appearance the year a player is in the draft results in his being selected about three to four slots earlier. However, if the player returns to school, that Final Four appearance now has no impact. Obviously, if appearing in the Final Four truly mattered, when that happened wouldn't make any difference. The empirical results suggest that decision makers in the NBA, however, only value the team's success most recently recorded.

It is important to emphasize that NBA teams are not just impressed by Final Four appearances; they also value team wins. Since 1991, the average team wins of a player selected out of college was 72%. And in related research, Greer, Price, and Berri (2015)[54] found that the probability of a player from a below 0.500 team being in the draft pool is essentially zero. From 2002–03 to 2016–17, the player who produced the most wins in NCAA Division I Men's College Basketball was Anthony Davis. As a freshman at the University of Kentucky in 2011–12, Davis produced 13.0 wins for a team that played 40 games. Obviously, Davis—by himself—was not enough for Kentucky to have a winning record.

This suggests that the NBA ignores a large sample of players (i.e., players on losing teams) that might be able to help its teams. In addition, its focus in compiling a sample appears to be incorrect. Again, NBA teams value young, tall scorers from winning college programs. Although such factors enhance how quickly a player is selected, players who possess these characteristics do not appear to be better NBA players.

---

[54]Tiffany Greer, Joshua Price, and David Berri, "Jumping in the Pool: What Determines Which Players the NBA Considers in the NBA Draft?," paper presented at the Western Economic Association, Honolulu, HI, July 2015.

What does predict future productivity are rebounding and shooting efficiency. This is not surprising. Wins in basketball are about gaining and keeping possession of the ball and turning those possessions into points, so it would be natural to assume that players who rebound well and hit their shots in college are more likely to produce wins in the NBA. But the impact of rebounding and shooting efficiency on draft position appears to be relatively small.

As for the nonbox-score factors, these don't appear to matter. Players from winning college teams do not make better NBA players. And the data collected in the NBA combine do not seem to tell decision makers anything at all.

Thus, decision making in the NBA draft is similar to what we see in the NBA free-agent market. Scoring is overemphasized. And the factors that lead to wins, like rebounds and shooting efficiency, are not emphasized enough.

Decision Making in the NFL Draft

Now we turn to the NFL draft. And our story begins in 2004.

The San Diego Chargers held the 1st pick in the 2004 NFL draft. The team's preference was to draft Eli Manning. But Manning made it clear that he did not wish to play for the Chargers. So after selecting Manning, the Chargers traded him to the New York Giants for the 4th pick in the 2004 draft, the 65th pick in the 2004 draft (a third-round pick), and the Giants, first-round pick in 2005 (which became the 12th pick).[55] Then with the 4th pick in the draft, the Chargers selected quarterback Phillip Rivers.

Tables 11.11 and 11.12 report the statistical production of Manning and Rivers for their respective teams through the 2016 season. Manning became the starting quarterback for the Giants midway through his rookie season. Rivers, though, sat behind Drew Brees for two seasons before assuming the starting position with the Chargers. Consequently, across the first 13 seasons of each player's career, Manning participated in 842 additional plays. Despite this difference in playing time, Manning's career statistical production of wins is actually lower. So obviously, Rivers has also produced more wins per 100 players (WP100).[56] And a similar story is told when we look at the NFL's traditional quarterback and ESPN's QBR metric.[57] No matter what metric is considered, it appears Rivers has been the better quarterback.

---

[55]http://www.cbssports.com/nfl/eye-on-football/22046030/eof-time-machine-eli-manning-really-didnt-want-chargers-to-draft-him.

[56]To put these numbers in perspective, all quarterbacks who attempted at least one pass from 2004 to 2012 participated in 174,910 plays. Across the plays, these quarterbacks offered a statistical production worth 1,168.9 wins. So across all quarterbacks, WP100 is 0.668.

[57]QBR considers the impact of all plays on outcomes, adjusting for where the play took place on the field and the time and conditions of the game. The metric, though, only goes back to 2006.

Year	All Yards	Plays	Interceptions	Fumbles[58]	Wins Produced[59]	WP100	QB Rating (NFL)	QBR (ESPN)
2004	995	216	9	3	0.66	0.308	55.4	NA
2005	3,658	614	17	9	4.04	0.657	75.9	NA
2006	3,079	572	18	9	2.96	0.518	77.0	43.5
2007	3,188	585	20	13	2.88	0.492	73.9	39.2
2008	3,074	526	10	5	3.72	0.707	86.4	60.4
2009	3,870	556	14	13	4.67	0.841	93.1	62.4
2010	3,955	587	25	7	4.25	0.724	85.3	56.4
2011	4,749	652	16	9	6.12	0.939	92.9	59.0
2012	3,842	575	15	5	4.76	0.828	87.2	66.0
2013	3,573	608	27	7	3.32	0.546	69.4	33.8
2014	4,254	641	14	7	5.38	0.839	92.1	65.9
2015	4,336	665	14	11	5.34	0.803	93.6	60.5
2016	3,876	640	16	7	4.52	0.706	86.0	60.2
Totals/ Averages[60]	46,449	7,437	215	104	52.66	0.708	83.7	55.2

Table 11.11 Eli Manning's Statistical Production: 2004–15

Fans of Manning, though, might cite these numbers for Manning and Rivers:

* playoff won-loss record (prior to 2017): Manning (8-3), Rivers (4-5)
* Super Bowls won (prior to 2017): Manning (2), Rivers (0)

Of course, these are team marks. Assigning wins to quarterbacks is a problem since outcomes in football depend on much more than just the quarterback. So perhaps we should rely more on player statistics? Then again, we also noted

---

[58]These are total fumbles. To calculate Wins Produced, only fumbles lost should be included. Whether a team loses a fumble, though, is essentially random. So in calculating Wins Produced, it was assumed half of fumbles were lost.

[59]Wins Produced for NFL quarterbacks was detailed in *The Wages of Wins*. It was also updated in David Berri and Brian Burke, "Measuring Performance in the NFL," in Kevin Quinn (ed.), *The Economics of the National Football League: The State of the Art* (New York: Springer, 2012), pp. 137–158. Essentially, this is derived from a series of regressions connecting box-score statistics in the NFL to team wins. As Berri and Burke (2012) noted, this measure is correlated with the NFL's quarterback rating and many measures at advancedfootballanalytics.com.

[60]In this last row are weighted averages for WP100 and QB Rating (i.e., these metrics are constructed based on the totals). QBR, though, only goes back to 2006. So the number seen is simply the average value from 2006 to 2016.

Year	All Yards	Plays	Interceptions	Fumbles	Wins Produced	WP100	QB Rating (NFL)	QBR (ESPN)
2004	28	12	0	1	−0.01	−0.097	110.9	NA
2005	98	26	1	2	−0.01	−0.041	50.4	NA
2006	3,293	535	9	8	4.09	0.764	92.0	62.3
2007	3,022	511	15	11	3.15	0.616	82.4	44.6
2008	3,942	534	11	8	5.23	0.979	105.5	66.9
2009	4,137	537	9	6	5.79	1.079	104.4	76.1
2010	4,535	608	13	7	6.08	1.001	101.8	62.5
2011	4,462	638	20	9	5.35	0.838	88.7	64.3
2012	3,335	603	15	15	3.37	0.559	88.6	46.2
2013	4,400	602	11	3	6.09	1.012	105.5	74.9
2014	4,199	643	18	8	4.98	0.774	93.8	70.5
2015	4,556	718	13	4	5.91	0.824	93.8	59.4
2016	4,233	628	21	9	4.86	0.775	87.9	74.4
Total/ Averages	44,240	6,595	156	91	54.89	0.775	94.7	63.8

Table 11.12 Phillip River's Statistical Production: 2004–15

that quarterbacks are not solely responsible for the stats we assign to their performance.

There is an additional issue. We are looking at these data 13 years after the trade occurred. On draft day in 2004, neither the Giants nor Chargers knew exactly whom they would be acquiring in this trade and how either player would perform. In the Chargers case, such was clearly true since they did not know whom they would select in the third round in 2004 or in the first round the following year. So how did the participants in this trade decide it was a "fair" one?

Although we cannot know for certain the process each team followed to reach its decision, we do have access to what is called "the Chart."[61] As Massey and Thaler (2013)[62] noted, the Chart was initially created by Mike McCoy (part-owner of the Dallas Cowboys) in 1991. McCoy examined trades from 1987 to

[61]http://sports.espn.go.com/nfl/draft06/news/story?id=2410670.

[62]Cade Massey and Richard H Thaler, "The Loser's Curse: Decision Making and Market Efficiency in the National Football League Draft," *Management Science* 59, no. 7 (July 2013): 1479–1495.

1990 and created a table, partially detailed in **Table 11.13**, showing the values that teams were apparently placing on draft picks.

Table 11.13	The NFL "Chart" (detailing value of draft picks)												
Rd. 1	Value	Rd. 2	Value	Rd. 3	Value	Rd. 4	Value	Rd. 5	Value	Rd. 6	Value	Rd. 7	Value
1	3000	33	580	65	265	97	112	129	43.0	161	28.0	193	15.2
2	2600	34	560	66	260	98	108	130	42.0	162	27.6	194	14.8
3	2200	35	550	67	255	99	104	131	41.0	163	27.2	195	14.4
4	1800	36	540	68	250	100	100	132	40.0	164	26.8	196	14.0
⋮	⋮	⋮	⋮	⋮	⋮	⋮	⋮	⋮	⋮	⋮	⋮	⋮	⋮
29	640	61	292	93	128	125	47	157	29.6	189	16.8	221	4.0
30	620	62	284	94	124	126	46	158	29.2	190	16.4	222	3.6
31	600	63	276	95	120	127	45	159	28.8	191	16.0	223	3.3
32	590	64	270	96	116	128	44	160	28.4	192	15.6	224	3.0

To illustrate, consider the Manning–Rivers trade with respect to the values listed in "the Chart." The Giants acquired the 1st pick in the draft, worth 3,000 points. In return, the Chargers received the 4th pick (worth 1,800 points), the 65th pick (worth 265 points), and the 12th pick in the next draft. Had the 12th pick been in the 2004 draft, it would have been worth 1,200 points, giving the Chargers a slight edge in this trade. But since the 12th pick in the first round would not take place until the following year, and when the trade was made, the Chargers did not know exactly where the pick would fall, one could argue this trade was approximately even.

Massey and Thaler (2013) examined trades from 1983 to 2008 and uncovered values quite similar to those originally reported by McCoy. This suggested that across the past 30 years, the prices teams place on draft picks have become somewhat standardized. But just as we wondered in the examination of the free-agent market in various sports, are the prices teams place on these picks "correct"?

The study offered by Massey and Thaler (2013) presents evidence that the chart detailed in Table 11.13 is not "correct." The evidence presented involves estimating the surplus value of each drafted player—or more specifically, the difference between each player's salary and the economic value of the player's production if he is allowed to be a free agent. Since the draft is supposed to reward the losers, we should expect to see the largest surplus value at the top of the first round. But Massey and Thaler (2013) pointed out that the highest surplus value is found at the top half of the second round. And given this result, Massey and Thaler (2013) argued that teams at the top of the draft should be trying to trade down.

Or as Massey and Thaler (2013) put it:

Our findings are strikingly strong. Rather than a treasure, the right to pick first appears to be a curse. If picks are valued by the surplus they produce, then the first pick in the first round is the worst pick in the round, not the best. In paying a steep price to trade up, teams are paying a lot to acquire a pick that is worth less than the ones they are giving up. We have conducted a wide range of empirical tests and every analysis gives qualitatively similar results. The same is true under the 2011 labor agreement. The new rookie salary cap reduced the cost of the very top draft picks, but not enough of them to alter our results. (p. 1493)

The difficulty with the Massey and Thaler (2013) study is that they attempted to evaluate all players at all positions. This limited their measurement of player performance to consider factors like games played, games started, and Pro Bowl appearances. In other words, Massey and Thaler (2013) could only consider factors common to all positions.

Another approach is to simply examine a specific position. This was the approach taken by Berri and Simmons (2011a).[63] Their paper specifically examined the drafting of NFL quarterbacks. From 1970 to 2014, a quarterback was selected with the 1st pick in the NFL draft 20 different times.[64] Some of these selected players went on to Hall-of-Fame careers. Others, like Tim Couch, David Carr, and JaMarcus Russell, have been far less successful. Of course, in hindsight, any draft pick could look like a poor decision. Teams do not have perfect information when they make their picks. So the fact that some do not work out does not indicate decision makers followed a flawed process.

To evaluate this process, Berri and Simmons (2011a) first examined which factors impact where a quarterback is selected in the draft. It then turned to how these factors related to future NFL performance. Ideally, the factors that predict draft position should also predict how a quarterback subsequently performs in the NFL.

That list of examined factors takes into account a variety of factors related to a quarterback's statistical production in college. In addition, the list includes factors related to a quarterback's physical dimensions (i.e., height and body mass

[63]David J. Berri and Rob Simmons, "Catching a Draft: On the Process of Selecting Quarterbacks in the National Football League Amateur Draft," *Journal of Productivity Analysis* 35, no. 1 (February 2011a): 37–49.

[64]According to pro-football-reference.com, of the 44 number one picks, 20 were quarterbacks, 9 defensive ends, 6 running backs, 3 offensive tackles, 2 defensive tackles, 2 linebackers, and 2 wide receivers.

index), speed (40 yard dash time), competition level (dummy for playing outside the top division of college football),[65] and intelligence.

This latter effect is measured via the Wonderlic test. According to Wonderlic.com, this test was developed by Eldon F. Wonderlic, an industrial psychologist, in 1937. The test consists of 50 questions that must be answered in 12 minutes. These questions, which are not about football, are designed to measure a person's mental agility. The average score for all people who take this test (i.e., not just football players) is 21.6. For the NFL quarterbacks in the Berri and Simmons (2011a) data set, the average score was 26.1 (with a range from 10 to 42).[66]

The model Berri and Simmons (2011a) estimated included a variety of measures of a quarterback's performance, and these estimates indicate that where a quarterback is drafted is statistically related to his height, Wonderlic test score, and 40-yard dash time. So NFL teams prefer quarterbacks that are fast, tall, and smart. Berri and Simmons (2011a) went on to note that the combine factors appear to dominate the decision-making process. Specifically, they reported that "nearly 20% of the variation in a quarterback's draft position is explained by just the combine factors" (p. 46). When the performance measures are considered, explanatory power rises by less than 3%. This suggests that scouts in the NFL "are more influenced by what they see when they meet the players at the combine than what the players actually did playing the game of football" (p. 46).[67]

Now it is possible that the combine factors isolate a quarterback from his teammates. So perhaps these factors are indeed better indicators of a quarterback's future production in the NFL. Berri and Simmons (2011a) addressed this possibility with a host of regressions employing different measures of an NFL quarterback's performance. As they noted, "In all of our formulations, we never found that the combine factors, or the college performance with respect to Wins Produced per 100 plays or QB rating, had a significant impact—of the expected sign—on NFL Wins Produced per play or NFL QB Rating at any level of experience in the NFL" (p. 47). These authors also noted after further analysis that "comparing two quarterbacks with same NFL experience, the player selected

---

[65]Historically, the top division was called Division I-A. Today, this division is referred to as the Football Bowl Subdivision (FBS). Division I-AA, or the second division in college football, is now referred to as the Football Championship Subdivision (FCS).

[66]The Wonderlic scores the authors utilized were taken from NFL Quarterback Wonderlic Scores (http://www.macmirabile.com/wonderlic.htm). This is a website maintained by Mac Mirabile.

[67]Berri and Simmons also looked explicitly at how college performance related to where a quarterback was drafted. The results suggest that performance on the field doesn't matter much.

earlier in the draft is not predicted to have significantly different NFL performance levels than a player picked later in the draft. Draft pick is not a significant predictor of NFL performance" (p. 48).

This last point can be illustrated, as in Appendix A of this chapter, with the correlation between where a player is selected and two factors: playing time and performance per play. One sees that better draft position definitely helps a quarterback get more playing time. And we have already observed—in our study of attractiveness and quarterback salaries—that draft position predicts a quarterback's pay well into his NFL career. But draft position does not predict how a quarterback will perform per play. This is not surprising since many of the factors the NFL considers in evaluating quarterbacks do not predict future performance. In sum, just as we learned in our review of the draft in baseball and basketball, decision making in the NFL draft is not very efficient.

11.5 Moneyball on the Field

Issues with decision making in sports extend beyond the labor market. Various studies have examined decision making on the field as well. And inefficiencies have been found in the study of coaches/managers in basketball, baseball, and American football.

Allocating Minutes in Basketball

Previously, in Chapter 7, we reviewed a study examining the role national identity played in the allocation of minutes in the NBA. This same study—by Berri, Deutscher, and Galletti (2015b)[68]—also looked at how various box-score statistics impacted the way in which coaches allocated minutes. As Table 11.14 notes, the results indicate that personal fouls per 48 minutes played has the largest impact on minutes. Such a result, though, simply reflects the rules of the game. After personal fouls, it is scoring that dominates how coaches allocate minutes.

Just as we saw with salaries and the NBA draft, scoring also dominates the coaches' evaluation of playing talent. Such a result is not confined to the NBA. A similar result was uncovered for how coaches allocated minutes in the Spanish

[68]David J. Berri, Christian Deutscher, and Arturo Galletti, "Born in the USA: National Origin Effects on Time Allocation in US and Spanish Professional Basketball," *Special Issue: National Institute Economic Review* (May 2015b): R41–R50.

Table 11.14   Impact of 1 Standard Deviation on Minutes per Game in NBA[69]

Independent Variable (statistics are per 48 minutes played)	Impact of a 1 Standard Deviation Change in NBA Sample
Personal fouls	−3.22
Points	2.48
Assists	1.30
Rebounds	0.63
Free-throw percentage	0.47
Adjusted field goal percentage	0.43
Steals	0.34
Turnover percentage	0.28
Blocked shots	0.22

Liga[70] and the WNBA.[71] In basketball, players who score more points per minute will see more minutes on the court. So it is not just the people hiring players who focus too much on scoring (i.e., general managers); coaches also tend to overvalue scoring.[72]

Stealing Wins in Baseball

Baseball teams have historically sought to "manufacture" runs. This process involves advancing runners via sacrifices and/or stolen bases. Of these two approaches, the stolen base gets far more attention. The all-time leader in stolen bases is Rickey Henderson. Across 25 major league seasons, the "Man of Steal" swiped 1,406 bases. Henderson is the only player to steal more than 1,000 bases in a career.[73] It is perhaps not surprising then that he was elected to the Hall of Fame in 2009.

---

[69]Berri *et al.* (2015b, Table 8). This is a linear model, so the elasticity is calculated by multiplying the coefficient from Table 11.14 by the ratio of the sample mean of the corresponding independent variable and the sample mean of minutes per game.

[70]Berri *et al.* (2015b).

[71]Jill Harris and David Berri, "If You Can't Pay Them, Play Them: Fan Preference and Own-Race Bias in the WNBA," *International Journal of Sport Finance* 11 (August 2016): 163–180.

[72]David Berri, Jennifer van Gilder, and Aju Fenn also found that the sports media overvalues scoring. See "Is the Sports Media Color-Blind?," *International Journal of Sport Finance* 9 (2014): 130–148.

[73]Lou Brock is second on the all-time list with 938 stolen bases.

Although each of these steals clearly provided a benefit to his respective teams, Henderson's efforts in this area also came at a cost. When his career ended, Henderson additionally held the all-time caught stealing mark. His mark of 335 means that on all of Henderson's attempts, he was successful 80.8% of the time.

Is this good? To answer the question, we need to consider costs and benefits. The benefit of stealing a base is that a team has moved a base runner one base closer to scoring.[74] The cost, though, is one more out if the runner is not successful. And since a team only has three outs in each innings—and 27 outs in a game—many have considered the loss of an out a substantial cost.

Certainly, Hall-of-Fame manager Earl Weaver seemed to make this argument in his seminal book *Weaver on Strategy: Classic Work on Art of Managing a Baseball Team*. As Weaver noted, a manager's "most precious possessions on offense are (his) twenty-seven outs."[75] For Weaver, advancing a runner in the hope of getting just one more run was not generally a good idea. As Weaver put it in his Fifth Rule of Strategy: "If you play for one run, that's all you will get."

To address the costs and benefits of this choice, we need to do more than appeal to authority. What we require are specific numbers. We already saw, back in Chapter 6, that regression analysis indicates each stolen base is worth 0.10 runs. Being caught stealing, though, reduces runs by 0.34. Given these values, a team breaks even with respect to stealing when it is successful 77.8% of the time. More sophisticated analysis—noted in the appendix to this chapter—indicates that the break-even point depends on what base a runner is trying to steal and how many outs exist when this happens. Such analysis shows that the break-even point ranges from 66.2% to 89.9%.

Let's just say the break-even point is 70%. Figure 11.1 reports the stolen base percentage for each year in MLB from 1951 to 2016. Again, a break-even point percentage is about 70%. The first time baseball reached this mark was 1987, when teams averaged a percentage of 70.1%. This success, though, was short-lived. From 1988 to 1995, the average percentage once again fell below 70%. And

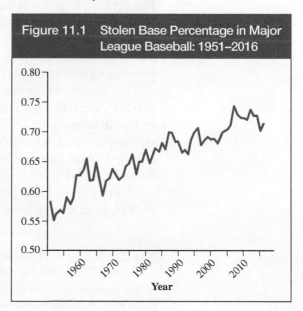

Figure 11.1   Stolen Base Percentage in Major League Baseball: 1951–2016

---

[74]Unless, of course, the runner steals home. This rarely happens in baseball.

[75]Terry Pluto and Earl Weaver, *Weaver on Strategy: Classic Work on Art of Managing a Baseball Team* (Lincoln, NE: Potomac Books, 1984).

then after reaching this threshold in 1995 and 1996, the percentage again dipped below 70% until 2004.

From 2006 to 2016, the average percentage has persistently exceeded 70%. In sum, it appears that baseball is now at least breaking even on stolen base attempts. What Figure 11.1 also makes clear, though, is that, historically, baseball did not break even with respect to stolen base attempts. In other words, the costs of stealing bases exceeded the benefits for much of baseball's history.

"Going for It" in the NFL

Baseball managers can at least argue that some learning has taken place in their sport. Back in 2006, David Romer[76] identified an important trend in the decision making of NFL coaches. Specifically, NFL coaches failed to "go for it" on fourth down as often as the data suggested they should. And in subsequent years, there is not much evidence that coaches have learned to "go for it."

Romer's study was similar to what we observed with respect to stolen bases. The decision to go for it on fourth down involves an examination of costs and benefits. The benefits of going for it are that the team keeps possession and continues to have a chance to score. The obvious cost is that the team loses possession of the ball. If the team punts, it almost definitely loses possession, but the other team's field position should be worse.

The analysis conducted by Romer was an extensive study of all the costs and benefits[77] associated with this decision. *The New York Times* employed Romer's analysis in creating the "NYT 4th Down Bot" that details what a team should do with respect to each fourth down at any point on the field.[78] For example, *The New York Times*, based on its analysis (which builds on Romer's work), offers the rules-of-thumb reported in Figure 11.2.

From Figure 11.2, one can see that the fourth down bot recommends an NFL team always "go for it" on fourth down if they have reached at least

---

[76]David H. Romer, "Do Firms Maximize: Evidence from Professional Football," *Journal of Political Economy* 114 (2006): 340–365.

[77]Brian Burke, an analyst at ESPN, put together a discussion of the fourth down decision:
http://www.advancednflstats.com/2009/09/4th-down-study-part-1.html
http://www.advancednflstats.com/2009/09/4th-down-study-part-2.html
http://www.advancednflstats.com/2009/09/4th-down-study-part-3.html
http://www.advancednflstats.com/2009/09/4th-down-study-part-4.html.
This series does a wonderful job of explaining the argument advanced in Romer (2006).

[78]https://www.nytimes.com/2014/09/05/upshot/4th-down-when-to-go-for-it-and-why.html.

their own 9-yard line and they only need 1 yard for a first down. If the team needs 2 yards for a first down, then the recommended rule-of-thumb is to "go for it" if the team has reached its own 28.

But the typical NFL coach does not follow the lesson taught by Figure 11.2. Furthermore, this does not appear to be changing over time. The Romer study received quite a bit of media attention prior to the 2004 season, and in subsequent seasons, this attention has persisted. *The New York Times* even allows one to analyze fourth down decisions throughout a season.[79] Nevertheless, despite more than 10 years of coverage and analysis, NFL coaches continue to be too conservative.[80]

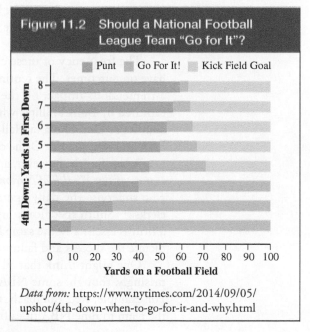

Figure 11.2   Should a National Football League Team "Go for It"?

Data from: https://www.nytimes.com/2014/09/05/upshot/4th-down-when-to-go-for-it-and-why.html

11.6 Adam Smith Versus NBA Coaches

There is evidence that coaches don't always get it right. That observation leads to a larger question. What is the value of a coach? Or more specifically, are some coaches better than others?

Let's begin by looking back at the NBA in 2012–13. The Denver Nuggets won 57 games in 2012–13, a mark that ranked fourth in the league. When the season ended, head coach George Karl was named NBA Coach of the Year by sportswriters. But after the Nuggets' first-round exit in the NBA playoffs, Karl was fired by the team.

A similar fate was suffered by the head coaches with the LA Clippers and Memphis Grizzlies. Each of these teams won 56 games in 2012–13. And each team fired its head coach when these teams exited the playoffs.

In all, 13 of the 30 teams in the NBA decided to let their head coach depart after the 2012–13 season. Such turnover was a bit higher than what had

[79]This is done at the following website: http://nyt4thdownbot.com/. In addition, one can follow the matter on Twitter: https://twitter.com/nyt4thdownbot.

[80]Brian Burke, who assists with *The New York Times* analysis, also recently agreed that NFL coaches continue to be too conservative (http://www.advancednflstats.com/2013/11/is-revolution-over-did-we-win.html#more).

previously been typical in the NBA. From 1995 to 2013, teams made 134 coaching changes.[81] Or on average, between six or seven head coaches were asked to depart each season.

The frequency of these changes leads one to wonder what impact coaches have on outcomes. The sentiment exists that coaches in professional sports have a tremendous impact on their team's ability to win games. This thought was captured by Bum Phillips, who offered the following comment on the coaching abilities of Don Shula (a Hall-of-Fame coach in the NFL): "Don Shula can take his'n and beat your'n. Or he can take your'n and beat his'n."[82]

Adam Smith, however, appeared to disagree. In *An Inquiry into Nature and Causes of The Wealth of Nations* (1776/1976), Smith suggested that the managers who supervise the daily operations of a firm are nothing more than "principal clerks."[83] Smith specifically argued that the job of "inspection and direction" for a firm is essentially the same for all firms. Consequently, daily managers do not dictate the success and failure of firms.[84]

One might think that all coaches would disagree with this assessment. Surprisingly, though, some NBA head coaches appear to agree with Adam Smith. For example, Red Auerbach, the legendary coach of the Boston Celtics who led the team to nine NBA titles from 1957 to 1966, had this to say about coaching:

> [Coaches] today want you to believe that what they're doing is some kind of science. Coaching is simple: you need good players who are good people. You have that, you win. You don't have that, you can be the greatest coach who ever lived and you aren't going to win.[85] (p. 273)

Auerbach seems to be arguing that it is players who produce wins. And if a coach doesn't have productive players, wins are not going to happen very often.

---

[81]Kevin Zimmerman, "The Unique Circumstance of NBA Coaching Turnover in 2013," 2013, http://www.sbnation.com/nba/2013/8/14/4614020/nba-coaches-doc-rivers-george-karl.

[82]This quote is taken from a *New York Times* article written by Dave Anderson, November 1, 1992. Others have argued that Phillips borrowed the quote. The original quote may have been about Bear Bryant, the legendary football coach at the University of Alabama. It has also been attributed to other coaches.

[83]The "principal clerk" observation was taken from chapter VI, "Of the Component Parts of the Price of Commodities," of *The Wealth of Nations* (Chicago: University of Chicago Press, 1976), pp. 54–55. The "principal clerk" argument was also noted by Ira Horowitz, "On the Manager as Principal Clerk," *Managerial and Decision Economics* 15 (1994): 187–194.

[84]The specific argument appears in Smith (1976, pp. 54–55).

[85]See John Feinstein and Red Auerbach, *Let Me Tell You a Story: A Lifetime in the Game* (New York: Little, Brown, 2004).

Of course, all coaches don't agree with Auerbach. NBA coaches have actually written books revealing their "leadership secrets" and touting the impact coaches have on team success. A nonrandom sample of such coaches would include Pat Riley, Rick Pitino, and Phil Jackson.[86]

In 1993, Riley authored the *The Winner Within: A Life Plan for Team Players*. In this book, Riley reveals his "formula for success," a formula drawn from his experiences as coach of the Los Angeles Lakers and New York Knicks.

At the time this book was published, Riley had coached parts of nine seasons and had a career regular-season winning percentage of 0.723. This mark—back in 1993—surpassed that of all NBA coaches in the history of the league. He also had led teams to four NBA championships. With such a record, it's not surprising that hundreds of corporations employed Riley as a public speaker. After all, who wouldn't want to awaken their own "winner within"?

After Riley's book was published, though, his own "winner within" became less visible. Riley coached parts of 13 seasons after the 1992–93 campaign. Across these seasons, his regular-season winning percentage was only 0.559 and his teams only managed to win one NBA championship. This title, with the Miami Heat in 2006, came in Riley's first season after leaving the bench in 2002–03. Why did Riley stop coaching in 2003? One suspects that the Heat's winning percentage of 0.305 that season—a mark bested by all but four NBA teams—played a major role in Riley's departure.

In 2004, though, the Heat acquired Shaquille O'Neal, one of the most productive "big" men in the history of the game. And in 2005, Riley decided to return to coaching. Although the Heat won Riley's fifth title in 2006, two years later, the team finished with a 15-67 record, the worst mark in Riley's career. After that season, Riley again stepped down as head coach.[87]

Despite Riley's disastrous final season as head coach, his career winning percentage still ranks 6th in the history of the NBA.[88] So although he did not find

---

[86]Pat Riley, *The Winner Within: A Life Plan for Team Players* (New York: Putnam, 1993). Rick Pitino's wrote two books: *Success Is a Choice: Ten Steps to Overachieving in Business and Life* (New York: Broadway Books, 1998) and *Lead to Succeed: 10 Great Traits of Leadership in Business and Life* (New York: 2000). Phil Jackson authored *Sacred Hoops: Spiritual Lessons of a Hardwood Warrior* (New York: Hyperion, 2006).

[87]Riley has apparently found success as a general manager. After stepping down as Heat head coach, Riley continued to lead the franchise. Under his leadership, the Heat advanced to the NBA Finals four times and won two championships. This success coincided with the team acquiring LeBron James in the free-agent market. Once James departed in 2014, the Heat's fortunes declined (the team missed the playoffs in 2014–15).

[88]Minimum 410 games coached (or 5 seasons). Coaching data can be found at http://www.basketball-reference.com/coaches/NBA_stats.html.

success every season he coached, over 23 seasons, his teams only failed to post a winning record three times.

One might believe that Riley's level of success was a prerequisite to write a book on leadership. But such is not the case. Rick Pitino coached only six seasons in the NBA. His teams never made it out of the second round of the playoffs and four of these teams finished with a losing record. With a career winning percentage of 0.466, one wouldn't think Pitino might author a single book on successful coaching. And you would be right. Pitino has actually written two books on the subject!

Pitino's first book, *Success Is a Choice: Ten Steps to Overachieving in Business and Life*, was published in 1998. At this point, Pitino had only coached two seasons in the NBA: the 1987–88 and 1989–90 seasons with the New York Knicks. Although these teams made the playoffs, Pitino's Knicks never made it very far in them. Pitino, though, was not known for his NBA coaching. In the college ranks, he led Providence College to the NCAA Final Four in 1987. After two years with the Knicks, he returned to the college arena, becoming the head coach at the University of Kentucky in 1989. Across the next eight seasons, Kentucky appeared in the Final Four three times and took the NCAA title in 1996.

Pitino departed from Kentucky in 1997 to become the head coach of the Boston Celtics. Pitino coached the Celtics for four seasons and never once led this team to a winning record. Despite this lack of success, Pitino published *Lead to Succeed: 10 Great Traits of Leadership in Business and Life* in 2001.

At about the time this book was released, Pitino left the Celtics and became head coach at the University of Louisville. Back in the college ranks, Pitino again found success. Under Pitino, the University of Louisville has won 74.4% of its games,[89] advanced to three Final Fours, and won the NCAA championship in 2013.

Obviously, it's Pitino's success in the college ranks that gives him credibility as an expert on leadership. Of course, as we observed in Chapter 9, in the college arena a coach does not face the same restrictions an NBA coach encounters in recruiting talent. NBA teams select talent via the draft and also must deal with salary restrictions in signing free agents. A college coach, on the other hand, is far less restrained in the recruitment of talent. In fact, the top teams often have more than one player with a future in the NBA. And these top teams get to play against teams that employ players who wouldn't even get to sit on the bench at an elite basketball school. Consequently, one suspects that a key reason why Pitino was so successful in the college ranks is simply because he was frequently able to coach better talent than the coaches he had to face. When Pitino's talent advantage was taken away — as often happens in the NBA — his ability to lead his

---

[89]As of the conclusion of the 2016–17 season.

teams to success faded away as well. In sum, Pitino's lack of success in the NBA was more about the quality of his NBA roster and less about his skills as a coach.

Turning this argument around, one might suspect that successful NBA coaches have simply been blessed with better talent. Certainly, Riley was a better coach with the Lakers, where he coached Magic Johnson, than he proved to be later in his career when his roster was less talented. And one suspects that the coach who currently boasts the best career winning percentage in NBA history may also owe his success to the wonderfully talented players on his roster.

At the conclusion of the 2010–11 season, Phil Jackson had coached for 20 NBA seasons. Over these years, Jackson's teams had won 70% of their regular-season contests and 11 NBA titles. Given all this success, it is not surprising that Jackson also wrote books detailing the lessons learned from basketball.

One of Jackson's books, though, is quite unlike the tomes offered by Riley and Pitino. Whereas Riley and Pitino have clearly tailored their discussions to people in business, Jackson's work, *Sacred Hoops*, is far more spiritual in its outlook. Jackson's writing, which draws on the teachings of Zen Buddhism, is not strictly intended for people who wear suits every day.

Just as one might have some skepticism in reviewing the advice of Riley and Pitino, one wonders if a basketball coach can truly advise on matters related to spirituality. Would we even listen to Jackson's views on spirituality if he didn't have the best coaching record in NBA history? In other words, if Jackson's career record in the NBA mirrored what Pitino posted, would anyone ask Jackson to share his thoughts on spirituality and hoops?

Jackson, though, doesn't have Pitino's record. His mark leads that of all coaches in NBA history.[90] Once again, we suspect that this record is really about the talent Jackson got to coach. To understand this point, let's quickly review Jackson's history in the NBA.

Jackson was named head coach of the Chicago Bulls in 1989. At that point, the Bulls had yet to make it to the NBA Finals. In Jackson's second year, however, the Bulls won the NBA title. And then they proceeded to win the next two titles as well.

After failing to win titles in 1994 and 1995, Jackson and the Bulls managed to win the NBA title in 1996, 1997, and 1998. After the 1998 season, Jackson left the Bulls. In 1999, he returned to the NBA with the Los Angeles Lakers. And just as we saw in Chicago, the Lakers proceeded to win three consecutive NBA championships. After losing in the NBA Finals in 2004, Jackson departed from the NBA once again. And again, he reemerged with the Lakers after a one-year hiatus. Although the Lakers failed to advance past the first round in both

---

[90]For such evaluations, a coach has to have a minimum of 410 games coached (or five seasons). Coaching data can be found at http://www.basketball-reference.com/coaches/NBA_stats.html.

2006 and 2007, in 2008, Jackson led the Lakers back to the NBA Finals. And in 2009 and 2010, Jackson's Lakers once more captured NBA titles.

Again, looking at the entire picture, we see that Jackson is the only coach to win 70% of his regular-season contests. Examining the playoffs, we note that Jackson's winning percentage of 0.688 also ranks first in NBA history[91]; and no one has ever led a team to 11 NBA titles.

Although Jackson's record is impressive, a skeptic might regard this record as less about "sacred hoops" and more about the wealth of talent he had at his disposal. Jackson's teams in Chicago were led by Michael Jordan. With the Lakers, he was able to coach Shaquille O'Neal. When these players were not available to him, Jackson's teams were not quite as dominant. Jordan retired in 1993 and then returned with 17 games remaining in the 1994–95 season. Across the 147 games Jordan was playing baseball, Jackson's teams only won 60.5% of their games. A similar story played out with the Lakers. With O'Neal, the Lakers won three titles and lost in the NBA Finals in 2004. After the 2003–04 season, Jackson retired and O'Neal was traded to the Miami Heat. Jackson returned to the Lakers for the 2005–06 season, and although the Lakers were still above average, the team's winning percentage from 2005–06 to 2007–08 was only 58.5%.

Overall, Phil Jackson's teams in the years without Jordan and O'Neal only won 59.3% of their games. When these two superstars were available, though, Jackson's teams won 74.4% of their games. In sum—just as we suspected when looking at the accomplishments of Pat Riley and Rick Pitino—it appears as if the quality of talent Jackson was able to coach had something to do with his record.

11.7 Systematically Evaluating Coaches

Views on coaches thus differ. Adam Smith and a few coaches seem to have thought the credit for success should go elsewhere. Other coaches have trumpeted the important role they have played in their organization's success.

To address this difference in opinions requires that we look at the evidence. Teams frequently change coaches in sports. And these changes, coupled with the fact that players also frequently switch teams, result in players often working for a variety of different coaches during the course of their career. So one wonders, do different coaches lead to different outcomes?

Not surprisingly, a variety of studies have addressed this very issue. We are going to focus on three specific studies examining coaches in soccer, basketball, and baseball.

---

[91]These data can be found at http://www.basketball-reference.com/coaches/NBA_stats.html. Again, only coaches who coached at least five seasons are considered.

Impact of Coaches in Soccer

We will begin our review with a study by Mario De Paola and Vincenzo Scoppa (2012)[92] that sought to understand how coaching turnover impacted outcomes for Italian soccer teams.[93]

The authors started out by noting that two econometric problems plague the study of coaching turnover:

1. Coaches are not randomly fired. Weaker teams are more likely to fire their coaches. Hence, the sample of teams that change coaches is not the same as the sample of teams that do not change coaches.

2. Researchers must also account for what is called "regression to the mean" or the "Ashenfelter dip."[94] There is a tendency for outcomes that are far from the mean to be followed by those that are closer to the mean. With respect to coaching, a tendency would exist for a team to fire its coach when the team is performing well below average. Once a new coach is on board, performance regresses back to the mean. If this tendency in the data is not accounted for, the researcher might conclude the new coach is the cause of the reversion.

Table 11.15 illustrates this second point. De Paola and Scoppa (2012) considered match-level data from 1997–98 to 2008–09. As the authors observed, 37% of the teams in the data set changed coaches during a season. And when this happened, those teams improved with respect to standing points and goals scored.

Table 11.15 Comparison of Team Performance Under a Former and New Coach in the Italian "Serie A"[95]			
	Points	Goals Scored	Goals Conceded
Old coach	0.994	1.023	1.509
New coach	1.122	1.15	1.455
Difference	0.128[a]	0.127[a]	−0.054

[a]Difference is statistically significant.

[92]Maria De Paola and Vincenzo Scoppa, "The Effects of Managerial Turnover: Evidence from Coach Dismissals in Italian Soccer Teams," *Journal of Sports Economics* 13, no. 2 (2012): 152–168.

[93]The study specifically looked at Italian "Serie A," the top division of Italian soccer and one of the top soccer leagues in the world (in terms of revenue, attendance, etc.).

[94]Orley Ashenfelter, "Estimating the Effect of Training Programs on Earnings," *Review of Economics and Statistics* 60 (1978): 47–57 studied the earnings of people in a training program. It determined that earnings tended to dip right before participants entered the program. So comparing earnings before and after the training program would overstate the value of the training program.

[95]De Paola and Scoppa (2012, Table 1, p. 156).

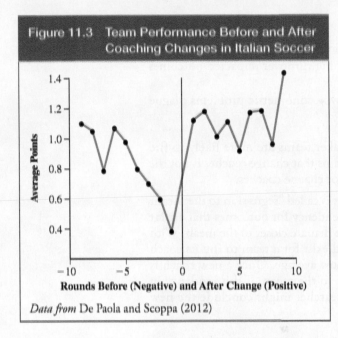

Figure 11.3   Team Performance Before and After Coaching Changes in Italian Soccer

Average Points

Rounds Before (Negative) and After Change (Positive)

Data from De Paola and Scoppa (2012)

This observation is also illustrated in Figure 11.3, which shows average team performance before and after a coaching change. Both Table 11.15 and Figure 11.3 suggest that changing coaches improves outcomes.

But again, we have the Ashenfelter dip. We might expect a team to change coaches when the team's performance is below average. And we also should expect below-average performances to be followed by improved outcomes, whether the coach changes or not.

To control for this impact, the De Paola and Scoppa (2012) study estimated a series of regressions that examined the impact of changing a coach after controlling for the quality of the two teams in the match. Once quality was controlled for, the impact of changing the coach — contrary to what we saw in Table 11.15 — was not statistically significant.[96]

The approach taken by De Paola and Scoppa (2012) is not the only approach one can adopt to investigate the impact of coaches. Another approach is to examine how a coach impacts individual player performance. In a sport like soccer, where individual performance measures are not widely available, gauging how a coach impacts the productivity of each player is difficult. But in sports like basketball and baseball, as we noted in Chapter 6, this can be done.

Impact of Coaches in Basketball

Berri, Leeds, Leeds, and Mondello (2009) specifically studied coaching in basketball.[97] Their study began by noting that, traditionally, we evaluate coaches by looking at winning percentage. The difficulty with such a traditional approach is that the quality of players with whom different coaches must work varies considerably. As previously observed, Phil Jackson and Pat Riley had the opportunity to coach some of the very best players in NBA history. And Rick Pitino did not.

---

[96]As De Paola and Scoppa (2012) noted, this result confirms studies of Belgium soccer and Dutch soccer. See A. Balduck and M. Buelens, "Does Sacking the Coach Help or Hinder the Team in the Short Term? Evidence from Belgian Soccer," working paper, Faculty of Economics and Business Administration, Ghent University, Belgium, 2007; A. Bruinshoofd and B. TerWeel, "Manager to Go? Performance Dips Reconsidered with Evidence from Dutch Football," *European Journal of Operational Research* 148 (2004): 233–246.

[97]David J. Berri, Michael Leeds, Eva Marikova Leeds, and Michael Mondello, "The Role of Managers in Team Performance," *International Journal of Sport Finance* 4, no. 2 (May 2009): 75–93.

A great coach can alter the performance of the players he coaches. But how often does a player's performance really change in response to his coach? To answer this question, we need to consider all the factors that can alter player performance. Such a list is provided in Table 11.16.

The table begins with the per-48-minute productivity of an NBA player.[98] The remaining factors are variables that might cause that performance to change. The list includes age of the player, games played (to control for injury), position played, the productivity of teammates (to control for diminishing returns),[99] the stability of a team's roster,[100] and then dummy variables for whether a player had a new team or a new coach.

Although each of these factors is important, none of the variables listed are the main focus of this model. The main focus is the impact of a new coach. This is controlled for by including dummy variables for each coach in the study, equal to 1 if the player came to the coach and zero otherwise.

Table 11.16 Average Value of NBA Player Performance and Various Factors that Could Cause Performance to Change[101]	
Variable	Mean
Productivity of player (ADJP48)	0.301
Age	27.141
Games played past two seasons	141.8
Center	0.207
Power forward	0.200
Small forward	0.196
Shooting guard	0.201
Productivity of teammates	0.097
Roster stability	0.690
New team	0.289
New coach	0.456

[98]ADJP48 refers to Adjusted Productivity per 48 minutes played. This is a player's performance adjusted for factors like team defense but not adjusted for position played. Wins Produced per 48 minutes (WP48) would be ADJP48 adjusted for position played. This is detailed in the appendix to this book and at http://wagesofwins.com/how-to-calculate-wins-produced/.

[99]Productivity of teammates is the team's Wins Produced per 48 minutes, minus the contribution of the player in question. This was included to control for diminishing returns. One should note, player performance was measured with Wins Produced, unadjusted for the diminishing returns effect of defensive rebounds. When this adjustment is made, the diminishing returns effect noted doesn't appear. In sum, diminishing returns appears to be primarily about defensive rebounds.

[100]Roster stability is measured as the percentage of minutes played by players employed by the team in both the current season and the previous season. A priori, greater roster stability makes players more comfortable with each other, and theoretically, this could enhance performance.

[101]Player data at basketball-reference.com.

Before we get to the impact of the coaches in the study, though, we begin with the impact of the other factors. The estimation of this model is reported in two tables. In **Table 11.17**, we see the noncoaching independent variables. This table indicates that a player's current performance is statistically impacted by his past performance, age, injury (again, games played past two seasons), and the productivity of teammates. More specifically, a player will tend to be more productive if he was productive in the past and avoids injury. He is less productive if his teammates are productive.

As for age, well it depends. When a player is younger, he can expect to improve. But eventually, age diminishes productivity. The results suggest that an NBA player peaks in performance around his mid-twenties.[102]

Table 11.17   Estimated Coefficient for Noncoaching Independent Variables[103]

Independent Variable	Coefficient	z-Statistic
ADJP48, lagged[a]	0.1588	4.47
Age[a]	0.0465	7.27
Age squared[a]	−0.0010	−8.38
Games past two seasons[a]	0.0006	8.18
Productivity of teammates (TMWP48)[a]	−0.2996	−6.68
Roster stability	0.0080	1.16
New team	−0.0025	−0.99
New coach	−0.0033	−0.93

p-Values not explicitly reported, but significance levels were noted as follows:
[a]Significant at the 1% level.

Although the results reported in Table 11.17 are interesting, the big question is whether coaching can alter any of this story. In all, 62 coaches were considered in the model. And again, the specific question is whether a player's performance changes when he begins to play for a new coach. The statistically significant results, as reported in **Table 11.18**, indicate that not many coaches

---

[102]The results reported here indicate that the peak age is about 24. Research by David J. Berri and Rob Simmons, "Mixing the Princes and the Paupers: Pay and Performance in the National Basketball Association," *Labour Economics* 18, no. 3 (June 2011b): 381–388 — based on data from 1991 to 2008 — suggests a peak of around 26 years of age. This may be because athletic training has improved over time. Such a result was consistent with what we reported for WNBA players in Chapter 8.

[103]Berri *et al.* (2009, Table 6A, p. 86). In addition to these variables, position dummies were employed.

have such an impact. As one can see, only 14 coaches—out of a sample of 62—had a statistically significant positive impact on a new player's per-minute performance. And only three coaches had an impact that was statistically significant at the 1% level.

Table 11.18	Coaches with a Statistically Significant Positive Impact on Player Performance[104]	
NBA Coaches	Coefficient	z-Statistic
Phil Jackson[a]	0.045	3.550
Gregg Popovich[a]	0.042	2.610
Cotton Fitzsimmons[a]	0.042	3.170
Jim O'Brien[b]	0.032	2.510
Gene Shue[a]	0.030	2.650
Don Nelson[b]	0.030	2.580
Flip Saunders[a]	0.028	2.700
Isiah Thomas[b]	0.028	2.000
Rick Pitino[c]	0.027	1.700
Stan Albeck[b]	0.026	2.240
Kevin Loughery[b]	0.026	2.520
Mike Fratello[b]	0.022	1.970
Chris Ford[b]	0.020	1.860
Larry Brown[b]	0.017	1.880

p-Values not explicitly reported, but significance levels were noted as follows:
[a]Significant at the 1% level.
[b]Significant at the 5% level.
[c]Significant at the 10% level.

The primary story of Table 11.18 tells us not the names listed, but again, the 48 coaches in the study who were not found to have a statistically significant impact on performance. It appears that when we control for the factors that cause a player's productivity to change, we find that most NBA coaches do not impact player performance.[105]

---

[104]Berri *et al.* (2009, Table 6B, p. 87).

[105]Berri *et al.* (2009) also looked at how performance might change in the second, and third, years with a new coach. Of the coaches examined, only three coaches had a positive statistically significant impact in the second year (Popovich, Jackson, and Nelson) and only Jackson had a positive statistically significant impact in the third year. The study also determined what happened when a player moved away from a coach. For 10 coaches, such a move caused performance to decline in a statistically significant fashion. In addition, one coach was found to have

The Impact of Coaches in Baseball

For the study of baseball managers, we turn to the work of Bradbury (2010).[106] The study began with a sample of baseball players, both hitters and pitchers,[107]—who played from 1980 to 2009.

With this sample, Bradbury estimated a model that links performance—OPS for hitters and ERA for pitchers—to dummy variables for the player's manager. In addition, the model considers league performance in a given year, the career performance of the player, the age of the player, and park effects.[108]

Like the aforementioned study of basketball, the factor we are most interested in is the impact of managers. Bradbury's study included 134 managers. Of these, just 21 had a statistically significant impact, at the "lenient ten-percent level benchmark,"[109]—on a hitter's performance.[110] For pitchers, only 15 managers had a statistically significant positive impact on performance.[111] And there was not a single manager found to have a positive statistically significant impact on hitters and pitchers.

Having presented evidence that most baseball managers do not alter the performance of players, Bradbury (2010) then asked if changing managers could impact consumer demand. The specific hypothesis was that by changing managers, a team sends a signal to its fans that the team will soon improve because

---

a negative statistically significant impact on a player when he came to the coach, while another had a negative statistically significant impact in the second year. For two coaches, performance improved in a statistical sense when the player departed. One should emphasize that this entire study utilized dummy variables to capture the impact of a coach. Such an approach is crude, and would not allow one to differentiate between the impact of a head coach or his assistants (or any other organizational issue present when the coach was employed). Obviously, this kind of approach does not tell us why a coach might have had the impact we observed.

[106]J. C. Bradbury, "Hired to Be Fired: The Publicity Value of Coaches," paper presented at the Southern Economic Association Meeting, November 2010.

[107]In Bradbury (2010), a hitter had to have 200 plate appearances and a pitcher 50 innings pitched to appear in the sample. In addition, players who had more than one manager in a given year were excluded from the sample.

[108]This list is similar to the one considered in the aforementioned study of basketball coaches. Like the basketball model, Bradbury (2010) considered age and past performance. League performance and park effects, though, are unique to the study of baseball, where league performance does not appear to be as constant across time and park effects matter.

[109]Bradbury (2010).

[110]Bradbury (2010) also reported that four managers had a statistically significant negative impact on a hitter's performance.

[111]Bradbury (2010) also indicated that nine managers had a statistically significant negative impact on a pitcher's performance.

(1) an inferior leader was removed and/or (2) a superior leader has been added. Again, Bradbury (2010) reported that most managers are not capable of changing outcomes. But it is entirely possible fans do not know and/or believe this, so therefore, changing a manager could change the fans' perceptions of the team.

To address this issue, a model was estimated that connects game-by-game attendance in baseball to a dummy variable for when a team changes its manager.[112] To ascertain the impact of such a change, the model also controls for a variety of additional factors that might impact attendance. The model was then estimated with games from the 1980s, 1990, and 2000s. The results indicated that changing a manager:

- in the 1980s was associated with a decline of about 1,100 fans per game

- in the 1990s did not statistically impact attendance

- in the 2000s was associated with an increase of about 1,000 fans per game

In sum, the impact of changing a manager in baseball has evolved over time, moving from an estimated negative impact in the 1980s to a positive impact in more recent years.

Bradbury's (2010) explanation of this finding is an excellent example of how to interpret results:

> The identified bump in attendance from hiring a new manager during the season in the 2000s offers some support for the managers-as-signals hypothesis. Fan interest in the game was certainly greater in the 2000s than in the preceding decades, and it is possible that the signaling effect did not manifest until recently as fans became more fervent in their demand for a winning team. However, the lack of the effect in the preceding decades makes it difficult to say for certain that the signaling effect was the primary cause for the rise in attendance associated with managerial turnover. (pp. 10–11)

Bradbury (2010) noted in his study that attendance in baseball has increased over time. And the above quote suggests that this increase in attention from fans might have changed how fans feel about winning. But Bradbury didn't stop with that conclusion. He also went on to note that the lack of an effect in the earlier sample casts some doubt on the entire signaling story.

---

[112]The obvious measures of team and managerial quality are listed in the equation. The equation, though, also reports three additional factors: month dummy variables, day-of-week dummy variables, and year dummy variables.

This brief discussion highlights an important issue regarding statistical evidence. What is reported in studies "suggests" a story. But we have to be very careful we do not leap to the conclusion that the results have "proven" a story.

11.8 So Do Teams Need a Coach?

Our discussion of "Moneyball on the field" has focused on coaching. This discussion has highlighted choices that coaches make on the field, including the inefficient choices NFL coaches frequently make on the fourth down. We also touched on the problem baseball managers historically have had with the stolen base decision. In addition, we noted the disconnect between what NBA coaches tell players to do to get playing time and how NBA coaches, in fact, allocate minutes.

The issues raised about coaches' choices on the field of play led to a much bigger question. Do coaches impact outcomes? Our review of research in soccer, basketball, and baseball suggested that coaches generally do not have much impact on the outcomes we observe.

And that leads us to an even bigger question. Do teams need coaches? Henry Abbott, of ESPN.com, had this reaction to the idea that most NBA coaches do not impact outcomes[113]:

> All those late nights of film study. All that competition for your job. All those tricks learned at conferences. All those books by the masters you have internalized. And now there is evidence to support the notion you could be replaced by a deck chair.

It is tempting to examine the impact of coaches in various sports and conclude that this research implies coaches are not necessary. But it is important to emphasize that none of the research cited can lead to such a conclusion. None of these studies have examined how a team performs with and without a coach. So none of these studies can tell us what a team would look like without a coach.

What these studies do seem to suggest is that the coaches and managers employed in sports are not tremendously different from each other.[114] And again,

---

[113]Henry Abbott, "Stat Geeks and Coaches," November 18, 2008 (http://myespn.go.com/blogs/truehoop/0-36-67/Stat-Geeks-and-Coaches.html). The posting came in response to Ryan McCarthy, "Change You Can't Believe In: Why Hiring a New Coach Won't Solve Your Favorite NBA Team's Problems (Unless the Old Coach Was Isaiah Thomas)," November 18, 2008 (http://www.slate.com/id/2204834). The McCarthy article detailed the aforementioned findings with respect to the impact NBA coaches have on player performance.

[114]One should add, none of this research tells us that coaches are the same as the fans in the stands. Again, not one of these studies looked at teams that were coached by fans in the stands. So these studies can't say that coaches are no better at their job than any random fan would be.

that is what the evidence "suggests." There are coaches who appear to make a difference. But, in general, the data suggest that when your favorite team changes coaches without changing players, the outcomes you will see are likely to be the same as those that caused the old coach to lose his or her job.

11.9 Moneyball? Well, It Depends . . .

The classic answer in economics is: "It depends." This certainly seems to apply to our study of decision making in the market for professional talent. In the baseball free-agent market—where the original *Moneyball* story was told—it appears that decision making is quite efficient. Perhaps this is not surprising since (1) the data have existed for more than 100 years and (2) these data are relatively easy to understand.

When we turn to complex invasion sports, like basketball and football, though, it appears decision making is less efficient. And that seems unsurprising as well. In complex invasion sports, we see that (1) the data have not existed for as long as data in baseball and (2) the data are harder to understand. And when we turn to the market for nonprofessional talent (i.e., the draft), we see inefficiencies in all sports. Again, that probably is not surprising. Projecting from the amateur ranks is much more difficult (relative to projecting veteran players). In sum, it appears decision making becomes less efficient as the data grow harder to understand.

Problems

Study Questions

1. Why have Milton Friedman and L. J. Savage argued that human beings do not need to be "lightning calculators" to make rational decisions?
2. What is the link between Batting Average, Isolated Power, and Eye (define these terms) and:
   a. runs scored per game?
   b. salary?
   What does this tell us about the *Moneyball* story?
3. Do we find *Moneyball* in the market for pitchers?
4. Is the evidence from baseball consistent with Veblen's critique or the view of Friedman and Savage?
5. What factor(s) primarily determine a free agent's salary in the NBA?
6. Is the evidence from the free-agent basketball market consistent with Veblen's critique or the view of Friedman and Savage?

7. What did Burgher and Walters (2003) report with respect to the drafting and performance of:
   a. college versus high school players?
   b. positional players versus pitchers?
   Have the trends these authors noted changed in recent years?
8. In the NBA, what three factors primarily dictate whether a player is drafted?
9. What does the NBA learn from the combine? What does an NBA team learn from a player's Final Four appearances? What does the NBA believe it learns from the combine and NCAA tournament?
10. According to Massey and Thaler (2013), what is the best draft pick to have in the NBA draft?
11. According to Berri and Simmons (2011a), how well do NFL teams do with respect to the drafting of quarterbacks?
12. Your favorite NFL team is facing fourth down and 3 yards to go at midfield. According to David Romer's research, should the team go for it? Do NFL teams tend to listen to this research?
13. Rickey Henderson set the record for stolen bases and walks (the latter record was eventually broken). Which record — in terms of wins in baseball — is the most impressive? Briefly explain your answer.
14. What is the impact of coaching in soccer, the NBA, and MLB? Does the research show that teams can do without coaches?
15. Is the sports labor market efficient?
16. Given what you learned about the NBA draft, what do you suspect is the actual value of a lottery pick (i.e., a pick at the top of the first round)?
17. At the conclusion of 2016–17 season, the San Antonio Spurs had yet to have a season in the 21st century when the team did not win at least 50 games and 60% of its contests (see http://www.basketball-reference.com/teams/SAS/). How many lottery picks have the Spurs employed in the 21st century? Why do you think the Spurs have achieved so much success with so few lottery picks?

Appendix A
Moneyball Models

Chapter 11 reviewed a variety of studies examining decision making in sports. Here, we report more details on the empirical evidence already discussed.

11A.1 Free-Agent Market in Basketball

As noted in the text, the evaluation of decision making in sports involves two steps:

1. Examine how various factors tracked for the players impact team outcomes.

2. Examine how various factors tracked for the players impact player salaries.

Wins in basketball are primarily about gaining and keeping possession of the ball (i.e., rebounds, steals, and turnovers) and turning those possessions into points (i.e., shooting efficiency). Is this what gets a player paid?

The model of salaries is taken from Berri, Leeds, and von Allmen (2015a). The model connects free-agent salaries[115] in the NBA to a collection of box-score statistics, as well as nonperformance factors such as games played (to control for injury), how much a player starts, whether a player resigned with the same team,[116] how many wins a player's team had before he went on the free-agent market, the age of the player, market size, plus three dummy variables designed to capture playoff success the year before free agency.[117]

The results, reported in Table 11A.1, indicate that NBA free agents are primarily paid for total points scored. How many points a player scores is more important than shooting efficiency (adjusted field goal percentage and free-throw percentage), rebounds, turnovers, and steals.[118] And that suggests teams are not evaluating players correctly.

---

[115]This is the log of average salary across the length of a player's contract. Only players who signed for more than a year are included in the sample.

[116]The NBA's collective bargaining agreement, as we noted before, gives the team that previously employed the player an advantage in negotiating with the player.

[117]This model also includes dummy variables for each year and fixed effects for the team signing the player. Additionally, dummy variables were included for position played and also for a collection of agents who negotiated these contracts (virtually all of these were insignificant, suggesting agents are not much different from each other). Finally, the size of any TV contract was included (this was also statistically insignificant). More details can be found in Berri *et al.* (2015a).

[118]Turnover percentage has the "wrong" sign since a higher mark (which is not helpful for wins) has a larger impact on salaries. And steals are not statistically significant.

Table 11A.1 Modeling NBA Free-Agent Salaries: 2001–11[119]			
Variable	Coefficient	t-Statistic	Elasticity[120]
Points scored	1.073[a]	10.33	0.428
Rebounds	1.202[a]	5.78	0.210
Steals	0.697	0.61	
Assists	1.234[a]	3.55	0.107
Blocked shots	1.552[a]	2.86	0.032
Turnover percentage	0.006[c]	2.03	0.074
Personal fouls	−2.022[a]	−3.24	−0.183
Adjusted field goal percentage	0.490[c]	2.00	0.242
Free-throw percentage	0.220[c]	1.87	0.166
Age of player	−0.016[a]	−5.72	−0.424
Whether player signed with same team	0.070[a]	3.92	
Ratio of games started to games played	0.203[a]	5.95	0.125
Team wins last season	0.004[a]	3.91	0.165
Percentage of games played in last two years	0.292[a]	4.26	0.247
Market population	0.021	0.89	
Played on title team in previous year	−0.035	−0.66	
Played on conference title team in previous year	0.096[b]	1.90	
Played in conference final in previous year	−0.053	−1.46	
R-squared	0.721		
Observations	483		

p-Values not explicitly reported, but significance levels were noted as follows:
[a]Significant at the 1% level.
[b]Significant at the 10% level.

In addition to scoring, players are paid more when they play for a winner. That suggests players are compensated for the quality of their teammates, something the player typically cannot control. We will observe this same result when looking at the NBA draft.

---

[119]Berri et al. (2015a, Table 9, p. 16).

[120]This is a semi-logged model. So the elasticity—at the point of means—is simply found by multiplying the estimated coefficient by the mean value of the variable. Elasticity is only reported for nondummy variables that were statistically significant (at a minimum of the 10% level).

11A.2 Star Power and Gate Revenue in Basketball

One might think that teams have an incentive to hire scorers since these players tend to be stars and stars—many believe—sell tickets. To assess whether or not this belief is true, we next turn to a model of an NBA team's gate revenue. The specific model is detailed in equation (11A.1)[121]:

$$GATE_{it} = d1_i + d2_t + a2 \times WINS_{it} + a3 \times WINS_{it-1} + a4$$
$$\times STARS_{it} + a5 \times SCAP_{it} + a6 \times DCAP_{it} + a7$$
$$\times DNEW_{it} + a9 \times DEXP_{it} + a10 \times WCHM_{it} + a11$$
$$\times DFT1_{it} + a12 \times DFT2_{it} + a13 \times DFT3_{it} + a14$$
$$\times DFT1_{it-1} + a15 \times DFT2_{it-1} + a16 \times DFT3_{it-1} + e_{it}$$

$$(11A.1)$$

where $GATE$ = log of real gate revenue[122]

$WINS$ = regular-season wins in the current season

$WINS_{t-1}$ = regular-season wins in the previous season

$STARS$ = number of All-Star votes received by players on the team in the current season

$SCAP$ = stadium capacity

$DCAP$ = dummy variable equal to 1 if team played at capacity

$DNEW$ = dummy variable equal to 1 if a team played in a stadium three years or less

$DEXP$ = dummy variable equal to 1 if a team was an expansion team in the current season

$WCHM$ = championships won in the past 20 years, weighted

[121]NBA gate revenue was examined in Joseph Price, Brian Soebbing, David Berri, and Brad Humphreys, "Tournament Incentives, League Policy, and NBA Team Performance Revisited," *Journal of Sports Economics* 11, no. 2 (April 2010): 117–135. The model created by Price *et al.* (2010) considered the value of additional draft picks (the 3rd pick in last year's draft, and the 2nd and 3rd pick from the previous draft; none of these additional picks were reported to be statistically significant) and was estimated with data from 1992–93 to 2007–08.

[122]Gate revenue is calculated as Average Ticket Price × Home Attendance. Average ticket price can be found at *Team Marketing Report* (https://www.teammarketing.com/). NBA attendance can be found at ESPN.com. Berri, Schmidt, and Brook (2004) discussed whether or not a revenue model should be linear or double-logged. A linear model would suggest that the value of a win is the same for all teams. A double-logged model indicates that the value of a win varies from team to team. The tests reported in this paper indicated the double-logged model is preferable.

$DFT1$ = dummy variable equal to 1 if a team employed the 1st pick in last year's NBA draft

$DFT2$ = dummy variable equal to 1 if a team employed the 2nd pick in last year's NBA draft

$DFT3$ = dummy variable equal to 1 if a team employed the 3rd pick in last year's NBA draft

$DFT1_{t-1}$ = dummy variable equal to 1 if a team employed the 1st pick in NBA draft from two years ago

$DFT2_{t-1}$ = dummy variable equal to 1 if a team employed the 2nd pick in NBA draft from two years ago

$DFT3_{t-1}$ = dummy variable equal to 1 if a team employed the 3rd pick in NBA draft from two years ago

This model was estimated with data from 1992–93 to 2007–08 (1998–99 was excluded since an All-Star game was not played that season). The results are reported in **Table 11A.2**. As one can see, both wins (current season and lagged) and All-Star votes are statistically significant. Team revenue thus responds to both success on the court and star power.[123]

Table 11A.2 Regression Results, Gate Revenue Model[124]

Variable	Coefficient	*t*-Statistic
Regular-season wins	0.099	3.72
Lagged regular-season wins	0.138	3.85
All-Star votes received	0.003	2.38
Stadium capacity	0.879	11.6

(continued)

[123]One might suspect that wins and star power are highly correlated. Of course, as this chapter argues, perceptions of star power and ability to produce wins are different. Beyond that story, though, one can look directly at the issue of multi-collinearity. One test is the Variation Inflation Factor (VIF). See A. H. Studenmund, *Using Econometrics: A Practical Guide* (New York: HarperCollins, 1992), pp. 274–276. The VIF requires that one first regress each independent variable in a model on all other independent variables. One then utilizes the *R*-squared from this model to calculate the VIF, which equals $(1)/(1 - R^2)$. Although there is no statistical test for what constitutes a "high" VIF, a general rule-of-thumb is that a value greater than 5 suggests a problem with multi-collinearity. The VIF for regular-season wins is 1.9, while the VIF for All-Star votes is 1.5. Those results suggest multi-collinearity is not a significant problem for wins and star power.

[124]These results were reported in Joseph Price, Brian Soebbing, David Berri, and Brad Humphreys, "Tournament Incentives, League Policy, and NBA Team Performance Revisited," *Journal of Sports Economics* 11, no. 2 (April 2010): Table 3, 125.

Table 11A.2 *(continued)*		
Variable	Coefficient	*t*-Statistic
Dummy variable, team at capacity	0.045	2.52
Dummy variable, expansion team	0.111	4.36
Dummy variable, age of stadium	0.054	6.81
Championships won, weighted	0.002	3.94
Dummy variable, 1st pick in draft	0.051	3.14
Dummy variable, 2nd pick in draft	0.048	3.81
Dummy variable, 3rd pick in draft	−0.005	−0.31
Dummy variable, 1st pick in draft, lagged	0.029	3.25
Dummy variable, 2nd pick in draft, lagged	0.006	0.42
Dummy variable, 3rd pick in draft, lagged	−0.017	−1.44
R-Squared	0.91	
Adjusted *R-Squared*	0.88	
N	315	

*p-Values not explicitly reported.

But what matters is which factor has the largest economic impact on gate revenue. This model addresses that issue with relative ease. This is because the above model was estimated as a double-logged model, and that means, as we have beforehand noted with respect to double-logged models, the coefficients reported in Table 11A.2 for regular-season wins, lagged regular-season wins, and All-Star votes received are the elasticities of gate revenue with respect to these variables. As one can see, the elasticity of gate revenue with respect to regular-season wins is 0.114. The elasticity of gate revenue with respect to All-Star votes is only 0.003. And that indicates that teams are better off hiring players who produce wins. Inefficient scorers, who do not produce wins or much revenue, are not very valuable. Yet, teams prefer veteran free agents who score over those who score less but produce more wins.

11A.3 Drafting Quarterbacks in the NFL

One issue highlighted in the text is that draft position and quarterback performance are not highly correlated in the NFL. This point—originally made by Berri and Simmons (2011a)—is illustrated in **Tables 11A.3** and **11A.4**.[125] The former reports how quarterbacks, selected at different points in the draft, have

---

[125]These tables originally appeared in Berri and Simmons (2011a).

Table 11A.3 Performance of NFL Quarterbacks Chosen at Different Points in NFL Draft Years: 1970–2007

Picks	Observations	Games	Plays	QB Score	Net Points	Wins
Picks 1–10	396	4,370	131,965	217,399	19,004	485.2
Picks 11–50	400	3,993	108,765	185,866	16,204	414.4
Picks 51–90	372	3,190	72,958	122,239	10,659	272.2
Picks 91–150	413	3,298	68,689	103,575	9,073	230.0
Picks 151–250	362	2,887	54,293	86,734	7,567	192.5

Picks	Observations			QB Score per Game	Net Points per Game	Wins per Game
Picks 1–10	396			49.7	4.3	0.111
Picks 11–50	400			46.5	4.1	0.104
Picks 51–90	372			38.3	3.3	0.085
Picks 91–150	413			31.4	2.8	0.070
Picks 151–250	362			30.0	2.6	0.067

Picks	Observations			QB Score per Play	Net Points per Play	Wins per Play
Picks 1–10	396			1.647	0.144	0.368
Picks 11–50	400			1.709	0.149	0.381
Picks 51–90	372			1.675	0.146	0.373
Picks 91–150	413			1.508	0.132	0.335
Picks 151–250	362			1.598	0.139	0.354

Picks	Observations	Completion Percentage	Passing Yards per Pass Attempt	Touchdowns per Pass Attempt	Interceptions per Pass Attempt	QB Rating
Picks 1–10	396	56.09%	6.78	0.0396	0.0381	74.4
Picks 11–50	400	56.73%	6.86	0.0419	0.0375	76.3
Picks 51–90	372	56.43%	6.86	0.0404	0.0392	74.8
Picks 91–150	413	55.26%	6.73	0.0386	0.0403	72.3
Picks 151–250	362	55.79%	6.77	0.0385	0.0402	72.9

performed in the NFL. Employing data from 1970 to 2007, we discern two clear stories. The first is that quarterbacks selected earlier in the draft spend far more time on the field of play. This makes sense since the quarterbacks picked first should be better performers.

Table 11A.4	Correlation Between Draft Position and Performance at Different Levels of Experience (1970–2007, minimum 100 plays in year examined)					
Experience	QB Score	Net Points	Wins	QB Score per Play	Net Points per Play	Wins per Play
1	−0.14	−0.15	−0.14	−0.03	−0.03	−0.03
2	−0.10	−0.11	−0.10	−0.04	−0.05	−0.05
3	−0.15	−0.16	−0.16	−0.05	−0.06	−0.06
4	−0.17	−0.17	−0.17	−0.04	−0.05	−0.05
5	−0.19	−0.20	−0.19	−0.03	−0.04	−0.04
6	−0.10	−0.11	−0.11	0.04	0.03	0.03
7	−0.08	−0.08	−0.08	−0.02	−0.03	−0.03
8	−0.22	−0.21	−0.21	−0.18	−0.18	−0.18
9	−0.20	−0.20	−0.20	−0.05	−0.06	−0.06
10	−0.16	−0.16	−0.16	−0.12	−0.13	−0.13

Experience	Plays	Completion Percentage	Passing Yards per Pass Attempt	Touchdowns per Pass Attempt	Interceptions per Pass Attempt	QB Rating
1	−0.26	0.03	−0.05	0.07	0.03	0.01
2	−0.21	−0.07	0.04	0.16	0.12	0.00
3	−0.29	−0.09	−0.02	−0.14	0.09	−0.12
4	−0.25	−0.07	−0.03	−0.19	0.10	−0.14
5	−0.32	−0.04	0.07	0.01	0.11	−0.04
6	−0.23	0.02	0.09	−0.05	0.09	−0.03
7	−0.14	0.02	0.02	−0.12	0.11	−0.09
8	−0.22	−0.20	−0.19	−0.15	0.05	−0.20
9	−0.31	−0.02	0.01	0.02	0.13	−0.07
10	−0.19	0.05	−0.06	−0.08	0.27	−0.16

But when we turn to the evaluation of quarterback performance, per play or per attempt, it doesn't appear that draft position predicts future performance. Specifically, quarterbacks taken with both picks 11 through 50 and 51 through 90, on average, deliver more per play or attempt than those selected with picks 1 through 10.

Table 11A.4 further illustrates this story. The correlation between draft pick and a variety of performance measures is quite low. In fact, of the factors considered, playing time has the highest correlation with draft position. But again, none of the per-play or per-attempt performance measures seem to be related to where a quarterback was selected in the NFL draft.

Draft position, however, definitely gets a quarterback played. We have already seen that draft position predicts a quarterback's pay well into his NFL career. In addition, quarterbacks historically have been paid very different amounts at the start of their career based on where they were selected in the draft. But because so much of what causes a quarterback to be drafted is not related to future NFL performance, those selected earlier do not seem to be consistently better quarterbacks.[126]

11A.4 Evaluating Stolen Bases in Baseball

In the text, we discussed the costs and benefits of stolen bases in baseball. Here, some more details are presented on how this calculation was performed.

We begin with the fact baseball has 24 defined states, or situations in the game. For example, one state is runner on 1st with 1 out. Another state would be runners on 2nd and 3rd with 2 outs. In each state, one is able to calculate how many runs a team can expect, on average, to score.[127]

Table 11A.5 presents such analysis from 2016.[128] The figures reported are the number of runs a typical team can expect to score given each of the 24 possible situations in a game (i.e., each state).

Table 11A.5 Value of each "State" in Baseball in 2016			
MLB in 2016	Outs		
Runners ON	0	1	2
NONE	0.506	0.274	0.103
1st ONLY	0.874	0.526	0.220
2nd ONLY	1.093	0.668	0.317

(continued)

---

[126]Berri and Burke (2012) noted that the performance of veteran NFL quarterbacks is difficult to predict. So it should not be surprising that the performance of future NFL quarterbacks is very difficult to forecast.

[127]John Thorn and Peter Palmer, *The Hidden Game of Baseball*, 3rd ed. (Chicago: University of Chicago Press, 2015) provided such analysis. One can also refer to similar analysis by Dan Levitt, "Empirical Analysis of Bunting," 2006, http://baseballanalysts.com/archives/2006/07/empirical_analy_1.php. Levitt offered values for each state from 1977 to 1992. The numbers presented here from 2016 are quite close to his, suggesting that the value of these states do not change much from season-to-season.

[128]These numbers come from *Baseball Prospectus* (http://www.baseballprospectus.com/sortable/index.php?cid=1918852).

Table 11A.5 (continued)			
MLB in 2016	Outs		
Runners ON	0	1	2
1st and 2nd	1.461	0.921	0.435
3rd ONLY	1.316	0.923	0.364
1st and 3rd	1.685	1.175	0.481
2nd and 3rd	1.903	1.317	0.578
1st, 2nd, and 3rd	2.272	1.569	0.696

From this table, we can see the costs and benefits of stealing a base. For example, a team that has a runner on 1st base with nobody out can expect to score 0.874 runs. If the runner on 1st steals 2nd, the team now has a runner on 2nd with nobody out. And the expected run value of that state is 1.093. This tells us that the benefit of stealing 2nd base with nobody out increases a team's expected runs by 0.219. But what if the runner is thrown out? If that happens, a team moves to a new state with nobody on base and 1 out. The expected runs in that state is 0.274. This means being caught stealing costs a team 0.601 expected runs.

The costs and benefits of stealing 2nd (i.e., 0.274 benefit vs. −0.601 cost) with nobody out tell us that a team needs to be successful 73.3% of the time to break even. If the team makes the same attempt with 1 out, the benefit of the stolen base is 0.142 and its cost is −0.424. These numbers give us a 74.9% break-even point.

Table 11A.6 reports the benefits, costs, and break-even points for stolen base attempts in these two states, as well as 10 additional states. The break-even points indicate that attempting to steal bases is a much better idea in certain states (and not a very good idea in others). For example, the break-even point for trying to steal 3rd when a team has a runner on 2nd with 1 out is 69.0%. In contrast, a team needs to be successful on 90.4% of its attempts to break even when trying to steal 3rd with runners on 1st and 2nd with 2 outs.

Table 11A.6 Break-Even Value of Stealing Bases in Baseball: 2013			
Stolen Base States	Benefit	Cost	Break-Even
Runner on 1st (0 outs), steal 2nd	0.219	−0.601	73.3%
Runner on 1st (1 out), steal 2nd	0.142	−0.424	74.9%
Runner on 1st (2 out), steal 2nd	0.098	−0.220	69.3%
Runner on 2nd (0 out), steal 3rd	0.223	−0.820	78.6%
Runner on 2nd (1 out), steal 3rd	0.255	−0.565	69.0%

(continued)

Table 11A.6 (continued)			
Stolen Base States	Benefit	Cost	Break-Even
Runner on 2nd (2 out), steal 3rd	0.046	−0.317	87.2%
Runner on 1st and 2nd (0 out), steal 3rd	0.223	−0.935	80.7%
Runner on 1st and 2nd (1 out), steal 3rd	0.255	−0.701	73.4%
Runner on 1st and 2nd (2 out), steal 3rd	0.046	−0.435	90.4%
Runner on 1st and 3rd (0 out), steal 2nd	0.219	−0.762	77.7%
Runner on 1st and 3rd (1 out), steal 2nd	0.142	−0.811	85.1%
Runner on 1st and 3rd (2 out), steal 2nd	0.098	−0.481	83.1%

In almost every case, a team has to do better than 70% to just break even. But as noted in the chapter, baseball did not reach a 70% success rate on stolen bases until the 1980s. So for much of baseball's history, teams were not breaking even on stolen bases.

Appendix A
Introduction to Performance Measures

One very important feature of studying *sports economics* is that it provides students with an opportunity to conduct empirical research. Many of these studies will take advantage of the wealth of player productivity data that sports has to offer. Although these studies can be a wonderful learning opportunity, there are some pitfalls that students should be aware of in employing the aforementioned player productivity data.

So far, we have already noted that any measure of player performance should be linked to wins. There should also be consistency in the measure across time, since inconsistency suggests the numbers are not actually about the player's performance. To demonstrate these issues, and others, a few performance measures will be reviewed. It is important to note that this review will be incomplete. The number of performance measures in sports is truly vast. Nevertheless, it is hoped this discussion will give students a sense of some general issues one must consider when adopting a specific measure of player performance for any study the student might conduct.

A.1 Wins Above Replacement and Marginal Productivity

Baseball comes with a host of measures. And many of these — at least for hitters — are adequate measures of marginal productivity. There is one particular approach, though, that is problematic.

Websites like baseball-reference.com or *Baseball Prospectus* (baseballprospectus .com) offer a lot of information on a measure called Wins Above Replacement[1] or WAR. The concept of WAR seems fairly common in sports analysis.[2] But

---

[1] It is important to define what is meant by "replacement." One definition is offered at *FanGraphs* (http://www.fangraphs.com/blogs/unifying-replacement-level/): "Replacement is defined very specifically for my purposes: it's the talent level for which you would pay the minimum salary on the open market. . . ."

[2] Kevin Pelton developed a WAR measure for basketball (http://www.sonicscentral.com/warp.html). And Brian Burke has used this concept for football players (http://www.advanced footballanalytics.com/2014/07/win-values-for-nfl.html). It has also been used by sports economists. For example, see Justin Sims and Vittorio Addona, "Hurdle Models and Age Effects in the Major League Baseball Draft," *Journal of Sports Economics* (2014) at http://jse.sagepub.com/content/early/2014/06/26/1527002514539516 and Russell Ormiston, "Attendance Effects of Star Pitchers in Major League Baseball," *Journal of Sports Economics* 15, no. 4 (2012): 338–364.

before one rushes in to use this measure, it is important to understand that WAR is not really a measure of marginal productivity.[3]

Let's begin by noting how WAR is calculated:

$$WAR = \text{Wins of Player} - \text{Wins of Replacement Player} \qquad (A6.1)$$

For much of Chapter 6, we discussed how to measure marginal productivity. Remember, this is defined as "the output from an additional worker."

Applying this concept to sports, if we assume a team is trying to maximize wins (and this is not always an assumption, as we have noted before, that matches a team's actions or performance), then the output we wish to measure is how many wins the additional player produces. These additional wins can be thought of as the player's "marginal product."

In calculating marginal product, we simply look at what the additional worker adds to the firm's output. WAR, though, does not take this approach. WAR is a player's production of wins minus a replacement player's production of wins. The calculation of marginal productivity, though, does not involve the consideration of a replacement worker's production.

Perhaps a non-sports example can illustrate the problem with WAR. Imagine you have a job selling cars. Let's say that you are able to sell five cars per month. But your employer believes that a "replacement worker" could sell two cars per month. Would it then be correct for an employer to decide that your actual productivity is three cars sold? One imagines you would prefer to be paid for all five sales. But if your employer believed in WAR, you might be compensated with a smaller paycheck than you would like.

Although WAR is not a measure of marginal productivity, it does have value. If we argue that a replacement player is worth the league's minimum wage, then WAR allows us to ascertain how much more a player produces beyond a minimum-wage player. And if we compare a player a team might hire to a hypothetical minimum-wage player, this might allow a team to figure out how much more it is willing to spend on a new worker.

This calculation, though, does require two assumptions. First, we obviously assume that "replacement player" is synonymous with "minimum-wage player." Replacement player is defined differently by different people. So this first assumption might not always be valid.

We also assume that there is a clear link between pay and productivity. We saw in Chapter 11 that in baseball this seems like a valid assumption. But in other sports—like basketball or football—such may not be true.

---

[3]The comment on WAR, marginal productivity, and the issue of minimum-wage players was derived from the following: http://wagesofwins.com/2014/07/23/wins-above-replacement-war-what-is-it-good-for-not-absolutely-nothing/.

So WAR might be a useful concept for a decision maker in baseball. But again, it is not a measure of marginal productivity. Therefore, you probably need a different measure if you are doing an economic study that requires a measure of marginal productivity of an athlete.

A.2 Statistical Measures in Basketball: A Collection of Cautionary Tales

Like baseball, basketball has a host of different measures (many — but not all — of these can be found at basketball-reference.com or NBA.com). Unfortunately, many of these either (1) do not explain wins very well and/or (2) are quite inconsistent over time. In addition, the construction of some measures, as we will see, is not entirely based on empirical evidence.

In the chapter, we discussed how Bill Gerrard's work on modeling complex invasion sports can help us build a productivity measure for a sport like basketball. The measure this approach leads us to is called Wins Produced.[4] This model has been used to analyze players in the NBA, WNBA, and men and women's college basketball. The analysis of basketball in each of these settings reveals that the analysis of player performance is remarkably the same in different leagues. But before we get to this observation — and other details regarding Wins Produced — we should briefly discuss some alternative measures students might encounter.

The "Efficiency" Approaches

Let's start with the "NBA Efficiency" measure:

$$NBA\ Efficiency = PTS + ORB + DRB + STL + BLK + AST - TO - MSFG - MSFT \tag{A6.2}$$

where
PTS = points scored
ORB = offensive rebounds
DRB = defensive rebounds
STL = steals
BLK = blocked shots
AST = assists

---

[4]Wins Produced was first laid forth in *The Wages of Wins* (Berri *et al.* 2006), and it builds on work initially published in the late 1990s.

$$TO = \text{turnovers}$$
$$MSFG = \text{missed field goals}$$
$$MSFT = \text{missed free throws}$$

The NBA Efficiency model is quite similar to the TENDEX model developed by Dave Heeran in 1959.[5] So this approach, which involves simply adding the positive actions a player takes and subtracting the negative, is perhaps the oldest attempt to aggregate the statistics tracked for an individual basketball player into a single number.

NBA Efficiency was originally reported at NBA.com. But more recently, that website has turned to Player Impact Estimate (PIE). PIE is a ratio, and the numerator seems quite similar to NBA Efficiency. Specifically, PIE adds together the positive factors a player brings to the court (PTS, DRB, ORB, AST, STL, and BLK) and subtracts missed shots, TO, and PF. Other than counting only one-half of ORB and BLK, the numerator is exactly the same as NBA Efficiency:

$$[PTS - (FGA - FGM) - (FTA - FTM) + DRB + 0.5 \times ORB + AST + STL + 0.5 \times BLK - PF - TO]$$

$$[TMPTS - (TMFGA - TMFGM) - (TMFTA - TMFTM) + TMDRB + 0.5 \times TMORB + TMAST + TMSTL + 0.5 \times TMBLK - TMPF - TMTO] \tag{A6.3}$$

where FGA = field goals attempted

FGM = field goals made

FTA = free throws attempted

FTM = free throws made

PF = personal fouls

TM = the team's accumulation of this factor

---

[5]Dave Heeren, *Basketball Abstract* (Englewood Cliffs, NJ: Prentice Hall, 1992). The simple TENDEX formula is as follows:

$$TENDEX = PTS + ORB + DRB + STL + AST + BLK - MSFG - MSFT/2 - TO - PF$$

In evaluating an individual player, one divides TENDEX by minutes played. One then also divides by game pace.

TENDEX and NBA Efficiency are also quite similar to the points created model developed by Robert Bellotti, *The Points Created Basketball Book, 1992–93* (New Brunswick, NJ: Night Work Publishing, 1993):

Points Created = $PTS + ORB + DRB + STL + AST + BLK - MSFG - MSFT - TO - PF/2$

Bellotti additionally presents a more complex measure that adjusts for game pace.

PIE looks more complicated than NBA Efficiency. But in terms of explanatory power, it really isn't an improvement. As Berri (2015) noted,[6] a team's NBA Efficiency only explains 34% of its winning percentage. The numerator for PIE explains 36% of a team's winning percentage.[7]

Although PIE looks a bit more complicated than NBA Efficiency, perhaps it is simply not complicated enough. Perhaps what we really need is something like John Hollinger's Player Efficiency Rating (PER)[8]:

$$
\begin{aligned}
PER = \ & (\text{League Pace/Team Pace}) \times (15/\text{League Average}) \times (1/\text{Minutes Played}) \\
& \times [3FGM + AST \times 0.67 + (FGM \times \{2 - [(\textit{Team AST}/\textit{Team FGM}) \\
& \times 0.588]\}) \\
& + (FTM \times 0.5 \times \{1+ [1 + (\textit{Team AST}/\textit{Team FGM})] + (\textit{Team AST}/ \\
& \textit{Team FGM}) \times 0.67]\}) \\
& - (VOP \times TO) - (MSFG \times VOP \times \textit{League DRB\%}) \\
& - \{MSFG \times VOP \times 0.44 \times [0.44 + (0.56 \times \textit{League DRB\%})]\} \\
& + [DRB \times VOP \times (1 - \textit{League DRB\%})] + (ORB \times VOP \times \textit{League} \\
& DRB\%) + (STL \times VOP) \\
& + (BLK \times VOP \times \textit{League DRB\%}) \\
& - \{PF \times [\textit{League FTM per PF} - (\textit{League FTA per PF} \\
& \times 0.44 \times VOP)]\}]
\end{aligned}
$$

(A6.4)

$$
\begin{aligned}
\text{where} \quad PACE = \ & [(\text{Offensive Possessions} + \text{Defensive Possessions}) \times \\
& 48]/(\text{Minutes Played}/2)
\end{aligned}
$$

$$\text{Possession} = FGA + 0.44 \times FTA + TO - ORB$$

League Average = average PERs value

$3FGM$ = 3-point field goals made

VOP = average points scored per possession for the league

League DRB% = average defensive rebounds divided by average total rebounds

[6]David J. Berri, "Think You Know Basketball? You Need to Know the Numbers to Know the Game," *Sports & Entertainment Review* 1, no. 1 (2015): 6–13.

[7]The specific regression used by Berri (2015) involved regressing team winning percentage on a team's NBA Efficiency or the numerator of PIE for the team. The data utilized began with 1987–88 and ended with the 2013–14 season (771 team observations were employed).

[8]PER was detailed in John Hollinger, *Pro Basketball Prospectus 2002* (Washington, DC: Brassey's Sports, 2002). Hollinger's work can also be found at ESPN.com and basketball-reference.com.

PER is definitely more complicated. But it turns out this complex model is essentially the same as Hollinger's "Game Score":

$$\text{Game Score} = PTS + 0.4 \times FGM - 0.7 \times FGA - 0.4 \times MSFT + 0.7 \times ORB$$
$$+ 0.3 \times DRB + STL + 0.7 \times AST + 0.7 \times BLK - 0.4$$
$$\times PF - TO \qquad \text{(A6.5)}$$

Although Game Score appears quite different from PER, Berri and Schmidt (2010) noted Game Score per 48 minutes and PER have a 0.99 correlation.[9] In addition, Game Score and NBA Efficiency have a 0.99 correlation.[10] Given this result, it is not surprising to see that a team's Game Score per game explains only 32% of the variation in its winning percentage.[11]

The primary problem with both "efficiency" measures is how each measures a player's shooting efficiency. A simple mathematical exercise can help illustrate the problem.[12]

Imagine a player takes 15 shots from the 2-point range and makes 5. This means the player has scored 10 points but also missed 10 shots. According to NBA Efficiency, which argues that the absolute value of missed shots and points is identical, this player has broken even on NBA Efficiency. In other words, a player who hits 33% of these 2-point shots breaks even and therefore any player who does better than this will see his NBA Efficiency value go up the more shots he takes.[13] A similar story can be told about 3-point shooting. If a player takes eight 3-point shots and makes 2, that player will have missed 6 shots and scored 6 points. So the break-even point on 3-point shooting, according to NBA Efficiency, is 25%.

---

[9]From 2005–06 to 2011–12, we have 3,182 player season observations. Across all these observations, there is a 0.99 correlation between a player's PER (which is a per-minute measure of performance) and his Game Score per 48 minutes (GS48).

[10]This finding is based on a sample of 3,182 player season observations from 2005–06 to 2011–12. There is also a 0.94 correlation between GS48 and NBA Efficiency per 48 minutes (NBA48).

[11]The specific regression involved regressing team winning percentage on a team's Game Score per game. The data utilized began with 1987–88 and ended with the 2011–12 season (711 team observations were employed).

[12]A similar exercise was originally reported in David J. Berri, "Measuring Performance in the National Basketball Association," in Stephen Shmanske and Leo Kahane (eds.), *The Handbook of Sports Economics*, Vol. 2 (New York: Oxford University Press, 2012), pp. 94–117.

[13]Imagine two players. The first takes five 2-point shots and makes 2, thus missing 3 shots and scoring 4 points. These 5 shots will increase NBA Efficiency by 1. A player who takes 20 shots and makes 8 will have the same shooting efficiency (i.e., 40%). But that player will see his NBA Efficiency increase by 4 from his shots. In sum, if you exceed the break-even threshold, the more shots you take, the better you look according to NBA Efficiency.

Berri (2012) also reported the break-even points for John Hollinger's Game Score. For the 2-point range, a player breaks even at 29.2%, while from the 3-point range, a player needs to hit 20.6% of his shots to break even. Any player who exceeds these thresholds will see his Game Score value rise the more shots he takes.

In sum, the "efficiency" metrics argue that an inefficient scorer could increase his value by simply taking more shots. But a team is not likely to be successful when an inefficient shooter takes more and more shots. Consequently, the link between wins and the "efficiency" metrics is quite poor.

It is not difficult to see the fundamental problem with all these measures. As we have noted, sports economists typically employ statistical analysis to uncover the link between two variables. But the value of each box score statistic we have reviewed was simply assigned by the person who invented the measure. Because these values are not based on empirical evidence, we cannot believe these measures capture the player's impact on outcomes. In sum, none of the box score "efficiency" measures reviewed can be regarded as a measure of a player's productivity.[14]

The Plus-Minus Approach

Perhaps because measures like NBA Efficiency, PIE, and PER do not explain wins very well, people have begun to look for an alternative approach. One of these involves a method first adopted in the NHL. Specifically, the NBA has begun tracking each player's "plus-minus,"[15] which Hollinger (2005)[16] described as follows:

> Add all the points the team scores when a player is on the court, and subtract all the points the team allows when he is on the court. Subtract the latter from the former, and you end up with the player's "plus-minus" — how many points better or worse (i.e., plus or minus) the team is with that man on the court.

[14]This criticism also applies to Win Shares. This is a measure reported at basketball-reference .com. It is based on the work of Dean Oliver and his measures of offensive and defensive ratings. As observed in *The Wages of Wins* (Berri *et al.*, 2006), Oliver did not connect each player's actions to wins. Instead, he ultimately assigned the value according to what he thought these measures were worth. And once again, assigning values does not give us a measure of each player's productivity.

[15]Berri and Schmidt (2010), in *Stumbling on Wins*, noted that only 9% of a hockey player's plus-minus is explained by the same player's plus-minus the previous season. So this is not a very good measure of performance in hockey.

[16]John Hollinger, "Hockey Stat, with a Twist, Useful in NBA, Too," ESPN.com, March 29, 2005, http://proxy.espn.go.com/nba/columns/story?id=2024296.

The problem with this approach should be obvious. As Hollinger has observed, a player's plus-minus is impacted by the quality of his teammates. So if you happen to play with a top performer, such as LeBron James, Chris Paul, and Anthony Davis, you will tend to have a higher plus-minus. Likewise, if your teammates play poorly, your plus-minus will suffer.

And this means the plus-minus statistic contradicts the purpose we noted for people to track statistics in the first place. Recall that we mentioned teams track stats to separate a player from his teammates. But the plus-minus approach results in a measure of performance for the player that is directly a function of his teammates' productivity.

The problems with a player's plus-minus measure have led researchers[17] to turn to a measure called adjusted plus-minus. This measure involves a regression designed to control for the impact of a player's teammates.[18]

There are quite a few problems with this approach:

- Arturo Galletti attempted to replicate the adjusted plus-minus approach and reported that the basic model explains less than 5% of outcomes.[19] Again, R-squared isn't everything. But the box score statistics can explain much of what happens on the court (as we will see). So if you create a model that ignores the basic box score statistics and it leaves more than 95% of the outcome unexplained, perhaps your model has some problems.

- Berri and Bradbury (2010)[20] analyzed the results reported at basketball-value.com[21] and noted that for most players the results were statistically insignificant. In other words, one could argue that most players, according to this model, did not have any impact on outcomes in basketball.

---

[17]Adjusted plus-minus was originally created by Wayne Winston and Jeff Sagarin [see Winston, *Mathletics: How Gamblers, Managers, and Sports Enthusiasts Use Mathematics in Baseball, Basketball, and Football* (Princeton, NJ: Princeton University Press, 2009)]. This metric is also offered at basketballvalue.com and discussed by Dan Rosenbaum at 82games.com (see http://www.82games.com/comm30.htm). In addition, Arturo Galletti (see http://arturogalletti.wordpress.com/2011/03/04/deconstructing-a-model/) has offered insights into how this model is constructed.

[18]Wayne Winston, who created this model (with Jeff Sagarin), has not published the specific model. Replications of the model, though, appear to argue that the basic model involves a regression of the point differential in a game when the line-ups of the two teams are fixed on dummy variables: equal to 1 if you are in the game (so 10 players get a 1) and 0 if you are not (400+ players are a zero). As Arturo Galletti found when he attempted to replicate the model, this approach doesn't actually explain much of the outcomes we observe. (See http://www.wagesofwins.com/2011/03/05/deconstructing-the-adjusted-plus-minus-model.)

[19]http://www.wagesofwins.com/2011/03/05/deconstructing-the-adjusted-plus-minus-model.

[20]David J. Berri and J. C. Bradbury, "Working in the Land of Metricians," *Journal of Sports Economics* 11, no. 1 (February 2010): 29–47.

[21]This site is still available online but has not been updated since 2012.

- Berri and Bradbury (2010) also noted that a player's adjusted plus-minus is quite inconsistent across time. Specifically, these authors reported that only 7% of a player's adjusted plus-minus in one year could be explained by that same player's adjusted plus-minus the previous year.

- Oliver (2004)[22] also noted that this measure does not look at the entire game but just segments within it. As Oliver observed, players are trying to win games and may choose to conserve energy at certain points in a contest in an effort to achieve final victory. Therefore, what we see in a specific segment of a game may not be a good barometer of a player's overall value.

- Oliver (2004) also noted the "black-box" nature of this measure. Decision makers need to know not only which players are helping a team achieve a specific outcome, but also why that is happening. Adjusted plus-minus might show a correlation between having a player on the court and a specific outcome, but because it can't explain why that correlation is observed, it does not provide us with evidence of causation.

This last point is especially important. No matter how a plus-minus measure is constructed, it cannot tell us causation. All it can do is provide us with a correlation. And that means we probably do not have—with this approach—a measure of a player's marginal productivity.

The Wins Produced Approach

Like the box score measures we have reviewed, the plus-minus approach doesn't seem to provide us with a measure of player productivity. Once again, what we need is a measure that connects what a player does to team wins. And the obvious approach is to simply look at the statistical relationship between the box score statistics and wins.

Such an approach begins with an observation made by both Hollinger (2002) and Oliver (2004). Both authors noted that team wins can be explained by a team's offensive efficiency and defensive efficiency. In other words, wins may be defined as follows[23]:

---

[22]Dean Oliver, *Basketball on Paper* (Washington, DC: Brassey's Sports, 2004).

[23]David J. Berri, "A Simple Measure of Worker Productivity in the National Basketball Association," in Brad Humphreys and Dennis Howard (eds.), *The Business of Sport*, 3 vols. (Westport, CT: Praeger), pp. 1–40 offers a discussion of why wins can be defined, as illustrated by equation A6.6. This discussion essentially follows the process outlined by Gerrard (2006). It should be noted that the model detailed in Berri (2008) was first put forth in *The Wages of Wins* (Berri *et al.*, 2006), and it builds on work initially published in the late 1990s. This was before Gerrard's work on complex invasion sports was published. So it is not entirely correct to say this model was constructed following Gerrard's example. To be chronologically correct, we should note that the approach taken by Gerrard was consistent with the approach adopted here.

$$\text{Winning Percentage} = a_1 + a_2 \times \text{Offensive Efficiency} + a_3$$
$$\times \text{Defensive Efficiency} + e_t \qquad \text{(A6.6)}$$

where   Offensive Efficiency = points scored per possession

Defensive Efficiency = points surrendered per possession

Hollinger (2002) and Oliver (2004) noted that possession can be defined by the following equation:

$$\text{Possession} = FGA + 0.44 \times FTA + TO - ORB \qquad \text{(A6.7)}$$

Berri (2008) relabeled this definition as "Possessions Employed (PE)." The factors that comprise PE are a list of actions a team can take once it has the ball. In sum, once a team has the ball, it can commit a turnover, take a field goal, or attempt free throws. Rebounding missed shots (i.e., ORB) allow a team to extend its possession.

In addition to PE, Berri (2008) offered another definition of possession. As detailed in equation A6.8, a team can acquire possession of the ball (i.e., Possessions Acquired or PA) by forcing its opponent to commit a turnover, rebounding a miss by the opponent (DRB or TMRB), or collecting the ball after a made shot by the opponent[24]:

$$PA = Opp.TO + DRB + TMRB + Opp.FGM + 0.44 \times Opp.FTM \qquad \text{(A6.8)}$$

With Possessions Employed and Possessions Acquired, we can now estimate equation A6.6. This was done with NBA team data from 1987–88 to 2015–16, WNBA team data from 1997 to 2016, each NCAA men's basketball season from 2002–03 to 2015–16, and each NCAA women's basketball season from 2012–13 to 2015–16.[25] The results are reported in Table A.1.

---

[24]As detailed in Berri (2008), team rebounds are defined as team rebounds that change possession. This is not the same as the team rebounds seen in a box score. Berri (2008) also explains how team rebounds that change possession are calculated. From this calculation, one derives the coefficient for FTA in equation A6.7 and Opp.FTM in equation A6.8. Utilizing NBA data from 1987–88 to 2015–16, the coefficient is 0.4423. For the WNBA from 1997 to 2016, the coefficient is 0.4464. And for NCAA men's basketball in 2015–16, the coefficient is 0.4531, while for NCAA women's basketball in 2015–16, the coefficient is 0.4460. Similar results are uncovered for each NCAA men's basketball season from 2002–03 to 2014–15 and NCAA women's basketball season from 2012–13 to 2014–15.

[25]Only the results for NCAA women and men's basketball for 2015–16 are reported. The results for the other seasons are quite similar.

Table A.1 Explaining Winning Percentage with Efficiency Measures in Basketball

	NCAA Women's		NCAA Men's		WNBA		NBA	
	Coefficient	t-Statistic	Coefficient	t-Statistic	Coefficient	t-Statistic	Coefficient	t-Statistic
Constant	0.550	6.89	0.555	5.55	0.568	6.41	0.474	9.09
Offensive efficiency	1.565	33.80	1.777	33.66	2.498	33.29	3.145	89.36
Defensive efficiency	−1.627	−27.98	−1.842	−27.19	−2.569	−33.75	−3.121	−78.25
Observations	349		351		256		831	
R-squared	0.90		0.88		0.89		0.95	

The results in Table A.1 suggest that perhaps there are some differences in how wins relate to the efficiency measures. Explanatory power differs across the leagues.[26] And it appears some differences exist in the magnitudes of the coefficients.

It is important to remember, though, that the purpose of this exercise is to ascertain the value of the various box score statistics. Offensive efficiency includes points scored, field goal attempts, free-throw attempts, turnovers, and offensive rebounds. Defensive efficiency includes defensive rebounds and opponent's turnovers, which includes steals. In addition, there are a variety of factors that are only tracked for the team. The results reported in Table A.1 allow us to ascertain the marginal value of each of these factors.[27] And the results of these calculations are offered in Table A.2.

When we compare the marginal value of each factor to the value determined for points, we suddenly see that the relative value of these box score stats — in terms of wins — is essentially the same across all four leagues. And that teaches an interesting lesson. We have noted that wins in basketball are primarily about gaining and keeping possession of the ball (i.e., rebounds and turnovers) and then turning those possessions into points (i.e., getting to the free-throw line and shooting efficiently). What we come to understand is that whether we are looking at the NCAA (women or men), WNBA, or NBA, basketball is essentially basketball.

[26]The difference in explanatory power partially reflects schedule length. As noted in the text, the longer the schedule, the more the impact of blowouts will be minimized.

[27]For example, the marginal value of an additional point scored (derived from the estimation of equation A6.6) equals a_2/Possessions Employed. And the marginal value of an additional possession employed is calculated as [a_2/Possessions Employed] × [Points Scored/Possessions Employed]. Because one often wishes to compare players across teams, league averages for points scored and possessions employed are used to calculate marginal values.

Table A.2 Impact of Various Player and Team Factors on Wins in National Collegiate Athletic Association Women's and Men's Basketball, the Women's National Basketball Association, and National Basketball Association

Player Factors	NCAA Women's, 2015–16		NCAA Men's, 2015–16		WNBA, 1997–2016		NBA, 1987–88 to 2015–16	
	Marginal Value	Value Relative to Points	Marginal Value	Value Relative to Points	Marginal Value	Value Relative to Points	Marginal Value	Value Relative to Points
PTS	0.022	1.0	0.025	1.0	0.033	1.0	0.033	1.0
FGA	−0.020	−0.9	−0.026	−1.0	−0.031	−0.9	−0.034	−1.0
FTA	−0.009	−0.4	−0.012	−0.5	−0.014	−0.4	−0.015	−0.5
ORB	0.020	0.9	0.026	1.0	0.031	0.9	0.034	1.0
TO	−0.020	−0.9	−0.026	−1.0	−0.031	−0.9	−0.034	−1.0
DRB	0.021	0.9	0.027	1.1	0.032	1.0	0.033	1.0
STL	0.021	0.9	0.027	1.1	0.032	1.0	0.033	1.0
Team Factors	Marginal Value	Value Relative to Points	Marginal Value	Value Relative to Points	Marginal Value	Value Relative to Points	Marginal Value	Value Relative to Points
Opp.PTS	−0.023	−1.0	−0.026	−1.0	−0.034	−1.0	−0.032	−1.0
Opp.FGM	0.021	0.9	0.027	1.1	0.032	1.0	0.033	1.0
Opp.FTM	0.009	0.4	0.012	0.5	0.014	0.4	0.015	0.5
Opp.TO[a]	0.021	0.9	0.027	1.1	0.032	1.0	0.033	1.0
TMREB	0.021	0.9	0.027	1.1	0.032	1.0	0.033	1.0

[a]Opp.TO includes steals. Steals are credited to the individual player. Opp.TO that are not steals are credited to the team.

We also learn another lesson. The value of most components of the box score can be empirically derived. We do not have to invent the weights. One can use simple regression analysis to ascertain what those weights would be in terms of wins.

One notes that there are three statistics commonly tracked for players not listed in Table A.2: personal fouls, blocked shots, and assists. Each of these factors impacts something else that has already been noted in offensive or defensive efficiency. Although one cannot include the three factors in the basic wins model, it is possible to still empirically determine a value for these variables.

For example, as noted in Berri (2008) and Berri and Krautmann (2013),[28] personal fouls lead directly to free throws by the opponent. So if a player is

[28]David J. Berri and Anthony Krautmann, (2013). "Understanding the WNBA On and Off the Court," in Eva Marikova Leeds and Michael Leeds (eds.), *Handbook on the Economics of Women in Sports* (Northampton, MA: Edward Elgar), pp. 132–155.

responsible for 10% of a team's personal fouls, that player can also be charged with 10% of the opponent's free throws made (a factor listed in Table A.2).

For blocked shots, a simple regression can be employed. As noted in Berri and Krautmann (2013), the opponent's made field goals may be regressed on both blocked shots and the opponent's field goals attempted. Utilizing team data from 1997 to 2016 from the WNBA, we see that this simple model explains 77% of the variation in the opponent's made field goals. In addition, each blocked shot reduces made field goals by the opponent by −0.656. Since a 2-point field goal by the opponent is worth −0.035 wins,[29] a blocked shot is worth 0.023 wins (or −0.656 × −0.035).[30]

Unlike everything done so far, the impact of assists is not ascertained at the team level but at the player level. As put forth in Berri and Schmidt (2010), a model was estimated with data for NBA veterans from 1974–75 to 2010–11. The dependent variable was the player's effective field goal percentage[31] in the current season. This was regressed on a player's effective field goal percentage last season, teammates' effective field goal percentage,[32] player age (and age squared), games played last year (as a percentage of possible games), dummy variables for position played, roster stability,[33] dummy variables for a new coach, new team, and season played. Finally, the teammates' assists per minute[34] were considered. The last factor is the primary focus of this model. The basic argument is that the more assists your teammates have, the higher will be a player's shooting efficiency.

---

[29]A point scored by the opponent is worth −0.034, while a made field goal by the opponent (which returns the ball to the team) is worth 0.032. Thus, the value of a 2-point shot by the opponents is calculated as (−0.034 × 2 + 0.032). There is some rounding to reach the value of −0.035.

[30]Similar results were uncovered for NCAA men's and women's basketball and the NBA. For NCAA women's basketball, the same regression for the WNBA was employed. The coefficient for blocked shots for the 2015–16 season was −0.802. Since a 2-point field goal by the opponent was worth −0.025, a blocked shot—in terms of wins – was estimated to be 0.020. For men's college basketball, it is a similar story. The resulting coefficient for blocked shots for the 2015–16 season was −0.751. Since a 2-point field goal by the opponent was worth −0.026, a blocked shot—in terms of wins—was valued at 0.019. For the NBA, a regression was estimated that connected the opponent's made field goals to opponent's field goal attempts, blocked shots, and dummy variables for teams, years (1987–88 to 2015–16 were the years considered in the model). This model indicates that each blocked shot in the NBA reduces the opponent's made shots by 0.617; hence, because a 2-point field goal by the opponent cost −0.031 a blocked shot is worth 0.019 wins in the NBA.

[31]Effective field goal percentage = $(FGM^* + TFGM \times 0.5)/FGA$. Where $TFGM$ = Three Point Field Goals Made.

This measure captures the player's ability to hit field goals from both the 2-point and 3-point range.

[32]This is the team's effective field goal percentage without the player being analyzed.

[33]Berri *et al.* (2006).

[34]These are assists of a team minus the assists of the player being examined.

This effect can be seen anecdotally with respect to LeBron James. As Reuben Fischer-Baum at 538.com noted,[35] the teammates of LeBron James shoot much better with him than without him. The model of effective field goal percentage discussed above offers a reason for this effect. Better passing teammates enhance a player's shooting efficiency.

The estimation of this model is consistent with such a hypothesis. The coefficient on teammate assists is both positive and statistically significant.[36] And with this coefficient in hand, we can now measure each player's Wins Produced.

The calculation of Wins Produced was detailed in Berri and Schmidt (2010) and Berri and Krautmann (2013).[37] The steps involved included adjustments for the team factors not assigned to individuals, the diminishing returns aspect of defensive rebounds, and position played. After all these steps, the results indicate, as Tables A.3 and A.4 report for the WNBA and NBA (in 2016 and 2015–16, respectively), team wins in basketball can be linked back to the actions of individual players.

Table A.3 Comparing Wins Produced and Wins in the Women's National Basketball Association: 2016			
WNBA Team	Wins	Summation of Wins Produced	Absolute Error
Atlanta Dream	17	14.7	2.3
Chicago Sky	18	17.6	0.4
Connecticut Sun	14	13.7	0.3
Dallas Wings	11	10.7	0.3
Indiana Fever	17	16.4	0.6
Los Angeles Sparks	26	24.9	1.1
Minnesota Lynx	28	27.0	1.0
New York Liberty	21	18.2	2.8
Phoenix Mercury	16	18.4	2.4
San Antonio Stars	7	7.7	0.7
Seattle Storm	16	19.1	3.1
Washington Mystics	13	15.5	2.5
		Average Error	**1.5**

[35]http://fivethirtyeight.com/datalab/lebron-is-going-to-make-his-cavs-teammates-woah-better/.

[36]As noted in Berri and Krautmann (2013), a similar result with respect to teammate assists was uncovered for the WNBA. And a similar model was estimated for NCAA women's and men's basketball.

[37]It can also be seen at http://wagesofwins.com/how-to-calculate-wins-produced/.

Table A.4 Comparing Wins Produced and Wins in the National Basketball Association: 2015–16

NBA Team	Wins	Summation of Wins Produced	Absolute Error
Atlanta Hawks	48	50.5	2.5
Boston Celtics	48	49.4	1.4
Brooklyn Nets	21	21.3	0.3
Charlotte Hornets	48	48.3	0.3
Chicago Bulls	42	37.2	4.8
Cleveland Cavaliers	57	57.1	0.1
Dallas Mavericks	42	40.6	1.4
Denver Nuggets	33	32.8	0.2
Detroit Pistons	44	42.7	1.3
Golden State Warriors	73	69.9	3.1
Houston Rockets	41	41.5	0.5
Indiana Pacers	45	45.6	0.6
Los Angeles Clippers	53	52.4	0.6
Los Angeles Lakers	17	15.3	1.7
Memphis Grizzlies	42	35.0	7.0
Miami Heat	48	45.4	2.6
Milwaukee Bucks	33	29.9	3.1
Minnesota Timberwolves	29	31.7	2.7
New Orleans Pelicans	30	30.8	0.8
New York Knicks	32	33.7	1.7
Oklahoma City Thunder	55	60.5	5.5
Orlando Magic	35	36.8	1.8
Philadelphia 76ers	10	13.6	3.6
Phoenix Suns	23	23.0	0.0
Portland Trail Blazers	44	43.2	0.8
Sacramento Kings	33	34.4	1.4
San Antonio Spurs	67	69.1	2.1
Toronto Raptors	56	52.9	3.1
Utah Jazz	40	46.0	6.0
Washington Wizards	41	39.5	1.5
		Average Error	**2.1**

Again, these results highlight an important story. Table A.2 indicates that an additional point scored and additional field goal attempt have essentially the same impact on team wins (in absolute terms). Such a result suggests that players must score 1 point per field goal attempt to break even. In other words, below-average shooting (i.e., inefficient scoring)—contrary to the aforementioned "efficiency" metrics—does not help a team win.[38]

Not only can one measure each player's production of wins, this measure appears to be quite consistent over time. Berri (2012) reported that a player's production per 48 minutes (unadjusted for position played) has a 0.83 correlation with the same player's production per 48 minutes the previous season. In sum, the numbers tabulated for the NBA—in terms of explanatory power and consistency across time—are as good as anything we see for baseball. And that means there is more than one sport where we can measure a player's marginal productivity.[39]

A.3 Statistical Measures in Football

We have seen that the data tracked for players in baseball and basketball can be employed to measure the marginal productivity of workers in those sports. What about football, the most popular American sport? Although data do exist, it seems as if player statistics in this sport don't quite capture the contribution of each individual player. In other words, it is not clear we can measure the marginal productivity of a football player.

To illustrate, let's talk about quarterbacks. In virtually every NFL broadcast, one will hear announcers mention a signal caller's quarterback rating. What isn't mentioned is how such a measure is, in fact, calculated.

The following is a "simple" step-by-step description of this measure.[40] First, you take a quarterback's completion percentage, then subtract 0.3 from that

---

[38]From 1987–88 to 2014–15, the average adjusted field goal percentage in the NBA was 48.8%. The average points-per-shot (PPS), which is simply twice the value of adjusted field goal percentage, was 0.98. So on average, players have to score about 1 point per field goal attempt to be average. Again, below-average marks should hurt a team's chances of winning.

[39]Wins Produced numbers can be found for the NBA at boxscoregeeks.com (a website created by Patrick Minton, Andres Alvarez, and Aruturo Galletti). For the WNBA, Wins Produced numbers can be found at theladiesleague.org (these data were created with the help of Lindsey Darvin and Taylor Cella). It is important to note that Wins Produced allows one to explain how productive a player has been in the past. If you attempt to predict performance, one would have to consider the fact that Wins Produced has various interaction effects built into the model. Predicting the future requires that one predicts these interactions.

[40]This was originally reported in Berri *et al.* (2006).

number, and divide by 0.2. You next take yards per attempts, subtract 3, and divide by 4. After that, you divide touchdowns per attempt by 0.05. For interceptions per attempt, you start with 0.095, subtract from this number interceptions per attempt, and then divide the result by 0.04. To get the quarterback rating, you add the values created from your first four steps, multiply this sum by 100, and divide the result by 6. Oh, and by the way, the sum from each of your first four steps cannot exceed 2.375 or be less than zero.

Here are all those words in a "simple" mathematical formula:

$$\left(\frac{\frac{COMP}{PASSATT} - 0.3}{0.2} + \frac{\frac{PASSYDS}{PASSATT} - 3}{4} + \frac{\frac{PASSTD}{PASSATT}}{0.05} + \frac{0.095 - \frac{INT}{PASSATT}}{0.04} \right) \cdot \frac{100}{6}$$

where $COMP$ = completions

$PASSYDS$ = yards passing

$PASSTD$ = touchdown passes thrown

INT = interceptions thrown

$PASSATT$ = passing attempts

Clearly, this formula is quite complicated. And it appears — at least on the surface — to be somewhat arbitrary. Finally, it isn't very clear that it is linked to actual outcomes.[41]

One alternative approach was offered in Berri (2007).[42] This paper presented a series of regressions linking the factors that comprise quarterback rating, as well as factors like rushing yards, rushing attempts, yards lost from sacks, and fumbles lost, to outcomes in football. This work was updated in Berri and Burke (2012),[43] where the marginal value of these factors was noted in terms of point differential and wins (see **Table A.5**).

---

[41]Don Steinberg, "How I Learned to Stop Worrying and Love the Bomb: A Survival Guide to the NFL's Quarterback Rating System," *GQ*, October 2001, http://www.donsteinberg.com/qbrating.htm.

[42]David Berri, "Back to Back Evaluation on the Gridiron," in James H. Albert and Ruud H. Konig (eds.), *Statistical Thinking in Sport* (Boca Raton, FL: Chapman & Hall/CRC Press, 2007), pp. 235–256.

[43]David Berri and Brian Burke, "Measuring Performance in the NFL," in Kevin Quinn (ed.), *The Economics of the National Football League: The State of the Art* (New York: Springer, 2012), pp. 137–158.

Table A.5 Marginal Value of Various Quarterback Statistics[44]

Variable	Impact of a 1-Unit Increase on Point Differential	Impact of a 1-Unit Increase on Wins
Yards (rushing yards, passing yards, and sack yards)	0.0739	0.0020
Plays (rushing attempts, passing attempts, and sacks)	−0.1063	−0.0028
Interceptions	−2.2793	−0.0636
Fumbles lost	−2.3395	−0.0652

As reported in Berri and Burke (2012), we can also simplify these numbers with a measure Berri (2007) and Berri *et al.* (2006) labeled the QB Score. Given these results, which differ somewhat from the results provided in Berri (2007), the QB Score metric would be calculated as follows:

$$\text{QB Score} = \text{All Yards} - 2 \times \text{All Plays} - 30 \times \text{All Turnovers}$$

If we look at a sample of quarterbacks with a minimum of 224 pass attempts in a season—or the number of attempts in an NFL season needed to qualify for the NFL's quarterback rating leaders—from 1998 to 2010 (421 observations), we observe a 0.9997 correlation between QB Score per play and wins per 100 plays.

There are alternatives to the regression approach. These alternatives rely on play-by-play data. For example, consider Expected Points Added (EPA).[45] This method begins by estimating how many points a team could expect at each point on the field and given the down and distance to a first down the team faces.

A simple example, from Berri and Burke (2012), can help illustrate this concept. Imagine a team has a first down on its own 30-yard line. A team in this situation can expect to score about 1.1 points. Now imagine the team throws a 15-yard pass. This team faces a first down on its own 45-yard line. A first down at this point on the field is generally worth about 1.9 points. And that means a 15-yard pass is worth 0.8 EPA.

---

[44]Berri and Burke (2012, p. 144).

[45]This method builds on the work of V. Carter and R. E. Machol, "Operations Research on Football," *Operations Research* 19, no. 2 (1971):541−544; Bob Carroll, Pete Palmer, and John Thorn, *The Hidden Game of Football* (New York: Warner, 1988); and David H. Romer, "Do Firms Maximize: Evidence from Professional Football," *Journal of Political Economy* 114 (2006): 340−365. It was also detailed in Berri and Burke (2012) and can be found as well at AdvancedNFLStat.com.

Unlike the regression approach detailed in Berri (2007), EPA doesn't treat all yards as the same. As Alok Pattani noted at ESPN.com[46] that "not all yards are created equal." The EPA of an 8-yard gain can vary drastically: at third-and-10, it's worth about -0.2 EPA, whereas at third-and-7, it's worth 1.4 EPA since the drive is still alive.

Similar to EPA, Wins Probability Added (WPA)[47] looks at each play and seeks to ascertain how it impacted the probability a team will win the game. Again, we turn to an example from Berri and Burke (2012). Imagine a team and the following scenario:

* It is the start of the second quarter.

* It is second-and-5.

* The team is down by 7 points.

In such a scenario, a team has wins probability of 36%. Now imagine this same team throws a 30-yard pass setting up a first down at the opponent's 45-yard line. This improves the team's wins probability to 39%. That means that play has a WPA of 0.03.

One can calculate EPA and WPA for any play and therefore use this measure to evaluate quarterbacks (and any other player on the field). And because these EPAs and WPAs capture everything a quarterback does on the field, both measures can be thought of as more comprehensive than the NFL's quarterback rating or Wins Produced.

But does "more comprehensive" suggest that these measures capture the contribution of an individual player? To answer this question, Berri and Burke (2012) examined the consistency of each measure.

The results, reported in Table A.6, indicate that no matter what metric we consider with respect to NFL quarterbacks, signal callers appear to be inconsistent.[48] And following the argument advanced by J. C. Bradbury in Chapter 6, that suggests these measures are not likely to capture a quarterback's marginal product.

---

[46]http://www.espn.com/nfl/story/_/id/8379024/nfl-explaining-expected-points-metric.

[47]WPA can be found at AdvancedNFLStats.com. It was also discussed in Berri and Burke (2012).

[48]ESPN.com introduced a quarterback metric called QBR. This measure was developed with the help of Dean Oliver (and based on the work of Brian Burke). ESPN.com reports QBR from 2008 to 2011. Across 101 quarterback observations, we see that 24% of a quarterback's total QBR in the current season is explained by the quarterback's total QBR the prior season.

Table A.6 Consistency of NFL Quarterbacks: 1998–2010; Minimum 224 Passing Attempts in Consecutive Seasons (256 observations)[49]	
Quarterback Statistic	Percentage of Current Performance Explained by Performance Last Season
NFL's QB rating	15.0%
Completion percentage	31.1%
Passing yards per attempt	22.1%
Touchdowns per attempt	10.1%
Interceptions per attempt[50]	0.6%
Wins Produced per 100	16.9%
Expected points per play[a]	21.0%
Wins probability added per play[a]	11.7%

[a]Data for these statistics are only for 2000 to 2010. Number of observations = 213.

The explanation for this is quite simple. No matter how we examine the actions of a quarterback, virtually all of them depend on his teammates. Receivers must catch his passes and linemen must block. In sum, it is very difficult to separate a quarterback from his teammates. Consequently, it is very hard for us to measure a quarterback's marginal productivity.

The ability to measure the marginal productivity of a worker is one of the main reasons economists are attracted to the study of sports. But as this brief introduction has indicated, although sports offers an abundance of productivity measures, not every one of these is truly a measure of marginal productivity. So, before you decided to use a particular measure in an economic study, think about whether that number truly captures the productivity of the individual. If so, then that measure might work for your study. If not, maybe you should keep looking for a better measure of marginal productivity.

[49]These data originally appeared in Berri and Burke (2012, p. 254).
[50]Fumbles lost per play are also quite inconsistent. Berri (2007) reported, a sample of quarterbacks taken from 2001 to 2005, that only 5.8% of the variation in a quarterback's fumbles lost per play this season is explained by quarterback's fumbles lost per play the previous season. For running backs, the variation explained was only 0.6%.

Glossary

Coase theorem When there are zero transaction costs, the application of legal rights has no effect upon the allocation of resources among economic enterprises—in baseball, the allocation of players will be the same under the reserve clause (whereby owners have the legal right to sell a player's talent) and a free market (whereby players have the legal right to sell their services).

competitive balance The distribution of wins in a league, so it is consistent with profit maximization across the league.

crowd out No change in output in spite of government spending in a fully employed economy.

crowding out effect What happens when the crowds associated with a sporting event lead other people to avoid the event, thus reducing its economic impact.

deductive reasoning Method whereby one begins with a general principle (or set of general principles) and then derives a theory.

demand To be in "demand" of a product, one must be willing and able to purchase a good or service (in different quantities at different prices).

demand curve Tells us how much of a good is demanded at various prices.

dependent variable What we wish to explain with a regression model, or the Y-variable.

discrimination coefficient (dc) A coefficient that measures how much discrimination exists in a market.

elasticity The ratio of the percentage change in a dependent variable to a percentage change in an independent variable.

explained sum of squares (ESS) How much variation in the dependent variable the model explained, or $\sum(\hat{Y} \text{ Mean of } Y)^2$.

explicit bias Positive or negative mental attitude toward a person, thing, or group that someone holds at a conscious level.

idealized standard deviation The ratio of the mean winning percentage in the league to the square root of

a league's schedule length; illustrates the importance of schedule length.

Implicit Association Test (IAT) To assess the existence of implicit bias, measures the strength of associations between concepts and evaluations or stereotypes.

implicit bias Positive or negative mental attitude toward a person, thing, or group that someone holds at an unconscious level.

income effect In general, a decrease in a good's price increases the purchasing power of a consumer (and an increase will decrease his or her purchasing power).

independent variable What we believe explains the dependent variable, or the X-variable.

inductive reasoning Method whereby one determines patterns in data and then derives a theory.

invariance principle The distribution of talent in sports leagues moves to its highest-valued use regardless of who (either the players or the owners) receives the revenue generated by the players.

law of demand As the price of a good increases, quantity demanded for the good will decline, holding all else constant.

law of diminishing returns As a firm hires more workers, holding all else constant, the amount of output from each additional worker a firm adds will eventually decline.

law of supply As the price of a good increases, quantity supplied for the good will increase, holding all else constant.

leakage effect What happens when professional athletes employed by sports teams tend to live elsewhere, with spending then leaking outside the city hosting the team.

lockout When employers refuse to allow workers to work.

Louis–Schmeling paradox In sports, the stronger the competition, the greater the interest of a paying customer—in contrast to what is observed outside of sports, where firms do better if their competition is weak or nonexistent.

marginal benefits The value derived from the decision being made.

marginal cost The cost per each additional unit.

marginal product (MP) The productivity of hiring that additional worker.

marginal revenue The amount of revenue a firm gains from an additional sale and also the slope of the total revenue curve.

marginal revenue product (MRP) Marginal product of labor multiplied by marginal revenue of output.

market period Period of time when firms cannot adjust supply, so prices are determined entirely by the level of demand.

Marshallian cross The standard supply and demand model.

monopoly A firm that is the sole seller in a market.

monopsony A market with only one buyer.

multi-collinearity The problem of two or more independent variables having a linear relationship.

multiplier The number by which the change in investment must be multiplied to calculate the resulting change in income.

multivariate model A model with more than one independent variable.

national origin bias (or **national origin discrimination**) A preformed negative opinion or attitude toward a group of persons of the same race or national origin who share common or similar traits, languages, customs, and traditions.

Noll–Scully measure Approach in constructing a competitive balance metric that compares the observed standard deviation of performance to an idealized standard deviation given a league's schedule length.

opportunity cost The value of the next best alternative cast aside in making a decision.

price ceiling A mandated price above which transactions cannot be made. Typically, it is the government that establishes such mandates (e.g., rent control laws in New York City). But we also find price ceilings in sports.

quantity demanded The amount consumers demand at each price, holding all else constant. We represent this by moving along the demand curve.

quantity supplied The amount producers supply at each price, holding all else constant. We represent this by moving along the supply curve.

regression analysis A statistical technique that uses a single equation to attempt to "explain" movements in the dependent variable as a function of movements in the independent (or explanatory) variables.

reserve clause A policy that allowed teams to retain the right to a player even when that player was not explicitly under contract.

residual sum of squares (RSS) How much variation in the dependent variable the model did not explain, or $\sum e^2$.

R-squared (R^2) The coefficient of determination, or the percentage of variation in the dependent variable (i.e., winning percentage), that is explained by all the independent variables (i.e., relative payroll).

short-run period Period when firms can change the supply of a good in response to a change in price.

strike When workers refuse to work in an effort to force employers to make changes to the worker–employer labor agreement.

substitution effect In general, an increase in a good's price makes other goods more attractive to the consumer (and a lower price makes other goods less attractive).

sunk costs Charges that are not impacted by the decision at hand.

supply To be in "supply" of a product, one must be willing and able to produce and sell a good or service (in different quantities at different prices).

total sum of squares (TSS) How much variation in the dependent variable there is to explain, or $\sum(Y_i - \text{Mean of } Y)^2$.

univariate model A model with one independent variable that tends to help students see the very basics of regression analysis, but does not help us understand much about the world.

utility The level of satisfaction or happiness a person is able to achieve.

winner's curse A tendency for the winner in a bidding process to be the person/group that most overvalues what is being bid on. This happens when value can only be estimated and not known with certainty.

x-inefficiency What happens when monopolies do not have an incentive to produce as efficiently as possible because they do not face competition.

References

Acosta, R. Vivian, and Linda J. Carpenter. 2014. "Women in Intercollegiate Sport: A Longitudinal, National Study, Thirty-Seven-Year Update, 1977–2014." Unpublished manuscript. http://www.acostacarpenter.org.

Adler, Joseph. 2006. *Baseball Hacks*. Sebastopol, CA: O'Reilly Media.

Albert, James, and Jay Bennett. 2003. *Curve Ball: Baseball, Statistics, and the Role of Chance in the Game*. New York: Copernicus Books.

Anderson, Deborah J., and John J. Cheslock. 2004. "Institutional Strategies to Achieve Gender Equity in Intercollegiate Athletics: Does Title IX Harm Male Athletes?" *American Economic Review* 94(2): 307–11.

Ariely, Dan. 2008. *Predictably Irrational: The Hidden Forces That Shape Our Decisions*. New York: HarperCollins.

Ashenfelter, Orley. 1978. "Estimating the Effect of Training Programs on Earnings." *Review of Economics and Statistics* 60: 47–57.

Averett, Susan L., and Sarah M. Estelle. 2013. "The Economics of Title IX Compliance in Intercollegiate Athletics." In *Handbook on the Economics of Women in Sports*, edited by Eva Marikova Leeds and Michael Leeds. Cheltenham, UK: Edward Elgar.

Baade, Robert, and Victor Matheson. 2012. "Financing Professional Sports Facilities." In *Financing Economic Development in the 21st Century*, edited by Zenia Kotval and Sammis White, 2nd ed., 323–42. Armonk, NY: M.E. Sharpe.

Balduck, A., and M. Buelens. 2007. "Does Sacking the Coach Help or Hinder the Team in the Short Term? Evidence from Belgian Soccer." Working paper, Faculty of Economics and Business Administration, Ghent University, Belgium.

Becker, Gary. 1957. *The Economics of Discrimination*. Chicago: University of Chicago Press.

Beckman, Elise M., Wenqiang Cai, Rebecca M. Esrock, and Robert J. Lemke. 2012. "Over Time Explaining Game-to-Game Ticket Sales for Major League Baseball Games." *Journal of Sports Economics* 13(5): 535–55.

Bellotti, Bob. 1992. *The Points Created Basketball Book, 1991–92*. New Brunswick, NJ: Night Work.

Bellotti, Robert. 1993. *The Points Created Basketball Book, 1992–93*. New Brunswick, NJ: Night Work.

Berger, Ken. 2014, September 24. "For Many NBA Assistants, the Road to Glory Is Well-Traveled." *CBS News*. http://www.cbssports.com/nba/writer/ken-berger/24723463/for-many-nba-assistants-the-road-to-glory-is-well-traveled.

Berri, David J. 2006. "Economics and the National Basketball Association: Surveying the Literature at the Tip-off." In *The Handbook of Sports Economics Research*, edited by John Fizel, 21–48. Armonk, NY: M.E. Sharpe.

Berri, David. 2007. "Back to Back Evaluation on the Gridiron." In *Statistical Thinking in Sport*, edited by James H. Albert and Ruud H. Konig, 235–56. Boca Raton, FL: Chapman & Hall/CRC Press.

Berri, David J. 2008. "A Simple Measure of Worker Productivity in the National Basketball Association." In *The Business of Sport*, edited by Brad Humphreys and Dennis Howard, 3 vols., 1–40. Westport, CT: Praeger.

Berri, David J. 2012a. "Did the Players Give Up Money to Make the NBA Better? Exploring the 2011 Collective Bargaining Agreement in the National Basketball Association." *International Journal of Sport Finance* 7: 158–75.

Berri, David J. 2012b. "Measuring Performance in the National Basketball Association." In *The Handbook of Sports Economics*, edited by Stephen Shmanske and Leo Kahane, Vol. 2, 94–117. New York: Oxford University Press.

Berri, David J. 2015. "Think You Know Basketball? You Need to Know the Numbers to Know the Game." *Sports & Entertainment Review* 1(1): 6–13.

Berri, David J. 2016. "Paying NCAA Athletes." *Marquette Sports Law Review* 26(2): 479–91.

Berri, David J., and J. C. Bradbury. 2010. "Working in the Land of Metricians." *Journal of Sports Economics* 11(1): 29–47.

Berri, David J., Stacey L. Brook, and Aju Fenn. 2011. "From College to the Pros: Predicting the NBA Amateur Player Draft." *Journal of Productivity Analysis* 35(1): 25–35.

Berri, David J., Stacey L. Brook, Aju Fenn, Bernd Frick, and Roberto Vicente-Mayoral. 2005. "The Short Supply of Tall People: Explaining Competitive Imbalance in the National Basketball Association." *Journal of Economics Issues* 39(4): 1029–41.

Berri, David, Stacey L. Brook, and Martin Schmidt. 2007. "Does One Simply Need to Score to Score?" *International Journal of Sport Finance* 2(4): 190–205.

Berri, David, Babatunde Buraimo, Giambattista Rossi, and Rob Simmons. 2016. "Pay and Performance in Italian Football." Paper presented at Western Economic Association meetings, Portland, OR.

Berri, David, and Brian Burke. 2012. "Measuring Performance in the NFL." In *The Economics of the National Football League: The State of the Art*, edited by Kevin Quinn, 137–58. New York: Springer.

Berri, David J., Christian Deutscher, and Arturo Galletti. 2015. "Born in the USA: National Origin Effects on Time Allocation in US and Spanish Professional Basketball." *Special Issue: National Institute Economic Review* 232: R41–R50.

Berri, David J., and Anthony Krautmann. 2013. "Understanding the WNBA On and Off the Court." In *Handbook on the Economics of Women in Sports*, edited by Eva Marikova Leeds and Michael Leeds, 132–55. Northampton, MA: Edward Elgar.

Berri, David J., and Anthony Krautmann. 2016. "Exploitation before Free Agency. Revisiting the Original Scully Model." Presented at the Western Economic Association, Portland, OR.

Berri, David, Michael Leeds, and Peter von Allmen. 2015. "Salary Determination in the Presence of Fixed Revenues." *International Journal of Sport Finance* 10(1): 5–25.

Berri, David J., Michael Leeds, Eva Marikova Leeds, and Michael Mondello. 2009. "The Role of Managers in Team Performance." *International Journal of Sport Finance* 4(2): 75–93.

Berri, David J., and Martin B. Schmidt. 2010. *Stumbling on Wins: Two Economists Explore the Pitfalls on the Road to Victory in Professional Sports*. Upper Saddle River, NJ: Financial Times Press.

Berri, David J., Martin B. Schmidt, and Stacey L. Brook. 2004. "Stars at the Gate: The Impact of Star Power on NBA Gate Revenues." *Journal of Sports Economics* 5(1): 33–50.

Berri, David J., Martin B. Schmidt, and Stacey L. Brook. 2006. *The Wages of Wins: Taking Measure of the Many Myths in Modern Sport*. Stanford, CA: Stanford University Press.

Berri, David J., and Rob Simmons. 2009. "Race and the Evaluation of Signal Callers in the National Football League." *Journal of Sports Economics* 10(1): 23–43.

Berri, David J., and Rob Simmons. 2011a. "Catching a Draft: On the Process of Selecting Quarterbacks in the National Football League Amateur Draft." *Journal of Productivity Analysis* 35(1): 37–49.

Berri, David J., and Rob Simmons. 2011b. "Mixing the Princes and the Paupers: Pay and Performance in the National Basketball Association." *Labour Economics* 18(3): 381–88.

Berri, David J., Rob Simmons, Jennifer Van Gilder, and Lisle O'Neill. 2011. "What Does It Mean to Find the Face of the Franchise? Physical Attractiveness and the Evaluation of Athletic Performance." *Economics Letters* 111: 200–02.

Berri, David J., Jennifer Van Gilder, and Aju Fenn. 2014. "Is the Sports Media Color-Blind?" *International Journal of Sport Finance* 9: 130–48.

Berri, David J., Steve Walters, and Jennifer Van Gilder. 2012. "Stereotypes and Hiring Decisions: Lessons from the NBA Draft." Paper presented at the Western Economic Association, San Francisco, CA.

Bertrand, Marianne, and Sendhil Mulainathan. 2004. "Are Emily and Greg More Employable Than Lakisha and Jamal? A Field Experiment on Labor Market Discrimination." *American Economic Review* 94(4): 991–1013.

Blair, Roger. 2012. *Sports Economics*. New York: Cambridge University Press.

Blass, Asher. 1992. "Does the Baseball Labor Market Contradict the Human Capital Model?" *Review of Economics and Statistics* 74: 261–68.

Blau, Francine, and Lawrence Kahn. 2016. "The Gender Wage Gap: Extent, Trends, and Explanation." IZA Discussion Paper No. 956.

Blaug, Mark. 1986. *Great Economists before Keynes.* Englewood Cliffs, NJ: Prentice Hall.

Borjas, George. 1996. *Labor Economics.* New York: McGraw-Hill.

Bowen, H. R. 1980. *The Costs of Higher Education.* San Francisco: Jossey-Bass.

Boyd, David, and Laura Boyd. 1998. "The Home Field Advantage: Implications for the Pricing of Tickets of Professional Team Sporting Events." *Journal of Economics and Finance* 22: 169–179.

Bradbury, J. C. 2007a. "Does the Baseball Player Labor Market Properly Value of Pitchers?" *Journal of Sports Economics* 8(6): 616–32.

Bradbury, J. C. 2007b. *The Baseball Economist: The Real Game Exposed.* New York: Dutton.

Bradbury, J. C. 2008. "Statistical Performance Analysis in Sport." In *The Business of Sport*, edited by Brad Humphreys and Dennis Howard, 3 vols., 41–56. Westport, CT: Praeger.

Bradbury, J. C. 2010. "Hired to Be Fired: The Publicity Value of Coaches." Paper presented at the Southern Economic Association Meeting.

Bradbury, J. C. 2011. *Hot Stove Economics: Understanding Baseball's Second Season.* New York: Copernicus Books.

Bradbury, J. C. 2013. "What Is Right with Scully's Estimates of Player's Marginal Revenue Product." *Journal of Sports Economics* 14(1): 87–96.

Brook, S. 2006. "Evaluating Inelastic Ticket Pricing Models." *International Journal of Sport Finance* 1: 140–50.

Brown, Eleanor, Richard Spiro, and Diane Keenan. 1991. "Wage and Non-Wage Discrimination in Professional Basketball: Do Fans Affect It?" *American Journal of Economics and Sociology* 50(3): 333–45.

Brown, Robert W. 1993. "An Estimate of the Rent Generated by a Premium College Football Player." *Economic Inquiry* 31: 671–84.

Brown, Robert W. 1994. "Measuring Cartel Rents in the College Basketball Player Recruitment Market." *Applied Economics* 26: 27–34.

Brown, Robert W. 2011. "Research Note: Estimate of College Football Rents." *Journal of Sports Economics* 12: 200–12.

Brown, Robert W., and R. Todd Jewell. 2004. "Measuring Marginal Revenue Product of College Athletics:

Updated Estimates." In *Economics of College Sports*, edited by F. Rodney and F. John. Westport, CT: Praeger.

Bruinshoofd, A., and B. TerWeel. 2004. "Manager to Go? Performance Dips Reconsidered with Evidence from Dutch Football." *European Journal of Operational Research* 148: 233–46.

Burger, John, and Stephen Walters. 2003. "Market Size, Pay, and Performance: A General Model and Application to Major League Baseball." *Journal of Sports Economics* 4(2): 108–25.

Burger, John D., and Stephen J. K. Walters. 2009. "Uncertain Prospects: Rates of Return in the Baseball Draft." *Journal of Sports Economics* 10(5): 485–501.

Callahan, Gerry. 1996, December 2. "Double Play: When He Signed Albert Belle, Jerry Reinsdorf Broke the Bank—and Maybe the Labor Impasse." *Sports Illustrated.* https://www.si.com/vault/1996/12/02/8109578/double-play-when-he-signed-albert-belle-jerry-reinsdorf-broke-the-bankand-maybe-the-labor-impasse.

Carroll, Bob, Pete Palmer, and John Thorn. 1988. *The Hidden Game of Football.* New York: Warner.

Carter, Susan B. 2006. "Labor Force, Employment, and Unemployment: 1890–1990." In *Historical Statistics of the United States, Earliest Times to the Present: Millennial Edition*, edited by Susan B. Carter, Scott Sigmund Gartner, Michael R. Haines, Alan L. Olmstead, Richard Sutch, and Gavin Wright. New York: Cambridge University Press.

Carter, V., and R. E. Machol. 1971. "Operations Research on Football." *Operations Research* 19(2): 541–44.

Cavalaris, Chuck. 2002, August 18. "Fans Warn Against Baseball Stoppage." *Knoxville News-Sentinel (Tennessee).* Sunday Final Edition, p. C2.

Clark, J. M. "J. M. Clark on J. B. Clark." In *The Development of Economic Thought*, edited by H. W. Spiegel, 610. New York: Wiley, 1952.

Clotfelter, Charles. 2011. *Big-Time Sports in American Universities.* New York: Cambridge University Press.

Coase, R. 1975. "Marshall on Method." *Journal of Law and Economics* 18(1): 30.

Coates, D., and T. Harrison. 2005. "Baseball Strikes and the Demand for Attendance." *Journal of Sports Economics* 6(3): 282–302.

Coates, Dennis, and Brad Humphreys. 2010. "Week to Week Attendance and Competitive Balance in the

National Football League." *International Journal of Sport Finance* 5: 239–52.

Coates, Dennis, and Brad R. Humphreys. 2012. "Game Attendance and Outcome Uncertainty in the National Hockey League." *Journal of Sports Economics* 13(4): 364–77.

Cohen-Zada, Danny, Alex Krumer, Mosi Rosenboim, and Offer Moshe Shapir. 2016. "Choking Under Pressure and Gender." Working paper. https://www.researchgate.net/publication/308901292_Choking_Under_Pressure_and_Gender.

Colander, David. 2017. *Principles of Microeconomics*. 10th ed. Dubuque, IA: McGraw-Hill.

Coletta, Amanda. 2015, June 5. "A League of Their Own: The Most Dominant Soccer Team in 1920 Was Full of Female Factory Workers." The New York Times. http://nytlive.nytimes.com/womenintheworld/2015/06/05/a-league-of-their-own-the-most-dominant-soccer-team-in-1920-was-full-of-female-factory-workers/.

Cooky, Cheryl, Michael A. Messner, and Michela Musto. 2015. "'It's Dude Time!' A Quarter Century of Excluding Women's Sports in Televised News and Highlight Shows." *Communication & Sport* 3(3): 1–27.

Coon, L. "NBA Salary Cap FAQ." http://www.cbafaq.com/salarycap.htm.

Cross, Patricia K. 1977. "Not Can, But Will College Teaching Improve?" *New Directions for Higher Education* 1977 (17): 1–15.

Darvin, Lindsey, Ann Pegoraro, and David Berri. 2016. "The Head Coach Role—Is It Only a Job for Men? An Investigation of Head Coach Gender and Player Performance in the WNBA and NCAA Women's Basketball." Working paper.

Davis, S. 2015, July 15. "NBA Commissioner Adam Silver Says a 'Significant Number' of Teams Are Losing Money." *Business Insider*. http://www.businessinsider.com/adam-silver-nba-teams-losing-money-2015-7.

DeGennaro, R. 2003. The Utility of Sport and Returns to Ownership." *Journal of Sports Economics* 4: 145–53.

Deli, D. 2013. "Assessing the Relative Importance of Inputs to a Production Function: Getting on Base vs Hitting for Power." *Journal of Sports Economics* 14(2): 203–17.

De Paola, Maria, and Vincenzo Scoppa. 2012. "The Effects of Managerial Turnover: Evidence from Coach Dismissals in Italian Soccer Teams." *Journal of Sports Economics* 13(2): 152–68.

Dietl, Helmut M., Martin Grossmann, and Markus Lang. 2011. "Competitive Balance and Revenue Sharing in Sports Leagues with Utility-Maximizing Teams." *Journal of Sports Economics* 3(12): 284–308.

Eckard, E. Woodrow. 2001. "The Origin of the Reserve Clause: Owner Collusion vs 'Public Interest.'" *Journal of Sports Economics* 2(2): 118.

Edmonds, Edmund. 1999. *The Curt Flood Act of 1998: A Hollow Gesture After All These Years?* Marquette Sports Law Journal 9: 315. http://scholarship.law.marquette.edu/sportslaw/vol9/iss2/8.

Ehrenberg, Ronald, and Robert S. Smith. 2000. *Modern Labor Economics*. Reading, MA: Addison Wesley Longman.

Fagan, Kate, and Luke Cyphers. 2015. "The Glass Wall: Women Continue to Shatter Stereotypes as Athletes. So How Come They Can't Catch a Break as Coaches?" *ESPN The Magazine*. http://sports.espn.go.com/espn/eticket/story?page=theGlassWall.

Feinstein, John, and Red Auerbach. 2004. *Let Me Tell You a Story: A Lifetime in the Game*. New York: Little, Brown.

Ferguson, D. G., K. Stewart, J. C. H. Jones, and A. Le Dressay. 1991. "The Pricing of Sports Events: Do Teams Maximize Profits?" *Journal of Industrial Economic* 39(3): 297–310.

"Football." 1934, November 26. *TIME Magazine*. http://content.time.com/time/magazine/article/0,9171,882323,00.html.

Ford, Rodney, and Andrew Gill. 2000. "Race and Ethnicity Assessment in Baseball Card Markets." *Journal of Sports Economics* 1(21): 21–38.

Forrest, D., R. Simmons, and B. Buraimo. 2005. "Outcome Uncertainty and the Couch Potato Audience." *Scottish Journal of Political Economy* 52: 641–61.

Fort, Rodney. 2000, Spring. "Stadiums and Public and Private Interests in Seattle." *Marquette Sports Law Journal* 10: 311–34.

Fort, Rodney. 2010. *Sports Economics*. 3rd ed. Upper Saddle River, NJ: Prentice Hall.

Friedman, Milton. 1966. "The Methodology of Positive Economics." In *Essays in Positive Economics*. Chicago: University of Chicago Press, 1966.

Friedman, Milton, and L. J. Savage. 1948. "The Utility Analysis of Choices Involving Risk." *Journal of Political Economy* 56(4): 279–304.

Gamrat, F., and R. Sauer. 2000. "The Utility of Sport and Returns to Ownership: Evidence from the Thoroughbred Market." *Journal of Sports Economics* 1: 219–35.

Gayer, Ted, Austin Drukker, and Alexander Gold. 2016. *Tax-Exempt Municipal Bonds and the Financing of Professional Sports Stadiums*. Economic Studies at Brookings. Washington, DC: Brookings Institution.

Gerrard, Bill. 2007. "Is the Moneyball Approach Transferable to Complex Invasion Team Sports?" *International Journal of Sports Finance* 2: 214–28.

Gladwell, Malcolm. 2007. *Blink*. New York: Back Bay Books.

Goff, Brian, H. Youn Kim, and Dennis Wilson. 2016. "Estimating the Market Value of Collegiate Football Players Using Professional Factor Shares." *Applied Economics Letters* 24(4): 233–37.

Gould, Stephen Jay. 1983. "Losing the Edge: The Extinction of the .400 Hitter." *Vanity Fair* 120: 264–78.

Gould, Stephen Jay. 1986, August. "Entropic Homogeneity Isn't Why No One Hits .400 Any More." *Discover* 7(8): 60–66.

Greer, Tiffany, Joshua Price, and David Berri. 2015. "Jumping in the Pool: What Determines Which Players the NBA Considers in the NBA Draft?" Paper presented at the Western Economic Association, Honolulu, HI.

Groothuis, Peter, and James Richard Hill. 2013. "Pay Discrimination, Exit Discrimination or Both? Another Look at an Old Issue Using NBA Data." *Journal of Sports Economics* 14(2): 171–85.

Hakes, Jahn K., and Raymond D. Sauer. 2006. "An Economic Evaluation of the Moneyball Hypothesis." *Journal of Economic Perspectives* 20: 173–86.

Hamermesh, D. S. 2011. *Beauty Pays: Why Attractive People Are More Successful*. Princeton, NJ: Princeton University.

Hamermesh, D. S., and J. Biddle. 1994. "Beauty and the Labor Market." *American Economic Review* 84: 1174–94.

Harris, Jill, and David Berri. 2016. "If You Can't Pay Them, Play Them: Fan Preference and Own-Race Bias in the WNBA." *International Journal of Sport Finance* 11: 163–80.

Haupert, Michael. 2007, December 3. "The Economic History of Major League Baseball." In *EH.Net Encyclopedia*, edited by Robert Whaples. https://eh.net/encyclopedia/the-economic-history-of-major-league-baseball/.

Heeren, Dave. 1992. *Basketball Abstract*. Englewood Cliffs, NJ: Prentice Hall.

Heilmann, Ronald L., and Wayne R. Wendling. 1976. "A Note on Optimum Pricing Strategies for Sports Events." In *Management Science in Sports*, edited by Robert Engel Machol and Shaul P. Ladany, 91–100. New York: North Holland.

Henderson, Joe. 2002, August 18. "Baseball Pushing Its Luck in Dispute?" *Tampa Tribune (Florida)*. Sunday Final Edition, Sports section, p. 1.

Hicks, John R. 1996. *The Theory of Wages*. 2nd ed. New York: St. Martin's Press.

Hollinger, John. 2002. *Pro Basketball Prospectus 2002*. Washington, DC: Brassey's Sports.

Hollinger, John. 2005, March 29. "Hockey Stat, with a Twist, Useful in NBA, Too." *ESPN.com*. http://proxy.espn.com/nba/columns/story?columnist=hollinger_john&id=2024296.

Holmes, Paul. 2011. "Win or Go Home: Why College Football Coaches Get Fired." *Journal of Sports Economics* 12(2): 157–78.

Holmes, Paul, Rob Simmons, and David Berri. 2014. "Moneyball and the Baseball Players' Labour Market." Paper presented at Western Economic Association meetings, Denver, CO.

Horowitz, Ira. 1994. "On the Manager as Principal Clerk." *Managerial and Decision Economics* 15: 187–94.

Humphreys, Brad. 2002. "Alternative Measures of Competitive Balance in Sports League." *Journal of Sports Economics* 3(2): 133–48.

Humphreys, Brad, and Jane Ruseski. 2009. "Estimates of the Dimensions of the Sports Market in the US." *International Journal of Sport Finance* 4: 94–113.

Iyengar, Shanto, Gaurav Sood, and Yphtach Lelkes. 2014. "Affect, Not Ideology: A Social Identity Perspective on Polarization." *Public Opinion Quarterly* 76(3): 405–31.

Jackson, Phil. 2006. *Sacred Hoops: Spiritual Lessons of a Hardwood Warrior.* New York: Hyperion.

Jenkins, Jeffery A. 1996. "A Reexamination of Salary Discrimination in Professional Basketball." *Social Science Quarterly* 77(3): 594–608.

Jennings, A. 2016, February 17. "The Super Bowl vs. the World Cup. What Is the Real Football?" *The Ladies League.* http://www.theladiesleague.org/#!The-Super-Bowl-vs-The-World-Cup-What-Is-The-Real-Football/n7e5e/56c506090cf25df9371d31cb.

Johnston, Louis, and Samuel H. Williamson. 2017. "What Was the U.S. GDP Then?" *MeasuringWorth.* https://www.measuringworth.com/usgdp/.

Kahn, L. 2000. "The Sports Business as a Labor Market Laboratory." *Journal of Economic Perspectives* 15(3): 74–94.

Kahn, Lawrence M. 1991. "Discrimination in Professional Sports: A Survey of the Literature." *Industrial Labor Relations Review* 44: 395–418.

Kahn, Lawrence M., and Peter D. Sherer. 1988. "Racial Differences in Professional Basketball Players' Compensation." *Journal of Labor Economics* 6(1): 40–61.

Karnitschnig, M., D. Solomon, L. Pleven, and J. Hilsenrath. 2008, September 16. "U.S. to Take Over AIG in $85 Billion Bailout; Central Banks Inject Cash as Credit Dries Up." *Wall Street Journal.*

Kavetsos, Georgios, and Stefan Szymanski. 2010. "National Well-Being and International Sports Events." *Journal of Economic Psychology* 31: 158–71.

Kennedy, Peter. 1996. *A Guide to Econometrics.* 3rd ed. Cambridge, MA: MIT Press.

Kesenne, Stefan. 2000. "Revenue Sharing and Competitive Balance in Professional Team Sports." *Journal of Sports Economics* 1(1): 56–65.

Kesenne, Stefan. 2005. "Revenue Sharing and Competitive Balance: Does the Invariance Proposition Hold?" *Journal of Sports Economics* 1(6): 98–106.

Kesenne, Stefan. 2007. "Revenue Sharing and Owner Profits in Professional Team Sports." *Journal of Sports Economics* 5(8): 519–29.

Keynes, J. M. 1924. "Alfred Marshall, 1842–1924." *The Economic Journal* 34(135): 342.

Keynes, J. N. 1999. *The Scope and Method of Political Economy.* Kitchener, ON: Batoche Books.

Kirwan, P. 2012, April 7. "Before Offensive Tackles Fly Off Draft Boards, Consider Supply and Demand." *CBS Sports.* http://www.cbssports.com/nfl/draft/story/18379951/before-offensive-tackles-fly-off-draft-boards-consider-supply-and-demand.

Koch, James V., and C. Warren Vander Hill. 1988. "Is There Discrimination in the Black Man's Game?" *Social Science Quarterly* 69(1): 83–94.

Krautmann, Anthony. 1999. "What's Wrong with Scully Estimates of a Player's MRP?" *Economic Inquiry* 37: 369–81.

Krautmann, Anthony, Peter von Allmen, and David J. Berri. 2009. "The Underpayment of Restricted Players in North American Sports Leagues." *International Journal of Sport Finance* 4(3): 155–69.

Krautmann, Anthony, and David J. Berri. 2007. "Can We Find It at the Concessions? Understanding Price Elasticity in Professional Sports." *Journal of Sports Economics* 8(2): 183–91.

Lambert, Peter J. 1993. *The Distribution and Redistribution of Income: A Mathematical Analysis.* Manchester, UK: Manchester University Press.

Landreth, Harry, and David Colander. 2002. *History of Economic Thought.* 4th ed. Boston: Houghton Mifflin.

Lane, Erin, Juan Nagel, and Janet Netz. 2012. "Alternative Approaches to Measuring MRP: Are All Men's College Basketball Players Exploited?" *Journal of Sports Economics* 15(3): 237–62.

Lecher, C. 2014, May 12. "Algorithm Reveals Link between Sour Cream and Traffic Accidents: Visualizing the Unexpected Correlations That Surround Us." https://www.popsci.com/article/science/algorithm-reveals-link-between-sour-cream-and-traffic-accidents.

Leeds, Michael, and Peter von Allmen. 2011. *The Economics of Sports.* 4th ed. Boston: Addison-Wesley.

Levitt, Dan. 2006. "Empirical Analysis of Bunting." http://baseballanalysts.com/archives/2006/07/empirical_analy_1.php.

Levitt, S. D., and S. J. Dubner. 2005. *Freakonomics: A Rogue Economist Explores the Hidden Side of Everything.* New York: William Morrow.

Lewis, Michael M. 2003. *Moneyball: The Art of Winning an Unfair Game.* New York: W.W Norton.

Lindsey, George. 1963. "An Investigation of Strategies in Baseball." *Operations Research* 11(4): 477–501.

Litke, Jim. 1994, November 16. "Big Dog's Big Push to Get Out of the Big Doghouse." *Associated Press.*

Marshall, Alfred. 1925/1885. "The Present Position of Economics." In *Memorials of Alfred Marshall,* edited by A. C. Pigou, 164. London: Macmillan.

Martin, Robert E. 2009. "The Revenue-to-Cost Spiral in Higher Education." *John William Pope Center for Higher Education Policy.* http://www.audibmw.info/pdf/revenue/8.pdf.

Massey, Cade, and Richard H. Thaler. 2013. "The Loser's Curse: Decision Making and Market Efficiency in the National Football League Draft." *Management Science* 59(7): 1479–95.

Matheson, Victor. 2008. "Mega-Events: The Effect of the World's Biggest Sporting Events on Local, Regional, and National Economies." In *The Business of Sport,* edited by Brad Humphreys and Dennis Howard, Vol. 1, 81–100. Westport, CT: Praeger.

McCarthy, Ryan. 2008, November 18. "Change You Can't Believe In: Why Hiring a New Coach Won't Solve Your Favorite NBA Team's Problems (Unless the Old Coach Was Isaiah Thomas)." http://www.slate.com/id/2204834.

McCloskey, Deidre. 1988. "Other Things Equal: The So-Called Coase Theorem." *Eastern Economic Journal* 24(3): 367–71.

McCracken, Voros. 2001, January 23. "Pitching and Defense? How Much Control Do Hurlers Have?" *Baseball Prospectus.* http://www.baseballprospectus.com/article.php?articleid=878.

McCulloch, Ron. 1995. *How Baseball Began.* Los Angeles: Warwick

McEvoy, Chad, Alan Morse, and Stephen Shapiro. 2013. "Factors Influencing Collegiate Athletic Department Revenues." *Journal of Issues in Intercollegiate Athletics* 6: 249–67.

Miller, Marvin. 1991. *A Whole Different Game: The Inside Story of Baseball's New Deal.* New York: Simon & Schuster.

Neale, Walter. 1964. "The Peculiar Economics of Professional Sports." *Quarterly Journal of Economics* 78(1): 1–14.

Noll, Roger. 1988. "Professional Basketball." *Stanford University Studies in Industrial Economics* (144).

Noll, Roger. 2013. "Endogeneity in Attendance Demand Models." In *The Econometrics of Sport,* edited by Placido Rodriguez, Stefan Kessenne, and Juame Garcia, 117–34. Northampton, MA: Edward Elgar.

North, Douglass. 1994. "Economic Performance through Time." *American Economic Review* 84(3): 359–68.

Oaxaca, Ronald. 1973. "Male-Female Wages Differentials in Urban Labor Markets." *International Economic Review* 14: 693–709.

Oliver, Dean. 2004. *Basketball on Paper.* Washington, DC: Brassey's Sports.

Onwuachi-Willig, Angela. 2015, June 17. "Race and Racial Identity Are Social Constructs." *New York Times.*

Ormiston, Russell. 2012. "Attendance Effects of Star Pitchers in Major League Baseball." *Journal of Sports Economics* 15(4): 338–64.

Owen, Dorian. 2015. "Measurement of Competitive Balance and Uncertainty of Outcome." In *Handbook on the Economics of Professional Football,* edited by John Goddard and Peter Sloan, 41–59. Cheltenham and Camberley, UK: Edward Elgar.

Owen, Dorian, and Nicholas King. 2015. "Competitive Balance Measures in Sports Leagues: The Effects of Variation in Season Length." *Economic Inquiry* 53(1): 731–44.

Palmer, P., and J. Thorn. 1984. *The Hidden Game of Baseball: A Revolutionary Approach to Baseball and Its Statistics.* Chicago: University of Chicago Press.

Peach, J. 2007. "College Athletics, Universities and the NCAA: Western Social Science Association Presidential Address." *Social Science Journal* 44(1): 11–22.

Perryman, Mark. 2012, July 7. "Do the Olympics Boost the Economy?" *Daily Beast,* p. 7.

Pitino, Rick. 1998. *Success Is a Choice: Ten Steps to Overachieving in Business and Life*. New York: Broadway Books.

Pitino, Rick. 2000. *Lead to Succeed: 10 Great Traits of Leadership in Business and Life*. New York: Random House.

Pluto, Terry, and Earl Weaver. 1984. *Weaver on Strategy: Classic Work on Art of Managing a Baseball Team*. Lincoln, NE: Potomac Books.

Pope, Devin, Joseph Price, and Justin Wolfers. Forthcoming. "Awareness Reduces Bias." *Management Science*.

Price, Joseph, and Justin Wolfers. 2010. "Racial Discrimination among NBA Referees." *Quarterly Journal of Economics* 125(4): 1859–87.

Price, Joseph., and Justin Wolfers. 2012. "Biased Referees?: Reconciling Results with the NBA's Analysis." *Contemporary Economic Policy* 30(3): 320–28.

Price, Joseph, Brian Soebbing, David Berri, and Brad Humphreys. 2010. "Tournament Incentives, League Policy, and NBA Team Performance Revisited." *Journal of Sports Economics* 11(2): 117–35.

Quinn, Kevin. 2012. "Getting to the 2011–12 National Football League Collective Bargaining Agreement." *International Journal of Sport Finance* 7: 141–57.

Quirk, James, and Rodney Fort. 1992. *Pay Dirt: The Business of Professional Team Sports*. Princeton, NJ: Princeton University Press.

Quirk, James, and Rodney Fort. 1999. *Hardball: The Abuse of Power in Pro Team Sports*. Princeton, NJ: Princeton University Press.

Rascher, Dan. 1999. "A Test of the Optimal Positive Production Network Externality in Major League Baseball." In *Sports Economics: Current Research*, edited by John Fizel, Elizabeth Gustafson, and Larry Hadley, 27–45. New York: Praeger.

Rascher, Daniel, and Timothy DeSchriver. 2012. "Smooth Operators: Recent Collective Bargaining in Major League Baseball." *International Journal of Sport Finance* 7: 176–208.

Riley, Pat. 1993. *The Winner Within: A Life Plan for Team Players*. New York: Putnam.

Robinson, Joan. 1969. *The Economics of Imperfect Competition*. 2nd ed. London: Palgrave Macmillan.

Robst, John, Jennifer Van Gilder, Corrine Coates, and David J. Berri. 2011. "Skin Tone and Wages: Evidence from NBA Free Agents." *Journal of Sports Economics* 12(2): 143–56.

Romer, David H. 2006. "Do Firms Maximize: Evidence from Professional Football." *Journal of Political Economy* 114: 340–65.

Ross, Charles. 1999. *Outside the Lines: African Americans and the Integration of the National Football League*. New York: New York University Press.

Rottenberg, Simon. 1956. "The Baseball Players' Labor Market." *Journal of Political Economy* 64(3): 242–58.

Rovell, D. 2013. "Honus Wagner Card Sells for $2.1 M." http://espn.go.com/mlb/story/_/id/9140901/t206-honus-wagner-baseball-card-sets-21m-auction-mark.

Samuelson, P. A. 1970. *Economics*. New York: McGraw-Hill.

Samuelson, Paul. 1995. "Some Uneasiness with the Coase Theorem." *Japan and the World Economy* 7: 2.

Schmidt, Martin B., and David J. Berri. 2001. "Competitive Balance and Attendance: The Case of Major League Baseball." *Journal of Sports Economics* 2(2): 145–67.

Schmidt, Martin B., and David J. Berri. 2003. "On the Evolution of Competitive Balance: The Impact of an Increasing Global Search." *Economic Inquiry* 41(4): 692–704.

Schmidt, Martin B., and David J. Berri. 2004. "The Impact of Labor Strikes on Consumer Demand: An Application to Professional Sports." *American Economic Review* 94(1): 344–57.

Schofield, Philip. 2003. "Jeremy Bentham's 'Nonsense Upon Stilts.'" *Utilitas* 15(1): 1–26.

Schumpeter, Joseph. 1954. *History of Economic Analysis*. New York: Oxford University Press.

Schwartz, Alan. 2004. *Numbers Game: Baseball's Lifelong Fascination with Statistics*. New York: Thomas Dunne Books/St. Martin's Press.

Scully, Gerald. 1974. "Pay and Performance in Major League Baseball." *American Economic Review* 64: 917–30.

Scully, Gerald. 1989. *The Business of Major League Baseball*. Chicago: University of Chicago Press.

Seymour, Harold. 1960. *Baseball: The Early Years*. New York: Oxford University Press.

Siegfried, John, and Andrew Zimbalist. 2002. "A Note on the Local Economic Impact of Sports Expenditures." *Journal of Sports Economics* 3(4): 361–66.

Siegfried, John J., and Andrew Zimbalist. 2000. "The Economics of Sports Facilities and Their Communities." *Journal of Economic Perspectives* 14(3): 95–114.

Sims, Justin, and Vittorio Addona. 2014. "Hurdle Models and Age Effects in the Major League Baseball Draft." *Journal of Sports Economics* 17(7): 672–87.

Smith, Adam. 1776. "Of the Component Parts of the Price of Commodities." In *The Wealth of Nations*, edited by Edwin Cannan, 54–55. Chicago: University of Chicago Press, 1976.

Spalding, A. G. 1911. *America's National Game*. San Francisco: Halo.

Staudohar, Paul. 1998, Spring. "Salary Caps in Professional Team Sports." *Compensation and Working Conditions* 3(1): 3–11.

Steinberg, Don. 2001. "How I Learned to Stop Worrying and Love the Bomb: A Survival Guide to the NFL's Quarterback Rating System." *GQ*.

Stigler, George. 1988. *Memoirs of an Unregulated Economist*. New York: Basic Books.

Studenmund, A. H. 1992. *Using Econometrics: A Practical Guide*. New York: HarperCollins.

Sullivan, D. A., ed. 1995. *Early Innings: A Documentary History of Baseball, 1825–1908*. Lincoln: University of Nebraska Press.

Szymanski, S. 2009. *Playbooks and Checkbooks: An Introduction to the Economics of Modern Sports*. Princeton, NJ: Princeton University Press.

Szymanski, Stefan, and Andrew Zimbalist. 2005. *National Pastime: How Americans Play Baseball and the Rest of the World Plays Soccer*. Washington, DC: Brookings Institution Press.

Thorn, John, and Peter Palmer. 2015. *The Hidden Game of Baseball*. 3rd ed. Chicago: University of Chicago Press.

Treber, Jaret, Rachel Levy, and Victor Matheson. 2013. "Gender Differences in Competitive Balance in Intercollegiate Basketball." In *Handbook on the Economics of Women in Sports*, edited by Eva Marikova Leeds and Michael Leeds, 251–68. Northampton, MA: Edward Elgar.

Utt, Joshua, and Rodney Fort. 2002. "Pitfalls to Measuring Competitive Balance with Gini Coefficients." *Journal of Sports Economics* 3(4): 367–73.

Veblen, T. 1898. "Why Is Economics Not an Evolutionary Science." *The Quarterly Journal of Economics* 12: 373–97.

Veblen, T. 1899. *The Theory of the Leisure Class*. New York: Macmillan.

von Allmen, Peter. 2013. "Coaching Women and Women Coaching: Pay Differentials in the Title IX Era." In *Handbook on the Economics of Women in Sports*, edited by Eva Marikova Leeds and Michael Leeds, 269–89. Northampton, MA: Edward Elgar.

Walker, Eric. 1982. *The Sinister First Baseman*. Millbrae, CA: Celestial Arts.

Wallace, Michael. 1988. "Labor Market Structure and Salary Determination among Professional Basketball Players." *Work and Occupations* 15(3): 294–312.

Weir, David R. 1992. "A Century of U.S. Unemployment, 1890–1990: Revised Estimates and Evidence for Stabilization." *Research in Economic History* 14: 301–46.

Winfree, Jason, and Chris Molitor. 2007. "The Value of College: Drafted High School Baseball Players." *Journal of Sports Economics* 8(4): 378–93.

Winston, Wayne. 2009. *Mathletics*. Princeton, NJ: Princeton University Press.

Winston, Wayne, and Jeff Sagarin. 2009. *Mathletics: How Gamblers, Managers, and Sports Enthusiasts Use Mathematics in Baseball, Basketball, and Football*. Princeton, NJ: Princeton University Press.

Wolohan, John T. 1999. "The Curt Flood Act of 1998 and Major League Baseball's Federal Antitrust Exemption." *Marquette Sports Law Journal* 9: 347. http://scholarship.law.marquette.edu/sportslaw/vol9/iss2/9.

Women's Media Center. 2015. "The Status of Women in the U.S. Media 2015." https://wmc.3cdn.net/83bf6082a319460eb1_hsrm680x2.pdf.

Wright, S. 2006. *Digital Compositing for Film and Video*. Burlington, MA: Focal Press.

Zimbalist, Andrew. 1992a. *Baseball and Billions*. New York: Basic Books.

Zimbalist, Andrew. 1992b. "Salaries and Performance: Beyond the Scully Model." In *Diamonds Are Forever: The Business of Baseball*, edited by Paul Sommers, 109–33. Washington, DC: The Brookings Institution.

Zimbalist, Andrew. 2001. *Unpaid Professionals*. Princeton, NJ: Princeton University Press.

Zimbalist, Andrew. 2003. "Labor Relations in Major League Baseball." *Journal of Sports Economics* 4(4): 333.

Zimbalist, Andrew. 2015. *Circus Maximus*. Washington, DC: Brookings Institution Press.

Zimmerman, Kevin. 2013. "The Unique Circumstance of NBA Coaching Turnover in 2013." http://www.sbnation.com/nba/2013/8/14/4614020/nba-coaches-doc-rivers-george-karl.

Index